Lecture Notes in Computer Science   14527

Founding Editors

Gerhard Goos
Juris Hartmanis

The series Lecture Notes in Computer Science (LNCS), including its subseries Lecture Notes in Artificial Intelligence (LNAI) and Lecture Notes in Bioinformatics (LNBI), has established itself as a medium for the publication of new developments in computer science and information technology research, teaching, and education.

LNCS enjoys close cooperation with the computer science R & D community, the series counts many renowned academics among its volume editors and paper authors, and collaborates with prestigious societies. Its mission is to serve this international community by providing an invaluable service, mainly focused on the publication of conference and workshop proceedings and postproceedings. LNCS commenced publication in 1973.

Chunpeng Ge · Moti Yung
Editors

Information Security and Cryptology

19th International Conference, Inscrypt 2023
Hangzhou, China, December 9–10, 2023
Revised Selected Papers, Part II

 Springer

Editors
Chunpeng Ge
Shandong University
Jinan, China

Moti Yung 🆔
Columbia University
New York, NY, USA

ISSN 0302-9743   ISSN 1611-3349 (electronic)
Lecture Notes in Computer Science
ISBN 978-981-97-0944-1   ISBN 978-981-97-0945-8 (eBook)
https://doi.org/10.1007/978-981-97-0945-8

This Springer imprint is published by the registered company Springer Nature Singapore Pte Ltd.
The registered company address is: 152 Beach Road, #21-01/04 Gateway East, Singapore 189721, Singapore

Paper in this product is recyclable.

Preface

The 19th International Conference on Information Security and Cryptology (Inscrypt 2022) was held December 9–10, 2023. The conference was hosted by Hangzhou Dianzi University and co-organized by Zhejiang Lab. Inscrypt is an international conference on information security, cryptology, and their applications. Inscrypt is designed to be a forum for theoreticians, scheme and application designers, protocol developers and practitioners to discuss and express their views on the current trends, challenges, and state-of-the-art solutions related to various issues in information security and cryptography. Topics of interests include, but are not limited to, information security and cryptography for asymmetric cryptography, symmetric cryptography, cryptography foundations, privacy and anonymity technologies, secure cryptographic protocols and applications, security notions, approaches, and paradigms, leakage-resilient cryptography, lattice-based cryptography and post-quantum cryptography, blockchain and cryptocurrency, IoT security, cloud security, and access control.

The conference received 152 submissions. Each submission was reviewed by at least three program committee members or external reviewers. The program committee members accepted 38 full papers, 7 short papers and 6 posters to be included in the conference program. The program committee members selected one best paper "Compact Ring Signatures with Post-Quantum Security in Standard Model" by Tuong Ngoc Nguyen, Willy Susilo, Dung Hoang Duong, Fuchun Guo, Kazuhide Fukushima and Shinsaku Kiyomoto, and one best student paper "Text Laundering: Mitigating Malicious Features through Knowledge Distillation from Language Foundation Models" by Yi Jiang, Chenghui Shi, Oubo Ma, Youliang Tian and Shouling Ji.

We thank the Program Committee members and the external reviewers for their hard work in reviewing the submissions. We thank the Organizing Committee and all volunteers for their time and effort dedicated to arranging the conference.

December 2023

Chunpeng Ge
Moti Yung

Organization

Honorary Co-chairs

Dongdai Lin   University of Chinese Academy of Sciences,
                               China
Guojin Ma   Hangzhou Dianzi University, China

General Co-chairs

Zhidong Zhao   Hangzhou Dianzi University, China
Zhe Liu   Zhejiang Lab, China

Program Co-chairs

Chunpeng Ge   Shandong University, China
Moti Yung   Columbia University, USA

Program Committee

Junqing Gong   East China Normal University, China
Long Yuan   Nanjing University of Science and Technology,
                               China
Jianchang Lai   Southeast University, China
Shi Bai   Florida Atlantic University, USA
Savio Sciancalepore   Eindhoven University of Technology (TU/e),
                               Netherlands
Shihui Fu   TU Delft, Netherlands
Aydin Abadi   University College London, UK
Thang Hoang   Virginia Tech, USA
Kirill Morozov   University of North Texas, USA
Hongbo Liu   University of Electronic Science and Technology
                               of China, China
Haoyu Ma   Zhejiang Lab, China
Tao Xiang   Chongqing University, China
Peng He   Hubei University, China

Hua Zhang	Beijing University of Posts and Telecommunications, China
Wenrui Diao	Shandong University, China
Hao Lin	Delft University of Technology, Netherlands
Zhenyu Wen	Zhejiang University of Technology, China
Wenting Li	Peking University, China
Junzuo Lai	Singapore Management University, Singapore
Yong Yu	Shaanxi Normal University, China
Florian Mendel	TU Graz, Austria
Rajat Subhra Chakraborty	IIT Kharagpur, India
David Jao	University of Waterloo, Canada
Lei Wang	Shanghai Jiao Tong University, China
Lf Zhang	Shanghaitech University, China
Yongjun Ren	Nanjing University of Information Science and Technology, China
Dongxi Liu	CSIRO, Australia
Weizhi Meng	Technical University of Denmark, Denmark
Huiwen Wu	Zhejiang Laboratory, China
Yanbin Li	Nanjing Agricultural University, China
Anmin Fu	Nanjing University of Science and Technology, China
Sebastian Berndt	University of Lübeck, Germany
Jianting Ning	Singapore Management University, Singapore
Cheng-Kang Chu	Institute for Infocomm Research, Singapore
Jie Chen	East China Normal University, China
Sebastian Ramacher	AIT Austrian Institute of Technology, Austria
Cong Zuo	Beijing Institute of Technology, China
Zhen Liu	Shanghai Jiao Tong University, China
Pierrick Meaux	Luxembourg University, Luxembourg
Jun Feng	Huazhong University of Science and Technology, China
Willy Susilo	University of Wollongong, Australia
Rupeng Yang	University of Wollongong, Australia
Michael Hutter	PQShield, UK
Rui Wang	TU Delft, Netherlands
Fangguo Zhang	Sun Yat-sen University, China
Yannan Li	University of Wollongong, Australia
Zhusen Liu	Zhejiang Lab, China

Publicity Chairs

Weizhi Meng   Technical University of Denmark, Denmark
Chuan Ma   Zhejiang Lab, China

Organizing Committee Co-chairs

Yizhi Ren   Hangzhou Dianzi University, China
Liming Fang   Nanjing University of Aeronautics and
                                     Astronautics, China

Contents – Part II

Cryptanalysis

Short Papers

Contents – Part I

Public Key Cryptography

Security and Privacy

System Security

Text Laundering: Mitigating Malicious Features Through Knowledge Distillation of Large Foundation Models

Yi Jiang[1,2], Chenghui Shi[1], Oubo Ma[1], Youliang Tian[3], and Shouling Ji[1(✉)]

[1] College of Computer Science and Technology, Zhejiang University, Hangzhou, China
{jiangyi2021,sji}@zju.edu.cn
[2] College of Renwu, Guizhou University, Guiyang, China
[3] College of Computer Science and Technology, Guizhou University, Guiyang, China

Abstract. Despite their efficacy in machine learning, Deep Neural Networks (DNNs) are notoriously susceptible to backdoor and adversarial attacks. These attacks are characterized by manipulated features within the input layer, which subsequently compromise the DNN's output. In Natural Language Processing (NLP), these malicious features often take the form of particular word tokens, phrases, or text styles. Defending against these harmful elements has proven challenging. Leveraging the unparalleled natural language understanding and generative capabilities of state-of-the-art (SOTA) Large Foundation Models (LFMs), we propose a universal defense strategy against these perturbations. Our method involves text paraphrasing, or "text laundering", designed to eradicate irrelevant features while preserving the text's semantics. Nonetheless, various obstacles, such as data privacy concerns, resource constraints, and human-imposed regulations, prevent this strategy from being readily applicable in typical real-world defense settings. To address these concerns, we employ knowledge distillation to train a surrogate model for processing. Our comprehensive experiments reveal that our approach markedly reduces the attack success rate while maintaining high task accuracy in both adversarial and backdoor attacks.

Keywords: backdoor · adversarial attack · defense · knowledge distillation

1 Introduction

Over the past decade, extensive research on Deep Neural Networks (DNNs) has consistently propelled technology to new heights. These advancements have led to successive breakthroughs in machine learning, setting new state-of-the-art (SOTA) records in various domains. Notable areas of impact include image classification, object detection, medical diagnosis, speech recognition, and Natural Language Processing (NLP).

One particularly noteworthy achievement has been witnessed recently, where DNN applications in the NLP field have achieved revolutionary breakthroughs.

The remarkable progress in large pre-trained language models highlights their unprecedented capabilities in natural language understanding and generation. These models, also known as Large Foundation Models (LFMs), have continuously demonstrated outstanding performance.

However, it is essential to recognize that alongside their impressive achievements, DNNs are susceptible to various security vulnerabilities including backdoor attacks [7,15,27,37], and adversarial attacks [21,32,33,43]. These security concerns are important considerations when deploying deep neural networks in real-world applications.

Early well-known adversarial and backdoor attacks initially surfaced within the realm of Computer Vision (CV). Researchers discovered that when carefully crafted noise was introduced into normal data samples, DNNs could yield incorrect predictions from a human perspective. These manipulated samples, known as adversarial examples, provided attackers with the means to execute model spoofing attacks. On the other hand, when DNN models were poisoned and the inputs tainted with specific triggers, whether perceptible to humans or not, normal data inputs could elicit predefined responses intended by attackers. Given the widespread integration of DNNs in real-world applications, this threat carries significant implications. For instance, prior studies demonstrated that in the context of autonomous driving, where human safety is paramount, an attacker could manipulate DNN models responsible for object recognition in vehicles by introducing backdoor triggers, such as attaching stickers to road signs [15]. Even when the model is initially free from contamination, attackers could employ adversarial attacks to deceive the critical model [21,48].

Extensive interest has been drawn to the research on defenses against adversarial and backdoor attacks. Unlike their counterparts in CV, the data samples in the NLP field are situated within discrete spaces and primarily originate from human sources. Common NLP malicious features often manifest as various sub-strings or distinct language styles that do not overtly modify the text's semantics [7,37]. These features are typically sensible by humans when ample effort is invested. Nevertheless, due to the inherent nature of human-generated text, some degree of noise is expected to be present and tolerated by DNNs; otherwise, their practical utility would be limited. Common occurrences such as misspellings, improper word usage, and peculiar language style compound the challenge of detecting malicious features within the text [16].

Existing defense frameworks exhibit two primary shortcomings.

The first issue is that, despite their effectiveness in countering certain categories of malicious features, they are vulnerable to the ones of various forms. As demonstrated in previous research [37], existing approaches can barely defend the features of text styles.

The second disadvantage is the lack of a unified framework for both adversarial and backdoor attacks. Both threats involve the introduction of additional features that can cause unexpected model responses. Consequently, defense frameworks should ideally address both of these threats.

In this paper, we present a straightforward yet highly effective approach that serves as a universal solution against both adversarial and backdoor attacks in

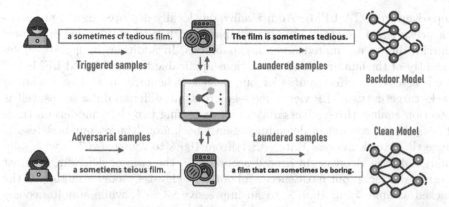

Fig. 1. The unified online defense against both backdoor and adversarial attacks.

the field of NLP. And it functions well with various forms of malicious features. We observed that in the last couple of years, the revolutionary breakthrough in pre-trained large language models [29,45] demonstrated incredible capabilities in natural language understanding and generating. They can play the role of a human expert to screen the suspicious items in the input text, alter them properly, and therefore compromise the malicious intention to activate the backdoor behaviors or malfunction. To be specific, we leverage the SOTA LFMs to paraphrase the input text into alternative sentences, a process we refer to as "text laundering". Thanks to the unprecedented capabilities of LFMs, the newly generated text remains coherent and retains the original semantic content, making it suitable for the intended tasks. As depicted in Fig. 1, our straightforward and united approach demonstrates superior performance compared to the majority of existing defense mechanisms designed to counter malicious text in universality.

Nonetheless, there are certain setbacks associated with relying on SOTA LFMs hosted in the cloud for standard defense:

1. **Privacy Concerns.** Outsourcing the data to the cloud side may not always be acceptable in most scenarios.
2. **Resource Constraints.** Even with open-sourced LFMs, the minimum requirement of computer hardware resources and computing power for deploying the LFMs can overwhelm most organizations.
3. **Utility Limitations.** The availability of the all-powerful language models is constrained by the legal and regulatory landscape in different countries.
4. **Extra Rules.** As public services, the LFMs are normally restricted by their publisher with content sensors, which would make them refuse to respond to certain inputs.

To address these challenges, we employ knowledge distillation [18] to train a surrogate student model for a cloud-side LFM. Focused specifically on sentence paraphrasing, our local student model adeptly overcomes these challenges. Notably, it demands significantly fewer storage and computational resources in comparison to SOTA LFMs. Additionally, our locally deployed model preserves data privacy and generally remains compliant with legal regulations in various countries due to its limited domain capabilities. In addition, it operates independently of the human-added restrictions applicable to cloud-based LFMs.

We assess the effectiveness of our defense scheme against two backdoor attacks targeting two NLP victim models across four different datasets, as well as protection against three adversarial attacks affecting two clean models on three datasets. In the context of defending against backdoor attacks, our best results reduce the Attack Success Rate (ASR) from 100% to a mere 2.67%, with only a marginal 3.3% decrease in overall accuracy. In the case of defending against adversarial attacks, our most successful outcome elevates model accuracy on the attacked samples from 16.97% to an impressive 93.85%, while simultaneously enhancing accuracy on clean samples by 1.39%[1].

Our contributions can be summarized as follows:

1. We propose a straightforward, effective, cross-dataset, and universally applicable strategy for online defense against agnostic text perturbations in the input layer, which would potentially trigger backdoor or adversarial attacks.
2. We exemplify the knowledge distillation of a huge cloud-side LFM to train a local small surrogate model. With the increasing concern over data privacy, it is possible to become a mainstream direction for utilizing LFMs.
3. We build the Paraphrased Sentence Pairs - 5 types (PSP5) dataset[2], comprising five fundamental categories of paraphrased English sentence pairs: declarative sentences (statements), interrogative sentences (questions), imperative sentences (commands), exclamatory sentences (exclamations), and sentence fragments (oral English). This dataset is expected to serve as a valuable resource for future research endeavors.

2   Related Work

2.1   Adversarial Attack and Defense

Adversarial examples in DNNs were initially demonstrated using images comprising imperceptible noise data to the human eye [43]. Despite their seemingly untainted appearance, these examples can deceive the model, leading to incorrect predictions. Subsequent research has delved into more advanced attack algorithms [14,32,33], alongside the introduction of defense strategies, including adversarial training [31,43], defensive distillation [5], and thermometer encoding [3]. The primary goal of most of these defense schemes is to bolster the models' resilience. Some of these defense approaches involve pre-processing at the input layer, such as techniques like feature squeezing [47], image compression, and bit-depth reduction [30].

---

[1] The code of this work is available at https://github.com/NESA-Lab/TextLaundering.
[2] The dataset is available at https://huggingface.co/datasets/jiangyige/PSP5.

DeepWordBug [13] extended the concept of adversarial perturbations from the CV domain to NLP, introducing perturbations in texts through word substitutions, deletions, and insertions. Textbugger [22] further refined this approach by introducing character-level perturbations. Similarly, TextFooler [1] employs a greedy search technique to craft adversarial examples by adding or replacing words in clean text. HotFlip [12] utilizes a gradient-based search to identify substitutions. Beyond word and character-level perturbations, SCPN [20] generates syntactically controlled paraphrases to create adversarial examples for deceiving NLP models.

In addition to borrowing defense strategies from the CV domain [3,5,31], the field of robust encoding explores various encoding techniques to enhance resilience against perturbations. ATfF [41] applies random insertion, deletion, or word substitution to mitigate the impact of adversarial perturbations. Unlike simply countering the perturbations by inserting extra noise randomly, ATINTER [17] trains a rewrite model to eliminate the influence of adversarial noise. While ATINTER shares some basic ideas with our approach, there are two notable distinctions. First, it necessitates training rewrite models for specific target databases, whereas our method is dataset-adaptive and doesn't rely on training data from specific datasets. Second, ATINTER is designed to address adversarial attacks, while our approach offers a unified solution for both backdoor and adversarial attacks.

2.2 Backdoor Attack and Defense

Backdoor attacks on DNNs have also emerged in the CV domain. Unlike adversarial attacks, which target clean models, backdoor attacks involve the insertion of malicious parameters into victim models. These parameters create a shortcut from a specific special feature, acting as a trigger, to a target class. The victim model performs correctly with normal samples, however, when the trigger is present in the input, the model's predictions are hijacked to output the target class, regardless of the sample's actual class. These attacks are typically carried out through data poisoning [4] or tampering with neural weights [27].

Much like the scenarios in adversarial attacks, backdoor triggers can be categorized into different levels, such as token level [7,23,38], sentence level [9,24], and semantic levels [34,37]. Representative attack methods include BadNL [7], which proposes triggers at three granularities: characters, words, and sentences, and StyleBKD [37], which innovatively uses language style as triggers.

Defense methods primarily focus on repairing victim models or implementing online defense at the input layer. Defense strategies for the input layer are often tailored to specific types of triggers. For instance, ONION [36] examines tokens in the text individually and assesses changes in perplexity to identify malicious tokens. To the best of our knowledge, there is still no effective defense approach against attacks involving language-style triggers.

2.3 Prompt Learning

The exponential growth in the number of parameters in pre-trained large language models has rendered the fine-tuning paradigm unsuitable for many practical use cases. As a response to this, the prompt learning paradigm has been introduced, effectively bridging the gap between the pre-training objective function and downstream NLP tasks [25]. Using carefully crafted prompt templates, transformed downstream tasks can be presented in a manner that aligns with the language model's familiarity from its pre-training stage. These workable prompts, whether human-recognizable or not, can be obtained through prompt-tuning or prompt engineering.

The tuning process involves training with a full dataset or using limited labeled samples, often referred to as few-shot learning. Prompt engineering, on the other hand, focuses on manually crafting prompts in natural language. These prompts may be paired with wrapped few-shot samples, known as in-context learning, or may not require any samples at all, as seen in zero-shot learning [2]. In the early stages of prompt learning in reality, particularly with relatively small language models like BERT and GPT2, it was common to utilize a full dataset, and the performance in few-shot and zero-shot settings was rather modest.

On the other hand, the recent proliferation of parameters in large language models, such as chatGPT [29] and LLaMA [45], has led to the emergence of remarkable abilities [26,46]. Models with a substantial number of parameters have demonstrated unprecedented performance in few-shot and even zero-shot learning scenarios. These remarkable emergent abilities enable the model to better comprehend human language and delve deeper into its semantics, even in the presence of various types of perturbations.

2.4 Knowledge Distillation

The increase of parameters in DNNs has proven to be beneficial for effectively capturing data structures in abundant datasets, yielding improved data representations, and achieving remarkable performance gains. Nevertheless, a significant real-world challenge lies in deploying these resource-intensive models in constrained environments, such as edge devices. Given that a substantial portion of these parameters is redundant for DNN model inference, a practical approach is to employ knowledge distillation, transferring knowledge from a large teacher model to a smaller student model [18].

Teacher models can convey "dark knowledge" to student models from three key aspects: the output [6], relationships among different layers [49], and features in hidden layers [50]. Depending on whether the teacher model's parameters are accessible or not, conventional knowledge distillation can be categorized as white-box distillation [40] and black-box distillation [19]. Conventional knowledge distillations have been primarily implemented in white-box settings, typically involving models with fewer than one billion parameters. However, in the era of LFMs, an increasing number of student models are trained through black-box knowledge distillation methods, such as Stanford Alpaca [44] and Vicuna

[8]. These student models emulate the behavior of SOTA models like ChatGPT via black-box APIs, delivering comparable performance in specific domains.

3 Methodology

The core concept of Text Laundering capitalizes on the remarkable natural language understanding and generation capabilities of SOTA LFMs to remove any malicious elements from the input text. To safeguard against both representative adversarial and backdoor attacks, we employ a zero-shot prompt learning approach for sentence paraphrasing with the LFM. Acknowledging the limitations of using LFMs, we also implement knowledge distillation to train a local surrogate model, as illustrated in Fig. 2.

3.1 Threat Model

Attackers' Capabilities and Goals. We assume attackers have white-box access to all the data they need in the whole life cycles of the victim models. For instance, the training datasets, the training process, and the models' structures and parameters. However, attackers do not have control over the inference pipeline and the communications between the model and the text-laundering module. Attackers hope to utilize certain malicious patterns in the input texts to stimulate the models to make wrong predictions.

Defenders' Capabilities and Goals. Defenders have full control over the inference pipeline of the models. Since text-laundering is an online defense, defenders can make sure all the inputs go through the text-laundering module and are then received by the input layers of the models. They hope to eradicate all the potentially malicious features in the inputs while maintaining their original semantics. In this way, even if the models were somehow poisoned or vulnerable to certain malicious features, the models are less likely to yield erroneous outputs.

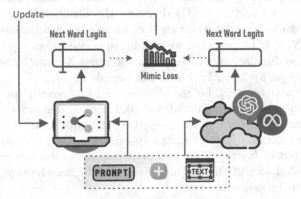

Fig. 2. The knowledge distillation process of building a local surrogate text laundering model.

3.2   Zero-Shot Prompt Learning

Recent SOTA LFMs have demonstrated impressive capabilities in zero-shot learning. However, it's essential to note that the choice of prompts can significantly impact the model's performance. For the specific task of paraphrasing, we employ a prompt engineering approach through trial and error to determine an optimal prompt for calling the LFM's API. By incorporating this optimal prompt into the original sentences and inputting them into the model, we obtain their paraphrased versions.

Figure 3 and Fig. 4 provide a visual representation of our fundamental defense methodologies against backdoor and adversarial attacks. Through the process of text laundering, the original texts are restructured, ensuring that the modified samples still reside on the same side of the decision boundary as the original ones.

3.3   Knowledge Distillation

To enable a student model Θ_s to partially acquire certain capabilities from a teacher model Θ_t, we can resort to knowledge distillation. In our case, the process happens between generative models rather than classification ones in conventional knowledge distillation applications.

We can formalize our procedure as follows:

With unsupervised sentence$X = x_0, x_2, ..., x_n$ as input, x_i as the ith token, generative model Θ can generate optimal sentence $Y = y_0, y_2, ..., y_m$ through maximize the likelihood:

$$p\left(X, \Theta_t\right) = \prod_i^m \left(y_i | x_0, ..., x_n, y_0, ... y_i, \Theta_t\right) \tag{1}$$

$$q\left(X, \Theta_s\right) = \prod_i^m \left(y_i' | x_0, ..., x_n, y_0', ... y_i', \Theta_s\right) \tag{2}$$

Accordingly, Θ_t and Θ_s are respectively the teacher model and the student model, with $p\left(X, \Theta_t\right)$ and $q\left(X, \Theta_s\right)$ denoting the likelihood from the teacher model and the student model, the target of knowledge distillation is to realize $q\left(X, \Theta_s\right) \approx p\left(X, \Theta_t\right)$. In practice, we use unsupervised text prompt as material for knowledge distillation, which means the input X above contains prompt tokens $Prompt = p_0, p_1, ..., p_n$ besides input sample x.

Let $logits_{i,k}^t$ and $logits_{i,k}^s$ be the ith row of logits vector for y_k from the teacher model and the student model, $i \in (0, 1, ...v)$, v denotes the vocabulary length of the language model. With the setting of temperature T in the knowledge distillation process, $p_{i,k}^T$ represents the softmax output of $logits_{i,k}^t$, and $q_{i,k}^T$ the softmax output of $logits_{i,k}^s$. The temperature affects the softmax output. It controls the randomness of the output token. The higher the temperature, the more diversity in the generated text.

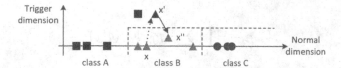

Fig. 3. Illustrating backdoor attacks and our defense: samples can be classified as A, B, or C on normal dimensions in clean models. Backdoor models were injected with a trigger dimension and shortcuts leading to a certain target class on this dimension. When regular sample x is added triggers and becomes x', it would be wrongly classified into targeted class A. Text laundering would reinvent x' into x'', which would be classified as class B like original x.

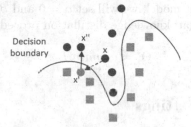

Fig. 4. The illustration of adversarial attack and our defense: to undermine its classification, a deliberately crafted perturbation is injected into sample x by the attacker, causing it to cross the decision boundary and transform into a modified version x'. Text laundering tries to convert the stained x' into x'', which is located at the same side of the decision boundary as the original x.

$$p_{i,k}^T = \frac{exp\left(logits_{i,k}^t/T\right)}{\sum_j^v exp\left(logits_{j,k}^t/T\right)} \tag{3}$$

$$q_{i,k}^T = \frac{exp\left(logits_{i,k}^s/T\right)}{\sum_j^v exp\left(logits_{j,k}^s/T\right)} \tag{4}$$

To train the student model to mimic the teacher model, we try to optimize Θ_s by minimizing the kullback-Leibler divergence between the output distribution of p and q.

$$\Theta_s^* = \underset{\Theta_s}{argmin} \; \mathbf{KL}\left[p||q\right] \tag{5}$$

We take into account L_{soft} and L_{hard} as factors of the mimic loss, the former loss considering the cross entropy between the output logits vector of 2 models, while the latter considers the loss between the hard label output c (one-hot vector with dimension of length of the vocabulary) of the teacher and the softmax output of the student model.

$$L_{soft} = -\prod_k^m \sum_j^v -p_{j,k}^T \log\left(q_{j,k}^T\right) \tag{6}$$

$$L_{hard} = -\prod_k^m \sum_j^N -c_j log q_{j,k}^1 \tag{7}$$

We use α and β as hyper-parameters adjusting the respect ratio weights of the 2 loss factors. $\alpha + \beta = 1$.

Where $\alpha + \beta = 1$. It is worthy to note that when the output logits of the teacher model is unavailable, only the output hard label would be the instruction knowledge for the student model, we will set $\alpha = 0$ and $\beta = 1$.

The ultimate goal of our knowledge distillation procedure is to minimize the loss L.

$$\Theta_s^* = \underset{\Theta_s}{argmin}\, L \tag{8}$$

4   Experimental Settings

4.1   Datasets and Victim Models

We examine the effect of our method on 2 popular NLP pre-trained language models, BERT [11] and ROBERTA [28], using 4 representative datasets involved in this work. We provide a brief introduction to these datasets below:

AG [51]: AG News is a 4-category text classification dataset. The news topic sentence in the dataset can be classified as 0 (world news), 1 (Sports news), 2 (Business news), and 3 (Sci/Tech news).

SST2 [42]: Standford Sentiment Treebank is a corpus for language sentiment analyzing, and SST2 is a version of 2-category sentiment analyzing. The samples in sst2 are mainly sentence fragments from oral English. The types of text are 1 (positive) and 0 (negative).

HS [10]: Hate Speech Detection dataset contains tweets labeled as hate speech or not. Labels are 1 (offensive) and 0 (non-offensive).

MR [35]: Rotten-tomatoes Movie Review is a famous text classification data set. It contains 2 types of samples. Labels are 1 (positive) and 0 (negative).

We implement 2 backdoor attacks named BadNL and StyleBKD towards BERT and ROBERTA on the 4 datasets, and defense against the malicious input to these victim models. And perform 3 adversarial attacks respectively on clean BERT and ROBERTA models on 3 datasets. We try to mitigate their effect by text laundering with the LFM and local surrogate model.

4.2   Attack Schemes

Adversarial and backdoor attacks on NLP models are typically classified into three categories based on the granularity of perturbation at the input layer: *character-level*, *word-level*, and *sentence-level*. In order to meet the criteria of being stealthy and preserving semantics, the malicious characteristics of backdoor triggers and noisy elements in adversarial examples in most existing research are introduced at either the word or character level. However, in a recent study [37], unique language styles have been employed as concealed triggers in backdoor attacks, enhancing the stealthiness of the malicious features.

In our evaluation of the defense approach, we consider two representative backdoor attacks: BadNL [7] (involving a *word-level* trigger) and StyleBKD [37] (utilizing a *language-style* trigger).

In the BadNL attack, the trigger consists of the randomly added "cf" into the input text, a common setting in various backdoor research endeavors.

In the StyleBKD attack, the original samples undergo transformation with a unique language style drawn from the Bible. This style is employed by the attacker to taint the training dataset, thereby introducing a backdoor into the model.

Furthermore, we assess our defense approach against three prominent adversarial attacks, each representing a primary style of adversarial perturbations in text: Textfooler (*word-level*) [1], DeepWordBug (*character-level*) [13], and Textbugger (*word&character-level*) [22].

Given that many attacking methods in current research employ similar perturbation styles at the input layer, we think our experiments are sufficient to demonstrate the effectiveness of our defense approach.

4.3 Defence Baseline

In the realm of defense against backdoor DNN models, a significant focus has been on mitigating tainted model parameters. However, since our defense operates in the input layer within a black-box model setting, we have selected ONION [36] as the baseline for backdoor defense in our experiments. ONION is a straightforward yet effective online defense method. It leverages the empirical observation that the inclusion of trigger tokens substantially increases sentence perplexity. ONION conducts online defense by examining the change in perplexity while systematically removing tokens from input samples with the assistance of GPT2. This defense is recognized for its simplicity and effectiveness in deployment.

When it comes to defending against adversarial attacks, the perturbations are inherent characteristics of the clean models rather than vulnerabilities. Existing defense methods typically revolve around enhancing the model's robustness, employing techniques such as adversarial training, gradient masking or obfuscation, and defensive distillation. For our experiments, we have chosen ATINTER [17], a recently published online defense method, as the baseline for addressing adversarial attacks.

4.4 Knowledge Distillation Setting

For our text laundering process, we have chosen the SOTA LFM chatGPT [29] as our LFM, and GPT2 [39] as our local surrogate model for the task of paraphrasing.

We crawled ten thousand unlabeled sentences from the internet, which serve as the training data for the knowledge distillation process. To create a comprehensive paraphrasing student model that mimics the teacher model chatGPT, our dataset encompasses all five basic types of English sentences:

1. Declarative Sentences (statements). 2. Interrogative Sentences (questions). 3. Imperative Sentences (commands). 4. Exclamatory Sentences (exclamations). 5. Sentence Fragments (oral English). Each text sample is augmented with a prompt: "The above can be paraphrased into". These samples, along with their prompts, are submitted through API calls to chatGPT for zero-shot learning. We then use the online feedback information to train our local student model, GPT2. Both the teacher model (chatGPT) and the student model (GPT2) are set to have temperatures of 0.8.

Throughout this process, we have generated a paraphrased sentence pair dataset. With the inclusion of the five-sentence structure mentioned above, this dataset can be valuable for training paraphrase models or for use in various NLP research areas, including sentence similarity, and the exploration of distribution variances between human-generated text and text produced by LFMs.

4.5   Metrics

Our evaluation metrics primarily focus on assessing the efficacy of the defense approach in eliminating malicious elements from poisoned inputs and its impact on the model's behavior when classifying clean samples. A successful defense scheme is characterized by a minimal drop in model accuracy on clean samples and a notable increase in model accuracy on poisoned samples.

Here are the key metrics we employ:

CA (Clean Accuracy): This metric measures the classification accuracy of the model when presented with clean samples.

CA_d (Clean Accuracy with Defense): Used to gauge the side effect of our text laundering scheme on clean samples.

ΔCA (Change in Clean Accuracy): This represents the difference in model accuracy on clean samples before and after the defense scheme is applied.

ASR (Attack Success Rate): This metric quantifies the portion of samples that are wrongly classified according to the attacker's target within the poisoned samples set. In this paper, ASR is primarily utilized as a metric in the context of backdoor attack experiments.

ASR_d (Attack Success Rate with Defense): Evaluates the ASR when defense schemes are applied, assessing the defense's effectiveness in thwarting backdoor attacks.

ΔASR (Change in Attack Success Rate): Represents the difference in ASR of a backdoor attack scheme before and after a defense scheme is applied.

AA (Attacked Accuracy): Assesses the model's accuracy on adversarial examples.

AA_d (Attacked Accuracy with Defense): Evaluates the defense's effectiveness against adversarial attacks by measuring the model's accuracy on adversarial examples when defense schemes are applied.

Δ *AA* (Change in Attacked Accuracy): Represents the difference in attacked accuracy before and after a defense scheme is applied.

5 Evaluation

5.1 Text Laundering Against Backdoor Attack

Our initial investigation examines the impact of our text laundering scheme on a backdoored BERT model fine-tuned with the SST2 dataset, as illustrated in Fig. 5. The victim model is trained with poisoned samples that include a special token "cf" as the trigger. The original performance of the victim model, represented by CA (the blue bar) and ASR (the orange bar), is notably high. The objective of the defense schemes is to reduce ASR while maintaining high CA.

When we use the performance of ONION as a baseline, we observe that the paraphrasing capabilities of chatGPT surpass ONION, resulting in a smaller ΔCA (change in clean accuracy) and a higher ΔASR (drop in attack success rate).

Locally deployed GPT2 exhibits more modest behavior but becomes comparable to the baseline after being trained with knowledge distillation from chatGPT.

To comprehensively assess the performance of text laundering across various text distributions and different forms of triggers, we extended our testing to include another backdoor attack involving three additional datasets.

The results presented in Table 1 demonstrate that chatGPT paraphrasing achieves satisfactory performance in terms of CA drop and significantly outperforms ONION in ASR reduction. Given that defense methods like ONION are designed exclusively for backdoor attacks, while text laundering is effective for scenarios involving semantically irrelevant perturbations, our approach can be considered a superior solution.

Furthermore, the student model GPT2, even though it sacrifices some accuracy on clean samples, exhibits a comparable ability to mitigate the impact of triggers through paraphrasing. This can be valuable in settings where positive identification takes precedence, and a certain level of negative-positive rate can be tolerated.

The text laundering tactic has proven highly effective in eliminating inserted special tokens in input. For instance, on the MR dataset, it reduces the ASR from 100% to 2.67%, surpassing the baseline ONION. In the case of style triggers, it's important to note that, to the best of our knowledge, there is no specialized defense scheme against this novel type of trigger. While the ONION defense demonstrates minimal mitigation effect in this scenario, our approach achieves a substantial ASR reduction of 65.69%.

Our defense approach exhibits its weakest performance when defending against StyleBKD on the SST2 dataset. This is primarily attributed to the composition of the SST2 dataset, which predominantly contains sentence fragments

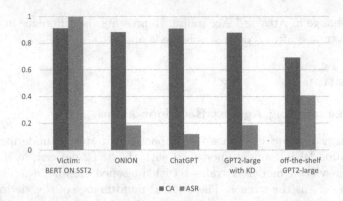

Fig. 5. Investigate the effect of text-laundering defense against representative backdoor attack.

rather than complete sentences. Since text laundering may have difficulty altering the language style of sentence fragments, its effectiveness is limited in this context.

However, on the HateSpeech and AGnews datasets, our defense approach consistently performs well. It achieves a substantial ASR reduction of approximately 50% in these cases.

5.2   Text Laundering Against Adversarial Attack

Following a similar rationale for removing noise in inputs, text laundering also holds significant promise in mitigating perturbations in adversarial examples.

In adversarial attacks, the model remains untouched by the attacker, and the success of NLP adversarial attacks is primarily achieved through query manipulation. Instead of solely considering the attack success rate of the attacking scheme, our focus lies in understanding how effectively the defense can reduce the ratio of workable adversarial examples identified by the attacker. This is reflected in the ΔAA metric, which measures the change in Attacked Accuracy before and after the defense is applied.

The results presented in Table 2 demonstrate that the text laundering approach can substantially enhance model accuracy under attack. In our experiments, the most significant mitigation result reaches up to 76.87%, illustrating the promising potential of text laundering in eliminating adversarial noise. Notably, the side effect of our defense scheme on clean samples is minimal, leading to a decrease in model accuracy of less than 1%. In some cases, such as the MR dataset, the text laundering scheme even enhances the model accuracy by 2.59%.

However, it's worth noting that while the student model GPT2, with knowledge distillation, achieves satisfying results in terms of both mitigation effectiveness and minimal side effects, it still has room for improvement to match the performance of the large teacher model for some optimized knowledge distillation process.

Table 1. Backdoor defense for 2 models respectively poisoned on 3 databases evaluated by ΔASR and ΔCA. CA_d and ASR_d are CA and backdoor ASR of the victim models after the defense. The less drop in ΔCA, the more in ΔASR, the better.

Attack	Dataset	Defense	Victim BERT						Victim ROBERTA					
			CA	ASR	CA_d	ASR_d	ΔCA	ΔASR	CA	ASR	CA_d	ASR_d	ΔCA	ΔASR
BadNL	AG	ONION	94.52	100	93.28	51.23	↓1.24	↓48.77	94.05	100	93.69	38.42	↓0.36	↓61.58
		ChatGPT			91.22	2.67	↓3.3	↓**97.33**			92.95	4.31	↓1.1	↓**95.69**
		GPT2			88.1	4.75	↓6.42	↓95.25			85.63	5.37	↓8.42	↓94.63
	SST2	ONION	94.67	100	90.86	18.37	↓**3.81**	↓81.63	94.22	100	92.19	42.54	↓**2.03**	↓57.46
		ChatGPT			91.81	11.82	↓5.86	↓**86.32**			90.25	17.09	↓3.97	↓**82.91**
		GPT2			85.2	12.82	↓9.47	↓87.18			87.73	17.09	↓6.49	↓82.91
	MR	ONION	83.39	100	81.37	48.2	↓2.02	↓51.8	86.28	100	82.09	52.03	↓4.19	↓47.97
		ChatGPT			85.92	17.05	↑**2.53**	↓**82.95**			87.73	20.16	↑**1.45**	↓**79.84**
		GPT2			80.87	24.81	↓2.52	↓75.19			79.78	27.13	↓6.5	↓72.87
StyleBKD	AG	ONION	91.26	89.67	88.39	84.51	↓**2.87**	↓5.16	89.32	83.10	87.31	80.12	↓**2.01**	↓2.97
		ChatGPT			87.38	37.09	↓3.88	↓**52.58**			85.44	35.68	↓3.88	↓**47.42**
		GPT2			80.58	65.73	↓10.67	↓23.94			77.67	63.85	↓11.65	↓19.25
	SST2	ONION	87.38	86.70	84.50	85.23	↓2.87	↓1.46	93.20	91.13	88.34	89.27	↓**4.86**	↓1.86
		ChatGPT			85.44	50.25	↓**1.94**	↓**36.45**			82.52	63.55	↓10.68	↓**27.59**
		GPT2			84.47	62.56	↓3.01	↓24.13			79.61	74.88	↓13.6	↓16.26
	HS	ONION	93.07	90.05	91.43	89.71	↓**1.64**	↓0.3363	90.10	99.52	88.33	95.42	↓1.77	↓4.1
		ChatGPT			86.14	36.32	↓6.93	↓**53.73**			89.11	33.83	↑0.99	↓**65.69**
		GPT2			84.16	57.71	↓8.91	↓32.33			86.14	49.25	↓3.96	↓50.27

5.3 Analyses of Knowledge Distillation of Text Laundering

In the process of training a surrogate model for text laundering, the choice of the pre-trained student model and the number of queries are hyperparameters. It's intuitive that a larger student model should benefit more from the knowledge distillation process. However, considering the real-world constraints on computational resources, it's crucial to strike a balance and obtain quantitative guidance. To address this, we conducted an experiment involving three versions of GPT2 (GPT2-small, GPT2-medium, GPT2-large) and employed varying numbers of queries from chatGPT to train them as student models. We then examined their performance in terms of CA and ASR.

The findings from the left part of Fig. 6 indicate that, when using the original CA of the victim model (represented by the purple dotted line) as the baseline, the model's accuracy on chatGPT paraphrased input closely aligns with it. This suggests that clean samples are minimally affected by text laundering. Moreover, when employing the same number of queries, GPT2-large outperforms the smaller versions. The paraphrasing accuracy steadily increases with a greater number of queries to the teacher model, up to a certain point. However, it's important to note that the performance of text laundering by student models doesn't always improve with additional queries. Once a maximum point is reached, further queries from the teacher model do not yield significant benefits for the student model.

Table 2. We defend 3 representative adversarial attacks to 2 models on 3 datasets: TF for TextFooler, DWB for DeepWordBug, TB for TextBugger. CA for model Clean Accuracy when samples are clean, AA for model Accuracy under Adversarial attack, CA_d for model clean Accuracy with defense methods, AA_d for model Accuracy under Adversarial attack with defense methods, and Δ CA for model Accuracy difference between w/wo defense.

Attack	Dataset	Defense	BERT						ROBERTA					
			CA	AA	CA_d	ΔCA	AA_d	ΔAA	CA	AA	CA_d	ΔCA	AA_d	ΔAA
TF	AG	ATINTER	94.18	19.86	**93.7**	↓**0.48**	71.80	↑51.94	94.68	14.54	**92.65**	↓**2.03**	72.32	↑57.78
		ChatGPT			92.89	↓1.28	**83.25**	↑**63.39**			90.36	↓4.33	**81.03**	↑**66.48**
		GPT2			89.35	↓4.83	70.41	↑50.55			85.86	↓8.83	73.60	↑59.06
	SST2	ATINTER	92.43	4.47	**92.04**	↓**0.39**	22.68	↑18.21	94.04	4.70	93.54	↓0.5	20.36	↑15.66
		ChatGPT			91.88	↓0.55	**77.16**	↑**72.68**			**95.43**	↑**1.39**	**72.59**	↑**67.89**
		GPT2			88.01	↓4.42	62.27	↑57.8			90.37	↓3.67	59.29	↑54.59
	MR	ATINTER	83.70	9.60	82.19	↓1.51	20.06	↑10.46	88.40	5.70	86.30	↓2.1	25.31	↑19.61
		ChatGPT			**86.29**	↑**2.59**	**73.98**	↑**64.38**			**90.31**	↑**1.91**	**73.47**	↑**67.77**
		GPT2			81.30	↓2.4	63.96	↑54.36			82.80	↓5.6	57.36	↑51.66
DWB	AG	ATINTER	94.18	37.41	**93.7**	↓**0.48**	67.23	↑29.82	94.68	40.82	**92.65**	↓**2.03**	70.44	↑29.62
		ChatGPT			92.89	↓1.29	**87.82**	↑**50.41**			90.36	↓4.33	**89.8**	↑**48.97**
		GPT2			89.35	↓4.83	75.73	↑38.31			85.86	↓8.83	78.17	↑37.35
	SST2	ATINTER	92.43	16.74	**92.04**	↓**0.39**	35.64	↑18.9	94.04	16.97	93.54	↓0.5	38.27	↑21.3
		ChatGPT			91.88	↓0.55	**85.28**	↑**68.54**			**95.43**	↑**1.39**	**93.85**	↑**76.87**
		GPT2			88.01	↓4.42	67.09	↑50.34			90.37	↓3.67	62.44	↑45.46
	MR	ATINTER	83.70	18.80	82.19	↓1.51	41.67	↑22.87	88.40	16.70	86.30	↓2.1	39.86	↑23.16
		ChatGPT			**86.29**	↑**2.59**	**82.9**	↑**64.1**			**90.31**	↑**1.91**	**84.92**	↑**68.22**
		GPT2			81.30	↓2.4	65.20	↑46.4			82.80	↓5.6	62.94	↑46.24
TB	AG	ATINTER	94.18	46.90	**93.7**	↓**0.48**	62.83	↑15.93	94.68	45.40	**92.65**	↓**2.03**	64.29	↑18.89
		ChatGPT			92.89	↓1.29	**89.8**	↑**42.9**			90.36	↓4.33	**88.54**	↑**43.14**
		GPT2			89.35	↓4.83	82.23	↑35.33			85.86	↓8.83	77.66	↑32.26
	SST2	ATINTER	92.43	29.13	**92.04**	↓**0.39**	40.50	↑11.37	94.04	36.70	93.54	↓0.5	51.23	↑14.53
		ChatGPT			91.88	↓0.55	**87.18**	↑**58.05**			**95.43**	↑**1.39**	**85.2**	↑**48.51**
		GPT2			88.01	↓4.42	72.82	↑43.69			90.37	↓3.67	68.46	↑31.77
	MR	ATINTER	83.70	30.80	82.19	↓1.51	45.70	↑14.9	88.40	29.80	86.30	↓2.1	45.29	↑15.49
		ChatGPT			**86.29**	↑**2.59**	**84.38**	↑**53.58**			**90.31**	↑**1.91**	**85.64**	↑**55.84**
		GPT2			81.30	↓2.4	68.50	↑37.7			82.80	↓5.6	66.60	↑36.8

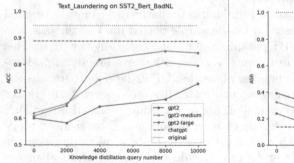
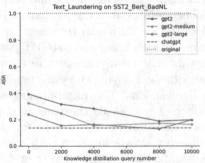

Fig. 6. Investigate the effect of query numbers in knowledge distillation for different student models.

The right part of Fig. 6 illustrates the substantial mitigation effect of chat-GPT paraphrasing on triggers in the input. The dotted line, representing the ASR of the victim model, is at 100% and remains significantly apart from the bottom red dashed line, which indicates the ASR of the attacker after text laundering by chatGPT. Furthermore, as the number of queries increases to 8000, the behavior of the student models closely approaches chatGPT's performance. However, when the number of queries surpasses 8000, the student models experience a slight decrease in their abilities.

Overall, as the number of queries increases, all student models demonstrate improved behavior in terms of maintaining CA and reducing ASR. This suggests that a smaller number of parameters can be compensated for by obtaining more knowledge through knowledge distillation from another model.

6 Discussion and Future Work

Latet SOTA LFMs demonstrate their natural language understanding and generation capabilities are unparalleled. Their capacity for paraphrasing is particularly impressive, making it exceedingly challenging for extraneous semantic noise to persist in their outputs.

Nevertheless, when it comes to outsourcing data and implementing online defense using cloud-side LFMs like ChatGPT, certain shortcomings cannot be disregarded. Concerns related to data privacy and cost are significant, and, in our experiments, the reliability is occasionally compromised due to the regulations imposed by the company developing these models. Consequently, a surrogate model may present a more viable solution.

One key aspect we aim to enhance is the paraphrasing proficiency of the student model. In our experiments, we encountered limitations in the knowledge obtained from ChatGPT due to limited quota, resulting in a lack of precise logits values for each generated word. This deficiency significantly impacts the mimic loss during the knowledge distillation process. In our forthcoming research, we plan to incorporate open-source LFMs (even if they may not match the performance of SOTA ChatGPT) to complement the loss by including logit values. Our findings indicate that the more queries made to the LFM for training knowledge, the more improved the student model's performance becomes. We will also explore the quantitative relationship regarding the number of queries for convergence in our future work.

Furthermore, during the paraphrasing process, the language model tends to transform the original text into a formal style, which can potentially alter the distribution of the original content. A superior paraphrasing model should not only retain the core meaning but also preserve the original style of language. Neglecting this consideration may exacerbate the out-of-distribution problem, leading to a decline in accuracy on clean samples. To address this concern, we introduce different sentence structures as training materials, although the impact is limited. We will further investigate methods to construct a more effective paraphrasing model for eliminating noisy features.

7   Conclusion

While DNNs have achieved remarkable success, they are also infamous for their susceptibility to backdoor and adversarial attacks. Defending against these attacks, which can exploit subtle features in the input to trigger unexpected behaviors or deceive the model, poses a significant challenge. Leveraging the powerful paraphrasing capabilities of SOTA LFM, we propose a straightforward and universal approach to mitigate malicious input noise. This approach involves paraphrasing input sentences into different but semantically equivalent forms. Our experiments, conducted across various datasets, victim models, and attack strategies, yielded highly satisfactory results, demonstrating that the paraphrasing procedure effectively eliminates most irrelevant input features.

To address the practical concerns surrounding the deployment of cloud-sided huge LFMs, we illustrate the knowledge distillation process for training a smaller, local surrogate generative model. This approach offers a cost-effective and lower-risk alternative to harness the benefits of paraphrasing while mitigating security concerns associated with large-scale LFM deployment.

References

1. Alzantot, M., Sharma, Y., Elgohary, A., Ho, B., Srivastava, M.B., Chang, K.: Generating natural language adversarial examples. In: Riloff, E., Chiang, D., Hockenmaier, J., Tsujii, J. (eds.) Proceedings of the 2018 Conference on Empirical Methods in Natural Language Processing, Brussels, Belgium, 31 October–4 November 2018, pp. 2890–2896. Association for Computational Linguistics (2018). https://doi.org/10.18653/v1/d18-1316
2. Brown, T., et al.: Language models are few-shot learners. In: Advances in Neural Information Processing Systems, vol. 33, pp. 1877–1901 (2020)
3. Buckman, J., Roy, A., Raffel, C., Goodfellow, I.J.: Thermometer encoding: one hot way to resist adversarial examples. In: 6th International Conference on Learning Representations, ICLR 2018, Vancouver, BC, Canada, 30 April–3 May 2018, Conference Track Proceedings. OpenReview.net (2018). https://openreview.net/forum?id=S18Su-CW
4. Carlini, N., Liu, C., Erlingsson, Ú., Kos, J., Song, D.: The secret sharer: evaluating and testing unintended memorization in neural networks. In: 28th USENIX Security Symposium (USENIX Security 2019), pp. 267–284 (2019)
5. Carlini, N., Wagner, D.: Defensive distillation is not robust to adversarial examples. arXiv preprint arXiv:1607.04311 (2016)
6. Chen, G., Choi, W., Yu, X., Han, T., Chandraker, M.: Learning efficient object detection models with knowledge distillation. In: Advances in Neural Information Processing Systems (2017)
7. Chen, X., et al.: BadNL: backdoor attacks against NLP models with semantic-preserving improvements. In: Annual Computer Security Applications Conference, pp. 554–569 (2021)
8. Chiang, W.L., et al.: Vicuna: an open-source chatbot impressing GPT-4 with 90%* ChatGPT quality (2023). https://vicuna.lmsys.org. Accessed 14 Apr 2023
9. Dai, J., Chen, C., Li, Y.: A backdoor attack against LSTM-based text classification systems. IEEE Access 7, 138872–138878 (2019)

10. De Gibert, O., Perez, N., García-Pablos, A., Cuadros, M.: Hate speech dataset from a white supremacy forum. arXiv preprint arXiv:1809.04444 (2018)
11. Devlin, J., Chang, M., Lee, K., Toutanova, K.: BERT: pre-training of deep bidirectional transformers for language understanding. In: Burstein, J., Doran, C., Solorio, T. (eds.) Proceedings of the 2019 Conference of the North American Chapter of the Association for Computational Linguistics: Human Language Technologies, NAACL-HLT 2019, Minneapolis, MN, USA, 2–7 June 2019 (Volume 1: Long and Short Papers), pp. 4171–4186. Association for Computational Linguistics (2019). https://doi.org/10.18653/v1/n19-1423
12. Ebrahimi, J., Rao, A., Lowd, D., Dou, D.: HotFlip: white-box adversarial examples for text classification. arXiv preprint arXiv:1712.06751 (2017)
13. Gao, J., Lanchantin, J., Soffa, M.L., Qi, Y.: Black-box generation of adversarial text sequences to evade deep learning classifiers. In: 2018 IEEE Security and Privacy Workshops (SPW), pp. 50–56. IEEE (2018)
14. Goodfellow, I.J., Shlens, J., Szegedy, C.: Explaining and harnessing adversarial examples. In: Bengio, Y., LeCun, Y. (eds.) 3rd International Conference on Learning Representations, ICLR 2015, San Diego, CA, USA, 7–9 May 2015, Conference Track Proceedings (2015). http://arxiv.org/abs/1412.6572
15. Gu, T., Dolan-Gavitt, B., Garg, S.: BadNets: identifying vulnerabilities in the machine learning model supply chain. arXiv preprint arXiv:1708.06733 (2017)
16. Guo, W., Tondi, B., Barni, M.: An overview of backdoor attacks against deep neural networks and possible defences. IEEE Open J. Signal Process. (2022)
17. Gupta, A., et al.: Don't retrain, just rewrite: countering adversarial perturbations by rewriting text. arXiv preprint arXiv:2305.16444 (2023)
18. Hinton, G., Vinyals, O., Dean, J.: Distilling the knowledge in a neural network. arXiv preprint arXiv:1503.02531 (2015)
19. Hsieh, C.Y., et al.: Distilling step-by-step! outperforming larger language models with less training data and smaller model sizes. arXiv preprint arXiv:2305.02301 (2023)
20. Iyyer, M., Wieting, J., Gimpel, K., Zettlemoyer, L.: Adversarial example generation with syntactically controlled paraphrase networks. arXiv preprint arXiv:1804.06059 (2018)
21. Jin, Z., Ji, X., Cheng, Y., Yang, B., Yan, C., Xu, W.: PLA-LiDAR: physical laser attacks against lidar-based 3D object detection in autonomous vehicle. In: 2023 IEEE Symposium on Security and Privacy (SP), pp. 1822–1839. IEEE (2023)
22. Li, J., Ji, S., Du, T., Li, B., Wang, T.: TextBugger: generating adversarial text against real-world applications. arXiv preprint arXiv:1812.05271 (2018)
23. Li, Y., Zhai, T., Wu, B., Jiang, Y., Li, Z., Xia, S.: Rethinking the trigger of backdoor attack. arXiv preprint arXiv:2004.04692 (2020)
24. Lin, J., Xu, L., Liu, Y., Zhang, X.: Composite backdoor attack for deep neural network by mixing existing benign features. In: Proceedings of the 2020 ACM SIGSAC Conference on Computer and Communications Security, pp. 113–131 (2020)
25. Liu, P., Yuan, W., Fu, J., Jiang, Z., Hayashi, H., Neubig, G.: Pre-train, prompt, and predict: a systematic survey of prompting methods in natural language processing. ACM Comput. Surv. 55(9), 1–35 (2023)
26. Liu, Y., et al.: Summary of ChatGPT-related research and perspective towards the future of large language models. Meta-Radiology 100017 (2023)
27. Liu, Y., et al.: Trojaning attack on neural networks. In: 25th Annual Network And Distributed System Security Symposium (NDSS 2018). Internet Soc. (2018)
28. Liu, Y., et al.: RoBERTa: a robustly optimized BERT pretraining approach. arXiv preprint arXiv:1907.11692 (2019)

29. Lund, B.D.: A brief review of ChatGPT: its value and the underlying GPT technology. Preprint. University of North Texas. Project: ChatGPT and Its Impact on Academia (2023)
30. Madry, A., Makelov, A., Schmidt, L., Tsipras, D., Vladu, A.: Towards deep learning models resistant to adversarial attacks. arXiv preprint arXiv:1706.06083 (2017)
31. Madry, A., Makelov, A., Schmidt, L., Tsipras, D., Vladu, A.: Towards deep learning models resistant to adversarial attacks. In: 6th International Conference on Learning Representations, ICLR 2018, Vancouver, BC, Canada, 30 April–3 May 2018, Conference Track Proceedings. OpenReview.net (2018). https://openreview.net/forum?id=rJzIBfZAb
32. Moosavi-Dezfooli, S.M., Fawzi, A., Fawzi, O., Frossard, P.: Universal adversarial perturbations. In: Proceedings of the IEEE Conference on Computer Vision and Pattern Recognition, pp. 1765–1773 (2017)
33. Moosavi-Dezfooli, S., Fawzi, A., Frossard, P.: DeepFool: a simple and accurate method to fool deep neural networks. In: 2016 IEEE Conference on Computer Vision and Pattern Recognition, CVPR 2016, Las Vegas, NV, USA, 27–30 June 2016, pp. 2574–2582. IEEE Computer Society (2016). https://doi.org/10.1109/CVPR.2016.282
34. Pan, X., Zhang, M., Sheng, B., Zhu, J., Yang, M.: Hidden trigger backdoor attack on NLP models via linguistic style manipulation. In: 31st USENIX Security Symposium (USENIX Security 2022), pp. 3611–3628. USENIX Association, Boston (2022). https://www.usenix.org/conference/usenixsecurity22/presentation/pan-hidden
35. Pang, B., Lee, L.: Seeing stars: exploiting class relationships for sentiment categorization with respect to rating scales. In: Proceedings of the ACL (2005)
36. Qi, F., Chen, Y., Li, M., Yao, Y., Liu, Z., Sun, M.: Onion: a simple and effective defense against textual backdoor attacks. arXiv preprint arXiv:2011.10369 (2020)
37. Qi, F., Chen, Y., Zhang, X., Li, M., Liu, Z., Sun, M.: Mind the style of text! adversarial and backdoor attacks based on text style transfer. arXiv preprint arXiv:2110.07139 (2021)
38. Qi, F., Yao, Y., Xu, S., Liu, Z., Sun, M.: Turn the combination lock: Learnable textual backdoor attacks via word substitution. arXiv preprint arXiv:2106.06361 (2021)
39. Radford, A., et al.: Language models are unsupervised multitask learners. OpenAI Blog 1(8), 9 (2019)
40. Sanh, V., Debut, L., Chaumond, J., Wolf, T.: DistilBERT, a distilled version of BERT: smaller, faster, cheaper and lighter. arXiv preprint arXiv:1910.01108 (2019)
41. Shafahi, A., et al.: Adversarial training for free! In: Wallach, H.M., Larochelle, H., Beygelzimer, A., d'Alché-Buc, F., Fox, E.B., Garnett, R. (eds.) Advances in Neural Information Processing Systems 32: Annual Conference on Neural Information Processing Systems 2019, NeurIPS 2019, Vancouver, BC, Canada, 8–14 December 2019, pp. 3353–3364 (2019). https://proceedings.neurips.cc/paper/2019/hash/7503cfacd12053d309b6bed5c89de212-Abstract.html
42. Socher, R., et al.: Recursive deep models for semantic compositionality over a sentiment treebank. In: Proceedings of the 2013 Conference on Empirical Methods in Natural Language Processing, Seattle, Washington, USA, pp. 1631–1642. Association for Computational Linguistics (2013). https://www.aclweb.org/anthology/D13-1170
43. Szegedy, C., et al.: Intriguing properties of neural networks. In: Bengio, Y., LeCun, Y. (eds.) 2nd International Conference on Learning Representations, ICLR 2014,

Banff, AB, Canada, 14–16 April 2014, Conference Track Proceedings (2014). http://arxiv.org/abs/1312.6199

44. Taori, R., et al.: Stanford alpaca: an instruction-following LLaMA model (2023)
45. Touvron, H., et al.: LLaMA: open and efficient foundation language models. arXiv preprint arXiv:2302.13971 (2023)
46. Wei, J., et al.: Emergent abilities of large language models. arXiv preprint arXiv:2206.07682 (2022)
47. Xu, W., Evans, D., Qi, Y.: Feature squeezing: detecting adversarial examples in deep neural networks. arXiv preprint arXiv:1704.01155 (2017)
48. Yan, C., Xu, Z., Yin, Z., Ji, X., Xu, W.: Rolling colors: adversarial laser exploits against traffic light recognition. In: 31st USENIX Security Symposium (USENIX Security 2022), pp. 1957–1974 (2022)
49. Yim, J., Joo, D., Bae, J., Kim, J.: A gift from knowledge distillation: fast optimization, network minimization and transfer learning. In: Proceedings of the IEEE Conference on Computer Vision and Pattern Recognition, pp. 4133–4141 (2017)
50. Zagoruyko, S., Komodakis, N.: Paying more attention to attention: improving the performance of convolutional neural networks via attention transfer. arXiv preprint arXiv:1612.03928 (2016)
51. Zhang, X., Zhao, J.J., LeCun, Y.: Character-level convolutional networks for text classification. In: NIPS (2015)

An Android Malware Detection Method Using Better API Contextual Information

Hongyu Yang[1], Youwei Wang[2], Liang Zhang[3(✉)], Ze Hu[1(✉)], Laiwei Jiang[2], and Xiang Cheng[4]

[1] School of Safety Science and Engineering, Civil Aviation University of China,
Tianjin 300300, China
zhu@cauc.edu.cn
[2] School of Computer Science and Technology, Civil Aviation University of China,
Tianjin 300300, China
[3] School of Information, University of Arizona, Tucson, AZ 85721, USA
liangzh@arizona.edu
[4] School of Information Engineering, Yangzhou University, Yangzhou 225127, China

Abstract. The vast popularity of the Android platform has fueled the rapid expansion of Android malware and existing detection methods are difficult to effectively detect malware. To address this issue, in this paper, we propose an Android malware detection method using better API contextual information (BACI). Firstly, BACI extracts the function call graph from each app. Then, we optimize the call graph by removing nodes of unknown functions while ensuring the connectivity between their predecessor and successor nodes. The optimized call graph can extract more robust API contextual information that accurately represents app behavior. Thirdly, we map the optimized call graph into a feature vector for malware detection, including three steps: call pairs extraction, call pairs abstraction, and one-hot mapping. Finally, machine learning classifiers are used for malware detection. The experimental results demonstrate that BACI greatly outperforms the existing state-of-the-art methods and can effectively detect Android malware.

Keywords: Malware detection · Function call graph · Machine learning

1 Introduction

The vast popularity of the Android platform has fueled the rapid expansion of Android malware and existing detection methods [16] are difficult to effectively detect malware. Different from the closed iOS system where users can

This research was supported by the National Natural Science Foundation of China (Grant No. 62201576, U1833107), the Scientific Research Project of the Tianjin Municipal Education Commission (Grant No. 2019KJ127), the Supporting Fund Project of the National Natural Science Foundation of China (Grant No. 3122023PT10), and the Discipline Development Funds of Civil Aviation University of China.

C. Ge and M. Yung (Eds.): Inscrypt 2023, LNCS 14527, pp. 24–36, 2024.
https://doi.org/10.1007/978-981-97-0945-8_2

only download manually reviewed apps from the app store, the Android system allows users to install unreviewed apps from any third-party platform, exposing users to a large amount of malware and causing huge losses.

Currently, most malware detection methods use the information of API invocations. The detection method using API frequency information exhibits a high false negative rate and is vulnerable to malicious attacks. The detection method that relies on the API contextual information demonstrates enhanced accuracy in identifying malicious behavior of apps. However, it faces a challenge in effectively extracting the API contextual information due to the absence of a suitable approach for handling a substantial volume of unknown function nodes within the call graph. In addition, these existing detection methods fail to consider the frequent changes of API, thereby posing challenges in effectively identifying Android malware.

Aiming at addressing the deficiencies in existing malware detection methods, we propose an Android malware detection method using better API contextual information (BACI), the contributions of this paper are summarized as follows:

- We propose a call graph optimization method. This method eliminates nodes of unknown methods that can hardly extract desired information while preserving the connectivity between their predecessor and successor nodes. If there exists a path consisting of all unknown function nodes between any two API nodes (e.g., APIx and APIy) in the call graph, APIx directly calls APIy in the optimized call graph. Call graph optimization allows the extracted API contextual information to more accurately represent the mode of app behavior.
- We propose an API abstraction method. By abstracting the API in the feature vector used for malware detection into the cluster centers, BACI is resilient to the frequent API changes in both the Android framework and malware.
- We present BACI, an Android malware detection method using better API contextual information. The average $F1$-Measure of BACI from 2012 to 2018 has reached 96.7%, which is 4.3% and 6.4% higher than MAMADROID [15] and MALSCAN [20], respectively. Our experimental results demonstrate that BACI greatly outperforms the existing state-of-the-art methods and can effectively detect Android malware.

2   Related Work

Currently, most malware detection methods are based on information of API invocations. The full name of API is the application programming interface, which is a special type of invocation that implements system functions such as network communication, Bluetooth utilization, camera operations, and so forth. API invocations' information describes the behavior of app, which is a suitable feature in learn-based malware detection.

According to different API forms in the feature vector of detection method, existing Android malware detection methods can be divided into two categories, including detection method using API frequency information and detection method using API contextual information.

2.1   Detection Method Using API Frequency Information

API frequency information is whether the API appears in the app. One-hot mapping is usually used to generate feature vectors of malware detection methods using API frequency information. The feature values corresponding to API that appear in the app to be detected are marked as 1, and the feature values corresponding to API that do not appear are marked as 0.

Arp [6] proposed Drebin, an interpretative malware detection method. Drebin uses the one-hot mapping of millions of features for malware detection, including hardware, permissions, components, API invocations, and network addresses used by the app. Daoudi [10] pointed out that 90% of the features used by Drebin are 'id-features', such as the name of components and network address. These features are named by software developers and can be changed easily at will. Therefore, Drebin is vulnerable to malicious attacks.

Aafer [3] proposed DroidAPIMiner, an Android malware detection method based on the frequency of sensitive APIs. This method performs statistical analysis on the APIs of the training set and uses APIs frequently called by malware as feature vectors for malware detection. However, many sensitive APIs are frequently used in both benign apps and malware, so DroidAPIMiner has a high false negative rate.

2.2   Detection Method Using API Contextual Information

API contextual information refers to the local information centered on API invocations in the call graph, including several callers and callees. There are many different ways to generate feature vectors for malware detection that using API contextual information.

Allen [4] proposed PikaDroid, an Android malware detection method based on the contextual information of API invocations. This paper believes that the malicious behavior of the app is the different events that sensitive APIs are invoked by. For example, when a user clicks the cancel dialog button, the probability of malware obtaining sensitive device information through the API *TelephoneManager.getDeviceID* is 11 times higher than benign apps.

MAMADROID [15] simulates the invocation relationship of the app's function call graph by constructing a Markov transfer matrix. MAMADROID also abstracts the API calls into its' packages to maintain resilience against newly introduced APIs that appeared in existing packages. However, APIs within the same package do not necessarily perform similar functions and MAMADROID cannot capture any information from APIs in the new package. Moreover, MAMADROID abstracts all unknown functions into *self-defined* methods or *obfuscated* methods, resulting in a serious loss of call graph structural information.

Wu [20] proposed MALSCAN, a malware detection method which uses the centrality information of more than 20,000 sensitive APIs listed by PScout [8] in the function call graph. However, the sensitive APIs listed by PScout were rarely used after 2016, which makes MALSCAN unable to effectively detect malware developed after 2016.

Feng [11] conducted a comparative analysis of the time overhead of different detection methods at each stage and pointed out that during the detection process, the time overhead of using FlowDroid [7] to extract function call graph from the app accounts for 95% of the total detection time cost. So that using complex neural networks will not significantly increase the time overhead of detection for detection methods based on function call graphs.

3 Android Malware Detection Method

BACI is a static malware detection method using API contextual information. Figure 1 illustrates the framework of BACI, including four steps.

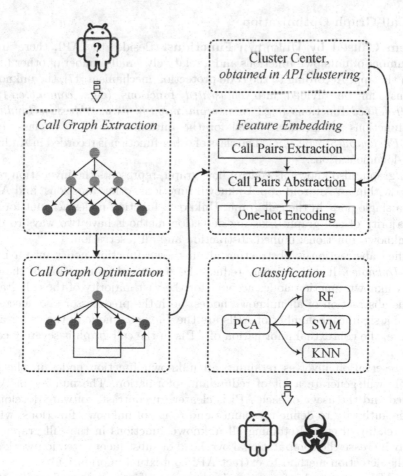

Fig. 1. Architecture of BACI.

- **Call Graph Extraction.** We employ FlowDroid [7], a widely utilized static analysis tool, to extract the function call graph from the apk file of each app to be detected.
- **Call Graph Optimization.** We optimize the call graph by deleting unknown function nodes while retaining the connectivity between their predecessor and successor nodes.
- **Feature Embedding.** Map the optimized call graph into a feature vector used for malware detection, including three steps: call pairs extraction, call pairs abstraction, and one-hot encoding.
- **Classification.** The last step is using the trained machine learning classifier to predict whether this app is benign or malicious. We select k-nearest neighbor (KNN) [12], support vector machines (SVM) [13], and random forests (RF) [9] as classifiers.

3.1 Call Graph Optimization

Problem Caused by Unknown Functions. Besides the API, there are a large number of unknown functions and a relatively small number of other functions in the app. According to the code protection mechanism [17], the unknown functions can be divided into *obfuscated* functions (e.g., *com.a.b.c.e123*) and *self-defined* functions (e.g., *com.xiaomi.mipush.sdk.pushMessageHandler*). Other functions are primarily used for the initialization of Java class (e.g., *java.io.FileOutputStream.init*). The class of other function is recorded in Android official documentations.

Call graph, also known as control flow graph, represents the invocation relationship within an Android app. Unknown functions, other functions, and APIs are all a single node in the call graph. Unknown function nodes account for the vast majority of call graph. Existing detection methods have two ways to deal with unknown functions: unified abstraction and all reservation.

Unified abstraction is abstracting all unknown function nodes into a node named *Unknown*. It will seriously reduce the structural information of the call graph. Unknown function nodes account for the vast majority of the call graph, after the abstraction of all unknown nodes, both the predecessor and successor nodes of a significant number of APIs are the *Unknown* node in the call graph. Therefore, the contextual information of APIs in the call graph is severely compromised.

All reservation involves retaining all unknown function nodes in the call graph. It will generate a lot of redundant information. The number of APIs is limited and the usage of each API is clearer. In contrast, software developers have the authority to define the names and usage of unknown functions, which can be readily altered. Retaining all unknown functions in the call graph will seriously increase the computational overhead of subsequent detection work and affect the detection method to extract API contextual information.

The API contextual information is the most effective feature in accurately representing the behavior of each app. In essence, the primary source of relevant data for malware detection lies in the local information pertaining to API invocations within a call graph. However, the large number of unknown function nodes greatly crippled the extraction of API contextual information.

Algorithm of Call Graph Optimization. In order to solve the serious difficulty in extracting API contextual information, we propose a call graph optimization method. This approach removes nodes of unknown functions that can hardly extract any useful information while preserving the connectivity between their predecessor and successor nodes. If there exists a path consisting of all unknown function nodes between any two API nodes (e.g., APIx and APIy) in the call graph, that is, APIx calls APIy by calling several unknown functions. In the optimized call graph, APIx directly calls APIy. The unknown function itself does not contain any information, or it contains a small amount of information that can hardly be extracted. However, its invocation relationship should be preserved because it reflects the behavior of app.

There are only three types of functions in the optimized call graph: entry function, API, and other functions. The invocation relationship between these three types of functions reflects the behavior of app more accurately and robustly.

Algorithm 1. Call Graph Optimization

Input: Call Graph $CG = (V, E)$, API Documents $AODs$

1: **for** each node n in nodes **do**
2:     **if** n is *entry function* **then**
3:         **continue**
4:     **end if**
5:     **if** n in $AODs$ or $n.class$ in $AODs$ **then**
6:         **continue**
7:     **end if**
8:     collect predecessor nodes of n as *callers*
9:     collect successor nodes of n as *callees*
10:     **for** each node *start* in nodes *callers* **do**
11:         **for** each node *end* in nodes *callees* **do**
12:             add edge (*start*, *end*) to CG
13:         **end for**
14:     **end for**
15:     remove node n from CG
16: **end for**
17: **return** CG

Algorithm 1 shows the pseudo-code of call graph optimization. The input of this algorithm is the call graph extracted from an app and Android official documentations. The output is the optimized call graph.

- Line 2 to 7 are used to filter the critical function nodes in the graph, including entry functions, APIs, and other functions.
- Line 8 to 9 are used to obtain the lists of predecessor nodes and successor nodes of the unknown node waiting to be deleted.

- line 10 to 14 serve the purpose of maintaining the connectivity between the lists of predecessor and successor nodes by traversing these two lists and adding a directed edge in the call graph. Every newly added edge is composed of two nodes each from these two lists respectively.
- Line 15 is used to remove the unknown node from the call graph.

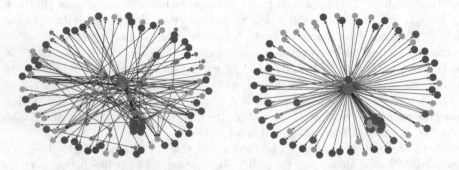

Fig. 2. Example of call graph and the optimized call graph for benign app.

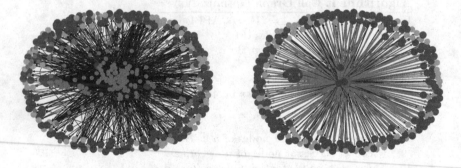

Fig. 3. Example of call graph and the optimized call graph for malicious app.

Examples of Call Graph Optimization. Figure 2 are the call graph (left) and the optimized call graph of benign app *app.eazi.ease126*. The MD5 of this app is 2149914d3284d4d0561f9d80dc1ad186. The green nodes in Fig. 2 represent entry functions, the gray nodes are unknown functions, the dark blue nodes represent the APIs recorded in Android official documents, and the light blue nodes are other functions. The red edges in Fig. 2 represent the newly discovered API cluster pairs after call graph optimization.

As shown in Fig. 2, unknown function nodes account for the majority of the call graph. These nodes seriously affect the extraction of API contextual information. Call graph optimization deletes all unknown function nodes that are difficult to identify in the graph while retaining the connectivity between API nodes. The optimized call graph enables the detection method to extract API contextual information that more accurately reflects the behavior of app.

Figure 3 shows the call graphs (left) and the optimized call graph (right) of the malicious app *de.android_telefonie.super.appmanager*. The MD5 of this app is 79a58748d8e346af229c60a6ed529ab8. This app hijacks phone calls received by device. Before optimization, a large number of APIs are invoked by gray nodes, which means that the critical APIs in the app that implement system functions, most of their local contextual information are unknown methods that are difficult to identify during the detection process.

After call graph optimization, many API call pairs that reflect the app behavior are added. Most of these call pairs are related to thread activities. Malware often disguises itself as benign app and implements malicious behavior through multi-thread activities. Figure 3 shows that the call graph optimization can enable the detection method to extract more features used in the identification of app categories.

3.2   Feature Embedding

Feature embedding is mapping the optimized call graph into a feature vector, which is finally used for classification. First, we extract function call pairs from the optimized call graph, each call pair has two functions: caller function and callee function. The functions in all function call pairs can be divided into three categories: API, entry function, and other function.

Then, each API is abstracted into its cluster center obtained in API clustering. API clustering is to generate API cluster centers representing the function of each API, which should be finished before Android malware detection. Figure 4 shows the architecture of API clustering, there are four steps in API clustering.

- **API Feature Extraction.** Extract features of each API from the Android official documentations. The features employed in our study encompass seven distinct categories: package, class name, method name, parameter, permission, exception, and return value.
- **API Sentence Generation.** Convert each API and its features into a sentence, called API sentence. For example, the API sentence of API named *android.telephony.TelephonyManager.getDeviceID* is 'method get device id from class telephony manager from package Android telephony use permission read phone state throw none exception use none parameter return none'.
- **API Sentence Encoding** We use the pre-trained Bert [14] model to encode each API sentence and take the encoding output of CLS as API semantic embedding. The 768-dimensional feature vector of CLS summarizes the semantic information of the entire sentence.

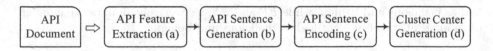

| API Document | ⇒ | API Feature Extraction (a) | → | API Sentence Generation (b) | → | API Sentence Encoding (c) | → | Cluster Center Generation (d) |

Fig. 4. Architecture of API clustering.

- **Cluster Centers Generation.** Elbow and k-Means [18] algorithms are used to generate cluster centers representing the function of API. During malware detection, API cluster centers are used to replace APIs in the feature vector of each app.

Feature embedding also involves the abstraction of other functions into their respective packages, with the entry function being designated as reserved. By abstracting APIs into the cluster centers, BACI is resilient to the API changes in both Android framework and malware. Finally, one-hot encoding is used to generate a feature vector for each app. The feature values of cluster call pairs in the optimized call graph are mapped to component one while the other components are set to zero.

4   Experiment and Analysis

4.1   Experimental Setup

Table 1 presents the summary of the datasets used in our experiment, including 42,450 malicious apps and 42,154 benign apps. The MD5 of apk we used was collected by the authors of APIGraph [21]. We downloaded malware from three open repositories, including AndroZoo [5], VirusTotal [2], and the AMD dataset [19]. All the malicious apps are marked as malicious by at least 15 antivirus engines in VirusTotal. We collect benign apps from Google Play Store [1] and download them with the help of AndroZoo. All the benign apps are marked as benign by every antivirus engine in VirusTotal.

Table 1. Summary of the datasets used in our experiments.

App	2012	2013	2014	2015	2016	2017	2018	All
Malicious (M)	4624	6519	6409	6494	6449	5388	6567	42450
Benign (B)	4418	6488	6364	6506	6474	5348	6556	42154
M + B	9042	13007	12773	13000	12923	10736	13123	84604
M/(M + B)	51.1%	50.1%	50.2%	50.0%	49.9%	50.2%	50.0%	50.2%

We choose the following widely used metrics to evaluate the performance of BACI, including *Precision, Recall*, and *F1*-Measure. $Precision = TP/(TP + FP)$, $Recall = TP/(TP + FN)$, and $F1 = 2 * Precision * Recall/(Precision + Recall)$. *TP* and *TN*, respectively, donate the number of samples correctly classified as malicious and benign, while *FP* and *FN*, respectively, donate the number of samples mistakenly identified as malicious and benign.

4.2   Malware Detection Performance

To evaluate the effectiveness of BACI on malware detection, we choose MAMADROID [15] and MALSCAN [20] as comparison methods. We conduct 10-fold cross-validations on each of the seven datasets depicted in Table 1. Figure 5 presents the detection performance achieved by different methods on each dataset, respectively.

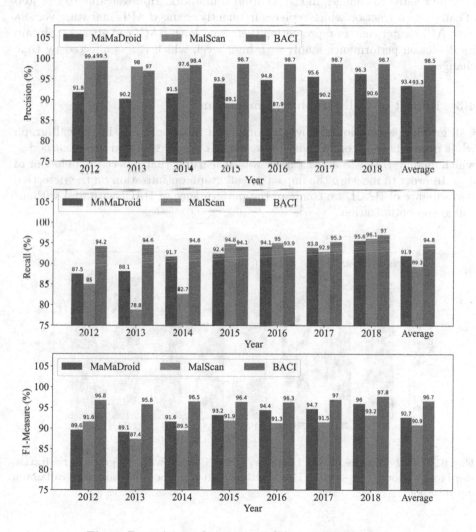

Fig. 5. Detection performance in the same period time.

Among SVM, RF, and KNN, BACI achieves the best performance with RF. The average *F1*-Measure of BACI in 7 years has reached 96.7%, which is 4.3% and 6.4% higher than MAMADROID (92.7%) and MALSCAN (90.9%), respectively; The average *Precision* of BACI is 98.5%, which is 5.5% and 5.6% higher than MAMADROID and MALSCAN respectively; The average *Recall* of BACI is 94.8%, which is 3.2% and 6.2% higher than MAMADROID and MALSCAN respectively.

It can be seen that all the metrics of MAMADROID increase slowly over time. MALSCAN has higher *Precision* and lower *Recall* between 2012 and 2014, but lower *Precision* and higher *Recall* between 2015 and 2018. Such phenomena may be related to changes in the Android framework. However, due to the step of call pair abstraction which replaces frequently changed APIs in feature vectors with API cluster centers representing their functions, BACI can always maintain its detection performance stably at a high level, which is less affected by time changes.

4.3   Impact of Call Graph Optimization

Call graph optimization removes all unknown function nodes in the call graph while preserving the connectivity between their predecessor and successor nodes, which enables BACI to extract more robust features that reflect the behavior of app. In order to measure the impact of call graph optimization on the detection performance of BACI, we compare the performance of BACI with and without call graph optimization.

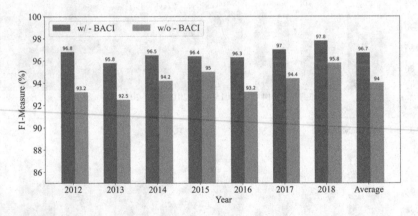

Fig. 6. The *F1*-Measure of BACI with (w/ - BACI: BACI with call graph optimization step) and without (w/o - BACI: BACI without call graph optimization step) call graph optimization

It can be seen from Fig. 6 that call graph optimization improves the detection performance of BACI. BACI has an average *F1*-measure of 96.7% from 2012 to 2018 with the step of call graph optimization, which is 2.9% higher than that without call graph optimization (94.0%). The experimental results show that call graph optimization is indispensable for malware detection.

5   Conclusion

The vast popularity of the Android platform has fueled the rapid expansion of Android malware and existing detection methods are difficult to effectively detect malware. We propose an Android malware detection method using better API contextual information (BACI). BACI is a static malware detection method using API contextual information. We optimize the function call graph by removing nodes corresponding to unknown functions, while ensuring the connectivity between their predecessor and successor nodes. The optimized call graph can extract more robust API contextual information that accurately represents app behavior.

We evaluate BACI on a dataset of 42K benign apps and 42K malicious apps developed over a seven-year period. The average F1-Measure of BACI in 7 seven years has reached 96.7%, which is 4.3% and 6.4% higher than MAMADROID and MALSCAN, respectively. The experimental results demonstrate that BACI greatly outperforms the existing state-of-the-art malware detection methods.

References

1. Google play store (2023). https://play.google.com/store
2. Virustotal (2023). https://www.virustotal.com/gui/home/upload
3. Aafer, Y., Du, W., Yin, H.: DroidAPIMiner: mining API-level features for robust malware detection in android. In: Zia, T., Zomaya, A., Varadharajan, V., Mao, M. (eds.) SecureComm 2013. LNICST, vol. 127, pp. 86–103. Springer, Cham (2013). https://doi.org/10.1007/978-3-319-04283-1_6
4. Allen, J., Landen, M., Chaba, S., Ji, Y., Chung, S.P.H., Lee, W.: Improving accuracy of android malware detection with lightweight contextual awareness. In: Proceedings of the 34th Annual Computer Security Applications Conference, pp. 210–221. Association for Computing Machinery (2018)
5. Allix, K., Bissyandé, T.F., Klein, J., Le Traon, Y.: AndroZoo: collecting millions of android apps for the research community. In: Proceedings of the 13th International Conference on Mining Software Repositories, pp. 468–471. Association for Computing Machinery (2016)
6. Arp, D., Spreitzenbarth, M., Hubner, M., Gascon, H., Rieck, K., Siemens, C.: DREBIN: effective and explainable detection of android malware in your pocket. In: Proceedings of the 2018 Network and Distributed Systems Security Symposium (2014)
7. Arzt, S., et al.: FlowDroid: precise context, flow, field, object-sensitive and lifecycle-aware taint analysis for android apps. ACM Sigplan Not. 49(6), 259–269 (2014)
8. Au, K.W.Y., Zhou, Y.F., Huang, Z., Lie, D.: PScout: analyzing the android permission specification. In: Proceedings of the 2012 ACM Conference on Computer and Communications Security, pp. 217–228. Association for Computing Machinery (2012)
9. Breiman, L.: Random forests. Mach. Learn. 45, 5–32 (2001)
10. Daoudi, N., Allix, K., Bissyandé, T.F., Klein, J.: A deep dive inside DREBIN: an explorative analysis beyond android malware detection scores. ACM Trans. Priv. Secur. 25(2), 1–28 (2022)

11. Feng, R., Chen, S., Xie, X., Meng, G., Lin, S., Liu, Y.: A performance-sensitive malware detection system using deep learning on mobile devices. IEEE Trans. Inf. Forensics Secur. **16**, 1563–1578 (2020)
12. Fix, E., Hodges, J.L.: Discriminatory analysis: nonparametric discrimination: small sample performance (1952)
13. Hearst, M.A., Dumais, S.T., Osuna, E., Platt, J., Scholkopf, B.: Support vector machines. IEEE Intell. Syst. Their Appl. **13**(4), 18–28 (1998)
14. Jacob, D., Ming-Wei, C., Kenton, L., Toutanova, K.: BERT: Pre-training of deep bidirectional transformers for language understanding. In: Proceedings of the 2019 NAACL-HLT, vol. 1, pp. 4171–4186. Association for Computational Linguistics (2019)
15. Mariconti, E., Onwuzurike, L., Andriotis, P., De Cristofaro, E., Ross, G., Stringhini, G.: MaMaDroid: detecting android malware by building Markov chains of behavioral models. arXiv preprint arXiv:1612.04433 (2016)
16. Qiu, J., Zhang, J., Luo, W., Pan, L., Nepal, S., Xiang, Y.: A survey of android malware detection with deep neural models. ACM Comput. Surv. **53**(6), 1–36 (2020)
17. Schulz, P.: Code protection in android. Insititute of Computer Science, Rheinische Friedrich-Wilhelms-Universitgt Bonn, Germany 110 (2012)
18. Syakur, M., Khotimah, B., Rochman, E., Satoto, B.D.: Integration k-means clustering method and elbow method for identification of the best customer profile cluster. In: Proceedings of the IOP Conference Series: Materials Science and Engineering, vol. 336, p. 012017. IOP Publishing (2018)
19. Wei, F., Li, Y., Roy, S., Ou, X., Zhou, W.: Deep ground truth analysis of current android malware. In: Polychronakis, M., Meier, M. (eds.) DIMVA 2017. LNCS, vol. 10327, pp. 252–276. Springer, Cham (2017). https://doi.org/10.1007/978-3-319-60876-1_12
20. Wu, Y., Li, X., Zou, D., Yang, W., Zhang, X., Jin, H.: MalScan: fast market-wide mobile malware scanning by social-network centrality analysis. In: Proceedings of the 34th IEEE/ACM International Conference on Automated Software Engineering, pp. 139–150. IEEE (2019)
21. Zhang, X., et al.: Enhancing state-of-the-art classifiers with API semantics to detect evolved android malware. In: Proceedings of the 2020 ACM SIGSAC Conference on Computer and Communications Security, pp. 757–770. Association for Computing Machinery (2020)

TAElog: A Novel Transformer AutoEncoder-Based Log Anomaly Detection Method

Changzhi Zhao[1,2], Kezhen Huang[3], Di Wu[4(✉)], Xueying Han[1,2], Dan Du[1,2], Yutian Zhou[5], Zhigang Lu[1,2], and Yuling Liu[1,2]

[1] Institute of Information Engineering, Chinese Academy of Sciences, Bejing 10085, China
{zhaochangzhi,hanxueying,luzhigang,liuyuling}@iie.ac.cn
[2] School of Cyber Security, University of Chinese Academy of Sciences, Beijing 100049, China
[3] Institute of Software, Chinese Academy of Sciences, Beijing 100190, China
kezhen@iscas.ac.cn
[4] China Cybersecurity Review Technology and Certification Center, Beijing, China
wudi_dlzl@163.com
[5] School of Data Science, Fudan University, Shanghai 200433, China
21300180031@m.fudan.edu.cn

Abstract. Log anomaly detection serves as an effective approach for identifying threats. Autoencoder-based detection methods address positive and negative sample imbalance issues and have been extensively adopted in practical applications. However, most existing methods necessitate a sliding window to adapt to the autoencoder's base network, leading to information confusion and diminished resilience. Furthermore, detection results may be worthless when a single log comprises numerous unbalanced log records. In response, we propose TAElog, a novel framework employing a transformer-based autoencoder designed to extract precise information from logs without the need for sliding windows. TAElog also incorporates a new loss calculation that computes both high-dimensional metrics and divergence information, enhancing detection performance in intricate situations with diverse and unbalanced log records. Moreover, our framework covers preprocessing to increase the compatibility between text and numeric logs. To verify the effectiveness of TAElog, we evaluate its performance against other methods on both textual and numerical logs. Additionally, we assess various preprocessing and loss computation approaches to determine the optimal configuration within our method. Experimental results demonstrate that TAElog not only achieves superior accuracy rates but also boasts increased processing speed.

Keywords: Self-supervised learning · Log anomaly detection · Autoencoder

1 Introduction

Log anomaly detection techniques have been widely used to discover threats in areas such as lateral movement and misapplied detection [2,3,10,11]. As

C. Ge and M. Yung (Eds.): Inscrypt 2023, LNCS 14527, pp. 37–52, 2024.
https://doi.org/10.1007/978-981-97-0945-8_3

systems and applications become more complex, the volume of log data generated increases, leading to a more diverse and imbalanced logging environment. This undermines the accuracy of current approaches in detecting anomalies. Therefore, developing automated log anomaly detection methods with a low false alarm rate is crucial. This is a vital area of research, as accurate detection is critical for identifying and responding to potential security threats, system failures, and operational issues promptly.

One branch of current solutions is the supervised learning method. It includes researches [1,8,14,16,20,21] using traditional machine learning such as SVM (Support Vector Machine), HMM (Hidden Markov Model), etc., which mainly analyze log events independently. However, features extracted through independent analysis may be limited in scope. Therefore, alternative approaches have been proposed, which focus on detecting anomalies by exploring the correlation information between log events. These approaches [13,15,22,25] choose deep learning methods, including CNN (Convolutional Neural Network) and RNN (Recurrent Neural Network) to perform contextual or graph correlation analysis on the logs.

In real-world scenarios, the data available for detecting log anomalies is often limited, leading to issues of imbalance and scarcity. The aforementioned methods typically do not account for these challenges, making it difficult for them to be effectively adapted and implemented in actual production environments. Then self-supervised learning methods [4,5,7,24] were introduced into the log anomaly detection field. Self-supervised learning-based methods can circumvent issues such as data imbalance, as they can detect anomalies by learning from only a limited subset of normal samples. These approaches assess the discrepancies between original log sequences and those reconstructed by the autoencoder to classify log sequences. While this strategy offers certain benefits, it still results in a notable false alarm rate.

Primarily, the issue stems from the existing autoencoders' dependence on a sliding window. To analyze lengthy and variable-length sequences, self-supervised learning methods for temporally correlated logs consistently utilize a sliding window. Although employing a sliding window can expand the dataset, it also introduces drawbacks that cannot be overlooked. When conducting anomaly detection on different logs, an optimal window size must be reselected, which adds complexity to the process. As mentioned in [23], the serial encoding and decoding processes in RNN-based autoencoder methods give rise to inconsistencies in the output, compromising the method's robustness. Besides, the use of sliding windows can lead to ambiguous event location information, as it only provides the model with the information contained within the window, rather than the global context. Consequently, critical global context information may be overlooked by existing methods

The current reconstruction error calculation processes may also pose challenges during anomaly detection. Autoencoder-based methods typically employ classification to compare the original sequence with the reconstructed one. For data exhibiting an imbalanced category distribution, the point-to-point comparison employed by classification methods inadequately accounts for the information at hand, yielding unsatisfactory results. This issue highlights the need for a novel comparison method in detecting anomalies.

Hence, we adopt an innovative method to address these two challenges. Our novel approach utilizes full-session input and self-attention to solve the lengthy or variable-length input without relying on sliding window. Moreover, our method augments the information involved in the reconstruction error operations and makes it more suited for anomaly detection in imbalanced log records. Overall, our contributions are as follows:

- In this paper, we introduce a novel framework, TAElog, designed for single-source log anomaly detection. With TAElog's transformer-based autoencoder, the realization of directly processing the entire *session* becomes a reality, effectively bypassing information confusion while using sliding windows. Additionally, the framework's preprocessing capabilities facilitate the application of the detection process across various log types, further enhancing its utility.
- We convert the idea of calculating reconstruction errors from single points into high-dimensional spaces, enabling the inclusion of more information for computing reconstruction errors. Our approach synergistically integrates the vector's distance and distribution calculations within the loss function. This combination not only relieves the problem of diversity and imbalance in log events but also enhances the robustness of the detection process.
- We evaluate TAElog and other existing methods on two distinct datasets, while also comparing the performance of various configurations on our framework. The experimental results conclusively demonstrate that TAElog outperforms other approaches in terms of both accuracy and efficiency.

2   Related Works

In recent years, deep learning-based anomaly detection methods have garnered significant interest. The LogRobust method [25] employs a BiLSTM (Bi-directional Long Short Term Memory) algorithm to manage unstable log events and sequences. This algorithm autonomously learns the importance of different log timings, enhancing the robustness and accuracy of log anomaly detection approaches. Lu et al. [15] utilized a log key and a CNN-based (Convolutional Neural Network) algorithm. Their study employed log key embedding as the input to the model, performing two-level parsing on raw log data to sequentially extract log keys and sequence features. This aimed to uncover complex connections hidden within the logs. LightLog [18], a lightweight temporal convolutional network, focuses on efficient and accurate log anomaly detection for edge devices. It carries out convolutional and pooling operations to ultimately generate a probability vector, which is used to detect anomalies by comparing predicted and true values. Yen et al. [22] successfully addressed the concept drift issue [6] in anomaly detection by leveraging the advantages of CNN in spatial feature extraction and LSTM in contextual feature extraction. However, these solutions did not discuss the problem of imbalanced positive and negative samples, limiting their applicability in real-world scenarios and hindering their transferability.

Self-supervised log anomaly detection approaches, similar to the one presented in this study, possess a natural advantage in addressing the issue of positive and negative sample imbalance and are better suited for deployment in new scenarios. DeepLog [7] is an LSTM-based log anomaly detection method that is trained on a subset of normal log sequences. The detection process employs a sliding window to predict the next log event, and if the subsequent event has a low probability in the predicted distribution, it is classified as an anomaly. This approach also supports online anomaly detection. Borghesi et al. [4] introduced an autoencoder-based anomaly detection method for identifying anomalous activity in high-performance computers. Yoo et al. [23] proposed a technique to mitigate the negative impact of input window size length by incorporating an enhanced self-attention mechanism, hidden state forcing, and skip transitions. DabLog [24] explores a log anomaly detection method that utilizes an LSTM autoencoder for prediction. This approach employs a word embedding technique to mine log data and improves log event prediction by considering not only preceding events but also subsequent ones, providing a direct probability distribution projection for each position. AutoLog [5] leverages a deep autoencoder instead of an RNN class to learn the typical behavior of syslogs and assess discrepancies. Most of these methods rely on the sliding window technique and do not address the imbalance of within log, which restrains their effectiveness in certain applications. So in our method, we deprecate the sliding windows and propose a new self-encoder using the transformer's structure to better handle the data after removing the sliding window.

3   Methods

3.1   Preliminaries

Our paper emphasizes the inherent relationships between various log records, and a single log entry might be perceived as normal in one sequence while appearing abnormal in another. Consequently, identifying anomalies based on individual log records is challenging. It necessitates an examination of the interconnected log records arising from a comprehensive activity. For better expression, we give the following definition. As illustrated in Fig. 1(a), we assign each log record to an explicit event. For Fig. 1(b), a set of log events with contextual associations is defined as a sequence. Figure 1(c) depicts the series of logs produced by a full act, which we refer to as a *session*. *Session* is the basic unit of our investigation.

3.2   Overview

Our detection framework consists of three main components, the Data processing module, the Transformer-based autoencoder module, and the Loss and Detection module, as shown in Fig. 2. In TAElog, the Data Processing module prepares

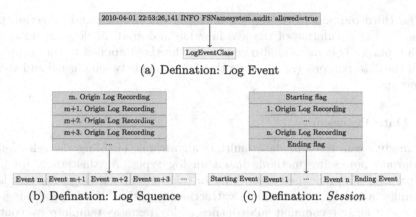

(a) Defination: Log Event

(b) Defination: Log Squence   (c) Defination: *Session*

Fig. 1. Definition: Log Sequence

input for the Transformer-based Autoencoder module, which then extracts features and creates representations that feed into the Loss and Detection module, effectively enabling a seamless flow for anomaly identification and quantification.

In our paper, we establish a data processing module to ensure uniform input for the autoencoder when analyzing various log entries. This step is crucial for achieving consistent and accurate detection of anomalies within the diverse log data.

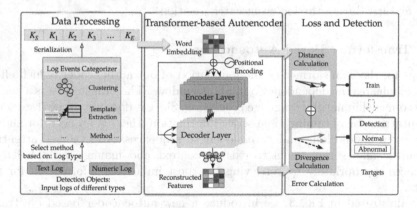

Fig. 2. The Overview of Detection TAElog

The autoencoder module is the core component of our detection method, which not only performs high-dimensional encoding but also reconstructs the *session* by extracting contextual information. The target of the autoencoder reconstruction is the set of features that the input *session* should have under normal behavior.

The third component of TAElog manages the training and detection processes, for the calculation of the loss function and gradient descent during the training phase. This module also employs a threshold applied to the computed loss in the detection process, enabling the distinction between normal and abnormal events.

3.3 Data Processing

This module can accommodate multiple algorithms, enabling the selection of appropriate processing methods based on log types. At this stage, we have incorporated two predefined algorithms for text and numeric logs. For text logs, we employ a widely used template extraction algorithm. While processing, we extract the longest common subsequence of log texts as template by content matching between log text. Then the algorithm groups log records with the same template into identical event types. And we apply clustering for numeric logs which contain various valuable features. We choose the features that have contributions to distinguish different events and feed them into Affinity Propagation Clustering [9] to get multiple log tags. The reason for choosing this clustering is that researcher don't need to know the number of kinds of data in advance and define it. Following the distinct processing phase, the representation of *session* is unified, facilitating consistent calculations and processing of different log types.

Although it may seem that our event key-based input representation disregards the original log features, the module has, in fact, already incorporated these features during the log event categorization.

3.4 Transformer Based Autoencoder

We opt for the Transformer as the foundation of our autoencoder, which effectively eliminates the dependency on sliding windows. The Transformer is a widely adopted model in natural language processing. Since it does not necessitate serial computations for obtaining time series information, there is no need for sliding windows to handle long and variable-length sequences. And the self-attention mechanism allows the model to extract context and manage variable-length sequences appropriately by retrieving the most influential information for the results.

As illustrated in Fig. 3, we introduce a new autoencoder based on Transformer. In our model, we deviate from the conventional transformer structure where the encoder and decoder handle separate source and target data. Instead, we adopt a self-supervised learning task to reconstruct sequences, resulting in the source and target data becoming identical. This allows us to seamlessly connect the input flow to both the encoder and decoder after word embedding and positional encoding, facilitating a unified learning process. So our model effectively utilizes self-supervised learning to converge the encoder and decoder, producing comprehensive and accurate representations of the input sequences. By maintaining this flow during the testing phase, we can keep parallelism because we

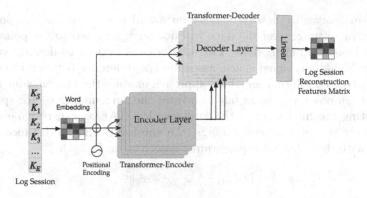

Fig. 3. The Structure of Transformer-based Encoder

still know the ground truth is the input. Furthermore, the model is designed to generate reconstructed features of the same shape as the word embedding. The specific computing of encoder is represented by Eq. (1) where X denotes the input matrix, A_e is the attention information, LN indicates the layer normalization and FFN (Feed Forward Network) function's details are provided in Eq. (2). In FFN equation, W_1 and W_2 are the weight matrices, and b_1 and b_2 are the bias.

$$KV = LN(FFN(LN(X + A_e) + A_e)) \tag{1}$$

$$FFN(x) = Relu(xW_1 + b_1)W_2 + b_2 \tag{2}$$

A slight distinction exists between the decoder and the encoder. In the decoder, the attention A_d is derived from the computation involving the encoder's output KV and the preceding layer's attention Q. The decoding process is shown in Eq. (3). And $\hat{X}$ represents the reconstructed features in Eq. (4), where W_o is the weight and b_o stands for the bias in the linear layer.

$$s = LN(FFN(LN(Q + A_d) + A_d)) \tag{3}$$

$$\hat{X} = sW_o + b_o \tag{4}$$

We use sine and cosine methods to encode position as shown in Eq. (5) and (6):

$$PE_{(pos,2i)} = sin(pos/10000^{2i/d_{model}}) \tag{5}$$

$$PE_{(pos,2i+1)} = cos(pos/10000^{2i/d_{model}}) \tag{6}$$

where *pos* represents the position, i is the dimension and d_{model} is the dimension of the word embedding vectors.

3.5   Loss and Detection

We adapt the reconstruction error calculation method from continuous data to discrete data by removing the original softmax layer. The original structure has a softmax layer to classify discrete data and makes the data to point. By removing the softmax layer the data will not be aggregated to the point, so we can treat it as continuous data. This allows this method to directly compute the loss in high-dimensional space, assessing the difference between the original and reconstructed information. This approach enables the autoencoder to learn not only from observed events but also from the surrounding vector space. By manipulating the final layer of the autoencoder, TAElog can reshape outputs to match the size of word embeddings. We employ Euclidean distance for this purpose, with the calculation procedures described in Eq. (7).

$$D_d(x_i, \hat{x}_i) = \|x - \hat{x}_i\|^2 \tag{7}$$

In high-dimensional computations, the autoencoder might generate multiple vectors with the same distance as the original vector, yet with inconsistent information across dimensions. This inconsistency could reduce robustness. For instance, as illustrated in Fig. 4, vectors α and γ have the same distance to vector β in two-dimensional space, but they exhibit different information in dimensions. To avoid this issue, we also use a different calculation for the distribution of vectors across individual dimensions. Kullback-Leibler divergence [12] is used to evaluate the error in this part, which can be expressed as follows:

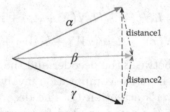

Fig. 4. Difference Vectors of Same Distance. In this 2D space, the distance between α and β is equal to the distance between γ and β, yet these two vectors are distinct. For a single log event, we aim for its reconstruction to be as unique as possible within the same distance range.

$$D_{KL}(x_i\|\hat{x}_i) = \Sigma_j^N x_{ij} log \frac{x_{ij}}{\hat{x}_{ij}} \tag{8}$$

We also make certain modifications to the final loss function to prevent averaging the losses at each position within one *session* and to accelerate training on lengthy *sessions*. So the largest loss in the *session* is considered as the actual loss for the entire *session*. Our final loss computation procedure is as follows:

$$Loss = max(D_d(X, \hat{X}) + D_{KL}(X\|\hat{X})) \tag{9}$$

4 Experiments

4.1 Datasets

Our experimental procedures strive to not only validate the effectiveness of TAElog but also to demonstrate its adaptability to various types of logs. Thus, our dataset originates from two sources: textual logs and numerical logs.

Text Log and Processing. For the textual log, we utilize the HDFS syslog dataset [21] for validation. This dataset was generated from map-reduce work, encompassing several operational anomalies. The log records in this dataset can be classified into 28 event categories, and we divide *sessions* based on distinct system operations, referencing previous work [19] on this dataset. To validate the transfer capability, we reduce the proportion of normal *sessions* used for training. The training *sessions* comprise approximately 6.

Numeric Log and Processing. We employ the UNSW-NB15 [17] traffic logs, selecting the logs from the first day as our dataset. This dataset monitors the transfer of network data streams between hosts and encompasses various cyber-attacks, such as exploits, DoS, reconnaissance, and more. The dataset provides 50 critical data stream features, from which we choose 'protocol', 'state', 'service', 'is ftp login', 'is sm ips ports', 'ct ftp cmd', 'ct flw http mthd', 'trans depth', and 'spkts' for clustering. Table 1 presents the event type statistics for each protocol. We also employ different time intervals, including 180 s, 300 s, and 600 s, to divide *sessions*.

Table 1. Log Event Types Statistics on Protocol

Protocols	arp	udp	tcp	ospf	sctp	mobile	pim	sun-nd	swipe	others	total
Count of Type	3	8	25	2	2	2	2	2	2	126	174

4.2 Setup and Evaluation Criteria

We establish various methods for comparison with the new autoencoder. Table 2 displays all the models involved in the experiments.

In assessing these methods, we use Precision, Recall, and F_1 scores as performance metrics. We opt not to use Accuracy due to the significant imbalance between positive and negative samples present in the dataset.

Table 2. The Methods and Descriptions

Method	Description	Datasets
Deeplog [7]	It originates from DeepLog [7] and it predicts the probability of the next event by sliding the window input LSTM	HDFS UNSW-NB15
DabLog [24]	This method predicts all the logs from the sliding window and is structurally formed by adding a softmax layer to the LSTM-Encoder method	UNSW-NB15
LSTM-Encoder	It is an autoencoder model explained by LSTM to reconstruct *session*	HDFS UNSW-NB15
TAElog-180 s TAElog-300 s TAElog-600 s	These three are used in traffic logs to distinguish distinct *session* division, with intervals of 180 s, 300 s, and 600 s	UNSW-NB15
TAElog$_{eu}$ TAElog$_{cos}$	These two represent the two different metrics given by the formulas (7) and (10) respectively	HDFS

Table 3. Evaluation on Different Datasets

Datasets	Methods	Precision	Recall	F_1
HDFS	DeepLog [7]	89.75%	91.56%	90.64%
	LSTM-Encoder	88.43%	99.51%	93.64%
	TAElog	**93.51%**	**99.54%**	**96.43%**
UNSW-NB15	DeepLog [7]	60.46%	82.17%	69.67%
	DabLog [24]	69.93%	**94.16%**	80.25%
	LSTM-Encoder	60.10%	80.22%	68.71%
	TAElog	**82.27%**	80.10%	**81.17%**

4.3 Results and Analysis

Validity Evaluation Experiments. First, we compare TAElog with other methods using two datasets. For the traffic data, we employ a 180-s interval to generate the *sessions*. The results, presented in Table 3, demonstrate that our approach outperforms the others on both datasets. This not only validates that our approach successfully eliminates the adverse effects brought about by the sliding window, but also confirms the efficacy of the method employed for addressing the issue of multi-class imbalance in log events.

Table 4. Evaluation of Different Configurations on TAElog

Datasets	Methods	Precision	Recall	F_1
HDFS	TAElog$_{cos}$	93.29%	92.02%	92.65%
	TAElog$_{eu}$	**93.51%**	**99.54%**	**96.43%**
UNSW-NB15	TAElog-180 s	**82.27%**	80.10%	**81.17%**
	TAElog-300 s	62.20%	80.47%	70.16%
	TAElog-600 s	57.48%	**81.21%**	67.31%

Configuration Experiments. Then we evaluate the performance of our method internally. Initially, we compare the Euclidean distance with Cosine distance (10) on the HDFS dataset. Additionally, we explore three *session* segmentation strategies on the traffic log data, utilizing a consistent Euclidean metric. The results are shown in Table 4. This table reveals that the Euclidean distance calculation tends to yield better detection outcomes. Moreover, our model exhibited the best performance on traffic log partitioned with a 180-s interval. We analyze that the reason for this is that the 180-s *session* segmentation interval for the traffic logs may more accurately reflect the division of true behavior. Furthermore, based on the evaluation metrics and classification outcomes, we can conclude that the ROC curves depicted in Fig. 5(b) offer limited insight when dealing with imbalanced data.

$$D_{cos}(x, \hat{x}) = 1 - \frac{x \cdot \hat{x}}{|x||\hat{x}|} \tag{10}$$

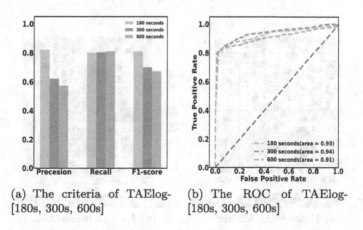

(a) The criteria of TAElog-[180s, 300s, 600s]

(b) The ROC of TAElog-[180s, 300s, 600s]

Fig. 5. Comparison of Different Divisions on UNSW-NB15

Visualisation Experiments. To demonstrate that our method is capable of classifying data, we create visual representations of the matrices for normal and abnormal *sessions*. We select a normal and an abnormal *session*'s embedding and output, then scale each dimension to the same range (0–255) so they can be displayed using gray-scale plots. Figure 6 and Fig. 7 depict a comparison of normal and abnormal *sessions*, respectively. Each row in these images represents a log event, while each column signifies a unique information level. As seen in Fig. 6, the normal sequence closely resembles the original sequence after reconstruction, whereas the abnormal sequence does not, as highlighted by the enlarged section within the red box in Fig. 7. This comparison shows the effectiveness of our approach in identifying anomalies through autoencoder reconstruction.

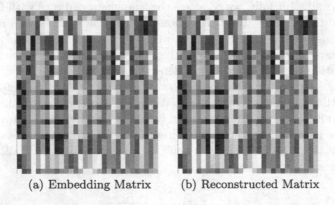

(a) Embedding Matrix   (b) Reconstructed Matrix

Fig. 6. Normal *Session* visualization. The embedding matrix is essentially equal to the output matrix.

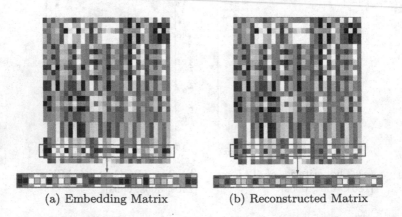

(a) Embedding Matrix   (b) Reconstructed Matrix

Fig. 7. Abnormal *Session* visualization. The embedding matrix differs from the output matrix in the red box. (Color figure online)

Detection Speed Experiments. The computational efficiency of our whole-*session*-input approach may be called into question due to the potentially lengthy inputs. To address this concern, we experiment with computational speed. We initialize several normal and abnormal *sessions*, then repeat each of these *sessions* 10,000 times as input to assess the effectiveness of each model's detection. Table 5 presents the average time cost for detecting these *sessions* 10,000 times, and Fig. 8 illustrates the detection speed of the various methods. Both the table and the figure demonstrate that our approach is high-speed. The speed improvement in our approach can be primarily attributed to the elimination of the sliding window, allowing for the detection of results in a single pass without multiple sliding iterations. Additionally, the parallel processing employed by the new autoencoder also contributes to this enhancement.

Table 5. Time Cost of Different Methods in Detection Speed Experiments

Methods	Normal Repeat Cost/s	Abnormal Repeat Cost/s
DeepLog [7]	110.23	45.55
DabLog [24]	11.15	12.74
LSTM-Encoder	10.68	12.17
TAElog	**3.99**	**3.85**

Analysis. Our model's Recall may not perform as well as other models on UNSW-NB15 shown in Table 3. Although the F_1 score is a more comprehensive representation of a method's overall performance compared to recall, we still delve into investigating this particular issue within the scope of our research.

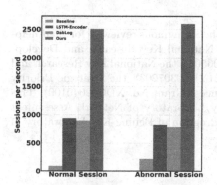

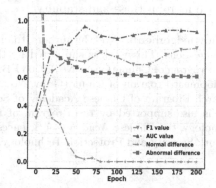

Fig. 8. Detection Speed of Different Methods

Fig. 9. Details of Each Epoch in TAElog-180 s. The 'difference' represents the average metric between original and reconstructed *session*

We believe this is partly due to the significant disparity in data proportions generated by our session segmentation and partly due to the model's mechanism or the nature of this detection method itself. To further investigate, we examine the model's training process on the optimal session segmentation with 180-second intervals, as illustrated in Fig. 9. The average loss of both normal and abnormal sessions decreases during the training process, indicating clear stratification and demonstrating that our model is capable of data separation. However, the AUC and F_1 score values fluctuate and often display a reverse trend. This may be because we use a threshold to differentiate between normal and abnormal sessions, but the model also automatically optimizes based on small changes in the loss. If the model is too strict in its detection, it will mistakenly classify normal data as abnormal, and if it is too lenient, the opposite will occur. As a result, during the self-supervised process, the model may fluctuate between strict and lenient states, causing oscillations in the metrics and preventing consistently excellent performance across all measures.

5   Conclusion and Future Works

In conclusion, our study presents TAElog, an anomaly detection method that uses a novel autoencoder and error calculation approach to address the sliding window and data imbalance issues. Through various experiments, we have shown that TAElog is effective in detecting anomalies and outperforms other methods. Additionally, our approach can be used with different log types and has a faster detection time than competing algorithms. However, we acknowledge that our current metrics are basic and plan to research more efficient metrics in the future. Moving forward, we intend to explore other models for anomaly detection that may provide better performance. Additionally, we plan to investigate the possibility of incorporating external knowledge into our model to further improve its accuracy. Lastly, we will continue to optimize our model's training process to enhance its robustness and stability.

Acknowledgements. We, the authors, thank the anonymous reviewers for their helpful suggestions. This work is supported by the National Key Research and Development Program of China (Grant No. 2020YFB1806504), the National Key Research and Development Program of China (Grant No. 2021YFF0307203), the Strategic Priority Research Program of Chinese Academy of Sciences (Grant No. XDC02040100). This work is also supported by the Program of Key Laboratory of Network Assessment Technology, the Chinese Academy of Sciences, Program of Beijing Key Laboratory of Network Security and Protection Technology.

References

1. Astekin, M., Özcan, S., Sözer, H.: Incremental analysis of large-scale system logs for anomaly detection. In: 2019 IEEE International Conference on Big Data (Big Data), pp. 2119–2127 (2019). https://doi.org/10.1109/BigData47090.2019.9006593
2. Berlin, K., Slater, D., Saxe, J.: Malicious behavior detection using windows audit logs. In: Proceedings of the 8th ACM Workshop on Artificial Intelligence and Security, pp. 35–44. Association for Computing Machinery (2015). https://doi.org/10.1145/2808769.2808773
3. Bian, H., Bai, T., Salahuddin, M.A., Limam, N., Daya, A.A., Boutaba, R.: Uncovering lateral movement using authentication logs. IEEE Trans. Netw. Serv. Manage. 18(1), 1049–1063 (2021). https://doi.org/10.1109/TNSM.2021.3054356
4. Borghesi, A., Bartolini, A., Lombardi, M., Milano, M., Benini, L.: Anomaly detection using autoencoders in high performance computing systems. In: Proceedings of the AAAI Conference on artificial intelligence, vol. 33, pp. 9428–9433 (2019). https://doi.org/10.1609/aaai.v33i01.33019428
5. Catillo, M., Pecchia, A., Villano, U.: AutoLog: anomaly detection by deep autoencoding of system logs. Expert Syst. Appl. 191, 116263 (2022). https://doi.org/10.1016/j.eswa.2021.116263
6. Dongre, P.B., Malik, L.G.: A review on real time data stream classification and adapting to various concept drift scenarios. In: 2014 IEEE International Advance Computing Conference (IACC), pp. 533–537 (2014). https://doi.org/10.1109/IAdCC.2014.6779381
7. Du, M., Li, F., Zheng, G., Srikumar, V.: DeepLog: anomaly detection and diagnosis from system logs through deep learning. In: Proceedings of the 2017 ACM SIGSAC Conference on Computer and Communications Security, CCS 2017, pp. 1285–1298. Association for Computing Machinery (2017). https://doi.org/10.1145/3133956.3134015
8. Dunia, R., Qin, S.J.: Multi-dimensional fault diagnosis using a subspace approach. In: American Control Conference, vol. 5. Citeseer (1997)
9. Frey, B.J., Dueck, D.: Clustering by passing messages between data points. Science 315(5814), 972–976 (2007)
10. Gao, Y., Ma, Y., Li, D.: Anomaly detection of malicious users' behaviors for web applications based on web logs. In: 2017 IEEE 17th International Conference on Communication Technology (ICCT), pp. 1352–1355 (2017). https://doi.org/10.1109/ICCT.2017.8359854
11. Ho, G., et al.: Hopper: modeling and detecting lateral movement. In: USENIX Security Symposium, pp. 3093–3110 (2021)
12. Kullback, S., Leibler, R.A.: On information and sufficiency. Ann. Math. Stat. 22(1), 79–86 (1951)
13. Kwon, D., Natarajan, K., Suh, S.C., Kim, H., Kim, J.: An empirical study on network anomaly detection using convolutional neural networks. In: 2018 IEEE 38th International Conference on Distributed Computing Systems (ICDCS), pp. 1595–1598 (2018). https://doi.org/10.1109/ICDCS.2018.00178
14. Li, T., Ma, J., Pei, Q., Shen, Y., Lin, C., Ma, S., Obaidat, M.S.: AClog: attack chain construction based on log correlation. In: 2019 IEEE Global Communications Conference (GLOBECOM), pp. 1–6 (2019)

15. Lu, S., Wei, X., Li, Y., Wang, L.: Detecting anomaly in big data system logs using convolutional neural network. In: 2018 IEEE 16th International Conference on Dependable, Autonomic and Secure Computing, 16th International Conference on Pervasive Intelligence and Computing, 4th International Conference on Big Data Intelligence and Computing and Cyber Science and Technology Congress (DASC/PiCom/DataCom/CyberSciTech), pp. 151–158 (2018)
16. Meng, W., et al.: Device-agnostic log anomaly classification with partial labels. In: 2018 IEEE/ACM 26th International Symposium on Quality of Service (IWQoS), pp. 1–6 (2018). https://doi.org/10.1109/IWQoS.2018.8624141
17. Moustafa, N., Slay, J.: UNSW-NB15: a comprehensive data set for network intrusion detection systems (UNSW-NB15 network data set). In: 2015 Military Communications and Information Systems Conference (MilCIS), pp. 1–6 (2015). https://doi.org/10.1109/MilCIS.2015.7348942
18. Wang, Z., Tian, J., Fang, H., Chen, L., Qin, J.: LightLog: a lightweight temporal convolutional network for log anomaly detection on the edge. Comput. Netw. **203**, 108616 (2022)
19. wuyifan18: Deeplog (2019). https://github.com/wuyifan18/DeepLog
20. Xu, W., Huang, L., Fox, A., Patterson, D., Jordan, M.: Online system problem detection by mining patterns of console logs. In: 2009 Ninth IEEE International Conference on Data Mining, pp. 588–597 (2009). https://doi.org/10.1109/ICDM.2009.19
21. Xu, W., Huang, L., Fox, A., Patterson, D., Jordan, M.I.: Detecting large-scale system problems by mining console logs. In: Proceedings of the ACM SIGOPS 22nd Symposium on Operating Systems Principles, SOSP 2009, pp. 117–132. Association for Computing Machinery, New York (2009). https://doi.org/10.1145/1629575.1629587
22. Yen, S., Moh, M., Moh, T.S.: CausalConvLSTM: semi-supervised log anomaly detection through sequence modeling. In: 2019 18th IEEE International Conference on Machine Learning and Applications (ICMLA), pp. 1334–1341 (2019). https://doi.org/10.1109/ICMLA.2019.00217
23. Yoo, Y.H., Kim, U.H., Kim, J.H.: Recurrent reconstructive network for sequential anomaly detection. IEEE Trans. Cybern. **51**(3), 1704–1715 (2021). https://doi.org/10.1109/TCYB.2019.2933548
24. Yuan, L.P., Liu, P., Zhu, S.: Recompose event sequences vs. predict next events: a novel anomaly detection approach for discrete event logs. In: Proceedings of the 2021 ACM Asia Conference on Computer and Communications Security, pp. 336–348. Association for Computing Machinery (2021). https://doi.org/10.1145/3433210.3453098
25. Zhang, X., et al.: Robust log-based anomaly detection on unstable log data. In: Proceedings of the 2019 27th ACM Joint Meeting on European Software Engineering Conference and Symposium on the Foundations of Software Engineering, pp. 807–817. Association for Computing Machinery (2019). https://doi.org/10.1145/3338906.3338931

EVFLR: Efficient Vertical Federated Logistic Regression Based on Batch Operations

Dong Chen[1,2], Zhiyuan Qiu[3], and Guangwu Xu[1,2,3,4]($\boxtimes$)

[1] Key Laboratory of Cryptologic Technology and Information Security of Ministry of Education, Qingdao 266237, China
gxu4sdq@sdu.edu.cn
[2] School of Cyber Science and Technology, Shandong University, Qingdao 266237, China
[3] Shandong Institute of Blockchain, Jinan 250101, China
[4] Quan Cheng Laboratory, Jinan 250103, China

Abstract. Vertical federated learning (VFL), where multiple partici pants with non-overlapping features for the same set of instances jointly train models, plays an increasingly important role in federated learning. This paper discusses vertical federated logistic regression (VFLR), one of the most popular VFL models. In existing VFLR solutions, homomor phic encryption (HE) is widely used to guarantee privacy. However, HE also entails huge communication and computation burdens. To solve this problem, we propose a method of packaging data by applying the Chinese remainder representation (CRR) to encode multiple smaller numbers into a single larger number through modulo operations. The classical Chinese Remainder Theorem shows that this process of packaging is a one-to-one correspondence in a certain range and preserves algebraic operations like addition and multiplication. Hence, it fits well with VFLR involving matrix multiplication. As far as we know, this is the first batch operation method that supports multiplication in federated learning. Additionally, the dACIQ clipping technique and the multiplicative symmetric quanti zation method are adopted to eliminate the obstacles in CRR application. The effectiveness of our method has also been confirmed through exten sive experiments, showing a reduction in traffic between participants of 32–54 times while achieving a training speedup of 3.6–14.6 times.

Keywords: Vertical federated learning · Logistic regression · Homomorphic encryption · Chinese remainder representation

1 Introduction

Machine learning models are widely used today due to their powerful functions, such as credit risk assessment in banks, disease detection in hospitals, and envi ronmental awareness in autonomous driving. The latest AIGC model, ChatGPT, has caused even more of a stir. However, training an accurate and robust machine learning model requires much data from diverse sources. Due to the sensitivity

C. Ge and M. Yung (Eds.): Inscrypt 2023, LNCS 14527, pp. 53–72, 2024.
https://doi.org/10.1007/978-981-97-0945-8_4

of the data and legal regulations [31], the data cannot be shared directly, which brings significant challenges to training high-quality machine learning models.

To address this challenge, federated learning (FL) was proposed [23]. FL allows multiple participants to train machine learning models collaboratively while keeping their private datasets locally. Participants only need to upload intermediate results (gradients, model parameters, or residuals) instead of raw data. Based on the distribution of data, FL can be divided into three broad categories: horizontal federated learning (HFL), vertical federated learning (VFL), and federated transfer learning (FTL) [35]. In HFL, participants' datasets share the same feature space but differ in sample space. In VFL, participants' datasets share the same sample space but different feature space. VFL has a broader application in the real world [19,33], especially when participants are from different types of organizations (hospitals and banks).

Logistic Regression (LR) [18] is an excellent classification model with strong interpretation and high efficiency. Vertical federated LR (VFLR) can combine data from different organizations so that the trained model is of higher quality while protecting the data privacy of each organization. For example, a bank works with a local Internet firm to obtain users' online characteristics, such as the number of investment software installations, to predict their creditworthiness more accurately. Therefore, it is of great significance to study VFLR.

In the existing VFLR solutions [16,17,30,36], HE is widely used to prevent privacy leakage from the intermediate results. It provides a high-level security guarantee and lossless computation. However, HE will bring a large amount of extra burden. On the one hand, the communication cost is very high, i.e., the data after HE will inflate significantly, Zhang et al. [37] have shown which is often tens or even hundreds of times the plaintext case. On the other hand, the computation burden is tremendous, i.e., HE causes a lot of modular exponentiation or other complex operations, which is very time-consuming. About eighty percent of the computing time is spent on HE [5,12]. Hence with HE, one has to investigate ways of reducing the extra computational burden and communication burden in order to be applied to VFLR realistically.

To deal with this problem, Cai et al. [5] leveraged principle component analysis (PCA) to reduce raw data dimensions to reduce the number of calls to various HE operations. Li et al. [21] proposed a double-end sparse compression (DESC) technique based on Top-K AllReduce sparse algorithm to save communication traffic volume by compressing the sparsity data transmitted between active party and passive parties. These two methods, however, have indeterminacy as PCA and DESC will reduce the amount of information, which may decrease model accuracy, which might not be acceptable in some scenarios since VFL (cross-silo FL) requires high model performance [19,35].

This paper proposes an almost lossless method based on Chinese remainder representation (CRR) to solve the efficiency problem when applying HE. Chinese Remainder Theorem (CRT) is a classical result in number theory that establishes a correspondence between regular integer representation and CRR that preserves mathematical operations. It has been used in many cryptographic applications to speed up encryption/decryption. A deeper level of fundamental duality revealed by CRT has been used by Beame, Cook, and Hoover in their framework of parallel arithmetic operations [3]. The rich algebraic structure of CRR is also used in our approach by encoding several pieces of (smaller) data into a single (bigger) data. This is essentially the CRR, and we call it packaging. It supports addition and multiplication. Although there have been some previous attempts [14, 38] to use CRR to improve FL efficiency, our treatments are different from them in two aspects. Firstly, prior works only used CRR for HFL involving vector addition, simply packaging gradients that needed to be transmitted. On this basis, we further explore the packaging scheme of using CRR for VFLR involving matrix multiplication. Specifically, we package both the raw data and the intermediate results according to specific rules so that they can be applied to VFLR. Secondly, the previous works only stated the idea of CRR packaging but did not give a viable implementation. CRR, for example, requires bounded positive integers, while data in FL are floating-point numbers without bounds. To bridge the gap, we use the state-of-the-art clipping technique dACIQ [37] and a multiplicative symmetric quantization method. Experiments show that our method is lossless when appropriate parameters are chosen.

The contributions of this paper can be summarized as follows:

- We propose a novel packaging method based on CRR for VFLR. To the best of our knowledge, this is the first batch calculation scheme that supports multiplication in FL.
- To make the data available for CRR encoding, we first use dACIQ to determine the range of datasets and intermediate results, then use multiplicative symmetric quantization to get bounded integers.
- We conduct a comprehensive experiment and analyze our scheme from multiple angles. The final experiments show that our scheme can achieve about 3.6–14.6 times training speedup and reduce 32–54 times communication burden between participants without at the expense of accuracy.

2   Related Work

2.1   Packaging Methods in FL

There are also batch operation approaches in other FL models. The authors of [12, 27, 37] proposed a packaging method for HFL, the core idea is to obtain quantized gradient values and then concatenate multiple (quantized) values to a single value, with values in concatenation being separated by a serial of zeros. For vertical federated XGBoost, the authors of [6, 34] encoded the first-order derivative and the second-order derivative into a single number for encryption. Fu et al. [15] analyzed the characteristics of GDBT and proposed a customized histogram packaging method based on re-ordered and polynomial transformation. However, all the above methods only support addition, not multiplication, so they cannot be used for VFLR.

Although some packaging methods in full homomorphic encryption support multiplication, such as SIMD in CKKS [7], they are only applicable to lattice-based cryptosystems. Our method is a general approach at the data processing level in FL and does not conflict with the use of SIMD.

2.2 Chinese Remainder Representation

One of the applications of CRR is to map a larger number as a vector of smaller numbers, and then perform parallel computation [3,8,10]. But in this article, we take the opposite approach, decrease the frequency of invoking HE operations by encoding multiple smaller numbers into one larger number.

2.3 Privacy Protection Methods in FL

In addition to HE, several other privacy protection methods are used in FL. Such as differential privacy (DP), pairwise additive mask (PAM), secret sharing (SS), and trusted execution environments (TEE). DP ensures privacy by adding noise to transmitted data. It can be used for HFL [32] and VFL [28]. Despite its high efficiency, the noise introduced can affect model performance, and even some recent works have shown that it does not provide a high level of security. The authors of [4] proposed PAM to protect participants' privacy. The idea is that every two participants negotiate a seed key, then generate a vector of random numbers with the same dimension as the gradient by the seed key and the pseudo-random generator (PRG). Such vectors are treated as masks to cover the original gradients, and the masks will be cancelled after aggregation. But PAM can only be used for HFL involving vector addition. The authors of [9,11] introduced SS, which splits the transmitted data into multiple shares and distributes them across multiple servers. But a big drawback is that its complex architecture demands several servers which leaves a greater potential risk. In some recent studies, TEE has also been used for FL [24,25]. It requires special hardware support and may be vulnerable to a certain attack, which couldn't provide a strong privacy guarantee to participants. Therefore, compared with them, HE is a better choice for VFLR.

3   Background and Preliminaries

3.1   Chinese Remainder Representation

Let $\mathcal{M} = \{m_1, m_2, \ldots, m_r\}$ be a set of pairwise co-prime integers and $M = \prod_{i=1}^{r} m_i$. For a set of integers $x_1, x_2, \ldots, x_r$ with $0 \leq x_i < m_i$, according to the CRT, the congruence system of equations

$$\begin{cases} x \equiv x_1 \pmod{m_1} \\ x \equiv x_2 \pmod{m_2} \\ \ldots \\ x \equiv x_r \pmod{m_r} \end{cases}$$

has a unique solution: $x = \sum_{i=1}^{r} x_i u_i \frac{M}{m_i} \pmod{M}$ with $0 \le x < M$, where $u_i = (M/m_i)^{-1} \pmod{m_i}$, u_i can be computed using the extended Euclidean algorithm.

The above system is called the Chinese remainder representation based on the CRT modulus set $\mathcal{M}$, denoted by $CRR(\mathcal{M})$.

Next, we consider the following scenario: suppose there are n sets of non-negative integers. Then give the CRT modulus set $\mathcal{M}$. For the t-th ($1 \le t \le n$) set $\mathcal{X}_t = \{x_1^{(t)}, x_2^{(t)}, \ldots, x_r^{(t)}\}$ with $0 \le x_i^{(t)} < m_i$, $1 \le i \le r$. By CRT, one obtains an integer $x^{(t)} = \sum_{i=1}^{r} x_i^{(t)} u_i \frac{M}{m_i} \pmod{M}$ that satisfies the following congruence system of equations:

$$\begin{cases} x^{(t)} \equiv x_1^{(t)} \pmod{m_1} \\ x^{(t)} \equiv x_2^{(t)} \pmod{m_2} \\ \cdots \\ x^{(t)} \equiv x_r^{(t)} \pmod{m_r}. \end{cases}$$

It is useful to remark that, if all sets perform the above, we can get $x^{(1)}, x^{(2)}, \ldots, x^{(n)}$. In essence, the CRT establishes an algebraic isomorphism. In particular, it preserves addition and multiplication. For example, $x^{(1)} \cdot (x^{(2)} + x^{(3)} + \cdots + x^{(n)}) \equiv x_i^{(1)} \cdot (x_i^{(2)} + x_i^{(3)} + \cdots + x_i^{(n)}) \pmod{m_i}$, for each $i = 1, 2, \ldots, r$. In our discussion later, situations like $x_i^{(1)} \cdot (x_i^{(2)} + x_i^{(3)} + \cdots + x_i^{(n)}) < m_i$ will be of particular interest.

3.2   Multiplicative Symmetric Quantization

In this paper, we employ a multiplicative symmetric quantization method. Suppose a floating-point number a in $[-\alpha, \alpha]$ is quantized to a signed integer that can be represented by s-bit. We proportionally map the number in the floating-point range $[-\alpha, \alpha]$ to the integer range $[-(2^{s-1} - 1), 2^{s-1} - 1]$ as:

$$Q(a, \alpha, s) = round[\frac{a}{\alpha} \cdot (2^{s-1} - 1)], \tag{1}$$

where $round[\cdot]$ is the stochastic rounding function.

The product of the quantized values can approximately restore the product of the original values, and the larger s, the higher the precision. For example, a_1, a_2 are quantized to q_{a_1}, q_{a_2}, respectively, we know $\frac{q_{a_1} \cdot q_{a_2} \cdot \alpha^2}{(2^{s-1}-1)^2} \approx a_1 \cdot a_2$.

3.3   Analytical Clipping for Integer Quantization

Analytical clipping for integer quantization (ACIQ) is a state-of-the-art clipping technique that minimizes the noise caused by quantization and clipping if the data obey a normal distribution. We review this method as follows.

Banner, Nahshan, and Soudry first proposed ACIQ in the case of standard rounding and generic asymmetric quantization [1]. Subsequently, Zhang et al.

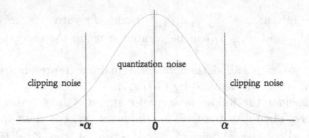

Fig. 1. Normal distribution.

extended it to dACIQ with stochastic rounding and symmetric quantization in distributed setting [37]. We adopt the extended method dACIQ.

As shown in Fig. 1, assume a set of floating-point numbers follows a normal distribution $X \sim N(0, \sigma^2)$, with a probability density function $f(x)$. The object is to quantize the floating-point numbers to s-bit integers uniformly with as small accumulated noise as possible. We know that quantization requires a range, so before quantization, the floating-point numbers are clipped to $[-\alpha, \alpha]$ according to $\text{clip}(x, \alpha)$ function:

$$\text{clip}(x, \alpha) = \begin{cases} x & \text{if } |x| \leq \alpha \\ \text{sign}(x) \cdot \alpha & \text{if } |x| > \alpha. \end{cases} \tag{2}$$

After determining the range $[-\alpha, \alpha]$, we can proportionally quantize the numbers in the floating-point range $[-\alpha, \alpha]$ to the integer range $[-(2^{s-1}-1), 2^{s-1}-1]$ just like Eq. (1).

In the above process, the accumulated noise comes from the clipping noise, which refers to the error caused by the clipped numbers outside $[-\alpha, \alpha]$, and the quantization noise, which refers to the error caused by the rounding of the numbers inside $[-\alpha, \alpha]$ during the quantization process. Let q_i be the i-th quantization level, $\Delta = \frac{2\alpha}{2^s}$. We evaluate the accumulated noise using the mean-square-error as follows:

$$E[(X - Q(X))^2] = \int_{-\infty}^{-\alpha} f(x) \cdot (x + \alpha)^2 \, dx + \int_{\alpha}^{\infty} f(x) \cdot (x - \alpha)^2 \, dx$$

$$+ \sum_{i=1}^{2^s-3} \int_{q_i}^{q_{i+1}} f(x) \cdot [(x - q_i)^2 \cdot (\frac{q_{i+1} - x}{\Delta}) + (x - q_{i+1})^2 \cdot (\frac{x - q_i}{\Delta})] \, dx \tag{3}$$

$$\approx (\alpha^2 + \sigma^2) \cdot [1 - \text{erf}(\frac{\alpha}{\sqrt{2}\sigma})] - \frac{\sqrt{2}\alpha \cdot \sigma \cdot e^{-\frac{\alpha^2}{2 \cdot \sigma^2}}}{\sqrt{\pi}} + \frac{2\alpha^2 \cdot (2^s - 2)}{3 \cdot 2^{3s}},$$

where the first term represents the quantization noise, and the second and the third terms represent the clipping noise.

Hence, as long as we know s, we can derive the optimal threshold α that minimizes the noise from Eq. (3). Specifically, when $s = 12, 16, 20$, the optimal clipping value of $\alpha = 4.89\sigma, 5.83\sigma, 6.66\sigma$, respectively.

For the details of dACIQ and the derivation of Eq. (3), refer to [1,37].

3.4 Paillier Homomorphic Encryption

Paillier HE [26] is a well-known HE method where the homomorphic property is with respect to the addition of plaintexts. Multiplication of plaintexts is also reflected by the exponentiation of ciphertext by a plaintext. This HE has been used in many FL algorithms. Let us describe the Paillier HE briefly:

- **Key generation and distribution.** One participant generates two random primes p, q (of about 1536 bits), then computes $n = pq$ and $\gamma = \text{lcm}(p-1, q-1)$. Choose $g = 1 + n$. Then the public key is set to be (n, g), and the private key is set to be γ. The public key and private key are distributed to other participants according to the agreement.
- **Encryption.** For any plaintext $c = m \in [0, n)$, using public key and a random number $r \in \mathbb{Z}_n^*$ compute ciphertext $[\![m]\!] = g^m r^n \pmod{n^2}$. We denote it as **Enc.**
- **Homomorphic operation.** Given two plaintexts m_1 and m_2, and their corresponding ciphertexts $[\![m_1]\!]$ and $[\![m_2]\!]$. There are two homomorphic operations in Paillier. Firstly, $[\![m_1]\!] \cdot [\![m_2]\!] \pmod{n^2} = [\![m_1 + m_2]\!]$, we call it **Madd.** Secondly, $[\![m_2]\!]^{m_1} \pmod{n^2} = [\![m_1 \cdot m_2]\!]$, we call it **Mmul.**
- **Decryption.** Given a ciphertext c, plaintext m can be recovered by $m = \frac{L(c^\lambda \bmod n^2)}{L(g^\lambda \bmod n^2)} \bmod n$, where $L(x) = \frac{x-1}{n}$. We denote it as **Dec.**

4 EVFLR

4.1 Problem Statement

In this paper, we focus on a typical HE-based VFLR framework [16], which is adopted by many real-world FL projects, such as FATE. As Fig. 2 shows, in this framework, there are three types of entities: the active party that has both a part of features and labels, the passive party that only has a part of features, and the Trusted Third Party (TTP) that is responsible for creating Paillier HE key pairs and decrypting.

Suppose K participants jointly train a logistic regression model, but only one participant has labels. Without loss of generality, we assume that the labels are located in participant K. We refer to participant K as the active party and the other participants as passive parties. The active party K has a dataset $\{\boldsymbol{x}_i^{(K)}, y_i\}_{i=1}^N, y_i \in \{-1, 1\}$, each passive party k $(k \neq K)$ has a dataset $\{\boldsymbol{x}_i^{(k)}\}_{i=1}^N$, where N is the number of training samples. Model parameters $\boldsymbol{\theta}_k$ corresponding to the feature space of $\boldsymbol{x}_i^{(k)} \in \mathbb{R}^{1 \times J_k}$, where J_k is the dimension of party k' features. Then the loss function L can be formulated as:

$$L = \frac{1}{N} \sum_{i=1}^N \log(1 + e^{-y_i \sum_{k=1}^K \boldsymbol{x}_i^{(k)} \boldsymbol{\theta}_k}) + \frac{\lambda}{2} \sum_{k=1}^K \|\boldsymbol{\theta}_k\|^2. \tag{4}$$

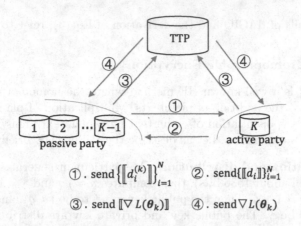

①. send $\left\{\left[\!\left[d_i^{(k)} \right]\!\right]\right\}_{i=1}^{N}$ ②. send$\{[\![d_i]\!]\}_{i=1}^{N}$

③. send $[\![\nabla L(\boldsymbol{\theta}_k)]\!]$ ④. send$\nabla L(\boldsymbol{\theta}_k)$

Fig. 2. The framework of VFLR.

Let $u_i^{(k)} = \boldsymbol{x}_i^{(k)}\boldsymbol{\theta}_k$, based on Taylor series expansion: $\log(1 + e^{-z}) \approx \log 2 - \frac{1}{2}z + \frac{1}{8}z^2 + O(z^4)$, we convert (4) into a linear function:

$$L \approx \frac{1}{N}\sum_{i=1}^{N}\left(\log 2 - \frac{1}{2}y_i\sum_{k=1}^{K} u_i^{(k)} + \frac{1}{8}(\sum_{k=1}^{K} u_i^{(k)})^2\right) + \frac{\lambda}{2}\sum_{k=1}^{K}\|\boldsymbol{\theta}_k\|^2. \qquad (5)$$

So, the gradient of each party k is:

$$\nabla L(\boldsymbol{\theta}_k) = \frac{1}{N}\sum_{i=1}^{N} d_i \boldsymbol{x}_i^{(k)} + \lambda\boldsymbol{\theta}_k = \frac{1}{N}\boldsymbol{g}^{(k)} + \lambda\boldsymbol{\theta}_k, \qquad (6)$$

where $d_i = d_i^{(K)} + \sum_{k=1}^{K-1} d_i^{(k)}$, $d_i^{(K)} = \frac{1}{4}u_i^{(K)} - \frac{1}{2}y_i$, $d_i^{(k)} = \frac{1}{4}u_i^{(k)}$. Then the model parameters updating can be expressed as:

$$\boldsymbol{\theta}_k = \boldsymbol{\theta}_k - \eta\nabla L(\boldsymbol{\theta}_k), \qquad (7)$$

until the termination condition is reached.

In VFLR framework, use Paillier HE [26] to encrypt $d_i^{(k)}$, $i = 1, 2, \ldots, N$, to prevent privacy leakage. The detail is shown in Algorithm 1.

Let's analyze the complexity of Algorithm 1. In each iteration, each passive party k ($k \neq K$) needs to call **Enc** N times, **Madd** $(N-1) \cdot J_k$ times, and **Mmul** $N \cdot J_k$ times. Active party K needs to call **Enc** N times, **Madd** $[(N-1)\cdot J_K + N\cdot(K-1)]$ times, and **Mmul** $N \cdot J_K$ times. These operations are very time-consuming, especially **Enc** and **Mmul**. They take up most of the time during the training process. Moreover, data inflation caused by Paillier HE is the main reason for increasing the communication burden. Therefore, reducing the number of calls to **Enc**, **Madd** and **Mmul** is the key to improving efficiency.

Algorithm 1: VFLR

---

1 **Initialization:**
2 the TTP creates a Paillier HE key pair and sends the public key to each party.
3 each party k initializes $\theta_1, \theta_2, \ldots, \theta_K$.
4 **for** *each iteration* $\psi = 1, 2, \ldots$ **do**
5   **for** *each party* $k = 1, 2, \ldots, K$ *in parallel* **do**
6   computes $\{[\![d_i^{(k)}]\!]\}_{i=1}^{N}$
7   **if** $k \neq K$ **then**
8   sends $\{[\![d_i^{(k)}]\!]\}_{i=1}^{N}$ to active party K
9   **end**
10   **end**
11   active party K computes and sends $\{[\![d_i]\!]\}_{i=1}^{N}$ to all passive parties
12   **for** *each party* $k = 1, 2, \ldots, K$ *in parallel* **do**
13   computes $[\![\nabla L(\theta_k)]\!]$, then sends it to TTP for decryption
14   receives $\nabla L(\theta_k)$, and updates local model according to Eq. (7)
15   **end**
16 **end**

Algorithm 2: Packaged matrix operations

    Input: $u = \{u_1, u_2, \ldots, u_r\}$, $v = \{v_1, v_2, \ldots, v_r\}$,
           $w = \{w_1, w_2, \ldots, w_r\}$, $\mathcal{M} = \{m_1, m_2, \ldots, m_r\}$
    Output: $z = \{z_1, z_2, \ldots, z_r\}$
1 $pu = \mathrm{enCRR}(u, \mathcal{M}, r)$
2 $pv = \mathrm{enCRR}(v, \mathcal{M}, r)$
3 $pw = \mathrm{enCRR}(w, \mathcal{M}, r)$
4 $z = (pu + pv) \cdot pw$
5 **for** $i = 1, 2, \ldots, r$ **do**
6      $z_i = \mathrm{deCRR}(z, m_i)$
7 **end**
8 **return** z

Algorithm 3: enCRR

    Input: a set of integers x, a CRT modulus set $\mathcal{M}$, set dimension r
    Output: x
1 **for** $i = 1, 2, \ldots, r$ **do**
2      $\tilde{x}_i = x_i \pmod{m_i}$
3 **end**

4 construct $\begin{cases} x \equiv \tilde{x}_1 \pmod{m_1} \\ x \equiv \tilde{x}_2 \pmod{m_2} \\ \ldots \\ x \equiv \tilde{x}_r \pmod{m_r} \end{cases}$

5 compute $x = \sum_{i=1}^{r} x_i u_i \frac{M}{m_i} \pmod{M}$
6 **return** x

Algorithm 4: deCRR

Input: x, modulus m
Output: y

1 $x = x \pmod{m}$

2 $y = \begin{cases} x - m & \text{if } x \geq \frac{m}{2} \\ x & \text{if } x < \frac{m}{2} \end{cases}$

3 **return** y

4.2 Packaged Matrix Operations

As described in Sect. 4.1, matrix multiplication and addition are the keys to VFLR. Hence, we propose packaged matrix operations (Algorithm 2) based on $CRR(\mathcal{M})$, which encodes multiple values into a single value to reduce the computational burden and communication burden in VFLR. In Algorithm 2, take three r-dimensional sets of integers, $\boldsymbol{u} = \{u_1, u_2, \ldots, u_r\}$, $\boldsymbol{v} = \{v_1, v_2, \ldots, v_r\}$, $\boldsymbol{w} = \{w_1, w_2, \ldots, w_r\}$, and a CRT modulus set $\mathcal{M} = \{m_1, m_2, \ldots, m_r\}$ as input. It is worthy to note that $|(u_i + v_i) \cdot w_i| < \frac{m_i}{2}$, for each $i = 1, 2, \ldots, r$. In lines 1–3, we package $\boldsymbol{u}$, $\boldsymbol{v}$, and $\boldsymbol{w}$ to pu, pv, and pw respectively based on $CRR(\mathcal{M})$. The details of the packaging process are described in Algorithm 3. In line 4, we compute $z = (pu + pv) \cdot pw$, then in lines 5–7, compute z_i based on Algorithm 4. According to Sect. 3.1, we know that $z_i = (u_i + v_i) \cdot w_i$, for each $i = 1, 2, \ldots, r$.

In the VFLR framework above, to cut down on the volume of requests made for diverse HE operations. We regard intermediate results $\{d_i^{(k)}\}_{i=1}^N$ as $\boldsymbol{u}$ or $\boldsymbol{v}$, each column $\{x_{i,j}^{(k)}\}_{i=1}^N$ of party k's dataset as $\boldsymbol{w}$, where $x_{i,j}^{(k)}$ is the j-th feature of party k's i-th sample, so that batch operations can be performed.

4.3 Data Conversion

At this point, all datasets and intermediate results are unbounded floating-point numbers that cannot be used for packaged matrix operations. So we need to convert unbounded floating-point data to bounded integer data ahead of time.

For the datasets, we know that data pre-processing will be performed before model training. In general, each party's dataset obeys a $(0, 1)$ normal distribution for the case of logistic regression, i.e., $x_{i,j}^{(k)} \sim N(0, 1)$, for each $i = 1, 2, \ldots, N$, $j = 1, 2, \ldots, J_k$. This is in line with the prerequisite required for dACIQ described earlier. Therefore, we can first use dACIQ to determine the range and then use a multiplicative quantization method, such as Eq. (1), to get bounded integers.

For the intermediate results, they are calculated according to datasets and model parameters, and the model parameters are between $[-1, 1]$ under the action of L_2 regularization. Therefore, we can easily calculate their ranges and then also scale them uniformly to bounded integers like Eq. (1).

Algorithm 5: EVFLR

---

1 **Initialization:**
2 the TTP creates a Paillier HE key pair and sends the public key to each party
3 negotiating a CRT modulus set $\mathcal{M}$ and a quantization parameter s among all participants
4 each party k initializes $\boldsymbol{\theta}_k$, $k = 1, 2, \ldots, K$
5 **Data preparation:**
6 **for** *each party* $k = 1, 2, \ldots, K$ *in parallel* **do**
7   derives α based on s and $\sigma = 1$
8   computes scaling factors $c_1 = \frac{2^{s-1}-1}{\alpha}$, $c_2 = \frac{2^{s-1}-1}{\alpha \cdot J_k}$
9   **for** $i = 1, 2, \ldots, N$ **do**
10   **for** $j = 1, 2, \ldots, J_k$ **do**
11           $\tilde{x}_{i,j}^{(k)} = \text{clip}(x_{i,j}^{(k)}, \alpha)$
12           $\overline{x}_{i,j}^{(k)} = Q(\tilde{x}_{i,j}^{(k)}, \alpha, s)$
13   **end**
14   **end**
15   gets a dataset $\widetilde{\boldsymbol{X}}^{(k)}$ of bounded floating-point numbers and a dataset $\overline{\boldsymbol{X}}^{(k)}$ of bounded integers, then packages $\overline{\boldsymbol{X}}^{(k)}$ to get $\boldsymbol{PX}^{(k)} \in \mathbb{R}^{t \times J_k}$
16 **end**
17 **Training:**
18 **for** *each iteration* $\psi = 1, 2, \ldots$ **do**
19   **for** *each party* $k = 1, 2, \ldots, K$ *in parallel* **do**
20   computes $\{d_i^{(k)}\}_{i=1}^{N}$
21        $\{d_i^{(k)}\}_{i=1}^{N} \rightarrow \{\overline{d}_i^{(k)}\}_{i=1}^{N}$
22        $\{\overline{d}_i^{(k)}\}_{i=1}^{N} \rightarrow \{pd_i^{(k)}\}_{i=1}^{t}$
23        $\{pd_i^{(k)}\}_{i-1}^{t} \rightarrow \{[\![pd_i^{(k)}]\!]\}_{i=1}^{t}$
24   **if** $k \neq K$ **then**
25   sends $\{[\![pd_i^{(k)}]\!]\}_{i=1}^{t}$ to active party K
26   **end**
27   **end**
28   active party K computes and sends $\{[\![pd_i]\!]\}_{i=1}^{t}$ to all passive parties
29   **for** *each party* $k = 1, 2, \ldots, K$ *in parallel* **do**
30   computes $[\![\boldsymbol{PG}^{(k)}]\!]$ and sends it to TTP for decryption
31   receives $\boldsymbol{PG}^{(k)}$
32   **for** *each feature* $j = 1, 2, \ldots, J_k$ *in parallel* **do**
33           $g_j^{(k)} = 0$
34   **for** *each* $i = 1, 2, \ldots, t$ *in parallel* **do**
35   **for** $l = 1, 2, \ldots r$ *in parallel* **do**
36                 $g_j^{(k)} += \text{deCRR}(pg_{i,j}^{(k)}, m_l)$
37   **end**
38   **end**
39   gets $g_j^{(k)} = \frac{1}{c_1 c_2} g_j^{(k)}$
40   **end**
41   gets $g^{(k)}$, then computes $\nabla L(\boldsymbol{\theta}_k)$ and updates local model $\boldsymbol{\theta}_k$
42   **end**
43 **end**

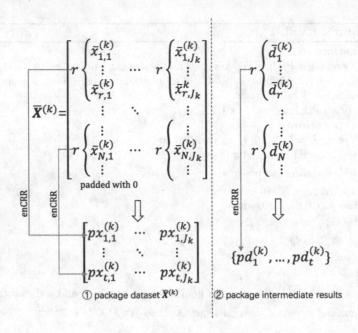

Fig. 3. Packaging process.

4.4   Design

After understanding packaged matrix operations and data conversion. We can construct efficient federated vertical logistic regression (EFVLF). EFVLR is composed of initialization, data preparation, and model training. We completely present it in Algorithm 5.

Initialization. In this phase, the TTP first creates a Paillier key pair and sends the public key to each party. Secondly, the active party K determines a quantization parameter s and an r-dimensional CRT modulus set $\mathcal{M}$, then sends them to each passive party. The generation of $\mathcal{M}$ will be discussed in detail in Sect. 4.4. Finally, each party k initializes the model parameters $\boldsymbol{\theta}_k \in [-1, 1]$.

Data Preparation. In this phase, each party generates some data used in the training phase. In lines 7–8, each party k derives the optimal threshold α based on s and $\sigma = 1$ from Eq. (3), and computes scaling factors $c_1 = (2^{s-1} - 1)/\alpha$, $c_2 = (2^{s-1}-1)/(\alpha \cdot J_k)$. In lines 9–15, each party k converts its dataset of floating-point numbers into a dataset $\widetilde{\boldsymbol{X}}^{(k)} \in \mathbb{R}^{N \times J_k}$ of bounded floating-point numbers and a dataset $\overline{\boldsymbol{X}}^{(k)} \in \mathbb{R}^{N \times J_k}$ of bounded integers, and then packages $\overline{\boldsymbol{X}}^{(k)}$ to get a compressed dataset $\boldsymbol{PX}^{(k)} \in \mathbb{R}^{t \times J_k}$ based on enCRR, where $t = \lceil \frac{N}{r} \rceil$. If N is not divisible by r, the dataset should be padded with 0. The packaging process is illustrated in Fig. 3 left.

Training. In this phase, in lines 19–27, each party k computes intermediate results $\{d_i^{(k)}\}_{i=1}^N$ based on $\widetilde{\boldsymbol{X}}^{(k)}$ and $\boldsymbol{\theta}_k$; converts each number in $\{d_i^{(k)}\}_{i=1}^N$ to a bounded integer $\overline{d}_i^{(k)}$ by $Q(d_i^{(k)}, \alpha \cdot J_k, s)$; packages $\{\overline{d}_i^{(k)}\}_{i=1}^N$ to get $\{pd_i^{(k)}\}_{i=1}^t$ by enCRR, the packaging process is shown in Fig. 3 right; then encrypts each number in $\{pd_i^{(k)}\}_{i=1}^t$ to get $\{[\![pd_i^{(k)}]\!]\}_{i=1}^t$ by the public key. If party k $(k \neq K)$ is the passive party, send $\{[\![pd_i^{(k)}]\!]\}_{i=1}^t$ to the active party K. In line 28, the active party receives encrypted intermediate results from all passive parties, and computes $\{[\![pd_i]\!]\}_{i=1}^t$,

$$[\![pd_i]\!] = \prod_{k=1}^{K} [\![pd_i^{(k)}]\!],$$

$i \in [1, t]$, then sends $\{[\![pd_i]\!]\}_{i=1}^t$ to all passive parties. In line 30, each party calculates a matrix $[\![\boldsymbol{PG}^{(k)}]\!] \in \mathbb{R}^{t \times J_k}$ of packaged gradients in ciphertext,

$$[\![\boldsymbol{PG}^{(k)}]\!] = \begin{bmatrix} \left(\prod_{k=1}^{K} [\![pd_1^{(k)}]\!] \right)^{px_{1,1}^{(k)}} & \cdots & \left(\prod_{k=1}^{K} [\![pd_1^{(k)}]\!] \right)^{px_{1,J_k}^{(k)}} \\ \vdots & \ddots & \vdots \\ \left(\prod_{k=1}^{K} [\![pd_t^{(k)}]\!] \right)^{px_{t,1}^{(k)}} & \cdots & \left(\prod_{k=1}^{K} [\![pd_t^{(k)}]\!] \right)^{px_{t,J_k}^{(k)}} \end{bmatrix},$$

then sends it to TTP for decryption. In line 31, receive the matrix $\boldsymbol{PG}^{(k)}$ of packaged gradients in plaintext, we know

$$\boldsymbol{PG}^{(k)} = \begin{bmatrix} px_{1,1}^{(k)} \sum_{k=1}^{K} pd_1^{(k)} & \cdots & px_{1,J_k}^{(k)} \sum_{k=1}^{K} pd_1^{(k)} \\ \vdots & \ddots & \vdots \\ px_{t,1}^{(k)} \sum_{k=1}^{K} pd_t^{(k)} & \cdots & px_{t,J_k}^{(k)} \sum_{k=1}^{K} pd_t^{(k)} \end{bmatrix}.$$

In lines 32–40, for the j-th value of $\boldsymbol{g}^{(k)}$, $j = 1, 2, \ldots, J_k$, it can be computed as follows:

$$\begin{aligned} g_j^{(k)} &\approx \frac{1}{c_1 c_2} \sum_{i=1}^{t} \sum_{l=1}^{r} deCRR(pg_{i,j}^{(k)}, m_l) \\ &\approx \frac{1}{c_1 c_2} \left(\overline{x}_{1,j}^{(k)} \sum_{k=1}^{K} \overline{d}_1^{(k)} + \cdots + \overline{x}_{N,j}^{(k)} \sum_{k=1}^{K} \overline{d}_N^{(k)} \right) \\ &\approx \frac{1}{c_1 c_2} \left(\overline{x}_{1,j}^{(k)} \overline{d}_1 + \cdots + \overline{x}_{N,j}^{(k)} \overline{d}_N \right) \\ &\approx \frac{1}{c_1 c_2} \sum_{i=1}^{N} \overline{x}_{i,j}^{(k)} \overline{d}_i \\ &\approx \sum_{i=1}^{N} x_{i,j}^{(k)} d_i. \end{aligned} \tag{8}$$

The process of calculating $g^{(k)}$ can be done in parallel. Finally, in line 41, each party k computes $\nabla L(\boldsymbol{\theta}_k)$ and updates local model $\boldsymbol{\theta}_k$.

Analysis. To ensure the validity of our scheme, it is necessary to ensure that $|\overline{x}_{i,j}^{(k)} \sum_{k=1}^{K} \overline{d}_i^{(k)}| < \frac{m_i}{2}$ and $pg_{i,j}^{(k)} < n$, where n is Paillier public key. Because $\overline{x}^{(k)}$ and $\overline{d}_i^{(k)}$ are bounded integers, we can easily figure out how many values we can package at once based on s, K, and n, which is the value of r. As shown in Table 1, we present several specific results and corresponding precision under certain s, K, and $len(n)$, where $len(n)$ is the bit length of n.

Therefore, for the communication burden, our scheme can theoretically reduce r (maximum 96) times the communication burden between the active party and each passive party. But we also find the communication burden between TTP and each party is t times higher than before. However, we can avoid it in the following two ways:

- In fact, for higher training efficiency, mini-batch stochastic gradient descent (SGD) is often used, i.e., instead of selecting one or all samples of data per iteration, a small batch of samples is selected randomly. We denote the selected samples as $\mathcal{B}$, $|\mathcal{B}|$ is the size of $\mathcal{B}$. Hence, if we set $|\mathcal{B}| = r$, the communication burden between TTP and each party remains the same as before.
- We can also set m_i to be larger, for example $t \cdot |\overline{x}_{i,j}^{(k)} \sum_{k=1}^{K} \overline{d}_i^{(k)}| < \frac{m_i}{2}$ and $t \cdot pg_{i,j}^{(k)} < n$, so that each column of the ciphertext matrix $[\![\boldsymbol{PG}^{(k)}]\!]$ can be added, and the added matrix is sent to TTP for decryption. In this way, the communication burden between TTP and each party also remains the same as before.

Obviously, our scheme also greatly reduces the calculation burden for every party. In the cnCRR and deCRR process, we only introduce some additional modulo operations, which are almost negligible compared with **Enc** and **Mmul**. Moreover, the CRT modulus set $\mathcal{M}$ does not need to be replaced after negotiation, so some values such as $u_i = (M/m_i)^{-1} \pmod{m_i}$ can be reused.

Table 1. The amount of data that can be packaged once.

	s	$len(n)$			
		1024	2048	3072	precision
$K = 2$	12	21	42	63	0.01
	16	16	32	48	0.0001
	20	12	25	38	0.00001
$K = 4$	12	20	40	61	0.01
	16	15	31	46	0.0001
	20	12	24	37	0.00001
$K = 8$	12	19	39	59	0.01
	16	15	30	45	0.0001
	20	12	24	36	0.00001

Table 2. Datasets information.

	Train samples	Test samples	P_1-features	P_2-features	P_3-features	P_4-features
breast-cancer	426	143	7	7	8	8
sklearn-digits	1347	450	8	12	20	24
census-income	32561	16281	12	22	32	42

5   Experients

5.1   Setting

Environment. Our experiments run on five computers that equipped with Intel(R) Core(TM) i7-8700 CPU @ 3.20 GHz and 32 GB memory in the LAN setting. Four computers as participants and one computer as TTP.

Datasets. We used three datasets breast-cancer [29], sklearn-digits [13], and census-income [20] to evaluate the effectiveness and efficiency of our approach. We divide them into four datasets with different features and assign them to four participants P_1, P_2, P_3, and P_4 (active party), respectively. Table 2 shows the information of them and the distribution of features on each party.

Parameters. We set $len(n) = 3072$ because 3072 can be considered as a safe length [2]. We fix the learning rate η to 0.05, and L_2 regularization parameter λ to 0.1. Let the batch sizes of breast-cancer, sklearn-digits and census-income be 426, 1347 and 2000 respectively.

5.2   Effectiveness

Method. By comparing with the plaintext centralized logistic regression, we evaluate the validity of our method under 12-bit, 16-bit, and 20-bit quantization respectively. We select Area Under the ROC Curve (AUC) and accuracy values (Acc) as evaluation metrics.

Result. Figure 4 depicts the convergence curves of AUC on test datasets. Table 3 also shows the results on test datasets after model convergence. We can find that the performance of the model in the case of 12-bit, 16-bit, and 20-bit quantization is comparable to or even slightly higher than that of the plaintext centralized LR.

Table 3. Comparison results.

Dataset	plain		12-bit		16-bit		20-bit	
	Acc	AUC	Acc	AUC	Acc	AUC	Acc	AUC
breast-cancer	0.9231	0.9768	0.9301	0.9761	0.9301	0.9759	0.9231	0.9759
sklearn-digits	0.8622	0.9313	0.8644	0.928	0.8622	0.9304	0.8622	0.9305
census-income	0.7207	0.889	0.7211	0.8783	0.7195	0.8853	0.7203	0.8861

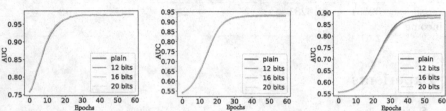

(a) breast-cancer test AUC   (b) sklearn-digits test AUC   (c) census-income test AUC

Fig. 4. The quality of the trained model with different quantization bit widths.

We can explain this result from two aspects. First, mini-batch SGD is a progressive optimization method, so the noise caused by quantization has little effect on it. Second, just like the dropout rate, quantization bit width can be regarded as a trade-off knob for how much information is retained and how much randomness is introduced. As long as the quantization bit width is not too small, it will not only not affect the accuracy, but also prevent overfitting.

5.3 Efficiency

Method. We test the efficiency of our method by comparing it with the typical VFLR framework (Hardy-LR). To assess the improvement in communication efficiency, we measure the traffic between the active party and each passive party (P-P traffic) and the communication amount between the active party and the TTP (P-T traffic) during an iteration. To evaluate the improvement in computational efficiency, we measure the time it takes to complete an iteration (lines 19–42 of Algorithm 5).

Communication. As shown in Fig. 5, using 12-bit quantization, 16-bit quantization and 20-bit quantization, we observe that the P-P traffic can be reduced by 54 times, 42 times and 34 times respectively on the breast-cancer dataset, 51 times, 40 times and 33 times respectively on the sklearn-digits dataset, and 50 times, 39 times and 32 times respectively on the census-income dataset. This is slightly lower than the values of the theoretical analysis in Table 1. This is because in our experiment, in order to avoid the increase in P-T traffic, we set m_i to be larger so that each column of $[\![PG^{(k)}]\!]$ can be added. As shown in Fig. 6, P-T traffic is proportional to the dimension of active party's features, which is consistent with our theoretical analysis.

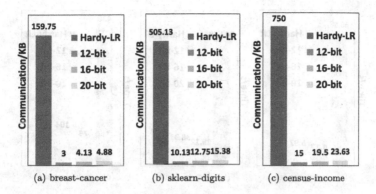

Fig. 5. P-P traffic during an iteration.

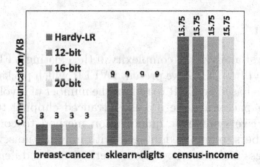

Fig. 6. P-T traffic during an iteration.

Computation. As shown in Fig. 7, our method can achieve 3.6×-14.6× training speedup. At the same time, we find that the acceleration factors obtained on breast-cancer, sklearn-digits and census-income are getting smaller and smaller. We think this is caused by the batch size, because the larger the batch size, not only the smaller r but also the more **Mmul** involved in one iteration, which pulls down the acceleration factor.

6   Discussion

- For vertical federated logistic regression without a third party [30,36], our scheme is also applicable since they also involve a large number of **Enc** and **Mmul**.
- Our scheme can also be extended to FTL [22] because the core of FTL is ciphertext matrix multiplication.
- Our approach does not reduce the traffic between participants and TTP, we leave it as a future job.

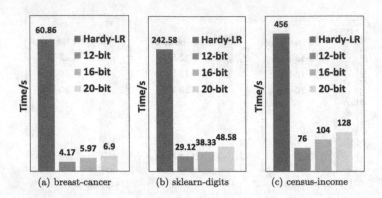

Fig. 7. Training time for one iteration.

7   Conclusion

In this paper, we first analyze the complexity of the existing VFLR scheme under homomorphic encryption. Then we present EVFLR which packages intermediate results and datasets based on CRR to reduce the number of invokes to various HE operations. During packaging, we use the advanced clipping technique dACIQ and the multiplicative symmetric quantization method to convert unbounded floating-point numbers to bounded integers with minimal noise. Finally, we analyze the effectiveness and efficiency of our method under different quantization bit widths and datasets.

Acknowledgements. This work is partially supported by the National Key R&D Program of China (No. 2022YFB2702804) and the National Natural Science Foundation of China (No. 12271306).

References

1. Banner, R., Nahshan, Y., Soudry, D.: Post training 4-bit quantization of convolutional networks for rapid-deployment. In: Advances in Neural Information Processing Systems, vol. 32 (2019)
2. Barker, E., Barker, E., Burr, W., Polk, W., Smid, M., et al.: Recommendation for key management: Part 1: General. National Institute of Standards and Technology, Technology Administration (2006)
3. Beame, P.W., Cook, S.A., Hoover, H.J.: Log depth circuits for division and related problems. SIAM J. Comput. **15**(4), 994–1003 (1986)
4. Bonawitz, K., et al.: Practical secure aggregation for privacy-preserving machine learning. In: Proceedings of the 2017 ACM SIGSAC Conference on Computer and Communications Security, pp. 1175–1191 (2017)
5. Cai, D., et al.: Accelerating vertical federated learning. CoRR abs/2207.11456 (2022). https://doi.org/10.48550/arXiv.2207.11456
6. Chen, W., Ma, G., Fan, T., Kang, Y., Xu, Q., Yang, Q.: SecureBoost+: a high performance gradient boosting tree framework for large scale vertical federated learning. CoRR abs/2110.10927 (2021). https://arxiv.org/abs/2110.10927

7. Cheon, J.H., Kim, A., Kim, M., Song, Y.: Homomorphic encryption for arithmetic of approximate numbers. In: Takagi, T., Peyrin, T. (eds.) ASIACRYPT 2017. LNCS, vol. 10624, pp. 409–437. Springer, Cham (2017). https://doi.org/10.1007/978-3-319-70694-8_15

8. Chiu, A., Davida, G., Litow, B.: Division in logspace-uniform NC1. RAIRO-Theoret. Inf. Appl. **35**(3), 259–275 (2001)

9. Corrigan-Gibbs, H., Boneh, D.: Prio: private, robust, and scalable computation of aggregate statistics. In: 14th USENIX Symposium on Networked Systems Design and Implementation (NSDI 2017), pp. 259–282 (2017)

10. Davida, G., Litow, B., Xu, G.: Fast arithmetics using Chinese remaindering. Inf. Process. Lett. **109**(13), 660–662 (2009)

11. Dong, Y., Chen, X., Shen, L., Wang, D.: Privacy-preserving distributed machine learning based on secret sharing. In: Zhou, J., Luo, X., Shen, Q., Xu, Z. (eds.) ICICS 2019. LNCS, vol. 11999, pp. 684–702. Springer, Cham (2020). https://doi.org/10.1007/978-3-030-41579-2_40

12. Dong, Y., Chen, X., Shen, L., Wang, D.: EaSTFly: efficient and secure ternary federated learning. Comput. Secur. **94**, 101824 (2020)

13. Dua, D., Graff, C.: UCI machine learning repository (2017). http://archive.ics.uci.edu/ml

14. Fu, A., Zhang, X., Xiong, N., Gao, Y., Wang, H., Zhang, J.: VFL: a verifiable federated learning with privacy-preserving for big data in industrial IoT. IEEE Trans. Industr. Inf. **18**(5), 3316–3326 (2020)

15. Fu, F., et al.: VF2Boost: very fast vertical federated gradient boosting for cross-enterprise learning. In: Proceedings of the 2021 International Conference on Management of Data, pp. 563–576 (2021)

16. Hardy, S., et al.: Private federated learning on vertically partitioned data via entity resolution and additively homomorphic encryption. CoRR abs/1711.10677 (2017). http://arxiv.org/abs/1711.10677

17. He, D., Du, R., Zhu, S., Zhang, M., Liang, K., Chan, S.: Secure logistic regression for vertical federated learning. IEEE Internet Comput. **26**(2), 61–68 (2021)

18. Hosmer, D.W., Jr., Lemeshow, S., Sturdivant, R.X.: Applied Logistic Regression, vol. 398. Wiley (2013)

19. Kairouz, P., et al.: Advances and open problems in federated learning. Found. Trends® Mach. Learn. **14**(1–2), 1–210 (2021)

20. Kohavi, R., et al.: Scaling up the accuracy of Naive-Bayes classifiers: a decision-tree hybrid. In: KDD, vol. 96, pp. 202–207 (1996)

21. Li, M., Chen, Y., Wang, Y., Pan, Y.: Efficient asynchronous vertical federated learning via gradient prediction and double-end sparse compression. In: 2020 16th International Conference on Control, Automation, Robotics and Vision (ICARCV), pp. 291–296. IEEE (2020)

22. Liu, Y., Kang, Y., Xing, C., Chen, T., Yang, Q.: A secure federated transfer learning framework. IEEE Intell. Syst. **35**(4), 70–82 (2020)

23. McMahan, B., Moore, E., Ramage, D., Hampson, S., Arcas, B.A.: Communication-efficient learning of deep networks from decentralized data. In: Artificial Intelligence and Statistics, pp. 1273–1282. PMLR (2017)

24. Mo, F., Haddadi, H., Katevas, K., Marin, E., Perino, D., Kourtellis, N.: PPFL: privacy-preserving federated learning with trusted execution environments. In: Proceedings of the 19th Annual International Conference on Mobile Systems, Applications, and Services, pp. 94–108 (2021)

25. Mondal, A., More, Y., Rooparaghunath, R.H., Gupta, D.: Poster: FLATEE: federated learning across trusted execution environments. In: 2021 IEEE European Symposium on Security and Privacy (EuroS&P), pp. 707–709. IEEE (2021)
26. Paillier, P.: Public-key cryptosystems based on composite degree residuosity classes. In: Stern, J. (ed.) EUROCRYPT 1999. LNCS, vol. 1592, pp. 223–238. Springer, Heidelberg (1999). https://doi.org/10.1007/3-540-48910-X_16
27. Phong, L.T., Aono, Y., Hayashi, T., Wang, L., Moriai, S.: Privacy-preserving deep learning via additively homomorphic encryption. IEEE Trans. Inf. Forensics Secur. **13**(5), 1333–1345 (2018). https://doi.org/10.1109/TIFS.2017.2787987
28. Ranbaduge, T., Ding, M.: Differentially private vertical federated learning. CoRR abs/2211.06782 (2022). https://doi.org/10.48550/arXiv.2211.06782
29. Street, W.N., Wolberg, W.H., Mangasarian, O.L.: Nuclear feature extraction for breast tumor diagnosis. In: Biomedical Image Processing and Biomedical Visualization, vol. 1905, pp. 861–870. SPIE (1993)
30. Sun, H., Wang, Z., Huang, Y., Ye, J.: Privacy-preserving vertical federated logistic regression without trusted third-party coordinator. In: ICMLSC 2022: The 6th International Conference on Machine Learning and Soft Computing, Haikou, China, 15–17 January 2022, pp. 132–138. ACM (2022). https://doi.org/10.1145/3523150.3523171
31. de la Torre, L.: A guide to the California consumer privacy act of 2018. Available at SSRN 3275571 (2018)
32. Wei, K.: Federated learning with differential privacy: algorithms and performance analysis. IEEE Trans. Inf. Forensics Secur. **15**, 3454–3469 (2020)
33. Xu, A., Huang, H.: Coordinating momenta for cross-silo federated learning. In: Proceedings of the AAAI Conference on Artificial Intelligence, vol. 36, pp. 8735–8743 (2022)
34. Xu, W., Fan, H., Li, K., Yang, K.: Efficient batch homomorphic encryption for vertically federated XGBoost. CoRR abs/2112.04261 (2021). https://arxiv.org/abs/2112.04261
35. Yang, Q., Liu, Y., Chen, T., Tong, Y.: Federated machine learning: concept and applications. ACM Trans. Intell. Syst. Technol. (TIST) **10**(2), 1–19 (2019)
36. Yang, S., Ren, B., Zhou, X., Liu, L.: Parallel distributed logistic regression for vertical federated learning without third-party coordinator. CoRR abs/1911.09824 (2019). http://arxiv.org/abs/1911.09824
37. Zhang, C., Li, S., Xia, J., Wang, W., Yan, F., Liu, Y.: BatchCrypt: efficient homomorphic encryption for Cross-Silo federated learning. In: 2020 USENIX Annual Technical Conference (USENIX ATC 2020), pp. 493–506 (2020)
38. Zhang, X., Fu, A., Wang, H., Zhou, C., Chen, Z.: A privacy-preserving and verifiable federated learning scheme. In: ICC 2020–2020 IEEE International Conference on Communications (ICC), pp. 1–6. IEEE (2020)

Clustered Federated Learning
with Inference Hash Codes Based Local
Sensitive Hashing

Zhou Tan[1], Ximeng Liu[1]([✉]), Yan Che[2], and Yuyang Wang[1]

[1] College of Computer Science and Big Data, Fuzhou University, Fuzhou 350108,
Fujian, China
snbnix@gmail.com
[2] College of Mechanical and Information Engineering, Putian University, Putian
351100, Fujian, China

Abstract. Federated Learning (FL) is a distributed paradigm enabling
clients to train a global model collaboratively while protecting client
privacy. During the FL training process, the statistical heterogeneity
between different clients can compromise the overall performance of the
global model and its generalization ability on each client, making it difficult for the training process to converge. This paper proposes an efficient
clustered FL (cFL) method called FedCC, which aims to cluster clients
based on their inference results on a public dataset. As inference results
may leak client data distribution, we use Locality Sensitive Hashing
(LSH) to transform inference results into Inference Hash Codes (IHC),
which are irreversible but can be used for similarity calculations. The
server compares the similarity of IHCs between clients and implements
dynamic clustering using the DBSCAN algorithm. FedCC also provides
an elegant method to quickly select the appropriate cluster model for
clients without downloading all cluster models. We evaluated FedCC on
four commonly used datasets and compared them against seven baselines. Experimental results show that FedCC achieves faster convergence
than other baselines while achieving an accuracy 1.66% higher than the
state-of-the-art baseline. Finally, we further validated the robustness of
FedCC against Byzantine attacks, where malicious clients upload negative gradients to reduce model accuracy and prevent convergence.

Keywords: Federated learning · Locality Sensitive Hashing ·
DBSCAN

1 Introduction

In traditional centralized machine learning, data is stored on a central server for
model training. However, this approach may not always be feasible or desirable
in real-world scenarios due to data siloing across different devices or organizations and privacy concerns. To address this issue, Federated Learning (FL) has
been proposed as a distributed machine learning technique that allows multiple
clients to collaboratively train a global model without leak data privacy [1,2].

C. Ge and M. Yung (Eds.): Inscrypt 2023, LNCS 14527, pp. 73–90, 2024.
https://doi.org/10.1007/978-981-97-0945-8_5

Nonetheless, FL may face the challenge of Non-IID data distribution among clients. In this situation, different clients may upload models with considerable differences in their parameters, which can reduce the accuracy and convergence speed of the global model and make it unable to meet all clients' needs [3,4].

Personalized federated learning (pFL) has been favoured by researchers as a method for addressing Non-IID problems from the client's perspective because it can provide personalized models tailored to the local data distribution of each client [5,6]. There are two ways to implement the personalized approach. The first way is to fine-tune the global model with each client's local data, such as Per-FedAvg [7]. This approach is highly dependent on the global model and requires high computation capability from clients. The second way involves clients interpolating between the global model and their local model, such as LG-FedAvg [5]. This approach has limitations, as the personalized model obtained by weighted aggregation may not fully adapt to the data distribution characteristics of a client or even perform worse than the original local model, especially when there are significant differences in data distribution among clients [8]. In addition, the limited amount of data available for each client and the personalization process only occurring within a single client without coordination with other clients can lead to a poor generalization ability of the personalized model.

Liu et al. [9] proposed in their research that there may be many clients with similar data distributions in the FL process. This implies that the models trained by these clients will also be similar, and aggregating these client models will outperform local adaptive solutions. Therefore, to better utilize the data from each client, clustered FL (cFL) [10] has been proposed to cluster clients with similar data distributions together for performing FL. This approach can effectively reduce the difference between models and improve the generalization ability and performance of the model [11,12].

However, previous cFL methods face challenges that limit their implementation in real-world scenarios: 1) pre-defining the number of clusters are required by methods such as IFCA [11], which limits flexibility and makes it difficult to adapt to changes in client data distribution and different scales of FL applications. 2) the clustering process may leak client privacy. As the server needs to cluster based on the identification sent by the client, the identification may contain private information. In the FLIS [13], the server conducts clustering based on client inference information, which may lead to the leakage of client data distribution. 3) taking PACFL [8] as an example, each client can only belong to one cluster. This approach may result in some clients being unable to aggregate effectively with others, thus failing to generate cluster models with good performance. 4) clients cannot quickly select a cluster model. Methods such as IFCA and FLIS require clients to download all cluster models and test them individually to find the most suitable one. This can increase communication and computation resource expenses and may reduce the method's efficiency.

We propose FedCC clustered federated learning algorithm to address these challenges. It can accurately partition clients with similar data distributions into one cluster while protecting client privacy. FedCC's clustering identification is based on the inference results of clients on the public dataset. To protect client privacy and minimize communication costs, we use Locality Sensitive Hashing (LSH) [14] for dimensionality reduction on the inference results, resulting in hash codes named Inference Hash Codes (IHC). On this basis, the server uses the Jaccard similarity coefficient to measure the similarity between IHCs and compare the similarity between clients. Finally, the DBSCAN algorithm [15] is used to achieve accurate client clustering. This method can effectively eliminate the problem of uneven data distribution and improve the performance and generalization ability of the model. In addition, in terms of model selection, we propose a fast method for selecting suitable models for clients. For cluster models, the IHC of the core point in the cluster is assigned. Clients only need to upload their IHC to the server, and the server can calculate the cluster model with the maximum similarity of IHC and give it to clients. To further protect clients' privacy, Secure multi-party computation [16] is adopted among clients to negotiate the public dataset and hash functions through secure communication before the training begins. This method can effectively prevent the server from reconstructing the client's inference results on the public dataset from IHC.

In summary, this paper makes the following main contributions:

- We propose a novel way to represent a client's data distribution based on the IHC, which ensures clustering efficiency and accuracy while protecting client privacy and reducing computational costs.
  We propose the FedCC algorithm, which clusters clients by calculating the IHC similarity between them without pre-defining cluster numbers and can quickly select the appropriate cluster model for clients.
- We conducted experiments on four datasets and baseline model architectures to verify the effectiveness of FedCC.

2   Related Work

2.1   Personalized Federated Learning

As previously mentioned, statistical heterogeneity poses a significant challenge in developing large-scale FL systems. This includes Non-IID datasets, imbalanced classes, and datasets with varying sizes [17,18]. The conventional approach involves training a single global model on heterogeneous data, which typically results in poor performance in highly heterogeneous settings [19]. Personalized federated learning (pFL) has become one of the research directions to address these challenges. Li et al. [20] first proposed the FedProx algorithm to handle Non-IID datasets. This algorithm constrains the difference between global and local models by adding a proximal term during iteration. The Per-FedAvg algorithm [7] is based on the Model-Agnostic Meta-Learning [21], where clients train the global model multiple times according to their data for pFL. The LG-FedAvg algorithm [5] focuses on reducing data and device distribution variance by combining local and global models to improve the generalization performance.

2.2 Clustered Federated Learning

Rather than providing personalized models, Clustered Federated Learning (cFL) leverages a pluralistic group architecture to divide the optimization objective into several sub-objectives [22]. By maintaining multiple specialized group or cluster models, cFL achieves high accuracy even in situations with varying data distributions. Ghosh et al. [11] propose IFCA, which optimizes the model by randomly generating cluster centres and dividing clients into clusters that minimize their loss values. IFCA can significantly improve the accuracy of client models. Still, it requires a fixed number of clusters, and in each global iteration, all cluster models must be sent to clients, reducing its flexibility and increasing communication costs. Mahdi et al. [13] propose FLIS, which clusters clients based on the inference similarity of public datasets on the client. While FLIS can achieve greater efficiency, it requires testing and downloading all cluster models on the local dataset to select the best model. This leads to significant communication costs and an increase in iteration time. Furthermore, the inference results sent by clients have not undergone any privacy processing, creating a risk of privacy leakage, as the server may infer the data distribution of the clients.

3 Preliminaries

3.1 Local Sensitive Hashing

Local Sensitive Hashing (LSH) is a commonly used method for quickly finding Approximate Nearest Neighbors (ANN) in large-scale datasets [14]. The basic idea is to project the original data into a low-dimensional space such that similar data points still have a high probability of being close to each other after the mapping. In contrast, different data points are likely to be separated. Specifically, LSH selects some special hash functions to achieve this mapping, designed to only conflict with similar data points. This means that they are more likely to map similar data points to the same bucket while less likely to map dissimilar ones to the same bucket. Therefore, when we need to find the approximate nearest neighbour of a particular data point, we only need to search in the adjacent buckets of the bucket where the data point is located, thereby significantly reducing the time and computation costs of the search. LSH is usually used to handle high-dimensional dense or sparse data and can substantially improve the search speed while ensuring search accuracy [23]. Due to its excellent performance and wide range of applications, LSH is widely used in machine learning, data mining, and privacy protection [24,25].

3.2 DBSCAN

DBSCAN [15] is a commonly used clustering algorithm in machine learning and data mining. Compared to other clustering algorithms, DBSCAN is especially suitable for noisy or outlier-prone datasets and can detect clusters of various shapes and sizes, offering robust performance in exploratory data analysis. Its

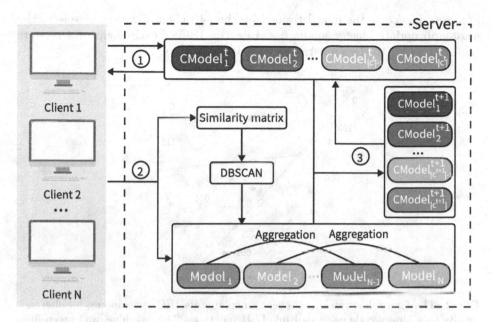

Fig. 1. This workflow consists of three steps: ① The client sends IHC to the server, and the server selects the cluster model with the highest similarity to the client's IHC and sends it to the client. ② The client sends updated IHC and models to the server. The server performs the DBSCAN clustering algorithm to cluster all clients' IHCs, grouping similar clients into the same cluster and generating corresponding cluster models for each cluster while assigning the core client's IHC to the corresponding cluster model. ③ The server removes the models from the previous round of cluster that is similar to the current round of cluster and then merges all cluster models.

primary benefit is that it does not require pre-defining the number of clusters because it automatically determines the number of clusters based on the density of data points. The algorithm is based on two key parameters, ϵ and $MinPts$ define the maximum distance between two points to be considered the same cluster and the minimum number of points needed to form a dense region. Its fundamental premise is that data points with densities greater than $MinPts$ are regarded as cluster cores, and data points within a proximity of ϵ to the cluster core are grouped into the same cluster. Furthermore, these parameters can be fine-tuned based on the distinctive properties of the dataset to achieve desirable clustering results. DBSCAN enables clients to belong to multiple clusters more in line with real-world scenarios.

4   Methodology

In this section, we introduced the design of the FedCC algorithm. The algorithm clusters clients based on the similarity of their IHCs, as illustrated in Fig. 1. Here, $CModel^t$ represents the set of cluster models in the t round, with a length of

$|c^t|$, and $Model_i$ is the model trained by the i-th client. The server selects the most appropriate cluster model based on the IHC of each client and clusters them according to the similarity of their IHC.

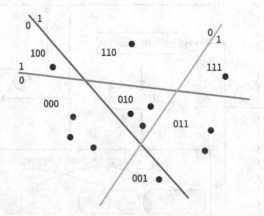

Fig. 2. The figure illustrates each client calculates its IHC by mapping its inference results to a binary code using multiple LSH functions. The red, blue, and green lines depict the LSH functions, while circular points represent the client's inference results. The IHC of the inference results for the centre triangle is 010. (Color figure online)

4.1   Design Goal

The design of FedCC aims to optimize and improve the problems that exist in the cFL, and we try to achieve the following four goals:

- Clustering Effectiveness: In a distributed dataset environment, FedCC requires superior clustering effectiveness, the ability to quickly and accurately complete clustering tasks, and dynamically determine the number of clusters to increase clustering flexibility.
- Privacy Protection: Clustering involves client data privacy. Therefore, FedCC must take measures to protect client privacy to ensure that client data privacy is not leaked. At the same time, it is also necessary to ensure the data security of all parties during the FL process.
- Communication Efficiency: To enhance communication efficiency, reduce costs, support large-scale clients, and promote distributed training in FL, FedCC requires a compact cluster identifier design and appropriate methods for clients to download their most suitable cluster model.
- Scalability: FedCC requires exceptional scalability and must adapt to different scales and types of datasets.

4.2   Inference Hash Codes

This section introduces Inference Hash Codes (IHC) as hashing codes generated by LSH of a model's inference results on a public dataset. IHC protects the privacy of inference results using the irreversible nature of LSH while still maintaining usability. Compared to FLIS, computing similarity between clients becomes faster, significantly reducing communication costs. Generating IHC and performing similarity calculations involve the following three steps:

First, clients collaborate to create a public dataset D^{public} of length n, and a set of LSH functions $S = (V_1, \ldots, V_k)$, where $V_i = (v_1^i, \ldots, v_n^i)$ is the i-th LSH function, and v_j^i $(1 \leq j \leq n)$ is a random value in the range of $[-1, 1]$. The inference result of client c can be represented as an n-dimensional vector $B_c = (b_1, \ldots, b_n)$, where $b_i = 1$ if client c correctly infers the i-th sample, otherwise $b_i = 0$.

Second, substitute all functions in set S and the inference results of client c into Eq. 1 in order [26], then concatenate the results to obtain the IHC of client c, denoted as $H_c = (h_1, \ldots, h_k)$. We depict generating IHC in Fig. 2.

$$h_i = LSH(B_c, V_i) = \begin{cases} 1 & \text{if } B_c \cdot V_i > 0 \\ 0 & \text{if } B_c \cdot V_i \leq 0 \end{cases} \tag{1}$$

where the symbol "·" represents the dot product between two vectors, i.e., the scalar product of their corresponding entries followed by a summation.

Third, after receiving the IHCs from participating clients, the server calculates the similarity between clients i and j using the following Jaccard similarity coefficient:

$$Jaccard(H_i, H_j) = \frac{|H_i \cap H_j|}{|H_i \cup H_j|} \tag{2}$$

4.3   Overview of FedCC

In FedCC, there is a prerequisite that all clients securely negotiate the public dataset and hash functions through secure multi-party computation [16]. Clients can generate public datasets using methods such as knowledge distillation [27, 28], prototype [29], and synthetic dataset [30], which only need to generate IHCs for clients. In the subsequent FL process, after the server receives the IHC sent by participating training clients, it calculates the similarity matrix using the Jaccard similarity coefficient, generates clusters using DBSCAN, and then aggregates the corresponding cluster models. Therefore, the time complexity of FedCC is $O(n^2)$.

To optimize the method of selecting cluster models for clients, an IHC is assigned to each cluster model. However, to protect client privacy and save server computing resources, We give the IHC of the core client in each cluster to the corresponding cluster model, denoted as F_i for the i-th cluster model. After this processing, clients only need to download the cluster model with the highest similarity to their IHC without downloading all cluster models and testing locally to select models. This method helps save communication costs and reduce the computing burden on clients.

Algorithm 1. FedCC

Input: Initial model θ^0; Clients set K; Total rounds T; Clustering threshold ϵ
Output: Cluster models θ^T
1: **for** each round $t = 1, 2, \ldots, T$ **do**
2:     $K_t \leftarrow$ random subset of K
3:     **for** each client k in K_t **do**
4:         **if** $t = 1$ **then**
5:             $\theta_k, H_k = ClientUpdate(k, \theta^0)$
6:         **else**
7:             $\widehat{j} = \arg\max(\text{Jaccard}(H_k, F_j^t)_{j=1}^{|F^t|})$
8:             $\theta_k, H_k = ClientUpdate(k, \theta_{\widehat{j}}^t)$
9:         **end if**
10:     **end for**
11:     $\{R_j\}_{j=1}^m = DBSCAN(\{H\}_1^{|K_t|}, \epsilon)$
12:     **for** each cluster $j = 1, 2, \ldots, m$ **do**
13:         $\theta_j^{t+1} = \sum_{i \in R_j} \frac{1}{|R_j|} \theta_i$
14:         $F_j^{t+1} = H_x$, x is a core client in the cluster R_j
15:     **end for**
16:     **if** $t > 1$ **then**
17:         Initialize empty set G
18:         **for** all $f \in F^t$ **do**
19:             **if** $\max(\text{Jaccard}(f, F_j^{t+1})_1^{|F^{t+1}|}) < \epsilon$ **then**
20:                 Add index of f to set G
21:             **end if**
22:         **end for**
23:         $F^{t+1} = F^{t+1} \cup F_i^t, i \in G$
24:         $\theta^{t+1} = \theta^{t+1} \cup \theta_i^t, i \in G$
25:     **end if**
26: **end for**

In addition, since the data distribution between clients is difficult to determine in real-world scenarios, the number of clusters is also uncertain. Therefore, pre-defining the number of clusters before training will reduce the algorithm's flexibility and the model's performance. The server saves not only the cluster models generated by DBSCAN but also the part of the previous round cluster model set whose Jaccard similarity coefficient with the current round cluster model is less than ϵ. This can more comprehensively and non-redundantly retain the cluster models, achieving global dynamic cluster numbers. The FedCC algorithm pseudocode is described in Algorithm 1.

During the initial stages of training, low-performing cluster models on the client can produce inaccurate IHC, leading to slower convergence speeds and unstable clustering effects. To tackle the issue, a local model was introduced to the client. We demonstrate in the following experiments that the local model can generate more accurate IHC early on while improving the accuracy and stability of clustering. However, due to the ceiling on the accuracy of the local model [31] and its computational burden, the local model is no longer trained when the

---

Algorithm 2. ClientUpdate

Input: Cluster model θ; Client k and local model θ_k^{local}; Train data D_k^{train} and test data D_k^{test}; Public data D^{public}; LSH function set S; Local train flag Ψ(default: True) and stop local train threshold $\mho$

Output: Trained model θ; Inference-Hash codes H_k

1: $\theta = Train(\theta, D_k^{train})$
2: $Acc = Eval(\theta, D_k^{test})$
3: **if** Ψ is $True$ **then**
4:     $\theta_k^{local} = Train(\theta_k^{local}, D_k^{train})$
5:     $Acc_k^{local} = Eval(\theta_k^{local}, D_k^{test})$
6:     $H_k = LSH(Inference(\theta_k^{local}, D^{public}), S)$
7: **end if**
8: **if** $Acc > Acc_k^{local}$ and $Acc > \mho$ **then**
9:     $H_k = LSH(Inference(\theta, D^{public}), S)$
10:     $\mho = Acc$
11:     $\Psi = False$
12: **end if**
13: **return** θ, H_k

---

cluster model surpasses its performance on the test set. In such situations, the cluster model is used to create IHC, and clients save the IHC generated by the best-performing model and send it to the server. Additionally, a hyperparameter $\mho$ was introduced to prevent premature stopping of the local model at low accuracies while also avoiding overtraining the model. The Client update algorithm pseudocode is described in Algorithm 2.

4.4 Security Analysis

In FedCC, attacks may come from semi-honest servers and malicious clients. The server may attempt to infer the client's local dataset distribution through the client's IHC. However, the IHC is processed by LSH and cannot be subjected to inversion attacks. Even if the server can obtain the hash function and the public dataset, reconstructing the result is still very difficult.

The time complexity of each LSH function is $O(n)$, where n is the length of the hash function and the size of the public dataset, and then the complexity of k hash functions is $O(kn)$. When the server reconstructs the n-bit inference results of the client's public dataset, it needs to enumerate all possible n bits and then hash them through each hash function separately, obtaining k hash codes that are compared with the known IHC. Therefore, the worst-case time complexity is $O(2^n kn)$. As n increases, 2^n grows very fast, which means that even with a relatively small value of k, it may take a very long time to reconstruct successfully. Therefore, more hash functions and larger public dataset sizes can be used to strengthen protection and make the reconstruction task more difficult.

In the following experiments, we have validated the robustness of FedCC against Byzantine attacks launched by malicious clients.

5 Experiments

5.1 Experimental Settings

Datasets and Non-IID Partitions. We conducted experiments on four commonly used datasets, including USPS, MNIST, FMNIST, and CIFAR10, using the 4-layer CNN [32]. For the MNIST, we kept only 25% of the training set. A public dataset is generated in [13], where 250 samples are selected from each class in the test set. To simulate heterogeneous settings, we employed two widely used scenarios. The first scenario was the pathological heterogeneous setting [32,33], where each client was randomly assigned two classes with an equal quantity of data for each class. We denoted this partitioning strategy as $\#C = 2$ for simplicity of presentation [4]. The second scenario was the practical heterogeneous setting [34,35], where each client was given a proportion of samples for each label based on the Dirichlet distribution. This distribution was represented as $Dir(\beta)$, with smaller values of β indicating more heterogeneous settings. For our heterogeneous default setting, we set β to 0.1 [36,37].

Baselines and Evaluation Metrics. We compare FedCC with seven FL baselines, including FedAvg [31], FedProx [20], LG-FedAvg [5], Per-FedAvg [7], FLIS (DC) [13], IFCA [11] and PACFL [8], as well as a Local baseline where clients only train on their local data. To simulate real-world FL settings, We use the same evaluation metrics as pFedMe [2], reporting the test accuracy of the best single global model for traditional FL, the average test accuracy of the personalized model for pFL and the cluster model for cFL.

Training Details. By default, our experiments follow the configuration below: we conduct 200 global iterations, with each client performing 10 epochs of iterations locally. For the Local baseline, each client performs 20 local iterations. The learning rate is set to 0.01, and there are 100 clients in total, with a participation ratio of 10% in each round. Since the number of clients is relatively small, we set $MinPts$ to 1. Randomly generate 500 LSH functions to form LSH function set S. We run all tasks three times and reported the average and standard deviation. **Implementation.** All clients and servers are simulated on a workstation with an RTX 3090 GPU, a 3.8-GHz Intel Xeon W-2235 CPU, and 64 GB of RAM. The implementation of all methods is done using PyTorch version 1.11.

5.2 Effect of Hyperparameters

Effect of ϵ. To compare the impact of different clustering thresholds on model performance, we tried seven different thresholds in the experiment under $\#C = 2$ and compared their effects as shown in Table 1. Through analysis of the experimental results, we found that in this experiment, the model achieved the best performance when $\epsilon = 0.7$, and the time cost was also relatively small. Furthermore, we observed that the model's performance would decline when the ϵ value is too high or too low. This can be attributed to the fact that when the ϵ value is too high, the clustering degree of the clients will be weakened, thus

Table 1. The test accuracy (%) and the average time per round of global iteration(s) for FedCC on CIFAR10 under $\#C = 2$

Items	$\mho = 80\%$						$\epsilon = 0.7$				
	$\epsilon = 0$	$\epsilon = 0.3$	$\epsilon = 0.5$	$\epsilon = 0.7$	$\epsilon = 0.9$	$\epsilon = 1.0$	$\mho = 50\%$	$\mho = 60\%$	$\mho = 70\%$	$\mho = 80\%$	$\mho = 90\%$
Acc	83.45	84.36	83.83	**86.57**	85.19	82.87	85.69	86.10	**87.51**	86.57	84.69
Time	56.46	54.59	51.79	42.72	42.81	**35.50**	**37.18**	37.71	38.71	42.72	52.82

Table 2. The test accuracy (%) in the pathological heterogeneous settings.

Settings	Pathological heterogeneous setting $\#C = 2$				
dataset	USPS	MNIST (25%)	FMNIST	Cifar10	Cifar10_R
Local	94.47 ± 0.25	97.50 ± 0.66	93.40 ± 0.53	82.57 ± 0.19	81.96 ± 0.50
FedAvg	92.86 ± 0.17	96.93 ± 1.93	78.99 ± 1.86	49.76 ± 3.90	49.45 ± 2.16
FedProx	97.22 ± 0.32	97.37 ± 2.05	97.04 ± 1.13	84.84 ± 2.34	84.80 ± 1.49
FedNova	93.58 ± 0.49	97.46 ± 1.69	96.14 ± 1.67	82.84 ± 0.33	84.35 ± 1.78
LG-FedAvg	96.05 ± 0.40	98.29 ± 0.10	96.92 ± 0.31	84.31 ± 0.83	82.99 ± 0.90
Per-FedAvg	94.02 ± 0.86	98.39 ± 0.63	96.08 ± 0.43	85.82 ± 0.56	86.64 ± 0.48
FLIS (DC)	97.13 ± 0.04	98.59 ± 0.15	97.38 ± 0.10	85.75 ± 0.47	86.18 ± 0.03
IFCA	97.17 ± 0.48	97.98 ± 0.18	97.17 ± 0.29	86.60 ± 0.15	84.38 ± 0.31
PACFL	96.77 ± 0.58	97.81 ± 0.64	97.28 ± 0.26	86.39 ± 0.38	85.88 ± 0.11
FedCC	$\mathbf{97.78 \pm 0.19}$	$\mathbf{98.97 \pm 0.12}$	$\mathbf{97.86 \pm 0.31}$	$\mathbf{87.51 \pm 0.44}$	$\mathbf{86.80 \pm 0.37}$

losing the meaning of clustering; on the other hand, when the ϵ value is too low, too many clients are clustered in the same cluster, which makes the clustering result not representative.

Effect of $\mho$. Increasing the hyperparameter $\mho$ increases the number of training iterations for the client's local model, allowing for more stable and efficient IHC generation in the early stages of training. Table 1 illustrates the effects of different values of $\mho$ on training time. We noticed that when $\mho = 50\%$, the time cost is the lowest because the local model terminates training too early, which results in poor IHC generation in the early stages of training and a reduction in model performance. On the other hand, when $\mho = 90\%$, the local model undergoes too much training, causing overfitting and burdening the client, mainly on resource-limited mobile devices. However, when $\mho$ reaches an appropriate value, such as $\mho = 70\%$, the local model achieves high performance after adequate training, and the required training time is shorter.

We chose $\epsilon = 0.7$ and $\mho = 70\%$ as the optimal parameter in the $\#C = 2$ setting.

5.3 Performance Comparison

Pathological Heterogeneous Setting. In this setting, there are obvious similarities between the clients, which facilitates using similarity metric methods to measure the similarity between clients. Table 2 shows the results when $\#C = 2$. The FedAvg algorithm is based on the average gradient method. When there are differences in the data distribution between clients, this averaging makes model training difficult, resulting in poor performance of the FedAvg algorithm in such cases. In contrast, the personalized and clustered methods perform better because they can improve the model's accuracy by fine-tuning it or utilizing the similarity between clients. FedCC can dynamically determine the number of clusters and utilize IHC to achieve more effective clustering, thus outperforming the baselines on each dataset.

To demonstrate our method's superiority, we added another Non-IID scenario, where images were randomly selected from CIFAR10 and rotated by 90 degrees to form the CIFAR10_R dataset [38]. In this case, the data heterogeneity between clients becomes more prominent, requiring stronger generalization capabilities to solve the problems of model drift and weight differences. The experimental results show that FedCC is minimally affected and has the highest accuracy, outperforming all other baselines.

Table 3. The test accuracy (%) in the practical heterogeneous settings.

Settings	Practical heterogeneous setting $Dir(0.1)$			
dataset	USPS	MNIST(25%)	FMNIST	Cifar10
Local	83.22 ± 0.94	81.86 ± 0.35	74.80 ± 0.69	46.09 ± 0.58
FedAvg	94.31 ± 0.20	97.01 ± 0.72	82.81 ± 0.79	43.69 ± 2.88
FedProx	93.82 ± 0.48	97.20 ± 0.19	85.35 ± 0.21	52.65 ± 2.37
FedNova	85.23 ± 2.34	94.23 ± 0.60	85.16 ± 0.54	44.23 ± 1.77
LG-FedAvg	85.19 ± 0.15	84.34 ± 0.50	76.12 ± 0.15	46.78 ± 0.27
Per-FedAvg	90.18 ± 0.12	96.14 ± 0.69	82.58 ± 0.31	53.19 ± 0.29
FLIS (DC)	94.05 ± 0.11	97.56 ± 0.20	85.26 ± 0.13	53.29 ± 0.66
IFCA	94.71 ± 0.45	97.09 ± 0.38	84.25 ± 0.36	52.06 ± 0.55
PACFL	84.86 ± 0.94	83.11 ± 0.68	85.21 ± 0.56	52.93 ± 1.97
FedCC	$\mathbf{95.06 \pm 0.79}$	$\mathbf{97.71 \pm 0.55}$	$\mathbf{85.73 \pm 0.98}$	$\mathbf{53.63 \pm 0.91}$

Practical Heterogeneous Setting. The experimental results under the $Dir(0.1)$ heterogeneous condition are shown in Table 3. It was observed that PACFL performs poorly on the USPS and MNIST (25%) datasets. This is primarily due to two reasons. Firstly, the limited size of training data and the high complexity of each client makes it challenging to capture the main features of the underlying distribution using SVD. This results in the server being unable to directly recognize the similarity between the distributions of the clients, thereby affecting PACFL's clustering accuracy on clients. Secondly, PACFL is a hard clustering method, restricting each client to be assigned to only one cluster. However, the experimental results demonstrate that soft clustering methods, such as FedCC and FLIS (DC), perform better.

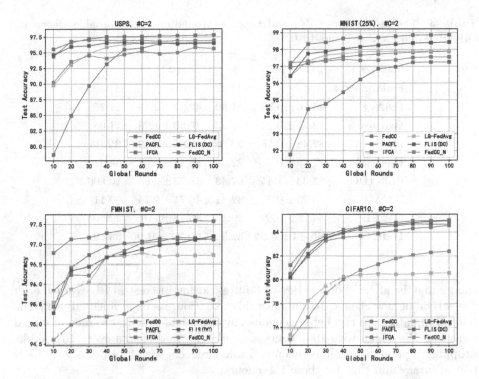

Fig. 3. The test accuracy versus number of communication rounds under $\#C = 2$.

Additionally, the experimental results indicate that IHC can more accurately represent the data distribution of clients, thereby achieving better clustering results.

Learning with Limited Communication. To evaluate the performance and stability of FedCC under different conditions, we imposed stricter constraints on the Pathological heterogeneous experiment in Table 2 [8]. We reduced the global iteration count by half and doubled the number of clients, which means that the amount of data per client was reduced by half. We compared FedCC with other baseline methods and conducted ablation experiments. In the ablation experiment, the client only uses a cluster model to generate IHC, named FedCC_N. As shown in Fig. 3, the experimental results display the average local test accuracy of all participating training clients every ten rounds.

FedCC outperforms other baselines on four datasets. Even when communication is restricted, our method's accuracy does not decrease too much, indicating that our method has low requirements for the amount of client data and communication rounds, significantly improving the performance of handling Non-IID data. Additionally, FedCC_N experimental results showed that introducing local models can accelerate convergence and significantly improve accuracy.

Dynamic Clients. Traditional FL assumes that the number of clients is static and can participate in training. However, in practical scenarios, the number of

Table 4. The test accuracy (%) and time per round(s) across variable clients on CIFAR10 under #C = 2 and dir(0.1)

Settings	#C = 2		$Dir(0.1)$	
Performances	Acc	Time	Acc	Time
FedAvg	46.10 ± 0.86	21.30	42.27 ± 2.18	31.75
FedProx	82.77 ± 0.34	31.53	45.00 ± 1.96	41.08
LG-FedAvg	82.48 ± 0.58	**21.16**	44.88 ± 0.99	**32.03**
Per-FedAvg	77.89 ± 0.41	22.62	48.43 ± 0.62	34.37
FLIS (DC)	83.33 ± 1.45	67.43	48.26 ± 0.85	109.06
IFCA	83.20 ± 0.25	32.41	49.71 ± 0.74	50.11
PACFL	84.18 ± 0.69	29.13	45.77 ± 1.31	42.50
FedCC	**85.84 ± 0.57**	32.34	**50.37 ± 0.90**	53.19

clients may be affected due to device failures, losing interest in FL over time, or the arrival of new clients. To simulate this situation, we experimented using the CIFAR10 dataset in two heterogeneous environments over 110 rounds of global iteration. We began with 100 clients and added 5 new clients every 10 rounds, dropping 5 previously trained clients. Table 4 reflects the absolute average local test accuracy and time for these 150 clients.

Our experimental results demonstrate that our method outperforms other methods, indicating its effectiveness in dynamically handling changing client numbers in FL. Furthermore, since clients in FLIS (DC) need to download all cluster models and perform local testing, the time overhead is significantly higher than other methods, resulting in substantial computational costs for the clients. Although our method performs poorly regarding the average time per round metric, there is still room for optimization to reduce training time further - a direction for future research endeavours.

Table 5. The test accuracy (%) for all clients with different numbers of malicious clients on CIFAR10 under #C = 2

Malicious clients	10	20	30
FedAvg	17.91 ± 0.86	9.00 ± 2.50	10.50 ± 3.50
FedProx	77.78 ± 2.05	50.00 ± 0.00	50.00 ± 0.00
LG-FedAvg	**82.21 ± 0.74**	**81.93 ± 1.05**	**82.97 ± 0.63**
Per-FedAvg	50.00 ± 0.00	50.00 ± 0.00	50.00 ± 0.00
FLIS (DC)	76.57 ± 0.78	70.20 ± 1.03	63.39 ± 2.45
IFCA	58.46 ± 2.39	52.53 ± 1.43	50.00 ± 0.00
PACFL	63.09 ± 2.39	51.39 ± 0.69	50.00 ± 0.00
FedCC	79.66 ± 0.45	73.94 ± 1.64	68.83 ± 2.04

Robustness. To evaluate the robustness and security of FedCC, we conducted byzantine attacks. Expressly, we set up 100 clients on the CIFAR10 dataset. We inserted 10, 20, and 30 malicious clients who attempted to upload negative gradients to the server to cause a decrease in model accuracy and prevent convergence. Table 5 shows all clients' average final local test accuracy.

The results indicate that malicious clients significantly impact FedAvg since their negative gradients cancel out with other clients' gradients, rendering the global model unusable with an accuracy of 0% for most clients. As the number of malicious clients increases, the model parameters become chaotic, making it meaningless for FedProx and PerFedAvg to fine-tune the model. IFCA and PACFL are also severely attacked by malicious clients. The final average accuracy of the clients in the method above is close to 50%, which we analyzed as being due to the loss of trainability in the model at this point and because there were only two classes of data among client samples - thus resulting in random guessing by the model with a probability of 50%. The FLIS(DC) retains some model performance because it tests all cluster models on each client's local test set and selects the one with the highest accuracy. In contrast, the accuracy of the LG-FedAvg was not affected by malicious clients because it only retains a portion of the global model's parameters on each client, equivalent to pruning the gradient of the global model, reducing the impact of malicious clients.

FedCC outperformed all baselines except LG-FedAvg. FedCC can resist Byzantine attacks because IHC efficiently represents the client's data distribution, enabling DBSCAN to achieve efficient clustering. Furthermore, we set relatively small $MinPts$ to generate more cluster models. Malicious clients typically only affect the local clusters around them with the negative gradients they send instead of acting on all clusters.

6 Conclusion

In this paper, we propose a cFL method called FedCC, based on Inference Hash Codes, aiming to achieve accurate and efficient clustering of clients. Unlike previous methods, FedCC does not require pre-defining the number of clusters, and clients do not need to download all cluster models while protecting client privacy. We conducted experimental comparisons, and the results showed that FedCC outperforms seven baseline methods in accuracy and is robust against Byzantine attacks. In the future, we will focus on minimizing the training time of FedCC as much as possible. We will further optimize the algorithm and explore new optimization approaches to achieve this.

Acknowledgements. We thank the anonymous reviewers for their helpful feedback. This work is supported by the National Key Research and Development Program of China (Grant No. 2021YFB0301100)

References

1. Reisizadeh, A., Mokhtari, A., Hassani, H., Jadbabaie, A., Pedarsani, R.: FedPAQ: a communication-efficient federated learning method with periodic averaging and quantization. In: International Conference on Artificial Intelligence and Statistics, pp. 2021–2031. PMLR (2020)
2. Dinh, C.T., Tran, N., Nguyen, J.: Personalized federated learning with Moreau envelopes. In: Advances in Neural Information Processing Systems, vol. 33, pp. 21394–21405 (2020)
3. Li, X., Huang, K., Yang, W., Wang, S., Zhang, Z.: On the convergence of FedAvg on Non-IID data. arXiv preprint arXiv:1907.02189 (2019)
4. Li, Q., Diao, Y., Chen, Q., He, B.: Federated learning on Non-IID data silos: an experimental study. In: 2022 IEEE 38th International Conference on Data Engineering (ICDE), pp. 965–978. IEEE (2022)
5. Liang, P.P., et al.: Think locally, act globally: federated learning with local and global representations. arXiv preprint arXiv:2001.01523 (2020)
6. Vahidian, S., Morafah, M., Lin, B.: Personalized federated learning by structured and unstructured pruning under data heterogeneity. In: 2021 IEEE 41st International Conference on Distributed Computing Systems Workshops (ICDCSW), pp. 27–34. IEEE (2021)
7. Fallah, A., Mokhtari, A., Ozdaglar, A.: Personalized federated learning with theoretical guarantees: a model-agnostic meta-learning approach. In: Advances in Neural Information Processing Systems, vol. 33, pp. 3557–3568 (2020)
8. Vahidian, S., et al.: Efficient distribution similarity identification in clustered federated learning via principal angles between client data subspaces. In: Proceedings of the AAAI Conference on Artificial Intelligence, vol. 37, pp. 10043–10052 (2023)
9. Liu, B., Guo, Y., Chen, X.: PFA: privacy-preserving federated adaptation for effective model personalization. In: Proceedings of the Web Conference 2021, pp. 923–934 (2021)
10. Sattler, F., Müller, K.-R., Samek, W.: Clustered federated learning: model-agnostic distributed multitask optimization under privacy constraints. IEEE Trans. Neural Netw. Learn. Syst. **32**(8), 3710–3722 (2020)
11. Ghosh, A., Chung, J., Yin, D., Ramchandran, K.: An efficient framework for clustered federated learning. In: Advances in Neural Information Processing Systems, vol. 33, pp. 19586–19597 (2020)
12. Mansour, Y., Mohri, M., Ro, J., Suresh, A.T.: Three approaches for personalization with applications to federated learning. arXiv preprint arXiv:2002.10619 (2020)
13. Morafah, M., Vahidian, S., Wang, W., Lin, B.: FLIS: clustered federated learning via inference similarity for Non-IID data distribution. IEEE Open J. Comput. Soc. **4**, 109–120 (2023)
14. Slaney, M., Casey, M.: Locality-sensitive hashing for finding nearest neighbors [lecture notes]. IEEE Signal Process. Mag. **25**(2), 128–131 (2008)
15. Bäcklund, H., Hedblom, A., Neijman, N.: A density-based spatial clustering of application with noise. Data Mining TNM033 **33**, 11–30 (2011)
16. Knott, B., Venkataraman, S., Hannun, A., Sengupta, S., Ibrahim, M., van der Maaten, L.: CrypTen: secure multi-party computation meets machine learning. In: Advances in Neural Information Processing Systems, vol. 34, pp. 4961–4973 (2021)
17. Bonawitz, K., et al.: Towards federated learning at scale: system design. Proc. Mach. Learn. Syst. **1**, 374–388 (2019)

18. Sattler, F., Wiedemann, S., Müller, K.-R., Samek, W.: Robust and communication-efficient federated learning from Non-IID data. IEEE Trans. Neural Netw. Learn. Syst. **31**(9), 3400–3413 (2019)
19. Zhao, Y., Li, M., Lai, L., Suda, N., Civin, D., Chandra, V.: Federated learning with Non-IID data. arXiv preprint arXiv:1806.00582 (2018)
20. Li, T., Sahu, A.K., Zaheer, M., Sanjabi, M., Talwalkar, A., Smith, V.: Federated optimization in heterogeneous networks. In: Proceedings of Machine Learning and Systems, vol. 2, pp. 429–450 (2020)
21. Finn, C., Abbeel, P., Levine, S.: Model-agnostic meta-learning for fast adaptation of deep networks. In: International Conference on Machine Learning, pp. 1126–1135. PMLR (2017)
22. Lee, J.-W., Oh, J., Lim, S., Yun, S.-Y., Lee, J.-G.: TornadoAggregate: accurate and scalable federated learning via the ring-based architecture. arXiv preprint arXiv:2012.03214 (2020)
23. Hu, H., Dobbie, G., Salcic, Z., Liu, M., Zhang, J., Zhang, X.: A locality sensitive hashing based approach for federated recommender system. In: 2020 20th IEEE/ACM International Symposium on Cluster, Cloud and Internet Computing (CCGRID), pp. 836–842. IEEE (2020)
24. Jafari, O., Maurya, P., Nagarkar, P., Islam, K.M., Crushev, C.: A survey on locality sensitive hashing algorithms and their applications. arXiv preprint arXiv:2102.08942 (2021)
25. He, W., Li, Y., Zhang, Y., Li, X.: A binary-search-based locality-sensitive hashing method for cross-site user identification. IEEE Trans. Comput. Soc. Syst. **10**(2), 480–491 (2022)
26. Qi, L., Zhang, X., Dou, W., Ni, Q.: A distributed locality-sensitive hashing-based approach for cloud service recommendation from multi-source data. IEEE J. Sel. Areas Commun. **35**(11), 2616–2624 (2017)
27. Liu, P., Yu, X., Zhou, J.T.: Meta knowledge condensation for federated learning. arXiv preprint arXiv:2209.14851 (2022)
28. Li, D., Wang, J.: FedMD: heterogenous federated learning via model distillation. arXiv preprint arXiv:1910.03581 (2019)
29. Tan, Y., Guodong Long, L., Liu, T.Z., Qinghua, L., Jiang, J., Zhang, C.: FedProto: federated prototype learning across heterogeneous clients. In: Proceedings of the AAAI Conference on Artificial Intelligence, vol. 36, pp. 8432–8440 (2022)
30. Liu, X.: Synthetic dataset generation for adversarial machine learning research. arXiv preprint arXiv:2207.10719 (2022)
31. McMahan, H.B., Moore, E., Ramage, D., Arcas, B.: Federated learning of deep networks using model averaging. arXiv preprint arXiv:1602.05629, vol. 2, p. 2 (2016)
32. McMahan, B., Moore, E., Ramage, D., Hampson, S., Arcas, B.A.: Communication-efficient learning of deep networks from decentralized data. In: Artificial Intelligence and Statistics, pp. 1273–1282. PMLR (2017)
33. Shamsian, A., Navon, A., Fetaya, E., Chechik, G.: Personalized federated learning using hypernetworks. In: International Conference on Machine Learning, pp. 9489–9502. PMLR (2021)
34. Li, Q., He, B., Song, D.: Model-contrastive federated learning. In: Proceedings of the IEEE/CVF Conference on Computer Vision and Pattern Recognition, pp. 10713–10722 (2021)
35. Li, T., Sahu, A.K., Talwalkar, A., Smith, V.: Federated learning: challenges, methods, and future directions. IEEE Sig. Process. Mag. **37**(3), 50–60 (2020)

36. Lin, T., Kong, L., Stich, S.U., Jaggi, M.: Ensemble distillation for robust model fusion in federated learning. In: Advances in Neural Information Processing Systems, vol. 33, pp. 2351–2363 (2020)
37. Wang, J., Liu, Q., Liang, H., Joshi, G., Vincent Poor, H.: Tackling the objective inconsistency problem in heterogeneous federated optimization. In: Advances in Neural Information Processing Systems, vol. 33, pp. 7611–7623 (2020)
38. Castellon, F.E., Mayoue, A., Sublemontier, J.-H., Gouy-Pailler, C.: Federated learning with incremental clustering for heterogeneous data. In: 2022 International Joint Conference on Neural Networks (IJCNN), pp. 1–8. IEEE (2022)

TIA: Token Importance Transferable Attack on Vision Transformers

Tingchao Fu[1], Fanxiao Li[1], Jinhong Zhang[2], Liang Zhu[3], Yuanyu Wang[3(✉)], and Wei Zhou[4(✉)]

[1] Engineering Research Center of Cyberspace, Yunnan University, Kunming, China
futingchao@stu.ynu.edu.cn, lifanxiao@mail.ynu.edu.cn
[2] School of Information Science and Engineering, Yunnan University, Kunming, China
zhangjinhong_vxnr@stu.ynu.edu.cn
[3] Kunming Institute of Physics, Kunming, China
wxyjin232425@163.com
[4] National Pilot School of Software, Yunnan University, Kunming, China
zwei@ynu.edu.cn

Abstract. Vision transformers (ViTs) have witnessed significant progress in the past few years. Recently, the latest research revealed that VITs are vulnerable to transfer-based attacks, in which attackers can use a local surrogate model to generate adversarial examples, then transfer these malicious examples to attack the target black-box ViT directly. Suffering from the threat of transfer-based attacks, it is challenging to deploy ViTs to security-critical tasks. Therefore, it becomes an exact need to explore the robustness of ViTs against transfer-based attacks. However, existing transfer-based attack methods do not fully consider the unique structure of ViT, and they indiscriminately attack the intermediate outputs token of ViTs, leading to the perturbations being focused on specific model information within the tokens, and further resulting in a limited transferability of the generated adversarial examples. To address the current limitations, we propose Token Importance Attack (TIA), a novel ViTs-oriented transfer-based attack method. Specifically, we introduce Randomly Shuffle Patches (RSP) strategy to expand the diversity of the input space. By applying RSP, we can generate multiple shuffled images from a single image, allowing us to obtain multiple token gradients. Then TIA ensembles these token gradients of shuffled images as a guide map to focus the perturbation on the model-independent information in the token rather than model-specific information. Benefiting from these two components, TIA can avoid overfitting to the surrogate model, thus enhancing the transferability of the crafted adversarial examples. Extensive experiments conducted on common datasets with different ViTs and CNNs have demonstrated the effectiveness of TIA.

Keywords: Adversarial Examples · Transfer-base Attacks · Vision Transformer · Model Vulnerability

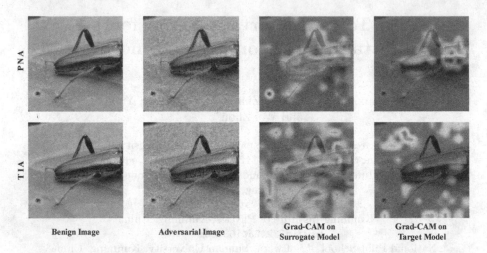

Fig. 1. Comparison of TIA and PNA, which indiscriminately perturbs the intermediate layer output tokens of ViTs. Adversarial examples generate by ViT-B16 to attack ConViT-B. By visualizing the model's attention using the Grad-CAM, it can observe that the adversarial examples generated by TIA cause both the surrogate model and the target model to focus their attention away from objects due to TIA perturbs the model-independent information within the intermediate output tokens.

1   Introduction

Vision Transformers (ViTs) [7] have shown superior performance in computer vision-related tasks, such as face recognition [26,29], semantic segmentation [1, 19], autonomous driving [17,35], medical diagnosis [14,22], etc. However, existing studies have shown that ViTs are vulnerable to adversarial examples [24], which can be crafted by adding imperceptible perturbation to the benign image and will mislead Deep Neural Networks (DNNs). Thus, it is vital to design effective attacks to explore the vulnerability of ViTs, which can help the community to improve the robustness of ViTs in some security-critical tasks.

Recently, many researchers have conducted considerable studies on generating adversarial examples to discover the vulnerability of DNNs. According to the accessible knowledge of the attackers about the victim model, attack methods can be roughly divided into two categories, i.e., white-box attacks and black-box attacks. Compared to white-box attacks which attackers know all the information of the target model, black-box attacks is more challenging and suitable in the real world [16]. In black-box attacks, query-based and transfer-based are two mainly methodologies. Query-based attacks require a large number of queries to the target black-box model, which is not feasible in practical scenarios [2]. In contrast, transfer-based attacks have been approved as one of the most threatening attack types [5], in which the attackers generate adversarial examples on a white-box surrogate model, then transfer these adversarial examples to attack the black-box target models without any queries, making it challenging to deploy

ViTs to security-critical tasks. Therefore, it is crucial to explore the vulnerability of ViTs through conducted studies on transfer-based attacks.

Transfer-based attacks on Convolution Neural Network (CNNs) have been extensively explored. These methods are designed based on the characteristics of CNNs to generate adversarial examples [6,8,14,18,20,32,34,36], e.g., the translation invariance property. However, they cannot achieve ideal attack performance when directly applied to ViTs due to the differences in structures between CNNs and ViTs. Specifically, unlike CNNs that extract image features for classification through convolution and pooling, ViTs crop one image into small patches and treat these patches as a sequence of input tokens to fit the architecture of the transformer. The output tokens of internal blocks in ViTs correspond to the extracted intermediate features in CNNs. Limited works attempt to enhance the transferability of adversarial examples by exploiting data augmentation or distorting intermediate layer output token based on the unique architecture of ViTs [21,33]. They have highlighted that attacking the ViTs intermediate layer output token can generate adversarial examples with high transferability. However, these methods are easily trapped into model-specific local optima since they indiscriminately perturbing tokens without considering their individual importance. It is obvious that if the attack focuses on model-specific information rather than model-independent information, it will lead to the adversarial examples overfitting to the surrogate model, and further restricting the transferability of the adversarial examples. Therefore, employing an appropriate guide map to guide the attack towards the model-independent information of tokens is crucial in enhancing the transferability of adversarial examples.

To address the limitation of existing transfer-based attacks easily trapping into model-specific local optima, we propose Token Importance Attack (TIA), which perturbs the model-independent information within the intermediate output tokens. Specifically, inspired by the observation that ViTs crop one image into small patches as a sequence of input tokens and how to encode spatial information is less critical in ViTs [7], we introduce a strategy called Randomly Shuffle Patches (RSP) to increase the diversity of the input space. By performing this operation, we can enhance the diversity of images by decomposing them into patches and reassembling them randomly without compromising the recognition performance of ViTs. As a result, multiple shuffled images can be generated from a single input image. These shuffled images are then fed into ViTs, and token gradients are computed through the process of backpropagation for each shuffled image. TIA subsequently ensembles these token gradients as a guide map so that suppress model-specific information and distort the model-independent information. Benefit from these processes, TIA allows adversarial examples to escape from model-specific local optima and improve transferability. Figure 1 illustrates the effectiveness of our proposed method. We utilize Grad-CAM [23] to visualize the interested regions of the adversarial examples in both the surrogate model and the black-box target model. Compared to advanced transfer-based attacks called Pay No Attention (PNA) [33], the adversarial examples generated by TIA demonstrate the inability of both the surrogate model ViT-B16 [7] and the black-box target model ConViT-B [4] to focus adequately on the objects in the image due to TIA perturbs the model-independent information within the intermediate output tokens. We follow the previous works to evaluate the performance of the proposed TIA against ViTs and CNNs. The experimental result demonstrate that the proposed TIA craft adversarial examples of remarkable transferability compared to the advanced transfer-based attacks. Our main contributions are summarized as follows:

- We propose Token Importance Attack (TIA), a novel method that enhances the transferability of adversarial examples by disrupting the model-independent information within the intermediate output token of ViTs.
- Inspired by the observation that ViTs crop one image into small patches as a sequence of input tokens and how to encode spatial information is less critical in ViTs, we propose a strategy namely Randomly Shuffle Patches (RSP) to enhance the diversity of input space.
- Extensive experiments are conducted on various ViTs and CNNs models to evaluate the effectiveness of TIA. Compared to the other advanced attack methods, the adversarial examples generate by TIA exhibit remarkable transferability.

2   Related Work

In transfer-based attacks, attackers can successfully attack other black-box target models using a surrogate model. In this section, we revisit the current transfer-based attacks against both CNNs and ViTs, while also discussing their limitations.

2.1   Transfer-Based Attacks on CNNs

Fast Gradient Sign Method (FGSM) [9] and Basic Iterative Method (BIM) [15] are fundamental attack methods. FGSM proposed a fast method for generating adversarial examples. It performs a one-step update in the direction of the sign of the gradient to generate the adversarial examples. BIM as an improved version of FGSM. It performs multiple iterations along the direction of the sign of gradient to find the optimal perturbation. However, BIM tends to overfit the source model, leading to poor transferability compared FGSM. Diversity Input Method (DIM) [34] is a data enhancement method that enriches the input space of samples by resize and padding, which solves the overfitting problem of adversarial examples to some extent and improves the transferability of adversarial examples. Momentum Iterative attack (MIM) [5] integrate the momentum term into the iterative attacks, which can stabilize update directions and escape from poor local maxima during the iterations, resulting in more transferable adversarial examples. In Translation-Invariant method (TIM) [6], the translation invariance property of CNNs is leveraged. It optimizes the perturbations for an ensemble of translated images by convolving the gradients with a linear or Gaussian kernel. Transferable Adversarial Perturbations (TAP) [36] maximizes the distance between benign images and their corresponding adversarial examples in the intermediate feature space while applying smooth regularization on adversarial perturbations to improve both white-box attacks and black-box attacks. Feature Importance-aware Attack (FIA) [32] is an advanced transfer-based attack on CNNs, which disrupts important object-aware features that dominate model decisions consistently. However, FIA utilizes a fixed aggregate gradient to attack the feature map, which can not consistently reflect the behavior of networks as the image is changed during iteration, limiting the transferability of adversarial examples. Moreover, it is important to note that the above approaches are designed based on the architecture and characteristics of CNNs. When these methods are directly applied to ViTs, their effectiveness is often compromised.

2.2   Transfer-Based Attacks on ViTs

In contrast to transfer-based attacks extensively studied on CNNs, there has been fewer effort in attacks on ViTs. ViTs exhibit more robustness compared to CNNs, making it challenging to achieve remarkable performance in transfer-base attacks on ViTs. Several related works have been proposed in recent years. Naseer et al. introduced the Self Ensemble method (SE) [21] to ensemble the class token from all blocks of the ViTs and feeds them into a shared classification head to extract information for generating adversarial examples. Additionally, Naseer et al. proposed Token Refinement (TR) [21] module to fine-tune the class tokens for further enhancing transferability. Although SE takes advantages of ViTs unique architecture, there are fewer ViTs have enough class token for SE to ensemble. Furthermore, TR suffers from significant time overhead as it requires training the TR module on ImageNet dataset. In order to destroy the self-attention in ViTs, Zhang et al. propose Pay No attention (PNA) [33] to view the attention map as a constant. Specifically, they change the gradient of the attention map to zero in the backpropagation. However, it is unreasonable to indiscriminately set all attention maps to a constant without considering their internal information, thus easily trapped into model-specific local optimum. In contrast, our method disrupt the model-independent information within the intermediate output token of ViTs, allowing adversarial examples to generalize better within ViTs.

In order to clearly position our study and highlight its unique contributions, we analyze the distinctions between our research and the existing studies as follows:

- Unlike existing transfer-based attacks on ViTs distorting intermediate layer output tokens indiscriminately, we propose TIA that specifically distorts the model-independent information within the tokens, allowing us to generate adversarial examples with high transferability.
- Unlike existing transfer-based attacks, we propose a novel approach specifically designed for ViTs, taking into account their unique architecture. We

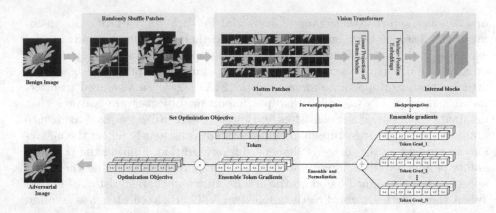

Fig. 2. Overview the overall framework of Token Importance Attack (TIA). Given a benign image, the first step is to apply the Random Shuffle Patches (RSP) to generate shuffled images. Next, tokens are extracted from the intermediate layers of ViTs. The token gradients are then computed via the backpropagation process. TIA further ensembles these gradients as a guide map to suppress model-specific information and distort the model-independent information. Through this framework, TIA effectively attacks model-independent information and enhances the transferability of adversarial examples.

introduce the strategy called Randomly Shuffle Patches (RSP) to enhance the diversity of the input space and avoid overfitting adversarial examples to the surrogate model.

3 Methodology

3.1 Problem Definition

We first set up some notations. We denote the surrogate model as $f_s : x \in X^{H \times W \times C} \rightarrow y \in Y^c$, where x and y denotes the benign image and the predicted label, respectively. And y is a c dimensional score vector containing pre-softmax scores for different classes. We aim to generate an adversarial example $x^{adv} = x + \epsilon$ to mislead model f_s and target model f_t, i.e., $f_s(x^{adv}) \neq y$ and $f_t(x^{adv}) \neq y$. ϵ is the perturbation we carefully designed constraint by L_∞ norm. Therefore, the objective of generating adversarial examples can be formulated as follows:

$$\arg \max_{x^{adv}} J(f_s(x^{adv}), y), s.t. \left\| x^{adv} - x \right\|_\infty \leq \epsilon, \tag{1}$$

where loss function J is the cross-entropy to measure the distance between the model out $f_s(x)$ and the ground-truth label y, $\left\| \cdot \right\|_\infty$ denotes the constraint L_∞ norm. Most existing attacks optimize this objective to generate adversarial examples, such as FGSM [9], BIM [15], MIM [5] and DIM [34]. They combine this optimization objective with techniques like momentum or input augmentation to generate highly transferable adversarial examples. Moreover, in transfer-based attacks, optimizing this objective only requires accessing a local surrogate model, without the need for any queries to the target model. This makes it more practical and feasible.

3.2   Overview

Our objective is to attack the model-independent information within the intermediate layer output tokens of ViTs in order to enhance the transferability of adversarial examples. As shown in the Fig. 2. We employ RSP to expand the diversity of the input space and get multiple shuffled images. Afterwards, these shuffled images and the benign image, are fed into ViTs, and the tokens are computed through forward propagation for the benign image. Token gradients are computed through backpropagation for the shuffled images. TIA ensembles these token gradients as a guide map, performing element-wise calculations with the tokens. This serves as the optimization objective to attack the model-independent information within the tokens.

3.3   Randomly Shuffle Patches

In order to attack the model-independent information within the intermediate output token of ViTs, we require a guide map to suggest the importance of information within the token. Gradients serves as an excellent weight for this purpose, which can be obtained as:

$$W_i^x = \frac{\partial J(f_s(x), y)}{\partial token_i(x)}, \tag{2}$$

where $J(\cdot)$ is the cross-entropy loss function to measures the distance between the output $f_s(x)$ of surrogate model and the label y, $token_i(x)$ denotes token output of the i-th layer of image x in ViTs.

Obviously, W_i^x is closely related to the contribution to the model's output. Higher element values in W_i^x indicate a larger contribution to the model's output, vice versa. However, over-reliance on gradient will lead the generated adversarial examples trapped in local optima of the model. Because the original token gradients contain model-specific information, reflecting the bias of the surrogate model towards the importance of specific tokens. Attacking these model-specific features will lead to overfitting to the surrogate model, thus reducing the transferability of adversarial examples.

To suppress the model-specific information, we use RSP to expand the diversity of input space. During each iteration, we perform N times RSP on the image $x \in X^{H \times W \times C}$, resulting in N shuffled images of size $x_n \in X^{M \times P \times P \times C}$, where H, W and C denotes the height, width and channel of the input image, M represents the number of patches and P represents the patch length. Our method calculates guide map for each of the N shuffled images by applying Eq. 2 during each iteration, and then ensemble them together as follows:

$$W = \sum_{n}^{N} \frac{1}{\|W_i^{x_n}\|_2} W_i^{x_n}, \tag{3}$$

where N represents the number of RSP performed for each iteration of the images, $\|\cdot\|_2$ denotes L_2 norm for normalizing.

Algorithm 1. Token Importance Attack

Input: A benign image x with its ground-truth class y, a white-box surrogate model f_s, the perturbation budge ϵ, iteration number T, the times of Randomly Shuffle Patches N, the number of patches in Randomly Shuffle Patches of a image M, initialize the momentum g, step size α, decay factor μ.

Output: Adversarial example x^{adv}

1: **for** $t = 1$ to T **do**
2:    **for** $n = 1$ to N **do**
3:      Randomly Shuffle Patches to get x_n and calculate $W_i^{x_n}$ according to Eq. 2.
4:    **end for**
5:    Ensemble the weights W according to Eq. 3.
6:    Set optimization objective:
     $L(token_i(x_t^{adv})) = \sum(W \cdot token_i(x_t^{adv}))$.
7:    Update x^{adv} by momentum iterative method:
     $g_{t+1} = \mu \cdot g_t + \frac{\nabla L(token_i(x_t^{adv}))}{\|L(token_i(x_t^{adv}))\|_1}$,
     $x_{t+1}^{adv} = Clip_{x,\epsilon}(x_t^{adv} + \alpha \cdot sign(g_{t+1}))$.
8: **end for**

3.4   Token Importance Attack

Our objective is to perturb the intermediate layers of ViTs to generate adversarial examples with enhanced transferability. We disrupt the model-independent information within the intermediate output token of ViTs by utilizing the guide map derived from Eq. 3. To achieve this, we consider the following optimization objective:

$$L(token_i(x)) = \sum(W \cdot token_i(x)), \tag{4}$$

where W guide the importance of information within the token. Higher element values in W represent regions of critical features that are model-independent in the token. Increasing lower element values and decreasing higher element values guide the adversarial examples towards more transferable directions.

Importantly, by ensembling the weights derived from the RSP, the importance score within W comes to be model-independent, thus enabling the shared knowledge across multiple models and further enhances the transferability of generated adversarial examples. Combined with Eq. 1, our optimization objective function can be defined as:

$$\arg\max_{x^{adv}} L(token_i(x^{adv})), s.t. \|x^{adv} - x\|_\infty \leq \epsilon. \tag{5}$$

We adopt the momentum optimization method to solve Eq. 5 [5], i.e., during the T iterations, the perturbation is added using the following formula:

$$x_{t+1}^{adv} = Clip_{x,\epsilon}(x_t^{adv} + \alpha \cdot sign(g_{t+1})), \tag{6}$$

where α represents the step size, $sign(\cdot)$ denotes the sign function applied to g_{t+1}, and $Clip_{x,\epsilon}$ operation constrains the pixel values of the adversarial image within a reasonable range, ensuring that the perturbation remains within the range of ϵ. g_{t+1} is the momentum at iteration $t+1$, calculated by the following formula:

$$g_{t+1} = \mu \cdot g_t + \frac{\nabla L(token_i(x_t^{adv}))}{\left\| L(token_i(x_t^{adv})) \right\|_1}, \tag{7}$$

where g_t is the momentum at iteration t, μ is the momentum decay factor, $\nabla L(token_i(x_t^{adv}))$ represents the gradient of the loss function $L(token_i(x_t^{adv}))$ with respect to adversarial image x_t^{adv} at iteration t, $\|\cdot\|_1$ denotes the L_1 norm.

The final adversarial examples can be obtained by iterating T times using these formulas. The details of our proposed method are outlined in Algorithm 1.

4   Experiments

4.1   Experimental Settings

- **Dataset.** We use an ImageNet-compatible dataset consisting of 1000 images, which has been previously used in the NIPS 2017 Adversarial Attack Competition.
- **Models.** In order to evaluate our attack performance, we conducted transferability attack tests on ViTs. In this experiment, we utilized the surrogate models ViT-B16 [7], PiT-B [13], and CaiT-S-24 [31] to generate adversarial examples. The ViTs target models included ViT-B16 [7], PiT-B [13], CaiT-S-24 [31], Visformer-S [3], DeiT-B [30], TNT-S [11], LeViT-256 [10], and ConViT-B [4], CNNs target models included VGG16 (Vgg-16) [25], VGG19 (Vgg-19) [25], ResNet-50 (Res-50) [12], ResNet-152 (Res-152) [12], Inc eption-V3 (Inc-v3) [28], Inception-V4 (Inc-v4) [27] and Inception-ResNet-V2 (IncRes-v2) [27]. All these models are pretrained on ImageNet and have achievement an average performance of over 90%.
- **Baseline Attacks.** To demonstrate the effectiveness of the our approach, we compared with advanced attack methods on both CNNs and ViTs. Specifically, we compared out method against the following attack methods: FGSM [9], BIM [15], MIM [5], TIM [6], TAP [36], and PNA [33].
- **Evaluation Metric.** In the experiments, the evaluation metric used is the Attack Success Rate (ASR), which is the ratio of successfully misleading the target model among all generated adversarial examples. ASR can be calculated as follows:

$$ASR = \frac{\sum_{l=1}^{L} \left\{ f_t(x_l^{adv}) \neq y_l \right\}}{\sum_{l=1}^{L} \left\{ f_s(x_l) = y_l \right\}}, \tag{8}$$

where x_l denotes the l-th images in a datasets of size L, y_l represents the label corresponding to the image x_l. The denominator represents the number of benign images in which the surrogate model f_s correctly predicts the label, while the numerator represents the number of adversarial examples generated from these benign images that cause the target model f_t to produce incorrect outputs.

– **Parameter Settings.** In all experiments, the maximum perturbation $\epsilon = 16/255$, the iteration $T = 10$, the decay factor $\mu = 1.0$, and step size $\alpha = \epsilon/T = 1.6/255$. In our method, the image was divided into $M = 16$ patches, and the ensemble number of RSP was set to $N = 30$. We choose to attack i-th layer as the output of the last layer-normalization module in ViTs, specifically the layer immediately preceding the final classification layer.

Table 1. ASR of different attacks against normally trained ViTs models.

Surrogate Model	Method	ViT-B16	PiT-B	CaiT-S-24	Visformer-S	DeiT-B	TNT-S	LeViT-256	ConViT-B
ViT-B16	FGSM	75.00%	28.28%	41.74%	31.89%	40.36%	35.70%	30.61%	44.92%
	BIM	100.00%	20.39%	52.54%	23.09%	49.26%	33.69%	21.50%	51.48%
	MIM	100.00%	42.80%	71.50%	45.55%	69.81%	55.93%	40.89%	73.52%
	TIM	99.79%	29.24%	37.50%	31.46%	36.97%	35.28%	24.26%	40.04%
	TAP	99.68%	20.87%	56.78%	23.31%	51.80%	36.55%	23.73%	54.87%
	PNA	98.13%	37.92%	70.55%	39.30%	68.11%	54.03%	37.39%	73.94%
	Ours	**100.00%**	**43.33%**	**72.56%**	**50.21%**	**71.50%**	**59.43%**	**44.60%**	**74.36%**
PiT-B	FGSM	20.85%	61.20%	27.77%	32.34%	25.85%	29.57%	28.09%	30.11%
	BIM	16.38%	100.00%	25.74%	37.23%	23.30%	33.09%	28.30%	26.81%
	MIM	**38.51%**	100.00%	52.34%	62.02%	50.53%	59.89%	53.19%	51.81%
	TIM	29.15%	97.45%	37.66%	50.64%	40.43%	47.55%	33.83%	43.94%
	TAP	16.38%	94.57%	26.91%	38.19%	25.96%	36.17%	29.04%	28.94%
	PNA	27.84%	100.00%	45.70%	61.96%	44.53%	57.39%	52.18%	45.16%
	Ours	36.81%	**100.00%**	**54.86%**	**63.94%**	**52.66%**	**62.02%**	**55.53%**	**55.11%**
CaiT-S-24	FGSM	35.39%	33.44%	67.59%	37.86%	48.97%	42.80%	36.32%	50.31%
	BIM	52.98%	38.79%	99.79%	44.14%	83.95%	68.11%	40.95%	80.35%
	MIM	79.32%	65.64%	99.90%	72.02%	93.62%	83.74%	64.30%	92.39%
	TIM	55.04%	55.45%	94.03%	62.04%	73.77%	74.07%	48.77%	74.59%
	TAP	43.83%	27.47%	99.59%	31.17%	74.59%	51.03%	32.61%	70.78%
	PNA	64.71%	49.28%	**100.00%**	57.00%	92.00%	78.50%	54.73%	88.79%
	Ours	**81.69%**	**67.49%**	99.59%	**73.25%**	**95.27%**	**86.52%**	**70.16%**	**93.72%**

4.2   Comparison of Transferability

Transferability on ViTs. We first evaluate the adversarial transferability of our method across different ViTs. Table 1 summarizes the results on various black-box ViT models. From the results, we have the following observations. First, it's observed that classical attack methods like FGSM and BIM do not achieve ideal transferability on ViTs. Even in the white-box scenario, FGSM fails to achieve a 100% ASR. MIM is an advanced gradient-based attack approach that effectively improves the challenge of overfitting and greatly enhances the transferability of adversarial examples by incorporating momentum. When applied to ViTs, MIM exhibits impressive transferability. Moreover, TIM exhibits poorer attack performances on ViTs compared to other method. This is because TIM is developed based on the translation invariance property of CNNs, which is not applicable to ViTs. TAP aims to maximize the distance between benign images and their corresponding adversarial examples in the intermediate feature space while applying smooth regularization on adversarial perturbations and has shown promising transferability on CNNs. However, in this experiment, the performance of TAP on ViTs was not satisfactory due to the structural differences between ViTs and CNNs. These differences result in distinct intermediate outputs, which hinder the effectiveness of TAP on ViTs. To demonstrate the effectiveness of our method, we employed the powerful PNA on ViTs, which drop the attention map calculated by Q and K in gradient backpropagation. However, it is worth noting that PNA attacks all attention maps indiscriminately, which limits its transferability. On the contrary, our method attacks the model-independent intermediate layer output tokens, ensuring that the perturbations are not focused on model-specific information. This enhances the transferability of adversarial examples.

Table 2. ASR of different attacks against normally trained CNNs models.

Surrogate Model	Method	Vgg-16	Vgg-19	Res-50	Res-152	Inc-v3	Inc-v4	IncRes-v2
ViT-B16	FGSM	63.14%	58.69%	44.49%	35.70%	45.02%	38.24%	33.69%
	BIM	31.89%	29.87%	21.93%	18.22%	28.18%	24.79%	20.23%
	MIM	62.61%	60.91%	49.89%	42.69%	49.15%	45.76%	38.03%
	TIM	34.53%	31.67%	29.87%	28.81%	35.91%	34.64%	24.36%
	TAP	38.56%	35.49%	27.97%	23.31%	34.85%	29.77%	22.35%
	PNA	43.64%	39.51%	34.53%	27.54%	38.88%	33.47%	26.80%
	Ours	**67.69%**	**64.41%**	**52.01%**	**46.08%**	**51.91%**	**46.29%**	**41.31%**
PiT-B	FGSM	61.38%	60.00%	46.06%	34.89%	45.00%	36.91%	33.30%
	BIM	40.96%	39.15%	30.53%	24.47%	28.94%	25.21%	19.79%
	MIM	74.04%	70.21%	59.57%	49.57%	54.57%	50.00%	42.98%
	TIM	41.38%	39.26%	35.74%	28.83%	37.02%	36.60%	25.11%
	TAP	45.74%	45.32%	31.06%	26.60%	34.15%	29.89%	23.40%
	PNA	57.70%	54.62%	47.50%	40.28%	41.87%	43.04%	32.94%
	Ours	**74.57%**	**71.49%**	**62.45%**	**49.89%**	**57.66%**	**51.60%**	**46.28%**
CaiT-S-24	FGSM	69.75%	67.08%	48.46%	40.74%	47.02%	38.99%	35.19%
	BIM	45.47%	43.83%	38.37%	33.13%	37.86%	34.57%	28.81%
	MIM	77.57%	76.54%	65.84%	61.01%	63.27%	57.30%	53.70%
	TIM	51.85%	48.46%	46.91%	45.27%	47.43%	48.05%	37.24%
	TAP	45.06%	43.72%	32.41%	28.29%	37.65%	33.54%	25.21%
	PNA	58.02%	55.86%	50.00%	42.39%	45.06%	45.06%	37.24%
	Ours	**80.97%**	**79.42%**	**70.88%**	**62.45%**	**64.71%**	**60.91%**	**56.07%**

Transferability on CNNs. We further evaluated the transferability of adversarial examples from ViTs to CNNs, the experimental results are shown in Table 2. We have the following observations. First, many existing adversarial example generation methods do not achieve high ASR when transferred to CNNs due to the structural differences between ViTs and CNNs. Secondly, several adversarial examples generation methods based on CNNs characteristics, such as TIM and TAP, exhibit poor transferability. The adversarial examples generated by MIM, which are independent of the model architecture, still demonstrate strong transferability. Moreover, TIA effectively utilizes the information extracted by ViTs based on the unique characteristics of ViTs, resulting in the best performance of the generated adversarial examples on CNNs.

4.3   Ablation Study

To provide a deeper analysis of our method, we conducted an investigation into the attack layer, the effectiveness of Randomly Shuffle Patches and effectiveness of attacking model-independent information.

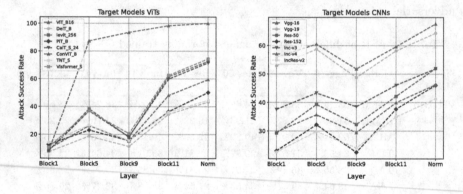

Fig. 3. The effectiveness of TIA by selecting various layers.

Attack Layer. We investigated which layer's output in the surrogate model achieves the best attack performance. Following the aforementioned experimental setup, we selected the outputs of the norm layer for Block1, Block5, Block9, Block11 in the surrogate model ViT-B16, as well as the last layer normalization before the classification layer. We computed the ASR of the generated adversarial examples on the target black-box models both ViTs and CNNs. The results are illustrated in Fig. 3, indicating that our attack performance improves as we choose deeper layers. We advocate that in the earlier layers of ViTs, insufficient information is extracted for effective classification. TIA achieved the best attack performance by selecting the last layer, which contains sufficient information extracted by ViTs. Although this information may include model-specific details, the presence of RSP ensures a greater focus on model-independent information, thereby mitigating the impact of model-specific details.

Table 3. The effectiveness of Randomly shuffle Patches

Surrogate Model	Target Model	No Randmly Shuffle Patches	Randmly Shuffle Patches
ViT-B16	ViTs	62.59%	**64.50%**
	CNNs	49.71%	**52.81%**
PiT-B	ViTs	58.19%	**60.05%**
	CNNs	57.69%	**59.13%**
CaiT-S-24	ViTs	81.38%	**83.46%**
	CNNs	65.06%	**67.92%**

Effectiveness of Randomly Shuffle Patches. We measure the transferability of adversarial examples generated from TIA under different conditions. Table 3 presents the average attack success rate of adversarial examples generated by TIA, both with and without using RSP, on the target model. The results show that TIA with RSP achieves an average attack success rate that is more than 2% higher compared to TIA without RSP, validating the effectiveness of RSP approach. Meanwhile, Figure 4 displays the shuffled images for different values of M in RSP. Figure 5 illustrates the average attack success rate of adversarial examples generated using the surrogate model ViT-B16 on both ViTs and CNNs, for different values of M in RSP. We can observe that the best results are achieved when $M = 16$. This is because choosing a larger M leads to smaller patch size $P \times P$, which results in more chaotic and unrecognizable images for both humans and models. This significant alteration of the spatial structure of the image not only decreases the model's classification accuracy but also reduces the effectiveness of our attack.

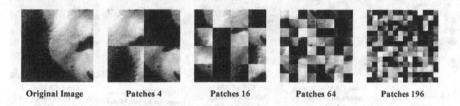

Original Image   Patches 4   Patches 16   Patches 64   Patches 196

Fig. 4. Shuffled images with different patches numbers.

Effectiveness of Attacking Model-Independent Information. To validate the effectiveness of TIA, we used Grad-CAM to visualize the regions of interest in the model for benign images and adversarial images generated by TIA. The highlighted regions in the heatmaps represent the areas that the model is focused on. Figure 6 shows that the adversarial examples generated by TIA successfully perturb the model-independent information. The regions of interest for both the surrogate model and the target model are shifted away from the intended object,

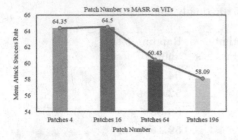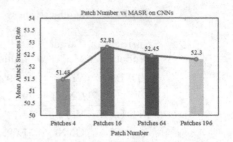

Fig. 5. Average success rate for different patches number M

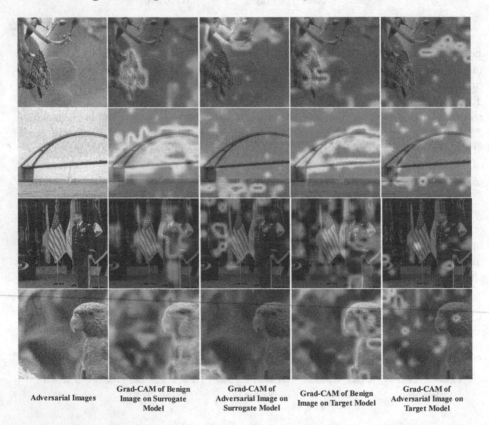

|Adversarial Images|Grad-CAM of Benign Image on Surrogate Model|Grad-CAM of Adversarial Image on Surrogate Model|Grad-CAM of Benign Image on Target Model|Grad-CAM of Adversarial Image on Target Model|

Fig. 6. Grad-CAM of adversarial images and benign images on the surrogate and target models.

indicating that the highlighted regions in the heatmaps for the adversarial images generated by TIA are significantly different from those of the clean benign. This demonstrates that TIA enables the generation of adversarial examples that escape the model-specific local optima, thereby enhancing the transferability of the adversarial examples.

5 Conclusion

In this paper, we analyzed the limitations of existing transfer-based attacks. These attacks did not consider the unique characteristics of ViTs and indiscriminately perturbed the intermediate layer output tokens, leading to adversarial examples generated by these methods overfitting the surrogate model. To generate adversarial examples with enhanced transferability, we proposed Token Importance Attack (TIA), a transfer-based attack on ViTs. Specifically, to effectively attack the model-independent information within the tokens, we introduced Randomly Shuffle Patches (RSP) inspired by the observation that how to encode spatial information is less critical in ViTs. We obtained multiple shuffled images from a single input image. These shuffled images are used as inputs to the ViTs, and token gradients are computed through backpropagation. TIA ensembles these token gradients as a guide map to suppress the model-specific information and direct the attack towards the model-independent information within the tokens. By these process, TIA can prevent overfitting to the surrogate model by attacking these model-independent information, thus enhancing the transferability. To validate the effectiveness of our proposed method, we conducted a comprehensive set of experiments. Compared to several advanced methods, TIA generates adversarial examples with high transferability. Additionally, we have demonstrated through using the visualization tool Grad-CAM that TIA perturbs model-independent information, helping adversarial examples to escape from model-specific local optima.

Acknowledgment. This work is supported in part by the National Natural Science Foundation of China under Grant 62162067 and 62101480, Research and Application of Object detection based on Artificial Intelligence, in part by the Yunnan Province expert workstations under Grant 202205AF150145.

References

1. Chen, L.C., Papandreou, G., Kokkinos, I., Murphy, K., Yuille, A.L.: DeepLab: semantic image segmentation with deep convolutional nets, atrous convolution, and fully connected CRFs. IEEE Trans. Pattern Anal. Mach. Intell. **40**(4), 834–848 (2017)
2. Chen, P.Y., Zhang, H., Sharma, Y., Yi, J., Hsieh, C.J.: ZOO: zeroth order optimization based black-box attacks to deep neural networks without training substitute models. In: Proceedings of the 10th ACM Workshop on Artificial Intelligence and Security, pp. 15–26 (2017)
3. Chen, Z., Xie, L., Niu, J., Liu, X., Wei, L., Tian, Q.: Visformer: the vision-friendly transformer. In: ICCV (2021)
4. d'Ascoli, S., Touvron, H., Leavitt, M.L., Morcos, A.S., Biroli, G., Sagun, L.: ConViT: improving vision transformers with soft convolutional inductive biases. In: ICML (2021)
5. Dong, Y., et al.: Boosting adversarial attacks with momentum. In: CVPR (2018)
6. Dong, Y., Pang, T., Su, H., Zhu, J.: Evading defenses to transferable adversarial examples by translation-invariant attacks. In: CVPR (2019)

7. Dosovitskiy, A., et al.: An image is worth 16x16 words: transformers for image recognition at scale. In: ICLR (2021)
8. Gao, L., Zhang, Q., Song, J., Liu, X., Shen, H.T.: Patch-wise attack for fooling deep neural network. In: Vedaldi, A., Bischof, H., Brox, T., Frahm, J.-M. (eds.) ECCV 2020. LNCS, vol. 12373, pp. 307–322. Springer, Cham (2020). https://doi.org/10.1007/978-3-030-58604-1_19
9. Goodfellow, I.J., Shlens, J., Szegedy, C.: Explaining and harnessing adversarial examples. In: Bengio, Y., LeCun, Y. (eds.) ICLR (2015)
10. Graham, B., et al.: LeViT: a vision transformer in convnet's clothing for faster inference. In: ICCV (2021)
11. Han, K., Xiao, A., Wu, E., Guo, J., Xu, C., Wang, Y.: Transformer in transformer. In: NIPS (2021)
12. He, K., Zhang, X., Ren, S., Sun, J.: Deep residual learning for image recognition. In: Proceedings of the IEEE Conference on Computer Vision and Pattern Recognition, pp. 770–778 (2016)
13. Heo, B., Yun, S., Han, D., Chun, S., Choe, J., Oh, S.J.: Rethinking spatial dimensions of vision transformers. In: ICCV (2021)
14. Kononenko, I.: Machine learning for medical diagnosis: history, state of the art and perspective. Artif. Intell. Med. **23**(1), 89–109 (2001)
15. Kurakin, A., Goodfellow, I.J., Bengio, S.: Adversarial examples in the physical world. In: ICLR (2017)
16. Li, Y., Li, Y., Xu, K., Yan, Q., Deng, R.H.: Empirical study of face authentication systems under OSNFD attacks. IEEE Trans. Dependable Secure Comput. **15**(2), 231–245 (2016)
17. Lillicrap, T.P., et al.: Continuous control with deep reinforcement learning. arXiv preprint arXiv:1509.02971 (2015)
18. Liu, R., et al.: DualFlow: generating imperceptible adversarial examples by flow field and normalize flow-based model. Front. Neurorobot. **17**, 1129720 (2023)
19. Long, J., Shelhamer, E., Darrell, T.: Fully convolutional networks for semantic segmentation. In: Proceedings of the IEEE Conference on Computer Vision and Pattern Recognition, pp. 3431–3440 (2015)
20. Naseer, M., Khan, S.H., Rahman, S., Porikli, F.: Task-generalizable adversarial attack based on perceptual metric. arXiv preprint arXiv:1811.09020 (2018)
21. Naseer, M., Ranasinghe, K., Khan, S., Khan, F.S., Porikli, F.: On improving adversarial transferability of vision transformers. In: ICLR (2022)
22. Papadakis, M.A., McPhee, S.J., Rabow, M.C.: Medical Diagnosis & Treatment. Mc Graw Hill, San Francisco, CA, USA (2019)
23. Selvaraju, R.R., Cogswell, M., Das, A., Vedantam, R., Parikh, D., Batra, D.: Grad-CAM: visual explanations from deep networks via gradient-based localization. In: Proceedings of the IEEE International Conference on Computer Vision, pp. 618–626 (2017)
24. Shao, R., Shi, Z., Yi, J., Chen, P.Y., Hsieh, C.J.: On the adversarial robustness of vision transformers. arXiv preprint arXiv:2103.15670 (2021)
25. Simonyan, K., Zisserman, A.: Very deep convolutional networks for large-scale image recognition. arXiv preprint arXiv:1409.1556 (2014)
26. Sun, Y., Wang, X., Tang, X.: Deeply learned face representations are sparse, selective, and robust. In: Proceedings of the IEEE Conference on Computer Vision and Pattern Recognition, pp. 2892–2900 (2015)
27. Szegedy, C., Ioffe, S., Vanhoucke, V., Alemi, A.: Inception-v4, inception-ResNet and the impact of residual connections on learning. In: Proceedings of the AAAI Conference on Artificial Intelligence, vol. 31 (2017)

28. Szegedy, C., Vanhoucke, V., Ioffe, S., Shlens, J., Wojna, Z.: Rethinking the inception architecture for computer vision. In: Proceedings of the IEEE Conference on Computer Vision and Pattern Recognition, pp. 2818–2826 (2016)
29. Taigman, Y., Yang, M., Ranzato, M., Wolf, L.: DeepFace: closing the gap to human-level performance in face verification. In: CVPR (2014)
30. Touvron, H., Cord, M., Douze, M., Massa, F., Sablayrolles, A., Jégou, H.: Training data-efficient image transformers & distillation through attention. In: ICML (2021)
31. Touvron, H., Cord, M., Sablayrolles, A., Synnaeve, G., Jégou, H.: Going deeper with image transformers. In: ICCV (2021)
32. Wang, Z., Guo, H., Zhang, Z., Liu, W., Qin, Z., Ren, K.: Feature importance-aware transferable adversarial attacks. In: Proceedings of the IEEE/CVF International Conference on Computer Vision, pp. 7639–7648 (2021)
33. Wei, Z., Chen, J., Goldblum, M., Wu, Z., Goldstein, T., Jiang, Y.: Towards transferable adversarial attacks on vision transformers. In: AAAI (2022)
34. Xie, C., et al.: Improving transferability of adversarial examples with input diversity. In: CVPR, pp. 2730–2739 (2019)
35. Yurtsever, E., Lambert, J., Carballo, A., Takeda, K.: A survey of autonomous driving: common practices and emerging technologies. IEEE Access 8, 58443–58469 (2020)
36. Zhou, W., et al.: Transferable adversarial perturbations. In: Ferrari, V., Hebert, M., Sminchisescu, C., Weiss, Y. (eds.) Computer Vision – ECCV 2018. LNCS, vol. 11218, pp. 471–486. Springer, Cham (2018). https://doi.org/10.1007/978-3-030-01264-9_28

Cryptography Engineering

Hardware Acceleration of NTT-Based Polynomial Multiplication in CRYSTALS-Kyber

Hang Yang, Rongmao Chen[✉], Qiong Wang[✉], Zixuan Wu, and Wei Peng[✉]

College of Computer Science and Technology, National University of Defense Technology, Changsha, China
{yanghang,chromao,wangqiong,wzxuan_,wpeng}@nudt.edu.cn

Abstract. CRYSTALS-Kyber is a promising post-quantum encryption candidate and has been selected for standardization. However, its operational efficiency faces challenges due to complex and time-consuming polynomial multiplication, which can be accelerated using number-theoretic transform (NTT). In this work, we propose a novel approach of hardware acceleration for NTT-based polynomial multiplication in CRYSTALS-Kyber on FPGA. Our approach leverages pipeline technology and optimized butterfly operation units with Montgomery and Barrott reductions, significantly improving computational efficiency. By running eight butterfly units in parallel, we achieve remarkably shorter computation cycles for key operations such as NTT, INTT, and PWM. Moreover, we introduce a dedicated Kyber algorithm PWM unit and optimized multi-RAM channel storage, greatly boosting memory access efficiency. This comprehensive optimization results in superior energy efficiency, surpassing other existing schemes and propelling the practical application of CRYSTALS-Kyber to new levels of efficiency.

Keywords: PQC · CRYSTALS-Kyber · NTT · FPGA

1 Introduction

Conventional public-key cryptographic systems rely on hardness assumptions such as integer factorization, discrete logarithm, and elliptic curve problems for security. However, the emergence of large-scale quantum computers poses a significant threat to these problems. Adversaries can exploit quantum algorithms like Shor's algorithm [1] or Grover's algorithm [2] to breach these traditionally hard problems. This development raises concerns and calls for the exploration of alternative cryptographic schemes resistant to quantum attacks, ensuring long-term security of sensitive information.

To address this challenge, extensive research has focused on post-quantum cryptography, developing cryptographic algorithms resistant to attacks from classical and quantum computers. The National Institute of Standards and Technology (NIST) in the United States has been standardizing post-quantum cryptography since 2016. Numerous post-quantum cryptographic schemes have

C. Ge and M. Yung (Eds.): Inscrypt 2023, LNCS 14527, pp. 111–129, 2024.
https://doi.org/10.1007/978-981-97-0945-8_7

been proposed, including lattice-based, code-based, multivariate polynomial-based, and hash-based systems. These schemes leverage mathematical structures believed to withstand attacks from classical and quantum computers. NIST recently released the fourth round of its Post-Quantum Cryptography Standardization process, featuring the CRYSTALS-Kyber algorithm [3].

In the context of Kyber lattice cipher schemes [4], polynomial multiplication plays a crucial role and often consumes substantial time and resources. To address this challenge, the Number-Theoretic Transform (NTT) is employed, significantly reducing the time complexity of polynomial multiplication and enhancing the overall efficiency of the Kyber algorithm. The NTT algorithm transforms polynomials into the number-theoretic domain, enabling efficient multiplication and subsequent inverse transformation. This approach empowers Kyber to offer robust security while maintaining reasonable computational overhead, ensuring its practicality and suitability for diverse applications.

When implementing the Kyber algorithm, achieving a balance between execution efficiency and resource consumption is crucial. FPGA platforms, known for their efficient parallel processing capabilities and high configurability [5,6], offer a well-suited solution for handling the cryptographic computations involved in Kyber. Leveraging FPGAs can significantly improve the algorithm's performance and efficiency, ensuring its practicality and suitability for resource-constrained environments. This becomes particularly important in rapidly evolving fields such as post-quantum cryptography. By harnessing the advantages of FPGA platforms, the Kyber algorithm can achieve optimal performance while effectively utilizing available resources.

1.1   Related Work

Previous works have primarily focused on optimizing the Kyber Key Encapsulation Mechanism (KEM) on FPGA devices. Researchers have explored various techniques, including innovative hardware designs and algorithmic enhancements, to optimize the core polynomial multiplication module, specifically the Number Theoretic Transform (NTT) algorithm.

An efficient hardware implementation of MLWE with $q = 7681$ based on a compact RLWE design was proposed by [7], however, it doesn't support the latest parameters. Mert et al. [8] optimized NTT operation at the word level using Montgomery modular multiplication, enabling software-hardware co-design via PCIe and DMA access. Zijlstra et al. [9] enhanced the Kyber algorithm using High-Level Synthesis (HLS), providing a detailed comparison of resource usage and time consumption. The Kyber algorithm's computation was accelerated by Fritzmann et al.'s [10] RISQ-V instruction set for FPGA. Chen et al. [7] mitigated RAM read-write conflicts using dual-column sequential storage and improved the butterfly operation with pipeline methods. Huang et al. [11] implemented a streamlined version of the Kyber algorithm on Xilinx Artix-7 and Virtex-7 FPGAs, realizing the NTT module in a pipelined form. However, the NTT computation cycle remained lengthy.

Mert et al. [12] utilized Montgomery modular multiplication to design butterfly operation units and allowed for parallel NTT computation by configuring parameters. In 2021, Mojtaba [13] applied a register-delay-free hardware unit, based on the K2-RED algorithm, for modulo 3329 reduction, enabling a high-speed design across four parallel NTT butterfly units. Although Yaman et al. [14] expedited NTT/INTT computation through 16 butterfly operation units, their modulo reduction module was complex, suggesting scope for improvement. Xing et al. [15] implemented the complete Kyber algorithm on Xilinx Artix-7, revealing potential for further enhancement in computation frequency. Ricci et al. [16] performed Kyber's NTT operation on the high-performance Xilinx Virtex UltraScale+ XCVU7P FPGA, achieving a computation period of 405. Ni et al. [17] balanced efficiency and resource consumption by implementing pipelined NTT/INTT and PWM algorithms on Artix XC7A200 and Zynq UltraScale+ XCZU7EV FPGAs. Lastly, Salarifard et al. [18] introduced a novel modulo reduction algorithm, leveraging pre-stored modular calculation values in BRAM, thus reducing DSP consumption and enhancing performance.

To enhance the FPGA implementation speed of the Kyber algorithm, two potential strategies could be employed: optimizing critical paths to improve computational efficiency and increasing parallelism between modules and data processing capability. Efforts to optimize critical paths play a crucial role in accelerating the Kyber algorithm on FPGA. By carefully examining and fine-tuning the most time-consuming operations, such as NTT-based polynomial multiplication, researchers can significantly improve computation speed. Furthermore, implementing specialized hardware modules tailored to exploit the unique features of lattice-based cryptography can lead to substantial performance gains. These optimizations aim to streamline the data flow and minimize delays caused by critical bottlenecks, ultimately enhancing the overall efficiency of the cryptographic scheme. Another avenue to boost FPGA implementation speed is by leveraging parallelism. Parallel processing allows multiple computations to take place simultaneously, thereby increasing throughput and reducing computation time. By exploring ways to efficiently distribute workloads among FPGA resources and exploiting parallelism within the Kyber algorithm's various components, researchers can unlock additional performance gains.

Despite these potential advantages, existing FPGA implementations of the Kyber algorithm have encountered challenges such as long NTT computation cycles and limited parallelism, thereby failing to meet the requirements of high-performance computing. Consequently, selecting the most suitable hardware implementation scheme under different performance and resource constraints remains an unresolved issue in the academic community.

1.2 Our Contributions

The prevailing solutions encounter difficulties like lengthy NTT computation rounds and limited parallelism. These shortcomings make them unsuitable for high-performance computing. Furthermore, some of these solutions do not support PWM computations. In response to these limitations, we propose algorithmic and hardware enhancements for the NTT core. These improvements are aimed at speeding up polynomial multiplication computations in hardware implementation. We offer a detailed examination of the NTT, INTT, and PWM stages of Kyber, selecting appropriate implementation methods based on computation, storage, and communication properties. Our goal is to augment the overall computational efficiency of Kyber, taking into account different aspects of the algorithm's computation stages. Here are the notable contributions and innovations of our work:

1. We put forward a specialized Montgomery modular reduction method for the NTT algorithm in Kyber. This technique surpasses the traditional Barrett reduction method in efficiency and resource utilization.
2. We suggest an innovative memory access optimization method for the Kyber algorithm. This approach ensures effective data storage, resolves read-write conflicts, and yields savings in coefficient storage space.
3. Our comprehensive FPGA architecture, which includes 8 parallel butterfly operation units, supports simultaneous NTT and INTT operations. This structure eliminates the necessity for preprocessing and postprocessing steps. We also design a pipelined PWM module that complements the architecture, further bolstering computational efficiency.

The remainder of the paper is organized as follows: Sect. 2 presents the theory of the Kyber algorithm and its associated NTT mathematical constructs. Section 3 elaborates on our hardware architecture and the optimization techniques employed. Section 4 displays our experimental outcomes and compares them with prior work. Section 5 concludes the paper with a summary and final thoughts on our work.

2 Preliminaries

2.1 Notation

The integer ring modulo a prime q is symbolized as Z_q whereas the polynomial ring takes the form $R_q = Z_q[X]/(X^n + 1)$. Throughout the Kyber protocol, distinct notations are utilized - unadorned lowercase letters denote single elements in R_q, while bold lowercase letters refer to k-element polynomial vectors. Bold uppercase letters correspond to $k \times k$ polynomial matrices. The n-th primitive root of unity in Z_q is represented by the Greek letter ζ, and its square by ω. In the Kyber system, values are designated for certain parameters: n is 256, q takes the value 3329, and ζ is set to 17. The variable k is flexible, with possible values ranging from 2 to 4.

2.2 CRYSTAL-KYBER

The parameters of the Kyber algorithm are shown in Table 1, where k is chosen to determine the dimensions of the polynomial matrix and adjust the algorithm's security level.

Table 1. Parameter sets for Kyber

	Security level	n	k	q
Kyber 512	1	256	2	3329
Kyber 768	2	256	3	3329
Kyber 1024	3	256	4	3329

The key generation, encryption, and decryption processes for the Kyber algorithm are as follows:

- **Key Generation:** $\mathbf{A} \in R_q^{k \times k}$, $\mathbf{s}$ and $\mathbf{e} \in R_q^k$. $\mathbf{pk} = \mathbf{A} \circ NTT(\mathbf{s}) + NTT(\mathbf{e})$, $\mathbf{sk} = NTT(\mathbf{s})$, where $\circ$ represents the polynomial matrix multiplication.

- **Encryption:** $\mathbf{A} \in R_q^{k \times k}$, $\mathbf{r}$ and $\mathbf{e}_1 \in R_q^k$, $e_2 \in R_q$. For a message msg, $\mathbf{u} = INTT(\mathbf{A}^T \circ NTT(\mathbf{r})) + \mathbf{e}_1$, $v = INTT(\mathbf{pk}^T \circ NTT(\mathbf{r})) + e_2 + msg$, where T represents the transpose operation.

- **Decryption:** $msg = v - INTT(\mathbf{sk}^T \circ NTT(\mathbf{u}))$.

During the key generation process, the public key $\mathbf{pk}$ and the private key $\mathbf{sk}$ are computed using $\mathbf{A}$, $\mathbf{s}$, and $\mathbf{e}$. For encryption, $\mathbf{A}$, $\mathbf{r}$, $\mathbf{e}_1$, and e_2 are utilized to calculate $\mathbf{u}$ and v. For decryption, the decrypted message msg is obtained by subtracting the NTT of the multiplication of $\mathbf{sk}$ and $\mathbf{u}$ from v.

2.3 NTT in KYBER

The Number Theoretic Transform (NTT) and its inverse transform (INTT) are highly efficient algorithms used for polynomial multiplication in the ring $R_q = Z_q[X]/(X^n + 1)$. These algorithms significantly reduce the computational complexity of polynomial multiplication from $O(n^2)$ to $O(n \log n)$. In the first edition of the Kyber standard, the prime modulus $q = 7681$ satisfies the condition $q \equiv 1 \mod 2n$. Moreover, the polynomial $X^n + 1 \equiv 0(\mod q)$ possesses a primitive 2n-th root in R_q.

The NTT and INTT algorithms for polynomial multiplication in $R_q[x]$ are defined as follows:

$$A_k = \sum_{j=0}^{n-1} a_j \zeta^{(2k+1)j} = \sum_{j=0}^{n-1} (a_j \zeta^j) \omega^{kj} \ (mod \ q) \tag{1}$$

$$a_j \equiv \frac{1}{n} \sum_{k=0}^{n-1} A_k \zeta^{-(2k+1)j} = \zeta^{-j} \cdot \frac{1}{n} \sum_{j=0}^{n-1} A_k \omega^{-kj} \ (mod \ q) \tag{2}$$

However, applying these formulas directly does not simplify the computational complexity associated with polynomial multiplication. To address this issue, we utilize elimination lemmas and half lemmas to break down the original n-point NTT into smaller sub-transforms based on the parity of the indices. This decomposition yields two new sequences, each with a size of n/2. The process continues recursively until reaching the two-point operations. These intermediate steps are commonly known as butterfly operations, where the NTT corresponds to the Cooley-Tukey butterflies, and the INTT corresponds to the Gentleman-Sande butterflies. The detailed calculation process is effectively illustrated in Fig. 1.

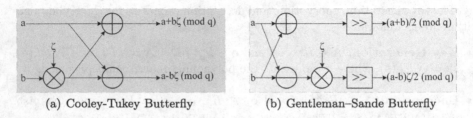

(a) Cooley-Tukey Butterfly   (b) Gentleman–Sande Butterfly

Fig. 1. Butterfly Unit

As an example, the complete operation of the 8-point NTT and INTT can be illustrated using three stages of butterfly transformations. Each stage is composed of four butterfly computation units, as depicted in Fig. 2.

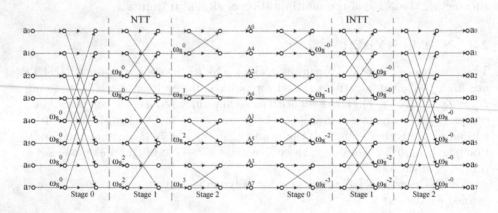

Fig. 2. Schematic Of NTT (left) And INTT (right)

In the latest round of the Kyber algorithm, the value of the modulus q has been reduced to 3329. Due to the fact that this prime number has only n distinct primitive roots but not $2n$ distinct primitive roots, direct calculations using formulas 1 and 2 are not viable. As stated in the official documentation, we can factorize the polynomial X^{256+1} over the ring, yielding the following result:

$$X^{256} + 1 = (X^2 - \zeta)(X^2 - \zeta^3) \dots (X^2 - \zeta^{2i+1}) \dots (X^2 - \zeta^{255}) \ (mod \ q) \quad (3)$$

Based on the Chinese Remainder Theorem (CRT), we can apply a mapping of the polynomial $a(x)$ to 128 individual polynomial rings $(X^2 - \zeta^{2i+1})$ over the given ring. Within these 128 polynomial rings, the congruence relation $(X^2 = \zeta 2i + 1) \ (mod \ q)$ can be obtained. Consequently, by distinguishing the parity of the coefficients in the polynomial $a(x)$, a novel approach for NTT can be derived:

$$NTT(a) = (A_0 + A_1 X, A_2 + A_3 X, \dots, A_{254} + A_{255} X) \quad (4)$$

$$A_{2i} = \sum_{j=0}^{127} a_{2j} \zeta^{(2i+1)j} = \sum_{j=0}^{127} (a_{2j} \zeta^j) \omega^{ij} \ (mod \ q) \quad (5)$$

$$A_{2i+1} = \sum_{j=0}^{127} a_{2j+1} \zeta^{(2i+1)j} = \sum_{j=0}^{127} (a_{2j+1} \zeta^j) \omega^{ij} \ (mod \ q) \quad (6)$$

Upon examining Eqs. 5 and 6, it is clear that they follow the principles of the conventional NTT. Thus, we can introduce a new twiddle factor, $\zeta = 17$, which enables the decomposition of the 256-point NTT into two separate NTT operations, each with 128 points. Following the polynomial NTT, a shift is made from conventional element-wise multiplication to point-wise multiplication. The computation procedure for this point-wise multiplication is as follows:

$$C_{2i} + C_{2i+1} X = (A_{2i} + A_{2i+} X)(B_{2i} + B_{2i+} X) \ (mod \ X^2 - \zeta^{2i+1}) \quad (7)$$

By simplifying Eq. 7, we obtain:

$$C_{2i} = A_{2i+1} \cdot B_{2i+1} \cdot \zeta^{2i+1} + A_{2i} \cdot B_{2i} \ (mod \ q) \quad (8)$$

$$C_{2i+1} = A_{2i} \cdot B_{2i+1} + A_{2i+1} \cdot B_{2i} \ (mod \ q) \quad (9)$$

The NTT, INTT, and PWM operations in the Kyber algorithm are presented in Algorithms 1, 2, and 3, respectively. In this context, we denote $br_k(i)$ as the reverse order representation of bit i in a k-bit sequence.

Algorithm 1. In-place DIT NTT

Input: $a(x) = (a_0, a_1, \ldots, a_{n-1})$ in standard order, ζ (s.t. $\zeta^n \equiv 1 \bmod q$)
Output: NTT of $a(x)$ in bit-reversed order
1: $k = 1$
2: $l = log_2^n$
3: $l = log_2^n$
4: **for** $i = 1$ to $l - 1$ **do**
5:     $m = 2^{l-i}$
6:     **for** $s = 0$ by m to n **do**
7:         **for** $j = s$ to $s + m$ **do**
8:             $u = a_j, v = a_{j+m}, w = \zeta^{br_{l-1}(k)} \ (mod \ q)$
9:             $t = v \cdot w \ (mod \ q)$
10:            $a_j = u + t \ (mod \ q), a_{j+m} = u - t \ (mod \ q)$
11:        **end for**
12:        $k = k + 1$
13:    **end for**
14: **end for**
15: **return** $A(x) = (A_0, A_1, \ldots, A_{n-1})$

Algorithm 2. In-place DIF INTT

Input: $A(x) = (A_0, A_1, \ldots, A_{n-1})$ in bit-reversed order, ζ^{-1} (s.t. $\zeta \times \zeta^{-1} \equiv 1 \bmod q$)
Output: INTT of $A(x)$ in standard order order
1: $k = 0$
2: $l = log_2^n$
3: **for** $i = l - 1$ to 1 **do**
4:     $m = 2^{l-i}$
5:     **for** $s = 0$ by m to n **do**
6:         **for** $j = s$ to $s + m$ **do**
7:             $u = A_j, v = A_{j+m}, w = \zeta^{-(br_{l-1}(k)+1)} \ (mod \ q)$
8:             $A_j = \frac{u+v}{2} \ (mod \ q), A_{j+m} = \frac{(u-v) \cdot w}{2} \ (mod \ q)$
9:         **end for**
10:        $k = k + 1$
11:    **end for**
12: **end for**
13: **return** $a(x) = (a_0, a_1, \ldots, a_{n-1})$

---

3   Proposed Design Overview

In this section, we propose our module design and the introduction of the core algorithms from the bottom up. Firstly, we introduce the module simplification units we use. This is followed by the introduction of the butterfly calculation units, then the hardware module introduction of PWM operations, and finally the RAM memory access design and the overall design scheme of the NTT module.

Algorithm 3. Point-wise Multiplication

Input: $A(x) = (A_0, A_1, \ldots, A_{n-1})$, $B(x) = (B_0, B_1, \ldots, B_{n-1})$ in bit-reversed order, ζ (s.t. $\zeta^n \equiv 1 \bmod q$)

Output: $C(x) = (C_0, C_1, \ldots, C_{n-1})$ in bit-reversed order

1: $l = log_2^n$
2: **for** $i = 1$ to $\frac{n}{2}$ **do**
3:     $w = \zeta^{br_{l-1}(i)+1} \ (mod \ q)$
4:     $C_{2i} = A_{2i+1} \cdot B_{2i+1} \cdot w + A_{2i} \cdot B_{2i} \ (mod \ q)$
5:     $C_{2i+1} = A_{2i} \cdot B_{2i+1} + A_{2i+1} \cdot B_{2i} \ (mod \ q)$
6: **end for**
7: **return** $C(x) = (C_0, C_1, \ldots, C_{n-1})$

3.1   Module Reduction Unit

Within the heart of our design, the butterfly unit, we strategically employ the Montgomery Reduction algorithm, adeptly customized to fit the unique needs of the Kyber algorithm where $q = 3329$. When contrasted with the Barrett Reduction [15], this specialized approach provides a tangible advantage, facilitating a reduction in resource expenditure of up to 25% during hardware implementation. The specifics of this algorithm are meticulously outlined in Algorithm 4. The schematic diagram of the circuit design is depicted in Fig. 3. In our design, DSP replaces the multiplier for rapid computation of two 12-bit data, and shift operations supplant multiplication operations in the original Montgomery Reduction algorithm. During the computation of NTT and INTT, we need to calculate $a + b \cdot \zeta$, $a - b \cdot \zeta$ and $\frac{(a-b)\cdot\zeta^{-1}}{2}$. To conserve hardware resources and optimize circuit design, we preprocess the twiddle factors in advance, storing $\zeta \cdot R \ (mod \ q)$ and $\zeta^{-1} \cdot R \ (mod \ q)$ in BROM. Consequently, the desired values can be obtained directly through the Montgomery Reduction module, thus eliminating the need for subsequent data processing that might otherwise lead to excessive time cycles and resource consumption.

Algorithm 4. Modified Montgomery Reduction

Input: $C[23 : 0] = A[11 : 0] \cdot B[11 : 0]$
Output: $res = C \cdot R^{-1} \ mod \ q$, $(q = 3329, R = 2^{12})$
1: $sum_0 = C[11 : 0] << 11 + C[11 : 0] << 10 + C[11 : 0] << 8 - C[11 : 0]$
2: $sum_1 = C + sum_0[11 : 0] << 11 + sum_0[11 : 0] << 10 + sum_0[11 : 0] << 8 + sum_0[11 : 0]$
3: $res = sum_1[24 : 12]$
4: **return** $res - q \geq 0 \ ? \ res - q : res$

However, every solution has its limitations. When the Montgomery Reduction algorithm is applied to PWM operations, it demands a substantial consumption of hardware resources and introduces complexity into the circuitry. To circumvent these challenges, we leverage the Barrett Reduction for the PWM units, a

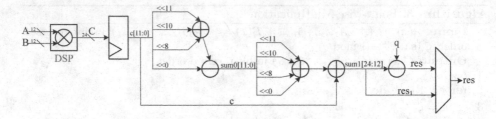

Fig. 3. The Hardware Structure Of Montgomery Reduction

choice justified by the detailed exposition in Algorithm 5. As depicted in Fig. 4, the hardware architecture employs a design logic analogous to the Montgomery reduction module. In the context of Algorithm 5, given that $diff$ falls within the range of $[-3q, 2q)$, the computation of the data difference is confined to the lower 15 bits, precluding the necessity for 24-bit addition/subtraction operations. This strategy proves to be a practical measure for the conservation of hardware resources.

Algorithm 5. Modified Barrett Reduction

    Input: $C[23 : 0] = A[11 : 0] \cdot B[11 : 0]$
    Output: $res = C \ mod \ q, \ (q = 3329)$
1: $sum = C[23 : 12] + C[23 : 14] - C[23 : 18] - C[23 : 20]$
2: $diff = C[14 : 0] - (sum + sum[6 : 0] << 8 + sum[4 : 0] << 10 + sum[3 : 0] << 11)$
3: **switch**($diff[14 : 12]$)
4:   **case** 0 : $q_{mux} = 0$
5:   **case** 1 : $q_{mux} = -q$
6:   **case** 5 : $q_{mux} = 3q$
7:   **case** 6 : $q_{mux} = 3q$
8:   **case** 7 : $q_{mux} = 2q$
9:   **default** : $q_{mux} = 0$
10: **end switch**
11: $res = diff + q_{mux}$
12: **return** $res - q \geq 0$? $res - q : res$

An alternative approach would be to harness the property of $q = 2^{11} + 2^{10} + 2^8 - 1$ through a series of iterative operations and shift registers [14]. However, this approach is resource-intensive, posing a challenge to efficient implementation. Consequently, after weighing the pros and cons, we affirm our decision to adopt the Montgomery and Barrett Reduction algorithms. This choice allows us to effectively execute the NTT, INTT, and PWM operations inherent in the Kyber algorithm, striking a balance between performance and resource utilization.

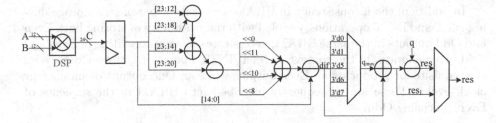

Fig. 4. The Hardware Structure Of Barrett Reduction

3.2 Butterfly Unit

Primarily, the butterfly unit is the pivotal module in both NTT and INTT operations. Our implementation strategy involves a pipelined structure, and the determination of the current computation process as either NTT (when CT=1) or INTT (when CT = 0) is guided by the control signal (CT). The schematic of the butterfly operation unit is presented in Fig. 5. Given that NTT and INTT differ in their computation sequences, with NTT performing modular multiplication before modular addition/subtraction, and INTT conducting modular addition/subtraction before modular multiplication, the integration of multiple buffer registers into the butterfly unit is crucial. These registers cache intermediate results and collaborate with control signals to orchestrate outputs. In addition, the application of caching minimizes the logic layer of butterfly operation, thereby preventing considerable path delays.

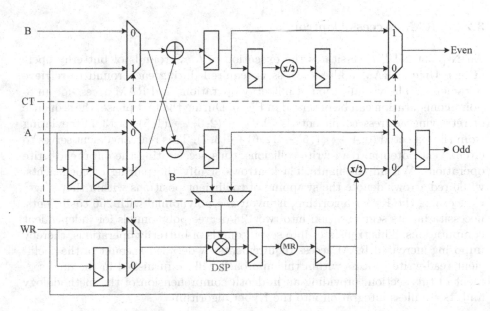

Fig. 5. The Unified Butterfly Unit

In addition, the inconsistency in BRAM accessed for parameter storage during NTT and INTT operations, coupled with the possibility of storing both Even and Odd outputs in the same BRAM, necessitates sequential writing of Even and Odd. To elaborate, in the context of NTT/INTT operations, three clock cycles are requisite for producing an Even output, while an Odd output demands four clock cycles. These are subsequently inscribed into BRAM in the sequence of Even preceding Odd.

3.2.1 $\frac{X}{2}$ Modulo Multiplication Optimization

In the process of INTT computation, it is imperative to calculate $n^{-1} \bmod q$. This calculation process can be fragmented into individual INTT stages as suggested in literature [19], thereby circumventing the need for modular multiplication. More specifically, for an odd prime q, the calculation can be accomplished using the formulation presented in Eq. 10:

$$\frac{X}{2} \ mod \ q = (X >> 1) + X[0] \& \frac{q+1}{2} \qquad (10)$$

Since q is a constant, the calculations of $\frac{A+B}{2} \ mod \ q$ and $\frac{A-B}{2} \ mod \ q$ in the INTT algorithm can be performed using right shifting, addition, and logical AND maneuvers. Consequently, this approach eases the operation of $\frac{X}{2} \ mod \ q$ and enhances the computational proficiency of the INTT algorithm. In summary, this strategy significantly mitigates the algorithmic complexity and computational burden, thereby fostering an overall enhancement in system efficiency.

3.2.2 RAM Access Control

An N-point NTT necessitates the execution of log_2^N rounds of butterfly operations. Unique RAM address access is required during each round to retrieve parameters. The visualization of butterfly operations and RAM access for an 8-point configuration can be observed in Fig. 6. During the first phase, the sequence of retrieving address coefficients is $(0, 4) \rightarrow (2, 6) \rightarrow (1, 5) \rightarrow (3, 7)$, deviating from the expected $(0, 4) \rightarrow (1, 5) \rightarrow (2, 6) \rightarrow (3, 7)$. This rearrangement serves to circumvent potential read-write collisions, thus accelerating the data read-write operations. Within the figure, black arrows signify the pairing of coefficients, while red arrows denote the swapping of coefficient positions within that stage. Concerning the Kyber algorithm, it involves a polynomial with 256 coefficients, necessitating its segmentation into two 128-degree polynomials for independent computations. This translates into seven rounds of butterfly operations, thereby imposing increased RAM access requirements. A detailed account of the coefficient read-write process within this approach will be furnished in the final segment of this section, providing an in-depth comprehension of the methodology and its seamless integration into the Kyber algorithm.

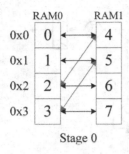
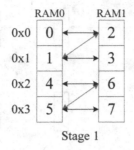
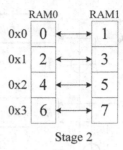

Fig. 6. Eight-point RAM Access

3.3 PWM Operation Unit

The process of calculating PWM in Kyber, as depicted in Algorithm 3, typically requires five multiplication operations. However, according to the literature [15], the Karatsuba algorithm has been utilized to diminish these operations to four. The specific computational methodology is detailed in Eqs. 11 and 12.

$$C_{2i} = A_{2i+1} \cdot B_{2i+1} \cdot \zeta^{2i+1} + A_{2i} \cdot B_{2i} \pmod{q} \tag{11}$$

$$C_{2i+1} = (A_{2i} + A_{2i+1})(B_{2i} + B_{2i+1}) - (A_{2i}B_{2i} + A_{2i}B_{2i}) \pmod{q} \tag{12}$$

Meanwhile, in Fig. 7, A_0, A_1, B_0, B_1, C_0, and C_1 correspond to the even and odd coefficients of the polynomials $A(x)$, $B(x)$, and $C(x)$, respectively. The twiddle factor ζ is pre-stored in BROM. The module employs one DSP, two 12x12 multipliers, and one 13x13 multiplier.

During the pipeline, the first clock cycle accomplishes two addition operations and three multiplication operations, while the second clock cycle conducts two subtraction operations and stores the results in a register. The Barrett Reduction occurs in the third clock cycle, prior to which the data is preprocessed to determine whether it falls within the range $[0, q^2 - 2q + 1]$. The fourth cycle carries out multiplication and addition operations, post which the data is again preprocessed, followed by Barrett reduction to obtain the desired results. This four-step process significantly optimizes the computational efficiency and resource allocation in the Kyber cryptographic system.

3.4 Overall Design Scheme

To bolster the overall flexibility and scalability of the hardware implementation of the Kyber algorithm, we have strategically placed 8 butterfly computational units within the FPGA. Each of these units possesses the capability to function independently, thereby significantly enhancing the efficiency and adaptability of the hardware. Subsequently, we incorporated 16 units of RAM to facilitate the storage of polynomial coefficients and the results of each iteration. This integration provides a convenient means for data access and management.

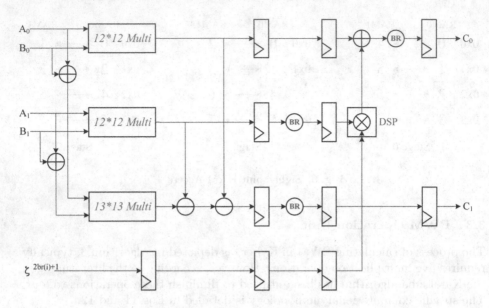

Fig. 7. The Piplined PWM Unit

Regarding the twiddle factor ζ, we employed a pre-computation approach, which is to perform $\zeta \cdot R^{-1} \pmod{q}$ calculations beforehand, and store the results in ROM. This method effectively reduces the complexity of real-time computations. Finally, we designed a control logic module responsible for managing the input and output of the butterfly computational units, controlling the access addresses in RAM, and regulating the retrieval of the parameter ζ. This seamless orchestration optimizes the overall performance of our hardware execution. The comprehensive structure is depicted in Fig. 8.

From the NTT and INTT algorithm processes, it's clear that each iteration involves distinct read and write parameters. This necessitates the use of arbitration for effective RAM operations. The FPGA design features a loosely-coupled interconnection, offering the flexibility to efficiently execute both NTT and INTT computations based on parameter configurations. This adaptable approach not only boosts performance but also streamlines the operations of these two complex computations. Through careful hardware integration and optimal resource utilization within the FPGA, we ensure streamlined execution of the NTT and INTT algorithms with minimal resource interference. This level of operational efficiency bolsters the overall system's performance.

The execution of PWM operations requires two sets of RAM to hold the polynomials $A(x)$ and $B(x)$, as depicted in Fig. 9. During these operations, the polynomial coefficients are directly accessed from both RAM sets, and the results of polynomial multiplication are stored back into one of them. Following this, a control signal initiates the INNT operation and records the outcome into one of the RAM sets. This clever reuse of both RAM sets not only curtails the need for numerous external communications but also conserves FPGA's on-chip RAM

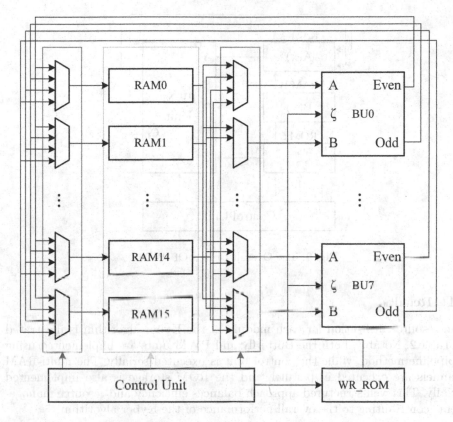

Fig. 8. The Overall Design Of NTT/INTT

resources. This resource-efficient strategy significantly boosts overall hardware performance while optimizing system memory usage.

4   Results and Comparison

In our study, we employed an FPGA accelerator card, specifically the Xilinx xc7a200tfbg484-2 chip, and Vivado 2017.3 software, a comprehensive tool that includes design, simulation, synthesis, and routing capabilities. Initially, we optimized each algorithmic module, allowing us to map out a synthesized and routed resource utilization. Then, through simulation, we analyzed the computational cycles of each module, and at the highest possible frequency, we evaluated the hardware's performance and energy efficiency ratio. This analysis also included a comprehensive comparison with other Kyber algorithm design schemes, providing valuable insights into the system's overall efficiency and performance.

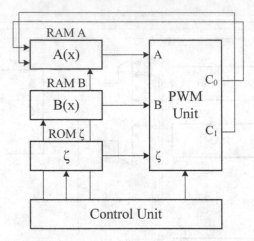

Fig. 9. The Overall Design Of PWM

4.1   Results

The resource utilization for each module in the Kyber algorithm is illustrated in Table 2. Notably, both the Butterfly and PWM units are implemented using a pipeline method, while the control unit is executed serially. The multi-RAM channels are executed in parallel, and the ROM storage is also implemented serially. This well-structured approach balances efficiency and resource management, contributing to the overall performance of the Kyber algorithm.

Table 2. Module Resource Consumption

Module	LUT	FF	DSP	BRAM
Butterfly Unit	160	109	1	0
PWM Unite	808	230	1	0
RAM	0	0	0	16
ROM	0	0	0	2
Address Unit	1384	80	0	0

As can be seen from Table 2, the Butterfly and PWM units consume fewer resources, while the Control unit requires more due to the calculation of various counts, addresses, and control signals. This includes parameters like the number of butterfly operation rounds, current round iterations, and RAM and ROM read/write addresses and controls. Additionally, the multi-RAM channels and ROM storage, which hold all parameters for the Kyber algorithm, consume only a part of the FPGA's BRAM resources, contributing to efficient resource management.

4.2   Comparisons

The proposed method in this work stands out when compared to other FPGA implementations of the Kyber algorithm, as evident from the comprehensive evaluation in Table 3. Notably, our approach achieves exceptional performance in terms of NTT, INTT, and PWM cycle counts, frequencies, and resource consumption.

Table 3. Comparison With Previous Works

Work	Platform	LUT/FF/DSP/BRAM	NTT/INTT/PWM(CC)
[13]	Artix-7	798/715/4/2	1591/1591/-
[14]	Artix-7	948/352/1/2.5	904/904/3359
[10]	Zynq-7000	2900/170/9/0	1935/1930/-
[20]	Virtex-7	2128/1144/8/3	922/1184/3812
Our Work	Artix-7	4969/1616/9/17.5	126/127/131

Our FPGA implementation boasts the shortest computation cycle, outperforming all other schemes under examination. This remarkable reduction in the overall computation cycle is attributed to the innovative integration of eight butterfly computation units operating in parallel, combined with the utilization of a dedicated PWM module. These parallelization techniques capitalize on the inherent capabilities of FPGA architectures, providing a substantial boost in computational efficiency.

Moreover, we have meticulously optimized the utilization of DSP and RAM resources on the chip, further contributing to the superior performance of our proposed scheme. By efficiently managing these resources, we strike an optimal balance between computational speed and resource consumption, setting our approach apart from other implementations.

While schemes [13] and [10] demonstrate modest savings in resource consumption compared to our proposed approach, it is crucial to note that neither of them incorporates a dedicated PWM module. In contrast, our approach encompasses this critical component, which plays a pivotal role in accelerating polynomial multiplication, resulting in superior overall performance.

Similarly, the implementations described in literature [14] and [20] exhibit reduced resource usage. However, they come at the cost of longer computation cycles for NTT, INTT, and PWM operations. If these schemes were to match the computational speed of our proposal through parallelism, their resource consumption would considerably surpass ours, rendering our approach more efficient in terms of both time and resource utilization.

In summary, our FPGA multi-channel parallel optimized implementation of the Kyber algorithm showcases an exemplary fusion of innovative techniques, effectively leveraging the logic resources of the chip. By achieving unparalleled computational speed while efficiently managing resources, our approach achieves a more efficient Kyber implementations on FPGA platforms. These compelling results affirm the practicality and potential of our proposed approach to advance the implementation of Kyber for practical applications.

5 Conclusion

Lattice-based cryptography is pivotal for future post-quantum cryptography standards and information system security. This study dissects the Kyber lattice cryptography, with in-depth analysis of NTT, INTT, and PWM algorithms. By leveraging pipeline technology, we optimized the butterfly computational units, used multi-channel RAM for efficient parameter access, and reduced computation latency. The eight butterfly units working together further enhanced the overall FPGA architecture and computational efficiency. Future work will extend the proposed NTT structure to the entire CRYSTALS-Kyber algorithm for more advanced computations.

Acknowledgements. This work is supported by the National Natural Science Foundation of China (Grant No. 62122092, No. 62032005).

References

1. Shor, P.: Algorithms for quantum computation: discrete logarithms and factoring. In: Proceedings of 35th Annual Symposium on the Foundations of Computer Science, Los Alamitos, CA, pp. 124–134. IEEE Computer Society Press (1994)
2. Gabriel, A.J., Alese, B.K., Adetunmbi, A.O., Adewale, O.S.: Post-quantum crystography: a combination of post-quantum cryptography and steganography. In: 2013 IEEE Third International Conference on Information Science and Technology (ICIST) (2014)
3. Alagic, G., et al.: Status report on the third round of the NIST post-quantum cryptography standardization process (2022). https://tsapps.nist.gov/publication/get_pdf.cfm?pub_id=935591
4. Avanzi, R.M., et al.: Crystals-kyber algorithm specifications and supporting documentation (2017)
5. Li, H., Guo, Y., Jia, R.: A hardware acceleration method for the normalized product correlation algorithm and its FPGA implementation. Comput. Eng. Sci./Jisuanji Gongcheng yu Kexue 1905–1910 (2019)
6. Han, Z., Jiang J., Qiao L., Dou, Y., Xu, J., Kan, Z.: Design and implementation of event extraction model and accelerator based on FPGA. Comput. Eng. Sci./Jisuanji Gongcheng yu Kexue 1941–1948 (2020)
7. Chen, Z., Ma, Y., Chen, T., Lin, J., Jing, J.: Towards efficient kyber on FPGAS: a processor for vector of polynomials. In: 2020 25th Asia and South Pacific Design Automation Conference (ASP-DAC), pp. 247–252 (2020). https://doi.org/10.1109/ASP-DAC47756.2020.9045459
8. Mert, A.C., Öztürk, E., Savaş, E.: Design and implementation of a fast and scalable NTT-based polynomial multiplier architecture. In: 2019 22nd Euromicro Conference on Digital System Design (DSD), pp. 253–260 (2019). https://doi.org/10.1109/DSD.2019.00045

9. Zijlstra, T., Bigou, K., Tisserand, A.: Lattice-based cryptosystems on FPGA: parallelization and comparison using HLS. IEEE Trans. Comput. **71**(8), 1916–1927 (2022). https://doi.org/10.1109/TC.2021.3112052
10. Fritzmann, T., Sigl, G., Sepúlveda, J.: RISQ-V: tightly coupled RISC-V accelerators for post-quantum cryptography. Cryptology ePrint Archive, Paper 2020/446 (2020). https://eprint.iacr.org/2020/446
11. Huang, Y., Huang, M., Lei, Z., Jiaxuan, W.: A pure hardware implementation of crystals-kyber PQC algorithm through resource reuse. IEICE Electron. Exp. **17**, 08 (2020). https://doi.org/10.1587/elex.17.20200234
12. Mert, A.C., Karabulut, E., Öztürk, E., Savaş, E., Aysu, A.: An extensive study of flexible design methods for the number theoretic transform. IEEE Trans. Comput. **71**(11), 2829–2843 (2022). https://doi.org/10.1109/TC.2020.3017930
13. Bisheh-Niasar, M., Azarderakhsh, R., Mozaffari-Kermani, M.: High-speed NTT-based polynomial multiplication accelerator for crystals-kyber post-quantum cryptography. Cryptology ePrint Archive, Paper 2021/563 (2021). https://eprint.iacr.org/2021/563
14. Yaman, F., Mert, A.C., Öztürk, E., Savaş, E.: A hardware accelerator for polynomial multiplication operation of crystals-kyber PQC scheme. In: 2021 Design, Automation & Test In Europe Conference & Exhibition (DATE), pp. 1020–1025 (2021). https://doi.org/10.23919/DATE51398.2021.9474139
15. Xing, Y., Li, S.: A compact hardware implementation of CCA-secure key exchange mechanism crystals-kyber on FPGA. IACR Trans. Cryptogr. Hardw. Embed. Syst. 328–356 (2021)
16. Ricci, S., Jedlicka, P., Cíbik, P., Dzurenda, P., Malina, L., Hajny, J.: Towards crystals-kyber VHDL implementation. In: International Conference on Security and Cryptography (2021)
17. Ni, Z., Khalid, A., O'Neill, M., Liu, W.: Efficient pipelining exploration for a high-performance crystals-kyber accelerator. Cryptology ePrint Archive, Paper 2022/1093 (2022). https://eprint.iacr.org/2022/1093
18. Salarifard, R., Soleimany, H.: Efficient accelerator for NTT-based polynomial multiplication. Cryptology ePrint Archive, Paper 2023/686 (2023). https://eprint.iacr.org/2023/686
19. Zhang, N., Yang, B., Chen, C., Yin, S., Wei, S., Liu, L.: Highly efficient architecture of NewHope-NIST on FPGA using low-complexity NTT/INTT. IACR Trans. Cryptogr. Hardw. Embed. Syst. **49–72**, 2020 (2020)
20. Derya, K., Mert, A.C., Öztürk, E., Savaş, E.: CoHA-NTT: a configurable hardware accelerator for NTT-based polynomial multiplication. Microprocess. Microsyst. **89**, 104451 (2022)

V-Curve25519: Efficient Implementation of Curve25519 on RISC-V Architecture

Qingguan Gao[1], Kaisheng Sun[2], Jiankuo Dong[2(✉)], Fangyu Zheng[3],
Jingqiang Lin[4], Yongjun Ren[5], and Zhe Liu[6]

[1] School of Cyber Science and Engineering, Southeast University, Nanjing, China
[2] School of Computer Science, Nanjing University of Posts and Telecommunications,
Nanjing, China
djiankuo@njupt.edu.cn
[3] School of Cryptology, University of Chinese Academy of Sciences, Beijing, China
[4] School of Cyber Security, University of Science and Technology of China, Hefei,
China
[5] Hangzhou Post Quantum Cryptography Technology Co., Ltd., Hangzhou, China
[6] Nanjing University of Aeronautics and Astronautics, Nanjing, China

Abstract. Internet of Everything technology has greatly promoted the
development of intelligent Internet of Vehicles (IoV) system. Similar to
the Internet of Things system, the Internet of Vehicles also faces the
problems of shortage of computing resources and weak security protection. Open-source RISC V is an important solution for Cloud-to-
Edge collaborative SoC chips in Vehicle Networking System. Research
on RISC-V based cryptography, especially public key cryptography with
high computational complexity, can provide efficient cryptographic support for security authentication, signature generation, data encryption
and so on. In this paper, based on the RISC-V 64-bit instruction set,
we propose several methods to improve the performance of Curve25519
public key cryptography algorithm, abbreviated as V-Curve25519. V-
Curve25519 optimizes the implementation of Curve25519 cryptography
from large integer representation, finite field, point arithmetic and scalar
multiplication, in which the large integer operation optimizations can be
extended to other elliptic curve public key cryptography schemes. Our V-
Cruve25519 also takes into account the side-channel protection security
implementation, which ultimately meets the constant-time computing
latency. On the same platform, the proposed V-Curve25519 improves by
35% compared to the state-of-the-art Curve25519 implementation.

Keywords: RISC-V · ECC · Curve25519 · Public Key Cryptography

This work was supported in part by the National Key R & D Program of China under
Grant No. 2022YFB2701400, in part by Major Science and Technology Demonstration
Project of Jiangsu Provincial Key R & D Program under Grant No. BE2022798, in
part by the National Natural Science Foundation of China under Grant No. 62302238,
in part by the Natural Science Foundation of Jiangsu Province under Grant No.
BK20220388, in part by the Natural Science Research Project of Colleges and Uni-
versities in Jiangsu Province under Grant No. 22KJB520004, in part by the China
Postdoctoral Science Foundation under Grant No. 2022M711689, in part by National
Cryptography Development Fund No. MMJJ20180105.

1   Introduction

With the rapid development of science and technology, the Internet of Things (IoT) technology has been widely used in all walks of life and infiltrated into all aspects of human life. The concept of IoT firstly appeared in the book "The Road Ahead" written by Bill Gates in 1995 [1]. It is the third information technology revolution after PC and Internet. It is a network that is expanded and extended on the basis of Internet. By combining various sensor devices with networks, the IoT forms a huge network to realize the interconnection between the physical world and the information world. As an important part of the new generation of information technology, the application fields of IoT technology have involved many aspects such as industry, agriculture, environment, medical treatment, transportation, and home, effectively promoting the intelligent development of all walks of life and greatly improving the quality of people's life. In recent years, the number of IoT devices has also shown explosive growth, and countries have invested huge costs in research and development of IoT technology.

Internet of Vehicles (IoV) has become an important intersection of the two areas of strategic emerging industries, the IoT and intelligent automobiles. The so-called IoV refers to the extraction and effective utilization of static and dynamic information of all vehicles on the information network platform through wireless technology through electronic devices loaded on vehicles. However, as shown in Fig. 1, compared with traditional IoT, the architecture of IoV is usually more complex, and because the physical location of the vehicle carrier itself is often in a high-speed moving state, while identity authentication has problems such as high communication costs, high computing costs, and low adaptability under IoV, so security issues become an urgent problem to be solved in IoV technology. It is very important to ensure personal information security, enterprise information security, and even national information security in the application of IoV technology, and to achieve a balance between informatization and security.

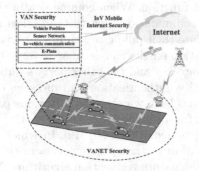

Fig. 1. The Architecture of IoV Security

Public key cryptography was born in 1976 [2], also known as asymmetric key cryptography. It is the core of modern cryptography and is widely used in many fields, such as public key encryption and decryption, key negotiation [3], digital signature [4], and secure multi-party computation [5]. Unlike symmetric cryptography, which uses the same key to perform encryption and decryption operations, public key cryptography divides the key into two parts: the public key and the private key. The public key is used for encryption and can be made public, while the private key is used for decryption and can only be held by the user. It needs to be kept strictly confidential. Although public key cryptography breaks the restriction that the encryption and decryption keys of traditional symmetric cryptography must be the same, the cost is that the key length and computational complexity are greatly increased compared with symmetric cryptography [6]. Therefore, it has an unbearable performance bottleneck when applied to the IoV devices with insufficient storage resources and computing resources. The security of public key cryptography originates from the mathematical difficulties used at the bottom. For example, the RSA algorithm officially released in 1978 is implemented based on the difficult problem of large integer decomposition. Due to the rapid improvement of computer performance in recent years, the key length of RSA mainstream must be more than 1024 bits [7], otherwise, there is a risk of exhaustive attack. The elliptic curve cryptosystem [8] proposed in 1985 is based on the difficulty of elliptic curve discrete logarithm problem. Compared with RSA, it has higher security, shorter key length, and better flexibility. It is very suitable for the IoT devices with limited resources and has attracted extensive attention from researchers.

Curve25519 is a Montgomery curve and one of the fastest elliptic curves at present. It was designed and published by Professor Daniel J. Bernstein in 2006 [9]. After Curve25519 was published, it received extensive attention from academic and industrial circles. Since the design parameters of Curve25519 are public, it is considered safe. On the other hand, due to its characteristics, Curve25519 has obvious performance advantages over NIST p-256 curve. In January 2018, the Internet Research Task Force (IRTF) released RFC 7748 [10], taking Curve25519 as the recommended curve of elliptic curve key negotiation protocol and naming it X25519 key negotiation function. When communicating on an insecure channel, through X25519, the communication parties can select a 32-byte private key by themselves, and calculate their public key through curve255119 scalar multiplication. The communication parties can calculate a 32-byte key shared by both parties through their private key and the other party's public key, which can be used for subsequent identity authentication and message encryption. Since the release of Curve25519, it has been widely used in various password libraries and security services. Starting from version 1.1.0, OpenSSL [11] supports the X25519 algorithm. In 2018, IRTF issued RFC 8446 [12], in which X25519 was used as the key negotiation algorithm of transport layer security (TLS) protocol, and ed25519 was added as the signature verification algorithm. Although Curve25519 is currently one of the fastest elliptic curves, its computational complexity is still too high to a certain extent, especially when used in some low-performance embedded devices. Therefore, there is an urgent need to optimize the Curve25519 calculation process from bottom to top to improve the overall performance, so as to drive the rapid development of this cryptographic algorithm in the field of IoT.

RISC-V is a free and open-source Instruction Set Architecture (ISA), which was initiated by University of California in 2010. RISC-V was founded as the RISC-V Foundation from 2015 and is incorporated today as RISC-V International Association [13]. Up to now, RISC-V can support 32-bit, 64 bit and even 128bit versions of secure microprocessors.

1.1 Contributions and Paper Organization

In this paper, based on 64-bit RISC-V platform, the key negotiation algorithm function X25519 based on Curve25519 is fully implemented, and the underlying finite field operation of Curve25519 scalar multiplication is carefully designed, including modulo addition, modulo subtraction, modulo multiplication, modulo square and modulo reduction, which greatly improves its operational efficiency. The implementation scheme (short for V-Cruve25519) has the advantages of high throughput, low delay, and high availability compared with existing works. The specific contributions are described in the following aspects:

- Firstly, based on RISC-V instruction set architecture, this paper fully implements the key negotiation function X25519 of efficient elliptic curve cryptography Curve25519. Based on the problem of insufficient authentication performance prevalent in the current IoV system, we select the RISC-V embedded development board VisionFive as the encryption computing accelerator platform, in order to improve the computing efficiency of message encryption and identity authentication in the IoV system. Compared with other related work, the various optimization methods in this paper can significantly improve the performance of scalar multiplication of elliptic curves. In addition, the work in this paper is not limited to Curve25519, which can also be used in other elliptic curve cryptography algorithm, thus bringing some performance improvement.
- Secondly, based on the 64-bit RISC-V architecture core, this paper optimizes the finite field layer operation of the elliptic curve Curve25519 to fully exploit the word length advantage of a 64-bit processor. To our knowledge, this paper is the first to fully implement X25519 key negotiation algorithm based on the 64-bit RISC-V kernel, which fills in the gap of insufficient optimization of related algorithms on the 64-bit RISC-V processor. In addition, this paper uses a constant computation delay scheme for the finite field large integer reduction method and uses the Montgomery Ladder algorithm with the same fixed delay to calculate the elliptic curve scalar multiplication, which makes the algorithm to some extent resistant to side-channel attacks.
- Finally, through the above optimization methods, we have mined the scalar multiplication performance of Curve25519 on the RISC-V architecture from the bottom to the top, reaching the latest performance record of 64-bit RISC-V processors. At 15W power consumption, our experimental device Vision-Five can provide scalar elliptic curve multiplication of 3378 ops/s with a delay of 0.296 ms, which is 1.35 times the implementation of OpenSSL on the same

platform. Our optimized scheme provides a more efficient choice for security in IoV devices.

The rest of this paper is organized as follows:

Section 2 explains some preliminaries including Curve25519, ECDH, RISC-V ISA, and our experimental platform, VisionFive development board. Section 3 describes the proposed strategies for the key negotiation algorithm function X25519 implementation. Section 4 performs our optimized implementation and compares it with related works. Section 5 concludes the paper and looks forward to future works.

2   Preliminaries

In this chapter, first, the basic knowledge of elliptic curve Curve25519 is briefly described, then the Diffie-Hellman key negotiation algorithm and ECDH algorithm are introduced. Finally, the RISC-V instruction set architecture and the embedded development board StarFive VisionFive based on RISC-V 64-bit processor are introduced in detail.

2.1   Curve25519

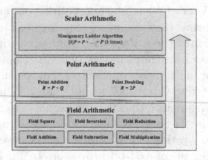

Fig. 2. The Architecture of ECC

As shown in Fig. 2, the architecture of ECC can be divided into finite field arithmetic layer, point arithmetic layer, and scalar multiplication arithmetic layer from bottom to top. Among them, the calculation of the upper layer needs to call the calculation of the lower layer to complete, so optimizing the calculation process at the arithmetic level of the lower finite field of the elliptic curve is the core of improving the efficiency of the elliptic curve cryptosystem.

Generally, the basic concept and operation principle of elliptic curve are introduced by taking Weierstrass curve as an example, because any elliptic curve can be written in the form of Weierstrass curve. In fact, elliptic curves also include many other types, such as Montgomery curve, twisted Edwards curve, and so on.

Weierstrass elliptic curve equation is as follows:

$$E/\mathbb{F}_p : y^2 = x^3 + Ax + B, \tag{1}$$

where $A, B \in \mathbb{F}_p$, $4A^3 + 27B^2 \neq 0$.

Montgomery elliptic curve equation is as follows:

$$E/\mathbb{F}_p : By^2 = x^3 + Ax^2 + x, \tag{2}$$

where $A, B \in \mathbb{F}_p$, $B(A^2 - 4) \neq 0$.

Edwards elliptic curve equation is as follows:

$$E/\mathbb{F}_p : ax^2 + y^2 = 1 + dx^2y^2, \tag{3}$$

where $a, d \neq 0$, $a \neq d$.

Curve25519 was proposed by the famous cryptographer Daniel J. Bornstein [9]. It is an elliptic curve defined on the Montgomery curve, where $p = 2^{255} - 19$, $A = 486662$, $B = 1$, base point is defined as:

$$(9, 14781619447589544791020593568409986887264606134616475288964881837755586237401) \tag{4}$$

2.2 Diffie-Hellman Key Negotiation Algorithm and ECDH

Diffie-Hellman key negotiation algorithm was first proposed by Diffie and Hellman in an original paper in 1976 [14]. It is used by communication parties to negotiate a symmetric key in an insecure channel so that messages can be encrypted using the key in subsequent communication. It has been widely used in many security-products.

ECDH applies elliptic curve to DH negotiation and exchanges the keys of communication parties through the mathematical problem of elliptic curve discrete logarithm. The main calculation flow of ECDH is shown in Fig. 3:

1. Alice and Bob determine the curve type E, the finite field $\mathbb{F}_p$, and the base point G on the elliptic curve. n is the order of the base point G, that is, the minimum positive integer satisfying $nG = 0$;
2. Alice generates a random number $k_A \in (0, n-1)$ and calculates the scalar multiplication of elliptic curve $P_A = k_A G$;
3. Bob generates a random number $k_B \in (0, n-1)$ and calculates the scalar multiplication of elliptic curve $P_B = k_B G$;
4. Alice and Bob exchange P_A and P_B;
5. Alice and Bob respectively calculate $K_{share} = k_A P_B = k_B P_A$.

Since then, Alice and Bob have negotiated the key K_{share} only known to them and can communicate securely on the insecure channel through symmetric cryptography.

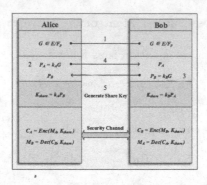

Fig. 3. The Diagram of ECDH

Table 1. Composition of RISC-V Basic ISA

Name	Numbers	Description
RV32I	47	Integer instruction, including arithmetic, branch, and memory access. 32 bits address space, 32-bit registers
RV32E	47	The instruction is the same as RV32I, but the number of registers is changed to 16, which is used in embedded environment
RV64I	59	Integer instruction, 64 bits addressing space, 32 64-bit registers
RV128I	71	Integer instruction, 128 bits address space, 32 128-bit registers

Table 2. Composition of RISC-V Extension ISA

Name	Numbers	Description
M	8	Contains 4 multiplication, 2 division, and 2 remainder operation instructions
A	11	Contains atomic operation instructions, such as read-modify-write, compare-exchange, etc
F	26	Contains single precision floating point instructions
D	26	Contains double precision floating point instructions
Q	26	Contains Quad Precision floating-point instructions
C	46	Compressed instruction set, in which the instruction length is 16 bits, the main purpose is to reduce the code size

X25519 is one of ECDH key negotiation protocols based on Curve255119 elliptic curve. Compared with the traditional ECDH key negotiation protocol, the most remarkable feature of X25519 protocol is that it can calculate the x coordinate of kP only by relying on the x coordinate of point P on the elliptic curve. The idea of constructing ECDH key negotiation protocol using only x-coordinate came from the foundational paper published by Victor Miller in 1985 [15].

Table 3. Operation Instructions

Instructions	Meanings
$ADD(a, b, c, s)$	$s = a + b$, and overflow value saved to c
$ADDC(a, b, c, s)$	$s = a + b + c$, and overflow value saved to c
$SUB(a, b, c, s)$	$s = a - b$, and underflow value saved to c
$SUBC(a, b, c, s)$	$s = a - b - c$, and overflow value saved to c
$MUL(a, b, h, l)$	$h = (a \times b)_{hi}$, $l = (a \times b)_{lo}$

2.3   RISC-V and VisionFive

RISC-V instruction set architecture (ISA) was proposed by Andrew Waterman and others at the University of California, Berkeley in 2010. At present, its application has covered many fields such as IoT devices, desktop computers, high-performance computers, and so on. RISC-V is an open-source instruction set architecture, and its goal is to become Linux in the field of instruction set architecture. Andrew Waterman mentioned in his doctoral dissertation [16] that the existing instruction sets are all commercial instruction sets protected by patents and are not open, which not only restricts competition, but also curbs innovation, and brings certain obstacles to the development of the chip industry; On the other hand, the existing instruction sets have a long history and have undergone several twists and turns in the development process. Therefore, most of them carry a lot of historical burdens, resulting in the instruction sets being quite complex and not suitable for academic research. In this case, an open new instruction set architecture can not only be freely used by more people but also avoid many historical problems.

At the beginning of design, RISC-V instruction set is considered to be applicable to education and scientific research as well as to meet the application requirements in industrial scenarios. In order to achieve the above two purposes, RISC-V instruction set adopts the form of combining a basic instruction set and extension instruction sets, taking a basic instruction set as the core, and then adding different extension instruction sets according to functional requirements, just like adding plug-ins to an application program, which fully embodies the idea of modularization. RISC-V ISA has four basic instruction sets, as shown in Table 1, and six standard extension instruction sets, as shown in Table 2.

VisionFive is a Linux single-board computer based on RISC-V ISA launched by the technology company StarFive. It can be widely used in edge computing, intelligent home appliances, intelligent monitoring, industrial robots, traffic management, intelligent logistics, wearable devices, network communications, and other fields. Visionfive embedded development board is equipped with 64-bit JH7100 CPU and 8GB LPDDR4 memory. The JH7100 processor is equipped with SiFive U74 dual-core and fully implements the RV64GC instruction set specification (where G is the initial letter of general and represents the specific combination of "IMAFD"). The operating frequency reaches 1GHz, which can provide strong computing capability for embedded intelligent devices such as edge computing, deep learning, and Internet of Things.

3   Methodology

This section describes our implementation method of the X25519 protocol based on RISC-V in detail. We first introduce the representation of large integers, including the concept and principle of radius limb. After that, we demonstrate how to calculate large integers at the finite field level under the representation method of radius limb, including addition, subtraction, multiplication, square, inverse, modular reduction, etc. Finally, we carry out scalar multiplication of Curve25519 elliptic curve in single coordinate by Montgomery Ladder algorithm to fully implement X25519 key agreement protocol.

3.1   Radix-2^{64} Limb Representation of Large Integer

At present, a large number of works have done relevant research on the representation scheme of large integers. Fundamentally, the large number representation scheme needs to fully consider the characteristics of the target platform, so as to select the appropriate digital representation scheme. For the 255-bit prime field elements used by curve25519, [2] initially proposed a scheme of Radix-$2^{25.5}$ to represent the field elements in the 32-bit architecture, which is widely spread and widely used in the industry. For the Radix-$2^{25.5}$ scheme, each 255-bit integer is composed of 10 limbs, including 5 length bits of 25 bits and the other 5 length bits of 26 bits. More formally, the field element f is represented by the following equation:

$$f = f_0 + 2^{26}f_1 + 2^{51}f_2 + 2^{77}f_3 + 2^{102}f_4 + 2^{128}f_5 + 2^{153}f_6 + 2^{179}f_7 + 2^{204}f_8 + 2^{230}f_9, \tag{5}$$

where $0 \leq f_{2i} < 2^{26}$ and $0 \leq f_{2i+1} < 2^{25}$ for $0 \leq i \leq 4$. For the calculation of a large integer represented by multiple limbs, if the lower limb exceeds the representable range, it is necessary to carry to the higher limb. This carry is generally highly continuous (called carry propagation), which is not conducive to the operation efficiency of modern CPU.

The Radix-$2^{25.5}$ representation scheme has significant advantages, because, for a 26-bit number a, $19a$ is still within the range of 32-bit integers, so that the carry propagation can be effectively delayed until the end of the whole multiplication, thereby improving the efficiency of the algorithm to a certain extent. However, considering our RV64GC instruction set architecture and the processing capability of SiFive U74 core, this representation is not necessarily the best choice. Therefore, we chose Radix-2^{64} to represent the domain elements. For any f belonging to $\mathbb{F}_p$, it is composed of four 64-bit limbs. The equation is as follows:

$$f = f_0 + 2^{64} f_1 + 2^{128} f_2 + 2^{192} f_3, \tag{6}$$

where $0 \le f_i < 2^{64}$ for $0 \le i \le 3$.

3.2 Implementation of Finite Field Arithmetic

As we all know, the underlying finite field arithmetic is the core that affects the efficiency of the entire elliptic curve cryptosystem. Therefore, optimizing the performance of X25519 key agreement algorithm is to optimize the underlying finite field arithmetic. In this paper, finite field addition, finite field subtraction, and finite field multiplication are implemented based on Radix-2^{64}, and fast modulo reduction in finite field is implemented according to the characteristics of modulo $p = 2^{255} - 19$.

In order to adapt to the Radix-2^{64} scheme used in this paper and improve the efficiency of the code, we have split up the calculation of finite field arithmetic and written the required calculation operations in the form of instructions in C language macro statements. The operation instructions involved in the experiment are shown in the Table 3.

Finite Field Addition. For the implementation of finite field arithmetic operation on the bottom of an elliptic curve, it is usually modified according to the specific large integer representation scheme to achieve a certain degree of optimization effect. For example, work [17] uses 8 32-bit fixed points to represent a large integer of 255 bits, thus redundant data of 1 bit. With the redundant bits of 1-bit, the input and output of the algorithm can be controlled at 256 bits. In the specific calculation process, only the large integer needs to be reduced to 256 bits, and only 256 bits can be reduced to $\mathbb{F}_p$, where $p = 2^{255} - 19$, when calculating the final scalar multiplication result. This technique can be used to cleverly simplify the rounds of reduction of large integers, thereby increasing the overall computational efficiency. However, this method requires an additional register to hold the overflow of 256-bit large integer addition results, which to some extent limits the overall performance. This paper uses 4 64-bit fixed-point numbers to represent a 255-bit large integer. Similar to the 8 32-bit fixed-point representation schemes, our representation scheme also has 1-bit redundancy, so we first tried the redundancy representation scheme in [17]. However, after many experiments, the performance of this scheme is not optimal on our RISC-V platform, so we simply chose the best implementation scheme.

Two 255-bit numbers are added in our finite-field addition algorithm, which means that the highest bit of the large integer addition input must be guaranteed to be zero to compute a 256-bit result. We don't need to immediately reduce the 256-bit calculation to 255-bit, but only when it is necessary to affect the correctness of the algorithm, in order to improve the overall efficiency. The flow chart for finite field addition is shown in the Fig. 4, where the large integer addition $C = A + B$ uses one $ADD()$ macro instruction, two $ADDC()$ macro instructions and two additional simple additions.

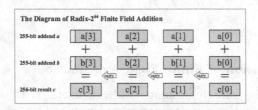

Fig. 4. Finite Field Addition

In addition, since RISC-V architecture does not provide the same functionality as CF in Program Status Word in X86 CPUs, programmers need to use software methods to determine whether data is overflowing or not. A common way to determine overflow is to compare the size of the operands and results. For example, as shown in Algorithm 1, in unsigned 64-bit integer addition $c = a + b$, if c is smaller than a or b instead, we can infer that a data overflow must have occurred. We can use a variable carry to hold the carry value, and when the carry occurs, it is set to 1, representing the 65th position of c. This makes it a carry operation in addition.

Algorithm 1. The carry generation method in addition
_____
Input:
    Two addends a, and b;
Output:
    The result c, and the carry cy generated by addition;
1: $c = a + b$
2: **if** $c < a$ **then**
3:      $cy = 1$
4: **else**
5:      $cy = 0$
6: **end if**

Finite Field Subtraction. Similar to finite field addition, to avoid introducing additional registers to handle the "debits" that result from the calculation, the input for finite field subtraction is limited to 255-bit so that the overflow from the subtraction process can be recorded using the redundant space of up to 1 bit. In large integer subtraction $C = A - B$, if A is less than B, the highest bit of the result will also be set to "1", indicating an underflow. However, unlike the addition that does not require immediate reduction of 256-bit to 255-bit, the underflow handling and reduction of finite-field subtraction is not common to addition, multiplication, etc. Therefore, we have separately integrated the steps of reduction in the calculation of finite-field subtraction to make the result $C \in \mathbb{F}_p$, that is, to output the result of a 255-bit calculation. The flow chart for finite-field subtraction is shown in the Fig. 5. First, use the conventional method to calculate the 255-bit large integer subtraction $C = A - B$, and get the 256-bit calculation result. Then, a $while()$ loop is used to eliminate the possible "1" generated by the highest bit, that is, simply set it to zero, and then subtract 19 from the remaining large integer (because $2^{256} \equiv 19 \pmod{2^{255} - 19}$). Since the remaining large integers may be less than 19, the $while()$ loop will execute a maximum of 2 times.

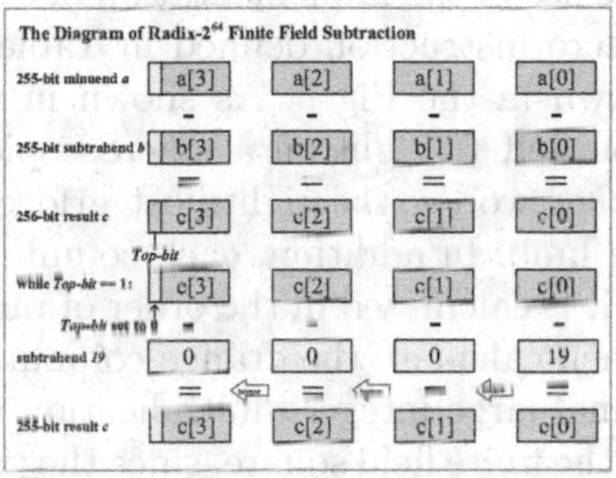

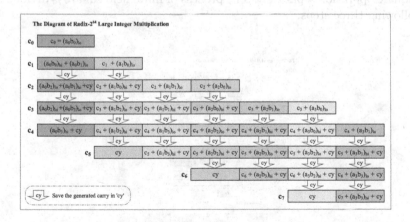

Fig. 5. Finite Field Subtraction

Fig. 6. Large Integer Multiplication

Finite Field Multiplication and Square. Finite field multiplication is the most computationally intensive and time-consuming underlying operation besides inversion, which has a significant impact on the performance of any elliptic curve cryptography system. Therefore, optimizing the calculation of multiplication is essential.

For the elliptic curve Curve25519, it is applied to the finite field $\mathbb{F}_p$, where $p = 2^{255} - 19$. As explained above, we use the Radix-2^{64} scheme, where a field element consists of four 64-bit numbers, to represent a large integer A, that is $A \in [0, 2^{256})$. Unlike finite field addition and subtraction, restricting the input of a finite field multiplication to 255-bit does not effectively reduce the use of additional variables, but rather results in some loss of efficiency due to additional reduction of the input. Therefore, in our multiplication calculation, the input can be 256-bit. For large integer multiplication $C = A \times B$ (where $A, B \in [0, 2^{256})$), there is $C \in [0, 2^{512})$.

The basic unit that we use in the implementation of finite-field multiplication is the $MUL(a, b, h, l)$ macro instruction defined in Table 3. The specific implementation process is shown in the Fig. 6. As shown in the figure, we perform iteration calculations from left to right on a macroscopic level and update the calculation results. In other words, the rightmost grid of each line is the final calculation result of each limb. In addition, each column is calculated from top to bottom. In a nutshell, it is calculated in the order of rainbow colors. First, calculate the red column, then calculate the orange column, and so on, and finally iterate to calculate the final large integer multiplication result.

For the calculation of the finite field square, since the two multiplier inputs are the same, that is, for the large integer multiplier $C = A \times B$ (where $A = B$), there is $A_i \times B_j = A_j \times B_i$. Therefore, there is a calculation method that can reduce the overall calculation steps by reusing intermediate results. To improve the overall performance of the algorithm, much literature [17,18] has implemented the finite field square operation separately. The process of finite field square is divided into the following three steps:

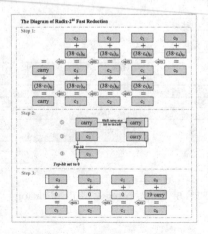

Fig. 7. Fast Reduction

- Firstly, when $i < j$, $A_i \times B_j$ (where $A = B$) is calculated, which is similar to the large integer multiplication mentioned above;
- Secondly, shift the above calculation result to the left by one bit. At this time, we have obtained the calculation result of $A_i \times B_j + A_j \times B_i$ $(i \neq j)$ (that is, twice as much as $A_i \times B_j$);
- Finally, for each i, compute $A_i \times A_i$, and add the results to the above results.

In the above calculation, the performance bottleneck lies in the left shift operation of the second step. Since the large integer representation scheme we use is Radix-2^{64} with 64-bit limb size, no redundant bits are reserved for each limb to use. Therefore, the left shift operation needs to receive the highest bit data from the lower level branch and send its highest bit data to the lowest level of the higher level branch, which has a huge performance impact. Our experimental results show that although the algorithm implemented for finite field squares alone can effectively reduce the number of simple multiplications, its overall performance is slightly weaker than that of using the multiplication algorithm directly for square calculations due to the influence of shift operation. In our experiment, calculating squares directly using the multiplication algorithm improves the performance of the algorithm by about 4% compared to implementing the algorithm for squares alone.

Fast Reduction. As we have learned from the previous section, the input of a large integer multiplication is two large 256-bit integers, which produce a 512-bit product output. For large integer multiplication $C = A \times B$ (where $A, B \in [0, 2^{256})$), there is $C \in [0, 2^{512})$. Further, C can be expressed as:

$$C \equiv \sum_{i=0}^{7} C_i \times 2^{64i} \pmod{p}$$
$$\equiv \sum_{i=4}^{7} C_i \times 2^{64i} + \sum_{i=0}^{3} C_i \times 2^{64i} \pmod{p} \tag{7}$$

From $p = 2^{255} - 19$, we can get: $2^{255} \equiv 19 \pmod{p}$ and $2^{256} \equiv 38 \pmod{p}$ Then, Eq. 7 can be further reduced to:

$$C \equiv \sum_{i=0}^{3} 38 \times C_{i+4} \times 2^{64i} + \sum_{i=0}^{3} C_i \times 2^{64i} \pmod{p}$$
$$\equiv \sum_{i=0}^{3} (C_i + 38 \times C_{i+4}) \times 2^{64i} \pmod{p} \tag{8}$$

It can be seen from Eq. 8 that the 512-bit large integer multiplication result C is composed of 8 64-bit fixed-point numbers. For the large integer multiplication result C, we can take the digit with the higher 256 bits ($c_4 c_5 c_6 c_7$), multiply it by 38, and add it to the lower 256 bits of C ($c_0c_1c_2c_3$). In this way, we get new calculation results, and it is obvious that the maximum length will not exceed 262 bits, of which the highest 6 bits are stored in a separate 32-bit variable, $carry$. At this time, we have made the first round of reduction for C, which is reduced from 512 bits to no more than 262 bits. Next, consider how to reduce 262 bits to 256 bits. If we continue to multiply the carry by 38 and add it to the lower 256 bits, a new 1-bit overflow will occur, which will trigger a new round of reduction. Therefore, we adopted an ingenious method, that is, we shifted the entire $carry$ to the left by one bit, and then moved the highest bit of the lower 256 bits part to the lowest bit of the $carry$. In this way, the lower 256 bits have 256 positions, but only 255 bits of information are saved. The value of carry cannot exceed 7 bits at most. According to equation $2^{255} \equiv 19 \pmod{p}$, carry can be multiplied by 19 and added to the lower 255 bits to obtain a calculation result not exceeding 256 bits. The overall fast reduction process is shown in Fig. 7.

3.3   Implementation of Scalar Multiplication Arithmetic

The most traditional scalar multiplication scheme for variable base points of elliptic curves is the Double-add scheme, which receives cache-timing side channel attacks easily and is inefficient due to the input-related computation delay. The Montgomery Ladder scheme can well resist side-channel attacks due to the fixed latency of the computation. This paper uses Montgomery Ladder algorithm to realize scalar multiplication of Curve25519 elliptic curve. The flow of the algorithm is shown in Algorithm 2, where cswap() is a conditional exchange function and $swap$ is 1 to exchange the values of two variables. This function is completed using the scheme of literature [10], which also guarantees fixed calculation delay. In the Montgomery Ladder algorithm, there is a fixed data variable a_{24}, whose specific value in Curve25519 elliptic curve is:

$$a_{24} = \frac{486662 - 2}{4} = 121665. \tag{9}$$

Since a large integer multiplication in the Curve25519 Montgomery Ladder algorithm process requires the fixed value $a_{24} + 1 = 121666$, which does not exceed the maximum length of 17 bits, the full $256bits \times 256bits$ multiplication is not required. In $step\ 22$ of Algorithm 2, we separately implemented a simplified version of the modular multi-add algorithm for calculating the large integer multiplication and addition algorithm $C(256bits) = A(256bits) \times B(64bits) + D(256bits)$, which omits the corresponding part of $A \times (b_1, b_2, b_3)$ calculation, and improves the overall efficiency of the algorithm. In addition, in order to improve the utilization of registers, reduce the swapping in and swapping out of memory, so as to make full use of the CPU pipeline and improve the computing efficiency, we fine tuned the order of some computing steps in the Montgomery Ladder algorithm, so that it can adapt to our RISC-V computing platform.

Algorithm 2. The X25519 key negotiation function based on Montgomery Ladder algorithm

---

Input:

The 255-bit length scalar k, and x coordinate of random point P: u;

Output:

The x coordinate of scalar multiplication $k \cdot P$;

1: $x_1 = u, x_2 = 1, x_3 = u$
2: $z_2 = 0, z_3 = 1, swap = 1$
3: **for** $i = 254$ to 0 **do**
4:    $k_i = (k >> 1)\&1$
5:    $swap = swap \oplus k_i$
6:    $(x_2, x_3) = \mathrm{cswap}(swap, x_2, x_3)$
7:    $(z_2, z_3) = \mathrm{cswap}(swap, z_2, z_3)$
8:    $swap = k_i$
9:    $tmp1 = x_2 - z_2$
10:    $x_2 = x_2 + z_2$
11:    $tmp0 = x_3 - z_3$
12:    $z_3 = x_3 + z_3$
13:    $z_3 = tmp0 \times x_2$
14:    $z_2 = tmp1 \times z_2$
15:    $tmp0 = tmp1^2$
16:    $tmp1 = x_2^2$
17:    $x_3 = z_3 + z_2$
18:    $z_2 = z_3 - z_2$
19:    $x_2 = tmp1 \times tmp0$
20:    $tmp1 = tmp1 - tmp0$
21:    $z_2 = z_2^2$
22:    $tmp0 = tmp1 \times 121666 + tmp0$
23:    $x_2 = x_2^2$
24:    $z_3 = x_1 \times z_2$
25:    $z_2 = tmp1 \times tmp0$
26: **end for**
27: $(x_2, x_3) = \mathrm{cswap}(swap, x_2, x_3)$
28: $(z_2, z_3) = \mathrm{cswap}(swap, z_2, z_3)$
29: **return** $x_2 \times (z_2^{-1})$

---

4   Performance Evaluation

In this section, the experimental results of the optimized X25519 function on the VisionFive RISC-V development board are presented and compared with other work. The necessary introduction to the VisionFive development board has been made earlier. Table 4 gives our hardware and software experimental environment, including system version, toolchain, hardware configuration parameters, etc.

Table 4. The Platform Configuration of V-Curve25519

Type	Model
OS	Linux Fedora release 33 (Rawhide)
Tool Chain	gcc (Red Hat 10.3.1-1)
CPU	SiFive U74 2-core 64-bit RV64GC @ 1.0GHz
Memory	8 GB LPDDR4
Power	About 15W

Table 5. Experiment Results

Operation Type	Cycles
Finite Field Addition	7
Finite Field Subtraction	10
Finite Field Multiplication	86
Finite Field Square	97
Finite Field Inversion	22304
Finite Field Mul121666AddNum	25
Curve25519 Scalar Multiplication	295967

Table 6. Scalar Multiplication Performance Comparison

	Platform	Curve	Cycles	TP (ops/s)	LAT (ms)
Liu et al. [19]	Cortex-M4F @ 400 MHz	FourQ	880,642	350	2.79
Wei et al. [20]	Cortex-M0 @ 48 MHz	FourQ	1,972,000	24	41.08
Nishinaga et al. [21]	Cortex-M0 @ 48 MHz	Curve25519	5,164,352	9	107.64
Nishinaga et al. [21]	Cortex-M0+ @ 72 MHz	Curve25519	4,209,866	17	58.48
Hayato et al. [22]	Cortex-M4 @ 48 MHz	Curve25519	907,240	52	18.90
Hayato et al. [22]	Cortex-M4 @ 72 MHz	Curve25519	1,003,707	71	13.94
Hayato et al. [22]	Cortex-M4 @ 84 MHz	Curve25519	894,391	93	10.65
Stefan [23]	Hifive1 @ 320MHz	Curve25519	5,389,988	59	16.84
OpenSSL [11]	VisionFive @ 1GHz	Curve25519	402,000	2,490	0.40
Ours	VisionFive @ 1GHz	Curve25519	**295,967**	**3,378**	**0.29**

4.1   Experiment Results

For the 64-bit RISC-V instruction set architecture, we completed the performance optimization of the key agreement algorithm based on Curve25519 curve from the bottom finite field to the top scalar multiplication. The scheme in this paper can be used for the identity authentication and security computing of the Internet of Vehicles, making up for the shortcomings of existing algorithms in the adaptation of RISC-V 64-bit platform.

As shown in Table 5, we show the number of *Cycles* consumed in each operation of our implementation scheme. It can be seen from the table that the finite field subtraction operation consumes 3 more instruction cycles than the addition operation. This is because the reduction of subtraction is different from addition and multiplication and needs to be implemented separately. In addition, the square of a finite field is implemented by simply passing two identical parameters to the multiplication of a finite field, and the compiler completes the corresponding optimization, which saves 11 instruction cycles compared with the multiplication of a finite field. The inversion of finite fields and the Montgomery ladder algorithm are based on the addition, subtraction, multiplication, and square of finite fields. Therefore, the focus of subsequent research is still to continue to explore the optimal implementation of finite field multiplication.

4.2   Performance Comparison

Table 6 summarizes the X25519 unknown point scalar multiplication we implemented based on the VisionFive development board for Diffie-Hellman key negotiation protocol, and compares it with other platforms. This paper mainly evaluates the performance of our scheme from the following three aspects:

- Cycles: It represents the number of instruction cycles required to calculate X25519 function once;
- Throughput (*ops/s*): It indicates the number of X25519 key negotiation functions completed by the RSIC-V 64-bit CPU in a unit time;
- Latency (*ms*): It refers to the time required for X25519 on the RSIC-V 64-bit CPU platform from the calculation request to the end of the calculation.

As can be seen from Table 6, due to the limited performance of computing platforms and the algorithm implementation itself, the number of instruction cycles of elliptic curve scalar multiplication on most embedded platforms ranges from hundreds of thousands to millions, and the throughput is about tens of times per second. Even the fastest elliptic curve FourQ is claimed to have a computing speed of only about 350 times per second on ARM Cortex-M4F platform, which shows that the computing performance of related cryptographic algorithms on specific resource-constrained platforms is still insufficient to support massive computing requests. After our test on the VisionFive development board, the overall computing performance of the X25519 open-source crypto library OpenSSL [11] shows that it is the implementation of the most advanced X25519 key agreement algorithm on the RISC-V 64-bit platform, with the minimum number of single computing instruction cycles and delay, and the maximum computing throughput.

OpenSSL [11] is currently the most popular and widely used tool for SSL cryptographic libraries, and it is also the state-of-the-art implementation of cryptography algorithm on our test platform. It provides a generic, robust, and fully functional tool suite to support the implementation of the SSL/TLS protocol. The X25519 key negotiation algorithm is also provided in OpenSSL and the performance of scalar multiplication can be tested using the command "*openssl speed ecdhx25519*".

In Table 6, the experimental results of the scheme and the implementation of OpenSSL on our experimental platform, VisionFive, are detailed. From the table, we can see that the performance of OpenSSL can be calculated approximately 2490 times per second by X25519 scalar multiplication. Compared with OpenSSL, our experimental results achieved higher throughput, reaching 3378 times per second, bringing about 35% performance improvement. Furthermore, our computing latency is smaller than that of OpenSSL implementation, and it can withstand the risk of side-channel attacks to some extent.

5   Conclusion

Since the introduction of the RISC-V instruction set architecture with open attributes, it has become a hot breeze in the IoT world. In this paper, based on RISC-V 64-bit processor, the X25519 key negotiation function is fully optimized, and the throughput reaches 1.35 times that of OpenSSL cryptographic library standard implementation, which has obvious performance advantages. On the other hand, it also takes into account a certain anti-side channel attack capability. In the future, we will focus on the computational performance of PQC on RISC-V architecture and continue to study the efficient implementation of related algorithms.

References

1. Gates, B., Myhrvold, N., Rinearson, P., Domonkos, D.: The road ahead (1995)
2. Diffie, W., Hellman, M.: New directions in cryptography. IEEE Trans. Inf. Theory **22**(6), 644–654 (1976)
3. Doyle, B., Bell, S., Smeaton, A.F., McCusker, K., O'Connor, N.E.: Security considerations and key negotiation techniques for power constrained sensor networks. Comput. J. **49**(4), 443–453 (2006)
4. Kerry, C.F., Gallagher, P.D.: Digital signature standard (DSS). FIPS PUB 186-4 (2013)
5. Goldreich, O.: Secure multi-party computation. Manuscript. Preliminary version, vol. 78, p. 110 (1998)
6. Chandra, S., Paira, S., Alam, S.S., Sanyal, G.: A comparative survey of symmetric and asymmetric key cryptography. In: 2014 International Conference on Electronics, Communication and Computational Engineering (ICECCE), pp. 83–93. IEEE (2014)
7. Suga, Y.: SSL/TLS status survey in japan-transitioning against the renegotiation vulnerability and short RSA key length problem. In: 2012 Seventh Asia Joint Conference on Information Security, pp. 17–24. IEEE (2012)
8. Koblitz, N.: Elliptic curve cryptosystems. Math. Comput. **48**(177), 203–209 (1987)
9. Bernstein, D.J.: Curve25519: new Diffie-Hellman speed records. In: Yung, M., Dodis, Y., Kiayias, A., Malkin, T. (eds.) PKC 2006. LNCS, vol. 3958, pp. 207–228. Springer, Heidelberg (2006). https://doi.org/10.1007/11745853_14

10. Langley, A., Hamburg, M.: Elliptic curves for security, order, vol. 500, p. 39081 (2016)
11. OpenSSL Software Foundation: OpenSSL Cryptography and SSL/TLS Toolkit (2016). http://www.openssl.org/
12. Rescorla, E.: The transport layer security (TLS) protocol version 1.3. Technical report (2018)
13. RISC-V International®. RISC-V international (2022). https://riscv.org/
14. Diffie, W., Hellman, M.E.: Multiuser cryptographic techniques. In: Proceedings of the 7–10 June 1976, National Computer Conference and Exposition, pp. 109–112 (1976)
15. Miller, V.S.: Use of elliptic curves in cryptography. In: Williams, H.C. (ed.) CRYPTO 1985. LNCS, vol. 218, pp. 417–426. Springer, Heidelberg (1985). https://doi.org/10.1007/3-540-39799-X_31
16. Waterman, A.S.: Design of the RISC-V instruction set architecture. University of California, Berkeley (2016)
17. Dong, J., Zheng, F., Cheng, J., Lin, J., Pan, W., Wang, Z.: Towards high-performance X25519/448 key agreement in general purpose GPUs. In: 2018 IEEE Conference on Communications and Network Security (CNS), pp. 1–9. IEEE (2018)
18. Düll, M., et al.: High-speed Curve25519 on 8-bit, 16-bit, and 32-bit microcontrollers. Des. Codes Crypt. 77(2–3), 493–514 (2015)
19. Liu, Z., Longa, P., Pereira, G.C., Reparaz, O., Seo, H.: FourQ on embedded devices with strong countermeasures against side-channel attacks. IEEE Trans. Dependable Secure Comput. 17(3), 536–549 (2018)
20. Zhang, W., Lin, D., Zhang, H., Zhou, X., Gao, Y.: A lightweight FourQ primitive on ARM cortex-M0. In: 2018 17th IEEE International Conference on Trust, Security and Privacy in Computing and Communications/12th IEEE International Conference on Big Data Science and Engineering (TrustCom/BigDataSE), pp. 699–704. IEEE (2018)
21. Nishinaga, T., Mambo, M.: Implementation of μNACL on 32-bit ARM cortex-M0. IEICE Trans. Inf. Syst. 99(8), 2056–2060 (2016)
22. Fujii, H., Aranha, D.F.: Curve25519 for the cortex-m4 and beyond. In: Lange, T., Dunkelman, O. (eds.) LATINCRYPT 2017. LNCS, vol. 11368, pp. 109–127. Springer, Cham (2017). https://doi.org/10.1007/978-3-030-25283-0_6
23. van den Berg, S.: RISC-V implementation of the NACL-library. Ph.D. dissertation, Master Thesis, vol. 1, no. 1 (2020)

Cryptanalysis

Improved Integral Cryptanalysis of Block Ciphers BORON and Khudra

Yi Guo[1,2], Danping Shi[1,2(✉)], Lei Hu[1,2], and Yin Lv[3]

[1] State Key Laboratory of Information Security, Institute of Information Engineering, Chinese Academy of Sciences, Beijing, China
shidanping@iie.ac.cn
[2] School of Cyber Security, University of Chinese Academy of Sciences, Beijing, China
[3] School of Computer Science, South China Normal University, Guangzhou, China

Abstract. Integral cryptanalysis is one of the frequently-used cryptanalytic methods of symmetric-key primitives. With the help of division property and the adoption of the automatic tool Mixed Integer Linear Programming (MILP), integral distinguishers can be found more efficiently. This paper uses MILP models to find integral distinguishers based on bit-based division property for block ciphers BORON and Khudra. It is worth noting that we used a combined technique to generate the according inequality set when describing the available division property propagation through the non-linear operation S-box. For one thing, we generate a larger inequality set based on the original set generated by the convex hull computation method. For another, we select a small but sufficient inequality subset from the larger set in the previous step. The numbers of linear constraints that describe the available division property propagation through S-boxes of BORON and Khudra are both reduced from 11 to 7 by our methods. Besides, the best 7-round integral distinguisher for BORON, and the best 9-round integral distinguisher with the smallest data complexity for Khudra are found based on the smaller scale of the whole MILP searching model.

Keywords: Integral cryptanalysis · Division property · MILP · BORON · Khudra

1 Introduction

Among the existing cryptanalysis techniques, differential cryptanalysis, linear cryptanalysis, and integral cryptanalysis are classical cryptanalytic technique for symmetric-key algorithms. Integral cryptanalysis was initially proposed by Deamen et al. when analyzing block cipher Square as a specified cryptanalysis method, which was firstly named as Square attack [4]. Through the years many variant cryptanalysis techniques emerged subsequently, including saturation attack [12], multiset attack [2] and so on.

© The Author(s), under exclusive license to Springer Nature Singapore Pte Ltd. 2024
C. Ge and M. Yung (Eds.): Inscrypt 2023, LNCS 14527, pp. 153–171, 2024.
https://doi.org/10.1007/978-981-97-0945-8_9

L.R. Knudsen and D. Wagner summarized these above methods extended from Square attack, and integral cryptanalysis was officially mentioned from then on [7].

Traditional integral distinguishers are based on unsophisticated properties on the word level: ALL (the word takes all the possible values), BALANCED (the sum of all the values which word takes is zero), and CONSTANT (the value of the word is constant). Division property, as an up-to-date technique, plays a considerable role in searching the integral property and was first proposed by Todo at EUROCRYPT 2015 [17]. Division property can figure out more characteristics about the multiset than traditional integral property.

With the help of division property, Todo presented some integral distinguishers for different versions of block ciphers SIMON and PRESENT. Subsequently, Todo found a 6-round integral distinguisher for MISTY1 in CRYPTO 2015, which is the first complete theoretical cryptanalysis of the full MISTY1 [16], demonstrating the division property's high efficiency in searching integral distinguisher.

All of the above achievements show the critical role that division property plays in integral cryptanalysis: division property helps cryptanalysts exploit the properties which may hide behind traditional integral properties. Moreover, the bit-based division property enables the cryptanalyst to find out the integral property on the more precise bit level, presenting a more sophisticated way to find balanced bits. Division property can improve the effect of integral cryptanalysis, finding better integral distinguishers or distinguishers which do not exist under the traditional integral cryptanalysis.

Formerly, cryptanalysts often established distinguishers for a symmetric primitive manually, which was time-consuming and skill-needed. Automatic tools like Boolean Satisfiability Problem (SAT)/Satisfiability Modulo Theories (SMT) and MILP make it more convenient to transform cryptanalysis problems into constraint program problems, which can be solved automatically and efficiently by some public solvers. For the past few years, describing an attack based on a symmetric primitive as an MILP problem and then solving it with some public solvers has been in vogue. Nowadays, MILP has been widely used in many types of cryptanalysis technologies. While not exceptional, it also has a good effect on bit-based division property integral cryptanalysis.

MILP was utilized by Mouha et al. in differential and linear attacks on several ciphers for the first time [13], and the results demonstrate that MILP is powerful and valuable. MILP models can turn cryptanalytic problems into linear constraints, which can be solved by the public solver Gurobi [6].

1.1   Our Contribution

In this paper, we use bit-based division property to find integral distinguishers and establish MILP models to solve this cryptanalysis problem automatically. We employ a combined technique to generate a inequality set describing the available division property propagation of the non-linear operation S-box.

We take two steps to attain a small but sufficient inequality set: On the one hand, we generate a larger set based on the original set given by the convex hull computation method. On the other hand, we choose a subset from the larger set, demanding that the subset is enough to describe all the available propagation. We demonstrate the effectiveness of our technique by applying it to S-boxes of block cipher BORON and Khudra. 11 inequalities are introduced in [10] to describe the available division property propagation through S-boxes of BORON and Khudra, while our techniques can reduce the inequalities from 11 to 7.

We can reduce the size of the entire division property search model because of the smaller inequality set used to describe the available division property through S-boxes, resulting in better integral distinguishers when analyzing block ciphers BORON and Khudra. The first application is BORON. We first show an improvement of the 6-round attack by [10] and [11]. We obtain a 7-round integral distinguisher of BORON, which is the known best integral distinguisher result for BORON so far. The second application is Khudra. We get a 9-round integral distinguisher, whose complexity is further reduced than [20]. Our 9-round integral distinguisher is with the smallest data complexity on Khudra heretofore. We use fewer inequalities to describe the division property propagation table of BORON's and Khudra's S-boxes, making the division property search model on a smaller scale. The compared results are presented in Table 1.

Table 1. Compared results of integral cyptanalysis of BORON and Khudra.

Target	#Rounds	Data	#Balanced bits	Reference
BORON	5	2^{36}	8	[10]
	6	2^{52}	2	[10,11]
	7	2^{63}	6	This paper
Khudra	6	2^{32}	16	[10]
	7	2^{56}	1	[10]
	8	2^{48}	16	This paper
	9	2^{63}	16	[20]
	9	2^{48}	38	This paper

1.2 Paper Outline

The organization of this paper is as follows. Section 2 gives notations and preliminaries. Section 3 explains our model to calculate the linear constraints of an available set. Section 4 establishes applications on block cipher BORON and Khudra. Finally, our conclusion of this paper is presented in Sect. 5.

2 Preliminaries

In this section, we will demonstrate the notations and definitions used in this paper, and also give a brief introduction of integral cryptanalysis and division property. For more details and rigorous proof, we recommend that interesting readers refer to [16–19].

2.1 Notations and Definitions

We denote the field with two elements as $\mathbb{F}_2$, i.e. a bit, and the n-dimensional vector space over it as $\mathbb{F}_2^n$. We use italic lowercase letters in order to stand for elements in $\mathbb{F}_{2^n}$, e.g. $a \in \mathbb{F}_{2^n}$. We use bold italic lowercase letters in order to stand for bit vector, e.g. $x \in \mathbb{F}_2^n$ and can also write as $x = (x_0, \cdots, x_{n-1})$, sometimes $x = x_0 \cdots x_{n-1}$ for short.

The Hamming Weight $W(a)$ of the vector a is defined as $W(a) = \sum_{i=1}^{n} a[i]$. Specially, we write the n-bit zero vector as 0, and use e_j to represent the unit vector whose coordinates are all equal to zero except for the jth coordinate which is one. We use bold blackboard capital letters to stand for vector set, e.g. $\mathbb{X}$. For convenience, we make a distinction between the addition of $\mathbb{F}_2^n$ and the addition of integer set $\mathbb{Z}$ by using $\oplus$ and $+$ respectively.

We denote $x = (x_0, \cdots, x_{n-1}) \in \mathbb{F}_2^n$ as an n-bit vector, where x_0 is the least significant bit. Also, we denote the ith bit x_i of x as $x[i]$, while $x[i : j]$ represents a truncated list composed of $j - i + 1$ bits, from the ith bit to the jth bit of x.

To discuss bit-based integral property, the following notations are needed in the paper:

- a (Active):
  all values appear same times in this bit position;
- b (Balanced):
  the XOR of all texts in this bit position is zero;
- c (Constant):
  the value is fixed to a constant for all texts in this position.
- ? (Unknown):
  the values of the texts in this position is not definite.

We define the function of obtaining the minimum value as $Min()$.

Definition 1 [16]. *A monomial m is said to contain a monomial n if and only if all of its variables are also members of n, or in other words if m is a divisor of n. We will write $m \preceq n$.*

For instance, $x_0 \preceq x_0 x_1$, but $x_2 \npreceq x_0 x_1$.

Definition 2 (Bit Product Function [16]). *Let $\pi_u : \mathbb{F}_2^n \to \mathbb{F}_2$ be a function for any $u \in \mathbb{F}_2^n$. The mathematical expression is defined as follows where x is the input, $\pi_u(x)$ is the AND value of $x[i]$ who satisfies $u[i] = 1$:*

$$\pi_u(x) := \prod_{i=1}^{n} x[i]^{u[i]}. \tag{1}$$

In this paper, we also use the notation x^u to represent $\pi_u(x)$. Every cipher can be mathematically seen as a Boolean functions $f : \mathbb{F}_2^m \to \mathbb{F}_2^n$, m represents the number of input bits while n of the output. But a cipher function may correspond to many types of algebraic representations, which can cause trouble in cryptanalysis. Based on this problem, Algebraic Normal Form was proposed in order to uniquely present the function.

Definition 3 (Algebraic Normal Form (ANF) [16]). *A Boolean function* $f :$ $\mathbb{F}_2^n \rightarrow \mathbb{F}_2$ *can be definitely and uniquely represented by a multivariate polynomial of field* $\frac{\mathbb{F}_2[x_0, \cdots, x_{n-1}]}{\langle x_0^2 + x_0, \cdots, x_{n-1}^2 + x_{n-1} \rangle}$, *which is named by its Algebraic Normal Form (ANF) and it can be defined as follows:*

$$f(\boldsymbol{x}) = f(x_0, \cdots, x_{n-1}) = \sum_{u \in \mathbb{F}_2^n} a_u \cdot \pi_u(\boldsymbol{x}) = \sum_{u \in \mathbb{F}_2^n} a_u \cdot \prod_{i=0}^{n-1} x_i^{u_i}, \quad where \quad a_u \in \mathbb{F}_2.$$

(2)

2.2 Integral Cryptanalysis

Integral cryptanalysis is a chosen-plaintext attack considering the propagation characteristic of sums of ciphertexts, and cryptanalyst intend to ultimately acquire key information utilizing an integral distinguishers. Assuming the attacking target cipher is a block cipher with n data blocks, and each block is of m bits length. Cryptanalyst typically chooses several blocks according to target cipher's specific integral characteristic. Without losing generality, we assume he chooses d blocks here. Then, the attacker chooses $2^{d \times m}$ plaintexts, which means plaintext set contains those plaintexts which taking all possible value (0 or 1) in the d blocks chosen before ($d \times m$ bits in all), and taking constant values in the other blocks ($(n - d) \times m$ bits in all). During an integral attack, attacker focuses on these $2^{d \times m}$ chosen plaintexts at a time. If he can predict the integral propagation characteristic in some certain ciphertext position(s) after some number rounds of encryption, which means there is an integral distinguisher to utilize.

Supposing $P_j = P(\boldsymbol{x}, \boldsymbol{y}) = (x_0, \cdots, x_{n-1}, k_0, \cdots, k_{m-1})$ is the polynomial expression of jth bit of the r-round ciphertext through block cipher E, which is a function of the plaintext $\boldsymbol{x} = (x_0, \cdots, x_{n-1})$ and master key $\boldsymbol{k} = (k_0, \cdots, k_{m-1})$. Whereas, it is obvious that if no monomial existing in the P_a is greater or equal to monomial $x_0 x_1 \cdots x_{i-1}$, then for all the values of tuple $(x_i, \cdots, x_{n-1}, k_0, \cdots, k_{m-1})$, there always holds:

$$\bigoplus_{x_0 \cdots x_{i-1} \in \{0,1\}^i} P_a(\boldsymbol{x}, \boldsymbol{k}) = 0.$$

(3)

This peculiarity makes an apparent distinction between the target cipher E and a random function. Theoretically, if we can get all the polynomial expressions of ciphertext bits through r-round block cipher E, then we can figure out all the integral characteristics of r-round output ciphertexts. Due to the limited computational resource, it is unpractical to concern all the output bits as the total number of terms in the polynomial expands too largely with the growth of round numbers.

We will show how division property works efficiently in figuring out the integral property by a simple instance. We suppose f and g as two n-bit functions: $y_i = f_i(x_0, \cdots, x_{n-1})$ and $z_i = g_i(y_0, \cdots, y_{n-1}) = g_i \circ f(x_0, \cdots, x_{n-1})$ are respectively the intermediate and final expressions of the coordinate functions of f and g. Division property focuses on estimating whether some certain monomial like x^a exists in z^c or not. It is natural to understand that if for every y^b in z^c, y^b does not involve a monomial greater than x^a, then z^c certainly does not either.

From this perspective, an efficient way to search for integral distinguishers is to follow the monomial through the round function of a cipher. In the following, we will present the definition of the division trail and the division property propagation rules through the basic operations. For more details, interesting readers can refer to [16–19].

2.3   Division Property

Definition 4 (Division Property [18]). *Suppose $\mathbb{X}$ to be a multiset whose elements take a value of $(\mathbb{F}_2^n)^m$, and $\mathbb{K}$ be a multiset composed of m-dimensional vectors whose coordinates take values between 0 and n. We say that the multiset set $\mathbb{X}$ has the division property $\mathcal{D}_{\mathbb{K}}^{n,m}$ if it fulfills the following conditions:*

$$\bigoplus_{x \in \mathbb{X}} \pi_u(x) = \begin{cases} unknown & \text{if there exists } \boldsymbol{k} \in \mathbb{K} \text{ s.t. } W(\boldsymbol{u}) \succeq \boldsymbol{k} \\ 0 & \text{otherwise.} \end{cases} \tag{4}$$

Noticing that if there are $\boldsymbol{k} \in \mathbb{K}$ and $\boldsymbol{k}' \in \mathbb{K}$ satisfying $\boldsymbol{k} \succeq \boldsymbol{k}'$, $\boldsymbol{k}$ can be removed because it is redundant.

Definition 5 (Division Trails [19]). *Let f denote the round function of an iterated block cipher, and $D_{\mathbb{K}_i}^n$ denote the division property propagating through after i applications of f. If the input set is with initial division property $D_{\mathbb{K}}^n$, then the chain of division property propagation is as follows:*

$$\mathbb{K}_0 \xrightarrow{f} \mathbb{K}_1 \xrightarrow{f} \cdots \xrightarrow{f} \mathbb{K}_i \xrightarrow{f} \cdots .$$

Moreover, for any vector $\boldsymbol{k}$ in $\mathbb{K}_i$ ($i \geq 1$), there must exist a vector $\boldsymbol{k}'$ in $\mathbb{K}_{i-1}$ such that $\boldsymbol{k}'$ can propagate to $\boldsymbol{k}$ by the division property propagation rules. Furthermore, for $(\boldsymbol{k}^0, \boldsymbol{k}^1, \cdots, \boldsymbol{k}^r) \in \mathbb{K}_0 \times \mathbb{K}_1 \times \cdots \times \mathbb{K}_r$, if $\boldsymbol{k}^{i-1}$ can propagate to $\boldsymbol{k}^i$ for all $i \in \{1, 2, \cdots, r\}$, then $(\boldsymbol{k}^0, \boldsymbol{k}^1, \cdots, \boldsymbol{k}^r)$ is called an r-round division trail.

In the rest of the paper, we will denote $\boldsymbol{k} \xrightarrow{f} \boldsymbol{k}'$ if the vector $\boldsymbol{k} \in \mathbb{F}_2^n$ can propagate to a vector $\boldsymbol{k}' \in \mathbb{F}_2^m$ through the n-bit to m-bit function f.

Thus, the set of the last vectors of all t-round division trails which start with $\boldsymbol{k}$ is equal to $\mathbb{K}_t$. If there exists a t-round division trail, it is equivalent that there exists a t-round integral distinguisher. So accurately describing the propagation pattern of division trails is essential in searching for an integral distinguisher. In the following, We will describe the propagation rules of some basic operations used in the ciphers.

2.4 Searching Division Trails

How to search the division property efficiently and feasibly means a lot in finding available integral distinguishers. In an attempt to settle the matter, many strategies and automatic models have been presented over the years, like Target-Oriented Cryptanalysis Strategy, SAT/SMT Model, and MILP Model.

Here in this paper, we settle the cryptanalysis problem with MILP model. Utilizing the MILP model to search division trails was initially adopted by Xiang et al. [18]. Sasaki and Todo [14] minimize the number of inequalities needed to model S-boxes with a developed MILP model. Then MILP was used for extended distinguishers considering the extra linear relationship of both the plaintexts and ciphertexts [9]. ElSheikh and Youssef [5] newly proposed to combine lossy modelization and lazy constraints for linear layers.

Modeling Basic Binary Operations. We will show how to model the division propagation rules through commonly used binary operations COPY and XOR with linear inequalities in the following.

Todo gave the propagation rules of some basic binary operations. Here we only present COPY and XOR. Linear constraints describing those operations are originally proposed by Xiang et al. [19]. We only present the conclusion here. For more detailed proofs and specific explanations, we recommend interesting readers to refer to papers [16,17,19].

Theorem 1. (COPY operation [16]). *Let* $\mathbb{X}$ *be an input multiset whose elements are selected from* $\mathbb{F}_2^n$, *and let* $x \in \mathbb{X}$. *The* COPY *function takes* x *as the input and outputs* (y_0, y_1), *where* $y_0 = x$ *and* $y_1 = x$. *Suppose the input multiset is with division property* D_k^n, *then the corresponding output multiset* $\mathbb{Y}$ *has division property* $D_{(0,k),(1,k-1),\cdots,(k,0)}^{n,2}$.

Theorem 2. (XOR operation [16]). *Let* $\mathbb{X}$ *be an input multiset whose elements are selected from* $\mathbb{F}_2^n \times \mathbb{F}_2^n$, *and let* $(x_0, x_1) \in \mathbb{X}$. *The* XOR *function takes* (x_0, x_1) *as the input and outputs* $y = x_0 \oplus x_1$. *Suppose the input multiset is with division property* $D_k^{n,2}$, *where* $\boldsymbol{k} = (k_0, k_1)$, *then the corresponding output multiset* $\mathbb{Y}$ *has division property* $D_{k'}^n$, *where* $k' = k_0 + k_1$.

Modeling COPY. Let $\mathbb{X}$ be an input multiset with division property $\mathbb{D}_k^1$. According to Theorem 1, the output multiset $\mathbb{Y}$ has division property $D_{(0,k),\cdots,(k,0)}^1$. Considering bit-based division property, input division property should satisfy $0 \leq k \leq 1$. So there are three available division trails: $(0) \xrightarrow{\text{COPY}} (0,0)$, $(1) \xrightarrow{\text{COPY}} (1,0)$, and $(1) \xrightarrow{\text{COPY}} (0,1)$.

Theorem 3. ([19]). *Let* $(a) \xrightarrow{\text{COPY}} (b_0, b_1)$ *be a division trail through* COPY *function. The following inequality describes the relationship of binaries* a, b_0, *and* b_1.

$$a - b_0 - b_1 = 0. \tag{5}$$

Proof. Apparently, all feasible solutions of the inequalities corresponding to (a, b_0, b_1) are $(0,0,0)$, $(1,0,1)$ and $(1,1,0)$, which are exactly the three available division trails of COPY function.

Modeling XOR. Let $\mathbb{X}$ be an input multiset with division property $\mathbb{D}_k^{1,2}$, where $k = (k_0, k_1)$. XOR operation takes $x = (x_0, x_1) \in \mathbb{X}$ and outputs $y = x_0 \oplus x_1$. According to Theorem 2, the output multiset $\mathbb{Y}$ has division property $D_{k_0+k_1}^1$. Considering bit-based division property, $k = (k_0, k_1)$ should satisfy $0 \leq k_0, k_1 \leq 1$ and the division property $D_{k_0+k_1}^1$ of $\mathbb{Y}$ must satisfy $k_0 + k_1 \leq 1$. So there are three available division trails: $(0,0) \xrightarrow{\text{XOR}} (0)$, $(0,1) \xrightarrow{\text{XOR}} (1)$, and $(1,0) \xrightarrow{\text{XOR}} (1)$.

Theorem 4. ([19]). *Let* $(a_0, a_1) \xrightarrow{\text{XOR}} (b)$ *denote a division trail through XOR function. The following inequality describes the relationship of binaries* a_0, a_1, *and* b.

$$a_0 + a_1 - b = 0. \tag{6}$$

Proof. All the feasible solutions of the above inequality corresponding to (a_0, a_1, b) are $(0,0,0)$, $(0,1,1)$ and $(1,0,1)$, which are exactly the division trails described above.

Modeling S-box. In this paper, we separate the model for S-box into two parts: calculating how the division trail propagates through the S-box for one thing, and representing the available division property propagation trails by linear inequality for another.

In the first place, we use the algorithm proposed in [19] to capture available bit-based division property propagation trails through S-box. We denote $x = (x_{n-1}, \cdots, x_0)$ and $y = (y_{n-1}, \cdots, y_0)$ as the input and output of an n-bit S-box respectively, where y_i is expressed as a boolean function of $(x_{n-1}, \cdots, x_0)$.

Due to length limitation, we only describe how to model some basic operations in this subsection, and we put the division trail search model methods into the Appendix A.1. How to describe the available division property propagation trails by linear inequality set will be presented latter in the Sect. 3.

Algorithm 1. Calculating division trails of S-box

Input: The input division property of an n-bit S-box $D_k^{1,n}$ where k is n-dimensional, $k = (k_{n-1}, \cdots, k_0)$.
Output: A set $\mathbb{K}$ such that the output multiset has division property $D_{\mathbb{K}}^{1,n}$.

1: $\overline{\mathbb{S}} = \{\overline{k} \mid \overline{k} \succeq k\}$
2: $F(x) = \{\pi_{\overline{k}}(x) \mid \overline{k} \in \overline{\mathbb{S}}\}$
3: $\overline{\mathbb{K}} = \emptyset$
4: **for** $u \in (\mathbb{F}_2)^n$ **do**
5:    **if** $\pi_u(y)$ contains any monomial in $F(x)$ **then**
6:        $\overline{\mathbb{K}} = \overline{\mathbb{K}} \cup \{u\}$
7:    **end if**
8: **end for**
9: $\mathbb{K} = \text{SizeReduce}(\overline{\mathbb{K}})$
10: **return** $\mathbb{K}$

2.5   A Brief Introduction of BORON and Khudra

Block cipher BORON [1] was proposed in 2017, which is a lightweight cipher based on SPN. BORON's blocksize is 64 bits, performing round function 25 times during encryption or decryption progress. BORON's round function consists of round key addition, S-box layer, and linear diffusion layer. The final round of iteration includes an extra round of key addition. The S-box layer consists of 16 identical 4-bit S-boxes. The linear diffusion layer comprises block shuffle, bit rotation and block XOR operation. The structure of BORON is shown in Fig. 2 in Appendix A.2.

Khudra is a block cipher based on the generalized type-2 Feistel structure, which was proposed by Kolay et al. [8] in 2014. Khudra's blocksize is 64-bit while its key length is 80-bit. Khudra has a two-layer design structure composed of inner and outer layers. Both layers are Feistel structures. Khudra performs 18 rounds in total. During every round, the inner round function iterates 6 times. Khudra's round function consists of round key addition, S-box layer, and linear diffusion layer. The outer structure and inner structure of Khudra are separately shown in Fig. 3 in Appendix A.2 and Fig. 4 in Appendix A.2.

3   Our Model to Calculate Linear Constraints

After applying Algorithm 1, we can get the set of all available division trail patterns through the target S-box. In the first place, each available division trail of an n-bit S-box can be treated as a 2n-dimensional vector in space $\{0,1\}^{2n}$. So all available division trails can be seen as a point set, referred to $\mathbb{P}$, whose elements come from $\{0,1\}^{2n}$. In the second place, we need to represent $\mathbb{P}$ by linear inequalities, turning the division trail search problem into a MILP model, which can be tackled by the public solver Gurobi [6].

The set of all available patterns can be represented by linear inequalities $\mathbb{L}$ using the convex hull computation method proposed by Sun et al. [15]. For the sake of efficiency, we want a reduced subset $\mathbb{L}'$, which is the subset of $\mathbb{L}$ but sufficient to describe the available point set $\mathbb{P}$. That is to say, $\mathbb{L}'$ contains fewer inequalities, but has the exact feasible solutions just as $\mathbb{L}$ does.

In this paper, we reach the goal through two steps. On the one hand, we generate a larger inequality set $\mathbb{L}^*$ based on $\mathbb{L}$. On the other hand, we choose a subset $\mathbb{L}'$ from $\mathbb{L}^*$. The method adopted in this paper is actually a combination of the method proposed by Yu Sasaki et al. [14] and the algorithm by Boura et al. [3].

3.1   Model for Generating More Inequalities

First, we wonder if generating more linear inequalities from the original set $\mathbb{L}$ is feasible. A more efficient inequality subset describing the available pattern set might be on the cards if chosen from a larger inequality set. Besides, a larger inequality set may contain inequality that performs a better exclusion effect, excluding more impossible points for one time.

Algorithm 2. Calculating A Larger Set of Inequalities from Original Inequalities

Input: The set $\mathbb{P}$ of all available patterns, the original linear inequality set $\mathbb{L}$, sum parameter l.

Output: A Larger inequality Set $\mathbb{L}^*$.

1: $\mathbb{L}^* \leftarrow \mathbb{L}$
2: **for** all $p \in \mathbb{P}$ **do**
3:     **for** all k-order subset of $\mathbb{L}$, $\mathbb{L}^i = \{c_{i_1}, \cdots, c_{i_l}\}$ **do**
4:         **if** p belongs to the hyperplanes of $c_{i_1}, \cdots, c_{i_l}$ **then**
5:             **if** c_{new} removes a new set of impossible points **then**
6:                 $c_{\text{new}} = c_{i_1} + \cdots + c_{i_l}$
7:                 $\mathbb{L}^* \leftarrow \mathbb{L}^* \cup \{c_{\text{new}}\}$
8:             **end if**
9:         **end if**
10:     **end for**
11: **end for**
12: **return** $\mathbb{L}^*$

In this paper, we adopt the Algorithm 2 proposed in [3] by summing up part of the original inequalities from $\mathbb{L}$, and the parameter l represents the number of inequalities summed up at a time. Of course, selecting l random inequalities from $\mathbb{L}$ and adding them together may produce an absurd inequality that could be satisfied by the entire space. What calls for special attention is to test whether the newly created inequality has a better exclusion effect. Boura et al. [3] discover that if l hyperplanes of the H-representation share a vertex with the entire space, implying a possible pattern, adding the l inequalities may be meaningful. If the new inequality can exclude a new set of impossible patterns than $\mathbb{L}$, we add it to $\mathbb{L}^*$. Then a new inequality set $\mathbb{L}^*$ can be obtained. The details of the algorithm are shown in the Algorithm 2.

3.2 MILP Method for Selecting Inequalities

The next step is to select a subset $\mathbb{L}'$ from the larger set $\mathbb{L}^*$ generated by Algorithm 2. For the purpose of reducing the runtime of solving the MILP, we want to minimize the number of inequalities describing the available propagation pattern set. In this work, we adopted the reduction algorithm proposed by Yu Sasaki in [14].

Just as we mentioned above, the set of all available division property propagation trails can be seen as a set $\mathbb{P}$, while the complementary set of $\mathbb{P}$ is denoted as $\mathbb{P}'$. For each impossible pattern $p' \in \mathbb{P}'$, we collect all the inequalities which can precluded p' from the solution space. Then, we set conditions to ensure that at least one inequality must exclude every p'.

Ultimately, we establish a MILP model like this: besides all the restricted conditions, we set the objective function to minimize the number of inequalities chosen by the algorithm.

Variables Used in the Model. The model includes N binary variables $z_1, z_2, \cdots, z_N$, and $z_i = 1$ means that ith inequality is selected while $z_i = 0$ means that ith inequality is not selected.

Constraints. All the constraints needed are to ensure that every impossible point can be excluded by at least one equality. So the number of constraints is precisely the number of patterns included by set $\mathbb{P}'$.

Objective Function. In order to choose the minimize subset of inequalities, the objective function is written as:

$$\text{Min}(\sum_{i=1}^{N} z_i).$$

The available division trails through the S-boxes of BORON and Khudra will be described using our model in the following section. As well a full division property search model finding integral distinguishers for BORON and Khudra.

4 Applications on BORON and Khudra

4.1 Describing Available Division Property Propagation Through S-Boxes of BORON and Khudra

An S-box, as a part of a cipher, is a function $S : \mathbb{F}_2^n \to \mathbb{F}_2^m$. Such functions can be either represented by a simple look-up table or its ANF.

We denote $\boldsymbol{i} = (i_3, i_2, i_1, i_0)$ and $\boldsymbol{o} = (o_3, o_2, o_1, o_0)$ as the input and output division property of 4-bit S-box separately, and we denote the division property propagation trail as $(i_3, i_2, i_1, i_0) \xrightarrow{\text{S-box}} (o_3, o_2, o_1, o_0)$.

Table 2. S-box of BORON.

x	0	1	2	3	4	5	6	7	8	9	a	b	c	d	e	f
$S(x)$	e	4	b	1	7	9	c	a	d	2	0	f	8	5	3	6

Table 3. S-box of Khudra.

x	0	1	2	3	4	5	6	7	8	9	a	b	c	d	e	f
$S(x)$	c	5	6	b	9	0	a	d	3	e	f	8	4	7	1	2

BORON's and Khudra's S-boxes are separately presented in Table 2 and Table 3 while the ANFs are presented in Eq. 7 and 8. Applying the Algorithm 1 according to the ANF, we can get all the available division trails through them.

BORON's and Khudra's available division trails are listed in Table 4 and Table 5 in the following.

$$\begin{cases} o_0 = i_1 \oplus i_2 \oplus i_3 \oplus i_0 i_3 \\ o_1 = 1 \oplus i_0 \oplus i_3 \oplus i_1 i_2 \oplus i_0 i_2 i_3 \\ o_2 = 1 \oplus i_1 \oplus i_0 i_2 \oplus i_0 i_3 \oplus i_1 i_2 \oplus i_0 i_2 i_3 \\ o_3 = 1 \oplus i_0 \oplus i_2 \oplus i_1 i_2 \oplus i_1 i_3 \oplus i_2 i_3 \oplus i_0 i_1 i_2 \oplus i_1 i_2 i_3 \end{cases} \tag{7}$$

$$\begin{cases} o_0 = i_0 \oplus i_2 \oplus i_3 \oplus i_1 i_2 \\ o_1 = i_1 \oplus i_3 \oplus i_1 i_3 \oplus i_2 i_3 \oplus i_0 i_1 i_2 \oplus i_0 i_1 i_3 \oplus i_0 i_2 i_3 \\ o_2 = 1 \oplus i_2 \oplus i_3 \oplus i_0 i_1 \oplus i_0 i_3 \oplus i_1 i_3 \oplus i_0 i_1 i_3 \oplus i_0 i_2 i_3 \\ o_3 = 1 \oplus i_0 \oplus i_1 \oplus i_3 \oplus i_1 i_2 \oplus i_0 i_1 i_2 \oplus i_0 i_1 i_3 \oplus i_0 i_2 i_3 \end{cases} \tag{8}$$

Table 4. Available division trails of BORON's S-box.

Input Division Property	Output Division Property
$(0,0,0,0)$	$(0,0,0,0)$
$(0,0,0,1)$	$(1,0,0,0), (0,1,0,0), (0,0,1,0), (0,0,0,1)$
$(0,0,1,0)$	$(1,0,0,0), (0,1,0,0), (0,0,1,0), (0,0,0,1)$
$(0,0,1,1)$	$(1,0,0,0), (0,1,1,0), (0,1,0,1), (0,0,1,1)$
$(0,1,0,0)$	$(1,0,0,0), (0,1,0,0), (0,0,1,0), (0,0,0,1)$
$(0,1,0,1)$	$(1,0,0,0), (0,1,0,0), (0,0,1,0)$
$(0,1,1,0)$	$(1,0,0,0), (0,0,1,0), (0,0,0,1)$
$(0,1,1,1)$	$(1,0,0,0), (0,1,0,1)$
$(1,0,0,0)$	$(1,0,0,0), (0,1,0,0), (0,0,1,0), (0,0,0,1)$
$(1,0,0,1)$	$(0,1,0,0), (0,0,1,0), (0,0,0,1)$
$(1,0,1,0)$	$(1,0,0,0), (0,1,1,0), (0,1,0,1), (0,0,1,1)$
$(1,0,1,1)$	$(1,1,0,0), (1,0,1,0), (1,0,0,1), (0,1,1,1)$
$(1,1,0,0)$	$(1,0,0,0), (0,1,0,0), (0,0,1,0)$
$(1,1,0,1)$	$(0,1,0,0), (0,0,1,0)$
$(1,1,1,0)$	$(0,0,1,1), (1,0,0,0)$
$(1,1,1,1)$	$(1,1,1,1)$

After applying our model in Sect. 3, we get a set of inequalities which describe the relationship of i and o. Compared with the work in [10], we get a smaller inequality set to describe the available division trail tables of BORON and Khudra's S-boxes. The work in [10] used 11 inequalities, while we both use 7 inequalities. The compared results of BORON and Khudra are separately listed in the Table 6 and Table 7.

4.2 Division Trail Search Model

For brevity, we only give a detailed description of search model on Khudra's inner round function here.

Table 5. Available division trails of Khudra's S-box.

Input Division Property	Output Division Property
$(0,0,0,0)$	$(0,0,0,0)$
$(0,0,0,1)$	$(1,0,0,0),(0,1,0,0),(0,0,1,0),(0,0,0,1)$
$(0,0,1,0)$	$(1,0,0,0),(0,1,0,0),(0,0,1,0),(0,0,0,1)$
$(0,0,1,1)$	$(1,0,0,0),(0,1,0,0),(0,0,1,0)$
$(0,1,0,0)$	$(1,0,0,0),(0,1,0,0),(0,0,1,0),(0,0,0,1)$
$(0,1,0,1)$	$(1,0,0,0),(0,1,0,0),(0,0,1,0)$
$(0,1,1,0)$	$(1,0,0,0),(0,0,1,0),(0,0,0,1)$
$(0,1,1,1)$	$(1,0,0,0),(0,0,1,0)$
$(1,0,0,0)$	$(1,0,0,0),(0,1,0,0),(0,0,1,0),(0,0,0,1)$
$(1,0,0,1)$	$(1,0,0,0),(0,1,0,0),(0,0,1,0)$
$(1,0,1,0)$	$(1,0,0,0),(0,1,0,0),(0,0,1,0)$
$(1,0,1,1)$	$(1,0,0,0),(0,1,0,0),(0,0,1,0)$
$(1,1,0,0)$	$(1,0,0,0),(0,1,0,0),(0,0,1,0)$
$(1,1,0,1)$	$(1,0,0,0),(0,1,0,0),(0,0,1,0)$
$(1,1,1,0)$	$(1,1,1,0),(1,0,1,1),(0,1,0,1)$
$(1,1,1,1)$	$(1,1,1,1)$

Table 6. Comparison of inequalities describing the available division trail tables of BORON's S-box

Results in [10]	Our results
$i_3+i_2+i_1+i_0-o_3-o_2-o_1-o_0 \geqslant 0,$	$2i_3+3i_2+2i_1+2i_0-3o_3-2o_2-2o_1-3o_0 \geqslant -1,$
$-i_3-2i_1-i_0+2o_3+o_2+o_1+o_0 \geqslant -1,$	$-i_3+4i_1-1o_0-2o_3-o_2-o_1-o_0 \geqslant -3$
$3i_1-o_3-o_2-o_1-o_0 \geqslant -1,$	$-2i_3-4i_1-2i_0+5o_3+3o_2+3o_1+3o_0 \geqslant -1,$
$-i_2+i_0-3o_3-2o_2+3o_1-2o_0 \geqslant -4,$	$-2i_3-4i_2-4i_1-2i_0+9o_3+7o_2+7o_1+3o_0 \geqslant -1,$
$i_3-i_2-3o_3-2o_2+3o_1-2o_0 \geqslant -4,$	$i_3-i_2+i_0-4o_3-3o_2-3o_1+4o_0 \geqslant -5,$
$-i_3-2i_2-i_0+3o_3+4o_2+4o_1+2o_0 \geqslant 0,$	$-3i_2-2i_1+i_0-2o_3+o_2+2o_1-4o_0 \geqslant -7,$
$-i_2-o_3-o_2-o_1-o_0 \geqslant -2,$	$i_3-2i_2+2i_1+2o_3-2o_2-3o_1-3o_0 \geqslant -5.$
$2i_3-i_2-i_1+2i_0-o_3-o_2-o_1-2o_0 \geqslant -3,$	
$i_3+i_0-3o_3-2o_2-2o_1+2o_0 \geqslant -3,$	
$-i_3-i_0+o_3+2o_2+2o_1+2o_0 \geqslant 0,$	
$-i_3-i_2-2i_1-i_0+o_3+o_0 \geqslant -3.$	

Table 7. Comparison of inequalities describing the available division trail table of Khudra's S-box

Results in [10]	Our results
$i_3+i_2+i_1+i_0-o_3-o_2-o_1-o_0 \geqslant 0,$	$-2i_3-i_2-i_1-2i_0+5o_3+5o_2+5o_1+2o_0 \geqslant 0,$
$-i_2-i_1-2i_0+o_3+o_1-o_0 \geqslant -3,$	$-i_0+3o_3-o_2-2o_1-2o_0 \geqslant -3,$
$-i_2-i_1-2i_0+4o_3+3o_2+4o_1+2o_0 \geqslant 0,$	$-i_0-2o_3-o_2+3o_1-2o_0 \geqslant -3,$
$-2i_3-i_2-i_1+2o_3+2o_2+2o_1+o_0 \geqslant -1,$	$i_2-i_0-3o_3+o_2-3o_1+o_0 \geqslant -4,$
$-2i_3-i_2-i_1+3o_3+3o_2+3o_1+2o_0 \geqslant 0,$	$i_3+i_2+i_1+i_0-3o_3-3o_2+2o_1-2o_0 \geqslant -2,$
$-o_3+o_2-o_1+o_0 \geqslant 0,$	$2i_3+2i_2+2i_1+3i_0-o_3-3o_2-3o_1-3o_0 \geqslant -1,$
$-2i_3-2i_2-2i_1-4i_0+o_3+4o_2+o_1-3o_0 \geqslant -7,$	$-3i_3-5i_2-5i_1+2o_3+o_2+2o_1+4o_0 \geqslant -8.$
$i_3+i_2+i_1+i_0-2o_3-2o_2+o_1-2o_0 \geqslant -1,$	
$-4i_2-4i_1-2i_0+o_3-3o_2+o_1+2o_0 \geqslant -9,$	
$-2i_0-o_3-o_2-o_1+2o_0 \geqslant -3,$	
$i_0+o_3-o_2-2o_1-o_0 \geqslant -2.$	

We denote 16-bit variables $u = (u_1^r, u_2^r, u_3^r, u_4^r)$ and $u^{r+1} = (u_1^{r+1}, u_2^{r+1}, u_3^{r+1}, u_4^{r+1})$ as the input and output division property through the rth inner round function f. Input data are seperated into 4 blocks, thus u_i^r and u_i^{r+1} ($1 \le i \le 4$) are all 4-bit variables. 8-bit variables $i^r = (i_1^r, i_2^r)$ and $o^r = (o_1^r, o_2^r)$ separately represent the input division property and output division property through two parallel S-boxes, while all i_s^r and o_s^r ($1 \le s \le 2$) are 4-bit variables. We establish the relationships between the variables like:

Two COPY operations: $(u_1^r) \xrightarrow{\text{COPY}} (i_1^r, u_4^{r+1})$, $(u_3^r) \xrightarrow{\text{COPY}} (i_2^r, u_2^{r+1})$.

Two S-box operations: $(i_1^r) \xrightarrow{\text{S-box}} (o_1^r)$, $(i_2^r) \xrightarrow{\text{S-box}} (o_2^r)$.

Two XOR operations: $(o_1^r, u_2^r) \xrightarrow{\text{XOR}} (u_1^{r+1})$, $(o_2^r, u_4^r) \xrightarrow{\text{XOR}} (u_3^{r+1})$.

How the variables are arranged is shown in the Fig. 1. According to Theorem 3, 4, and the seven inequalities that describe the relationship between input and output division property through Khudra's S-box, we can describe the division property propagation through the inner round function using linear constraints. In the interest of brevity, how to put the initial setting in the model and the algorithm how to search the division trail are presented in the Appendix A.2.

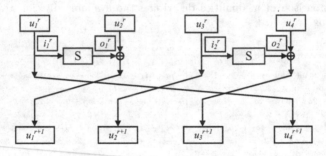

Fig. 1. Variables arrangement of Khudra's inner round function

4.3   Results

7-round Integral Distinguisher of BORON. Utilizing the model described in the last paragraph, we gain a 7-round integral distinguisher, whose initial division property is $D_{7ffffffffffffffff}^{1,64}$. The 2nd to 64th (the leftmost bit is the 1st bit) input bits are selected as active bits (taking all values, 0 and 1) while the rest are set as inactive bits (taking fixed value). After 7 rounds of BORON encryption, we can get an integral distinguisher listed as follows:

The input is set as: (caaa, aaaa, aaaa, aaaa, aaaa, aaaa, aaaa, aaaa, aaaa, aaaa, aaaa, aaaa, aaaa, aaaa, aaaa, aaaa).

After 7 rounds of BORON encryption, the output will be: (????, ?b??, ?b??, ?b??, ????, ?b??, ?b??, ?b??, ????, ????, ????, ????, ????, ????, ????, ????).

This integral distinguisher demands that input values take all possibilities (both 0 and 1) from the 2nd to the 64th bits, which refers to the positions where the input division property is a. There are 63 active bits in total, so the data complexity is 2^{63}. Other positions where the integral property is c take constant values, referring to the 1st bit in this distinguisher. After 7 rounds of BORON encryption, the sum values of positions whose integral property is b must be 0, while other positions whose integral property are denoted as ? are unknown.

8-round Integral Distinguisher of Khudra. We gain an 8-round integral distinguisher of Khudra, whose initial division property is $D^{1,64}_{0000ffffffffffff}$. The 17th to the 64th input bits are selected as active bits, while the rest are set as inactive bits.

The integral distinguisher is listed as follows:

The input is set as: (cccc, cccc, cccc, cccc, aaaa, aaaa, aaaa, aaaa, aaaa, aaaa, aaaa, aaaa, aaaa, aaaa, aaaa, aaaa).

After 8 rounds of Khudra encryption, the output will be: (????, ????, ????, ????, ????, ????, ????, ????, bbbb, bbbb, bbbb, bbbb, ????, ????, ????, ????).

The data complexity of this 8-round distinguisher for Khudra is 2^{48}.

9-round Integral Distinguisher of Khudra. We gain a 9-round integral distinguisher, whose initial division property is $D^{1,64}_{000000ffffffffff}$, the 25th to the 64th input bits are selected as active bits while the rest are set as inactive bits.

The integral distinguisher is listed as follows:

The input is set as (cccc, cccc, cccc, cccc, cccc, cccc, aaaa, aaaa, aaaa, aaaa, aaaa, aaaa, aaaa, aaaa, aaaa, aaaa).

After 9 rounds of Khudra encryption, the output will be (????, ??bb, ??b?, bbbb, bbbb, bbbb, bbbb, ?b?b, ?b??, b??b, ?b??, ??bb, bb?b, b???, bbbb, bbb?).

The data complexity of this 9-round distinguisher for Khudra is 2^{40}.

5 Conclusion

In this work, we combine the technique to generate more inequalities and the algorithm to select a small but sufficient set to describe the division property propagation tables of block cipher BORON and Khudra's S-boxes. In this way, we reduce the number of linear constraints, attaining the best 7-round integral distinguisher for block cipher BORON and the best 9-round integral distinguisher with the smallest data complexity on block cipher Khudra.

In the future, we will consider utilizing our model on some other block ciphers for one thing and searching for better key recovery attacks based on distinguisher for another.

Acknowledgments. We would like to thank the anonymous reviewers for their helpful comments and suggestions. The work of this paper was supported by the National Key Research and Development Project (No. 2018YFA0704704, No. 2022YFB2701900, No. 2022YFB2703003), the National Natural Science Foundation of China (No. 62172410, No. 62202460) and the Youth Innovation Promotion Association of Chinese Academy of Sciences.

A   Appendix

A.1   Division Trail Search Model

Initial Setting and Stopping Rule. Since the propagation rules through all the basic operations used in the cipher can be expressed by linear inequalities. So the integral search problem can completely described by a linear inequality system.

We denote a t-round division trail as $\left(a_{n-1}^0, \cdots, a_0^0\right) \xrightarrow{f} \cdots \xrightarrow{f} \left(a_{n-1}^t, \cdots, a_0^t\right)$. f is the round function.

An integral distinguisher search model always starts with an initial setting, and the presence of an available solution indicates the presence of an integral distinguisher. Thus, we should add the initial setting in the model. For example, if the initial input division property is $D_k^{1,n}$, where $k = (k_{n-1}, \cdots, k_0)$. When searching for a t-round division trail denoted as $\left(a_{n-1}^0, \cdots, a_0^0\right) \to \cdots \to \left(a_{n-1}^t, \cdots, a_0^t\right)$, we put the initial setting $a_i^0 = k_i$ ($i = 0, 1, \cdots, n-1$). In this way, the model will output all available division trails which starts from input division property k.

Theorem 5. (Set without Integral Property [19]). *If the multiset $\mathbb{X}$ is with division property $D_{\mathbb{K}}^{1,n}$, then $\mathbb{X}$ has no integral property if and only if $\mathbb{K}$ contains all the n unit vectors: $e_1, e_2, \cdots, e_n$.*

We denote the output division property after t-round encryption by $D_{\mathbb{K}_t}^{1,n}$. If $\mathbb{K}_{t+1}$ for the first time contains all the n unit vectors while $\mathbb{K}_t$ does not, the search progress can terminate, and we obtain an r-round distinguisher. Therefore, we only need to focus on detecting whether $\mathbb{K}_i$ contains all the n unit vectors during every round, and it is equal to check every tail-end vector of all t-round division trails. So we set the objective function as:

$$\text{Min}(a_0^t + a_1^t + \cdots + a_{n-1}^t).$$

Division Trail Search Algorithm. From the above description, we can get a MILP model with a constraint set and an objective function. Note that $\mathbb{K}_i$ does not contain a zero vector during every round. Thus, there is no probability that the objective function takes a zero value. The MILP problem will return an objective value greater than zero when feasible. We use the algorithm proposed in [6]. Details are shown in Algorithm 3.

A.2   BORON and Khudra's Structure

Algorithm 3. Determine whether there exists a t-round division property trail

---

Input: $M = (\mathbb{L}, o)$ is an MILP model
Output: A set $\mathbb{B}$ of all balanced bit positions
1: $\mathbb{B} = \{a_0^r, a_1^r, \cdots, a_{n-1}^r\}$
2: **if** M is feasible **then**
3:    $M.optimize()$
4:    **if** o=1 **then**
5:       **for** i in range (0,n) **do**
6:          **if** a_i^t=1 **then**
7:             $\mathbb{B} \backslash \{a_i^t\}$
8:             add constraint $a_i^t = 0$ into constraint set $\mathbb{L}$;
9:             *break*
10:         **end if**
11:      **end for**
12:   **end if**
13: **end if**
14: **return** $\mathbb{B}$

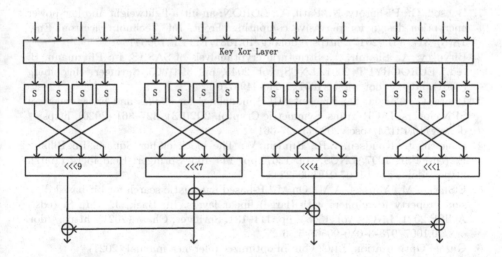

Fig. 2. The round function of BORON.

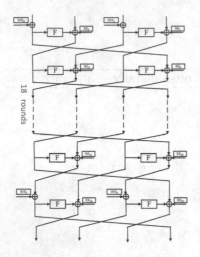

Fig. 3. The outer structure of Khudra   **Fig. 4.** The inner structure of Khudra

References

1. Bansod, G., Pisharoty, N., Patil, A.: BORON: an ultra-lightweight and low power encryption design for pervasive computing. Front. Inf. Technol. Electron. Eng. **18**(3), 317–331 (2017). https://doi.org/10.1631/FITEE.1500415
2. Biryukov, A., Shamir, A.: Structural cryptanalysis of SASAS. In: Pfitzmann, B. (ed.) EUROCRYPT 2001. LNCS, vol. 2045, pp. 394–405. Springer, Heidelberg (2001). https://doi.org/10.1007/3-540-44987-6_24
3. Boura, C., Coggia, D.: Efficient MILP modelings for sboxes and linear layers of SPN ciphers. IACR Trans. Symmetric Cryptol. **2020**(3), 327–361 (2020). https://doi.org/10.13154/tosc.v2020.i3.327-361
4. Daemen, J., Knudsen, L.R., Rijmen, V.: The block cipher Square. In: Biham, E. (ed.) FSE 1997. LNCS, vol. 1267, pp. 149–165. Springer, Heidelberg (1997). https://doi.org/10.1007/BFb0052343
5. ElSheikh, M., Youssef, A.M.: On MILP-based automatic search for bit-based division property for ciphers with (large) linear layers. In: Baek, J., Ruj, S. (eds.) ACISP 2021. LNCS, vol. 13083, pp. 111–131. Springer, Cham (2021). https://doi.org/10.1007/978-3-030-90567-5_6
6. Gurobi Optimization, LLC: Gurobi optimizer reference manual (2021)
7. Knudsen, L.R., Wagner, D.A.: Integral cryptanalysis. In: Daemen, J., Rijmen, V. (eds.) FSE 2002. LNCS, vol. 2365, pp. 112–127. Springer, Heidelberg (2002). https://doi.org/10.1007/3-540-45661-9_9
8. Kolay, S., Mukhopadhyay, D.: Khudra: a new lightweight block cipher for FPGAS. In: Chakraborty, R.S., Matyas, V., Schaumont, P. (eds.) SPACE 2014. LNCS, vol. 8804, pp. 126–145. Springer, Heidelberg (2014). https://doi.org/10.1007/978-3-319-12060-7_9
9. Lambin, B., Derbez, P., Fouque, P.: Linearly equivalent s-boxes and the division property. Des. Codes Cryptogr. **88**(10), 2207–2231 (2020). https://doi.org/10.1007/s10623-020-00773-4

10. Li, J., Liang, M.: Integral distinguisher search of BORON and Khudra based on bit-based division property. Appl. Res. Comput. **37**(10), 3063–3067 (2020). https://doi.org/10.19734/j.issn.1001-3695.2019.05.0235. https://www.arocmag.com/article/01-2020-10-037.html

11. Li, Y., Liang, M., Lin, H., Wang, S.: Integral attack on reduced-round BORON based on bit-based division property. J. Phys. Conf. Ser. **1486**, 022016 (2020). https://doi.org/10.1088/1742-6596/1486/2/022016

12. Lucks, S.: The saturation attack - a bait for twofish. In: Matsui, M. (ed.) FSE 2001. LNCS, vol. 2355, pp. 1–15. Springer, Heidelberg (2001). https://doi.org/10.1007/3-540-45473-X_1

13. Mouha, N., Wang, Q., Gu, D., Preneel, B.: Differential and linear cryptanalysis using mixed-integer linear programming. In: Wu, C., Yung, M., Lin, D. (eds.) Inscrypt 2011. LNCS, vol. 7537, pp. 57–76. Springer, Heidelberg (2011). https://doi.org/10.1007/978-3-642-34704-7_5

14. Sasaki, Y., Todo, Y.: New algorithm for modeling S-box in MILP-based differential and division trail search. In: Farshim, P., Simion, E. (eds.) SecITC 2017. LNCS, vol. 10543, pp. 150–165. Springer, Heidelberg (2017). https://doi.org/10.1007/978-3-319-69284-5_11

15. Sun, S., et. al.: Towards finding the best characteristics of some bit-oriented block ciphers and automatic enumeration of (related-key) differential and linear characteristics with predefined properties. Cryptology ePrint Archive, Paper 2014/747 (2014). https://eprint.iacr.org/2014/747

16. Todo, Y.: Integral cryptanalysis on full MISTY1. In: Gennaro, R., Robshaw, M. (eds.) CRYPTO 2015, Part I. LNCS, vol. 9215, pp. 413–432. Springer, Heidelberg (2015). https://doi.org/10.1007/978-3-662-47989-6_20

17. Todo, Y.: Structural evaluation by generalized integral property. In: Oswald, E., Fischlin, M. (eds.) EUROCRYPT 2015, Part I. LNCS, vol. 9056, pp. 287–314. Springer, Heidelberg (2015). https://doi.org/10.1007/978-3-662-46800-5_12

18. Todo, Y., Morii, M.: Bit-based division property and application to Simon family. In: Peyrin, T. (ed.) FSE 2016. LNCS, vol. 9783, pp. 357–377. Springer, Heidelberg (2016). https://doi.org/10.1007/978-3-662-52993-5_18

19. Xiang, Z., Zhang, W., Bao, Z., Lin, D.: Applying MILP method to searching integral distinguishers based on division property for 6 lightweight block ciphers. In: Cheon, J.H., Takagi, T. (eds.) ASIACRYPT 2016, Part I. LNCS, vol. 10031, pp. 648–678. Springer, Heidelberg (2016). https://doi.org/10.1007/978-3-662-53887-6_24

20. Zhu, S., Wang, G., He, Y., Qian, H.: Integral attacks on some lightweight block ciphers. KSII Trans. Internet Inf. Syst. **14**(11), 4502–4521 (2020). https://doi.org/10.3837/tiis.2020.11.014

Automatic Search of Linear Structure: Applications to KECCAK and ASCON

Huina Li[1], Guozhen Liu[2], Haochen Zhang[1], Peng Tang[1], and Weidong Qiu[1(✉)]

[1] School of Cyber Science and Engineering, Shanghai Jiao Tong University,
Shanghai, China
qiuwd@sjtu.edu.cn
[2] School of Physical and Mathematical Sciences, Nanyang Technological University,
Singapore, Singapore

Abstract. The linear structure technique was developed by Guo *et al.* at ASIACRYPT 2016, notably boosting the preimage attacks on KECCAK. This technique transforming the preimage attack into solving algebraic systems allows entire linearization of the underlying permutation of KECCAK for up to 2.5 rounds with significant degrees of freedom left. A linear structure with a larger degree of freedom left refers to a more powerful preimage attack, as it can substantially reduce the complexity of solving algebraic systems. However, previous linear structures on KECCAK relied solely on manual design. They impose restrictions on specific lanes, requiring each of them to have exactly 64 variables, which may lead to some better linear structures without this restriction being ignored.

In this paper, we remove such restrictions, formulate the essential ideas of designing linear structures for preimage attacks in well-defined ways, and translate the problem of finding the best preimage attacks into searching for optimal linear structure problems. We propose a new bit-level SAT-based automatic tool to search for optimal linear structures. The SAT model captures a large solution space of linear structures. Based on our tool, we find Guo *et al.*'s structures on KECCAK-224/-256/-384/-512, which proves the correctness of our model. Furthermore, we improve Guo *et al.*'s preimage attacks on 2-/3-round KECCAK-512 from $2^{384}/2^{482}$ to $2^{365}/2^{478}$ by identifying a new 1.5-round linear structure on KECCAK-512 with $147°C$ of freedom left. Since a similar nonlinear layer exists in the final winner of the lightweight cryptography standardization competition ASCON, we make a study of linear structures on ASCON as an independent interest. As a result, we discover a 2-round linear structure with $102°C$ of freedom left. Based on this 2-round structure, we construct a full-round zero-sum distinguisher with a time complexity of 2^{82}.

Keywords: KECCAK · ASCON · SAT · Linear structure · Preimage attack · Zero-sum distinguisher

1 Introduction

In 2007, the National Institute of Standards and Technology (NIST) initiated a competition to select the SHA-3 standard. The KECCAK hash function family

C. Ge and M. Yung (Eds.): Inscrypt 2023, LNCS 14527, pp. 172–192, 2024.
https://doi.org/10.1007/978-981-97-0945-8_10

designed by Bertoni *et al.* [4] was selected as the final winner of the competition in 2012. Since KECCAK was announced as the SHA-3 standard, it has attracted intensive third-party cryptanalysis in both its hash and keyed modes.

Specifically, at ASIACRYPT 2016, Guo *et al.* [13] made a breakthrough in preimage attacks on Keccak by developing the linear structure technique. Building on a 1.5-round linear structure of KECCAK-224/256, they presented the first practical preimage attacks on 2-round KECCAK-224/256. Subsequently, several preimage attacks on round-reduced KECCAK using linear structure were presented [14,21–23]. At EUROCRYPT 2019, Li *et al.* [21] proposed a 2-block model named allocating model to further improve the linear structure technique. With the allocating model, more degrees of freedom (DF) can be left in their structure after 2-round entire linearization. Consequently, they significantly improved preimage attacks on 3-/4-round KECCAK-224 and KECCAK-256. Especially, they presented the first practical 3-round preimage attack for KECCAK-224. At 2021 FSE, Lin *et al.* [23] improved the first stage of Li *et al.*'s allocating model. As a result, the complexity of finding a preimage for 3-round KECCAK-224/256 can be decreased to $2^{32}/2^{65}$. In the same year, He *et al.* [14] proposed the partial linearization method and improved preimage attacks on 4-round KECCAK-224/256. Apart from preimage attacks on KECCAK based on the linear structure technique, there are several other techniques, such as rotational cryptanalysis [30], solving multivariate equation systems [8,45], and non-linear structures [15,19,24,26,36][1]. We would not list them all here, since they are less relevant to our work. In this paper, we focus on more in-depth study of round-reduced KECCAK preimage attacks using the linear structure technique.

In recent years, a series of automatic methods have been invented to boost cryptanalysis of symmetric-key primitives. The most popular automated tools are the Boolean satisfiability problem (SAT) [32] and Mixed Integer Linear Programming (MILP) [33]. The main difference between them is the forms of describing constraints and objective functions, such as clausal normal form (CNF) in SAT tools and linear inequality form in MILP tools. Several automatic methods have been proposed to search for differential characteristics [12,41,43], which provide more flexibility and better efficiency in searching differential characteristics compared to dedicated search strategies [7,28]. However, these automated tool-based methods for searching differential characteristics mainly rely on Markov assumptions[2], which may result in an invalid differential returned, *i.e.*, there may not be a valid right pair following this differential due to contradictions in the conditions imposed by the differential. To address this problem, several automatic search and verification methods were proposed [20,25,37]. They were used to verify the validity of differential characteristics and to search

---

[1] Till now, in [15], preimage attacks based on non-linear structure with *extra linear dependence* on 2-/3-round KECCAK-512 perform best.

[2] With the tacit assumption that differentials of two consecutive rounds are independent, these local differentials for all rounds could be chained into one so-called differential characteristic, for the sake of simplicity, we generally refer to all these underlying assumptions as the Markov assumption here.

for a conforming right pair simultaneously. Automatic tools were also introduced for other attacks, such as meet-in-the-middle attacks [2,3,35], collision attacks [10,12,27], and cube-attack-like cryptanalysis [17,38,39].

Till now, few works have studied preimage attacks on KECCAK using SAT. Compared to MILP, SAT is well suited for bitwise descriptions of behaviour. In 2013, a practical SAT-based preimage attack introduced by Morawiecki *et al.* [31] was proposed on a simplified KECCAK using parameters different from the recommended ones. Apart from that, there has been no prior work on KECCAK preimage attacks based on SAT. To fill this void, in this paper, we present a new SAT tool to search for better or even optimal linear structures on KECCAK and further improve previous preimage attacks.

Our Contributions. Our contributions are summarized below.

– We propose a new bit-level SAT model to search for linear structures on KECCAK by exploiting the structural properties of KECCAK-f permutation, *i.e.*, the limited diffusion of its internal mappings and the algebraic properties of its nonlinear layer. Moreover, we eliminate the restriction that mandates a specific number of variables in a given lane, allowing for arbitrary variable counts in each lane. Hence, our model searches optimal linear structures in terms of the whole space. To reduce the scale of bit-level model and make it solvable in reasonable time, we optimize several aspects of our SAT model, such as taking into account the rotational symmetry property of KECCAK-f, minimizing the size[3] of cardinality encoding model and model solving with multi threads. With regard to attack complexities, the linear structures found in our model are almost optimal.
– We apply our SAT model to KECCAK-224/256/384/512. As a result, we find previous 2.5-round linear structures on KECCAK-224/256 with 194 DF left, and 1.5-round linear structures on KECCAK-384 with 128 DF left, which well demonstrate the correctness of our model and the validity of the previous linear structures. Moreover, we find some 2.5-round linear structures on KEC-CAK-384 with 64 DF left. However, for 2.5-round linear structures on KEC-CAK-512, we find no such solutions that the DF are greater than zero exist, yet one 1.5-round linear structure with 147 DF left is obtained, which improves the previous complexity of finding a 2-/3-round preimage from $2^{384}/2^{482}$ to $2^{365}/2^{478}$ [13].
– In particular, a good n-round linear structure with a larger linear space that can extend a longer zero-sum distinguisher [6,13] by n rounds without increasing the complexity. In February 2023, ASCON [9] was selected as the final winner of the lightweight cryptography standardization competition, and as an independent interest, we apply our modified SAT model to search 2-round linear structures on ASCON permutation. Consequently, we get one linear structure with 102 DF left. Based on this linear structure, we construct a

---

[3] The minimum or compact size refers to one SAT model with as small as possible number of clauses.

Table 1. Summary of linear structures on KECCAK and ASCON. LS.rnd: Round Number of the Linear Structure. LS.df: Degrees of freedom of the Linear Structure.

Target	LS.rnd	LS.df	Ref.
KECCAK-224	2.5	128	[13]
			Sec. 4.1
KECCAK-256		64	[13]
			Sec. 4.1
KECCAK-224/256		194	[21]
			Sec. 4.1
KECCAK-384	1.5	256	[13]
			Sec. 4.1
		64	Sec. 4.1
KECCAK-512	1.5	128	[13]
		147	Sec. 4.2
ASCON	2	102	Sec. 5.2

better zero sum distinguisher[4] for the full permutation of ASCON with a time complexity of 2^{82} than the designers' 2^{130}.

All our results are summarized in Table 1 and solved by `CryptoMiniSat` solver (version 5.8.0). For the source code, please refer to https://github.com/HuinaLi/Automatic-Search-of-Linear-Structure.

Organization. This paper is organized as follows. Section 2 gives a brief description of KECCAK and ASCON, and the linear structure technique. The SAT model is presented in Sect. 3. The application of our tool to preimage attacks on KECCAK and to zero-sum distinguishers on ASCON permutation are presented in Sect. 4 and Sect. 5, respectively. Our conclusions are given in Sect. 6.

2 Preliminaries

In this section, we introduce some notations and descriptions of KECCAK and ASCON, as well as the linear structure technique utilized in the preimage attack.

2.1 Notations

Most of the notations to be used in this paper are listed below.

---

[4] Noted that our zero-sum distinguisher is not the best so far, a novel higher-order differential technique was presented in [16] published on the ePrint, which offers a more efficient zero-sum distinguisher for full-round ASCON with a time complexity of only 2^{55}, yet we first provide an internally better 2-round linear structure combined with automated tools from an algebraic aspect.

≪:   The logic operations rotate left, for bit rotation towards the most significant (MSB) bit of the 64-bit word.

≫:   The logic operations rotate right, or bit rotation towards the least significant (LSB) of the 64-bit word.

c: Capacity of a sponge function.

r: Rate of a sponge function.

b: Size of state for KECCAK-$p[b, n_r]$, $b = r + c$.

n_r: Number of rounds for KECCAK-p, $n_r = 12 + 2log_2(\frac{b}{25})$.

d: Length of digest for KECCAK hash function, $c = 2d$, $r = b - 2d$.

2.2 Description of KECCAK-p Permutation

KECCAK-$p[b, n_r]$ is the underlying permutation of KECCAK hash functions, where $b \in \{25, 50, 100, 200, 400, 800, 1600\}$ and n_r. The b-bit state of KECCAK can be seen as a three-dimensional array, namely A[5][5][w], where $w = \frac{b}{25}$. Each bit of the array is located by (x, y, z) coordinates where $0 \leq x < 5$, $0 \leq y < 5$ and $0 \leq z < w$. At one-dimensional level, A[*][y][z] is represented as a row, A[x][*][z] is called a column, and A[x][y][*] is called a lane. The KECCAK-$p[b, n_r]$ permutation consists of the iteration of a round function R with n_r rounds that includes five step mappings $i.e.$, θ, ρ, π, χ, and ι, denoted by $R = \iota \circ \chi \circ \pi \circ \rho \circ \theta$.

Mixing Layer θ. θ is a column parity mixer. If all column sums are constant, then state A is in the column-parity-like (CP-like) kernel.

$$A[x][y][z] = A[x][y][z] + \sum_{y=0}^{4} A[x-1][y][z] + \sum_{y=0}^{4} A[x+1][y][z-1] \qquad (1)$$

Diffusion Layer ρ **and** π. The effect of ρ to rotate the bits of each lane by a length, called the rotation constants $r_{x,y}$ (please refer to [4]) π is used to rearrange the positions of lanes.

$$\rho: \qquad A[x][y][z] = A[x][y][z - r_{x,y}]$$
$$\pi: \qquad A[y][2x + 3y][z] = A[x][y][z]$$

Non-linear Layer χ. χ operates in parallel on 5-bit rows. Suppose the input of one 5-bit S-box A[*][y][z] = $(a_0, a_1, a_2, a_3, a_4)$. The algebraic degree of χ mapping is 2, and can be easily deduced from its algebraic normal form (ANF):

$$
\begin{aligned}
b_0 &= a_0 + (1 + a_1)a_2 \\
b_1 &= a_1 + (1 + a_2)a_3 \\
b_2 &= a_2 + (1 + a_3)a_4 \\
b_3 &= a_3 + (1 + a_4)a_0 \\
b_4 &= a_4 + (1 + a_0)a_1
\end{aligned}
\qquad (2)
$$

Addition of Constants ι. ι adds a constant to lane $A[0][0][*]$ for each round. We ignore the details of round constants since it does not affect our attacks.

2.3 Description of KECCAK Hash Function

The KECCAK-d hash functions ($d \in \{224, 256, 384, 512\}$ is our study target) are built using the sponge construction. They employ KECCAK-$p[1600, 24]$ (also called KECCAK-$f[1600]$) as the underlying permutation and use pad $10**1$ as the padding rule. Firstly, the message is padded to be a new form $M\|10 * *1$ whose length is a multiple of r. Then, the padded message can be divided into $\frac{len(M\|10**1)}{r}$ blocks. In this paper, we consider at most two-block messages. Secondly, the starting state is initialized to zero. In the subsequent processing of the blocks, the r-bit block is absorbed by XORing them to the output state, followed by KECCAK-f until no message block needs to be processed. Finally, d-bit hash value is squeezed out of its output state. The whole process is illustrated in Fig. 1.

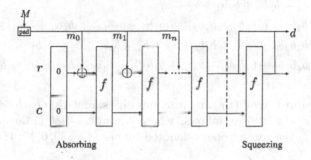

Fig. 1. Illustration of the sponge construction

2.4 Description of ASCON

ASCON [9] including AEAD and Hash schemes, has been announced by NIST as the final winner in the lightweight cryptography standardization competition. Both schemes operate on a 320-bit state B which updates with two permutations p^a (12 rounds) and p^b (6 rounds). Each bit is denoted by $B[y][z], 0 \leq y < 5, 0 \leq z < 64$. The state B is arranged into 5 rows or 64 columns, each row is a 64-bit register word, denoted by $B[y][*]$. Each column denoted by $B[*][z]$ can be seen as a 5-bit S-box, for example, a 5-bit S-box ($B[0][0], B[1][0], B[2][0], B[3][0], B[4][0]$). The underlying permutations p^a and p^b are iterative designs and consist of three steps p_C, p_S, and p_L. The round function is denoted by $p = p_L \circ p_S \circ p_C$.

Addition of Constants (p_C). p_C adds a round constant c_i to register word w_2 of the state B in i-th round. We ignore the details of c_i since it does not affect our attacks to be presented.

Substitution Layer (p_S). p_S operates the state B with 64 parallel applications of the 5-bit S-box to each bit-slice of the five register words $B[0][*], B[1][*], B[2][*], B[3][*], B[4][*]$, which is affine equivalent to the non-linear operation, *i.e.*, χ mapping of KECCAK. We suppose the input of a 5-bit

Sbox $B[*][z] = (a_0, a_1, a_2, a_3, a_4)$, and its output is $(b_0, b_1, b_2, b_3, b_4)$. The ANF of the S-box is given by

$$b_0 = a_4a_1 + a_3 + a_2a_1 + a_2 + a_1a_0 + a_1 + a_0$$
$$b_1 = a_4 + a_3a_2 + a_3a_1 + a_3 + a_2a_1 + a_2 + a_1 + a_0$$
$$b_2 = a_4a_3 + a_4 + a_2 + a_1 + 1 \qquad (3)$$
$$b_3 = a_4a_0 + a_4 + a_3a_0 + a_3 + a_2 + a_1 + a_0$$
$$b_4 = a_4a_1 + a_4 + a_3 + a_1a_0 + a_1$$

The algebraic degree of the inverse of the S-box is 3, and can be easily determined from its ANF:

$$a_0 = b_4b_3b_2 + b_4b_3b_1 + b_4b_3b_0 + b_3b_2b_0 + b_3b_2 + b_3 + b_2 + b_1b_0 + b_1 + 1$$
$$a_1 = b_4b_2b_0 + b_4 + b_3b_2 + b_2b_0 + b_1 + b_0$$
$$a_2 = b_4b_3b_1 + b_4b_3 + b_4b_2b_1 + b_4b_2 + b_3b_1b_0 + b_3b_1 + b_2b_1b_0 + b_2b_1 + b_2 + 1 + a_1$$
$$a_3 = b_4b_2b_1 + b_4b_2b_0 + b_4b_2 + b_4b_1 + b_4 + b_3 + b_2b_1 + b_2b_0 + b_1$$
$$a_4 = b_4b_3b_2 + b_4b_2b_1 + b_4b_2b_0 + b_4b_2 + b_3b_2b_0 + b_3b_2 + b_3 + b_2b_1 + b_2b_0 + b_1b_0$$
$$(4)$$

Linear Diffusion Layer (p_L). p_L provides diffusion within each 64-bit register word $B[y][*], 0 \le y < 5$ as follows, where the first offset is denoted by $r_0 \in \{19, 61, 1, 10, 7\}$, the second one is denoted by $r_1 \in \{28, 39, 6, 17, 41\}$.

$$B[0][*] \leftarrow \Sigma_0(B[0][*]) = B[0][*] + (B[0][*] \ggg 19) + (B[0][*] \ggg 28)$$
$$B[1][*] \leftarrow \Sigma_1(B[1][*]) = B[1][*] + (B[1][*] \ggg 61) + (B[1][*] \ggg 39)$$
$$B[2][*] \leftarrow \Sigma_2(B[2][*]) = B[2][*] + (B[2][*] \ggg 1) + (B[2][*] \ggg 6) \qquad (5)$$
$$B[3][*] \leftarrow \Sigma_3(B[3][*]) = B[3][*] + (B[3][*] \ggg 10) + (B[3][*] \ggg 17)$$
$$B[4][*] \leftarrow \Sigma_4(B[4][*]) = B[4][*] + (B[4][*] \ggg 7) + (B[4][*] \ggg 41)$$

2.5   Linear Structures

Linear structure technique was first formalized and developed by Guo *et al.* [13] in 2016. Based on this novel technique, a series of cryptanalysis records of preimage attacks on KECCAK and zero-sum distinguishers of the underlying permutation KECCAK-f[1600] were broken. Generally, the main idea is to construct algebraic systems with an adequate number of remaining degrees of freedom based on one known linear structure. One linear structure with a larger number of remaining degrees of freedom indicates a more effective preimage attack, as it decreases the complexity of solving the entire algebraic system. Let us consider a 1.5-round linear structure used in the preimage attack on 2-round KECCAK-384 (see Fig. 2).

Let A be a starting state, where each bit $A[x][y][z]$ is either a linear bit that includes the linear polynomial of variables with the algebraic degree-1 or a constant bit. Figure 2 gives a 1.5-round linear structure on KECCAK-f[1600]

with 384 variables and 256 DF remaining. Suppose $A[x][y][*]$ for $x = 0, 2$ and $y = 0, 1, 2$ be linear bits (each specified lane has 64 linear bits.). To limit these linear bits not be diffused by θ mapping, 128 linear conditions such as $A[x][2][z] = \sum_{y=0}^{1} A[x][y][z] + c_{x,z}$ with $c_{x,z} = 0$ or $c_{x,z} = 1$ are set up, such that these linear bits in each column sum to a constant. Thus, the left DF is calculated as $384 - 128 = 256$, where each linear equation costs one DF.

In Fig. 2, we can see how the propagations of linear bits through the round function of KECCAK-$f[1600]$. Each bit of lanes with yellow represents a linear bit. The other lanes are all constants where gray and white bits stand for value 0 and arbitrary constants, respectively. Note that ρ and π linear mappings only re-arrange the location of linear bits, while ι mapping adds one round constant, thus the linear bits will not be diffused by these linear mappings. The algebraic degree of the nonlinear mapping χ is 2 determined by Eq. 2. Only when all linear bits before χ are not adjacent to each other, the algebraic degree of each bit keeps at most 1. Thus, it makes sure that the algebraic degrees of the state bits remain linear after 1.5 rounds. Otherwise, the output bits are quadratic ones. Based on this 1.5-round linear structure, the preimage attack on 2-round KECCAK-384 can be mounted. For simplify, we give some properties related to this paper without any proof. For more proof details, please refer to [13].

Property 1. [13] Given 5 bits b_i ($0 \le i < 5$) of the output of χ, 5 linear equations can be set up on the 5 input bits a_i[5] as $b_i = a_i + (b_{i+1} + 1)a_{i+2}$.

Property 2. [13] Given 3 consecutive bits b_i, b_{i+1}, b_{i+2} of the output of χ, 2 linear equations can be set up on the input bits [5] as $b_i = a_i + (b_{i+1} + 1)a_{i+2}$.

According to Property 1, we have 256 linear equations with $256°C$ of freedom for KECCAK-384, and solve this system just once. The search complexity of preimage attack on 2-round KECCAK-384 is calculated as $2^{384-256+1} = 2^{129}$ after dealing with paddings.

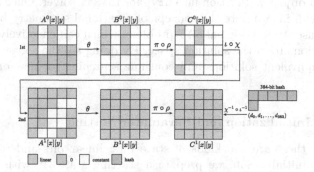

Fig. 2. 1.5-round linear structure with $256°C$ of freedom left used in preimage attack on 2-round KECCAK-384.

---

[5] Their algebraic degrees are at most 1..

2.6   SAT-Based Cryptanalysis

Given a Boolean formula $f(x_1, x_2, \ldots, x_n)$, the Boolean satisfiability problem (SAT) is to determine whether there is any assignment of values to these Boolean variables which makes the formula true. A Boolean formula in conjunctive normal form (CNF) consists of one or more clauses joined by *conjunctions* ($\land$), where each clause is a *disjunction* ($\lor$) of *literals*, each literal represents a positive or negative variable, *e.g.*, x_i or $\neg x_i$. The basic idea of the SAT-based cryptanalysis method is encoding the cryptanalysis problem such as the search for optimal differential characteristics as a SAT Model in CNF [12,41,42], and then invokes off-the-shelf SAT solver to solve it. In recent years, several SAT solvers are presented in public community, such as the CryptoMiniSat [40] and CaDiCaL [5]. All of these SAT solvers based on *conflict-driven clause learning* (CDCL) [29] support CNF (in DIMAC format) as their input. Since CryptoMiniSat shows outstanding performance in SAT solving with multi threads, and this is the main reason that we choose this SAT solver.

3   SAT Model for Linear Structure Search

Instead of controlling and tracing the propagation of linear bits manually, in this section, we develop a new bit-level SAT model for searching new better, or even optimal linear structures on KECCAK-d hash functions under different parameter d variants. Generally, an optimal SAT model refers to a model with the minimum number of clauses and variables which have a significant impact on the solver runtime, so we aim to minimize both.

First, we model the propagation of linear bits through the round function R. The linear layer of R of the underlying permutation KECCAK-$f[1600]$ is defined as $\lambda = \pi \circ \rho \circ \theta$ (we ignore ι mapping here since it does not affect our model). Then, the objective function is set to maximize the value of DF. After that, we input our model and objective function into CryptoMiniSat solver. Once a solution is returned, we will incorporate the concept of rotational symmetry by adding 64 additional clauses to the original SAT problem, which can effectively restrict the acquired solutions from the solution space. By doing so, the solver will exclude rotationally-equivalent solutions and continue searching for new ones that are distinct.

3.1   Model Initialization and Parameter Setting

In our model, there are two kinds of state bits: linear bits and constant bits. At the model initialization, we prepare a starting state A^0 with 1600 model variables, denoted by $A^0_{x,y,z}$. If $A^0[x][y][z]$ is a linear bit, $A^0_{x,y,z} = 1$; otherwise $A^0_{x,y,z} = 0$, *i.e.*, $A^0[x][y][z]$ is a constant. Since the last c bits of the initial state of KECCAK-d are all fixed constant '0', the last c variables are initialized as 0. As shown in Fig. 3.

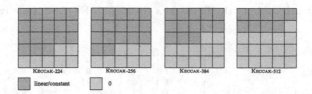

Fig. 3. Model initialization state for KECCAK-224/256/384/512. Orange stands for either linear bits or constant bits. Gray stands for constant 0. (Color figure online)

3.2 Propagation of Linear Bits in the Linear Layer

Let A^i, B^i, C^i be the input of $i+1$-th round, the output of $i+1$-th ($0 \le i < n_r$) θ and $\pi \circ \rho$, respectively. Since the effect of $\pi \circ \rho$ just re-arranges the location of the state bits, we only need to simulate the update of the 1600-bit state using $C^i = \pi \circ \rho(B^i)$ to obtain the output state C^i in ANFs, which is easy to handle by symbolic computation. We take SageMath [44] as the symbolic computation tool, which supports ANFs to CNFs conversion by invoking *CNFEncoder()* function.

To model the propagation of linear bits through θ, we introduce $G^i_{x,z}$ and $D^i_{x,z}$ with 320 model variables, respectively. $G^i_{x,z} = 1$ if the sum of column $A^i[x][*][z]$ contains linear bits, otherwise $G^i_{x,z} = 0$; $D^i_{x,z} = 1$ if $A^i[x][*][z]$ contains linear bits and the sum of these linear bits is a constant $c_{x,z}$, and the corresponding linear condition will be created to the system as shown in Eq. 6, which costs 1 DF; otherwise $D^i_{x,z} = 0$.

$$\sum_{y=0}^{4} A^i_{x,y,z} = c_{x,z} \tag{6}$$

We take $A^0[0][*][0]$ as an example, the relations among variables ($A^0_{0,0,0}$, $A^0_{0,1,0}$, $A^0_{0,2,0}$, $A^0_{0,3,0}$, $A^0_{0,4,0}$, $G^0_{0,0}$, $D^0_{0,0}$) can be described by Table 2. Based on this table, 11 clauses can be generated via *POSform()* function. The *POSform()* function employs simplified pairs and a redundant group elimination algorithm to convert the list of all input combinations that generate the minterms into the smallest Product-Of-Sums (POS) form. For more details please refer to https://docs.sympy.org/latest/modules/logic.html.

Besides, another constraint through θ should be taken into consideration according to Eq. 1. If any of $G^i_{x-1,z}$, $G^i_{x+1,z-1}$, and $A^i_{x,y,z}$ equal to 1, $B^i[x][y][z]$ will be a linear bit, *i.e.*, $B^i_{x,y,z} = 1$, which can be described by Table 3. All minterms are described with 4 clauses accurately by invoking *POSform()* function.

3.3 Propagation of Linear Bits in the Non-Linear Layer

Suppose $C^i[*][y][z]$ are the input of the χ mapping. According to Eq. 2, we know that there are at most 2 linear bits in $C^i[*][y][z]$ and these two linear bits must not be consecutive as well. Thus, only 11 possible patterns for $C^i[*][y][z]$. This can be described by Table 4 with 5 variables ($C^i_{0,y,z}$, $C^i_{1,y,z}$, $C^i_{2,y,z}$, $C^i_{3,y,z}$, $C^i_{4,y,z}$).

Table 2. The truth table of the linear bits through θ. F: the output value is true if $F = 1$.

$A^0_{0,0,0}$	$A^0_{0,1,0}$	$A^0_{0,2,0}$	$A^0_{0,3,0}$	$A^0_{0,4,0}$	$G^0_{0,0}$	$D^0_{0,0}$	F	$A^0_{0,0,0}$	$A^0_{0,1,0}$	$A^0_{0,2,0}$	$A^0_{0,3,0}$	$A^0_{0,4,0}$	$G^0_{0,0}$	$D^0_{0,0}$	F
0	0	0	0	0	0	0	1	1	0	0	0	0	1	0	1
0	1	0	0	0	1	0	1	1	1	0	0	0	1	0	1
0	0	1	0	0	1	0	1	1	0	1	0	0	1	0	1
0	1	1	0	0	1	0	1	1	1	1	0	0	1	0	1
0	0	0	1	0	1	0	1	1	0	0	1	0	1	0	1
0	1	0	1	0	1	0	1	1	1	0	1	0	1	0	1
0	0	1	1	0	1	0	1	1	0	1	1	0	1	0	1
0	1	1	1	0	1	0	1	1	1	1	1	0	1	0	1
0	0	0	0	1	1	0	1	1	0	0	0	1	1	0	1
0	1	0	0	1	1	0	1	1	1	0	0	1	1	0	1
0	0	1	0	1	1	0	1	1	0	1	0	1	1	0	1
0	1	1	0	1	1	0	1	1	1	1	0	1	1	0	1
0	0	0	1	1	1	0	1	1	0	0	1	1	1	0	1
0	1	0	1	1	1	0	1	1	1	0	1	1	1	0	1
0	0	1	1	1	1	0	1	1	0	1	1	1	1	0	1
0	1	1	1	1	1	0	1	1	1	1	1	1	1	0	1
1	1	0	0	0	0	1	1	1	0	1	0	0	0	1	1
0	1	1	0	0	0	1	1	1	1	1	0	0	0	1	1
1	0	0	1	0	0	1	1	0	0	1	1	0	0	1	1
1	1	0	1	0	0	1	1	0	0	0	1	0	0	1	1
1	0	1	1	0	0	1	1	0	1	1	1	0	0	1	1
1	1	1	1	0	0	1	1	1	0	0	0	1	0	1	1
0	1	0	0	1	0	1	1	1	1	0	0	1	0	1	1
0	0	1	0	1	0	1	1	1	0	1	0	1	0	1	1
0	1	1	0	1	0	1	1	1	0	0	1	1	0	1	1
0	0	0	1	1	0	1	1	1	1	0	1	1	0	1	1
0	1	0	1	1	0	1	1	1	0	1	1	1	0	1	1
0	0	1	1	1	0	1	1	1	1	0	1	1	0	1	1
0	1	1	1	1	0	1	1	1	1	1	1	1	0	1	1

Table 3. The truth table of determining the value of $B^i_{0,0,0}$. F: the output value is true if $F = 1$.

$A^i_{0,0,0}$	$G^i_{63,0}$	$G^i_{1,63}$	$B^i_{0,0,0}$	F	$A^i_{0,0,0}$	$G^i_{63,0}$	$G^i_{1,63}$	$B^i_{0,0,0}$	F
0	0	0	0	1	0	0	1	1	1
0	1	0	1	1	0	1	1	1	1
1	0	0	1	1	1	0	1	1	1
1	1	0	1	1	1	1	1	1	1

Similarly, adding all minterms of this truth table into *POSform()* function, 5 clauses are generated.

Let $A^{i+1}[*][y][z]$ be the inputs of the next round, *i.e.*, the outputs of the nonlinear mapping χ. Given $C^i[*][y][z]$, the corresponding outputs $A^{i+1}[*][y][z]$ can be easily determined based on Eq. 2. Let '?' and c stand for the linear bit and constant bit, respectively. For example, if $C^i[*][0][0] = (?cccc)$, then there are 4 possible outputs: $A^{i+1}[*][0][0] = \{(?cc?c), (?cccc), (?cc??), (?ccc?)\}$.

All of them and their corresponding outputs construct a truth table with 10 variables $(C^i_{0,0,0}, C^i_{0,1,0}, C^i_{0,2,0}, C^i_{0,3,0}, C^i_{0,4,0}, A^{i+1}_{0,0,0}, A^{i+1}_{0,1,0}, A^{i+1}_{0,2,0}, A^{i+1}_{0,3,0}, A^{i+1}_{0,4,0})$ is listed in Table 5. Overall, 15 clauses are generated to describe χ mapping.

Table 4. The truth table of 11 possible patterns for $C^i[*][y][z]$. F: the output value is true if F = 1.

$C_{0,y,z}^i$	$C_{1,y,z}^i$	$C_{2,y,z}^i$	$C_{3,y,z}^i$	$C_{4,y,z}^i$	F	$C_{0,y,z}^i$	$C_{1,y,z}^i$	$C_{2,y,z}^i$	$C_{3,y,z}^i$	$C_{4,y,z}^i$	F
1	0	1	0	0	1	0	1	0	0	0	1
0	1	0	0	1	1	0	0	1	0	0	1
1	0	0	1	0	1	0	0	0	1	0	1
0	0	1	0	1	1	0	0	0	0	1	1
0	1	0	1	0	1	0	0	0	0	0	1
1	0	0	0	0	1						

3.4 Objective Function

One good linear structure means with the larger DF left, we set the value of DF as our objective function. The DF is computed using Eq. 7, where N is the round number of preimage attack, and the corresponding round number of linear structure is $N-1$ in our model. Encoding a limit on the maximum number of active variables in a given set is commonly referred to as a cardinality constraint encoding.

$$Maximize: \quad DF = \sum_{x,y,z} A_{x,y,z}^0 - \sum_{0 \le i < N-1} \sum_{x,z} D_{x,z}^i \tag{7}$$

Inspired by [11,41], we evaluate the performance of different encodings using implementations by the PySAT project [18] (see Table 6). The *kmTotalizer* [34] performs well with the least number of clauses and variables. In this way, we significantly reduce the size of SAT model by taking *kmTotalizer* as our cardinality encoding.

4   SAT-Based Automatic Linear Structure Analysis on KECCAK

In this section, we apply our SAT model to KECCAK-224/256/384/512, respectively.

4.1 Linear Structures of KECCAK-d Hash Functions

For KECCAK-224/256, Li *et al.* [21] proposed a 2.5-round linear structure with 194 DF left. To verify the correctness of our SAT model, we apply it to search for the same or even better linear structure with DF larger than 194. As a result, it just takes a few seconds to search for the same linear structure, but after 10 days it still does not output any better solution. Thus, this 2.5-round linear structure with 194 DF left is the best one so far for KECCAK-224/256. Besides, we also find Guo *et al.*'s linear structure on KECCAK-224/256/512 [13],

Table 5. The truth table of the linear bits through χ (take $C^i[*][0][0]$ as an example). F: the output value is true if $F = 1$.

$C^i_{0,0,0}$	$C^i_{1,0,0}$	$C^i_{2,0,0}$	$C^i_{3,0,0}$	$C^i_{4,0,0}$	$A^{i+1}_{0,0,0}$	$A^{i+1}_{1,0,0}$	$A^{i+1}_{2,0,0}$	$A^{i+1}_{3,0,0}$	$A^{i+1}_{4,0,0}$	F
1	0	1	0	0	1	0	1	0	0	1
1	0	1	0	0	1	0	1	1	0	1
1	0	1	0	0	1	1	1	0	0	1
1	0	1	0	0	1	0	1	0	1	1
1	0	1	0	0	1	1	1	1	0	1
1	0	1	0	0	1	0	1	1	1	1
1	0	1	0	0	1	1	1	0	1	1
1	0	1	0	0	1	1	1	1	1	1
0	1	0	1	0	0	1	0	1	0	1
0	1	0	1	0	0	1	0	1	1	1
0	1	0	1	0	0	1	1	1	0	1
0	1	0	1	0	1	1	0	1	0	1
0	1	0	1	0	0	1	1	1	1	1
0	1	0	1	0	1	1	0	1	1	1
0	1	0	1	0	1	1	1	1	0	1
0	1	0	1	0	1	1	1	1	1	1
0	0	1	0	1	0	0	1	0	1	1
0	0	1	0	1	1	0	1	0	1	1
0	0	1	0	1	0	0	1	1	1	1
0	0	1	0	1	0	1	1	0	1	1
0	0	1	0	1	1	0	1	1	1	1
0	0	1	0	1	1	1	1	0	1	1
0	0	1	0	1	0	1	1	1	1	1
0	0	1	0	1	1	1	1	1	1	1
1	0	0	1	0	1	0	0	1	0	1
1	0	0	1	0	1	1	0	1	0	1
1	0	0	1	0	1	0	0	1	1	1
1	0	0	1	0	1	0	1	1	0	1
1	0	0	1	0	1	1	0	1	1	1
1	0	0	1	0	1	1	1	1	0	1
1	0	0	1	0	1	0	1	1	1	1
1	0	0	1	0	1	1	1	1	1	1
0	1	0	0	1	0	1	0	0	1	1
0	1	0	0	1	0	1	1	0	1	1
0	1	0	0	1	1	1	0	0	1	1
0	1	0	0	1	0	1	0	1	1	1
0	1	0	0	1	1	1	1	0	1	1
0	1	0	0	1	0	1	1	1	1	1
0	1	0	0	1	1	1	0	1	1	1
0	1	0	0	1	1	1	1	1	1	1
1	0	0	0	0	1	0	0	1	0	1
1	0	0	0	0	1	0	0	0	0	1
1	0	0	0	0	1	0	0	1	1	1
1	0	0	0	0	1	0	0	0	1	1
0	0	0	0	1	0	0	1	0	1	1
0	0	0	0	1	0	0	0	0	1	1
0	0	0	0	1	0	0	1	1	1	1
0	0	0	0	1	0	0	0	1	1	1
0	0	0	1	0	0	1	0	1	0	1
0	0	0	1	0	0	0	0	1	0	1

continued

Table 5. continued

$C^i_{0,0,0}$	$C^i_{1,0,0}$	$C^i_{2,0,0}$	$C^i_{3,0,0}$	$C^i_{4,0,0}$	$A^{i+1}_{0,0,0}$	$A^{i+1}_{1,0,0}$	$A^{i+1}_{2,0,0}$	$A^{i+1}_{3,0,0}$	$A^{i+1}_{4,0,0}$	F
0	0	0	1	0	0	1	1	1	0	1
0	0	0	1	0	0	0	1	1	0	1
0	0	1	0	0	1	0	1	0	0	1
0	0	1	0	0	0	0	1	0	0	1
0	0	1	0	0	1	1	1	0	0	1
0	0	1	0	0	0	1	1	0	0	1
0	1	0	0	0	0	1	0	0	1	1
0	1	0	0	0	0	1	0	0	0	1
0	1	0	0	0	1	1	0	0	1	1
0	1	0	0	0	1	1	0	0	0	1
0	0	0	0	0	0	0	0	0	0	1

Table 6. Comparison of cardinality encodings of models for KECCAK 224/256/384/512 with $|A^0_{x,y,z}| = r \geq k$ (since the last c variables are initialized as 0, we only consider r model variables here for simplify). $\#C$: the number of clauses. $\#V$: the number of auxiliary boolean variables.

Encoding	$r = 1152 \geq 512$		$r = 1088 \geq 512$		$r = 832 \geq 256$		$r = 576 \geq 256$	
Encoding	$\#C$	$\#V$	$\#C$	$\#V$	$\#C$	$\#V$	$\#C$	$\#V$
seqcounter	655232	327680	589760	294912	294592	147456	163770	81920
totalizer	674753	11776	602337	11008	353825	8182	170913	5312
mTotalizer	61383	7139	56725	6692	38680	4961	22466	3288
CardNet	162812	108541	162812	108541	72191	48127	66812	44541
kmTotalizer	47818	6658	43563	6208	33661	4834	17633	3105
sortnetwrk	175103	116735	175103	116735	72191	48127	72191	48127

which well demonstrate the previous linear structures are optimal so far and the corresponding preimage attacks are also valid.

For KECCAK-384/512, we search the best 1.5-round linear structure with 128 DF left for KECCAK-384, which has the same setting as the previous one [13]. Based on our SAT model, we successfully seek some 2.5-round linear structures with 64 DF on KECCAK-384. For KECCAK-512, we find no such 2.5-round structure with DF greater than 0 exists. However, we find some best 1.5-round linear structures on KECCAK-512 with 147 DF left. Based on this new linear structure, we improve Guo *et al.*'s preimage attack on 2-/3-round KECCAK-512.

4.2 Improved Preimage Attacks on KECCAK-512

In [13], Guo *et al.* proposed a preimage attack on 2-/3-round KECCAK-512. The basic idea is to make full use of the leaked linear/non-linear relations from the hash value and then construct a quadratic Boolean equation system. For 3-round preimage attacks on KECCAK-512, according to Theorem 2, there are 448 linear equations and 64 quadratic ones. The complexity of 2-round KECCAK-512 given in [13] can be formalized by $2^{448-DF+64}$. For 3-round preimage attacks, Guo *et al.* proposed an improved technique by partially linearizing the inputs of the last χ, and the complexity of 3-round KECCAK-512 is $2^{448-2\lfloor\frac{DF-5}{8}\rfloor+64}$.

Once a new better linear structure is found with a larger DF left, the complexity of a preimage attack based on this linear structure can further decrease. Thus, we exploit our new better 1.5-round linear structure with 147 DF left to improve preimage attacks on 2-/3-round KECCAK-512. In this way, we obtain improved preimage attacks on 2-/3-round KECCAK-512 with $2^{365}/2^{478}$ time complexity, respectively.

5   SAT-Based Automatic Linear Structure Analysis on ASCON

Our SAT model can further be extended to other similar cryptographic primitives, such as ASCON. In this section, we modify the SAT model slightly to search the linear structures of ASCON permutation. As an independent interest, we make a study of constructing zero-sum distinguishers based on searched linear structures.

5.1   Modified SAT Model

The Constraints on the Starting State B. As mentioned in Equation 4, the algebraic degree of the inverse of nonlinear operation p_S is 3. Let B be the starting state, with 320 model variables, denoted by $B_{y,z}$, $0 \le y < 5$, and $0 \le z < 64$. If $B[y][z]$ is a linear bit, $B_{y,z} = 1$; otherwise $B_{y,z} = 0$, *i.e.*, $B[y][z]$ is a constant bit. We aim to search for 2-round linear structures of ASCON, for one round in both forward and backward directions, as figured in Fig. 4. To ensure the algebraic degree of one forward round and one backward round is at most 1(only p_S and p_S^{-1} affect the algebraic degree), some constraints on B must be added.

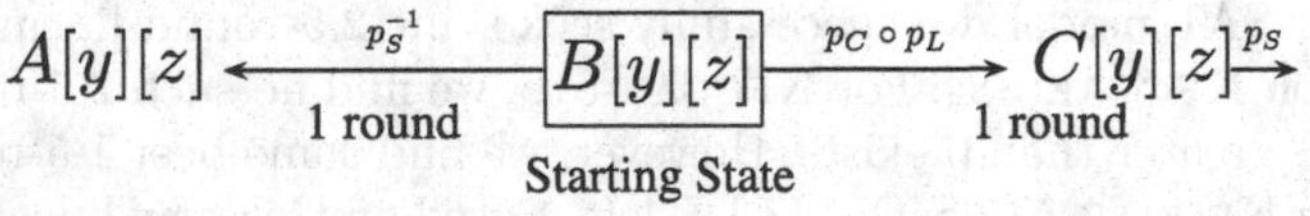

$$A[y][z] \xleftarrow[\text{1 round}]{p_S^{-1}} \boxed{B[y][z]} \xrightarrow[\text{1 round}]{p_C \circ p_L} C[y][z] \xrightarrow{p_S}$$

Starting State

Fig. 4. One backward round and one forward round for ASCON.

Observation 1 *According to Equation 4, if there are two linear bits in the inputs $(b_0, b_1, b_2, b_3, b_4)$, only 10 possible patterns as below can ensure the outputs of the inverse of p_S are linear bits or constant bits.*

$$
\begin{cases}
p_S^{-1}(b_0, 0, 0, b_3, 0) = (b_3 + 1, b_0, b_0 + 1, b_3, b_3) \\
p_S^{-1}(b_0, 0, 0, 0, b_4) = (1, b_0 + b_4, b_0 + b_4 + 1, b_4, 0) \\
p_S^{-1}(b_0, 1, 0, 0, b_4) = (b_0, b_0 + b_4 + 1, b_0 + b_4, 1, b_0) \\
p_S^{-1}(1, 1, 0, b_3, b_4) = (b_3 + 1, b_4, b_4 + 1, b_3 + 1, b_3 + 1) \\
p_S^{-1}(0, 1, b_2, 0, b_4) = (b_2, b_4 + 1, b_4, b_2 + 1, b_2) \\
p_S^{-1}(1, b_1, 1, b_3, 0) = (b_3, b_1 + b_3, b_1 + b_3, b_3 + 1, b_3 + 1) \\
p_S^{-1}(1, b_1, 0, b_3, 0) = (b_3 + 1, b_1 + 1, b_1, b_1 + b_3, b_1 + b_3) \\
p_S^{-1}(0, b_1, b_2, 0, 1) = (b_1 + b_2 + 1, b_1 + 1, b_1, b_2 + 1, b_2) \\
p_S^{-1}(0, b_1, b_2, 1, 1) = (b_2, b_1 + b_2 + 1, b_1 + b_2 + 1, b_2, b_2 + 1) \\
p_S^{-1}(b_0, 0, b_2, 0, 1) = (b_2 + 1, b_0 + 1, b_0, b_2 + 1, b_2)
\end{cases}
$$

Together with Observation 1 and considering the inputs with at most 1 linear bit, there are 13 possible patterns for $B[*][z]$ that satisfy the condition that the algebraic degrees of the outputs of p_S^{-1} are at most 1, i.e., $B_{*,z} \in \{(10010), (10001), (00011), (00101), (01010), (01100), (10100), (10000), (01000), (00100), (00010), (00001), (00000)\}$, as shown in Table 7. After putting this truth table into $POSform()$ function, 10 clauses are generated.

The Constraints on State $C[y][z]$. Suppose $C[y][z]$ is the output of the nonlinear operation p_S. Based on Eq. 3, we deduce that there are 8 possible patterns for $C[*][z]$ that ensure the outputs of one round are linear bits or constant bits, i.e., $C_{*,z} \in \{(00000), (10000), (01000), (00100), (00010), (00001), (10100), (00101)\}$ and the truth table is listed in Table 8. After feeding this truth table into $POSform()$ function, 8 clauses are obtained.

The Constraints on the p_L. Based on a similar idea of KECCAK's model, we introduce 320 model variables, denoted by $D_{y,z}, 0 \le y < 5, 0 \le z < 64$. According to Eq. 5, $C_{y,z} = 1$ if the sum of $B[y][z], B[y][z - r_0], B[y][z - r_1]$ is not a constant; otherwise $C_{y,z} = 0$. $D_{y,z} = 1$ if the sum of $B[y][z], B[y][z - r_0], B[y][z - r_1]$ contains linear bits and the sum of these linear bits is a constant;

Table 7. The truth table of 13 possible patterns for $B[*][z]$. F: the output value is true if F = 1.

$B_{0,z}$	$B_{1,z}$	$B_{2,z}$	$B_{3,z}$	$B_{4,z}$	F	$B_{0,z}$	$B_{1,z}$	$B_{2,z}$	$B_{3,z}$	$B_{4,z}$	F
1	0	0	1	0	1	1	0	0	0	0	1
1	0	0	0	1	1	0	1	0	0	0	1
0	0	0	1	1	1	0	0	1	0	0	1
0	0	1	0	1	1	0	0	0	1	0	1
0	1	0	1	0	1	0	0	0	0	1	1
0	1	1	0	0	1	0	0	0	0	0	1
1	0	1	0	0	1						

Table 8. The truth table of 8 possible patterns for $C[*][z]$. F: the output value is true if F = 1.

$C_{0,z}$	$C_{1,z}$	$C_{2,z}$	$C_{3,z}$	$C_{4,z}$	F	$C_{0,z}$	$C_{1,z}$	$C_{2,z}$	$C_{3,z}$	$C_{4,z}$	F
0	0	0	0	0	1	0	0	0	1	0	1
1	0	0	0	0	1	0	0	0	0	1	1
0	1	0	0	0	1	1	0	1	0	0	1
0	0	1	0	0	1	0	0	1	0	1	1

otherwise $D_{y,z} = 1$. All constraints are listed in Table 9. 7 clauses can accurately describe this table.

Table 9. The truth table of the linear bits through p_L. (take $C[0][0]$ as an example, $r_0 = 19$ and $r_1 = 28$). F: the output value is true if F = 1.

$B_{0,0}$	$B_{0,45}$	$B_{0,36}$	$C_{0,0}$	$D_{0,0}$	F	$B_{0,0}$	$B_{0,45}$	$B_{0,36}$	$C_{0,0}$	$D_{0,0}$	F
0	0	0	0	0	1	0	1	1	1	0	1
1	0	0	1	0	1	1	1	1	1	0	1
0	1	0	1	0	1	1	1	0	0	1	1
1	1	0	1	0	1	1	0	1	0	1	1
0	0	1	1	0	1	0	1	1	0	1	1
1	0	1	1	0	1	1	1	1	0	1	1

5.2   Zero-Sum Distinguishers

In 2016, the designers of ASCON [9] presented a full 12-round zero-sum distinguisher (4 inverse rounds, free middle round, and 7 forward rounds) of ASCON permutation with the complexity of 2^{130}. We apply our modified model to ASCON, as a result, we find one 2-round linear structure with 102 DF left. As a direct application, two rounds can be inserted without increasing the complexities for constructing better full 12-round zero-sum distinguishers.

Suppose the full 12 rounds of ASCON include 4 inverse rounds, 2 free middle rounds, and 6 forward rounds. Combined with Aumasson *et al.*'s technique [1] for zero-sum distinguisher, the complexity is calculated as $2^{1+max(3^4, 2^6)} = 2^{82}$. The round of the zero-sum distinguisher is limited by the size of the linear structures, and the largest linear space that we find for a 2-round linear structure is $2^{102} > 2^{82}$. Therefore, the 12-round distinguisher can be constructed theoretically with 2^{82} complexity.

6   Conclusion

In this paper, we develop a generic automatic tool for search linear structures by transforming the propagation of linear bits through the round function into an exact SAT model. We successfully apply this model to KECCAK-224/256/384/512 hash function. As a result, we verify previous best 2.5-round linear structures with 194 DF left on KECCAK-224/256. Moreover, we find a 1.5-round linear structure on KECCAK-512 with 147 DF left, and further improve the preimage attacks on 2-/3-round KECCAK-512. Besides, we modify the SAT model slightly to search the linear structure of ASCON. Consequently, we obtain a 2-round linear structure with 102 DF left. As an independent interest, we further extend this linear structure to a 12-round zero-sum distinguisher of ASCON permutation with the complexity of 2^{82}.

At the end, we briefly overview future work: our model demonstrates feasibility for large-state-size ciphers by utilizing a combined linear structure technique for preimage attacks. Considering the nonlinear structures in addition to the linear structures could provide more degrees of freedom and significantly enhance the overall effectiveness of the attack, it might also be interesting to consider nonlinear structures using SAT. Our optimization strategy significantly reduces the scale of the model, but we still do not guarantee optimal solutions with respect to huge search space, even with advanced cardinality encoding. Another future work is to consider more advanced search strategy for improving efficiency.

Acknowledgments. We are grateful to the anonymous reviewers for their valuable feedback and comments that improved the quality of the paper. This research is supported by the National Natural Science Foundation of China under (Grants No. 61972249) and the State Scholarship Fund (No. 202106230206) organized by China Scholarship Council.

References

1. Aumasson, J.P., Meier, W.: Zero-sum distinguishers for reduced Keccak-f and for the core functions of luffa and Hamsi. rump session of Cryptographic Hardware and Embedded Systems-CHES 2009, p. 67 (2009)
2. Bao, Z., et al.: Automatic search of meet-in-the-middle preimage attacks on AES-like hashing. In: Canteaut, A., Standaert, F.-X. (eds.) EUROCRYPT 2021. LNCS, vol. 12696, pp. 771–804. Springer, Cham (2021). https://doi.org/10.1007/978-3-030-77870-5_27
3. Bao, Z., Guo, J., Shi, D., Tu, Y.: Superposition meet-in-the-middle attacks: updates on fundamental security of AES-like hashing. In: Dodis, Y., Shrimpton, T. (eds.) Advances in Cryptology - CRYPTO 2022, CRYPTO 2022. LNCS, vol. 13507, pp. 64–93. Springer, Cham (2022). https://doi.org/10.1007/978-3-031-15802-5_3
4. Bertoni, G., Peeters, M., Van Assche, G., et al.: The keccak reference (2011). http://keccak.noekeon.org
5. Biere, A.: CADICAL at the SAT Race 2019 (2019). https://github.com/arminbiere/cadical

6. Boura, C., Canteaut, A.: Zero-sum distinguishers for iterated permutations and application to KECCAK-f and Hamsi-256. In: Biryukov, A., Gong, G., Stinson, D.R. (eds.) SAC 2010. LNCS, vol. 6544, pp. 1–17. Springer, Heidelberg (2011). https://doi.org/10.1007/978-3-642-19574-7_1

7. Daemen, J., Van Assche, G.: Differential propagation analysis of Keccak. In: Canteaut, A. (ed.) FSE 2012. LNCS, vol. 7549, pp. 422–441. Springer, Heidelberg (2012). https://doi.org/10.1007/978-3-642-34047-5_24

8. Dinur, I.: Cryptanalytic applications of the polynomial method for solving multivariate equation systems over GF(2). In: Canteaut, A., Standaert, F.-X. (eds.) EUROCRYPT 2021. LNCS, vol. 12696, pp. 374–403. Springer, Cham (2021). https://doi.org/10.1007/978-3-030-77870-5_14

9. Dobraunig, C., Eichlseder, M., Mendel, F., Schläffer, M.: Ascon v1. 2 submission to the caesar competition, September 15 2016. submission to the caesar competition

10. Dong, X., Hua, J., Sun, S., Li, Z., Wang, X., Hu, L.: Meet-in-the-middle attacks revisited: key-recovery, collision, and preimage attacks. In: Malkin, T., Peikert, C. (eds.) CRYPTO 2021. LNCS, vol. 12827, pp. 278–308. Springer, Cham (2021). https://doi.org/10.1007/978-3-030-84252-9_10

11. Erlacher, J., Mendel, F., Eichlseder, M.: Bounds for the security of ascon against differential and linear cryptanalysis. IACR Trans. Symmetric Cryptol. **2022**(1), 64–87 (2022)

12. Guo, J., Liu, G., Song, L., Tu, Y.: Exploring SAT for cryptanalysis: (Quantum) collision attacks against 6-round SHA-3. In: Agrawal, S., Lin, D. (eds.) Advances in Cryptology - ASIACRYPT 2022, ASIACRYPT 2022, LNCS, vol. 13793, pp. 645–674. Springer, Cham (2022). https://doi.org/10.1007/978-3-031-22969-5_22

13. Guo, J., Liu, M., Song, L.: Linear structures: applications to cryptanalysis of round-reduced KECCAK. In: Cheon, J.H., Takagi, T. (eds.) ASIACRYPT 2016. LNCS, vol. 10031, pp. 249–274. Springer, Heidelberg (2016). https://doi.org/10.1007/978-3-662-53887-6_9

14. He, L., Lin, X., Yu, H.: Improved preimage attacks on 4-round keccak-224/256. IACR Trans. Symmetric Cryptol. **2021**(1), 217–238 (2021). https://doi.org/10.46586/tosc.v2021.i1.217-238

15. He, L., Lin, X., Yu, H.: Improved preimage attacks on round-reduced keccak-384/512 via restricted linear structures. IACR Cryptol. ePrint Arch. p. 788 (2022)

16. Hu, K., Peyrin, T.: Revisiting higher-order differential(-Linear) attacks from an Algebraic perspective - applications to Ascon, Grain v1, Xoodoo, and ChaCha. IACR Cryptol. ePrint Arch. p. 1335 (2022)

17. Huang, S., Wang, X., Xu, G., Wang, M., Zhao, J.: Conditional cube attack on reduced-round keccak sponge function. In: Coron, J.-S., Nielsen, J.B. (eds.) EUROCRYPT 2017. LNCS, vol. 10211, pp. 259–288. Springer, Cham (2017). https://doi.org/10.1007/978-3-319-56614-6_9

18. Ignatiev, A., Morgado, A., Marques-Silva, J.: PySAT: a python toolkit for prototyping with SAT oracles. In: SAT, pp. 428–437 (2018). https://doi.org/10.1007/978-3-319-94144-8_26

19. Li, H., He, L., Chen, S., Guo, J., Qiu, W.: Automatic preimage attack framework on ascon using a linearize-and-guess approach **2023**(3), 74–100 (2023). https://doi.org/10.46586/tosc.v2023.i3.74-100

20. Li, H., Liu, G., Zhang, H., Hu, K., Guo, J., Qiu, W.: AlgSAT – a SAT method for search and verification of differential characteristics from algebraic perspective. Cryptology ePrint Archive, Report 2022/1641 (2022). https://eprint.iacr.org/2022/1641

21. Li, T., Sun, Y.: Preimage attacks on round-reduced KECCAK-224/256 via an allocating approach. In: Ishai, Y., Rijmen, V. (eds.) EUROCRYPT 2019. LNCS, vol. 11478, pp. 556–584. Springer, Cham (2019). https://doi.org/10.1007/978-3-030-17659-4_19

22. Li, T., Sun, Y., Liao, M., Wang, D.: Preimage attacks on the round-reduced Keccak with cross-linear structures 2017(4), 39–57 (2017). https://doi.org/10.13154/tosc.v2017.i4.39-57

23. Lin, X., He, L., Yu, H.: Improved preimage attacks on 3-round Keccak-224/256. IACR Trans. Symmetric Cryptol. 2021(3), 84–101 (2021). https://doi.org/10.46586/tosc.v2021.i3.84-101

24. Lin, X., He, L., Yu, H.: Practical preimage attack on 3-round keccak-256. IACR Cryptol. ePrint Arch. p. 101 (2023)

25. Liu, F., Isobe, T., Meier, W.: Automatic verification of differential characteristics: application to reduced Gimli. In: Micciancio, D., Ristenpart, T. (eds.) CRYPTO 2020. LNCS, vol. 12172, pp. 219–248. Springer, Cham (2020). https://doi.org/10.1007/978-3-030-56877-1_8

26. Liu, F., Isobe, T., Meier, W., Yang, Z.: Algebraic attacks on round-reduced Keccak. In: Baek, J., Ruj, S. (eds.) ACISP 2021. LNCS, vol. 13083, pp. 91–110. Springer, Cham (2021). https://doi.org/10.1007/978-3-030-90567-5_5

27. Liu, F., et al.: Analysis of RIPEMD-160: new collision attacks and finding characteristics with MILP. In: Hazay, C., Stam, M. (eds.) Advances in Cryptology - EUROCRYPT 2023, EUROCRYPT 2023. LNCS, vol. 14007, pp. 189–219. Springer, Cham (2023). https://doi.org/10.1007/978-3-031-30634-1_7

28. Liu, G., Qiu, W., Tu, Y.: New techniques for searching differential trails in Keccak. IACR Trans. Symmetric Cryptol. 2019(4), 407–437 (2019)

29. Marques-Silva, J., Lynce, I., Malik, S.: Conflict-driven clause learning sat solvers. In: Handbook of Satisfiability -. Frontiers in Artificial Intelligence and Applications, vol. 336, 2nd edn., pp. 133–182. IOS Press, Ohmsha (2021)

30. Morawiecki, P., Pieprzyk, J., Srebrny, M.: Rotational cryptanalysis of round-reduced KECCAK. In: Moriai, S. (ed.) FSE 2013. LNCS, vol. 8424, pp. 241–262. Springer, Heidelberg (2014). https://doi.org/10.1007/978-3-662-43933-3_13

31. Morawiecki, P., Srebrny, M.: A SAT-based preimage analysis of reduced Keccak hash functions. Inf. Process. Lett. 113(10–11), 392–397 (2013)

32. Mouha, N., Preneel, B.: Towards finding optimal differential characteristics for ARX: application to Salsa20. IACR Cryptol. 2013, 328 (2013). https://eprint.iacr.org/2013/328

33. Mouha, N., Wang, Q., Gu, D., Preneel, B.: Differential and linear cryptanalysis using mixed-integer linear programming. In: Wu, C.-K., Yung, M., Lin, D. (eds.) Inscrypt 2011. LNCS, vol. 7537, pp. 57–76. Springer, Heidelberg (2012). https://doi.org/10.1007/978-3-642-34704-7_5

34. Ogawa, T., Liu, Y., Hasegawa, R., Koshimura, M., Fujita, H.: Modulo based CNF encoding of cardinality constraints and its application to maxsat solvers. In: ICTAI, pp. 9–17. IEEE Computer Society (2013)

35. Qin, L., Hua, J., Dong, X., Yan, H., Wang, X.: Meet-in-the-middle preimage attacks on sponge-based hashing. In: Hazay, C., Stam, M. (eds.) Advances in Cryptology - EUROCRYPT 2023, EUROCRYPT 2023, LNCS, vol. 14007, pp. 158–188. Springer, Cham (2023). https://doi.org/10.1007/978-3-031-30634-1_6

36. Rajasree, M.S.: Cryptanalysis of round-reduced KECCAK using non-linear structures. In: Hao, F., Ruj, S., Sen Gupta, S. (eds.) INDOCRYPT 2019. LNCS, vol. 11898, pp. 175–192. Springer, Cham (2019). https://doi.org/10.1007/978-3-030-35423-7_9

37. Sadeghi, S., Rijmen, V., Bagheri, N.: Proposing an MILP-based method for the experimental verification of difference-based trails: application to SPECK. SIMECK. Des. Codes Cryptogr. **89**(9), 2113–2155 (2021). https://doi.org/10.1007/s10623-021-00904-5

38. Song, L., Guo, J.: Cube-attack-like cryptanalysis of round-reduced keccak using MILP. IACR Trans. Symmetric Cryptol. **2018**(3), 182–214 (2018)

39. Song, L., Guo, J., Shi, D., Ling, S.: New MILP modeling: improved conditional cube attacks on Keccak-based constructions. In: Peyrin, T., Galbraith, S. (eds.) ASIACRYPT 2018. LNCS, vol. 11273, pp. 65–95. Springer, Cham (2018). https://doi.org/10.1007/978-3-030-03329-3_3

40. Soos, M., Nohl, K., Castelluccia, C.: Extending SAT solvers to cryptographic problems. In: Kullmann, O. (ed.) SAT 2009. LNCS, vol. 5584, pp. 244–257. Springer, Heidelberg (2009). https://doi.org/10.1007/978-3-642-02777-2_24

41. Sun, L., Wang, W., Wang, M.: More accurate differential properties of LED64 and Midori64. IACR Trans. Symmetric Cryptol. **2018**(3), 93–123 (2018). https://doi.org/10.13154/tosc.v2018.i3.93-123

42. Sun, L., Wang, W., Wang, M.: Accelerating the search of differential and linear characteristics with the SAT Method. IACR Trans. Symmetric Cryptol. **2021**(1), 269–315 (2021). https://doi.org/10.46586/tosc.v2021.i1.269-315

43. Sun, S., Hu, L., Wang, P., Qiao, K., Ma, X., Song, L.: Automatic security evaluation and (related-key) differential characteristic search: application to SIMON, PRESENT, LBlock, DES(L) and other bit-oriented block ciphers, pp. 158–178 (2014). https://doi.org/10.1007/978-3-662-45611-8_9

44. The sage developers: SageMath, the sage mathematics software system (Version 9.5s) (2022). https://www.sagemath.org

45. Wei, C., et al.: Preimage attacks on 4-round Keccak by solving multivariate quadratic systems. In: Park, J.H., Seo, SH. (eds.) Information Security and Cryptology - ICISC 2021. ICISC 2021, LNCS, vol. 13218, pp 195–216. Springer, Cham (2022). https://doi.org/10.1007/978-3-031-08896-4_10

Differential-Linear Cryptanalysis of Round-Reduced SPARX-64/128

Zhichao Xu, Hong Xu$^{(\boxtimes)}$, Lin Tan, and Wenfeng Qi

Information Engineering University, Zhengzhou, China
xuhong0504@163.com

Abstract. SPARX is a family of ARX-based block ciphers introduced at ASIACRYPT 2016, which is designed according to the long-trail strategy (LTS). For SPARX-64/128 with block size 64 and key size 128, the best known attack is a differential cryptanalysis of 16-round SPARX-64/128. In this paper, we further present a differential-linear cryptanalysis of SPARX-64/128. Due to the special structure of the round function, we first present some 6-round differential-linear characteristics of SPARX-64/128, then obtain two 14-round differential-linear characteristics of SPARX-64/128 by adding a 7-round differential characteristic before and a one-round linear approximation after the characteristics. By extending backwards three rounds before the 14 round differential-linear characteristics, we present a differential-linear cryptanalysis of 17-round SPARX-64/128, which covers one more round than previous work.

Keywords: ARX · Block cipher · SPARX · Differential-linear cryptanalysis

1 Introduction

ARX ciphers are cryptographic primitives composed of modular addition, rotation, and XOR. Many symmetric primitives are designed based on the ARX structure due to its efficiency in software and good security properties, including SPARX [11], SPECK [4], Chaskey [20], ChaCha [7] and so on.

SPARX is a family of ARX-based block ciphers that was introduced at ASIACRYPT 2016 [11]. It was designed with the goal of provable security against differential and linear cryptanalysis. As a dual to the wide trail strategy adopted by many block ciphers, the designers proposed the long trail strategy, which allows the designers to bound the maximum differential probability and linear correlation for any number of rounds for a block cipher.

In the design paper of SPARX [11], three iterations of SPECK-like S-box and a linear layer are applied to ensure the fast diffusion and confusion of the block cipher. The family contains three types of block ciphers: SPARX-64/128, SPARX-128/128, and SPARX-128/256. For SPARX-64/128 with block size 64 and key size 128, known cryptanalysis includes integral cryptanalysis [11], differential cryptanalysis [2], impossible differential cryptanalysis [1], *etc.* In this paper, we further consider the differential-linear cryptanalysis of SPARX-64/128.

© The Author(s), under exclusive license to Springer Nature Singapore Pte Ltd. 2024
C. Ge and M. Yung (Eds.): Inscrypt 2023, LNCS 14527, pp. 193–208, 2024.
https://doi.org/10.1007/978-981-97-0945-8_11

Differential-linear cryptanalysis was proposed based on differential crypt-analysis and linear cryptanalysis by Langford and Hellman [14], which has been used to attack many ciphers such as DES, ICEPOLE, and Serpent [9,13,19]. Differential-linear cryptanalysis is also a hot topic in the analysis of block ciphers recently. At EUROCRYPT 2019, Bar-On *et al.* [3] introduced the Differential-Linear Connectivity Table (DLCT), and present differential-linear cryptanalysis of ICEPOLE and DES. At CRYPTO 2021, Liu *et al.* [17] studied differential-linear cryptanalysis from an algebraic perspective and improved the cryptanalysis of Ascon, Serpent, and Grain v1. At EUROCRYPT 2021, Liu *et al.* [18] proposed the rotational differential-linear cryptanalysis and improved the crypt-analysis of FRIET, Xoodoo, and Alzette. At CRYPTO 2022, Niu *et al.* [21] further improved the technique and presented improved (rotational) differential-linear characteristics of Alzette, SipHash, SPECK32, and ChaCha.

For differential-linear cryptanalysis of ARX ciphers, Leurent [15] presented at EUROCRYPT 2016 the differential-linear cryptanalysis of 7-round Chaskey with the improved partitioning technique [8]. Later, Beierle *et al.* [5,6] further presented improved differential-linear cryptanalysis of 7-round and 7.5-round Chaskey. At EUROCRYPT 2022, Dey *et al.* [10] presented improved differential-linear cryptanalysis of 7-round ChaCha256.

1.1 Our Contribution

In this paper, we consider the differential-linear cryptanalysis of SPARX-64/128. We first construct multiple 6-round differential-linear characteristics based on the structure of SPARX-64/128. Then two 14-round differential-linear charac-teristics are further constructed by adding a 7-round differential characteristic before and a one-round linear approximation after the characteristics. Finally, a differential-linear cryptanalysis of 17-round SPARX-64/128 is presented based on the 14-round differential-linear characteristics, which covers one more round than previous work.

A summary of known cryptanalysis for SPARX-64/128 is listed in Table 1.

Table 1. Summary of cryptanalysis for SPARX-64/128.

Rounds	Cryptanalysis type	Data	Time	Source
15	Integral	2^{37}	$2^{101.0}$	[11]
16	Impossible differential	$2^{51.0}$	$2^{94.1}$	[1]
16	Truncated differential	2^{32}	2^{93}	[2]
16	Rectangle	$2^{59.6}$	2^{122}	[2]
16	Yoyo	2^{64}	2^{126}	[2]
17	Differential-linear	2^{63}	$2^{125.6}$	this paper

1.2   Organization

Some notations, a brief review of SPARX-64/128, differential-linear cryptanalysis, and some basic properties of modular addition are presented in Sect. 2. The details for the construction of differential-linear characteristics of 14-round SPARX-64/128 are presented in Sect. 3, and a differential-linear cryptanalysis of 17-round SPARX-64/128 is proposed in Sect. 4. Finally, a short conclusion is presented in Sect. 5.

2   Preliminaries

2.1   Notations

In this paper, we use the following symbols:

$X_{i,j}$: the j-th word of the output state of the i-round SPARX-64/128.

$\Delta_{i,j}$: the j-th word of the output difference of the i-round SPARX-64/128.

$\Gamma_{i,j}$: the j-th word of the output linear mask of the i-round SPARX-64/128.

$k_{i,j}$: the j-th word of the subkey of the i-th round SPARX-64/128.

$X \lll r$: left rotation of X by r bits.

$X \ggg r$: right rotation of X by r bits.

$\oplus$: bitwise XOR operation.

wt(x): Hamming weight of the n-bit vector x, i.e. $\text{wt}(x) = \sum_{i=0}^{n-1} x[i]$.

$x \cdot y$: the inner product of n-bit vectors x and y, i.e. $x \cdot y = \oplus_{i=0}^{n-1} x[i]y[i]$.

$\text{Cor}_{x \in F_2^n}(f(x))$: correlation of a Boolean function $f(x)$, where

$$\text{Cor}_{x \in F_2^n}(f(x)) = 2\text{Pr}_{x \in F_2^n}(f(x) = 0) - 1.$$

For simplicity, the internal states X_i, differences Δ_i, linear masks Γ_i and the subkeys k_i of SPARX-64/128 are expressed in hexadecimal.

2.2   Description of SPARX-64/128

SPARX [11] is a family of ARX-based block ciphers proposed in ASIACRYPT 2016. The ARX-based S-box SPECKEY is applied in SPARX, and only XOR, rotation, and modular addition are used in S-box SPECKEY.

SPARX-64/128 is a member of the SPARX family. SPARX-64/128 operates on 64-bit blocks using 128-bit keys. The step structure of SPARX-64/128 is shown in Fig. 1. Suppose $X_{3i-3} = (X_{3i-3,0}, X_{3i-3,1}, X_{3i-3,2}, X_{3i-3,3})$ be the input of the i-th step of SPARX-64/128, where $X_{3i-3,j}$ is a 16-bit word, $0 \leq j \leq 3$. In each step, the input X_{3i-3} is first divided into two 32-bit words $(X_{3i-3,0}, X_{3i-3,1})$ and $(X_{3i-3,2}, X_{3i-3,3})$, three iterations of key addition and SPECKEY S-box are applied to these two words in parallel, and an extra linear layer is applied to ensure diffusion between the words. Such steps are iterated eight times for SPARX-64/128.

The three iterations of key addition and SPECKEY S-box in the i-th step are the $(3i - 2)$-th round, $(3i - 1)$-th round, and $3i$-th round, respectively. Thus the total round of SPARX-64/128 is 24. The linear layer consists of a Feistel round with a Feistel function L_2. In this paper, the linear layer after the i-th step or the $3i$-th round is taken as the $(3i)'$-th round function.

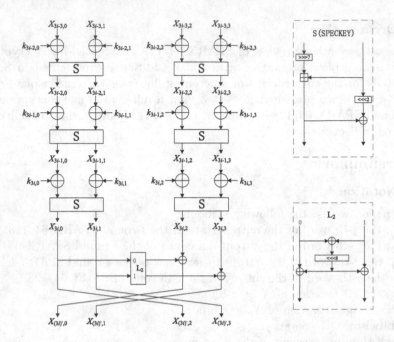

Fig. 1. Step structure of SPARX-64/128

Key Schedule of SPARX-64/128. The permutation used in the key schedule is shown in Fig. 2, where j is initialized to 0. When the permutation is applied every time, j will increase by 1. The 128-bit master key is denoted by $(K_0^0, K_1^0, K_2^0, K_3^0, K_4^0, K_5^0, K_6^0, K_7^0)$. Then, the keys $(K_0^0, K_1^0, K_2^0, K_3^0, K_4^0, K_5^0)$ are extracted and used in the left branch of the first step, $i.e.$

$$(k_{1,0}, k_{1,1}, k_{2,0}, k_{2,1}, k_{3,0}, k_{3,1}) = (K_0^0, K_1^0, K_2^0, K_3^0, K_4^0, K_5^0).$$

Afterwards, the permutation illustrated in Fig. 2 is applied and then the keys $(K_0^1, K_1^1, K_2^1, K_3^1, K_4^1, K_5^1)$ are extracted and used in the right branch of the first step, $i.e.$

$$(k_{1,2}, k_{1,3}, k_{2,2}, k_{2,3}, k_{3,2}, k_{3,3}) = (K_0^1, K_1^1, K_2^1, K_3^1, K_4^1, K_5^1).$$

The application of the permutation and the extraction of the keys are interleaved until all the round keys encompassing the post-whitening ones are generated.

In [1,2], the following proposition was observed by the key schedule of SPARX-64/128.

Proposition 1. [1,2] *Given the* 64-*bit subkey* k_{3r} *of the* 3r-*th round of SPARX-64/128, one can directly derive the right* 32-*bit subkeys of the* $(3r + 1)$-*th and* $(3r + 2)$-*th rounds, i.e. the subkeys* $(k_{3r+1,2}, k_{3r+1,3})$ *and* $(k_{3r+2,2}, k_{3r+2,3})$.

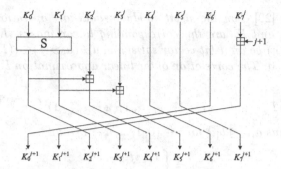

Fig. 2. SPARX-64/128 key schedule permutation

2.3 Differential Characteristic and Linear Approximation of Modular Addition

Assume $x \in F_2^n$, $y = F(x)$, where $F(\cdot)$ is a vectorial Boolean function. If there exist an input difference Δ_x, and an output difference Δ_y, such that $p = \Pr_{x \in F_2^n} (F(x) \oplus F(x \oplus \Delta x) = \Delta y) \neq 0$, then say $\Delta x \xrightarrow{F} \Delta y$ is a differential characteristic of F with differential probability p.

For the n-bit modular addition operation $x + y = z \mod 2^n$, Lipmaa et al. [12,16] presented an algorithm to compute the differential probability of modular addition, which is shown in Proposition 2 and Proposition 3.

Proposition 2. [12,16] *For the n-bit modular addition operation $x + y = z \mod 2^n$, Δ_x, Δ_y and Δ_z are the possible difference if and only if $\Delta_x[0] \oplus \Delta_y[0] \oplus \Delta_z[0] = 0$ and $\Delta_x[i-1] = \Delta_y[i-1] = \Delta_z[i-1] = \Delta_x[i] \oplus \Delta_y[i] \oplus \Delta_z[i]$ for $\Delta_x[i-1] = \Delta_y[i-1] = \Delta_z[i-1]$, $i \in \{1, 2, ..., n-1\}$.*

Proposition 3. [12,16] *For the n-bit modular addition operation $x + y = z \mod 2^n$, if Δ_x, Δ_y and Δ_z are the possible difference, then the differential probability is $2^{-\sum_{i=0}^{n-2} neq(\Delta_x[i], \Delta_y[i], \Delta_z[i])}$, where*

$$neq(\Delta_x[i], \Delta_y[i], \Delta_z[i]) = \begin{cases} 0, & if \ \Delta_x[i] = \Delta_y[i] = \Delta_z[i], \\ 1, & otherwise. \end{cases}$$

Assume $x \in F_2^n$, $y = F(x)$, where $F(\cdot)$ is a vectorial Boolean function. If there exist an input linear mask Γ_x and an output linear mask Γ_y, such that $q = \Pr_{x \in F_2^n} (\Gamma_x \cdot x \oplus \Gamma_y \cdot y = 0) \neq \frac{1}{2}$, then say $\Gamma_x \cdot x \oplus \Gamma_y \cdot y$ or $\Gamma_x \xrightarrow{F} \Gamma_y$ is a linear approximation of F with probability q or correlation $c = 2q - 1$.

For the n-bit XOR operation $x \oplus y = z$, Γ_x, Γ_y and Γ_z are the corresponding linear masks if and only if $\Gamma_x = \Gamma_y = \Gamma_z$.

For the n-bit branching operation $x = y = z$, Γ_x, Γ_y and Γ_z are the corresponding n-bit linear masks if and only if $\Gamma_x \oplus \Gamma_y = \Gamma_z$.

For the n-bit modular addition operation $x + y = z \mod 2^n$, Schulte-Geers [22] proposed a method to calculate the correlation of linear approximations. Proposition 4 gives the formula to calculate the correlation.

Proposition 4. [22] *For the n-bit modular addition operation* $x + y = z$ *mod* 2^n, Γ_x, Γ_y *and* Γ_z *are the corresponding linear masks. Let* $u = (u[n-1], u[n-2], ..., u[0])$ *be an n-bit vector satisfying* $u \oplus (u \gg 1) \oplus ((\Gamma_x \oplus \Gamma_y \oplus \Gamma_z) \gg 1) = 0$, $u[n-1] = 0$. *The correlation of the linear approximation* $\Gamma_x \cdot x \oplus \Gamma_y \cdot y \oplus \Gamma_z \cdot z$ *is given by*

$$\mathrm{Cor}_{x \in F_2^n}(\Gamma_x \cdot x \oplus \Gamma_y \cdot y \oplus \Gamma_z \cdot z) = 1_{\Gamma_z \oplus \Gamma_y \preceq u} 1_{\Gamma_z \oplus \Gamma_x \preceq u}(-1)^{(\Gamma_z \oplus \Gamma_y) \cdot (\Gamma_z \oplus \Gamma_x)} 2^{-\mathrm{wt}(u)},$$

where $a \preceq b$ *means* $a[i] \leq b[i]$ *for* $i \in \{0, 1, ..., n-1\}$ *and*

$$1_{a \preceq b} = \begin{cases} 1, & if \ \ a \preceq b, \\ 0, & otherwise. \end{cases}$$

2.4   Differential-Linear Cryptanalysis

Differential-linear cryptanalysis [14] was introduced by Langford and Hellman. For given input difference Δ_{in} and output mask Γ_{out} of cipher E, the correlation of the differential-linear characteristic $\Delta_{in} \xrightarrow{E} \Gamma_{out}$ is defined as

$$c = \mathrm{Cor}_{x \in F_2^n}(\Gamma_{out} \cdot E(x) \oplus \Gamma_{out} \cdot E(x \oplus \Delta_{in})).$$

By preparing ϵc^{-2} input pairs $(x, x \oplus \Delta_{in})$, the cipher E can be distinguished from a pseudorandom permutation.

Differential-linear characteristics can be constructed by differential characteristics and linear approximations. Assume that cipher E can be divided into two sub-ciphers E_1 and E_2, such that $E = E_2 \circ E_1$, and there exists a differential characteristic $\Delta_{in} \xrightarrow{E_1} \Delta_m$ for sub-cipher E_1 and a linear approximation $\Gamma_m \xrightarrow{E_2} \Gamma_{out}$ for sub-cipher E_2. The differential probability and linear correlation are p and q respectively, *i.e.*

$$\mathrm{Pr}_{x \in F_2^n}(E_1(x) \oplus E_1(x \oplus \Delta_{in}) = \Delta_m) = p,$$

$$\mathrm{Cor}_{x \in F_2^n}(\Gamma_m \cdot x \oplus \Gamma_{out} \cdot E_2(x)) = q.$$

Assume that $E_1(x)$ and $E_2(x)$ are independent, then there exists a differential-linear characteristic $\Delta_{in} \xrightarrow{E} \Gamma_{out}$ with correlation pq^2, *i.e.*

$$\mathrm{Cor}_{x \in F_2^n}(\langle \Gamma_{out}, E(x) \rangle \oplus \langle \Gamma_{out}, E(x \oplus \Delta_{in}) \rangle) = pq^2.$$

In practice, $E_1(x)$ and $E_2(x)$ may not be independent, which may lead to wrong estimates of the correlation. In order to provide a better estimates, Bar-On *et al.* [3] presented the Differential-Linear Connectivity Table (DLCT). Based on the DLCT, cipher E is divided into three sub-ciphers E_1, E_m and E_2, such that $E = E_2 \circ E_m \circ E_1$. If there exists a differential characteristic, a differential-linear characteristic and a linear approximation for E_1, E_m and E_2 with probability p, correlation r and correlation q, respectively, *i.e.*

$$\mathrm{Pr}_{x \in F_2^n}(E_1(x) \oplus E_1(x \oplus \Delta_{in}) = \Delta_m) = p,$$

$$\mathrm{Cor}_{x \in F_2^n}(\Gamma_m \cdot E_m(x) \oplus \Gamma_m \cdot E_m(x \oplus \Delta_m)) = r,$$

$$\mathrm{Cor}_{x \in F_2^n}(\Gamma_m \cdot x \oplus \Gamma_{out} \cdot E_2(x)) = q.$$

then there exists a differential-linear characteristic for E with correlation prq^2, i.e.

$$\mathrm{Cor}_{x \in F_2^n} \left(\Gamma_{out} \cdot E(x) \oplus \Gamma_{out} \cdot E(x \oplus \Delta_{in}) \right) = prq^2.$$

Complexity Analysis. In order to measure the effectiveness of differential and linear attack, Selçuk introduced the notion of advantage [23]. If the right key ranks among the best 2^{k-a} key candidates when k-bit key is guessed, then the attack achieves an advantage of a bits. Given a desired advantage a, the probability of success P_S is the probability that the actual advantage surpasses a.

Let N, c, and a denote the number of known plaintext pairs, the correlation of differential-linear characteristic, and the number of advantage bits, respectively. The success probability P_S is estimated as follows,

$$P_S = \Phi \left(\sqrt{N} |c| - \Phi^{-1}(1 - 2^{-a-1}) \right),$$

where Φ and Φ^{-1} are the normal distribution and its inverse, respectively.

3   Differential-Linear Characteristic of 14-Round SPARX-64/128

In this section, we will present two 14-round differential-linear characteristics from the third round to the 20th round. Denote by $E = E_3 \circ E_2 \circ E_1$ the corresponding cipher, where E_1 denote the 7-round SPARX-64/128 from the sixth round to the 12th round, E_2 denote the 6-round SPARX-64/128 from the 13th round to the 18th round without the last linear mixing layer, and E_3 denote the one-round SPARX-64/128 from the 18'-th round to the 19th round.

In the following, we first transform a 6-round truncated differential of E_2 into a 6-round differential-linear characteristic. Then extend the characteristic to construct a 14-round differential-linear characteristic of SPARX-64/128 by adding a 7-round differential of E_1 before and a one-round linear approximation of E_3 after the characteristic. The detailed construction for the characteristics is presented as follows.

3.1   6-Round Differential-Linear Characteristic of E_2

The Feistel-like structure of SPARX-64/128 allows some generic differential characteristics that pass through almost two steps such that only one branch is active. For example, there exists a 6-round truncated differential

$$(0000, 0000, ****, ****) \xrightarrow{E_2} (****, ****, 0000, 0000)$$

for E_2 with probability 1. The truncated differential is shown in Fig. 3, where Δ_i is the output difference of the i-th round SPARX-64/128.

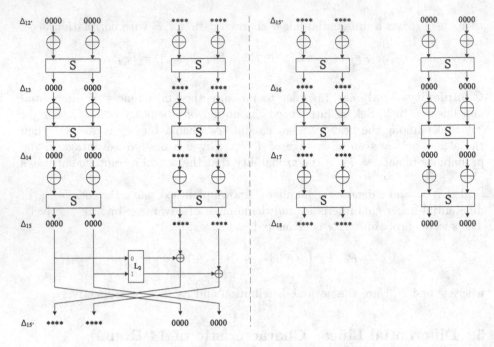

Fig. 3. 6-round truncated differential of E_2

Suppose $\Delta_{12'} = (0000, 0000, a_7a_6a_5a_4, a_3a_2a_1a_0)$ be the input difference of E_2, where $(a_7a_6a_5a_4, a_3a_2a_1a_0)$ can be any nonzero vector of F_2^{32}. From Fig. 3 we know that the output differences Δ_{18} of E_2 always satisfy $\Delta_{18,2} = \Delta_{18,3} = 0000$. Let $\Gamma_{18} = (0000, 0000, b_7b_6b_5b_4, b_3b_2b_1b_0)$ denote the output mask of E_2, where $(b_7b_6b_5b_4, b_3b_2b_1b_0)$ can be any nonzero vector of F_2^{32}. Then $\Gamma_{18} \cdot \Delta_{18}$ always equal to 0. A differential-linear characteristic $\Delta_{12'} \xrightarrow{E_2} \Gamma_{18}$ exists, and the correlation can be calculated as follows.

$$\text{Cor}_{X_{12'} \in F_2^{64}} \left(\Gamma_{18} \cdot E_2(X_{12'}) \oplus \Gamma_{18} \cdot E_2(X_{12'} \oplus \Delta_{12'}) \right)$$
$$= 2\text{Pr}_{X_{12'} \in F_2^{64}} \left(\Gamma_{18} \cdot E_2(X_{12'}) \oplus \Gamma_{18} \cdot E_2(X_{12'} \oplus \Delta_{12'}) = 0 \right) - 1$$
$$= 2\text{Pr}_{X_{12'} \in F_2^{64}} \left(\Gamma_{18} \cdot \Delta_{18} = 0 \right) - 1$$
$$= 1.$$

Thus there exist many 6-round differential-linear characteristics of the form

$$\Delta_{12'} \xrightarrow{E_2} \Gamma_{18}$$

with correlation 1, where

$$\Delta_{12'} = (0000, 0000, a_7a_6a_5a_4, a_3a_2a_1a_0),$$
$$\Gamma_{18} = (0000, 0000, b_7b_6b_5b_4, b_3b_2b_1b_0).$$

We can extend the characteristics by adding some differential characteristics before and some linear approximations after the characteristics.

The linear mask Γ_{18} is fixed as $(0000, 0000, 0000, 8000)$ because it's easier to extend the differential-linear characteristics with this linear mask. There are multiple different input differences. Thus the differential-linear characteristics are denoted by

$$\Delta_{12'} \xrightarrow{E_2} \Gamma_{18},$$

where

$$\Delta_{12'} = (0000, 0000, ****, ****),$$
$$\Gamma_{18} = (0000, 0000, 0000, 8000).$$

3.2 7-Round Truncated Differential Characteristic of E_1

In [2], Ankele et al. presented a 7-round truncated differential $\Delta_5 \xrightarrow{E_1} \Delta_{12'}$, where

$$\Delta_5 = (0000, 0000, 0a20, 4205),$$
$$\Gamma_{12'} = (0000, 0000, ****, ****).$$

with probability $2^{-28.36}$ from the sixth round to the 12'-th round, which is shown in Table 2, where p_i is the probability of the corresponding round.

Table 2. 7-round truncated differential of E_1

Round i	$\Delta_{i,0}$	$\Delta_{i,1}$	$\Delta_{i,2}$	$\Delta_{i,3}$	$-\log_2 p_i$
5	0000	0000	0a20	4205	
6	0000	0000	0211	0a04	5
6'	0211	0a04	0000	0000	0
7	2800	0010	0000	0000	4
8	0040	0000	0000	0000	2
9	8000	8000	0000	0000	0
9'	8000	8000	8000	8000	0
10	****	****	****	****	17.36
11	****	****	****	****	
12	****	****	****	****	
12'	0000	0000	****	****	

The probability of the first 4-round differential is 2^{-11}, and the output difference of the 9th round is $(8000, 8000, 8000, 8000)$. The last 3-round truncated differential is obtained by experiments with probability $2^{-17.36}$, and the output differences are $(0000, 0000, ****, ****)$, which means the right branch of output differential traverses all values. This 7-round truncated differential is applied to E_1 from the sixth round to the 12th round.

We use the automatic tool SAT [24] to search for the differential characteristic of the first 4-round for E_1, and find another differential characteristic with the same output difference $(8000, 8000, 8000, 8000)$ and the same differential probability 2^{-11}, while the input difference is $(0000, 0000, 0a60, 4205)$. Therefore, we can use two different input differences $(0000, 0000, 0a20, 4205)$ and $(0000, 0000, 0a60, 4205)$ of the 7-round truncated differential, which will result in a decrease in data complexity.

3.3   One-Round Linear Approximation of E_3

The output linear mask of E_2 is $\Gamma_{18} = (0000, 0000, 0000, 8000)$, and then a one-round linear approximation is applied to E_3 from the 18'-th round to the 19th round with correlation 1. The detailed linear masks are shown in Table 3, where c_i is the correlation of the corresponding round, and the propagation of the linear mask is presented in Fig. 4.

Table 3. One-round linear approximation of E_3

Round i	$\Gamma_{i,0}$	$\Gamma_{i,1}$	$\Gamma_{i,2}$	$\Gamma_{i,3}$	$\log_2|c_i|$
18	0000	0000	0000	8000	
18'	0000	8000	0080	8080	0
19	0002	0002	0207	0206	0

We also use the automatic tool SAT [24] to search for longer linear approximation after E_2. However, the maximal correlation for two-round linear approximation after E_2 is 2^{-4}, which will result in a significant increase in complexity. Therefore, it is not suitable to adopt the two-round linear approximation.

3.4   Differential-Linear Characteristic of 14-Round SPARX-64/128

By splicing the 7-round differential characteristics of E_1, 6-round differential-linear characteristics of E_2, and one-round linear approximation of E_3, we can obtain two 14-round differential-linear characteristics $\Delta_5 \xrightarrow{E_3 \circ E_2 \circ E_1} \Gamma_{19}$ from the 6th round to the 19th round, where

$$\Delta_5 \in \{(0000, 0000, 0a20, 4205), (0000, 0000, 0a60, 4205)\},$$

and $\Gamma_{19} = (0002, 0002, 0207, 0206)$. The correlation is $prq_0^2 = (2^{-11} \cdot 2^{-17.36}) \cdot 1 \cdot 1^2 = 2^{-28.36}$, where $p = 2^{-11} \cdot 2^{-17.36}$ is the probability of the 7-round truncated differential for E_1, $r = 1$ is the correlation of the 6-round truncated differential-linear characteristic for E_2, and $q_0 = 1$ is the correlation of the one-round linear approximation for E_3.

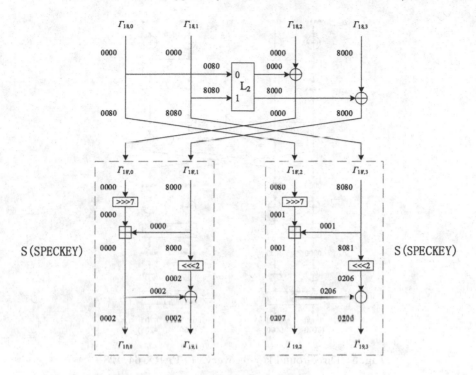

Fig. 4. One-round linear approximation of E_3

4   Differential-Linear Cryptanalysis of SPARX-64/128

In this section, we will present the 17-round cryptanalysis of SPARX-64/128 from the third round to the 19th round based on the 14-round difference-linear characteristic from the sixth round to the 19th round.

The subkeys of the third round are guessed to produce data pairs (X_5, X_5') satisfying the output differences after the fifth round, that is, $X_5 \oplus X_5' = \Delta_5$. The three-round key-recovery is shown in Fig. 5 from the third round to the fifth round.

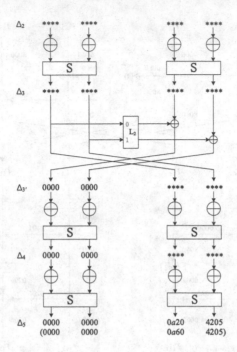

Fig. 5. Three-round key-recovery of SPARX-64/128

Let C and C' denote a pair of ciphertexts. $C = X_{19} \oplus k_{20}$, $C' = X'_{19} \oplus k_{20}$, where k_{20} is the post-whitening key.

4.1   Selection of Input Pairs

Inspired by Leurent *et al.*'s work [2,15], we also use the linear function to construct input pairs with certain differences.

Proposition 5. [2,15] *Assume $\Delta \in F_2^n$ is a fixed difference, and $x^0, x^1, ..., x^{m-1}$ represent m values for which the goal is to find pairs (x^i, x^j) that result in $x^i \oplus x^j = \Delta$. Then, one can define a linear function $L : F_2^n \to F_2^n$ with rank $n-1$, s.t. $L(\Delta) = 0$; thus, all pairs (x^i, x^j) with $x^i \oplus x^j = \Delta$ will collide in $L(x^i) = L(x^j)$.*

For each output difference Δ_5 of the fifth round, define a linear function $L : \{0,1\}^{64} \to \{0,1\}^{64}$ with rank 63, such that $L(\Delta_5) = 0^{64}$. From Proposition 5 we know that $X_5 \oplus X'_5 = \Delta_5$ if and only if $L(X_5) = L(X'_5)$. Therefore the selection of difference pairs can be converted into the collision of data, and the process of selecting input pairs can be accelerated.

There are two differential-linear characteristics with different input differences, that is, $(0000, 0000, 0a20, 4205)$ and $(0000, 0000, 0a60, 4205)$. Thus two such linear functions are required.

4.2   Key-Recovery

In this Subsection, we will present the 17-round cryptanalysis of SPARX-64/128. L_0 and L_1 are two linear functions as described in Subsect. 4.1 with rank 63, *i.e.* $L_0(\Delta_0) = L_1(\Delta_1) = 0$, where $\Delta_0 = (0000, 0000, 0a20, 4205)$ and $\Delta_1 = (0000, 0000, 0a60, 4205)$. Assuming that N data are used, the details of the cryptanalysis are as follows.

1. Select N plaintexts $(X_{2,0}, X_{2,1}, X_{2,2}, X_{2,3})$ for the input of the third round and request the corresponding N ciphertexts.
2. Guess the subkey k_3 for the third round, and the subkey $(k_{4,2}, k_{4,3})$ and $(k_{5,2}, k_{5,3})$ can be obtained by Proposition 1.
   2.1 Encrypt all plaintexts $(X_{2,0}, X_{2,1}, X_{2,2}, X_{2,3})$ over one round, and get the value $X_{3'} = (X_{3',0}, X_{3',1}, X_{3',2}, X_{3',3})$. $(X_{4,2}, X_{4,3})$ and $(X_{5,2}, X_{5,3})$ can be further obtained by encrypting the right branch of $X_{3'}$ with subkey $(k_{4,2}, k_{4,3})$ and $(k_{5,2}, k_{5,3})$.
   2.2 For all $(X_{3',0}, X_{3',1}, X_{5,2}, X_{5,3})$, evaluate the value of L_0 and L_1, store the value in Table T_0^0 and T_1^0 respectively.
   2.3 Consider the values that collide in T_0^0 or T_1^0. Each collision will produce a difference pair. There are about $N^* = \frac{N \cdot (N-1)}{2} \cdot \frac{1}{2^{64}} \cdot 2$ pairs satisfying the output differences of the fifth round. For each pair, request the corresponding ciphertexts pairs $C = (C_0, C_1, C_2, C_3)$ and $C' = (C_0', C_1', C_2', C_3')$.
3. Calculate $t = \Gamma_{19} \cdot (C \oplus C')$. Denote N_c the number that t takes 0.
4. Compute $\eta = |2N_c/N^* - 1|$. Sort η by value in descending order. For the first 2^{64-a} value of η, output the corresponding values of the guessed subkey bits of k_3 as the candidate right subkeys.
5. Check the remaining $2^{64-a} \cdot 2^{64}$ keys to obtain the unique right master key.

Success Probability. When $N = 2^{63}$ chosen plaintexts are used, the number of valid ciphertext pairs for each subkey k_3 is $N^* = \frac{N \cdot (N-1)}{2} \cdot \frac{1}{2^{64}} \cdot 2 \approx 2^{62}$. Let $a = 23$ be the number of advantage bits, then from Subsect. 2.4 we know that the success probability is

$$P_S = \Phi\left(\sqrt{N^*}|c| - \Phi^{-1}(1 - 2^{-a-1})\right) \approx 82.6\%,$$

and the expected number of wrong keys of k_3 is $2^{64} \cdot 2^{-a} = 2^{41}$. Then there are $2^{41} \cdot 2^{64} = 2^{105}$ candidate master keys, which can be checked using plaintext-ciphertext pairs with complexity 2^{105}.

Complexity Analysis.

- The time complexity of step 2.1 is $2^{64} \cdot N \cdot 2 = 2^{65} \cdot N$ one-round encryptions, *i.e.* $2^{65} \cdot N/17 \approx 2^{123.91}$ 17-round encryptions.
- The cost of a call to L_0 or L_1 is approximated by the one-round encryption. The time complexity of step 2.2 is about $2^{64} \cdot N \cdot 2 \cdot 1/17 \approx 2^{123.91}$ 17-round encryptions.

- The cost of the collision for T_0^0 or T_1^0 is approximated by N one-round encryption. The time complexity of step 2.3 is $2^{64} \cdot N \cdot 2 \cdot 1/17 \approx 2^{123.91}$ 17-round encryptions.
- The calculation of $\Gamma_{19} \cdot (C \oplus C')$ is approximated by the one-round encryption. The time complexity of step 3 is $2^{64} \cdot N^* \cdot 1/17 \approx 2^{121.91}$ 17-round encryptions.
- Checking the remaining candidate master keys needs 2^{105} 17-round encryptions.

The total time complexity of the key-recovery process is

$$2^{123.91} + 2^{123.91} + 2^{123.91} + 2^{121.91} + 2^{105} \approx 2^{125.6}.$$

The memory complexity is $2^{63} + 2^{63} + 2^{63} \cdot 2 + 2^{41} \approx 2^{65}$, which is used to store plaintexts, ciphertexts, tables T_0^0, T_1^0 and the candidate subkeys k_3 of step 4.

5   Conclusions

Differential-linear cryptanalysis is an important cryptanalysis method for block ciphers. In this paper, we consider the differential-linear cryptanalysis of an ARX cipher SPARX-64/128. Using the special property of the round function, we construct two 14-round differential-linear characteristics of SPARX-64/128, and present a 17-round differential-linear cryptanalysis of SPARX-64/128, which covers one more round than previous work.

Acknowledgements. We thank the anonymous reviewers for their careful reading and helpful comments.

References

1. Abdelkhalek, A., Tolba, M., Youssef, A.M.: Impossible differential attack on reduced round SPARX-64/128. In: Joye, M., Nitaj, A. (eds.) AFRICACRYPT 2017. LNCS, vol. 10239, pp. 135–146. Springer, Cham (2017). https://doi.org/10.1007/978-3-319-57339-7_8
2. Ankele, R., List, E.: Differential cryptanalysis of round-reduced Sparx-64/128. In: Preneel, B., Vercauteren, F. (eds.) ACNS 2018. LNCS, vol. 10892, pp. 459–475. Springer, Cham (2018). https://doi.org/10.1007/978-3-319-93387-0_24
3. Bar-On, A., Dunkelman, O., Keller, N., Weizman, A.: DLCT: a new tool for differential-linear cryptanalysis. In: Ishai, Y., Rijmen, V. (eds.) EUROCRYPT 2019. LNCS, vol. 11476, pp. 313–342. Springer, Cham (2019). https://doi.org/10.1007/978-3-030-17653-2_11
4. Beaulieu, R., Shors, D., Smith, J., Treatman-Clark, S., Weeks, B., Wingers, L.: The SIMON and SPECK lightweight block ciphers. In: Proceedings of the 52nd Annual Design Automation Conference, San Francisco, CA, USA, June 7–11, 2015. pp. 175:1–175:6. ACM (2015). https://doi.org/10.1145/2744769.2747946
5. Beierle, C.: Improved differential-linear attacks with applications to ARX ciphers. J. Cryptol. **35**(4), 29 (2022). https://doi.org/10.1007/s00145-022-09437-z

6. Beierle, C., Leander, G., Todo, Y.: Improved differential-linear attacks with applications to ARX ciphers. In: Micciancio, D., Ristenpart, T. (eds.) CRYPTO 2020. LNCS, vol. 12172, pp. 329–358. Springer, Cham (2020). https://doi.org/10.1007/978-3-030-56877-1_12

7. Bernstein, D.J.: Chacha, a variant of salsa20 (2008). https://cr.yp.to/chacha.html

8. Biham, E., Carmeli, Y.: An improvement of linear cryptanalysis with addition operations with applications to FEAL-8X. In: Joux, A., Youssef, A. (eds.) SAC 2014. LNCS, vol. 8781, pp. 59–76. Springer, Cham (2014). https://doi.org/10.1007/978-3-319-13051-4_4

9. Biham, E., Dunkelman, O., Keller, N.: Enhancing differential-linear cryptanalysis. In: Zheng, Y. (ed.) ASIACRYPT 2002. LNCS, vol. 2501, pp. 254–266. Springer, Heidelberg (2002). https://doi.org/10.1007/3-540-36178-2_16

10. Dey, S., Garai, H.K., Sarkar, S., Sharma, N.K.: Revamped differential-linear cryptanalysis on reduced round ChaCha. In: Dunkelman, O., Dziembowski, S. (eds.) Advances in Cryptology - EUROCRYPT 2022–41st Annual International Conference on the Theory and Applications of Cryptographic Techniques, Trondheim, Norway, May 30 - June 3, 2022, Proceedings, Part III. LNCS, vol. 13277, pp. 86–114. Springer, Cham (2022). https://doi.org/10.1007/978-3-031-07082-2_4

11. Dinu, D., Perrin, L., Udovenko, A., Velichkov, V., Großschädl, J., Biryukov, A.: Design strategies for ARX with provable bounds: SPARX and LAX. In: Cheon, J.H., Takagi, T. (eds.) ASIACRYPT 2016. LNCS, vol. 10031, pp. 484–513. Springer, Heidelberg (2016). https://doi.org/10.1007/978-3-662-53887-6_18

12. Fu, K., Wang, M., Guo, Y., Sun, S., Hu, L.: MILP-based automatic search algorithms for differential and linear trails for speck. In: Peyrin, T. (ed.) FSE 2016. LNCS, vol. 9783, pp. 268–288. Springer, Heidelberg (2016). https://doi.org/10.1007/978-3-662-52993-5_14

13. Huang, T., Tjuawinata, I., Wu, H.: Differential-linear cryptanalysis of ICEPOLE. In: Leander, G. (ed.) FSE 2015. LNCS, vol. 9054, pp. 243–263. Springer, Heidelberg (2015). https://doi.org/10.1007/978-3-662-48116-5_12

14. Langford, S.K., Hellman, M.E.: Differential-linear cryptanalysis. In: Desmedt, Y.G. (ed.) CRYPTO 1994. LNCS, vol. 839, pp. 17–25. Springer, Heidelberg (1994). https://doi.org/10.1007/3-540-48658-5_3

15. Leurent, G.: Improved differential-linear cryptanalysis of 7-round Chaskey with partitioning. In: Fischlin, M., Coron, J.-S. (eds.) EUROCRYPT 2016. LNCS, vol. 9665, pp. 344–371. Springer, Heidelberg (2016). https://doi.org/10.1007/978-3-662-49890-3_14

16. Lipmaa, H., Moriai, S.: Efficient algorithms for computing differential properties of addition. In: Matsui, M. (ed.) FSE 2001. LNCS, vol. 2355, pp. 336–350. Springer, Heidelberg (2002). https://doi.org/10.1007/3-540-45473-X_28

17. Liu, M., Lu, X., Lin, D.: Differential-linear cryptanalysis from an Algebraic perspective. In: Malkin, T., Peikert, C. (eds.) CRYPTO 2021. LNCS, vol. 12827, pp. 247–277. Springer, Cham (2021). https://doi.org/10.1007/978-3-030-84252-9_9

18. Liu, Y., Sun, S., Li, C.: Rotational cryptanalysis from a differential-linear perspective. In: Canteaut, A., Standaert, F.-X. (eds.) EUROCRYPT 2021, Part 1. LNCS, vol. 12696, pp. 741–770. Springer, Cham (2021). https://doi.org/10.1007/978-3-030-77870-5_26

19. Lu, J.: A methodology for differential-linear cryptanalysis and its applications. In: Canteaut, A. (ed.) FSE 2012. LNCS, vol. 7549, pp. 69–89. Springer, Heidelberg (2012). https://doi.org/10.1007/978-3-642-34047-5_5

20. Mouha, N., Mennink, B., Van Herrewege, A., Watanabe, D., Preneel, B., Verbauwhede, I.: Chaskey: an efficient MAC algorithm for 32-bit microcontrollers. In: Joux, A., Youssef, A. (eds.) SAC 2014. LNCS, vol. 8781, pp. 306–323. Springer, Cham (2014). https://doi.org/10.1007/978-3-319-13051-4_19
21. Niu, Z., Sun, S., Liu, Y., Li, C.: Rotational differential-linear distinguishers of ARX ciphers with arbitrary output linear masks. In: Dodis, Y., Shrimpton, T. (eds.) Advances in Cryptology - CRYPTO 2022. CRYPTO 2022, LNCS, vol. 13507, pp 3–32. Springer, Cham (2022). https://doi.org/10.1007/978-3-031-15802-5_1
22. Schulte-Geers, E.: On CCZ-equivalence of addition mod 2^n. Des. Codes Cryptogr. **66**(1–3), 111–127 (2013). https://doi.org/10.1007/s10623-012-9668-4
23. Selçuk, A.A.: On probability of success in linear and differential cryptanalysis. J. Cryptol. **21**(1), 131–147 (2008). https://doi.org/10.1007/s00145-007-9013-7
24. Sun, L., Wang, W., Wang, M.: Accelerating the search of differential and linear characteristics with the SAT method. IACR Trans. Symmetric Cryptol. **2021**(1), 269–315 (2021). https://doi.org/10.46586/tosc.v2021.i1.269-315

Improved Herrmann-May's Attack with Merging Variables and Lower LLL Bound

Qingfeng Cheng[iD], Chunzhi Zhao[✉], Jinzheng Cao[iD], and Fushan Wei[iD]

Information Engineering University, Zhengzhou 450001, China
zhaochunzhi2022@126.com

Abstract. Using side information to attack RSA is a practical method. In reality, it's possible to intercept some bits of an unknown divisor p of a known composite integer N for us. Then we can utilize Coppersmith's method to recover the whole p in polynomial time according to the work of Herrmann and May (Asiacrypt'08). In this paper, we analyze the idea of merging unknown bit blocks proposed by Herrmann and May in detail and indicate the cases where the blocks can be merged with a considerable reduction in the complexity of Herrmann-May's attack. In fact, the complexity of this attack depends on the output quality of the LLL algorithm. For this, we purposely propose a lower upper bound of the length of LLL-reduced vectors using probabilistic statistical methods. To be specific, considering the $\|v_i^*\|/\|v_{i+1}^*\|$'s as continuous random variables, we find that the middle $\|v_i^*\|/\|v_{i+1}^*\|$'s after LLL-reduction are almost independently and identically distributed. Then we utilize the central limit theorem to present a lower LLL bound holding with probability close to 1. We have shown the advantages of merging variables and applying new bound by experiments. Finally, we combine these two points to propose the improved Herrmann-May's attack.

Keywords: RSA · Lattice · LLL algorithm · Coppersmith's method

1 Introduction

In 1978, Rivest, Shamir, and Aldeman [17] at MIT proposed the famous public-key cryptographic algorithm RSA, whose security relies on the difficulty of decomposing integers $N = pq$, where p and q are two large prime numbers. In general, to crack RSA system, we have to decompose N directly, and it's almost impossible to achieve with traditional computers for large N. However, if we are informed about the RSA system in part, we may be able to crack it effectively. For instance, if we know the partial bits of p, we can equate the decomposition of N to solving an equation $a_1 x_1 + a_2 x_2 + \cdots + a_n x_n = p$ where x_i denotes the value of unknown block and a_i denotes the known coefficient for $i = 1, ..., n$. Furthermore, with both sides of the equation modulo p at the same time, we can obtain the modular equation $a_1 x_1 + a_2 x_2 + \cdots + a_n x_n \equiv 0 \bmod p$. Then we only need to solve this modular equation to recover p. One efficient way for solving modular equations is Coppersmith's method.

© The Author(s), under exclusive license to Springer Nature Singapore Pte Ltd. 2024
C. Ge and M. Yung (Eds.): Inscrypt 2023, LNCS 14527, pp. 209–229, 2024.
https://doi.org/10.1007/978-981-97-0945-8_12

In 1996, Coppersmith [2] proposed an efficient algorithm for solving the small roots of the single-variable modular equation for the case of partial plaintext leakage of RSA with the small public exponent and gave the following conclusion. For polynomial $f(x) = 1 + a_1x + \cdots + a_\omega x^\omega \in Z[x]$ and constant $X \leq N^{\frac{1}{\omega}}$, we can find all integer solutions x_0 ($|x_0| \leq X$) of $f \equiv 0 \bmod N$ in polynomial time. In 2008, Herrmann and May [7] studied how to recover p with several consecutive pieces of p unknown. They introduced a heuristic algorithm to solve the modular linear equations. They showed that it's enough to factor N with $\ln(2) \approx 70\%$ of the bits of p known. However, their algorithm is in polynomial time only for $n = \mathcal{O}(\log\log N)$ blocks. In 2015, Lu et al. [12] extended Herrmann-May's attack for solving multivariate linear modular equations to $N = p^r q$, $r \geq 1$ and proposed some new techniques to find the small root of these equations. For instance, when $\beta = 0.5, f(x_1, x_2) = a_1x_1 + a_2x_2 \bmod p^v$ ($v \leq r, p \geq N^\beta$), their method improves the upper bound of x_1x_2 from $N^{0.207}$ to $N^{0.25}$. Eventually, they experimentally presented the advantage of their algorithm. In fact, the efficiency of Coppersmith's method mainly depends on the quality of the short vector we can find in a lattice. In 1982, Lenstra et al. [10] proposed the LLL algorithm to find short vectors in lattice. In fact, this algorithm is an extension of Gaussian algorithm in high dimension, which is an integer Gram-Schmidt orthogonalization process with additional conditions. The LLL algorithm has since been improved in many ways. In 1994, the deep-LLL algorithm was proposed in [18]. In deep-LLL, it's supposed that $\|v_j^* + \mu_{j,j-1}v_{j-1}^* + \ldots + \mu_{j,i}v_i^*\|^2 \geq \delta\|v_i^*\|^2$ for all pairs (i, j) with $j > i$ instead of applying the original Lovász condition. This new constraint is stronger than Lovász condition so that the deep-LLL algorithm could get better vectors. In 2005, Nguyen and Stehlé [14] proposed the L^2 algorithm, which is a floating-point variant of LLL. The L^2 algorithm can output LLL-reduced basis in polynomial time up to $\mathcal{O}(d^5(d + \log B)\log B)$. Then Nguyen and Stehlé improved the floating-point LLL algorithm and controlled the floating-point errors in [16]. So far, the L^2 algorithm is the most widely used variant of the LLL algorithm for large entries. Actually, the well-known open-source project fplll [19] has implemented the L^2 algorithm. On the other hand, the precise description of the output quality of the LLL algorithm has always remained mysterious. Although the authors give an upper bound of the length of LLL-reduced vectors in [10], the actual vectors' length is much smaller than the theoretical bound in practice as shown in [4,15]. Interestingly, these two papers both show that it almost always holds that the first vector of a d-dimensional random LLL-reduced basis has length $\approx 1.02^d \det(\mathcal{L})^{1/d}$. This phenomenon is surprising for the work of Kim and Venkatesh [9] which indicates that for almost every lattice, nearly all of its LLL-reduced bases have root Hermite factor (RHF) nearly reaching the worst bound.

Our Contribution. We revisit the problem of solving linear modular polynomials for recovering $p \geq N^\beta$ where the known integer $N = pq$, and p, q are both large unknown prime. Herrmann and May achieved a breakthrough in this problem in Asiacrypt'08, they presented a method to solve the problem with an arbitrary number of n variables. In this paper, we delve into the idea of merging variables and give the cases where the merging can be done with a considerable reduction in the complexity of Herrmann-May's attack. Specifically, we show that the complexity of Herrmann-May's attack is reduced from $\mathcal{O}((\frac{e}{\epsilon})^{7n}(1+\log N)\log N)$ to $\mathcal{O}((\frac{e}{\epsilon})^{7(n-m+1)}(1+\log N)\log N)$ as m adjacent variables in n variables are merged where e is the Euler's number. Moreover, we propose a heuristic algorithm to merge variables more efficiently. In addition, we propose a lower upper bound of the length of LLL-reduced vectors. To be specific, considering the r_i's := $\|v_i^*\|/\|v_{i+1}^*\|$'s (ratios of two adjacent Gram-Schmidt orthogonal vectors of LLL-reduced basis) as random variables, we have tested four types of Coppersmith lattices and find that the r_i's after LLL-reduction are all almost independently and identically distributed except for the first and last individual variables which are both stochastically dominated by the middle ones. Therefore we make an assumption, then we use the central limit theorem to present a lower upper bound of the length of LLL-reduced vectors which holds with probability close to 1. In fact, our method to improve the LLL bound can be generalized to other types of lattices and one only needs to know the mean and variance of the r_i's. We have verified the validity of merging variables and applying new bound by experiments in the end and combining those two improvements, we propose the improved Herrmann-May's attack.

The paper is managed as follows. In Sect. 2, we introduce some basic theorics. In Sect. 3, we give the analysis of merging variables and our new LLL bound, then we propose the improved Herrmann-May's attack by combining these two points. In Sect. 4, we show the experimental results supporting Assumption 2 in Subsect. 3.2 and verify the validity of merging variables and the new LLL bound by experiments. We summarize this paper in Sect. 5.

2   Preliminaries

Let $v_1, v_2, ..., v_d \in R^{d \times d}$ be d linearly independent vectors, we call $\mathcal{L}$ the lattice spanned by $\{v_1, v_2, ..., v_d\}$ if $\mathcal{L} = \sum_{i=1}^{d} z_i \cdot v_i$, where $z_i \in Z$ for $i = 1, ..., d$. How to efficiently find short vectors in a lattice is what scholars have been investigating. The lattice basis reduction algorithm is one of the most popular algorithms for finding short vectors in a lattice. As one of the most widely used lattice basis reduction algorithms, the LLL algorithm can find approximate shortest vectors in polynomial time which is a significant tool for cryptanalysis. Before describing the LLL algorithm, we will describe the Gram-Schmidt orthogonalization which is one of the most important parts of the LLL algorithm.

Definition 1 (Gram-Schmidt Orthogonalization (GSO) [3]). *Let* $B = (v_1, ..., v_d) \in R^{d \times d}$ *be a lattice basis. The Gram-Schmidt orthogonal basis of* B *is* $B^* = (v_1^*, ..., v_d^*)$, *where* $v_i^* = \pi_i(v_i)$ *for* $i = 1, ..., d$. *The function* π_i *is defined as*

$$v_1^* = v_1, \ v_i^* = v_i - \sum_{j=1}^{i-1} \mu_{i,j} \cdot v_j^*,$$

for $i = 2, ..., d$, *where* $\mu_{i,j} = <v_i, v_j^*>/\|v_j^*\|^2$.

Definition 2 (LLL-Reduced Basis [3]**).** *Let* $\{v_1, ..., v_d\}$ *be a d-dimensional lattice basis, and* $\{v_1^*, ..., v_d^*\}$ *be the Gram-Schmidt orthogonal basis. We call* $\{v_1, ..., v_d\}$ *a LLL-reduced basis if it satisfies two conditions*

1. $\|\mu_{i,j}\| \leq \frac{1}{2}$, *for* $1 \leq j < i \leq d$,
2. $\|v_{i+1}^* + \mu_{i+1,i}v_i^*\|^2 \geq \delta\|v_i^*\|^2$, *for* $1 \leq i \leq d-1$.

Algorithm 1: LLL algorithm

Input: A basis $\{v_1, \ldots, v_d\}$, and $\delta \in (1/4, 1)$
Output: A LLL-reduced basis
1 Compute the Gram-Schmidt basis $v_1^*, ..., v_d^*$, coefficients $\mu_{i,j}$ and
   $V_i = <v_i^*, v_i^*>$ for $1 \leq j < i \leq d$. Let $k=2$.
2 **while** $k \leq d$ **do**
3   **for** $i = k-1$ *to* 1 **do**
4          $v_k = v_k - \lfloor \mu_{i,j} \rceil v_i$.
5   **for** $j = 1$ *to* i **do**
6              $\mu_{k,j} = \mu_{k,j} - \lfloor \mu_{k,i} \rceil \mu_{i,j}$.
7   **if** $V_k \geq (\delta - \mu_{k,k-1}^2)V_{k-1}$ **then**
8          $k = k+1$.
9   **else**
10   Swap v_k with v_{k-1}. Update the values v_k^*, v_{k-1}^*, V_k, V_{k-1}, $\mu_{k-1,i}$
           and $\mu_{k,i}$ for $1 \leq i < k$ and $\mu_{j,k}$ and $\mu_{j,k-1}$ for $k < j \leq d$. Let
           $k=\max\{2, k-1\}$.
11 **return** $\{v_1, \ldots, v_d\}$.

Algorithm 1 describes the operation process of the LLL algorithm and the following conclusion is about the length of vectors the LLL algorithm outputs.

Theorem 1 (LLL [13]**).** *Let* $\mathcal{L}$ *be an d-dimensional integer lattice. The LLL algorithm outputs a reduced basis* $\{v_1, ..., v_d\}$ *where*

$$\|v_1\| \leq \|v_2\| \leq \cdots \leq \|v_i\| \leq 2^{\frac{d(d-1)}{4(d+1-i)}} \det(\mathcal{L})^{\frac{1}{d+1-i}}, \quad i = 1, ..., d$$

in polynomial time.

In Sect. 3 we use probabilistic statistical methods to give a lower LLL bound. When we study the relationship between the distributions of multiple random variables, the following definition has been used.

Definition 3 (Stochastic Dominance [11]**).** *A cumulative distribution* $F(\cdot)$ *is said to stochastically dominate cumulative distribution* $G(\cdot)$ *if for any* $x \in R$, *there is*

$$F(x) \leq G(x).$$

Coppersmith's method can only get the correct solution if the length of the vector is small enough because of the following theorem Howgrave and Graham have proposed.

Theorem 2 (Howgrave-Graham [8]). *Let* $f(y_1, ..., y_n) \in Z[y_1, ..., y_n]$ *be an integer polynomial with* ω *monomials. Suppose that*

1. $f(u_1, ...u_n) \equiv 0 \bmod p^t$ *for* $|u_1| \leq Y_1, ...|u_n| \leq Y_n$,
2. $\|f(y_1 Y_1, ..., y_n Y_n)\| < \frac{p^t}{\sqrt{\omega}}$,

then $f(u_1, ..., u_n) = 0$ *holds over the integers.*

Herrmann-May's attack is based on the following heuristic assumptions for computations with multivariate polynomials.

Assumption 1. *Herrmann-May's lattice-based construction for solving linear modular equations yields algebraically independent polynomials.*

Assumption 1 guarantees that we can efficiently solve linear modular equations using numerical methods such as Gröbner basis. Given the parameters m, t, Herrmann and May define the following cluster of polynomials

$$g_{i_2, ..., i_n, k} = x_2^{i_2} ... x_n^{i_n} f^k N^{\max\{t-k, 0\}},$$

where $i_j \in 0, ...m$ such that $\sum_{j=2}^{n} i_j \leq m - k$. It's easy to verify that these polynomials share one root modulo p^t. They construct a lattice consisting of the coefficient vectors of the $g_{i_2, ..., i_n, k}$'s. Then they apply the LLL algorithm to reduce the lattice for solving linear modular equations. Based on the structure of this lattice, Theorems 1, 2 and Assumption 1, Herrmann and May proposed the following theorem.

Theorem 3 (Herrmann-May [7]). *Let* $\epsilon > 0$ *and let* $N = pq$ *where* $p \geq N^\beta$ *and* p, q *are both large prime number. Let* $g(y_1, ..., y_n) \in Z[y_1, ..., y_n]$ *be a monic linear polynomial with* n *variables. Under Assumption 1, we can obtain all solutions* $(u_1, ..., u_n)$ *of the equation* $g(y_1, ..., y_n) = 0 \bmod p$ *with* $|u_1| \leq N^{\alpha_1}, ..., |u_n| \leq N^{\alpha_n}$ *if*

$$\sum_{i=1}^{n} \alpha_i \leq 1 - (1-\beta)^{\frac{n+1}{n}} - (n+1)(1 - \sqrt[n]{1-\beta})(1-\beta) - \epsilon.$$

3   Improvements on Herrmann-May's Attack

In this section, we present the details of our new approach to improve the Herrmann-May's attack. First, we show how to merge variables, then we indicate the cases where the merging can be done with considerable reduction in the complexity. In addition, we theoretically propose a lower LLL bound with a high probability using the central limit theorem [5].

3.1 Merging Variables

We consider that there are n variables $x_1, ..., x_n$ in the linear equation. Let $X_1, ..., X_n$ be the upper bounds for variables $x_1, ..., x_n$. According to Theorem 3, we can recover p in polynomial time only if $\prod_{i=1}^{n} X_i$ is less than

$$N^{1-(1-\beta)\frac{n+1}{n}-(n+1)(1-\sqrt[n]{1-\beta})(1-\beta)}.$$

At the end of Herrmann and May's paper, they argued that if two unknown blocks are close to each other, we can merge them to get a higher efficiency in attack. Here we delve into the idea of merging variables. We are able to combine n unknown bit blocks into a single bit block (see Fig. 1), i.e. let

$$x = x_n + \sum_{m=1}^{n-1} 2^{\sum_{i=m}^{n-1} j_i + t_{i+1}} x_m + \sum_{m=1}^{n-1} 2^{(\sum_{i=m}^{n-1} j_i + t_{i+1}) - j_m} Y_m,$$

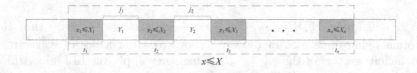

Fig. 1. Merging variables

where X_i and t_i are the upper bound of x_i and the number of bits of the unknown block for $i = 1, ...n$, respectively, and j_i and Y_i are the number of bits of the known block and the value of the known blocks for $i = 1, ..., n-1$, respectively. We know that the upper bound of the product of all unknown quantities before merging is $\prod_{i=1}^{n} X_i$, while this bound after merging is

$$X_n + \sum_{m=1}^{n-1} 2^{\sum_{i=m}^{n-1} j_i + t_{i+1}} X_m + \sum_{m=1}^{n-1} 2^{(\sum_{i=m}^{n-1} j_i + t_{i+1}) - j_m} Y_m.$$

Then the ratio of the upper bound between post-merged and pre-merged satisfies

$$\frac{X_n + \sum_{m=1}^{n-1} 2^{\sum_{i=m}^{n-1} j_i + t_{i+1}} X_m + \sum_{m=1}^{n-1} 2^{(\sum_{i=m}^{n-1} j_i + t_{i+1}) - j_m} Y_m}{\prod_{i=1}^{n} X_i}$$

$$\leq \frac{1}{\prod_{i \neq n} X_i} + \sum_{m=1}^{n-1} \frac{2^{\sum_{i=m}^{n-1} j_i + t_{i+1}}}{\prod_{i \neq m} X_i} + \sum_{m=1}^{n-1} \frac{(2^{j_m} - 1) 2^{(\sum_{i=m}^{n-1} j_i + t_{i+1}) - j_m}}{\prod_{i=1}^{n} X_i} \quad (1)$$

$$\leq \sum_{m=1}^{n-1} \frac{2^{\sum_{i=m}^{n-1} j_i + t_{i+1}}}{\prod_{i \neq m} X_i} + \sum_{m=1}^{n-1} \frac{2^{\sum_{i=m}^{n-1} j_i + t_{i+1}}}{\prod_{i=1}^{n} X_i}.$$

Generally we set $X_i = 2^{t_i}$, so that the ratio is less than

$$2^{j_1 + \cdots + j_{n-1}} + \frac{2^{j_1 + \cdots + j_{n-1}+1}}{X_1}.$$

Further, if $X_1 \geq 2$, the ratio is less than $2^{j_1 + \cdots + j_{n-1}+1}$ (in practice, most values are smaller than this bound). We set $f(n) = 1 - (1 - \beta)^{\frac{n+1}{n}} - (n+1)(1 - \sqrt[n]{1 - \beta})(1 - \beta)$, where $f(x)$ is a monotonically decreasing convex function. It's obvious that the value of the unknown quantity will increase after merging, and by the above analysis we also know that when the number of the unknown bit blocks decreases, the maximum value of unknown quantity that can be solved in polynomial time will increase. Therefore, the variables can be merged as long as the increase in the unknown quantity is less than or equal to the increase in the maximum value of the unknown quantity that can be solved in polynomial time. From this idea, we propose the following theorem.

Theorem 4. *Let $\epsilon > 0$ and let N be a RSA modulus of r bits. We assume that the divisor p ($p \geq N^\beta$) have n unknown bit blocks $x_1, x_2, \ldots, x_n$ where l_i is the bit size of x_i and j_i is the number of bits between r_i and x_{i+1} for $i = 1, \ldots, n - 1$. We set $X_i = 2^{t_i}$ as the upper bound of x_i and assume $\prod_{i=1}^n X_i = N^{f(n)-\epsilon}$. Let $x_v, x_{v+1}, \ldots, x_{v+m-1}$ be m neighboring bit blocks where $X_v \geq 2$. Under Assumption 1, if $1 + \sum_{i=v}^{v+m-2} j_i \leq (r - 1)[f(n - m + 1) - f(n)]$, we can recover p in time complexity $\mathcal{O}((\frac{e}{\epsilon})^{7(n-m+1)} (1 + \log N) \log N)$ after merging $x_v, \ldots, x_{v+m-1}$ which is smaller than $\mathcal{O}((\frac{e}{\epsilon})^{7n} (1 + \log N) \log N)$ before merging.*

Proof. Since N is an r-bit RSA modulus and at the same time an odd number, we can derive that $N > 2^{r-1}$. According to

$$X_i = 2^{t_i}, X_v \geq 2 \text{ and Eq. (1)},$$

the ratio of the upper bound between post-merged and pre-merged is less than $2^{j_v + \cdots + j_{v+m-2}+1}$. Meanwhile, after the m neighboring blocks $x_v, x_{v+1}, \ldots, x_{v+m-1}$ are merged, due to the reduction in the number of blocks, the threshold in Theorem 3 becomes larger, and the ratio of this threshold between post-merged and pre-merged is

$$N^{f(n-m+1)-f(n)} > 2^{(r-1)(f(n-m+1)-f(n))}.$$

Knowing $\prod_{i=1}^n X_i = N^{f(n)-\epsilon}$, if $1 + \sum_{i=v}^{v+m-2} j_i \leq (r-1)(f(n-m+1)-f(n))$, the product of variables after merging will be less than $N^{f(n-m+1)-\epsilon}$ which means that we can recover p in polynomial time due to Theorem 3. The dimension of the lattice in [7] is $d = \mathcal{O}((\frac{e}{\epsilon})^n)$, and the maximal bitsize of an entry in the lattice is $B \approx d \cdot \log N$. According to [12], the time complexity of the L^2 algorithm is $\mathcal{O}(d^5(d + B)B)$, and the running time of Herrmann-May's attack mainly depends on the running time of the L^2 algorithm, thereby the time complexity of Herrmann-May's attack is about

$$\mathcal{O}\left(\left(\frac{e}{\epsilon}\right)^{7n} (1 + \log N) \log N \right).$$

Therefore, the time complexity of Herrmann-May's attack before and after merging is $\mathcal{O}((\frac{e}{\epsilon})^{7n}(1+\log N)\log N)$ and $\mathcal{O}((\frac{e}{\epsilon})^{7(n-m+1)}(1+\log N)\log N)$, respectively. It is obvious that the time complexity of the algorithm after merging is significantly reduced, so we can obtain the Theorem 4's result.   □

Algorithm 2: Merge variables

Input: Variable sequence $(x_1, x_2, \ldots, x_n)$
Output: New variable sequence $(y_1, y_2, \ldots, y_m)$

1 $y_i \leftarrow x_i, i = 1, 2, \ldots, n$.
2 **for** $i = n$ **to** 2 **do**
3 $\quad$ $a \leftarrow 0, z \leftarrow 0$.
4 $\quad$ **for** $j = 1$ **to** $n - i + 1$ **do**
5 $\quad\quad$ **if** $1 + \sum_{t=j}^{j+i-2} j_t \leq (r-1)(f(n) - f(n-i+1))$ and $\sum_{t=j}^{j+i-2} j_t \geq a$ **then**
6 $\quad\quad\quad$ $a \leftarrow \sum_{t=j}^{j+i-2} j_t, z \leftarrow j$.
7 $\quad$ **if** $z \neq 0$ **then**
8 $\quad\quad$ Merge $(y_z, \ldots, y_{z+i-1})$.
9 $\quad\quad$ $(y_1, y_2, \ldots, y_{n-i+1}) \leftarrow$ update $(y_1, y_2, \ldots, y_n)$.
10 $\quad\quad$ $n \leftarrow n - i + 1$.
11 $m \leftarrow n - i + 1$.
12 **return** $(y_1, y_2, \ldots, y_m)$.

Interestingly, after a merging is done, due to the reduction in the number of blocks, we can merge some blocks that we could't merge before. Specifically, let $x_s, \ldots, x_{s+k-1}$ be k adjacent unknown blocks, and $x_t, \ldots, x_{t+l-1}$ be another l adjacent unknown blocks that don't share bits with $x_s, \ldots, x_{s+k-1}$. In the beginning, we assume that $1 + \sum_{i=t}^{t+l-2} j_i \leq (r-1)(f(n-l+1) - f(n))$, but $1 + \sum_{i=s}^{s+k-2} j_i > (r-1)(f(n-k+1) - f(n))$. Therefore, we can merge $x_t, \ldots, x_{t+l-1}$ instead of $x_s, \ldots, x_{s+k-1}$. Because f is a convex function, we can obtain $f(n-l-k+2) - f(n-l+1) \geq f(n-k+1) - f(n)$. So after merging $x_t, \ldots, x_{t+l-1}$, we can potentially to merge $x_s, \ldots, x_{s+k-1}$ which we can't merge before. Thus we need to reduce the number of unknown blocks as many as possible by fully merging variables. To merge variables more efficiently, we propose Algorithm 2 to merge variables which uses a "greedy" strategy to merge as many variables and bits as possible at each step. By experiments, we learn that merging variables can greatly enhance the efficiency of Herrmann-May's attack in some cases.

3.2   Implementing New LLL Bound

We collect extensive samples of the r_i's of different types of Coppersmith lattices to investigate the relationship between the r_i's. Let $S_1, \ldots, S_n$ be n random variables. $S_1, \ldots, S_n$ are independent if and only if $F(x_1, \ldots, x_n) = F_{s_1}(x_1) \cdots F_{s_n}(x_n)$ where $F(x_1, \ldots, x_n)$ is the joint distribution function of $(S_1, \ldots, S_n)$, and $F_{s_i}(x_i)$ is the distribution functions of S_i for $i = 1, \ldots, n$. In fact, the r_i's are considered independent in [15] for random bases. To be more rigorous, we test the independence of the r_i's using the definition and figure out whether the r_i's are identically distributed or not using the Kolmogorov-Smirnov test [6]. Interestingly, we don't observe any significant change in the behaviour of the r_i's of random LLL-reduced bases for different types of Coppersmith lattices. We show the relevant data in Subsect. 4.1 to conclude the following assumption.

Assumption 2. *Considered as continuous random variables, the r_i's of the random bases of Coppersmith lattice (dimension d is large than 40) after LLL reduction are independently and identically distributed except for the first and last individual variables which are both stochastically dominated by the middle ones.*

A possible explanation for Assumption 2 is that the basis matrixes of all types of Coppersmith lattices have a common lower triangular structure coming from the shift polynomials generated with a series of nonlinear operations on the initial polynomial including the power operation and shift operation which lead to a diffusion and confusion of the coefficients of the initial polynomial in the entries of basis matrixes. This structure is similar to the structure of the random bases used in [15]. On the other hand, the large range of the coefficients of the initial polynomial might make the selection of entries appear to be truly random because the selection approximates a selection in the whole space. Both of them could make the LLL-reduced bases behave random.

Theorem 5. *Assume that $x_1, ..., x_n$ and $y_1, ..., y_n$ are both n random variables where x_i and y_i have continuous probability density functions $f_i(x)$ and $g_i(x)$ $(x \geq 0)$ for $i = 1, ..., n$, respectively. If y_i stochastically dominates the x_i for $i = 1, ..., n$, then for the closed area $D : 0 \leq \frac{\sum_{i=1}^{n} x_i}{n} \leq x \subset R^n$, we have*

$$\int \cdots \int_D f_1(x_1) \cdots f_n(x_n) \, dx_1 \cdots dx_n \geq \int \cdots \int_D g_1(x_1) \cdots g_n(x_n) \, dx_1 \cdots dx_n.$$

Proof. The closed area $D : 0 \leq \frac{\sum_{i=1}^{n} x_i}{n} \leq x$ can be denoted by such as

$$0 \leq x_1 \leq nx, \ 0 \leq x_2 \leq x_2'(x_1), ..., 0 \leq x_n \leq x_n'(x_1, x_2, ..., x_{n-1}).$$

Then we can convert the multiple integral into an iterated integral

$$\int \cdots \int_D f_1(x_1) \cdots f_n(x_n) \, dx_1 \cdots dx_n$$

$$= \int_0^{nx} dx_1 \int_0^{x_2'(x_1)} dx_2 \cdots \int_0^{x_n'(x_1, x_2, ..., x_{n-1})} f_1(x_1) \cdots f_n(x_n) \, dx_n$$

$$= \int_0^{nx} f_1(x_1) \, dx_1 \int_0^{x_2'(x_1)} f_2(x_2) \, dx_2 \cdots \int_0^{x_n'(x_1, x_2, ..., x_{n-1})} f_n(x_n) \, dx_n.$$

We know y_i stochastically dominates x_i, so for any $x \in R$, there is $F_i(x) \geq G_i(x)$, i.e.

$$\int_0^x f_i(x_i) \, dx_i \geq \int_0^x g_i(x_i) \, dx_i,$$

where $F_i(x)$ and $G_i(x)$ are the distribution functions of x_i and y_i, respectively, for $i = 1, ..., n$. Therefore we have

$$\int \cdots \int_D f_1(x_1) \cdots f_n(x_n) \, dx_1 \cdots dx_n$$

$$= \int_0^{nx} f_1(x_1) \, dx_1 \int_0^{x_2'(x_1)} f_2(x_2) \, dx_2 \cdots \int_0^{x_n'(x_1, x_2, ..., x_{n-1})} f_n(x_n) \, dx_n$$

$$\geq \int_0^{nx} g_1(x_1) \, dx_1 \int_0^{x_2'(x_1)} g_2(x_2) \, dx_2 \cdots \int_0^{x_n'(x_1, x_2, ..., x_{n-1})} g_n(x_n) \, dx_n$$

$$= \int \cdots \int_D g_1(x_1) \cdots g_n(x_n) \, dx_1 \cdots dx_n.$$

This terminates the proof. □

According to Assumption 2, the middle r_i's stochastically dominate the first-tail ones. This means that by letting $f_i(x)$ be the probability density function of r_i and $f(x)$ be the probability density function of the middle ones, we have

$$\Pr_2 \left\{ \frac{\sum_{i=1}^{d-1} x_i}{d-1} < x \right\} = \int \cdots \int_{D : \frac{\sum_{i=1}^{d-1} x_i}{d-1} < x} f(x_1) \cdots f(x_{d-1}) \, dx_1 \cdots dx_{d-1}$$

$$\leq \int \cdots \int_{D : \frac{\sum_{i=1}^{d-1} x_i}{d-1} < x} f_1(x_1) \cdots f_{d-1}(x_{d-1}) \, dx_1 \cdots dx_{d-1} = \Pr_1 \left\{ \frac{\sum_{i=1}^{d-1} x_i}{d-1} < x \right\},$$

where $\Pr_1$ denotes the real probability, and $\Pr_2$ denotes the probability when the first-tail variables are considered as the middle ones. So we can treat all the random variables as the middle random variables which has no negative impact on the LLL bound we have proposed. And according to Assumption 2, we have the following theorem.

Theorem 6. *Let w and s be the parameters that need to be determined. Assume that $\{v_1, ..., v_d\}$ ($d > 40$) is a random LLL-reduced basis of Coppersmith lattice, and let the mean and variance of the middle r_i's of $\{v_1, ..., v_d\}$ be a and σ^2, respectively. Under Assumption 2, we have*

$$\|v_z\| \leq \sqrt{1 + \frac{T^z - T}{4(T-1)}} \left(T^{\frac{(z-1)(z-2) + s(s+1)}{4}} e^{\frac{(d-s-z)\sqrt{T}}{a}} \prod_{i=s+1}^{d-z} \beta_i{}^i \right)^{\frac{1}{d-z+1}} \det(L)^{\frac{1}{d-z+1}},$$

for $z = 1, ..., d$, with probability at least $\Phi(w)^{\lfloor (d-s-z)/3 \rfloor + 2}$ where $T = 1/(\delta - 0.25)$, $\beta_i = w\sigma/\sqrt{i} + a$, and δ is the parameter of LLL algorithm,

$$\Phi(x) = \frac{1}{\sqrt{2\pi}} \int_{-\infty}^x e^{-\frac{t^2}{2}} \, dt.$$

Proof. Let $X_{i,j} := \prod_{k=j}^{i-1} r_k$. From the proof of Theorem 1 in [13], we know

$$\|v_j\| \leq \sqrt{1 + \frac{T^j - T}{4(T-1)}} \|v_j^*\| = \sqrt{1 + \frac{T^j - T}{4(T-1)}} X_{i,j} \|v_i^*\|, \; X_{i,1} \|v_i^*\| = \|v_1^*\| \geq 1,$$

for $1 \le j < i \le d$. Therefore, we can obtain

$$\|v_z\|^{d-z+1} \le \left(1 + \frac{T^z - T}{4(T-1)}\right)^{\frac{d-z+1}{2}} \|v_z^*\| \prod_{i=z+1}^{d} X_{i,z} \|v_i^*\|$$

$$\le \left(1 + \frac{T^z - T}{4(T-1)}\right)^{\frac{d-z+1}{2}} \left(\prod_{i=2}^{z-1} X_{i,1} \cdot \prod_{i=z+1}^{d} X_{i,z}\right) \prod_{i=1}^{d} \|v_i^*\|$$

$$\le \left(1 + \frac{T^z - T}{4(T-1)}\right)^{\frac{d-z+1}{2}} T^{\frac{(z-1)(z-2)}{4}} \left(\prod_{i=z+1}^{d} X_{i,z}\right) \det(L),$$

for $1 \le z \le d$, i.e.

$$\|v_z\| \le \sqrt{1 + \frac{T^z - T}{4(T-1)}} \left(T^{\frac{(z-1)(z-2)}{4}} \prod_{i=z}^{d-1} \prod_{j=z}^{i} r_j\right)^{\frac{1}{d-z+1}} \det(L)^{\frac{1}{d-z+1}}.$$

Let $Z_i = \frac{\sum_{j=z}^{i+z-1} r_j}{i}$ for $i - 1, ..., d - z$, according to the fundamental inequality $\frac{x_1 + x_2 + \cdots + x_n}{n} \ge \sqrt[n]{x_1 x_2 \cdots x_n}$, we have $\prod_{j=z}^{i+z-1} r_j \le \left(\frac{\sum_{j=z}^{i+z-1} r_j}{i}\right)^i = Z_i^{\,i}$

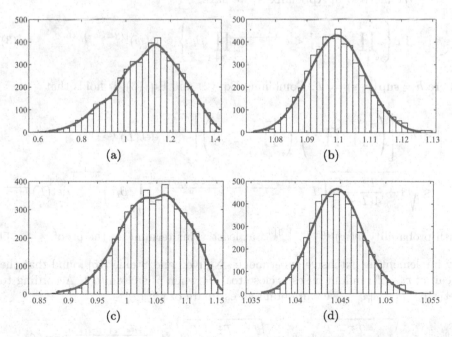

Fig. 2. (a), (c) are the distributions of r_i's in the middle with $\delta = 0.75, 0.999$, respectively, and (b), (d) are the distributions of $X_{60,30}$ with $\delta = 0.75, 0.999$, respectively. The data come from a 84-dimensional lattice used in low public exponent attack [2], and other lattices with different type and dimension have a similar behavior

Obviously, the mean a and variance σ^2 of r_i ($1 \leq i \leq d-1$) exist and $\sigma^2 \neq 0$, so the sequence of r_i ($1 \leq i \leq d-1$) obeys the central limit theorem according to Assumption 2. I.e. let $\eta_i = \frac{1}{\sigma/\sqrt{i}}(Z_i - a)$ for $1 \leq i \leq d-z$, then for $x \in R$, the agreement is consistently

$$\lim_{i \to \infty} \Pr\{\eta_i < x\} = \Pr\left\{\frac{Z_i - a}{\sigma/\sqrt{i}} < x\right\} = \Pr\left\{Z_i < \frac{x\sigma}{\sqrt{i}} + a\right\} = \Phi(x).$$

This means that given a large number s, we can consider Z_{s+1} to be normally distributed (see Fig. 2). Then we have

$$\|v_z\| \leq K \cdot \left[\left(\prod_{i=z}^{z+s-1} \prod_{j=z}^{i} r_j\right)\left(\prod_{i=z+s}^{d-1} Z_{i-z+1}^{i-z+1}\right)\right]^{\frac{1}{d-z+1}} \det(L)^{\frac{1}{d-z+1}}. \tag{2}$$

where $K = \sqrt{1 + (T^z - T)/(4T - 4)} \cdot T^{\frac{(z-1)(z-2)}{4(d-z+1)}}$. For the first half of the coefficient, we have $\prod_{i=z}^{z+s-1} \prod_{j=z}^{i} r_j \leq T^{\frac{s(s+1)}{4}}$. As for the second half, given a positive number w, let $P_i(w) = \Pr\{\eta_i < w\}$, we can get

$$\Pr\left\{Z_i^{\,i} < \beta_i^i\right\} = \Pr\{Z_i < \beta_i\} = P_i(w).$$

So with the method in Appendix A, we have

$$\Pr\left\{\prod_{i=z+s}^{d-1} Z_{i-z+1}^{i-z+1} < e^{\frac{(d-s-z)h}{a}} \prod_{i=s+1}^{d-z} \beta_i^{\,i}\right\} > \Phi(w)^{\lfloor(d-s-z)/3\rfloor+2}, \tag{3}$$

where $h = \sup\{r_i\text{'s}\} = \sqrt{T}$. Combining Eq. (2) and Eq. (3), it holds that

$$\|v_z\| \leq K \cdot \left[\left(\prod_{i=z}^{z+s-1} \prod_{j=z}^{i} r_j\right)\left(\prod_{i=z+s}^{d-1} Z_{i-z+1}^{i-z+1}\right)\right]^{\frac{1}{d-z+1}} \det(L)^{\frac{1}{d-z+1}}$$

$$\leq \sqrt{1 + \frac{T^z - T}{4(T-1)}} \left(T^{\frac{(z-1)(z-2)+s(s+1)}{4}} e^{\frac{(d-s-z)\sqrt{T}}{a}} \prod_{i=s+1}^{d-z} \beta_i^{\,i}\right)^{\frac{1}{d-z+1}} \det(L)^{\frac{1}{d-z+1}},$$

with probability $\Phi(w)^{\lfloor(d-s-z)/3\rfloor+2}$ at least. This terminates the proof. $\quad\square$

By implementing extensive experiments, Nguyen and Stehlé [15] found that the mean of r_i's of random bases is close to 1.04 when δ is close to 1. According to $\det(\mathcal{L}) = \prod_{i=1}^{d} \|v_i^*\|$, we can obtain an estimate of $\|v_z\|$

$$\|v_z\| \leq \sqrt{1 + \frac{T^z - T}{4(T-1)}} \|v_z^*\| \approx \sqrt{1 + \frac{T^z - T}{4(T-1)}} 1.04^{\frac{(d-z)(d-z+1)-z(z-1)}{2d}} \det(\mathcal{L})^{\frac{1}{d}},$$

for $z = 1, ..., d$. In our experiments, when $\delta = 0.999$, we notice that a stabilizes at 1.045 matching the result in [4] but slightly higher than the "1.04" of [15], and σ^2 stabilizes at 0.003. Meanwhile, when $\delta = 0.75$, we observe that a and σ^2 are stable at 1.1 and 0.025, respectively (see Fig. 3).

Let $\mathcal{L}$ be a Coppersmith lattice. We generally determine the dimension d in the following way. We compute the determinant $\det(\mathcal{L})$ of $\mathcal{L}$, and according to Theorem 1, 2, we can obtain the minimum value of d which satisfies $T^{\frac{d(d-1)}{4(d-i+1)}} \cdot \det(\mathcal{L})^{\frac{1}{d-i+1}} \leq \frac{p^m}{\sqrt{d}}$, for $1 \leq i \leq d$. After applying our new bound, we can obtain a lower dimension d' which happens to satisfy $NC \cdot \det(\mathcal{L})^{\frac{1}{d'-i+1}} \leq \frac{p^m}{\sqrt{d'}}$ where NC is the coefficient of our LLL bound for $1 \leq i \leq d'$. Though NC remains exponential, it is indeed far smaller than the worst-case, especially under high dimension. Therefore, we are able to improve the efficiency of Coppersmith's method to some extent.

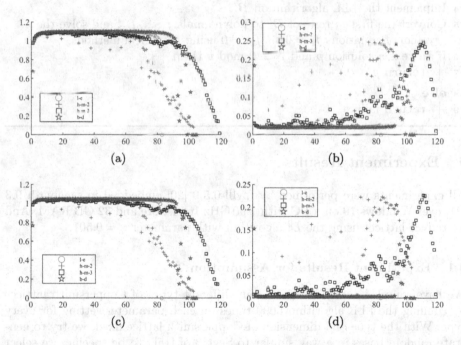

(a)

(b)

(c)

(d)

Fig. 3. The mean and variance of r_i's. "l-e" indicates low public exponent attack, "h-m-2" indicates Herrmann-May's attack [7] with 2 variables, "h-m-3" indicates Herrmann-May's attack with 3 variables, and "b-d" indicates Boneh-Durfee's attack [1]

3.3   Improved Herrmann-May's Attack

In Subsect. 3.1 we analyze the merging of variables in detail. Then we propose a lower LLL bound that holds with a high probability in Subsect. 3.2. As a result, these two improvements both enhance the efficiency of Herrmann-May's attack. Combining these two points, we present the improved Herrmann-May's attack.

Algorithm 3: The improved Herrmann-May's attack

Input: The modulus N, variable sequence $(x_1, x_2, \ldots, x_n)$ and new bound NC

Output: The divisor p

1 $(y_1, y_2, \ldots, y_m) \leftarrow$ implement the Algorithm 2 on $(x_1, x_2, \ldots, x_n)$.
2 Construct basis matrix B using the method of[7] with $(y_1, \ldots, y_m)$.
3 $d \leftarrow$ dimension of lattice after applying NC, $B' \leftarrow$ submatrix consisting of the first d rows and columns of B.
4 Implement the LLL algorithm on B'.
5 Convert the first m rows of B' to polynomials $f_1, \ldots, f_m$, and solve the system of equations $f_1 = 0, \ldots, f_m = 0$ using numerical methods.
6 **if** there is a solution p and $N \equiv 0 \bmod p$ **then**
7 $\quad\lfloor$ **return** p.
8 **else**
9 $\quad\lfloor$ **return** failure.

---

4   Experiment Results

All experiments were performed by fpylll-0.5.9 [20] embedded in sagemath 9.3 [21] over Windows 10 on a PC with 2.90 GHz Intel Core and 32 GB RAM. And we reduce lattices using the L^2 algorithm with parameter $\eta = 0.501$.

4.1   Experiment Results for Assumption 2

We have sampled extensive r_i's of four different types of Coppersmith lattices by running the LLL algorithm 5000 times on each parameter setting for every type. With the type and dimension of Coppersmith lattice fixed, we try to generate random bases in a way similar to Sect. 3 of [15]. To be specific, we select the inputs of Coppersmith's algorithm uniformly at random within their value ranges, respectively, including the modulus, the upper bounds and positions of unknown variables. Then we run the LLL algorithm on the bases to obtain random LLL-reduced bases. Interestingly, we have found that the distribution characteristics of local bases of different types of Coppersmith lattices behave surprisingly consistently.

Let $\{x_i\text{'s}\}$ be the dataset of r_i for $i = 1, \ldots, d-1$. For each i ($1 \le i \le d-1$), we perform the Kolmogorov-Smirnov test on r_i and r_j for $j = 1, \ldots, i-1, i+1, \ldots, d-1$, and if the significance level is greater than 0.05, we consider r_i and r_j to be identically distributed and record the maximum number of variables having the same distribution. We let these variables form the set A, and the remaining variables form the set B. We have observed that for any r_i (in the middle) in set A and any r_j in set B, there is $|\{x_i|x_i \leq l\}| \leq |\{x_j|x_j \leq l\}|$ for $0 \leq l \leq \sqrt{T}$, which means that each r_i's in A stochastically dominate every r_j's in B. Such a phenomenon is shown in Fig. 4. In addition, to verify the independence of $r_1, ..., r_{d-1}$, we randomly select a large number of points $(t_1, ..., t_{d-1}) \in R^{d-1}$ with $0 \leq t_i \leq \sqrt{T}$ for $i = 0, ..., d-1$ to consist the set S. Then we set

$$F(t_1, ..., t_{d-1}) = |\{(x_1, ..., x_{d-1})|0 < x_i \leq t_i, \ i = 1, ..., d-1\}|/|S|,$$
$$F_i(t_i) = |\{(x_1, ..., x_{d-1})|0 < x_i \leq t_i\}|/|S|, \text{ for } i = 1, ..., d-1,$$

and we consider these random variables to be independent as long as

$$\max\left\{ \left| F(t_1, ..., t_{d-1}) - \prod_{i=1}^{d-1} F_i(t_i) \right|, \ (t_1, ..., t_{d-1}) \in S \right\}, \tag{4}$$

is sufficiently small. We have documented the maximum number of the middle variables that have the same distribution and the value of Eq. (4) in Table 1 4, where "Id" indicates the number of the middle variables which are identically distributed, while "In" represents the value of Eq. (4). We construct the lattices used in Herrmann-May's attack [7] of 2 variables with $d = 55, 78, 105$ by uniformly selecting the modulus of 1024 bits and the unknown variables (their sizes and locations). Similarly, we construct the lattices used in Herrmann-May's attack of 3 variables with $d = 56, 84, 120$. The results are presented in Table 1 and Table 2, respectively. Then we construct the lattices used in Boneh-Durfee's attack [1] with $d = 48, 75, 106$ by uniformly selecting the modulus of 1024 bits, parameter γ, and secret key $d < N^\gamma$. We select $\gamma \leq 0.273, 0.276, 0.279$ corresponding to $d = 48, 75, 106$, according to the maximum value which can be solved theoretically with different dimensional lattices. The results are shown in Table 3. Likely, we construct the lattices used in low public exponent attack [2]

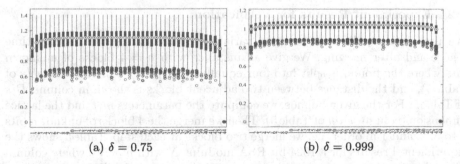

(a) $\delta = 0.75$ (b) $\delta = 0.999$

Fig. 4. The distributions of r_i's of a 45-dimensional lattice used in low public exponent attack [2] with $\delta = 0.75, 0.999$. Similar behavior occurs in other lattices with different type and dimension

Table 1. Herrmann-May's attack, 2 variables

δ	d		
	55	78	105
In	0.75	0.012	0.015	0.011
	0.999	0.037	0.05	0.045
Id	0.75	14	25	39
	0.999	16	20	35

Table 2. Herrmann-May's attack, 3 variables

δ	d		
	56	84	120
In	0.75	0.006	0.01	0.017
	0.999	0.035	0.05	0.02
Id	0.75	8	31	46
	0.999	8	34	45

Table 3. Boneh-Durfee's attack

δ	d		
	48	75	106
In	0.75	0.005	0.012	0.017
	0.999	0.02	0.02	0.03
Id	0.75	20	43	73
	0.999	18	41	69

Table 4. Low public exponent attack

δ	d		
	45	63	84
In	0.75	0.015	0.011	0.014
	0.999	0.038	0.033	0.021
Id	0.75	26	42	58
	0.999	25	40	58

with public key $e = 3$ by uniformly selecting the modulus of 1024 bits, plaintext and leaked bits. We set $d = 45, 63, 84$. The results are shown in Table 4. In all experiments, the values of "In" are lower than 0.05 so that we can consider the r_i's to be independent no matter the type and dimension of lattice. Moreover, the number of the r_i's in the middle which have the same distribution is about half the number of all the r_i's for every lattice. And we observe that the middle r_i's all stochastically dominate the first-tail r_i's which has been described before. These explain why all our experiments with new LLL bound are successful in Subsect. 4.2.

4.2   Experiment Results for Verification

We present the validity of merging variables by comparing the running time before and after merging. We give an instance with $n = 4$ blocks of unknown bits where the bound is split into four equally sized pieces (column *Variable* of Table 5), and the distance between two adjacent blocks is shown in column *Dis* of Table 5. For the given bounds, we compute the parameters m, t and the lattice dimension (column *Dim* of Table 5). Then we merge the 4 blocks of unknown bits into 3, 2, and 1 in order, i.e. we merge two blocks at each step. Table 5 shows the experimental results for a 1024-bit RSA modulus N with $p \geq N^{\frac{1}{2}}$ where column *Time* denotes the running time of Herrmann-May's attack. In all experiments, we successfully recover the small root we want after each merging. With Table 5, we can learn that merging variables will greatly enhance the efficiency of Herrmann-May's attack in some cases.

Table 5. The results of merging variables

n	m	t	Dim	Variable	Dis	Time (min)
4	9	1	715	27/27/26/26	17/8/45	>1000
3	7	1	120	27/61/26	17/45	0.2
2	5	1	21	105/26	45	<0.1
1	8	1	9	176	—	<0.1

Furthermore, with increasing dimension d, we show the trend of $T^{\frac{d(d-1)}{4(d-i+1)}}/NC$, i.e. the ratio of the worse-case bound to our new bound. In our experiments, we have observed a rough exponential increase in the ratio as d increases (see Fig. 5). The results show that our new bound on Herrmann-May's attack is more effective as d is larger. Moreover, we demonstrate the advantages of the improved Herrmann-May's attack by comparing the effects of the attack with different LLL bounds, including our new bound, the bound deduced with [15], and the original bound provided by Theorem 1. Specifically, we set $m = 17, t = 5$ for the 2 variables case, and $m = 8, t = 2$ for 3 variables case. The corresponding lattice dimensions are 171 and 165, respectively (column *O-Dim*). Then we present the probabilities (column *Pr* of Table 6) that different bounds hold successfully in practice. Given the parameters m, t, we compute the number of bits (column *Bit* of Table 6) that one can theoretically recover p under different bounds and the number of bits (column *O-Bit* of Table 6) under the original bound in Theorem 1. Moreover, column *Dim* indicates the dimension of lattices that one can theoretically recover p under our new bound and the bound deduced by [15] with *O-Bit*. The experiment results are shown in Table 6. In all experiments with our new bound, we successfully recover the small roots we want, thereby we can factor N. This proves that our new bound is more accurate than the estimate in [15]. So that we can theoretically recover more unknown bits or reduce the lattice dimension after applying our new bound. According to Fig. 5, we could predict that as the lattice dimension increases, we are able to reduce more dimensions but still succeed in recovering p.

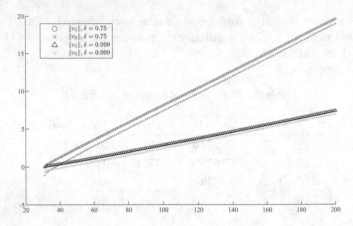

Fig. 5. $T^{\frac{d(d-1)}{4(d-i+1)}}/NC$ with $i = 1, 5$ and $\delta = 0.75, 0.999$. The parameters $s = 30, w = 3$

Table 6. The results of Herrmann-May's attack with different bounds

n	δ	Bound	Pr	Dim	O-Dim	Bit	O-Bit
2	0.75	our new bound	100%	167	171	91/90	89/88
	0.999	our new bound	100%	169		92/91	91/90
		bound with [15]	93%	166		93/93	
3	0.75	our new bound	100%	160	165	35/34/34	31/31/31
	0.999	our new bound	100%	163		37/36/36	35/35/35
		bound with [15]	94%	160		39/39/39	

5   Conclusion

In this paper, we revisit the work of Herrmann and May in Asiacrypt'08 for solving linear equations modulo unknown divisors. To be specific, we delve into the idea of merging variables proposed by Herrmann and May and give the cases where the merging can be done with a considerable reduction in the complexity of Herrmann-May's attack. Moreover, we have proposed a lower LLL bound using the central limit theorem so that we can also enhance the efficiency of Herrmann-May's attack. Finally, we combine these two improvements to propose the improved Herrmann-May's attack. Furthermore, our method to improve the LLL bound could be generalized to other types of random bases and one only needs to know the mean and variance of their r_i's. This is also the direction of our future work.

Acknowledgements. This work was supported by the National Key Research and Development Program of China (Grant No. 2022YFB3102900), the National Natural Science Foundation of China (Grant Nos. 61872449, 62172433, 62172435) and the Science Foundation for the Excellent Youth Scholars of Henan Province (Grant No. 222300420099).

A   Probability

Let $h = \sup\{r_i\text{'s}\}$. We can write Z_{i+n} as $Z_{i+n} = \frac{i \cdot Z_i}{i+n} + \frac{\prod_{j=i+1}^{i+n} r_{j+z-1}}{i+n}$, for $i = 1 \leq i < i + n \leq d - z$. Knowing $Z_i^i < \beta_i^i$, i.e. $Z_i < \beta_i$, we can obtain

$$Z_{i+n}^{i+n} = \left(\frac{i \cdot Z_i}{i+n} + \frac{\prod_{j=i+1}^{i+n} r_{j+z-1}}{i+n} \right)^{i+n} < \left(\beta_{i+n} + \frac{nh}{i+n} \right)^{i+n},$$

i.e. $\Pr\{Z_{i+n}^{i+n} < (\beta_{i+n} + \frac{nh}{i+n})^{i+n}, ..., Z_{i+1}^{i+1} < (\beta_{i+1} + \frac{h}{i+1})^{i+1}, Z_i^i < \beta_i^i\} = \Pr\{Z_i^i < \beta_i^i\}$, for $i = 1 \leq i < i + n \leq d - z$.

Let $c_i = s + 3i + 1$ and $A_i = \left\{ Z_{c_i} < \beta_{c_i}, Z_{c_i+1} < \beta_{c_i+1} + \frac{h}{c_i+1}, Z_{c_i+2} < \beta_{c_i+2} + \frac{2h}{c_i+2} \right\}$, for $i = 0, ..., b$, and let $A_{b+1} = \{Z_{d-z-1} < \beta_{d-z-1}\}, A_{b+2} = \{Z_{d-z} < \beta_{d-z}\}$, then we can obtain

$$\Pr\left\{ \prod_{i=s+1}^{d-z} Z_i^i < M \right\} > \Pr\{A_0, A_1, ..., A_{b+2}\} = \Pr\{A_0\} \cdot \prod_{i-1}^{b+2} \Pr\{A_i | A_0, ..., A_{i-1}\}$$

$$> \prod_{i=0}^{h+?} \Pr\{A_i\} = \prod_{i=b+1}^{b+2} \Pr\{A_i\} \cdot \prod_{i=0}^{b} \Pr\left\{ Z_{c_i} < \beta_{c_i} \right\} = \Phi(w)^{\lfloor (d-s-z)/3 \rfloor + 2},$$

where $m_2 = \lceil ((d - s - z) \bmod 3)/3 \rceil, m_1 = ((d - s - z) \bmod 3) - m_2, b = \lfloor (d - s - z)/3 \rfloor - 1$ and

$$M = \left(\prod_{i=0}^{b} \beta_{c_i}^{c_i} \cdot \left(\beta_{c_i+1} + \frac{h}{c_i+1} \right)^{c_i+1} \cdot \left(\beta_{c_i+2} + \frac{2h}{c_i+2} \right)^{c_i+2} \right) \cdot \beta_{d-z-1}^{(d-z-1)m_1} \beta_{d-z}^{(d-z)m_2}.$$

On the other hand, there is $\left(1 + \frac{h}{x}\right)^x \xrightarrow{increasing} e^h$ as x $(x > 0)$ increases, therefore, we have

$$\beta_i^i < \left(\beta_i + \frac{nh}{i} \right)^i = \beta_i^i \left(1 + \frac{nh/\beta_i}{i} \right)^i < \beta_i^i e^{nh/\beta_i} < \beta_i^i e^{nh/a},$$

for $i = s + 1, ...d - z$. After simplification, we can obtain

$$\prod_{i=s+1}^{d-z} Z_i^i < M \leq e^{\frac{(d-s-z)h}{a}} \prod_{i=s+1}^{d-z} \beta_i^i.$$

with a probability $\Phi(w)^{\lfloor (d-s-z)/3 \rfloor + 2}$ at least.

References

1. Boneh, D., Durfee, G.: Cryptanalysis of RSA with private key d less than $N^{0.292}$. In: Stern, J. (ed.) EUROCRYPT 1999. LNCS, vol. 1592, pp. 1–11. Springer, Heidelberg (1999). https://doi.org/10.1007/3-540-48910-X_1
2. Coppersmith, D.: Finding a small root of a univariate modular equation. In: Maurer, U. (ed.) EUROCRYPT 1996. LNCS, vol. 1070, pp. 155–165. Springer, Heidelberg (1996). https://doi.org/10.1007/3-540-68339-9_14
3. Deng, X.: An Introduction to lenstra-lenstra-lovasz Lattice Basis Reduction Algorithm. Massachusetts Institute of Technology (MIT) (2016)
4. Ding, J., Kim, S., Takagi, T., Wang, Y., Yang, B.Y.: A physical study of the LLL algorithm. J. Number Theor. **244**, 339–368 (2023). https://doi.org/10.1016/j.jnt.2022.09.013
5. Dodge, Y.: Central limit theorem, pp. 66–68. Springer, New York (2008). https://doi.org/10.1007/978-0-387-32833-1_50
6. Dodge, Y.: Kolmogorov-Smirnov Test, pp. 283–287. Springer, New York (2008). https://doi.org/10.1007/978-0-387-32833-1_214
7. Herrmann, M., May, A.: Solving linear equations modulo divisors: on factoring given any bits. In: Pieprzyk, J. (ed.) ASIACRYPT 2008. LNCS, vol. 5350, pp. 406–424. Springer, Heidelberg (2008). https://doi.org/10.1007/978-3-540-89255-7_25
8. Howgrave-Graham, N.: Finding small roots of univariate modular equations revisited. In: Darnell, M. (ed.) Cryptography and Coding 1997. LNCS, vol. 1355, pp. 131–142. Springer, Heidelberg (1997). https://doi.org/10.1007/BFb0024458
9. Kim, S., Venkatesh, A.: The behavior of random reduced bases. Int. Math. Res. Notices **2018**(20), 6442–6480 (2017). https://doi.org/10.1093/imrn/rnx074
10. Lenstra, H, W., Lenstra, A, K., Lovász, L.: Factoring polynomials with rational coefficients. Math. Ann. **261**, 515–534 (1982). https://doi.org/10.1007/BF01457454
11. Levy, H.: Stochastic dominance and expected utility: survey and analysis. Manage. Sci. **38**(4), 555–593 (1992). https://doi.org/10.5555/2783639.2783646
12. Lu, Y., Zhang, R., Peng, L., Lin, D.: Solving linear equations modulo unknown divisors: revisited. In: Iwata, T., Cheon, J.H. (eds.) ASIACRYPT 2015. LNCS, vol. 9452, pp. 189–213. Springer, Heidelberg (2015). https://doi.org/10.1007/978-3-662-48797-6_9
13. May, A.: New RSA vulnerabilities using lattice reduction methods. Ph.D. thesis, Citeseer (2003)
14. Nguên, P.Q., Stehlé, D.: Floating-point LLL revisited. In: Cramer, R. (ed.) EUROCRYPT 2005. LNCS, vol. 3494, pp. 215–233. Springer, Heidelberg (2005). https://doi.org/10.1007/11426639_13
15. Nguyen, P.Q., Stehlé, D.: LLL on the average. In: Hess, F., Pauli, S., Pohst, M. (eds.) ANTS 2006. LNCS, vol. 4076, pp. 238–256. Springer, Heidelberg (2006). https://doi.org/10.1007/11792086_18
16. Nguyen, P.Q., Stehlé, D.: An LLL algorithm with quadratic complexity. SIAM J. Comput. **39**(3), 874–903 (2009). https://doi.org/10.1137/070705702
17. Rivest, R.L., Shamir, A., Adleman, L.: A method for obtaining digital signatures and public-key cryptosystems. Commun. ACM **21**(2), 120–126 (1978). https://doi.org/10.1145/359340.359342
18. Schnorr, C.P., Euchner, M.: Lattice basis reduction: improved practical algorithms and solving subset sum problems. Math. Program. **66**(2), 181–199 (1994). https://doi.org/10.1007/BF01581144

19. development team, T.F.: fplll, a lattice reduction library, Version: 5.4.4 (2023). https://github.com/fplll/fplll
20. development team, T.F.: fpylll, a Python wrapper for the fplll lattice reduction library, Version: 0.5.9 (2023). https://github.com/fplll/fpylll
21. The Sage Developers: SageMath, the Sage Mathematics Software System (Version 9.3) (2021). https://www.sagemath.org

Full Round Distinguishing
and Key-Recovery Attacks on SAND-2

Zhuolong Zhang[1], Shiyao Chen[2], Wei Wang[1,3,4($\boxtimes$)], and Meiqin Wang[1,3,4]

[1] School of Cyber Science and Technology, Shandong University, Qingdao, China
zhuolongzhang@mail.sdu.edu.cn, {weiwangsdu,mqwang}@sdu.edu.cn
[2] Nanyang Technological University, Singapore, Singapore
shiyao.chen@ntu.edu.sg
[3] Quan Cheng Laboratory, Jinan, China
[4] Key Laboratory of Cryptologic Technology and Information Security,
Ministry of Education, Shandong University, Jinan, China

Abstract. This paper presents full round distinguishing and key recovery attacks on lightweight block cipher SAND-2 with 64-bit block size and 128-bit key size, which appears to be a mixture of the AND-Rotation-XOR (AND-RX) based ciphers SAND and ANT. However, the security arguments against linear and some other attacks are not fully provided. In this paper, we find that the combination of a SAND-like nibble-based round function and ANT-like bit-based permutations will cause dependencies and lead to iterative linear and differential trails with high probabilities. By exploiting these, full round distinguishing attacks on SAND-2 work with 2^{46} queries for linear and $2^{58.60}$ queries for differential in the single-key setting. Then, full round key recovery attacks are also mounted, which work with the time complexity $2^{48.23}$ for linear and $2^{64.10}$ for differential. It should be noted that the dependency observed in this paper only works for SAND-2 and will not threaten SAND and ANT. From the point of designers, our attacks show the risk of mixing the parts of different designs, even though each of them is well-studied to be secure.

Keywords: Linear Cryptanalysis · Differential Cryptanalysis · Distinguishing Attack · Key Recovery Attack · SAND-2

1 Introduction

With strong demands of lightweight symmetric-key primitives, the design and cryptanalysis of lightweight ciphers (*e.g.,* block cipher and hash function) has been one of the most productive lines of research in recent years. As one of the most important building blocks of symmetric primitives, lightweight block cipher has motivated and inspired many important research directions and works.

Taking a variety of cost metrics into considerations under lightweight scenarios, it is naturally a challenge to balance different perspectives when designing the block cipher, including security level, hardware cost and software efficiency.

© The Author(s), under exclusive license to Springer Nature Singapore Pte Ltd. 2024
C. Ge and M. Yung (Eds.): Inscrypt 2023, LNCS 14527, pp. 230–250, 2024.
https://doi.org/10.1007/978-981-97-0945-8_13

For instance, SIMON and SPECK proposed by NSA [3] are two quite elegant and competitive algorithms but without any design rationale and security analysis in the design paper, where the former is hardware-oriented and the latter is software-oriented. SKINNY [4] is then proposed by Beierle *et al.* at CRYPTO 2016 as a competitor to SIMON in terms of performance, and it provides stronger security guarantees with regard to differential [6] and linear [12] attacks, which are the most classical and powerful cryptanalytic methods. Later, Chen *et al.* [9] proposed a new family of AND-RX block ciphers SAND at DCC 2022, which admits an equivalent nibble-based structure, this makes SAND both software and hardware efficient. They also introduced a novel approach to analyze the security, which allows for high security in both single-key and related-key [5,11] scenarios.

Recently, Chen and Li *et al.* [10] follows SAND and ANT [8] block ciphers to design a new cipher called SAND-2[1], which adopts almost all SAND cipher and bit-based permutations similar to that in ANT cipher. They aim to achieve a better diffusion and security bounds of differential, however, the designers only evaluate the resistance against differential attack and do not provide other common cryptanalysis. Especially considering that the bit-based permutations totally break the nibble-based structure, it seems that the designers of SAND-2 did not take care of the dependency existing in the round function, which has already been discussed by the designers of SAND [9, Section 3]. And it is worth noting that this similar dependency has already been observed by Sasaki [13] to break full round ANU cipher [2] under related-key setting. Naturally, we wonder that *whether there are some dependencies in SAND-2?* and if there exists, *whether we can make full use of such dependencies to provide more in-depth security evaluations of SAND-2?*

Contributions. In this paper, we answer the above two questions positively. By carefully observing the bit-based round function of SAND-2, we firstly find some dependencies that can be used to construct linear and differential trails, which help us derive two-round iterative differential and linear characteristics. Then, we mount longer number of rounds distinguishers from these iterative trails. Based on which, we finally launch full round key recovery attacks on SAND-2, our results are given in Table 1.

Dependencies in the Round Function of SAND-2. Although the designers of SAND-2 adopted bit-based permutations P_0/P_1 to mix bits in G_0/G_1 as complicated as possible, considering the software implementation, it still preserves some properties (like the partial rotation invariant property of P_0 and P_1 in ANT cipher). Based on these properties, for SAND-2 round function, we can easily derive the same input bit for two parallel non-linear components G_0 and G_1 after regrouping by rotations and bit permutations P_0/P_1.

Iterative Linear and Differential Trails of SAND-2. Based on the observed dependencies, we then construct two-round iterative linear and differential characteristics of SAND-2. For linear $(0x0, 0x2) \xrightarrow{2r} (0x0, 0x2)$, it has

---

[1] SAND-2 uses the name of SAND, but it is designed by totally different designers.

the linear bias with 2^{-2}. For differential $(0x8, 0x0) \xrightarrow{2r} (0x8, 0x0)$, it has the differential probability with 2^{-3}. Both only have one active bit and have other seven rotation equivalent trails due to the partial rotation invariant of bit-based permutations.

Then, we mount longer linear and differential distinguishers based on these iterative characteristics, the clustering effect is also considered, SAT/SMT based automatic search method clustering and experiments of these distinguishers are performed as verifications. For linear, these iterative based longer number of rounds distinguishers has no significant clustering effect. For differential, we develop a formula based method to approximately evaluate the clustering differential probability, especially for longer number of rounds where SAT/SMT based method is inefficient. The experiment results show that our method is effective and efficient to approximate these iterative differential distinguishers.

Full Round Attacks on SAND-2. With these carefully constructed and evaluated iterative trails, full round distinguishers can be mounted: $(0x2, 0x0) \xrightarrow{47r} (0x0, 0x2)$ for linear with linear probability 2^{-46} and $(0x0, 0x8) \xrightarrow{47r} (0x8, 0x0)$ for differential with differential probability $2^{-58.60}$. These distinguishers not only lead to full round distinguishing attacks on SAND-2, but also they have a high probability, especially for linear with a practical complexity 2^{46}. Then, we launch linear and differential *full round key recovery attacks* on SAND-2, which are summarized in Table 1. It is worth noting that the time and data complexity of linear full round key recovery attack are even *practical* (both under 2^{50}).

Table 1. Distinguishing and key recovery attacks on SAND-2 (the total rounds of SAND-2 are 47).

Attack Method	Rounds	Time[†]	Data	Memory	Success Prob.	Source
Distinguisher						
Differential	6	–	–	–	–	[10]
Linear	47	$2^{46.00}$	$2^{46.00}$	1	–	Sect. 3.1
Differential	47	$2^{58.60}$	$2^{58.60}$	1	–	Sect. 3.2
Key Recovery						
Linear	47 (41)[‡]	$2^{48.23}$	$2^{45.50}$	$2^{35.00}$	83.24%	Sect. 4.1
Differential	47 (43)	$2^{64.10}$	$2^{60.20}$	$2^{57.20}$	92.61%	Sect. 4.2
Differential	47 (41)	$2^{73.70}$	$2^{53.13}$	$2^{53.13}$	90.65%	Full version

† Time complexity is evaluated by one full round encryption of SAND-2.
‡ The number of rounds of the distinguisher used for key recovery attack are 41.

Outline of the Paper. In Sect. 2, we firstly give a brief introduction of SAND and SAND-2 block ciphers. In Sect. 3, we show the dependencies in the round function of SAND-2, which are used to construct differential and linear distinguishers. Based on the distinguishers we mount, full round linear and differential key recovery attacks on SAND-2 are provided in Sect. 4. Finally, we conclude the paper.

2 Preliminary

The design of SAND-2 almost follows SAND block cipher, except that the designers of SAND-2 break the nibble-based equivalent structure of SAND by adopting bit-based permutations in the middle of two parallel expanding round functions, which may incur dependency problems as discussed in the design rationales of SAND [9, Section 3]. This also makes the security analysis of SAND-2 more difficult, that is, the cipher cannot be analyzed under nibble-level like SAND. We note that SAND-2 still lacks enough cryptanalysis and the designers only provide a rough security bound against differential attack. Since SAND-2 directly uses the same key schedule and the similar round function of SAND, we will first give an introduction to SAND and then briefly introduce SAND-2.

2.1 Specification of SAND Block Cipher

SAND is an AND-RX block cipher with Feistel construction, which has two versions SAND-64 and SAND-128. As SAND-2 only has 64-bit version, we only introduce SAND 64 here, It has 48 total rounds and 128-bit keysize.

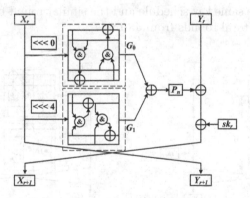

Fig. 1. Round Function of SAND-64.

Round Function of SAND. As shown in Fig. 1, the left branch X_r firstly has a double expanding process and rotates with rotation constants (s_0, s_1), where $(s_0, s_1) = (0, 4)$ for its *Synthetic S-box* (SSb) equivalent representation. Non-linear components G_0 and G_1 are then applied parallelly. Before applying a nibble equivalent permutation P_n and adding to the right branch Y_r, the outputs of G_0 and G_1 are compressed by XOR operations. For more details, we refer the reader to SAND design paper [9].

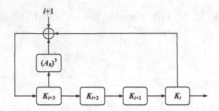
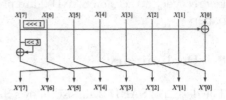

Fig. 2. Key schedule of SAND-64.   **Fig. 3.** Operation A_8 of SAND-64.

Key Schedule. The 128-bit master key K can be viewed as four 32-bit words, i.e., $K = K_3||K_2||K_1||K_0$. The update function of key schedule is shown in Fig. 2, and K_{i+4} can be calculated as below

$$K_{i+4} \leftarrow (A_8)^3(K_{i+3}) \oplus K_i \oplus (i+1),\ 0 \leq i \leq 43,$$

where $(A_8)^3$ denotes that the operation A_8 is applied to K_{i+3} for three times iteratively. A_8 is a nibble-based function and depicted in Fig. 3 where $X[j]$ denotes the j-th $(0 \leq j < 8)$ nibble of input X, i.e., $K_r(\ 0 \leq r \leq 47)$ can be divided into eight nibbles. Finally, the r-th round subkey sk_r will be loaded from K_r and added to the encryption state.

2.2 Specification of SAND-2 Block Cipher

SAND-2 adopts the same key schedule and the similar round function of SAND, it also changes the total rounds from 48 to 47.

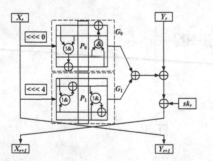
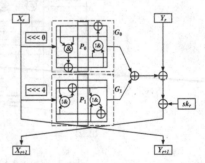

Fig. 4. Round function for even round.   **Fig. 5.** Round function for odd round.

For the round function of SAND-2, as shown in Fig. 4, it firstly replaces some AND operations to NAND operations in G_0 and G_1. Then it uses two different bit permutations P_0 and P_1, as shown in Table 2, which are similar to the bit-based permutation adopted in ANT [8] block cipher. Finally, SAND-2 alternatively swaps NAND and AND operations in two layers of G_0 for even round and odd round (see in Fig. 5). For more details of SAND-2, please refer to its design paper [10].

Table 2. Bit permutations P_0 and P_1.

i	0	1	2	3	4	5	6	7	8	9	10	11	12	13	14	15
$P_0(i)$	28	23	26	1	0	27	30	5	4	31	2	9	8	3	6	13
i	16	17	18	19	20	21	22	23	24	25	26	27	28	29	30	31
$P_0(i)$	12	7	10	17	16	11	14	21	20	15	18	25	24	19	22	29
i	0	1	2	3	4	5	6	7	8	9	10	11	12	13	14	15
$P_1(i)$	20	27	2	29	24	31	6	1	28	3	10	5	0	7	14	9
i	16	17	18	19	20	21	22	23	24	25	26	27	28	29	30	31
$P_1(i)$	4	11	18	13	8	15	22	17	12	19	26	21	16	23	30	25

3   Iterative and Full Round Distinguishers of SAND-2

In this section, we show how to exploit dependency properties existing in the round function of SAND-2 to construct iterative linear and differential characteristics. Then, full round linear and differential distinguishers can be both mounted. To enhance the probability of distinguishers, we evaluate the clustering effect for these distinguishers, experiments are also performed for verifications.

3.1   Linear Distinguishers of SAND-2

We firstly present a two-round iterative linear characteristic of SAND-2, as shown in Fig. 6, this is obtained by carefully observing two bit permutations P_0/P_1 and the rotation, then we have the following property.

Property 1. For the input bit with index $i_0 = 4 \times t + 3^2$ ($0 \le t < 8$) of G_0 and the input bit with index $i_1 = 4 \times (t + 1) + 3$ of G_1, these two bits are derived from the same bit in X_r with index $4 \times t + 3$ and have a linear relation with $(4 \times t + 1)$-th output bit of G_0 and G_1 respectively.

We now give an example of this property as follows, and it should be noted that it has *other seven equivalent cases* for different choices of t. Also, this property is independent of the odd or even round.

Example 1. For $i_0 = 31$, $P_0(i_0) = 29$, and $P_1(i_1) = 29$ when $i_1 = 3$. Due to the rotation $X_r \lll 0$ before G_0 and $X_r \lll 4$ before G_1, then the bit with index $i_0 = 31$ in G_0 and the bit with index $i_1 = 3$ in G_1 are derived from the same bit in X_r, which are marked as yellow in Fig. 6. Coincidentally, both these bits are linear related to the 29-th bit of the outputs of G_0 and G_1 respectively.

With Property 1, the two-round linear characteristic depicted in Fig. 6 with linear bias 2^{-2} (equivalent to linear probability 2^{-2}) is now constructed as below.

---

[2] For simplicity, all bit indices are taken modulo 32 in the rest of the paper.

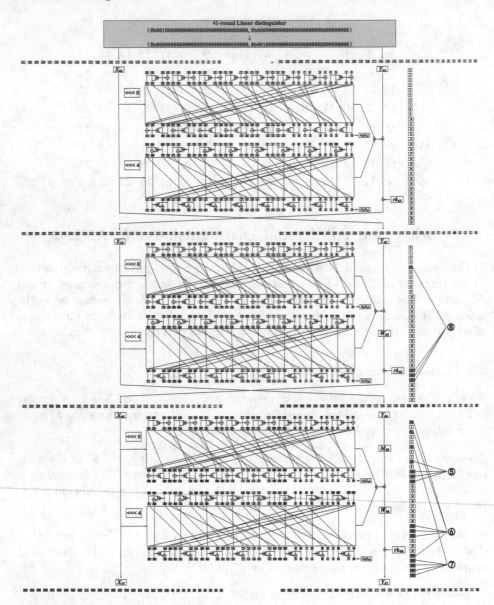

Fig. 6. Two-round iterative linear characteristic (active bit is marked as yellow). (Color figure online)

1. Let only the 29-th bit mask of the right branch of the input be active, *i.e.*, $\Gamma Y_r[29] = 1$. All the rest bits of ΓY_r and ΓX_r are set to be zero mask. So, the input mask is $(\Gamma X_r, \Gamma Y_r) = (0x00000000, 0x20000000)$;
2. According to the propagation rule of linear mask, the output masks of G_0 and G_1 of the first round function are both with $0x20000000$;

3. In order to make the trail iterative, we let the mask $\Gamma Y_{r+1} = 0x00000000$. Then according to Property 1, the input masks of G_0 and G_1 of the first round function can be set to be $0x80000000$ and $0x00000008$ respectively;

4. With $\Gamma X_{r+1} = 0x20000000$, it leads to the output mask of the second round $(\Gamma X_{r+2}, \Gamma Y_{r+2}) = (\Gamma X_r, \Gamma Y_r) = (0x00000000, 0x20000000)$.

For the linear bias of this two-round trail, only the step 3 mentioned above produces the probability, that is, the second layer of G_1 of the first round function, as the 29-th output bit mask is non-zero, then the output mask of the corresponding NAND operation is also non-zero, which makes this NAND operation active with linear bias 2^{-2}. Thus, this two-round iterative linear characteristic[3] $(0x00000000, 0x20000000) \rightarrow (0x00000000, 0x20000000)$ has the linear bias with 2^{-2} and can start from both even or odd round number.

Longer Trails, the Clustering Effect and Experiments. With the presented two-round iterative trail above, longer number of rounds linear distinguishers can be naturally mounted. Especially, a *47-round (full round)* linear characteristic of SAND-2 can be obtained by iterating the two-round trail 23 times and appending one free round at the beginning, which has the linear bias with 2^{-24}. Not only does this trail invalidates the security of SAND-2 against linear attacks, but also its bias is even high enough to be a *practical full round distinguisher* with the complexity 2^{46}.

To verify these iterative trails, we firstly cluster the trails of different numbers of iterative times by the mature SAT/SMT automatic search method [1]. The results show that this kind of two-round iterative based linear trails has no significant clustering effect. Then, we perform experiments to evaluate the linear bias of these trails, which are given in Table 3 and match the results of clustering. In next section, we will use the 41-round linear distinguisher with the bias 2^{-21} to mount full round key recovery attack on SAND-2.

Table 3. Experiments of the iterative linear characteristics.

Round	Theoretical linear bias	Experimental linear bias	Test data
2	2^{-2}	$2^{-2.00}$	2^{26}
4	2^{-3}	$2^{-3.00}$	2^{26}
6	2^{-4}	$2^{-4.00}$	2^{26}
8	2^{-5}	$2^{-4.99}$	2^{26}
16	2^{-9}	$2^{-9.02}$	2^{26}
24	2^{-13}	$2^{-12.91}$	2^{26}
26	2^{-14}	$2^{-13.89}$	2^{28}

---

[3] Note that this trail also has other seven equivalent cases, all these can be used to mount longer distinguishers and key recovery attacks. In the rest of the paper, we will only focus on evaluating one case, but the other seven cases will be similar.

3.2   Differential Distinguishers of SAND-2

Similar to finding linear distinguishers of SAND-2, we now show how to construct iterative differential trails of SAND-2 and then try to approximate differential probability by considering the clustering effect.

We firstly divide the input bits of G_0 (G_1) by its 4-bit output, as shown in Table 4 and Table 5, where the six bit indices of each row is derived from the left branch state X_r and $G_0[3-0]$ represents the lowest nibble of the output of G_0 (similarly for G_1). Then, still by carefully observing the inputs of G_0 and G_1, it has the following property.

Property 2. When all input bit differences of X_r are zero, except the $(4 \times t+3)$-th $(0 \leq t < 8)$ bit, that is $\Delta X_r[4 \times t + 3] = 1$, it then has

- For the $(t-1)$-th[4] nibble of G_0, its input difference is $0b001000$ (binary representation). Then, its possible 4-bit output differences are $0b0000$ with probability $\frac{1}{2}$, $0b0001$ with probability $\frac{1}{4}$ or $0b1001$ with probability $\frac{1}{4}$;
- For the t-th nibble of G_0, its input difference is $0b000001$. Then, its possible 4-bit output differences are $0b0010$ with probability $\frac{1}{2}$ or $0b1010$ with probability $\frac{1}{2}$;
- For the $(t-7)$-th nibble of G_1, its input difference is $0b000100$. Then, its possible 4-bit output differences are $0b0000$ with probability $\frac{1}{2}$, $0b0110$ with probability $\frac{1}{4}$ or $0b0100$ with probability $\frac{1}{4}$;
- For the t-th nibble of G_1, its input difference is $0b001000$, its 4-bit output difference must be $0b0010$.

Table 4. Grouping input bit index of G_0.   **Table 5.** Grouping input bit index of G_1.

Nibbles	Bit index of X_r					
$G_0[3-0]$	13	10	7	6	4	3
$G_0[7-4]$	17	14	11	10	8	7
$G_0[11-8]$	21	18	15	14	12	11
$G_0[15-12]$	25	22	19	18	16	15
$G_0[19-16]$	29	26	23	22	20	19
$G_0[23-20]$	1	30	27	26	24	23
$G_0[27-24]$	5	2	31	30	28	27
$G_0[31-28]$	9	6	3	2	0	31

Nibbles	Bit index of X_r					
$G_1[3-0]$	8	5	3	31	30	29
$G_1[7-4]$	12	9	7	3	2	1
$G_1[11-8]$	16	13	11	7	6	5
$G_1[15-12]$	20	17	15	11	10	9
$G_1[19-16]$	24	21	19	15	14	13
$G_1[23-20]$	28	25	23	19	18	17
$G_1[27-24]$	0	29	27	23	22	21
$G_1[31-28]$	4	1	31	27	26	25

With Property 2, we can easily construct an iterative two-round differential characteristic with probability 2^{-3} as below.

1. Let only the 31-th bit difference ($t = 7$) of the left branch of the input be active, *i.e.*, $\Delta X_r[31] = 1$. All the rest bits of ΔX_r and ΔY_r are set to be zero difference. So, the input difference is $(\Delta X_r, \Delta Y_r) = (0x80000000, 0x00000000)$;

---

[4] For simplicity, the index number of the nibble takes modulo 8.

2. In order to make this trail iterative, according to Property 2, we let the 4-bit output differences of the 6-th nibble of G_0 and the 0-th nibble of G_1 be both zero, and 4-bit output difference of the 7-th nibbles of G_0 be $0b0010$, which then can cancel the difference of the corresponding nibble of G_1;

3. With $\Delta X_{r+1} = 0x00000000$, it leads to the output difference of the second round $(\Delta X_{r+2}, \Delta Y_{r+2}) = (\Delta X_r, \Delta Y_r) = (0x80000000, 0x00000000)$.

For the differential probability of this two-round trail, only the step 2 mentioned above produces the probability 2^{-3}, that is, cancelling all differences at the compression. Thus, this two-round differential trail[5] $(0x80000000, 0x00000000) \rightarrow (0x80000000, 0x00000000)$ has the differential probability 2^{-3} and can start from both even or odd round number.

Approximation of Differential Probabilities. In order to obtain a more accurate differential probability of the iterative based distinguishers for later attacks, we try to approximate the probability of these iterative distinguishers, however, the method we proposed in the following still cannot capture all trails for the given differential, but it can effectively cluster the differential with high probability, which usually dominates the final probability of a differential. We then also use SAT/SMT automatic search method to evaluate the clustering effect, which shows our method is efficient and effective to approximate the probability of such iterative differentials of SAND-2. The following property is firstly introduced, which can be partly derived from Property 2.

Property 3. For one round of SAND-2, it has the following differential characteristics and corresponding probability P:

- $(0x80000000, 0x00000000) \xrightarrow{1-round} (0x00000000, 0x80000000)$, $P = 2^{-3}$;
- $(0x80000000, 0x00000000) \xrightarrow{1-round} (0x80000000, 0x80000000)$, $P = 2^{-3}$;
- $(0x80000000, 0x80000000) \xrightarrow{1-round} (0x00000000, 0x80000000)$, $P = 2^{-3}$;
- $(0x80000000, 0x80000000) \xrightarrow{1-round} (0x80000000, 0x80000000)$, $P = 2^{-3}$;
- $(0x00000000, 0x80000000) \xrightarrow{1-round} (0x80000000, 0x00000000)$, $P = 1$.

We note that the case in Property 3 is also just one of the eight equivalent cases. Based on Property 3, except the above presented two-round iterative trail with probability 2^{-3}, we can also construct an $(m+3)$-round differential trail with probability $2^{-3(m+2)}$ as below:

$$(0x8, 0x0) \rightarrow (0x8, 0x8) \xrightarrow{m-round} (0x8, 0x8) \rightarrow (0x0, 0x8) \rightarrow (0x8, 0x0).$$

With this configurable trail, it may bring us many different characteristics that can be clustered to enhance the final probability. Thus, we provide the following formulas to do such clustering process.

---

[5] Similarly, this trail also has other seven equivalent cases, which can be both used to mount longer distinguishers and key recovery attacks.

Proposition 1. *For a given even number of rounds* $N_r = 2n_r$ $(n_r \in \mathbf{Z}^+)$, *for a fixed probability* $P = 2^{-p}$ $(p \in \mathbf{Z}^+)$, *it has*

$$2j + \sum_{i=0, m_i=i}^{min(N_r-3, \lfloor \frac{p}{3}-2 \rfloor)} (m_i + 3)k_i = N_r,$$

$$3j + \sum_{i=0, m_i=i}^{min(N_r-3, \lfloor \frac{p}{3}-2 \rfloor)} 3(m_i + 2)k_i = p,$$

where j $(0 \le j \le n_r)$ *denotes the iterative times of the two-round iterative differential characteristic and* k_i $(0 \le k_i \le \lfloor \frac{p}{3(m_i+2)} \rfloor)$ *denotes the number of* $(m_i + 3)$-*round iterative differential. We can obtain a set of values for* $(j, k_0, k_1, ...)$ *which denotes the number of different short-round iterative differential characteristic. Then we iterate the position of these short-round iterative differential characteristic, equivalent to calculating a permutation combination number, which corresponds to different trails that can be clustered.*

In order to check whether the method presented above can effectively approximate the probability of longer rounds iterative distinguishers, we also apply the SAT/SMT based search method to do the clustering for 8-round and 16-round iterative differential trails with probability greater than 2^{-30} and match the results clustered by Proposition 1. Then the experiments to compare the theoretical and experimental probabilities are also performed for several distinguishers, which shows the effectiveness of our proposed method and are given in Table 6. It can be observed that these iterative differential trails have slight clustering effect.

Table 6. Experiments of the iterative differentials of SAND-2.

Round	Theoretical probability	Experimental probability	Test data
2	$2^{-3.00}$	$2^{-3.00}$	2^{27}
4	$2^{-5.83}$	$2^{-5.81}$	2^{27}
8	$2^{-11.13}$	$2^{-11.08}$	2^{27}
16	$2^{-21.21}$	$2^{-21.02}$	2^{27}

Distinguishers for Full Round Attacks. With the effective and efficient evaluation method presented above, we then mount 40-round, 42-round and 46-round iterative distinguishers. It should be noted that for such longer rounds, SAT/SMT based method is already very inefficient due to the size of models thus cannot provide tight bounds of the final probability. For the formulas in Proposition 1, we also limit and select part m_i for the calculation considering the efficiency, thus just providing a lower bound of the probability. However, it is still high enough to launch full round attacks and invalidate security bounds given in SAND-2 design paper [10, Table 17].

- For 46-round distinguisher, it has the probability $2^{-58.60}$. When one round is added to its head with probability 1, this can lead to a *full round differential distinguisher* of SAND-2.
- In order to launch *full round key recovery attacks* on SAND-2, we mount a 43-round (extended from 42-round) and a 41-round (extended from 40-round) distinguisher with probability $2^{-53.62}$ and $2^{-51.13}$ respectively.

Remark: In this section, we construct iterative differential and linear distinguishers, which already lead to full round distinguish attacks. Some distinguishers will be later used to mount full round key recovery attacks, and we summarize these distinguishers in Table 7. It should be noted that we only perform experiments on some short rounds distinguishers of SAND-2 due to our inefficient software implementation[6] of SAND-2 and the limited computing resources.

Table 7. Summary of the differential and linear distinguishers of SAND-2.

Type	Distinguisher	Probability	Usage
Linear	$(0x2, 0x0) \xrightarrow{47\text{-round}} (0x0, 0x2)$	2^{-46}	Distinguishing attack
Linear	$(0x2, 0x0) \xrightarrow{41\text{-round}} (0x0, 0x2)$	2^{-40}	Key recovery attack
Differential	$(0x0, 0x8) \xrightarrow{47\text{-round}} (0x8, 0x0)$	$2^{-50.00}$	Distinguishing attack
Differential	$(0x0, 0x8) \xrightarrow{43\text{-round}} (0x8, 0x0)$	$2^{-53.62}$	Key recovery attack
Differential	$(0x0, 0x8) \xrightarrow{41\text{-round}} (0x8, 0x0)$	$2^{-51.13}$	Key recovery attack

4 Key Recovery Attacks on SAND-2

In this section, we give the *full round key recovery attacks* based on the 41-round linear distinguisher and 43-round differential distinguisher presented above. For linear attack, the time, data and memory complexities are $2^{48.23}$ full round encryptions, $2^{45.50}$ known-plaintexts and $2^{35.00}$ respectively. For differential attack, the time, data and memory complexities are $2^{64.10}$ full round encryptions, $2^{60.20}$ chosen-plaintexts and $2^{57.20}$ respectively.

It should be noted that a full round key recovery attack based on 41-round differential distinguisher is also mounted, which has a lower data complexity $2^{53.13}$ but a higher time complexity $2^{73.70}$. Thus, we just list this result in Table 1, which may can be provided in a final full version.

---

[6] Because SAND-2 adopts two different bit permutation layers P_0/P_1 and different round functions in even or odd round.

4.1   Full Round Linear Attack

In the attack, we both append three rounds before and after the 41-round linear distinguisher. The key recovery attack is illustrated in Fig. 7 and Fig. 8, where X_i and Y_i denote the 32-bit input to the left and right branches, $G_0(X_i)$ and $G_1(X_i)$ represent the 32-bit output of function G_0 and G_1 in the i-th round, W_i records the XOR value of output of G_0, G_1 and Y_i in the head(resp. Y_{i+1} in the tail), rk_i stands for the i-th round key and M_i is the XOR value of W_i and rk_i. In the following, we use $X_i[j]$ to represent the j-th bit of X_i and the least significant bit is $X_i[0]$. And the white cell denotes the linear mask of the bit is zero, the yellow cell represents the linear mask of the bit is non-zero, the blue cell denotes the value of the bit should be computed, the red cell represents the subkey bits that are involved in the partial encryption and decryption phases and the sequence numbers represent the order in which the key bits are guessed.

Suppose that the number of required plaintext-ciphertext pairs is N_L. The attack is realised with the following steps.

1. Guess 4-bit subkey value $rk_0[8, 10\text{-}12]$ and allocate a counter $C_1^L[z_1]$ for each of 2^{35} possible values of

$$z_1 = X_{46}[4, 25\text{-}27]||W_0[0, 2, 5, 21\text{-}23, 27\text{-}31]||W_1[4, 25\text{-}27]||$$
$$W_{46}[0, 2, 5, 8, 10\text{-}12, 21\text{-}23, 27\text{-}31]||t_0,$$

where $t_0 = G_0(X_0)[29] \oplus G_1(X_0)[29] \oplus Y_0[29] \oplus G_0(X_{46})[29] \oplus G_1(X_{46})[29] \oplus Y_{47}[29]$. Then, for each possible 4-bit subkey value $rk_0[8, 10\text{-}12]$, we compute the value of z_1 and update $C_1^L[z_1]$ with $C_1^L[z_1] + 1$, thus the dominant time complexity is $N_L \cdot 2^4$ memory accesses to a table with 2^{35} elements.

2. Guess 6-bit subkey value $rk_0[0, 2, 21\text{-}23, 27]$ and allocate a counter $C_2^L[z_2]$ for each of 2^{30} possible values of

$$z_2 = X_{46}[4, 25\text{-}27]||W_0[5, 28\text{-}31]||M_0[27]||W_1[4, 25\text{-}27]||$$
$$W_{46}[0, 2, 5, 8, 10\text{-}12, 21\text{-}23, 27\text{-}31]||t_1,$$

where $t_1 = t_0$ and $M_0[27]$ records the value of $rk_0[27]$. For each possible 6-bit subkey value $rk_0[0, 2, 21\text{-}23, 27]$, we compute the value of z_2 and update $C_2^L[z_2]$ with $C_2^L[z_2] + C_1^L[z_1]$, thus the dominant time complexity of this step is $2^{35} \cdot 2^4 \cdot 2^6 = 2^{45}$ memory accesses to a table with 2^{30} elements.

3. Guess 5-bit subkey value $rk_0[5, 28\text{-}31]$ and allocate a counter $C_3^L[z_3]$ for each of 2^{24} possible values of

$$z_3 = X_{46}[4, 25\text{-}27]||W_1[4, 25\text{-}27]||W_{46}[0, 2, 5, 8, 10\text{-}12, 21\text{-}23, 27\text{-}31]||t_2,$$

where $t_2 = t_1$. For each possible 5-bit subkey value $rk_0[5, 28\text{-}31]$, we compute the value of z_3 and update $C_3^L[z_3]$ with $C_3^L[z_3] + C_2^L[z_2]$, thus the dominant time complexity of this step is $2^{30} \cdot 2^{10} \cdot 2^5 = 2^{45}$ memory accesses to a table with 2^{24} elements.

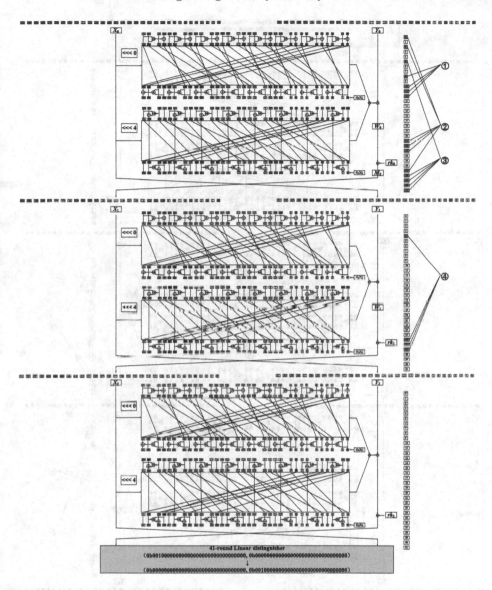

Fig. 7. The head of Linear key recovery attack on full round SAND-2.

4. Guess 4-bit subkey value $rk_1[4, 25\text{-}27]$ and allocate a counter $C_4^L[z_4]$ for each of 2^{20} possible values of

$$z_4 = X_{46}[4, 25\text{-}27]||W_{46}[0, 2, 5, 8, 10\text{-}12, 21\text{-}23, 27\text{-}31]||t_3,$$

where $t_3 = t_2 \oplus G_1(X_2)[29]$. For each possible 4-bit subkey value $rk_1[4, 25\text{-}27]$, we compute the value of z_3 and update $C_4^L[z_4]$ with $C_4^L[z_4] +$

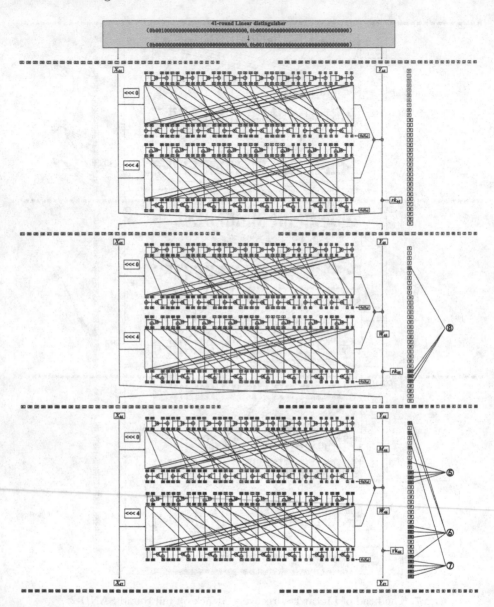

Fig. 8. The tail of Linear key recovery attack on full round SAND-2.

$C_3^L[z_3]$. The dominant time complexity of this step is $2^{24} \cdot 2^{15} \cdot 2^4 = 2^{43}$ memory accesses to a table with 2^{20} elements.

5. Guess 4-bit subkey value $rk_{46}[8, 10\text{-}12]$ and allocate a counter $C_5^L[z_5]$ for each of 2^{16} possible values of

$$z_5 = W_{46}[0, 2, 5, 21\text{-}23, 27\text{-}31] || W_{45}[4, 25\text{-}27] || t_4,$$

where $t_4 = t_3$. For each possible 4-bit subkey value $rk_{46}[8, 10\text{-}12]$, we compute the value of z_5 and update $C_5^L[z_5]$ with $C_5^L[z_5] + C_4^L[z_4]$. The dominant time complexity of this step is $2^{20} \cdot 2^{19} \cdot 2^4 = 2^{43}$ memory accesses to a table with 2^{16} elements.

6. Guess 6-bit subkey value $rk_{46}[0, 2, 21\text{-}23, 27]$ and allocate a counter $C_6^L[z_6]$ for each of 2^{11} possible values of

$$z_6 = W_{46}[5, 28\text{-}31] || M_{46}[27] || W_{45}[4, 25\text{-}27] || t_5,$$

where $t_5 = t_4$. For each possible 6-bit subkey value $rk_{46}[0, 2, 21\text{-}23, 27]$, we compute the value of z_6 and update $C_6^L[z_6]$ with $C_6^L[z_6] + C_5^L[z_5]$. The dominant time complexity of this step is $2^{16} \cdot 2^{23} \cdot 2^6 = 2^{45}$ memory accesses to a table with 2^{11} elements.

7. Guess 5-bit subkey value $rk_{46}[5, 28\text{-}31]$ and allocate a counter $C_7^L[z_7]$ for each of 2^5 possible values of

$$z_7 = W_{45}[4, 25\text{-}27] || t_6,$$

where $t_6 = t_5$. For each possible 5-bit subkey value $rk_{46}[5, 28\text{-}31]$, we compute the value of z_7 and update $C_7^L[z_7]$ with $C_7^L[z_7] + C_6^L[z_6]$. The number of memory accesses in this step is $2^{11} \cdot 2^{20} \cdot 2^5 = 2^{45}$.

8. Guess 4-bit subkey value $rk_{45}[4, 25\text{-}27]$ and initialize a counter $Counter_L$. Then compute the value of $t_7 = t_6 \oplus G_1(X_{44})[29]$ for each possible 4-bit subkey value $rk_{45}[4, 25\text{-}27]$. If $t_7 = 0$, we update $Counter_L$ with $Counter_L + C_7^L[z_7]$. The number of memory accesses in this step is $2^5 \cdot 2^{34} \cdot 2^4 = 2^{43}$.

9. The key guess will be accepted as a candidate if the counter $Counter_L$ satisfies $|Counter_L/N_L - 0.5| > \tau_L$, where τ_L is the threshold used in [16].

10. As mentioned above, the mask "2" of linear distinguisher can be placed in the remaining 7 position. Thus we can use three of them to recover key. Each distinguisher involves 38-bit key and can recover 84 bits when considering them together (30 bits are overlapped), which are shown in the Table 8.

11. Then do exhaustive search for all keys that correspond to the guessed 84-bit subkey bits against a maximum of two plaintext-ciphertext pairs.

Complexity Analysis. As we leave 2^{16} candidates, that means the advantage [14] of the attack as $a = 22$. For three distinguishers, there are a total of $2^{16} \cdot 2^{16} \cdot 2^{16}$ candidate keys remaining. Then we set the number of pairs N_L as $2^{45.5}$, so the data complexity of this attack is $2^{45.5}$. And according to [15], we consider one memory access as a half round encryption. So, the time complexity of this attack can be computed as follows.

$$3 \times (N_L \cdot 2^4 + 2^{45} \times 4 + 2^{43} \times 3) \times \frac{1}{2} \times \frac{1}{47} + ((2^{16})^3 + 2^{128-84}) \times (1 + 2^{-64}),$$

where $((2^{16})^3 + 2^{128-84}) \times (1 + 2^{-64})$ denotes the time complexity of step 11. Then, the time complexity of the attack is about $2^{48.23}$ full round encryptions.

Table 8. Key bits involved in the 41-round distinguishers.

Distinguisher	Key bits involved in the distinguisher	All 84-bit key
(0x20000000,0x00000000) ↓ (0x00000000,0x20000000)	$rk_0[0, 2, 5, 8, 10\text{-}12, 21\text{-}23, 27\text{-}31]$ $rk_{46}[0, 2, 5, 8, 10\text{-}12, 21\text{-}23, 27\text{-}31]$ $rk_1[4, 25\text{-}27]$ $rk_{45}[4, 25\text{-}27]$	rk_0 [0-8, 10-15, 17-31] rk_{46} [0-8, 10-15, 17-31] $rk_1[0, 4, 17\text{-}19$ 21-23, 25-28] $rk_{45}[0, 4, 17\text{-}19$ 21-23, 25-28]
(0x02000000,0x00000000) ↓ (0x00000000,0x02000000)	$rk_0[1, 4, 6\text{-}8, 17\text{-}19, 23\text{-}28, 30]$ $rk_{46}[1, 4, 6\text{-}8, 17\text{-}19, 23\text{-}28, 30]$ $rk_1[0, 21\text{-}23]$ $rk_{45}[0, 21\text{-}23]$	
(0x00200000,0x00000000) ↓ (0x00000000,0x00200000)	$rk_0[0, 2\text{-}4, 13\text{-}15, 19\text{-}24, 26, 29]$ $rk_{46}[0, 2\text{-}4, 13\text{-}15, 19\text{-}24, 26, 29]$ $rk_1[17\text{-}19, 28]$ $rk_{45}[17\text{-}19, 28]$	

$C_1^L[z_1]$ dominates the memory complexity which is roughly 2^{35}. We calculate the success probability by the following formula in [7]:

$$P_s \approx \Phi\Big(\frac{c \cdot \sqrt{N_L} - \Phi^{-1}(1 - 2^{-(a+1)}) \cdot \sqrt{1 + N_L \cdot 2^{-n}}}{\sqrt{1 + N_L \cdot (ELP - c^2)}}\Big),$$

where $\Phi(\cdot)$ is the normal distribution and n is block size. The variable c denotes the approximation of the absolute value of the correlation related to the dominant linear characteristic and the expected linear potential, denoted as ELP, of the approximation is calculated as the sum of squared correlations across all characteristics associated with it. In our attack, $ELP = c^2$, thus the success probability for one such attack is $P_s = 94.07\%$ and $(94.07\%)^3 = 83.24\%$.

4.2 Full Round Differential Attack

In the attack, we both append two rounds before and after the 43-round distinguisher. The key recovery attack is illustrated in Fig. 9, where the white cell denotes the difference of the bit is zero, the yellow cell represents the difference of the bit is non-zero, the blue cell denotes the difference of the bit can be zero or non-zero and the red cell represents the value of the bit needs to be computed for the intermediate states and for the round key that denotes being guessed.

Data Collection. We can construct structures at the position of (X_0, Y_0). In each structure, the 43 bits

$$X_0[0, 3\text{-}23, 25\text{-}26, 28\text{-}30]\|Y_0[0, 3\text{-}4, 7\text{-}15, 18\text{-}19, 21\text{-}22]$$

with the difference being zero in Fig. 9 are fixed, and the value of the remaining 21 bits are traversed. Thus, 2^{41} pairs can be generated with one structure composed of 2^{21} plaintexts.

Key Recovery. In the attack, we prepare N_s structures and obtain $N_1 = N_s \cdot 2^{41}$ pairs. Thus, the data complexity of the attack is $N_s \cdot 2^{21}$. The detailed

Table 9. Conditions for key recovery and filter probabilities on SAND-2.

Condition	Filter	Probability
(C1)	$\Delta X_{47}[0, 3\text{-}23, 25\text{-}26, 28\text{-}30] \| \Delta Y_{47}[0, 3\text{-}4, 7\text{-}15, 18\text{-}19, 21\text{-}22] = 0$	2^{-43}
(C2)	$\Delta X_1[1\text{-}2, 5\text{-}6, 16\text{-}17, 20, 23\text{-}30] = 0, \Delta X_1[31] = 1$	2^{-16}
(C3)	$\Delta Y_{46}[1\text{-}2, 5\text{-}6, 16\text{-}17, 20, 23\text{-}30] = 0, \Delta Y_{46}[31] = 1$	2^{-16}
(C4)	$\Delta X_2[1\text{-}2, 24, 27, 31] = 0$	2^{-5}
(C5)	$\Delta Y_{45}[1\text{-}2, 24, 27, 31] = 0$	2^{-5}

attack is realised with the following steps and we list all filter conditions in Table 9.

1. For each pair $P = (X_0, Y_0)$ and $P' = (X_0', Y_0')$, we obtain the corresponding values of the ciphertexts $C = (X_{47}, Y_{47})$ and $C' = (X_{47}', Y_{47}')$ by querying the oracle. The time complexity of this step is $N_s \cdot 2^{21}$ full round encryptions.
2. Denoising over ciphertexts: the 43 bits of ciphertexts with the difference being zero and check the condition (C1), $N_1 \cdot 2^{-43}$ pairs will be left;
3. For each pair $P = (X_0, Y_0)$ and $P' = (X_0', Y_0')$, we first calculate $\Delta X_1 = X_1 \oplus X_1'$ without guessing any key bits and check the condition (C2), then $N_1 \cdot 2^{-43} \cdot 2^{-16}$ pairs will be left. This step involves 18 S-box operation, thus the time complexity is $2 \cdot N_1 \cdot 2^{-43} \times 18 \times 1/32 \times 1/47$ full round encryptions.
4. For each pair $C = (X_{47}, Y_{47})$ and $C' = (X_{47}', Y_{47}')$, we can calculate ΔY_{46} without guessing key bits and check the condition (C3), then $N_1 \cdot 2^{-43} \cdot 2^{-16} \cdot 2^{-16}$ pairs will be left. Similarly, this step involves 18 S-box operation, thus the time complexity is $2 \cdot N_1 \cdot 2^{-43} \cdot 2^{-16} \times 18 \times 1/32 \times 1/47$ full round encryptions.
5. Guess 7 bits of rk_0. We can compute $X_2[1\text{-}2, 24, 27, 31]$ and $X_2'[1\text{-}2, 24, 27, 31]$ for each possible 7-bit subkey value $rk_0[0, 2\text{-}3, 8, 27, 29\text{-}30]$ and check the condition (C4), then $N_1 \cdot 2^{-43} \cdot 2^{-16} \cdot 2^{-16} \cdot 2^{-5}$ pairs will be left. This step involves 6 S-box operation, thus the time complexity is $2 \cdot N_1 \cdot 2^{-43} \cdot 2^{-16} \cdot 2^{-16} \cdot 2^7 \times 6 \times 1/32 \times 1/47$ full round encryptions.
6. Guess 7 bits of rk_{46}. We can compute $\Delta Y_{45}[1\text{-}2, 24, 27, 31]$ for each possible 7-bit subkey value $rk_{46}[0, 2\text{-}3, 8, 27, 29\text{-}30]$ and check the condition (C5), then $N_1 \cdot 2^{-43} \cdot 2^{-16} \cdot 2^{-16} \cdot 2^{-5} \cdot 2^{-5}$ pairs will be left. Similarly, the time complexity is $2 \cdot N_1 \cdot 2^{-43} \cdot 2^{-16} \cdot 2^{-16} \cdot 2^{-5} \cdot 2^7 \times 6 \times 1/32 \times 1/47$ full round encryptions.
7. As mentioned above, the difference "8" of Differential distinguisher can be placed in the remaining 7 position. Thus we can use all of them to recover key. Each distinguisher involves the 14-bit key, and the all can recover a total of 64 bits which cover exactly rk_0 and rk_{46}.
8. Then do exhaustive search for all keys which correspond to the guessed 64-bit subkey bits against a maximum of two plaintext-ciphertext pairs.

Complexity Analysis. We set a counter to record the number of right pairs that validate the input and output differences of the 43-round distinguisher. With the analysis above, for random key guesses, the number of right pairs is

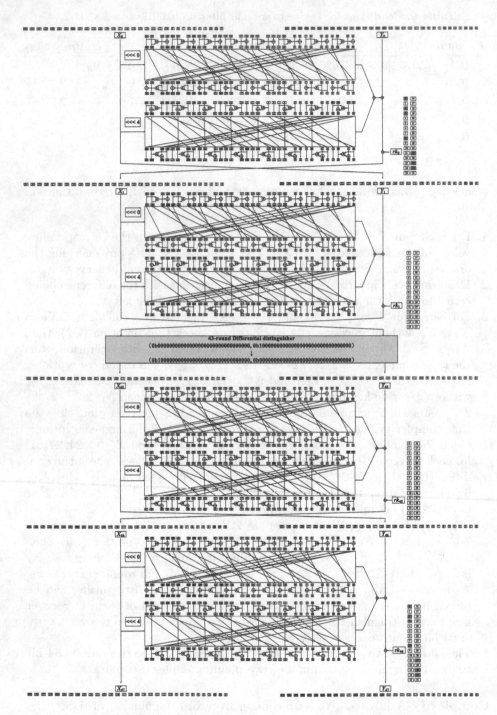

Fig. 9. Differential key recovery attack on full round SAND-2.

about $N_1 \cdot 2^{-85}$. For the right key guess, the number of right pairs is expected to be $N_1 \cdot 2^{-21} \cdot 2^{-53.62}$, where 2^{-21} is the probability of the difference of plaintext to the head of the distinguisher and $2^{-53.62}$ is the probability of the distinguisher. In order to get higher success probability we set the number of right pair μ is 6 and the signal-to-noise ratio $S_N = \frac{N_1 \cdot 2^{-21} \cdot 2^{-53.62}}{N_1 \cdot 2^{-85}} = 2^{10.38}$. So the pairs N_1 is $2^{77.20}$ and corresponding N_s is $2^{36.20}$. For eight distinguishers, the data requirement of the attack is $8 \times 2^{36.20} \cdot 2^{21} = 2^{60.20}$ chosen plaintexts. As we leave only one best candidate, that means advantage a is 14. So the time complexity of this attack can be computed as follows.

$$8 \times (2^{36.20} \cdot 2^{21} + N_1 \cdot 2^{-42.97}) + (1 + 2^{64}) \times (1 + 2^{-64}),$$

where $(1 + 2^{64}) \times (1 + 2^{-64})$ denotes the time complexity of step 8. Then, the time complexity of this attack is about $2^{64.10}$ full round encryptions. We calculate the success probability by the following formula in [14]:

$$P_s = \Phi\left(\frac{\sqrt{\mu S_N} - \Phi^{-1}(1 - 2^{-a})}{\sqrt{S_N + 1}}\right),$$

thus the success probability for one such attack is $P_s = 99.04\%$ and $(99.04\%)^8 = 92.61\%$ for the whole attack. Since we should record the right pairs, the memory complexity of this attack is roughly $2^{57.20}$.

5   Conclusion

In this paper, we present full round distinguishing and key recovery attacks on lightweight block cipher SAND-2 in single-key setting. Our attacks exploit iterative distinguishers with high probability (*e.g.*, the time complexities of linear distinguishing and key recovery attacks are both even lower than 2^{50}), which are derived from the dependencies of the round function of SAND-2. Moreover, we believe that our attacks provide the insight for designers about the importance of applying extensive and in-depth security analysis under designers' responsibility.

Acknowledgments. We sincerely thank the anonymous reviewers for providing valuable comments to help us improve the overall quality of the paper. This work is supported by the National Key Research and Development Program of China (Grant No. 2018YFA0704702 & 2022YFB2701700), the National Natural Science Foundation of China (Grant No. 62032014), the Shandong Provincial Natural Science Foundation (Grant No. ZR2020MF053), the Major Basic Research Project of Natural Science Foundation of Shandong Province (Grant No. ZR202010220025), Department of Science & Technology of Shandong Province (Grant No. SYS202201), and Quan Cheng Laboratory (Grant No. QCLZD202306).

References

1. Ankele, R., Kölbl, S.: Mind the gap - a closer look at the security of block ciphers against differential cryptanalysis. In: Cid, C., Jacobson, M., Jr. (eds.) Selected Areas in Cryptography - SAC 2018. LNCS, vol. 11349, pp. 163–190. Springer, Cham (2018). https://doi.org/10.1007/978-3-030-10970-7_8

2. Bansod, G., Patil, A., Sutar, S., Pisharoty, N.: ANU: an ultra lightweight cipher design for security in IoT. Secur. Commun. Netw. **9**(18), 5238–5251 (2016)
3. Beaulieu, R., Shors, D., Smith, J., Treatman-Clark, S., Weeks, B., Wingers, L.: The SIMON and SPECK families of lightweight block ciphers. IACR Cryptol. ePrint Arch., p. 404 (2013)
4. Beierle, C., et al.: The SKINNY family of block ciphers and its low-latency variant MANTIS. In: Robshaw, M., Katz, J. (eds.) CRYPTO 2016, Part II. LNCS, vol. 9815, pp. 123–153. Springer, Heidelberg (2016). https://doi.org/10.1007/978-3-662-53008-5_5
5. Biham, E.: New types of cryptanalytic attacks using related keys. J. Cryptology **7**(4), 229–246 (1994)
6. Biham, E., Shamir, A.: Differential cryptanalysis of des-like cryptosystems. J. Cryptology **4**(1), 3–72 (1991)
7. Blondeau, C., Nyberg, K.: Joint data and key distribution of simple, multiple, and multidimensional linear cryptanalysis test statistic and its impact to data complexity. Des. Codes Cryptogr. **82**(1–2), 319–349 (2017)
8. Chen, S., Fan, Y., Fu, Y., Huang, L., Wang, M.: On the design of ant family block ciphers. J. Cryptol. Res. **6**(6), 748 (2019)
9. Chen, S., et al.: SAND: an AND-RX Feistel lightweight block cipher supporting S-box-based security evaluations. Des. Codes Cryptogr. **90**(1), 155–198 (2022)
10. Chen, W., Li, L., Guo, Y., Huang, Y.: SAND-2: an optimized implementation of lightweight block cipher. Integr. **91**, 23–34 (2023)
11. Knudsen, L.R.: Cryptanalysis of LOKI. In: Imai, H., Rivest, R.L., Matsumoto, T. (eds.) ASIACRYPT 1991. LNCS, vol. 739, pp. 22–35. Springer, Heidelberg (1993). https://doi.org/10.1007/3-540-57332-1_2
12. Matsui, M.: Linear cryptanalysis method for DES cipher. In: Helleseth, T. (ed.) EUROCRYPT 1993. LNCS, vol. 765, pp. 386–397. Springer, Heidelberg (1994). https://doi.org/10.1007/3-540-48285-7_33
13. Sasaki, Yu.: Related-key boomerang attacks on full ANU lightweight block cipher. In: Preneel, B., Vercauteren, F. (eds.) ACNS 2018. LNCS, vol. 10892, pp. 421–439. Springer, Cham (2018). https://doi.org/10.1007/978-3-319-93387-0_22
14. Selçuk, A.A.: On probability of success in linear and differential cryptanalysis. J. Cryptol. **21**(1), 131–147 (2008)
15. Soleimany, H., Nyberg, K.: Zero-correlation linear cryptanalysis of reduced-round Lblock. Des. Codes Cryptogr. **73**(2), 683–698 (2014)
16. Sun, L., Wang, W., Wang, M.: Improved attacks on GIFT-64. In: AlTawy, R., Hülsing, A. (eds.) SAC 2021. LNCS, vol. 13203, pp. 246–265. Springer, Cham (2022). https://doi.org/10.1007/978-3-030-99277-4_12

Real-Time Symbolic Reasoning Framework for Cryptojacking Detection Based on Netflow-Plus Analysis

Zhen Yang[1,2](✉), Jing Li[1,2], Fei Cui[3], Jia Qi Liu[4], Yu Cheng[2], Xi Nan Tang[4], and Shuai Gui[4]

[1] School of Computer Science and Technology, University of Science and Technology of China, Hefei, Anhui, China
yangzhen007@mail.ustc.edu.cn
[2] Anhui Province Key Laboratory of Cyberspace Security Situation Awareness and Evaluation, Hefei, Anhui, China
[3] Hangzhou Eastcom Network Technology Co., Ltd., Hangzhou, China
[4] Nanjing Yunlilai Software Technology Co., Ltd., Nanjing, China

Abstract. Cryptojacking is a cybersecurity threat in which cybercriminals use unauthorized computing resources for cryptocurrency mining. This kind of illegal activity is showing an intensifying trend when cryptocurrency becomes widely acceptable. However, the machine learning (ML) based detection approaches cannot be applied in real-time yet due to low performance.

First, compared with domain experts the ML researchers have a tendency to extend feature set with statistical functions, which are very computational heavy. Second, in network security research analyzed metadata are hardly collected if the targeted traffic is a kind of *mice-flow* (1–2% of total traffic). *Netflow* is a sampling technique and statistically it cannot be applied in such a case. Third, the ML community usually *ignores* data *preprocessing* costs which may take more time than the inference itself. These three types of fundamental weakness prevent the ML based detection algorithms from being applied to a large network in *real-time*.

We propose a novel *symbolic reasoning* framework to accurately detect such illegal cryptojacking in real-time. To deal with *mice-flows*, *Netflow-plus* traffic analyzing technique is proposed to compute TCP *metadata* using a *parallel* protocol parser in which every TCP flow is analyzed but the TCP payload. High performance is maintained by only addition based aggregation is allowed. Feature set selection is done by domain experts without using any STD and VAR statistic functions. Building upon the aforementioned foundations, a symbolic reasoning frame is designed to capture cryptojacking activities based on a behavior model. A series of Boolean-expression based filters is applied first to significantly reduce solution search space by three orders of magnitude. The fixed-packet-length communication behavior of *Stratum* protocol is then model by using linear *diophantine* equations. Since Stratum is predominantly used in cryptojacking, detection Stratum equals to finding out cryptojacking. By combining Netflow-plus traffic analysis and symbolic reasoning framework our system can deal with not only clear-text but encrypted traffic, and it achieved satisfactory detection results in a large campus network in real-time.

Keywords: cryptomining · cryptojacking · anomaly detection · network traffic analysis · network security

1   Introduction

Cryptojacking is an illegal activity in which cybercriminals steal user's computing resources for cryptocurrency mining operations and obtain benefits without the user's consent. In cryptojacking the cybercriminals could get very lucrative returns by avoiding to pay for expensive mining hardware and high electricity bills. The more computing machines are infected and the longer they are used for mining, the more profit the cybercriminal can make. Therefore, detecting such illegal activities in real-time can not only prevent economic loss in time but stop potential collateral damage caused by being hacked.

There are two general detection approaches to monitor abnormal cryptocurrency mining activities. The first is the host based approach in which CPU, Memory, OS, and Browser's activities are closely monitored to detect each host's mining behaviour [7]. The second is network based [3] in which the network traffic is analyzed to detect mining communication behaviour. Since the network based approach is of easy deployment, easy management, and non-intrusive, it is preferred in practice for a large enterprise network consisting of tens of thousands of IP addresses. Furthermore, since the pool mining is widely used, the miners and the pool server have to use a network protocol to communicate. In practice, Stratum is the default communication protocol [15] used in the mining community and almost every cryptocurrency builds various applications on top of it. Therefore, it is more efficient to detect Stratum protocol usage than to detect other mining activities and we will rely on network traffic analysis to detect Stratum communication protocol.

The detection studies of cryptocurrency mining activity focus on various machine learning (ML) algorithms in which training data are usually collected by the Netflow sampling approach [9,12,16].

First, from a domain expert's point of view the feature set selection in ML is kind of *arbitrary* and *complex*. The ML researchers normally use advanced statistic function such as STD (Standard Deviation) and VAR (Variance) to make *artificial* attributes. For example, from packet length they derive AVE (length), VAR (length) and STD (length), and then add them into the feature set. However such derived statistic features are of computational heavy. Using them frequently makes the analysis unable to reach real-time performance.

Second, the data are statistically hardly to be collected in a 10 Gbps *thick* port if any *sampling* approach is used for a *mice-flow* (1–2% of total traffic).

This makes the ML approach only applied to a simple LAN environment in which traffic is small and 100% sampling is possible.

Third, a ML approach actually spends most of time in data *preprocessing* such as combining two-way Netflow TCP flows into one TCP connection. In general a data preprocessing task takes more time than the inference itself.

These three types of weakness make the ML detection algorithms run inefficiently, and thus they can only be applied to *off-line* analysis. A better approach is needed to make detecting cryptojacking accurately in real-time.

The main contributions of this paper are as follows:

- We design a *Netflow-plus*, simply $Netflow+$, traffic analysis to calculate TCP metadata using more fine-grained per-flow analysis than *Netflow* sampling approach. Unlike DPI (*Deep Packet Inspection*), $Netflow+$ skips to inspect TCP payload for improving analytic performance. And it is designed for high-performance in which only amortized $O(1)$ aggregation is allowed to reduce computation overhead. Thus, $Netflow+$ can be very effective in handling *mice-flow* traffic.
- We use symbolic reasoning to capture cryptojacking behaviour. The Boolean expression based filtering processing is designed to make solution space smaller after each pipelined filtering stage. In the meantime *aggregation* and *sorting* analytic are effectively applied to further reduce the TCP metadata. Most importantly the feature selection relies on domain expert's input [2] and the minimal feature set is used in order to reduce computational overhead. In star contrast to the ML approach there is neither STD nor VAR derived features used in our symbolic reasoning framework. In doing so, the computational cost is further reduced.
- We build an analytic behaviour model using a set of linear *diophantine* equations for capturing the fixed-packet-length characteristics of *Stratum* protocol that is widely and dominantly used in cryptocurrency mining communication. By eliminating the impact of TCP retransmission, we have reduced the number of unknown variables in the equation, resulting in a faster equation solving speed.

The rest of the paper is organized as follows. Section 2 discusses related work. Section 3 gives problem statement. Section 4 defines Netflow-plus analysis and describes Boolean expression based filters. Section 5 uses *diophantine* equations to characterize the packet-fixed-length of Stratum protocol communication. Section 6 shows our experimental results. Section 7 discusses the interference of noisy traffic. Section 8 concludes.

2   Related Work

Detection of cryptocurrency mining activity has aroused the research community interest since the Bitcoin became popular [9,12,16]. The host based approach focuses on collecting data on each host by analyzing the behavior characteristics of illegal mining. Such detection approach, however, requires a proxy to be installed on each host, which is only the first step. Maintenance in the future requires more effort, making it expensive and unsuitable for large networks. Therefore, we prefer to use a non-intrusive approach for detecting cryptojacking behavior through network traffic analysis, which is easy to install and manage. Cryptojacking detection is a traffic classification problem, for which pattern-based IDS (Intrusion Detection System) has been used for quite some time. However, due to reasons such as increasing encryption of payloads, pattern-based methods are becoming increasingly unsuitable for detecting cryptojacking.

Recently machine learning (ML) is introduced to compensate the IDS weakness by focusing on network behaviour analysis. In order to better illustrate the differences between our work and previous research, we summarize the characteristics of each in Table 1.

Table 1. Related work comparison

Approach	Classification	Data Collection
Muoz [12]	ML	NetFlow/IPFIX
Pastor [14]	ML+Deep Learning	Modified Tstat
Gomes [8]	Unsupervised ML	CICFlowmeter
Hu [9]	ML	Not mentioned
Russo [16]	ML+preprocessing	Netflow
Netflow+	Symbolic Reasoning	Parallel Parser

Muoz [12] proposed to monitor the mining communication protocol in which only 8 traffic features are used through the ML based classification. However, it does not deal with the encrypted traffic, nor does it consider the interference of other noises that exist widely in a real network environment. Pastor's [14] modified Tstat tool to handle the encrypted traffic but the feature set size is expanded to 51, and thus it used more complex models to detect encrypted mining traffic. Gomes [8] created an artificial hybrid data set that leverages both host and traffic features to detect mining activity through unsupervised machine learning algorithms. The extraction of traffic feature is through the open source tool Cicflowmeter [11]. However, this tool is unstable yet and cannot handle the high traffic data. Hu's [9] work focuses on extracting network traffic features from the first four packets of a flow, and then uses ML methods to detect the cryptojacking traffic. Only Bitcoin detection was implemented and the high cost of analyzing the first four packets in a large network environment is not mentioned.

Most relevant work to ours is Russo [16], in which it lists 100+ references. Interested readers are referred to its bibliographic section for more background coverage. Russo's contributions are as shown below.

First, it promoted one-class ML classifier to detect communication behaviour using the Stratum protocol. Since it does not consider other types of traffic noises, it may have high false-positive in practice. Even though it only detects one network protocol, it is still an *off-line* algorithm due to the high cost of ML detection algorithm.

Second, it used Netflow approach to collect *mice-flow* mining traffic. However, it sets the Netflow's sampling rate to 100%. Firstly, this is not a common practice used by most network operators [4]. Secondly, it exceeds the performance capabilities of most switch hardware.

Third, it recognized the importance of data pre-processing and introduced the *speculative reconstruction* method to clean up the data. I.e., the 2-way Netflow records are combined into one TCP-connection to facilitate the later ML algorithm's processing. However, our experiences indicate that the cost of speculative reconstruction is far more than that of the ML based detection. Therefore, in terms of performance, enhancing ML detection algorithms may have detrimental effect if the preprocessing step is not significantly improved.

Fourth, it collected a total of 500-million TCP flows in a month. However, this amount of traffic is dwarfed by our data collection in one day, in which 3.4-billion TCP collections (2-way TCP flows) were collected on a campus network.

In summary, the ML based detection is still far from the real-time processing in terms of performance. A better detection algorithm is needed in practice.

3   Problem Statement

Our work focuses on developing a high-performance detection frameworks in real time. First, we notice there are two dilemmas in the existing ML detection algorithms: *data collection* and *data preprocessing* [10].

On the one hand, data collection for mice-flow traffic (1–2% of total traffic) is hard to get and a better scheme than Netflow is required in practice. Netflow is indeed a sampling-based data collection method. However, if the sampling rate is set below 100%, such as 1 out of 100 (typically used in practice), any mice-flow traffic will be normally skipped and network traffic-based detection will be failed badly [1]. If the sampling rate is set to 100%, the needed processing power is prohibitively expensive and beyond hardware capability of most switches, and thus it is not recommended in practice.

On the other hand, data pre-processing is the most important and time-consuming step in any ML detection algorithm and its cost is much higher than the inference step itself. It is more profitable to improve data preprocessing efficiency than to enhance an ML detection algorithm in terms of real-time processing.

Therefore, we design a symbolic reasoning framework to address:

- data collection and preprocessing: *Netflow+* is a *parallel* protocol parser for computing the TCP metadata (features) by performing network traffic analysis, in which it takes live traffic as input and outputs TCP metadata as shown in Fig. 1. *Netflow+* is designed to address the two dilemmas, in which TCP per-flow analysis can capture *mice-flow* and most of the data preprocessing tasks are performed by the parser at runtime [19].

– symbolic filtering: the Boolean expression based filters are applied to reduce search space. This filtering process is performed on top of the *structured* TCP metadata and outputs qualified TCP connections, which are described in: source IP (SIP), destination IP (DIP), destination port (Dport), Bytes, Packets, Flows, and TCP retransmission, etc. The filtering process is performed by a modified open-source tool Nfdump [13].

– behavior analytic model: a set of linear *diophantine* equations are derived based on the remaining TCP connections, and an *integer* solution is searched to capture the fixed-packet-length communication behavior of the Stratum protocol, which is dominantly used in cryptocurrency mining.

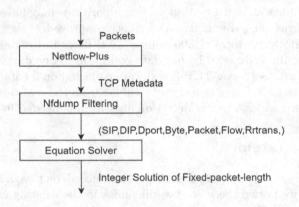

Fig. 1. Framework for detection cryptocurrency mining

In contrast to other ML algorithms, our framework is of high-performance in design:

– the three stages described in Fig. 1 can run in parallel to exploit the multi-core scale-up feature;
– high-performance design carries over to all three stages:
  1. in $Netflow+$ analysis: (1) the TCP payload is avoided to speed up traffic analysis; (2) only amortized $O(1)$ addition aggregation is allowed to further reduce computation cost;
  2. in feature selection, neither STD nor VAR is allowed for the minimized feature set;
  3. in the filtering process, a RB tree is used in Nfdump to speed up Boolean expression evaluation;
  4. in building *diophantine* equations, a dimensional reduction technique is applied to use fewer variables to reduce the equation's search space.

Furthermore, such a framework can be implemented by *one* server through the CPU-core *affinity* optimization technique. Therefore it can be easily deployed in a large network environment to process high-volume traffic in real time.

4   Netflow-Plus Traffic Analysis

4.1   Netflow-Plus for High-Performance

To overcome the Netflow shortcomings and avoid performing computational heavy operations in the DPI analysis, we propose a new Netflow-plus traffic analysis technique.

We define $Netflow+$ as the following:

- it is the same as Netflow but the sampling rate is set at 100%. Since sampling at the rate of 100% is beyond most of the switch's capability, the traffic could be mirrored out and then a parallel protocol parser is applied to analyze the mirrored traffic. The parallelizing techniques for such a parallel parser is beyond the scope of this paper and interested readers can refer to [5,18,19] for details;
- it is unlike DPI and it does not inspect the TCP payload;
- it is an extension to Netflow by computing:
  1. accumulated counters of the TCP flags such as total SYN/ACK/PSH/ FIN bits seen per TCP flow;
  2. the TCP retransmission packets;
  3. the TCP keep-alive packets;
  4. the TCP connections by combining two related TCP flows into one TCP connection by default;
  5. the TCP long connections that last more than 360-s.

First, please note that $Netflow+$ is a per-flow analysis due to 100% sampling. Therefore, it can handle *mice-flow* traffic such as in Stratum communication if computation is fast enough. And the TCP payload is actually skipped to reduce computation cost. It is designed for high performance and aggregations with only an amortized $O(1)$ complexity per packet is allowed. For instance, packet aggregation analysis allows only *addition* (1-cycle) but *division* (tens of cycles). However, the *average* operation is allowed for an entire TCP connection because a division is only used once per TCP connection, and thus its amortized per packet cost is still $O(1)$. Second, the 5-extensions listed above are designed to facilitate detecting Stratum communication in which certain packets have fixed packet lengths and the keep-alive packets are widely used in Stratum communication. Third, by combing related two TCP flows into one TCP connection in traffic analysis it can perform such preprocessing task efficiently and simplify future efforts in modeling Stratum communication.

The $Netflow+$ analysis stage is implemented by modifying a parallel TCP/IP protocol parser written in C, in which all main protocols such as TCP/UDP/DNS are analyzed [19]. If it were tailed for Stratum protocol alone, higher performance could be achieved [18].

The advantages of $Netflow+$ are as follows:

- To capture mice-flow, it requires 100% sampling of Netflow analysis. Otherwise, the analyzed results are inaccurate; Therefore, per-flow analysis is a must requirement in modeling Stratum communication;

- data preprocessing takes a significant amount of time in any big data analysis including in ML. By exploiting TCP flow-based parallelism and parallelizing data preprocessing operations, it opens a door to detect Stratum communication in real time;
- TCP flags seen in a TCP connection are aggregated to facilitate filtering of required TCP long connection. Since only operations with amortized $O(1)$ complexity are allowed, they can runs very efficiently.

4.2 Feature Selection

Table 2. TCP feature set for Stratum detection

Name	Description
In byte	bytes observed from client to sever
Out byte	bytes observed from sever to client
In packet	total packets observed from client to sever
Out packet	total packets observed from sever to client
Psh_in	packets with PSH flag sent by the client
Psh_out	packets with PSH flag sent by the sever
Ack_in	packets with ACK flag sent by the client
Ack_out	packets with ACK flag sent by the sever

The TCP features listed in Table 2 is used in our analysis in which PSH/ACK are TCP header flags and they cannot be obtained by Netflow analysis. Please note that all features can be computed at the transport layer, and encryption technologies such as TLS will not affect $Netflow+$ to compute these features. Only addition is used in the feature aggregation and thus their amortized computation cost is of $O(1)$. Neither statistic function STD nor VAR is used in our feature set to further reduce its size.

To the best of our knowledge, this feature set is the minimal in Stratum protocol detection since no single statistic derived feature is included in our feature set. Meanwhile, since IPv6 does not affect the TCP flags, our feature set is also applicable to IPv6 traffic.

4.3 Pipelined Filtering Process

The real network environment is full of various and yet noise traffic, and we cannot directly apply an analytic model to the noise traffic. In Fig. 1, a filtering process is designed to reduce the traffic to an acceptable level. In order to filter out traffic as much as possible, this section discusses several conditions for identifying mining traffic. The effectiveness of the filtering process will be reported in Sect. 6.

At present, communication between the miner and the pool generally adopts the Stratum protocol, which always maintains a stable long TCP connection.

Therefore, the mining traffic using the Stratum protocol must be the long TCP connection; otherwise it will enter the subscribe stage more often. The first thing we need to do is to filter out the traffic that is of short TCP connection.

After filtering the short connections, it is necessary to distinguish between the internal and external TCP connections. An obvious fact is that the IP address of the miner is inside the campus network, and the address of the mining pool is outside the campus network. Therefore, the connection that contains illegal mining behavior must have an internal IP as a SIP and an external public IP as DIP for communication.

The third step involves setting filtering conditions based on the relationships between TCP flags. According to the characteristics of the Stratum protocol, the specific filtering condition of this stage is that (1) the total number of PSH flags of the TCP packets transmitted in the connection is greater than 0; (2) the number of PSH flags carried by the incoming data packets is always greater than the number carried by the outbound TCP packets (the direction is based on the mining pool). The information of the TCP flags for each connection is obtained through the Netflow+ analysis and saved as TCP features in the (SIP, DIP, Dport) triple. Therefore, after this stage we filter out TCP connections that do not hold such PSH conditions.

The final filtering stage is to use TCP retransmission for cleaning data. This is because modeling Stratum communication requires *pure* communication process in which packets caused by TCP retransmission are not considered; otherwise an extra unknown variable must be introduced to denote the number of retransmission packets to model the exact communication process. Adding more unknown variables into our next model building step will significantly add computational cost. Therefore, we try to eliminate such cases in practice.

Through such pipelined filtering process, we can reduce the TCP metadata to a level in which only small set of TCP connections remain for further processing.

5 Model Stratum with Equations

After filtering, the number of TCP connections has significantly decreased, with only a few remaining. In the final stage of the symbolic analysis framework shown in Fig. 1, we can afford to model Stratum communication with a set of linear *diophantine* equations for the remaining TCP connections.

5.1 Mining Machine to Mining Pool

Except for the establishment of the TCP three-way handshake before the official mining starts, in the stable mining stage the mining machine will send two kinds of TCP packets:

- the empty payload with only the ACK flag packet (hereinafter referred to as submission ACK);
- the resulting submission packet with the ACK+PSH flags (hereinafter referred to as submission packet)

The size of the empty-payload packet depends on the miner's operating system, but it is fixed for a miner. The size of the submission depends on the number of the task. The length of two adjacent tasks does not differ by more than 1, and thus the size of the submission packet is relatively fixed. Therefore, the total number of bytes inbound (relative to the mining pool) is equal to the sum of the number of bytes in the submission packet and that of in the ACK packet. From this we can get the following equation.

$$INBYTE = INBYTE_{sub} \times INPACKET_{sub} \\ + INBYTE_{ACK} \times INPACKET_{ACK} \tag{1}$$

5.2 Mining Pool to Mining Machine Direction

Similarly, after entering the stable communication stage, the mining pool will send out three types of TCP packets:

- empty payload packets with only ACK flags (called ACK packet);
- result response packets with ACK and PSH flags (called result packet);
- task delivery packets with ACK and PSH flags (called job packet).

The size of the empty-payload packet depends on the operating system of the mining pool, but its size is fixed for a pool. The size of both the result and delivery packets is contingent upon the number of tasks. Moreover, as the difference in length between any two adjacent tasks is no more than 1, the result and delivery packets' sizes are relatively fixed. Even in the case of TLS protocol encryption, the sizes of result and delivery packets are relatively fixed. So the total number of bytes outbound (relative to the mining pool) is equal to the sum of the number of bytes in the ACK packet, the number of bytes in the delivery packet and the number of bytes in the result packet. We can have the following equation.

$$OUTBYTE = OUTBYTE_{ACK} \times OUTPACKET_{ACK} \\ + OUTBYTE_{res} \times OUTPACKET_{res} \\ + OUTBYTE_{job} \times OUTPACKET_{job} \tag{2}$$

5.3 Equations Capturing Fixed Packet Length

According to previous discussion, the fixed-length packets containing the PSH flag are job delivery, result, and submission. In rare cases the length will vary. Disregarding these exceptional cases, we set up the followings:

- Delivery: the job delivery packet length is x, and the number of packets is $t1$.
- Submit: the submit packet length is y, and the number of packets is $t2$.
- Result: the result packet length is z, and the number of packets is $t3$.

The relationship among the lengths of three packets satisfies:
$x > y > z$. We also set the number of PSH packets, the number of ACK packets, and the total number of bytes transmitted in each direction as follows:

- PSH_in: the number of inbound packets with the PSH flag, recorded as $p1$;
- PSH_out: the number of outbound packets with the PSH flag, recorded as $p2$;
- ACK_in: the number of inbound packets with the ACK flag, recorded as $a1$;
- ACK_out: the number of outbound packets with the ACK flag, recorded as $a2$;
- Inbyte: the total number of bytes inbound, recorded as $s1$;
- Outbyte: the total number of bytes outbound, recorded as $s2$.

Among the outbound packet types, only delivery and result packets carry the PSH flag, so the following equation can be obtained.

$$t1 + t3 = p2 \tag{3}$$

Similarly, in the incoming data packet type, only the submit packets carry the PSH flag, and the following equation can be obtained.

$$t2 = p1 \tag{4}$$

Every time when the miner uploads a solution result, the mining pool returns a corresponding result for verification. So the following equation can be obtained

$$t2 = t3 \tag{5}$$

During the experiment, we found that the packet length with empty payload is 60-bytes, which is less than 64bytes, the minimal length of an Ethernet packet. This is because the last 4-bytes of CRC is dropped. Therefore, the packet length of empty payload used to keep alive in the mining connection is fixed to $60 + 4 * n(n < 10)$. Combining Eq. 1, we can get the following equation:

$$y * t2 + 60 * (a1 - p1) = s1 \tag{6}$$

Likewise, combining Eq. 2 we can get the following equation:

$$x * t1 + z * t3 + 60 * (a2 - p2) = s2 \tag{7}$$

The formulas obtained by combining and simplifying the above formulas (3)–(7) are as follows:

$$y = (s1 - 60 * (a1 - p1))/p1 \tag{8}$$

$$x * p1 + z * (p2 - p1) = s1 - 60 * (a2 - p2) \tag{9}$$

In Eq. 8 and 9, only x, y, and z are unknown variables, and the rest of the values can be computed by the $Netflow+$ technology through aggregation. Equation 8 can be directly solved to get the value of y, that is, the packet length of the submit type. Equation 9 has two unknown variables, x and z. If a pair of integers that satisfy the packet length constraints can be identified, it indicates that the TCP connection in question uses fixed-packet-length for message exchange. Therefore, we successfully detect the communication behavior of the Stratum protocol. Please note the TCP connections with TCP retransmission have been already eliminated by a previous filter. Therefore, we only consider *pure* communication process between a miner and the pool. Eliminating one unknown variable in these equations could significantly speed up the search of integer solution process.

6   Experimental Results

In this section, we present the experiment setup and report the experimental results. In Subsect. 6.1, we discuss the dilemma in evaluating the accuracy of detection of cryptocurrency mining activities because there lacks of public testing data. Subsection 6.2 describes the campus network environment. Subsection 6.3 to 6.5 demonstrate through several experiments that the detection framework proposed in this paper can achieve real-time detection of cryptojacking in high-traffic environments.

6.1   Testing Dilemma

Since there is still no publicly available authoritative mining traffic (i.e., complete, raw traffic data spanning several consecutive days or even months), we spent 6-months in the early stage of research to collect mining traffic. Because the collection and processing of original packet data can significantly impact the subsequent analysis, we must determine which types of cryptojacking traffic to collect.

Monero is the cryptocurrency that causes the most widespread cryptojacking damage. Since it is specifically designed to run on the CPU, we collect its traffic first. Even though Ethereum is anti-ASIC, it still can be mined with a GPU. We collected Ethereum mining traffic as well. Our mining machine has a decent GPU, NVIDIA GeForce RTX 2080. We mine Monero on CPU with xmrig and Ethereum on GPU with excavator software. Traffic data is collected through Wireshark and then the corresponding IP addresses are manipulated for privacy concerns. In order to benefit other researchers, the mining traffic collected will be made public in the future at [20].

For Ethereum and Monero mining, we collected Pcap trace files for the learning purpose. Table 3 lists those trace files described by cryptocurrency name, date collected, Pcap size, and packet number.

Due to the current lack of a large amount of authoritative public cryptocurrency mining test data (trace files), each research group collects its own test data and then evaluates the detection accuracy against those data. In so doing, it introduces testing dilemmas:

- Even if the test result were good against the collected data, it would fail badly in practice if the detection algorithm were used in the traffic with much noise. I.e., the one-class-fit-all approach did not work well in practice [16];

Table 3. Mining traffic collection

Name	Date	Bytes (MB)	Packets
Ethereum	2022.10.8	33.73	261, 133
Ethereum	2022.11.27	15.35	190, 802
Ethereum	2022.12.17	12.31	154, 377
Monero	2022.12.23	0.39	3, 658
Monero	2022.12.30	0.48	4, 643
Ethereum	2023.1.11	7.05	85, 650
Monero	2023.4.8	0.39	3, 499

- Even if some selected noise traffic were added into the test data, the detection algorithm would still fail since there are unlimited types of noise traffic.

Therefore, we use collected data for learning mining characteristics and rely on lively traffic for our testing purpose.

6.2 Lively Traffic Testing Setup

We perform lively traffic testing to detect cryptocurrency mining in a large campus network environment with more than 32,000 IPs. The 24-h traffic characteristics are described in Table 4.

Table 4. 24-h traffic characteristics of the campus network

Characteristics	Value
Total Packets	89 Billion
Total Bytes	59 TB
Total Flows	3B
Ave. packet length	144 Bytes
Re-transmission rate	3.3%
TCP vs. UDP	66.5% vs. 33.5%
Scan traffic	20.96%
IPs	32, 877

Please note:
- compared to the 500-Million flows in one month, we deal with 3-Billion flows in one day, which is almost three orders of magnitude more than that reported in [16];
- compared to [18] which uses traffic from a campus for lively testing, we see that:

- there is large amount of UDP traffic 33.5% in campus, the same trend as reported in [18]; however, $Netflow+$ still performs the UDP traffic analysis because the UDP metadata is needed to help resolve *false-positive* cases in later stage. For example, the UDP metadata can be used to detect if an IP launched any UDP DDoS attack.
- a scan TCP traffic is a TCP flow in which the TCP three-way handshake has not been successfully finished. Maximally there are around 21% traffic are of scan type, only 1/3 of reported in [18];

The above two differences make the $Netflow+$ analysis doing more computation than reported in [16,18]. If $Netflow+$ did the same early traffic filtering as described in [18], performance would be much higher.

6.3   Detection Performance

Since a long TCP connection is defined as lasting at least 5 min, our analysis time window is set to 6 min. The first alarm will be triggered if two integer solutions to variables x and z in Eq. 9 are found, indicating that two types of messages used fixed-length packets to communicate. Subsequently, the alarm will be reported every 6 min if the TCP connection continues to be used for mining until a throttling threshold is reached.

Table 5. Time to solve formulated equations

Name	Max	Min	Ave
Total	39.38 s	23.26 s	30.22 s
Single	0.72 ms	0.81 ms	0.78 ms
Equations	54,121	28,629	38,918
Period	day	evening	24-h

Table 5 shows how fast we can solve those equations within a 6-min time-window, in which row Single gives average execution time (mili-seconds) for solving a single equation, row Total lists execution time (seconds) for all equations, row Equation reports the number of total equations to be solved, and row Period tells when the event will usually appear. Column Max and Min are for row Total and Equation.

From the table, we can see that on average, there are about 39,000 equations within a 6-min window, and they could be solved around 30 s, using only $30/360 = 1/12$ of allowed time budget. And there are more equations in day time since there is more traffic in the day than in the evening. In the following, we will show the effectiveness of *Boolean filtering* process, which enables us to run the solver against significantly smaller set of equations.

6.4   Boolean Filtering Effects

We discuss the effectiveness of the filter process, including filtering

- by long vs. short TCP connections can reduce the TCP connections by two orders of magnitude;
- by direction can further reduce size by almost half;
- by header bits can further reduce size by 40%;
- by TCP retrainmission can further reduce size by 13%.

To reach the aforementioned conclusion, we used one week of campus network traffic to calculate daily TCP metrics. Tables 6, 7, 8 and 9 present more specific data results for each filtering step, where "B" is the abbreviation for "billion" and "M" is the abbreviation for "million".

Table 6. TCP daily connections: Long vs. short

Connection	Max	Min	Average	Percentage
Short	3.5B	1.9B	2.8B	98.56%
Long	49M	34M	41M	1.44%

Table 7. TCP daily connections: external vs. internal

Connection	Max	Min	Average	Percentage
External	26M	17M	22M	53.66%
Internal	23M	16M	19M	46.34%

Table 8. TCP daily connections: with vs. without flags

Type	Max	Min	Average	Percentage
Without	11M	7M	9M	40.91%
With	15M	10M	13M	59.09%

The final results before and after filtering can be found in Table 10. After a series of filtering, we finally reduced the actual number of TCP connections by almost 3-orders of magnitude (0.43%).

The total number of TCP connections that need to be processed is reduced from 2.8 billions to 11 millions. I.e., on average the TCP long connections that require to be modelled by equations are reduced to 8,333 per minute. Therefore, each equation must be solved by 7 ms. Since each *diophantine* equation has only two unknowns, whose integer range is within [60, 1024], and thus the integer solution space is $O(1024*1024 = 1M)$. Any modern CPU running at Ghz should easily solve such an equation in a few of macro-seconds, which is much less that the 8-ms budget. From Table 5 we can see that each equation takes around 0.8 ms

Table 9. TCP connections: Retransmission or Not

Retrans	Max	Min	Average	Percentage
Yes	2.1M	1.4M	1.8M	13.04%
No	14M	9M	12M	86.96%

Table 10. TCP connections: Filtered vs. Remaining

Type	Connection	Percentage
Filtered	2.8B	99.57%
Remained	12M	0.43%

to be solved, which is one order of magnitude less than the allowed budget. Therefore, those *diophantine* equations can be solved comfortably in real-time. Once a pair of integer solution is found, we can infer that Stratum protocol is indeed used two types of the fixed-length of packets to exchange messages. Then an alarm message with TCP meta data (SIP, DIP, Dport) will be generated.

6.5   Detection Results

As we pointed out previously, the 7-traces listed in Table 3 are used as the learning purpose. They can be 100% identified as having Stratum communication by our symbolic analysis framework. Therefore, we put our framework into a campus environment for lively traffic testing. We identity 5 pool IPs within one month period. Table 11 shows those IPs, the country belong to, encryption method. Please note that we did not show source IPs (SIP) for the privacy reason. Since an internal SIP may connect to many pool DIPs and many SIPs may connect to one pool DIP, the number of TCP connections (SIP,DIP,Dport) reported as having mining behaviour is much more than 5.

Table 11. Detection mining traffic lively in a campus

DIP	Country	Encryption
142.132.147.187	Germany	NO
141.94.96.71	France	NO
107.191.99.221	USA	NO
45.77.240.51	Singapore	YES
172.86.75.2	Netherlands	YES

To confirm the framework's alarmed results are actually having mining activities, we seek the *ground truth* as follows:

– for the clear-text traffic, it is automatically triggered to collect the SIP's *mining* traffic (SIP, DIP, Dport) as soon as the framework generated an alarming report. And then we manually analyzed the TCP payload and verified it indeed contains Stratum protocol messages;

- for the encrypted traffic, we avoid to collect the SIP's *all* traffic (SIP,*,*), in which * means all DIP and all Dport since it would significantly increase storage space. Instead, we rely on already collected traffic *metadata*:

  1. verifying if the DIP is used as a mining pool IP through a third-party's threat intelligence;
  2. investing other evidence showing this SIP has been hacked already by analyzing its traffic behaviour, including TCP, UDP, HTTP, HTTPs, DNS etc.;

The reported 5-DIP listed in Table 11 has been verified by this process as pool mining IPs.

6.6 Experimental Evaluation

Section 2 explains why other methods [9,11,12,14] can only achieve detection under offline or low-flow conditions, while Subsects. 6.2 to 6.4 demonstrate through experiments why the proposed method in this paper is capable of real-time detection. The ML community has a tendency to *arbitrarily* extend a metric feature into a series of statistic derived ones using $MIN/MAX/AVE/STD/VAR$ functions. We use a simple experiment to explain that rashly introducing these statistic functions will lead to a significant increase in time costs.

A Pcap file with 18-MB size and 197,989 packets is selected to test function's performance. The amount of this data is about the size of the traffic transmitted by a machine to mining half a month. First, the file is loaded into memory to avoid measuring the IO overhead, we run a processing loop with 5,000 times. The machine used is an Intel CPU: Core(TM) i7-9750H with 12 MB of L3 cache. Since the file size is larger than L3 cache size, cache misses occur to reflect the real application running environment.

Table 12. Execution time of statistic functions

Name	Time(s)	Ratio
MAX	0.49	1.0
MIN	0.54	1.1
AVE	4.08	8.4
VAR	12.25	25.2
STD	15.16	31.2

Table 12 lists function name, function execution time, and the ratio of execution time against MAX's, which is the base line. Please note that column *Ratio* is more important than column *Time* since the relative computational cost is compared. The key to achieving high-performance in our framework is that we have not used any STD or VAR or AVE statistic function in purpose to reduce computation cost, and thus we can use a *low-end* server to reach 10Gbps linerate processing.

As mentioned in Subsect. 6.1, there is currently a lack of authoritative open-source mining traffic datasets (or in other words, scattered traffic data spanning only a few hours). A small portion of pure mining traffic datasets were made public by Feng [6]. Therefore, we combined this datasets with a authoritative benign dataset CIC-IDS [17], creating a hybrid dataset that was used to evaluate the accuracy of the detection method proposed in this paper. The hybrid dataset (Pcap trace files) is approximately 10 GB in size, with mining traffic accounting for around 1% of the total. This proportion of data matches the characteristics of mouse flows in real networks.

We retransmitted the hybrid dataset in the campus network environment to allow $Netflow+$ to capture and detect it. Based on the source and destination IP, there are a total of 23 instances of mining connections in the hybrid dataset. When the one-way fixed-packet met the conditions, the system alert level is set to "information". When the two-way fixed-packet met the conditions, the system alert level is set to "critical". At the same time as the alert, the system will list the source IP and destination IP addresses of the suspected mining connection. Dividing into two alert levels can improve the robustness of the system and provide network security personnel with more options. The $Netflow+$ system generated 28 "information" level alerts and 23 "critical" level alerts for the aforementioned hybrid dataset. The results of evaluating the model accuracy are shown in the following Table 13.

Table 13. Experimental Results of "info" level alert.

Name	"info" level alert	"critical" level alert
Accuracy	99.85%	100%
Precision	100%	100%
Recall	45%	100%
F1	0.6	1

Please note that the experimental results in the first column of Table 13 represent the results for "information" level alerts, obtained using one-way fixed equations. This means that a small portion of benign traffic with characteristics that match the one-way equation model may be misclassified as mining traffic. However, by employing a two-way equation model, the accuracy of the model on this dataset can reach 100% (as shown in the second column of the table). Therefore, it can be said that the detection method proposed in this paper is excellent on existing open-source mining datasets.

7 Discussion

There are many rich applications similar to the mining TCP flows, and thus this may generate *false-positive* alarm. The common characteristics of these flows are that (1) they maintain a long TCP connection; (2) there is regular communication behavior using the fixed-packet-length; (3) they use encryption for transmission. We study what would happen if we only relied on finding one-way fixed-packet-length for detecting Stratum communication. Table 14 shows three typical applications that generate false-positive alarms.

Table 14. Noisy network traffic

APP Name	Vendor
IBM Force	IBM intelligence group
Windows-update	Microsoft Windows
Ding-Talk	Alibaba Inc

We successfully addressed this issue by modeling bidirectional communication with fixed packet length. Of course, some applications may occasionally exhibit two-way fixed-packet-length communication behaviour. To solve this, we discuss a solution that extends the detection time window. Since the Stratum protocol uses bidirectional fixed packet length to exchange messages persistently, while other applications only occasionally exhibit this behavior. I.e., if more time budget is allocated, more false-positive cases could be potentially eliminated.

8 Conclusion

To address the serious network security threat posed by cryptojacking, we propose a real-time detection framework based on Netflow-plus traffic analysis. This framework can detect illegal cryptocurrency mining activities from both cleartext and encrypted traffic. It also can be applied to detect the mining traffic for both IPv4 and IPv6. In order to extract necessary features from network traffic, we create *Netflow-plus* analysis technique to derive TCP metadata for analyzing *mice-flow* communication behaviour. We first apply a series of pipelined based Boolean filters to reduce the search space, and then model Stratum communication with *diophantine* equations. By solving the corresponding equations in the symbolic way, we can infer a TCP long connection with fixed-packet-length communication has used the Stratum protocol for mining. Finally, we deployed the detection system in a large campus network environment and obtained good detection results. Future work will include dealing with more cryptocurrencies and make the collected mining traffic open source.

Acknowledgments. The project was supported by Open Fund of Anhui Province Key Laboratory of Cyberspace Security Situation Awareness and Evaluation.

References

1. Alikhanov, J., Jang, R., Abuhamad, M., Mohaisen, D., Nyang, D., Noh, Y.: Investigating the effect of traffic sampling on machine learning-based network intrusion detection approaches. IEEE Access **10**, 5801–5823 (2021)
2. Campazas-Vega, A., Crespo-Martínez, I.S., Guerrero-Higueras, Á.M., Álvarez-Aparicio, C., Matellán, V.: Analysis of NetFlow features' importance in malicious network traffic detection. In: Gude Prego, J.J., de la Puerta, J.G., García Bringas, P., Quintián, H., Corchado, E. (eds.) CISIS - ICEUTE 2021. AISC, vol. 1400, pp. 52–61. Springer, Cham (2022). https://doi.org/10.1007/978-3-030-87872-6_6
3. Caprolu, M., Raponi, S., Oligeri, G., Di Pietro, R.: Cryptomining makes noise: a machine learning approach for cryptojacking detection. arXiv preprint arXiv:1910.09272 (2019)
4. Cisco-Netflow: Using netflow sampling to select the network traffic to track. https://www.cisco.com/c/en/us/td/docs/ios-xml/ios/netflow/configuration/xe-3s/asr1000/nf-xe-3s-asr1000-book/nflow-filt-samp-traff-xe.pdf. Accessed 29 July 2022
5. Clearclouds: Network traffic visualization. http://www.ido-net.net. Accessed 29 July 2022
6. Feng, Y., Li, J., Sisodia, D.: CJ-Sniffer: measurement and content-agnostic detection of cryptojacking traffic. In: Proceedings of the 25th International Symposium on Research in Attacks, Intrusions and Defenses, pp. 482–494 (2022)
7. Gomes, F., Correia, M.: Cryptojacking detection with CPU usage metrics. In: 2020 IEEE 19th International Symposium on Network Computing and Applications (NCA), pp. 1–10. IEEE (2020)
8. Gomes, G., Dias, L., Correia, M.: CryingJackpot: network flows and performance counters against cryptojacking. In: 2020 IEEE 19th International Symposium on Network Computing and Applications (NCA), pp. 1–10. IEEE (2020)
9. Hu, X., Shu, Z., Song, X., Cheng, G., Gong, J.: Detecting cryptojacking traffic based on network behavior features. In: 2021 IEEE Global Communications Conference (GLOBECOM), pp. 01–06. IEEE (2021)
10. Huang, J., Li, Y.F., Xie, M.: An empirical analysis of data preprocessing for machine learning-based software cost estimation. Inf. Softw. Technol. **67**, 108–127 (2015)
11. Lashkari, A.H., Zang, Y., Owhuo, G., Mamun, M., Gil, G.: CICFlowmeter (2017)
12. i Muñoz, J.Z., Suárez-Varela, J., Barlet-Ros, P.: Detecting cryptocurrency miners with netFlow/IPFIX network measurements. In: 2019 IEEE International Symposium on Measurements & Networking (M&N), pp. 1–6. IEEE (2019)
13. Nfdump: Nfdump- toolset in order to collect and process netflow data. https://github.com/phaag/nfdump. Accessed 1 Oct 2022
14. Pastor, A., et al.: Detection of encrypted cryptomining malware connections with machine and deep learning. IEEE Access **8**, 158036–158055 (2020)
15. Recabarren, R., Carbunar, B.: Hardening stratum, the bitcoin pool mining protocol. arXiv preprint arXiv:1703.06545 (2017)
16. Russo, M., Šrndić, N., Laskov, P.: Detection of illicit cryptomining using network metadata. EURASIP J. Inf. Secur. **2021**(1), 1–20 (2021)
17. Sharafaldin, I., Lashkari, A.H., Ghorbani, A.A.: Toward generating a new intrusion detection dataset and intrusion traffic characterization. In: International Conference on Information Systems Security & Privacy (2018)

18. Wan, G., Gong, F., Barbette, T., Durumeric, Z.: Retina: analyzing 100GbE traffic on commodity hardware. In: Proceedings of ACM 36th SIGCOMM Conference, pp. 530–544. ACM (2022)
19. Wang, J., Cheng, H., Hua, B., Tang, X.: Practice of parallelizing network applications on multi-core architectures. In: Proceedings of the 23rd International Conference on Supercomputing, 2009, Yorktown Heights, NY, USA, 8–12 June 2009, pp. 204–213. ACM (2009). https://doi.org/10.1145/1542275.1542307
20. Yang, Z.: Mining traffic data (2023). https://github.com/banzhuanle/Mining-traffic-datasets

Non-malleable Codes from Leakage Resilient Cryptographic Primitives

Anit Kumar Ghosal$^{(\boxtimes)}$ ⓘ and Dipanwita Roy chowdhury ⓘ

Department of Computer Science and Engineering, IIT Kharagpur, Kharagpur, India
anit.ghosal@gmail.com

Abstract. Non-malleable codes (NMC) are used as a relaxation of error correction and error detection codes to guarantee strong privacy where correctness is not the main concern. Usually, a coding scheme is said to be non-malleable with respect to a class of tampering function if any tampering with the codeword, the underlying function changes the codeword to a *completely unrelated one*, i.e., $\perp$ or *same*, in case of unsuccessful tampering. The real life application of such codeword is to provide security against leakage and tampering attacks on the memory, which is also called *active physical attacks or hardware attacks*. Standard version of non-malleable codes are used to protect highly sensitive data (i.e., secret key of any cryptographic scheme) on private memory of the device. In literature, leakage resilient authenticated encryptions (AE) are used to design such codeword. We show a generic framework to design leakage resilient authenticated encryption and prove it non-malleable with respect to *one-time* tampering attack. The instantiation of such codeword is based on leakage resilient IV-based encryption scheme along with leakage resilient CBC-MAC and 1-more weakly extractable leakage-resilient hash function (wECRH). When the tampering experiment of our strong NMC returns $\perp$, the security is reduced to the security of authenticated encryption and 1-more weakly extractable leakage-resilient hash function.

Keywords: Leakage resilient authenticated encryption · Extractable hash · Non-malleable codes · Tamper resilient cryptography

1 Introduction

In cryptography, various algorithms are designed under the so-called black-box model, where an attacker receives the black-box access to the hardware implementation. Though such model covers a wide range of attacks but it fails to capture the real life scenario. An adversary can use the physical weakness of the hardware implementation and it can mount attacks on the cryptographic system. An instance of such cryptographic system is a *smart-card* which are light-weight hardware devices, used in various payment gateways to enable the authenticity of the user, by requiring them to ensure proof of knowledge of the secret code or pin, stored in the devices private memory. The attacker can physically tamper with the device to know the *pin or secret code* which is considered to be a

C. Ge and M. Yung (Eds.): Inscrypt 2023, LNCS 14527, pp. 272–290, 2024.
https://doi.org/10.1007/978-981-97-0945-8_15

real threat to the security of any crypto-module. One of the most efficient way to introduce such attack by using fault during run-time of cryptographic algorithm on the memory of hardware module [1,5]. To protect cryptographic memory against *physical attacks or tampering attacks*, non-malleable codes (NMC) [10,21] are developed which ensures strong privacy. Now, rather than storing the secret data in clear form, it is encoded via non-malleable codes and the underlying codeword is stored into the private memory. An attacker can use the *tampering function* on the codeword, and non-malleability property guarantees that output is either *completely same as original message* or *essentially destroyed*, i.e., $\perp$. Hence, the adversary can not perform any harmful activity on the tampered codeword and security of the cryptosystem is preserved. In literature, it is shown that NMC designs are restricted to the particular classes of tampering functions. Consider a tampering experiment. Let m be the secret information. First, the non-malleable encoding of m is computed as $\mathsf{Enc}(m)$. An attacker can tamper the encoded message in the following way $f_{tamper}(\mathsf{Enc}(m))$. The output generated by the tampering experiment is $\mathsf{Enc}(m)+1$. Moreover, the decoding of the codeword is performed as $\mathsf{Dec}(\mathsf{Enc}(m)+1)$. The expected output at the end of tampering experiment is m+1. It is clear that an adversary can easily find some relation between m+1 and original secret message m. The model which has gained attention to the research community, is the *split-state* model where the actual codeword is stored into two halves of the memory M_L, M_R. The attacker can use two different tampering functions f_L and f_R on the codeword in an independent and arbitrary way [11,13,16,18,19,22,23,26,28].

Table 1. Various constructions of NMC in split-state model [28]. Here, I.T. implies *Information-theoretic* and Comp. denotes *computational*

Reference	Codeword length	Model	Assumption
[15]	$\mathcal{O}((|m| + \tau)^7 \log^7(|m| + \tau))$	I.T	NA
[16]	$\mathcal{O}(max(|m|, \tau))$	I.T	NA
[15] + [19]	$|m| + \mathcal{O}(\tau^7)$	Comp	Authenticated Encryption
[6] + [8] + [11] + [19]	$|m| + \mathcal{O}(\tau^2)$	Comp., CRS	Leakage resilient PKE + Robust NIZK
[18]	$|m| + 18\tau$	Comp., CRS	Leakage resilient AE + KEA
[22]	$|m| + 2\tau$	Comp	Pseudorandom permutation with leakage + Fixed related-key
[25]	$|m| + 5\tau$	Comp	Entropic fixed related-key
[26]	$\mathcal{O}(|m| + 2\tau)$ [a]	Comp	Related-key + PRP with leakage + Leakage resilient CBC-MAC
[28]	$|m| + 2\tau + 2log^2(\tau)$	Comp	Leakage resilient AE + 1-more extractable hash
This work	$|m| + 7\tau + 2log^2(\tau)$	**Comp.**	**Leakage resilient AE + 1-more weakly extractable leakage-resilient hash**

[a] $|m|$ and τ denote the message and security parameter.

In literature, the design of non-malleable codes are broadly classified into two domains as *computational* [19] and *information-theoretic* [13]. In [15], authors propose an information-theoretic construction of non-malleable code of size $\mathcal{O}((|m| + \tau)^7 log^7(|m| + \tau))$. The first computational split-state non-malleable code [11] is proposed from public key primitives [8] with *robust non interactive Zero knowledge* (NIZK) proof [3]. Later, the codeword length is optimized into $|m| + \mathcal{O}(\tau^7)$ by combining the idea of [15] and [19]. Further, the length of NMC is improved to $|m| + \mathcal{O}(\tau^2)$ [6,8,11,19]. Usually, the encoding scheme of NMC is considered to be *keyless* [10,21]. Later, it is observed that such codeword can be designed from various *symmetric-key primitives*. In [18], authors propose a construction of non-malleable code from *one-time leakage-resilient* AE with *l-more extractable hash function* in *common reference string* (CRS) model. Unfortunately, they use *knowledge of exponent assumption* (KEA) in the design of codeword which is non-standard. Fehr et al. [22] show first an optimal NMC construction from *related-key* secure cipher in the plain model. Unfortunately, their assumptions are not satisfied by *cipher-dependent* tampering function. Later, a different construction of codeword is proposed by introducing a new security notion, called *entropic fixed-related-key* but the NMC is not optimal in codeword length. In [26], authors show an alternative way of designing close to optimal length codeword from authenticated encryption. Table 1 illustrates various constructions of non-malleable codes in split-state model as available in the literature.

Motivation of Our NMC Design. In literature, it is shown that leakage resilient authenticated encryption (AE) can be used to construct computationally secure non-malleable codes [15,19,26]. Kiayias et al. [18] show a non-malleable code from AE of codeword length $|m| + 18\tau$ with CRS based setup. Later, the codeword length is optimized in [26,28] using a similar kind of AE based scheme without any CRS based setup. Unfortunately, they use a specific kind of authenticated encryption in the design of non-malleable codes. We show a framework to design leakage resilient authenticated encryption, i.e., *encrypt then MAC based authenticated encryption* [2] and further prove it non-malleable. The work of Barwell et al. [20] is more relevant in the construction of leakage resilient authenticated encryption. They show that an encrypt-then-MAC paradigm yields a leakage-resilient scheme when the underlying encryption scheme and MAC both are leakage resilient [24]. The same approach can be used to construct a leakage resilient authenticated encryption. Moreover, there are some cryptographic primitives like hash function, which is secure in general but it becomes insecure in presence of side channel leakage [20]. Hence, the hash function of [18] may not provide adequate security in presence of leakage. So the construction of [28] can be attacked when an adversary has access to some arbitrary leakage function. To overcome all these limitations, we propose a construction of non-malleable code from stronger hash primitives [27]. As an example, we instantiate our non-malleable code using *leakage resilient IV-based encryption scheme* of [20] along with *leakage resilient CBC-MAC* [17] and *1-more weakly extractable leakage-resilient hash function* (wECRH) [27]. Moreover, there are also alternative ways to instantiate such AE to design the codeword.

Our Contribution. In this work, we propose a construction of computationally secure NMC from *leakage authenticated encryption* along with *1-more weakly extractable leakage-resilient hash function* [27] in split-state model. The security notion of *1-more weakly extractable leakage-resilient hash function* is even more stronger than *1-more extractable hash function* [18] when an adversary has access to some leakage function. To design the codeword, *encrypt then MAC* based authenticated encryption is used where the underlying encryption scheme and MAC both are leakage resilient.

In [11], authors show that the equality between $f_L(\hat{sk})$ and $f_L(sk)$ can be checked by an adversary through the leakage of a universal hash function which outputs $log^2 \tau^1$ bits in total (where $|sk| = |\tau|$). Further, Kiayias et al. [18] observe that using the leakage of a universal hash, the comparison of $f_L(\hat{r}, \hat{sk})$ and $f_L(r, sk)$ can be done by generating $2\tau + log^2 \tau$ bits of output. Our split-state codeword is constructed as $\mathsf{Enc}_{sk} : m \rightarrow \{r, sk\} || \{c, tag, h_1\}$. The codeword length is calculated as message length $|m|$ and additional $|security\text{-}bits|$. In the construction of our codeword, we set $\lambda = 2\tau + log^2 \tau$ (Subsect. 3.2) and the length of codeword is $|m| + |sk| + |r| + |tag| + |h_1|$, i.e., $|m| + 7\tau + 2log^2(\tau)$ (where $|c| = |m|$), assuming the total length of $|tag|$, $|sk|$, r are τ bits each.

In a nutshell, the major goals of our work are illustrated as follows:

(a) A provably secure construction of NMC is described from *leakage resilient AE* along with *1-more weakly extractable leakage-resilient hash function* without any CRS based setup. The NMC provides security against one-time tampering attack and leakage attack.

(b) The codeword size is $|m| + 7\tau + 2log^2(\tau)$ compared to other non-malleable codes as available in the literature. On the other hand, the proposed construction of AE in this paper is generic in the sense that any *leakage resilient encryption* can be combined with *leakage resilient authentication* as illustrated in [20].

Organization. The organization of the paper is described as follows: Sect. 2 explains the preliminaries of non-malleable code and various definitions. In Sect. 3, we illustrate the codeword construction while the security analysis of the codeword is explained in Sect. 4. Finally, our work concludes in Sect. 5.

2 Preliminaries

Basic Notations. Let A be a computationally bounded adversary. Two different tampering functions are f_L and f_R. We represent the memory as $\mathbf{M} = \{M_L || M_R\}$ which is split into two halves, i.e., the left half M_L and the right half M_R. The secret key set is denoted as SK. When a uniformly random key is selected, it is represented by $sk \leftarrow SK$ as a shorthand notation. The set of message is denoted by M whereas C is the ciphertext set. We write τ to denote

---

[1] τ is the security parameter.

the security parameter. When a particular message m from the message set M is selected, we write it as m ← M. In the same way, a ciphertext c is selected from the set of ciphertext C as c ← C. The ciphertext c is broken into chunks as $c_1, c_2, \ldots, c_n$. The final codeword set is denoted as $\mathcal{C}$. When a particular codeword $\mathfrak{C}$ is selected from $\mathcal{C}$, we denote it as $\mathfrak{C} \leftarrow \mathcal{C}$. Two different messages are represented by m^0, m^1. The leakage function is l_v. sk is the intermediate key of leakage resilient CBC-MAC algorithm whereas k is the key of pseudorandom function $\mathcal{F}_k$. r represents the randomness. Let E be an event and we denote that the event is not occurred by $\sim E$. A function $\epsilon : \mathcal{N} \to [0, 1]$ is called negligible in τ if it vanishes faster than the inverse of any polynomial in τ. In Table 2, the description of various notations are shown.

Table 2. Summary of notations

Notation	Terminology
A	Computationally bounded adversary
M	Split-state memory module
M_L, M_R	Left and right half of a memory
$\mathfrak{C}_L, \mathfrak{C}_R$	Left and right half of a codeword
$\mathcal{F}_k$	Pseudorandom function
f_L, f_R	Two tampering functions
SK	Key set
$sk \xleftarrow{\$} SK$	When a key is chosen
l_v	Leakage function
ϵ	A negligible function
τ	Security parameter
sk	Intermediate key of CBC-MAC
H_τ	1-more weakly extractable leakage-resilient hash function
m ← M	A particular message is selected
PRG	Pseudorandom generator
$\epsilon(\tau)$	A negligible function
k	Key of $\mathcal{F}_k$
$\widetilde{h} \leftarrow \widetilde{H_{\lambda-1}}$	Universal hash function
$Pr[F]$	Denotes the probability that event F has occurred
$Pr[\sim F]$	Denotes the probability that event F has not occurred
$E_v()$	Extractor of 1-more hash function
r	Randomness
$\mathcal{C}$	Codeword set
C	Ciphertext space
c ← C	A ciphertext is selected
$c = \{c_1, c_2, .., c_n\}$	Ciphertext is broken into chunks
$l_v^{h_z}$	Leakage function on h_z
$l_v^{\widetilde{h}, h_z}$	Leakage function on universal hash $\widetilde{h}$

Definition 2.1 (Coding Scheme). *Let (Enc$_{sk}$, Dec) be a coding scheme in the split state model where Enc$_{sk}$ algorithm inputs a message* m $\in$ M *with a*

secret key sk $\in$ SK *and produces a codeword* $\mathfrak{C} \in C$. *The final codeword* $\mathfrak{C}$ *is split into two halves* $\mathfrak{C}_L, \mathfrak{C}_R$ *and stored into memory* M_L *and* M_R *respectively. On the other hand,* Dec *algorithm inputs the codeword from* M_L, M_R *and produces the plaintext* m.

Definition 2.2 (Non-malleable Codes). *Let* F *be a split-state tampering function. For any* f $= (f_L, f_R) \in$ F, *the coding scheme (Enc$_{sk}$, Dec) is said to be non-malleable if* Dec(f($\mathfrak{C}$)) *outputs* m', *where* m' *can be* m, $\perp$ *or completely independent of* m.

Definition 2.3 (Strong Non-malleability). *The coding scheme (Enc$_{sk}$, Dec) is said to be strongly non-malleable with respect to tampering function* f $\in$ F *if* $\textbf{Tamper}_m^f(m^0) \underset{c}{\approx} \textbf{Tamper}_m^f(m^1)$ *are computationally indistinguishable for two arbitrarily chosen messages* m^0 *and* m^1, *where* $\textbf{Tamper}_m^f$ *is defined as follows:*

$$\textbf{Tamper}_m^f = \left\{ \begin{array}{c} \mathfrak{C} \leftarrow \text{Enc}_{sk}(m), \mathfrak{C} = \{M_L, M_R\} \\ \{M'_L, M'_R\} = \{f_L(M_L), f_R(M_R)\} \\ \mathfrak{C}' = \{M'_L, M'_R\}, m' = \text{Dec}(\mathfrak{C}') \\ output : same^*, if \mathfrak{C}' = \mathfrak{C}, else \ m'. \end{array} \right\},$$

where randomness comes from the encoding algorithm. Here same* refers to the situation when the codeword is not modified by the tampering experiment and it is same as original codeword.

Definition 2.4 (Extractable Hash). *Let* H_τ *be a hash function. The hash is said to be extractable [12] if for any probabilistic polynomial time algorithm* A, *there exists a probabilistic polynomial time extractor* E_A, *such that for all* $\tau \in$ N, *for any input* $p \in \{0,1\}^\tau$ *and a negligible function* $\epsilon(\tau)$:

$$Pr_{h \leftarrow H_\tau}[y \leftarrow A(h,p), \exists x : h(x) = y, x' \leftarrow E_A(h,p) \wedge h(x') \neq y] \leq \epsilon(\tau).$$

Definition 2.5 (1-more Weakly Extractable Leakage Resilient Hash). *The hash function* H_τ *is said to be 1-more weakly extractable leakage resilient hash [27] against* λ *bits of leakage if for any probabilistic polynomial time algorithm* A_{h_1} *and any* $p_{h_1} \in \{0,1\}^\tau$, *there exists a probabilistic polynomial time extractor* E_{h_1} *and* $p_E \in \{0,1\}^\tau$, *such that for all PPT algorithm* A_{sk}, $\tau \in$ N, *for any input message* sk $\in \{0,1\}^\tau$ *and a negligible function* $\epsilon(\tau)$:

$$Pr_{h_z \leftarrow H_\tau}[\textbf{Exp}_{A_{h_1}, A_{sk}, E_{h_1}}^{sk, h_z}(1, p_{h_1}, p_E) = 1] \leq \epsilon(\tau),$$

where $\textbf{Exp}_{A_{h_1}, A_{sk}, E_{h_1}}^{sk, h_z}(1, p_{h_1}, p_E)$ *consists of four properties [27] as follows:*

- **(Hash computation)** : $(h_1) \leftarrow h_z(r, sk)$, *randomness* $r \leftarrow \{0,1\}^\tau$
- **(Hash tampering)** : $(h'_1, t) \leftarrow A_{h_1}(h_z, h_1, l_v(r), p_{h_1})$
- **(Preimage extraction)** : $(\hat{sk}, \hat{r}) \leftarrow E_{h_1}(h_z, h_1, p_E)$
- **(Preimage tampering)** : $(sk', r') \leftarrow A_{sk}(h_z, r, sk, t)$

If $h_z(\mathsf{sk}', r') = h_1' \wedge h_z(\hat{\mathsf{sk}}, \hat{r}) \neq h_1'$, return 1

else, return 0

The experiment $\mathbf{Exp}^{sk,h_z}_{\mathsf{A}_{h_1},\mathsf{A}_{sk},\mathsf{E}_{h_1}}(1, p_{h_1}, p_\mathsf{E})$ works in the following way: we use the randomized hash function. An attacker A_{h_1} wants to generate a tampered hash h_1', given some additional information, i.e., a hash h_1 with auxiliary information p_{h_1} and leakage function $l_v()$ on randomness r. Further, the extractor E_{h_1} produces the preimage, given h_1 and auxiliary input p_E. Finally, the attacker A_{sk} tries to generate the preimage of h_1' with the help of additional information gathered during the experiment. The output of the experiment is 1, if A_{h_1} is able to successfully produce a valid hash h_1', and a valid preimage of h_1' is generated by A_{sk}, while the extractor algorithm is unable to generate the output properly.

Let $h_z \leftarrow \mathsf{H}_\tau$ is sampled from the set of collision resistant, efficiently samplable, 1-more weakly extractable leakage resilient hash function family as described in [27]. The adversary selects $\widetilde{h} \leftarrow \widetilde{H_{\lambda-1}}$ from the family of universal hash function where $\widetilde{h} : \{0,1\}^\tau \rightarrow \{0,1\}^{\lambda-1}$. The output generated by the hash function consists of $\lambda - 1$ bits. The leakage function $l_v^{\widetilde{h},h_z}$ is defined in the following way:

Set $l_v^{\widetilde{h},h_z}(\mathsf{sk}, r) = (0, \widetilde{h}(\mathsf{f}_L(\mathsf{sk}, r), h_z(\mathsf{sk}, r))$ if $(\mathsf{f}_L(\mathsf{sk}, r) = (\mathsf{sk}, r))$.

else, set $l_v^{\widetilde{h},h_z}(\mathsf{sk}, r) = (1, \widetilde{h}(\mathsf{f}_L(\mathsf{sk}, r), h_z(\mathsf{sk}, r))$, if $(\mathsf{f}_L(\mathsf{sk}, r) \neq (\mathsf{sk}, r))$.

The maximum leakages are λ bits where $\lambda = \omega(log\tau) + \rho(\tau)$ and $\rho(\tau) = poly(\tau)$. The experiment finds the leakage value rather than the output generated by f_L.

Definition 2.6 (Authenticated Encryption). An *authenticated encryption* (AE) scheme (SK, Enc, Dec) contains the following algorithms:

- Enc : SK × M → C The encoding algorithm takes a key sk ← SK and message m ← M as input which in turn produces ciphertext c ← C. We write the encoding as c ← Enc(sk, m).
- Dec : SK × C → M ∪ {⊥} The decoding algorithm inputs a key sk ← SK and ciphertext c ← C pair. Finally, it outputs m ← M or ⊥, if decryption fails. We write the decoding as m ← Dec(sk, c).

Moreover, any AE should satisfy the *correctness* property that Dec(sk, Enc (sk, m)) = m, for all sk ← SK, m ← M and c ← C.

Definition 2.7 (Semantically Secure One-time Leakage Resilient AE). Let $l_v : \{0,1\}^\tau \rightarrow \{0,1\}^\lambda$ be the leakage function that generates λ bits of output. An *authenticated encryption* (AE) scheme is *semantically secure* in presence of leakage l_v if $\{Enc(\mathsf{sk}, \mathsf{m}^0), l_v(\mathsf{sk})\}$ and $\{Enc(\mathsf{sk}, \mathsf{m}^1), l_v(\mathsf{sk})\}$ are computationally indistinguishable, i.e., $\{Enc(\mathsf{sk}, \mathsf{m}^0), l_v(\mathsf{sk})\} \underset{c}{\approx} \{Enc(\mathsf{sk}, \mathsf{m}^1), l_v(\mathsf{sk})\}$, for any m^0, m^1. The leakage function should be defined by the adversary before it can get access to the challenge ciphertext. Moreover, the probability of unforgeability of the AE should be negligible.

Definition 2.8 (Pseudorandom Generator). A *deterministic function PRG* is said to be *pseudorandom generator* [7, 9] in presence of an adversary A if $\forall \mathsf{A} \in$

A, $\exists$ a length increasing function $f : \mathsf{N} \to \mathsf{N}$ (domain of f, i.e., $|\mathsf{N}| = 2\lambda$ and co-domain of f, i.e., $|\mathsf{N}| = |m| + \tau$) such that $\{PRG_\tau\}_{\tau \in \mathsf{N}} \underset{c}{\approx} \{U_\tau\}_{\tau \in \mathsf{N}}$, where U_τ denotes the uniform distribution in $\{0,1\}^\tau$.

Definition 2.9 (Pseudorandom Function). A function $\mathcal{F} : \{0,1\}^k \times \{0,1\}^\tau \to \{0,1\}^\tau$ is said to be **pseudorandom function (PRF)** in presence of an adversary A [14] if the below security advantage holds:

$$\mathbf{Adv}^{prf}_{\mathcal{F}_k}(\mathsf{A}) = [Pr[\mathsf{A}(\mathcal{F}_k,.) = 1] - Pr[\mathsf{A}(R(.)) = 1]]$$

Moreover, the underlying **pseudorandom function** is said to be **leakage-resilient** if the PRF security advantage $\mathbf{Adv}^{prf}_{\mathcal{F}_k}$ still holds when the adversary has access to some arbitrary leakage function l_v on $\mathcal{F}_k$.

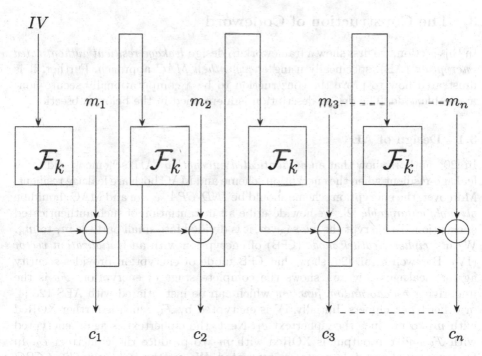

Fig. 1. CFB Mode of Encryption

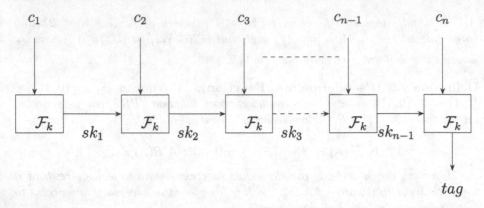

Fig. 2. Leakage resilient CBC-MAC [17]

3   The Construction of Codeword

In this section, we first show a framework to design *leakage resilient authenticated encryption* (AE), specifically using *encrypt then MAC* approach. Further, it is illustrated how to prove the construction to be a computationally secure non-malleable code. The design description is mentioned in the below subsection.

3.1   Design of AE

In [20], authors show that an *authenticated encryption* (AE) scheme is said to be leakage-resilient when the encryption scheme and MAC both are leakage resilient. Moreover, the encryption scheme should be *IND-CPA secure* and MAC should be *strongly unforgeable* [2]. We now describe an instantiation of such authenticated encryption. To encrypt the message m, it is divided into small parts as m_1 to m_n. We use *cipher feedback mode* (CFB) of encryption with an *initialization vector* (IV). Barewell et al. [20] show that CFB mode of encryption provides security against leakages. Figure 1 shows the complete stage of encryption. $\mathcal{F}_k$ is the underlying *pseudorandom function* which can be instantiated with AES-128 [4] or other block ciphers. Initially, IV is encrypted by $\mathcal{F}_k$ which is further XORed with m_1 to produce the ciphertext c_1. Next, the ciphertext is again encrypted with $\mathcal{F}_k$ and the output is XORed with m_2 to produce the ciphertext c_2. In this way, all of the ciphertexts are generated. We use the *leakage resilient CBC-MAC* [17] to output the *tag* as shown in Fig. 2. The *pseudorandom function* of CBC-MAC algorithm is instantiated with AES-128 algorithm. In the construction of AE, the main advantage of using CFB is that only forward direction of the encryption algorithm is invoked in encryption and decryption.

3.2   Design of Non-malleable Code

To design the codeword, we use *leakage resilient pseudorandom generator* (PRG) of [7,9]. The purpose of PRG is to encode the secret key in such a way that it protects the key against bounded leakages. The *leakage resilient pseudorandom generator* : $\{0,1\}^{2\lambda} \rightarrow \{0,1\}^{|m|+\tau}$ of [7] considers the length of secret key $|sk|$ = $2\lambda/\rho$, and the maximum leakages are upper bounded by $\rho\lambda$ bits [9], where $\rho \in [0,1]$ and the value depends on underlying assumption. In the instantiation of our codeword, the strongest assumption is considered, i.e., $\rho = 1$ which implies that the length of secret key is $|sk| = 2\lambda$. We prove further the non-malleability of the codeword with respect to one-time tampering attack. To encode the message m, *leakage resilient authenticated encryption* is used along with *1-more weakly extractable leakage resilient hash*. The encoding and decoding process are illustrated as follows:

- **Encoding.** In order to encode a message m using the NMC, the first step is to break m into m_1 to m_n. The CFB mode of encryption is invoked as discussed in the Subsect. 3.1 with the input $IV = r$ (where $r \leftarrow \{0,1\}^{\tau}$) and message m that generates the output c = $\{c_1, c_2, ..., c_n\}$. We use a *pseudorandom generator* which takes the secret key sk and produces r_1, r_2, where the length of $|r_1| = |m|$ and $|r_2| - |k|$, i.e., $(r_1, r_2) \leftarrow$ PRG(sk) and we set $k = r_2$. The key k is used in the pseudorandom permutation $\mathcal{F}_k$ which is instantiated with AES-128 in our case. Further, in the generation of *tag*, we invoke the *leakage resilient CBC-MAC* as described in Fig. 2. The *1-more weakly extractable leakage resilient hash* function $h_z \leftarrow H$, is invoked with randomness $r \leftarrow \{0,1\}^{\tau}$ which outputs a hash value for (sk, r), i.e., $h_1 \leftarrow h_z(r, sk)$. Finally, the codeword $\mathfrak{C} = (\mathfrak{C}_L || \mathfrak{C}_R)$ is stored into the memory $(M_L || M_R)$ in the following fashion: $M_L = \{r, sk\}$, $M_R = \{c, tag, h_1\}$.
KeyGen(1^{τ}): sk $\leftarrow \{0,1\}^{2\lambda}$
Enc$_{sk}$(m):
  - $(r_1, r_2) \leftarrow$ PRG(sk)
  - $|r_1| = |m|$, $|r_2| = |k|$
  - $r \leftarrow \{0,1\}^{\tau}$
  - Set $k = r_2$ and $IV = r$
  - Split $m \oplus r_1$ into $(m_1, m_2, ..., m_n)$
  - c = $\{c_1, c_2, ..., c_n\} \leftarrow$ CFB$_k(IV, m \oplus r_1)$
  - CFB$_k(IV, m \oplus r_1)$
    - $c_1 \leftarrow \mathcal{F}_k(IV) \oplus m_1$
    - $\forall i = 2$ to n
    - $c_i \leftarrow \mathcal{F}_k(c_{i-1}) \oplus m_i$
    - c = $\{c_1, ..., c_n\}$
  - $sk \leftarrow$ CBC-MAC(c_1, k)
    - $\forall i = 2$ to $n - 1$
    - $sk_i \leftarrow$ CBC-MAC(c_i, sk_{i-1})
  - $tag \leftarrow$ CBC-MAC(c_n, sk_{n-1})
  - $(h_1) \leftarrow h_z(r, sk)$,
  - Left part of codeword $\mathfrak{C}_L = \{r, sk\}$ and right part of codeword $\mathfrak{C}_R = \{c, tag, h_1\}$
  - Set the codeword $\mathfrak{C} = (\mathfrak{C}_L || \mathfrak{C}_R)$
  - Set left part of memory $M_L = \mathfrak{C}_L$ and right part of memory $M_R = \mathfrak{C}_R$

– **Decoding.** In order to decode the codeword $\mathfrak{C} = (\mathfrak{C}_L \| \mathfrak{C}_R)$, the *1-more weakly extractable leakage resilient hash* is invoked to extract the hash value of the secret key sk and randomness r, i.e., $(\hat{sk}, \hat{r}) \leftarrow \mathsf{E}_{h_1}(h_z, h_1, p_\mathsf{E})$. Then extracted key, randomness $(\hat{sk}, \hat{r})$ are compared with (sk, r) and if output is *same*, the *tag* is regenerated again using CBC-MAC($\mathsf{c} = \{c_1, \ldots, c_n\}, k$). Whenever the *tag* matches with the tampered *tag'*, the CFB mode of decryption is performed to retrieve m. We describe the decoding steps of our NMC as below:

Dec($\mathfrak{C}$):

- Parse $\mathfrak{C} = (r, \mathsf{sk}, \mathsf{c}, tag, h_1)$
- $(r_1, r_2) \leftarrow \mathsf{PRG}(\mathsf{sk})$
- Set $k = r_2$ and $IV = r$
- Calculate again $(h_1') \leftarrow h_z(r, \mathsf{sk})$
- If $(h_1') \neq (h_1)$, return $\perp$
- $(\hat{sk}, \hat{r}) \leftarrow \mathsf{E}_{h_1}(h_z, h_1, p_\mathsf{E})$
- If $(\hat{sk}, \hat{r}) \neq (\mathsf{sk}, r)$, return $\perp$
- Regenerate the *tag* using CBC-MAC($\mathsf{c} = \{c_1, \ldots, c_n\}, k$)
- If $tag' \neq tag$, return $\perp$
- Invoke decoding of $\mathsf{CFB}_k(IV, \mathsf{c} = \{c_1, \ldots, c_n\})$ to get $\mathsf{m} \oplus r_1$
- Perform xoring between $\mathsf{m} \oplus r_1$ and r_1
- Return m

3.3 Security Proof Idea of the Construction

Let A be a computationally bounded adversary that performs the experiment $\mathbf{Tamper}_m^f$ using the function $\mathsf{f} = (\mathsf{f}_L, \mathsf{f}_R)$ on the codeword $\mathfrak{C}$. Our goal is to show that for any two messages m^0, m^1, the experiment $\mathbf{Tamper}_m^f(\mathsf{m}^0)$ and $\mathbf{Tamper}_m^f(\mathsf{m}^1)$ are computationally indistinguishable, i.e., $\mathbf{Tamper}_m^f(\mathsf{m}^0) \underset{c}{\approx} \mathbf{Tamper}_m^f(\mathsf{m}^0)$. To prove the non-malleability, the experiment $\mathbf{TamperNMC}_{A,0}^{f,m}()$ is defined in Algorithm 1. It is almost same as the $\mathbf{Tamper}_m^f$ with the message m and tampering function $\mathsf{f} = (\mathsf{f}_L, \mathsf{f}_R) \in \mathsf{F}$. Moreover, we define the hybrid experiments $\mathbf{TamperNMC}_{A,1}^{f,m}()$, $\mathbf{TamperNMC}_{A,2}^{f,m}()$, $\mathbf{TamperNMC}_{A,3}^{f,m}()$ by incrementally changing the operation of various primitives that are used in the security game. In each experiment, a negligible amount of change is introduced and subsequently, the $\mathbf{Tamper}_m^f$ game is modified.

The Algorithm 2 illustrates the $\mathbf{TamperNMC}_{A,1}^{f,m}()$ experiment where we check whether the secret key sk, randomness r and ciphertext c are modified by f or not. If the values are equal, we compare *tag* with *tag'* and it produces $\perp$ as output in case $(tag \neq tag')$. Otherwise, the authenticity property under leakage is violated. Whenever the comparison is successful and if the hash is not modified, i.e., $(h_1 = h_1')$ the output is set to *same**. Finally, if $(r, \mathsf{sk}, \mathsf{c}) \neq (r', \mathsf{sk}', \mathsf{c}')$, the decoding of codeword is generated, i.e., $\mathsf{m}' = \mathsf{Dec}(\mathfrak{C}')$.

In $\mathbf{TamperNMC}_{A,2}^{f,m}()$ experiment (Algorithm 3), instead of using real decoding, the extractor algorithm of 1-more weakly extractable leakage resilient hash function $\mathsf{E}_{h_1}()$ is invoked to retrieve the preimage of the hash h_1, i.e., $(\hat{sk}, \hat{r})$. When the extracted value is consistent with (sk', r'), the hash $h_z(\hat{\mathsf{sk}}, \hat{r})$ is calculated again using the preimage $(\hat{\mathsf{sk}}, \hat{r})$ and subsequently, it is checked with the tampered hash h_1'. Finally, $\mathsf{m}' = \mathsf{Dec}(\mathfrak{C}')$ is performed. The main difference between $\mathbf{TamperNMC}_{\mathsf{A},2}^{\mathsf{f},\mathsf{m}}()$ experiment and earlier one is the use of 1-more extractability property of 1-more weakly extractable leakage resilient hash function which guarantees that if $\mathfrak{C}'$ is a valid codeword, $\mathsf{E}_{h_1}()$ should produce a valid preimage with overwhelming probability. In any circumstances, if the preimage generated by $\mathsf{E}_{h_1}()$ is not valid, it should return $\perp$. Now we describe the behaviour of extractor $\mathsf{E}_{h_1}()$ with the hash h_z, (c, tag), h_1, and the tampering function $\mathsf{f} = (\mathsf{f}_L, \mathsf{f}_R)$:

- (**Define** A_{h_1}) : $\mathsf{A}_{h_1}(h_z, h_1, p_{h_1}) = ([\mathsf{f}_R(h_1, p_{h_1})])$
- (**Select auxiliary information for** A_{h_1}) : $p_{h_1} = (\mathsf{c}, tag)$
- (**Role of extractor** E_{h_1} **and auxiliary input** p_E): Given the following information A_{h_1} and p_{h_1}, with the help of 1-more extractability property of the hash function H_τ, an extractor E_{h_1} can be designed, with additional hardwired auxiliary info p_E. The extractor finds the preimage from the hash value h_1 and finally, it computes $(\hat{\mathsf{sk}}, \hat{r}) \leftarrow \mathsf{E}_{h_1}(h_z, h_1, p_\mathsf{E})$.

Algorithm 1 Experiment $\mathbf{TamperNMC}_{\mathsf{A},0}^{\mathsf{f},\mathsf{m}}()$

1: $\mathsf{sk} \leftarrow \{0,1\}^{2\lambda}$
2: $(r, \mathsf{sk}, \mathsf{c}, tag, h_1) \leftarrow \mathsf{Enc}_{\mathsf{sk}}(\mathsf{m})$
3: $\mathfrak{C} = (r, \mathsf{sk}, \mathsf{c}, tag, h_1)$
4: $\mathsf{M}_L = (r, \mathsf{sk})$
5: $\mathsf{M}_R = (\mathsf{c}, tag, h_1)$
6: $(r', \mathsf{sk}') = \mathsf{f}_L(r, \mathsf{sk})$
7: $(\mathsf{c}', tag', h_1') = \mathsf{f}_R(\mathsf{c}, tag, h_1)$
8: $\mathfrak{C}' = (r', \mathsf{sk}', \mathsf{c}', tag', h_1')$
9: **if** $\mathfrak{C} = \mathfrak{C}'$ **then**
10:     output $same^*$
11: **else**
12:     output $\mathsf{m}' = \mathsf{Dec}(\mathfrak{C}')$
13: **end if**

The experiment $\mathbf{TamperNMC}_{\mathsf{A},3}^{\mathsf{f},\mathsf{m}}()$ differs from the previous one in the following way: Here the comparison of secret key sk and randomness r is performed via the leakage of a universal hash function $\widetilde{h} \leftarrow \widetilde{H_{\lambda-1}}$. The output of such hash produces $\lambda - 1$ bits. The description of the leakage function $l_v^{\widetilde{h}, h_z}$ is mentioned as follows:

$l_v^{\widetilde{h}, h_z}(\mathsf{sk}, r) = (0, \widetilde{h}(\mathsf{f}_L(\mathsf{sk}, r), h_z(\mathsf{sk}, r))$ if $(\mathsf{f}_L(\mathsf{sk}, r) = (\mathsf{sk}, r))$.

else, $l_v^{\widetilde{h}, h_z}(\mathsf{sk}, r) = (1, \widetilde{h}(\mathsf{f}_L(\mathsf{sk}, r), h_z(\mathsf{sk}, r)), (\mathsf{f}_L(\mathsf{sk}, r) \neq (\mathsf{sk}, r))$.

With access to the leakage function $l_v^{\widetilde{h}, h_z}$, an attacker can compute the hash $(\mathsf{b}, h_1') \leftarrow l_v^{\widetilde{h}}(r, \mathsf{sk})$. A random variable indicates whether the comparison of $(\mathsf{f}_L(\mathsf{sk}, r) = (\mathsf{sk}, r))$ is successful or not. When the comparison is true, b is set to 0. The main difference between this experiment with the earlier one is the statement $(\widetilde{h}(\hat{r}, \hat{\mathsf{sk}}) \neq h_1')$. Since the universal hash function $\widetilde{h}$ is collision resistant, it induces statistical difference only when a collision is occurred. The probability of such collision is negligible since $\tilde{h}$ is selected independently. Further, the hash of $h_z(\hat{r}, \hat{sk})$ is retrieved, and also it is compared, i.e., $h_1' = h_z(\hat{r}, \hat{sk})$. Finally, it outputs $\mathsf{Dec}(\mathfrak{C}')$, if they are equal. Otherwise, the experiment generates $\perp$.

It is also clear from the brief introduction of security proof that whenever the tampering experiment returns $\perp$, the security of strong NMC reduces to the security of semantically secure authenticated encryption scheme and extractable hash function.

At the end, we show that for any m^0 and m^1, the experiment $\mathbf{TamperNMC}_{A,3}^{f,\mathsf{m}^0}()$ and $\mathbf{TamperNMC}_{A,3}^{f,\mathsf{m}^1}()$ are computationally indistinguishable.

Algorithm 2 Experiment $\mathbf{TamperNMC}_{A,1}^{f,\mathsf{m}}()$

1: $\mathsf{sk} \leftarrow \{0,1\}^{2\lambda}$
2: $(r, \mathsf{sk}, \mathsf{c}, tag, h_1) \leftarrow \mathsf{Enc}_{\mathsf{sk}}(\mathsf{m})$
3: $\mathfrak{C} = (r, \mathsf{sk}, \mathsf{c}, tag, h_1)$
4: $M_L = (r, \mathsf{sk})$
5: $M_R = (\mathsf{c}, tag, h_1)$
6: $(r', \mathsf{sk}') = \mathsf{f}_L(r, \mathsf{sk})$
7: $(\mathsf{c}', tag', h_1') = \mathsf{f}_R(\mathsf{c}, tag, h_1)$
8: $\mathfrak{C}' = (r', \mathsf{sk}', \mathsf{c}', tag', h_1')$
9: **if** $(r, \mathsf{sk}, \mathsf{c}) = (r', \mathsf{sk}', \mathsf{c}')$ **then** $\triangleright$ Algo 2 is different from Algo 1 from this part
10:     **if** $tag \neq tag'$ **then**
11:         output $\perp$
12:     **else**
13:         **if** $h_1 = h_1'$ **then**
14:             output $same^*$
15:         **else**
16:             output $\perp$
17: **else**
18:     output $\mathsf{m}' = \mathsf{Dec}(\mathfrak{C}')$
19: **end if**

---

4   Security Proof of the Construction

To prove the non-malleability of our proposed design, we first prove some lemmas which is directly related to the Theorem 1.

Lemma 1. Let (SK, Enc, Dec) be a one-time leakage resilient authenticated encryption scheme, H_τ is the family of collision resistant, preimage resistant, 1-more extractable leakage resilient hash function, $f = (f_L, f_R) \in F$ be a tampering function and for any message m, the two experiments $TamperNMC_{A,0}^{f,\mathsf{m}}()$ and $TamperNMC_{A,1}^{f,\mathsf{m}}()$ are computationally indistinguishable.

Proof. The major difference between the experiment $\mathbf{TamperNMC}_{A,0}^{f,\mathsf{m}}()$ and $\mathbf{TamperNMC}_{A,1}^{f,\mathsf{m}}()$ are the way branch condition is performed in the experiment $\mathbf{TamperNMC}_{A,1}^{f,\mathsf{m}}()$:

(a) $((r, \mathsf{sk}, \mathsf{c}) = (r', \mathsf{sk}', \mathsf{c}') \wedge (tag = tag'))$
(b) $((r, \mathsf{sk}, \mathsf{c}) = (r', \mathsf{sk}', \mathsf{c}') \wedge (tag \neq tag'))$
(c) $((r, \mathsf{sk}, \mathsf{c}) = (r', \mathsf{sk}', \mathsf{c}') \wedge (tag = tag') \wedge (h_1 \neq h_1'))$
(d) $(h_1 = h_1')$

In the description of branching above, if we consider (a) and (d) only, two experiments $\mathbf{TamperNMC}_{A,0}^{f,m}()$ and $\mathbf{TamperNMC}_{A,1}^{f,m}()$ are exactly identical. Let E be the event that represents the branch condition $((r, \mathsf{sk}, \mathsf{c}) = (r', \mathsf{sk}', \mathsf{c}') \wedge (tag = tag') \wedge (h_1 \neq h_1'))$ is occured and the output of $\mathbf{TamperNMC}_{A,0}^{f,m}()$ is not $\perp$. Moreover, let F be the event $((r, \mathsf{sk}, \mathsf{c}) = (r', \mathsf{sk}', \mathsf{c}') \wedge (tag \neq tag'))$. The experiment $\mathbf{TamperNMC}_{A,0}^{f,m}()$ and $\mathbf{TamperNMC}_{A,1}^{f,m}()$ output $same^*$ conditioned on the event $\sim E, \sim F$. From the probability distribution, the statistical distance between two experiments are bounded by $Pr[E]$ and $Pr[F]$. We need to show that the occurrence of $Pr[E]$ and $Pr[F]$ should be negligible. Let us consider $Pr[E] > \epsilon(\tau)$, where ϵ is a negligible function. Then, there exists a PPT adversary A that breaks the collision resistance property of the underlying hash function H_τ.

The adversary can simulate $\mathbf{TamperNMC}_{A,1}^{f,m}()$ and produces the output $(r, \mathsf{sk}, \mathsf{c}), (r', \mathsf{sk}', \mathsf{c}'), h_1$ and h_1' (where $h_1' \leftarrow h_z(r, \mathsf{sk})$). The computation time of tampering function $f = (f_L, f_R) \in F$ is polynomial. Hence, the adversary runs for polynomial time and wins the event, where it is assumed that $Pr[E] > \epsilon(\tau)$. It implies that the collision resistance property of the underlying hash function is not satisfied with non-negligible probability. So, we arrive at the contradiction that hash function is not collision resistant. On the other hand, let us consider $Pr[F] > \epsilon(\tau)$. Then, we have an attacker A that breaks authenticity property under leakage. It uses the leakage function $l_v^{h_z} = h_z(r, \mathsf{sk})$ against the secret key of the encryption algorithm. Moreover, it receives $(h_1 \leftarrow h_z(r, \mathsf{sk}))$, and invokes the encoding of NMC to get the codeword $\mathfrak{C} \leftarrow \mathsf{Enc}_{\mathsf{sk}}(m)$. Further, the tampering function f_R is used in the following way $(\mathsf{c}', tag', h_1') = f_R(c, tag, h_1)$ and outputs tag. Now, assuming $Pr[F] > \epsilon(\tau)$, we get $(tag \neq tag')$ and the experiment produces a valid ciphertext by taking the secret input sk. Hence, the authenticity property breaks with non-negligible probability under leakage. Finally, we arrive at the contradiction and the lemma is proved.

Lemma 2. *Considering H_τ to be a family of 1-more weakly extractable leakage resilient hash function, for any tampering function $f = (f_L, f_R)$ and any message m, and $TamperNMC_{A,1}^{f,m}() \underset{c}{\approx} TamperNMC_{A,2}^{f,m}()$.*

Proof. Instead of using real decoding procedure, the $\mathbf{TamperNMC}_{A,2}^{f,m}()$ experiment uses the extractor of 1-more weakly extractable leakage resilient hash to retrieve the secret key and randomness, i.e., $(\hat{\mathsf{sk}}, \hat{r}) \leftarrow \mathsf{E}_{h_1}(h_z, h_1, p_\mathsf{E})$ if $(h_1 \neq h_1')$ is satisfied. Then, it is compared with the tampered key (sk', r'). Whenever the comparison is successful, the hash is regenerated using the extracted key and it is checked with the tampered hash as $h_1' = h_z(\hat{r}, \hat{\mathsf{sk}})$. This is the only difference between this experiment and earlier one. To prove that $\mathbf{TamperNMC}_{A,1}^{f,m}() \underset{c}{\approx}$

TamperNMC$_{A,2}^{f,m}$(), we need to show that probability of occurrence of the events $((\text{sk}', r') \neq (\hat{\text{sk}}, \hat{r}) \wedge (h_1' = h_z(\hat{\text{sk}}, \hat{r})))$ and $((\text{sk}', r') = (\hat{\text{sk}}, \hat{r}) \wedge (h_1' \neq h_z(\hat{\text{sk}}, \hat{r})))$ are negligible. Since we are using 1-more weakly extractable leakage resilient hash, which is deterministic in nature and the extracted value matches with (sk', r'), the inequality $((\text{sk}', r') = (\hat{\text{sk}}, \hat{r}) \wedge (h_1' \neq h_z(\hat{\text{sk}}, \hat{r})))$ should occur with negligible probability. Let us consider T be the event $(\text{sk}', r') \neq (\hat{\text{sk}}, \hat{r})$. Moreover, T_1, T_2 be the following events:

- T_1 : $T \wedge (h_z(\text{sk}', r') = h_z(\hat{\text{sk}}, \hat{r}) = h_1') \rightarrow$ This is possible only when collision is present and from the property of 1-more weakly extractable leakage resilient hash $Pr[T_1] \leq \epsilon(\tau)$.
- T_2 : $T \wedge (h_z(\text{sk}', r') = h_1' \wedge h_z(\hat{\text{sk}}, \hat{r}) \neq h_1') \rightarrow$ From the property of hash function, we can conclude that $Pr[T_2] \leq \epsilon(k)$. Now, we can find the relation between **TamperNMC**$_{A,2}^{f,m}$() and **Exp**$_{A_{h_1}, A_{\text{sk}}, E_{h_1}}^{\text{sk}, h_z}$$(1, p_{h_1}, p_E)$, for some message m', algorithm A_{h_1}, A_{sk}, extractor E_{h_1} and inputs p_{h_1}, p_E.

Therefore, from the above analysis, it is proved that $Pr[T_1] + Pr[T_2] \leq \epsilon(\tau)$. Hence, **TamperNMC**$_{A,1}^{f,m}$() $\underset{c}{\approx}$ **TamperNMC**$_{A,2}^{f,m}$().

Algorithm 3 Experiment **TamperNMC**$_{A,2}^{f,m}$()

1: $\text{sk} \leftarrow \{0,1\}^{2\lambda}$
2: $(r, \text{sk}, c, tag, h_1) \leftarrow \text{Enc}_{\text{sk}}(m)$
3: $\mathfrak{C} = (r, \text{sk}, c, tag, h_1)$
4: $M_L = (r, \text{sk})$
5: $M_R = (c, tag, h_1)$
6: $(r', \text{sk}') = f_L(r, \text{sk})$
7: $(c', tag', h_1') = f_R(c, tag, h_1)$
8: **if** $(r, \text{sk}, c) = (r', \text{sk}', c')$ **then**
9:      **if** $tag \neq tag'$ **then**
10:         output $\perp$
11:     **else**
12:         **if** $h_1 = h_1'$ **then**
13:             output $same^*$
14: **if** $h_1 \neq h_1'$ **then**
15:     $(\hat{\text{sk}}, \hat{r}) \leftarrow E_{h_1}(h_z, h_1, p_E)$ ▷ Algo 3 is different from Algo 2 from this part
16:     **if** $(\text{sk}', r') = (\hat{r}, \hat{\text{sk}})$ **then**
17:         **if** $h_1' = h_z(\hat{r}, \hat{\text{sk}})$ **then**
18:             output $m' = \text{Dec}(\mathfrak{C}')$
19:         **else**
20:             output $\perp$
21:     **else**
22:         output $\perp$
23: **end if**

Algorithm 4 Experiment $\mathbf{TamperNMC}_{A,3}^{f,m}()$

1: $\mathsf{sk} \leftarrow \{0,1\}^{2\lambda}$
2: $(r, \mathsf{sk}, \mathsf{c}, tag, h_1) \leftarrow \mathsf{Enc}_{\mathsf{sk}}(\mathsf{m})$
3: $\mathfrak{C} = (r, \mathsf{sk}, \mathsf{c}, tag, h_1)$
4: $M_L = (r, \mathsf{sk})$
5: $M_R = (\mathsf{c}, tag, h_1)$
6: $(r', \mathsf{sk}') = f_L(r, \mathsf{sk})$
7: $(\mathsf{c}', tag', h_1') = f_R(\mathsf{c}, tag, h_1)$
8: $(\mathsf{b}, h_1^l) \leftarrow l_v^{\tilde{h}, h_z}(\mathsf{sk}, r)$
9: **if** $(r, \mathsf{sk}, \mathsf{c}) = (r', \mathsf{sk}', \mathsf{c}')$ **then**
10:      **if** $tag = tag'$ **then**   ▷ Algo 4 is different from Algo 3 from this part
11:          **if** $h_1^l = h_1'$ **then**
12:              output $same^*$
13:      **else**
14:          output $\perp$
15: $(\hat{\mathsf{sk}}, \hat{r}) \leftarrow E_v(h_z, h_1, p_E)$
16: **if** $\tilde{h}(\hat{r}, \hat{\mathsf{sk}}) \neq h_1^l$ **then**
17:      **if** $(\mathsf{sk}', r) = (\hat{\mathsf{sk}}, r)$ **then**
18:          **if** $h_1' = h_z(r, \hat{\mathsf{sk}})$ **then**
19:              output $m' = \mathsf{Dec}(\mathfrak{C}')$
20:          **else**
21:              output $\perp$
22:      **else**
23:          output $\perp$
24: **end if**

Lemma 3. *Let $\tilde{h} \leftarrow \widetilde{H_{\lambda-1}}$ be a universal hash function that generates $\lambda-1$ bits as output, where $\lambda = \omega(log\tau)$ and H_τ is a collision resistant hash function, for any message m, $\mathbf{TamperNMC}_{A,2}^{f,m}() \underset{c}{\approx} \mathbf{TamperNMC}_{A,3}^{f,m}()$.*

Proof. $\mathbf{TamperNMC}_{A,3}^{f,m}()$ experiment selects $\tilde{h} \leftarrow \widetilde{H_{\lambda-1}}$ from a universal hash function and calculates the hash by taking the secret key sk and randomness r as input. We notice the difference between this experiment and the earlier one is the calculation of hash value, i.e., $h_1^l = h_1'$ where $(\mathsf{b}, h_1^l) \leftarrow l_v^{\tilde{h}, h_z}(\mathsf{sk}, r)$. When such condition is met, output is set to $same^*$. Let C_1 be the event $((\tilde{h}(\hat{\mathsf{sk}}, \hat{r}) = h_1^l) \wedge (\mathsf{sk}', r') \neq (\hat{\mathsf{sk}}, \hat{r}))$. From the collision resistance property of universal hash, we get $Pr[C_1] \leq \epsilon(\tau)$. The statistical difference of the above experiments are bounded by $Pr[C_1]$ and the universal hash $\tilde{h}$ is selected in an independent way from its input and for any two inputs, the maximum collision probability is upper bounded by $2^{\lambda-1} \leq \epsilon(\tau)$. Moreover, let C_2 be the event that $(\tilde{h}(\hat{\mathsf{sk}}, \hat{r}) \neq h_1^l) \wedge (\mathsf{sk}', r') = (\hat{\mathsf{sk}}, \hat{r}))$. We observe that $Pr[C_2] \leq \epsilon(\tau)$ due to the deterministic nature of the underlying hash. Hence, we can conclude that $\mathbf{TamperNMC}_{A,2}^{f,m}()$ and $\mathbf{TamperNMC}_{A,3}^{f,m}()$ are computationally indistinguishable.

Lemma 4. *Let (SK, Enc, Dec) be a one-time semantically secure leakage resilient authenticated encryption scheme, for any* $f = (f_L, f_R)$ *and for any two messages* m^0 *and* m^1, $\mathbf{TamperNMC}_{A,3}^{f,m^0}() \approx_c \mathbf{TamperNMC}_{A,3}^{f,m^1}()$.

Proof. For any two messages m^0, m^1 and for any $f = (f_L, f_R)$, we can construct a PPT distinguisher D in such a way that satisfies $|Pr[D(\mathbf{TamperNMC}_{A,3}^{f,m^0}()) = 1] - Pr[D(\mathbf{TamperNMC}_{A,3}^{f,m^1}()) = 1]| > \epsilon$, where $\epsilon = 1/poly(\tau)$. The adversary can break the semantic security of the authenticated encryption by picking the leakage function $l_v^{\tilde{h},h_z}()$. Moreover, it can hardwire the leakage function and simulates the experiment $\mathbf{TamperNMC}_{A,3}^{f,m}()$ for any pair of messages m^0 and m^1. An adversary breaks the semantic security of the encryption scheme with the same advantage of D by distinguishing $\mathbf{TamperNMC}_{A,3}^{f,m^0}()$ and $\mathbf{TamperNMC}_{A,3}^{f,m^1}()$, which is negligible by assumption. Hence, we reach at the contradiction and the lemma is proved.

The complete analysis shows that for any $f = (f_L, f_R)$ and for any messages m^0 and m^1, we get $\mathbf{TamperNMC}_{A,3}^{f,m^0}() \approx_c \mathbf{TamperNMC}_{A,3}^{f,m^1}()$. Finally, we can derive the Theorem 1 as follows:

Theorem 1. *Let* $\tilde{h} : \{0,1\}^\tau \to \{0,1\}^{\lambda-1}$ *be sampled from the family of universal hash function* $\widehat{H_{\lambda-1}}$ *and* H_τ *be 1-more weakly extractable leakage resilient hash function that outputs* $\rho(\tau)$ *bits. Suppose the authenticated encryption* (SK, Enc, Dec) *be a semantically secure against one-time leakage that can handle* $\lambda = \omega(log\tau) + \rho(\tau)$ *bits of leakage at most. Then the coding scheme* (Enc$_{sk}$, Dec) *is said to be strongly non-malleable with respect to* $f = (f_L, f_R) \in F$ *and leakage resilient with respect to* l_v.

5   Conclusion

In this work, we describe a framework to design leakage resilient AE. Further, an instantiation of such AE is shown using CFB mode of encryption with a CBC-MAC. Moreover, we design a computationally secure NMC with the underlying AE and hash function in the split-state model. The requirement of CRS based setup is completely removed in our construction. Further research work can be pursued to design such NMC by decreasing the length of codeword, and from minimal cryptographic assumptions while maintaining the same security against one-time tampering attack. Another interesting direction of this work is to construct continuous version of the NMC which provides security against polynomial number of tampering and continual leakage attacks. These constructions can applied to design tamper resilient signature scheme etc. in the various real life settings.

References

1. Boneh, D., DeMillo, R.A., Lipton, R.J.: On the importance of eliminating errors in cryptographic computations. J. Cryptol. **14**(2), 101–119 (2001)
2. Bellare, M., Namprempre, C.: Authenticated encryption: relations among notions and analysis of the generic composition paradigm. In: Okamoto, T. (ed.) ASIACRYPT 2000. LNCS, vol. 1976, pp. 531–545. Springer, Heidelberg (2000). https://doi.org/10.1007/3-540-44448-3_41
3. De Santis, A., Di Crescenzo, G., Ostrovsky, R., Persiano, G., Sahai, A.: Robust non-interactive zero knowledge. In: Kilian, J. (ed.) CRYPTO 2001. LNCS, vol. 2139, pp. 566–598. Springer, Heidelberg (2001). https://doi.org/10.1007/3-540-44647-8_33
4. Joan, D., Vincent, R.: The Design of Rijndael. Springer, New York (2002). https://doi.org/10.1007/978-3-662-04722-4
5. Agrawal, D., Archambeault, B., Rao, J.R., Rohatgi, P.: The EM side channel(s): attacks and assessment methodologies. In: Kaliski, B.S., Jr., Koc, C.K., Paar, C. (eds.) CHES 2002. LNCS, vol. 2523, pp. 29–45. Springer, Heidelberg (2003). https://doi.org/10.1007/3-540-36400-5_4
6. Groth, J., Sahai, A.: Efficient non-interactive proof systems for bilinear groups. In: Smart, N.P. (ed.) EUROCRYPT 2008. LNCS, vol. 4965, pp. 415–432. Springer, Heidelberg (2008). https://doi.org/10.1007/978-3-540-78067-3_24
7. Pietrzak, K.: A leakage-resilient mode of operation. In: Joux, A (ed.) EUROCRYPT 2009. LNCS, vol. 5479, pp. 462–482. Springer, Heidelberg (2009). https://doi.org/10.1007/978-3-642-01001-9_27
8. Naor, M., Segev, G.: Public-key cryptosystems resilient to key leakage. In: Halevi, S. (ed.) CRYPTO 2009. LNCS, vol. 5677, pp. 18–35. Springer, Heidelberg (2009). https://doi.org/10.1007/978-3-642-03356_8_2
9. Standaert, F.-X., Pereira, O., Yu, Y., Quisquater, J.-J., Yung, M., Oswald, E.: Leakage resilient cryptography in practice. In: Sadeghi, A.R., Naccache, D. (eds.) Towards Hardware-Intrinsic Security, pp. 99–134. Springer, Heidelberg (2010). https://doi.org/10.1007/978-3-642-14452-3_5
10. Dziembowski, S., Pietrzak, K., Wichs, D.: Non-malleable codes. In: Yao, A.C.-C. (ed.) ICS 2010, Beijing, China, 5–7 January, pp. 434–452. Tsinghua University Press (2010)
11. Liu, F.-H., Lysyanskaya, A.: Tamper and leakage resilience in the split-state model. In: Safavi-Naini, R. (ed.) CRYPTO 2012. LNCS, vol. 7417, pp. 517–532. Springer, Heidelberg (2012). https://doi.org/10.1007/978-3-642-32009-5_30
12. Bitansky, N., Canetti, R., Chiesa, A., Tromer, E.: From extractable collision resistance to succinct non-interactive arguments of knowledge, and back again. In: ITCS, pp. 326–349 (2012)
13. Dziembowski, S., Kazana, T., Obremski, M.: Non-malleable codes from two-source extractors. In: Canetti, R., Garay, J.A. (eds.) CRYPTO 2013. LNCS, vol. 8043, pp. 239–257. Springer, Heidelberg (2013). https://doi.org/10.1007/978-3-642-40084-1_14
14. Abdalla, M., Belaïd, S., Fouque, P.-A.: Leakage-resilient symmetric encryption via re-keying. In: Bertoni, G., Coron, J.-S. (eds.) CHES 2013. LNCS, vol. 8086, pp. 471–488. Springer, Heidelberg (2013). https://doi.org/10.1007/978-3-642-40349-1_27
15. Aggarwal, D., Dodis, Y., Lovett, S.: Non-malleable codes from additive combinatorics. In: STOC, pp. 774–783 (2014)

16. Aggarwal, D., Dodis, Y., Kazana, T., Obremski, M.: Non-malleable reductions and applications. In: Proceedings of the Forty-Seventh Annual ACM on Symposium on Theory of Computing, pp. 459–468. ACM (2015)

17. Pereira, O., Standaert, F., Vivek, S.: Leakage-resilient authentication and encryption from symmetric cryptographic primitives. In: CCS 2015, pp. 96–108 (2015)

18. Kiayias, A., Liu, F., Tselekounis, Y.: Practical non-malleable codes from l-more extractable hash functions. In: CCS, pp. 1317–1328 (2016)

19. Aggarwal, D., Agrawal, S., Gupta, D., Maji, H.K., Pandey, O., Prabhakaran, M.: Optimal computational split-state non-malleable codes. In: Kushilevitz, E., Malkin, T. (eds.) TCC 2016. LNCS, vol. 9563, pp. 393–417. Springer, Heidelberg (2016). https://doi.org/10.1007/978-3-662-49099-0_15

20. Barwell, G., Martin, D.P., Oswald, E., Stam, M.: Authenticated encryption in the face of protocol and side channel leakage. In: Takagi, T., Peyrin, T. (eds.) ASIACRYPT 2017. LNCS, vol. 10624, pp. 693–723. Springer, Cham (2017). https://doi.org/10.1007/978-3-319-70694-8_24

21. Dziembowski, S., Pietrzak, K., Wichs, D.: Non-malleable codes. J. ACM **65**(4), 20:1–20:32 (2018)

22. Fehr, S., Karpman, P., Mennink, B.: Short non-malleable codes from related-key secure block ciphers. IACR Trans. Symmetric Cryptol. 336–352 (2018)

23. Aggarwal, D., Obremski, M.: A constant-rate non-malleable code in the split-state model. In: IEEE 61st Annual Symposium on Foundations of Computer Science, FOCS (2020)

24. Krämer, J., Struck, P.: Leakage-resilient authenticated encryption from leakage-resilient pseudorandom functions. In: Bertoni, G.M., Regazzoni, F. (eds.) COSADE 2020. LNCS, vol. 12244, pp. 315–337. Springer, Cham (2021). https://doi.org/10.1007/978-3-030-68773-1_15

25. Brian, G., Faonio, A., Ribeiro, L., Venturi, D.: Short non-malleable codes from related-key secure block ciphers, revisited. IACR Trans. Symmetric Cryptol. 1–19 (2022)

26. Ghosal, A.K., Ghosh, S., Roychowdhury, D.: Practical non-malleable codes from symmetric-key primitives in 2-split-state model. In: Ge, C., Guo, F. (eds.) Provable and Practical Security (2022)

27. Kiayias, A., Liu, F.H., Tselekounis, Y.: Leakage Resilient l-more Extractable Hash and Applications to Non-Malleable Cryptography. Cryptology ePrint Archive, Report 2022/1745 (2022)

28. Ghosal, A.K., Roychowdhury, D.: Non-malleable codes from authenticated encryption in split-state model. In: Prabhu, S., Pokhrel, S.R., Li, G. (eds.) Applications and Techniques in Information Security (2022)

Short Papers

DP-Loc: A Differential Privacy-Based Indoor Localization Scheme with Bilateral Privacy Protection

Yinghui Zhang[1,2(✉)], Haorui Du[1,2], Jin Cao[3], Gang Han[1,2],
and Dong Zheng[1,2,4]

[1] School of Cyberspace Security, Xi'an University of Posts and Telecommunications,
Xi'an 710121, China
yhzhaang@163.com

[2] National Engineering Research Center for Secured Wireless, Xi'an University of
Posts and Telecommunications, Xi'an 710121, China

[3] School of Cyber Engineering, Xidian University, Xi'an 710071, China

[4] Westone Cryptologic Research Center, Beijing 100070, China

Abstract. Among indoor localization services, WiFi fingerprint tech nology has attracted much attention because of its wide coverage area and high positioning accuracy. However, concerns arise regarding the vulnerability of users' personal sensitive information to malicious attacks during location queries. Existing differential privacy (DP) indoor local ization techniques encounter challenges when iterating the collected user fingerprints into the clustering process, as the addition of noise to cluster centroids during iterative operations can lead to increasing deviations, adversely affecting clustering results and causing localization errors. In this paper, we put forward a differential privacy indoor localization scheme (DP-Loc) that supports bilateral privacy protection. It mainly protects the privacy of the user's personal location when querying in the online localization phase, as well as the privacy of the fingerprint database on the server side. The online stage server-side fingerprint clus tering reduces the error in the fingerprint clustering stage by selecting the centroids, dividing the similarity between clusters and clusters, adding noise to cluster centers based on differential privacy, masking the true position by fingerprint replacement, and returning the results to the client to complete the localization. Experimental simulations and tests conducted on an existing dataset demonstrate that the DP-Loc scheme enhances localization accuracy within the same privacy budget while also providing more robust protection for user location privacy compared to existing approaches.

Keywords: WiFi fingerprint · Indoor localization · Privacy protection · Differential privacy · Fingerprint clustering

1 Introduction

With the increasing development of mobile communication technology, location-based services (LBS) technology has become pervasive in various domains [10].

However, due to the confined indoor space and lack of GPS signals, WiFi fingerprint-based indoor localization technology has become one of the most promising indoor localization technologies characterized by its advantages of extensive coverage area and cost-effectiveness. It uses WiFi access points (AP) to determine the received signal strength (RSS) value as a specific fingerprint location. The localization process involves two distinct stages: offline and online [13]. In the offline stage, RSS valued from different AP in the reference points (RP) are gathered and deposited in the fingerprint database of the location service provider (LSP) [4]. The user's location can be assessed by the RSS value they sends during the online stage. However, when users obtain their location by querying the location server, their location can be leaked to untrustworthy location servers or stolen from the transmission by malicious attackers.

To protect user privacy more effectively when the client sends the query location and to ensure the privacy of the LSP fingerprint database from malicious attacks, we propose the DP-Loc scheme based on the existing differential privacy WiFi fingerprint-based indoor localization scheme. Our contributions are as follows:

Existing differential privacy-based indoor localization schemes either cause localization errors due to poor fingerprint clustering or poor privacy protection due to inappropriate selection of privacy budget. In this regard, we propose an online stage localization framework, which includes three steps: initial center selection, sample points division into clusters, and calculation of new clustering center from the fingerprint clustering process, to solve the problem of poor clustering due to the new cluster centers deviating from the true cluster centers. We measure the utility of the scheme by the change in the average distance error under different privacy budgets, and then compare the localization accuracy with that of the existing scheme, and simultaneously compare the localization accuracy of those scheme without privacy protection. The experimental results confirm that our proposed DP-Loc online stage localization scheme can effectively guarantee the localization accuracy while protecting the user location privacy during the localization process.

2   Related Work

In recent years, the issue of privacy protection in WiFi indoor localization has been gradually taken into account. Li et al. [9] proposes to protect location privacy by homomorphic encrypted measurement of RSS, named PriWFL, but the drawback is that the computational overhead is too large and can be too demanding for the client terminal device because of the resource consumption of encryption and decryption. Konstantinidis A et al. [8] put forward a privacy-preserving location scheme using k-anonymity, where the client sends a location request using WiFi fingerprint features of multiple locations instead of real-time WiFi fingerprint features of a single point to be located, so the server cannot determine the true location of the client user and thus achieve privacy protection. Unfortunately, the k-anonymity scheme can indirectly infer the true location of the client by using some historical data. Järvinen K et al. [6] combines a secure two-party computing protocol with a size- and depth-optimized circuit designed for PPIL, but the drawback is that a secure system for multi-party computation requires a lot of processing and high communication overhead.

Similarly, differential privacy is also used to protect privacy in indoor localization, first proposed by Dwork [2], and can be used against attackers with arbitrary background knowledge. Specifically, existing studies based on differential privacy are more likely to use differential privacy techniques to protect location privacy by adding noise to fingerprint data. Zhao et al. [14] put forward a privacy-preserving paradigm-driven indoor localization framework based on differential privacy, motivated by the fact that indoor localization systems share a common two-phase localization paradigm. In addition, Kim et al. [7] combined localized differential privacy and optimal data coding to interfere with user data. Similarly, Wang et al. [12] put forward a differential privacy-based indoor privacy-preserving localization scheme DP3 by Laplace noise and clustering of fingerprints to preserve privacy. However, in the existing indoor localization schemes on differential privacy, it is difficult to take into account the localization accuracy while protecting the location privacy.

3   System Model and Attack Model

In this section we will introduce the system model and the attack model for the whole scenario.

3.1   System Model

The whole indoor localization privacy preserving system of DP-Loc is divided into two phases: offline sampling phase and online localization phase. Considering the length requirements of the paper, we will not focus on privacy protection during fingerprinting in the offline phase here.

The online stage user sends AP sample to the already collected fingerprint database to form a new fingerprint database. Using the DP-based k-means++ clustering algorithm, the k clusters with the closest positions are divided by multiple iterations. The exponential mechanism is then used to replace each location in the same cluster in a probabilistic manner, and finally the processed dataset was returned to the client, which uses the location matching algorithm to locate it.

3.2   Attacker Model

Throughout the program, we not only consider the privacy issue when the client user sends query personal location information in the online stage but also focus on the privacy issue when the fingerprint database LSP collects reference point AP fingerprints in the offline stage.

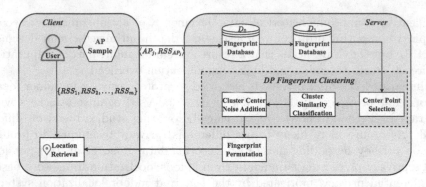

Fig. 1. The online stage system framework of DP-Loc.

Attacks on client users: The attacker could be a service provider that makes a profit by collecting user location information or an outside attacker who can intercept the location results sent by the server to the client or the real-time fingerprint of the client and get the location result of the client by online stage query.

4   Design of DP-Loc

In this section, we will describe the specific realization process of the DP-Loc scheme. The online stage process is shown in Fig. 1. The client to be located collects the instantaneous WiFi fingerprint, including the name of the AP and the Counterpart RSS value, noting $\langle AP_j, RSS_{AP_j} \rangle_{AP_j \subseteq Sample}$. The client only needs to send the AP sample to the server to initiate the location request. The complete WiFi fingerprint is easily intercepted by attackers to obtain the location of the client to be located by querying the server. Upon receipt of the AP sample, the server extracts the reports in the fingerprint database D_0 with even values of AP sample to form a certain dataset D_1. Through centroid selection, inter-cluster similarity division within clusters, and finally, the cluster center noise addition based on differential privacy is used to calculate the new cluster centers to achieve privacy protection for the fingerprint clustering phase. Considering that the location is still real, we introduce fingerprint permutation with the purpose of perturbing dataset D_1 to ensure that the fingerprints in dataset D_1 will not be re-identified. Finally, the fingerprint permutation data is updated, and the updated data set will be delivered back to the client, and the user can complete the query by entering the real-time WiFi fingerprint.

4.1   DP Fingerprint Clustering

Upon receipt of the AP sample, the server extracts the reports in the fingerprint database D_0 with even values of AP sample to form a certain dataset D_1. A DP-based fingerprint clustering algorithm partitions sampled points into k clusters while incorporating differential privacy to conceal the actual centroid of each cluster, preventing the inference of cluster membership for a location from the clustering output. The Laplace mechanism is used in the fingerprint clustering phase, and global sensitivity is used throughout the process, which is determined by the maximum distance between any pair of positions in the dataset D_1. The whole fingerprint clustering stage includes the selection of initial centroids, the similarity division between clusters within clusters, and the noise addition to the cluster centers, and the scheme is described as follows:

In the selection of the initial centroids, we improve and optimize the k-means++ roulette wheel method [1]. Considering the distribution characteristics of the sample selected probabilities in the calculation of the cumulative probabilities, the selection probabilities are sorted in reverse order from largest to smallest. Thus the method enhances the probability of the more distant sample as the next initial center, increases the stability and accuracy of the initial center selection, and reduces the sensitivity of the DP k-means algorithm to the initial center selection. The whole procedure is shown in Algorithm 1.

Algorithm 1. Cluster initial center selection

Input: The original data set, D_1; the number of clusters, k;
Output: Cluster initial center, u;
1: Randomly select the first initial center u_0, $j = 0$, $u \in D_1$;
2: **while** $j < k$ **do**
3:   **for** $i : D_1$ **do**
4:     $dist(x_i, u_j) = argmin\| x_i, u_j \|_2$, $u_j \in u$;
5:     $p(x_i) = \frac{dist(x_i, u_j)^2}{\sum_{x_i \in D_1} dist(x_i, u_j)^2}$;
6:   $reversedSort(d)$;
7:   $pr = rand(0, 1)$;
8:   **for** $q : D_1$ **do**
9:     **if** $pr \leq \sum_{i=0}^{q} p(x_i)$ **then**
10:       $u_j := x_q$;
11:       $j = j + 1$;
12:       $break$;
13:     **end if**
14:   **end for**
15:   **end for**
16: **end while**
17: **return** u;

While optimizing the selection of the initial center improves the clustering effect to some extent, it does not solve the cluster center deviation problem. As the number of iterations increases, the possibility and degree of cluster center deviation will become larger and larger, leading to inaccurate final classification of clusters. Based on this idea, we redefine the similarity metric when dividing clusters, i.e., consider the intra-cluster and inter-cluster similarity. First, calculate the similarity of each sample to each cluster set, and then the product of

---

Algorithm 2. Intra-cluster inter-cluster clustering division

Input: The original data set D_1, the cluster centroid u
Output: Cluster set C
1: **for** $i : D_1$ **do**
2:     $similarity(x_i, C_z) = \frac{1}{|C_z|}\sum_{y \in C_z} \| x_i, y \|_2^2$;
3:     $dist(x_i, u_j)' = dist(x_i, u_j) * similarity(x_i, C_z)$;
4:     $C_z \Leftarrow argmin_j \; dist(x_i, u_j)'$;
5: **end for**
6: **return** C;

---

this similarity and the traditional euclidean distance is calculated as the distance when the sample is divided into clusters. The intra-cluster similarity of the sample to the cluster it belongs to is higher than the other inter-cluster similarity and is numerically the smallest, so calculating the product of this similarity and the traditional Euclidean distance, as the distance when dividing the clusters, can indirectly increase the possibility that the sample still belongs to the original cluster when reclassifying the clusters, which also disguisedly offsets a certain degree of cluster center deviation. The whole procedure is shown in Algorithm 2.

Considering Laplace noise has randomness, it is possible that the absolute value of the added noise $\frac{sum'}{num'}$ is so large that it deviates completely from the $[0, 1]^d$-space range. Based on the transformation invariance of differential privacy, a clustering center correction mechanism is proposed to deal with the clustering center bias issue. Transforming the deviated cluster center coordinates to the $[0, 1]^d$-space range can essentially solve the cluster center deviation problem caused by adding Laplace random noise and also prevent the extreme case where the deviated cluster center divides no samples or all samples are divided into a certain cluster. Similarly, since the privacy-preserving budget is a pre-given fixed value, how to allocate the privacy-preserving budget reasonably is a key issue. Dwork proposed two ways of allocating the privacy budget to protect the cluster centers by adding Laplace random noise to sum and num, respectively. Adding or removing a sample in a d-dimensional dataset with a maximum change of 1 in each dimension results in a global sensitivity $\Delta f_{sum} = d$ for sum, a global sensitivity $\Delta f_{num} = 1$ for num, and an overall global sensitivity $GS = d + 1$. If the total iteration count T is known, then each privacy budget consumption can be set to $\frac{\varepsilon}{T}$ and each added Laplace noise to $Lap(\frac{T \cdot GS}{\varepsilon})$. If the total iteration count T is unknown, then each privacy budget consumption is set to $\frac{1}{2}$ of the remaining privacy budget and the random noise added in the t-th iteration to $Lap(\frac{GS \cdot 2^t}{\varepsilon})$. In the fingerprint clustering phase, we use the method with unknown number of iterations to allocate the privacy protection budget of $\frac{\varepsilon}{2}$. The whole procedure is shown in Algorithm 3.

Algorithm 3. Cluster center noise addition

Input: Cluster set C, number of clusters k, global sensitivity GS, privacy-preserving budget $\frac{\varepsilon}{2}$

Output: Cluster set u'

1: **for** $j : k$ **do**
2:     $sum = \sum_{x \in C_z} x$;
3:     $num = \mid C_z \mid$;
4:     $sum' = sum + Lap(\frac{2 \cdot GS}{\varepsilon})$;
5:     $num' = num + Lap(\frac{2 \cdot GS}{\varepsilon})$;
6:     $new\ u = \frac{sum'}{num'}$;
7:     **if** $new\ u \notin [0,1]^d$ **then**
8:         $u_j' = corrMechanism(new\ u)$;
9:     **else**
10:         $u_j' = new\ u$;
11:     **end if**
12: **end for**
13: **return** u';

4.2   Fingerprint Permutation

Although after the DP fingerprint clustering phase, the location and WiFi fingerprints are still true for the fingerprint dataset, and the fingerprint permutation phase aims to perturb the dataset D_1 and ensure that the fingerprints in the dataset D_1 are not re-identified. The privacy budget of this phase assigns $\frac{\varepsilon}{2}$. The scheme uses an exponential mechanism to permute the sampling points, and for a specific location t_i in the cluster u', all of the locations in the cluster u' are composed with different probabilities to replace the candidate set I_l at a specific location t_i.

From exponential mechanism [3], it is clear that the mechanism M can satisfy ε−differential privacy as long as it satisfies $Pr[M(I) = t_j] \propto exp\frac{\varepsilon \cdot q(I, t_j)}{2 \Delta q}$, where $q(I, t_j)$ is the scoring function used to calculate location t_j in I as the output. It can be observed that the probability of permutation t_i for each position in the candidate set I_l in cluster u' is related to the scoring function $q(I, t_j)$ and the sensitivity of the scoring function. The formula for the probability of replacing $t_i(t_j, t_i \subseteq I_l)$ with t_j is as follows:

$$Pr_{t_j, t_i \subseteq I_l}(t_j) = \frac{exp\frac{\varepsilon \cdot q_i(I_l, t_j)}{4 \cdot GS}}{\sum_{t_j, t_i \subseteq I_l} exp(\frac{\varepsilon \cdot q_i(I_l, t_j)}{4 \cdot GS})} \tag{1}$$

We define the scoring function $q_i(I_l, t_j)$ by the distance between sampling points:

$$q_i(I_l, t_j) = GS - \| (x_i, y_i) - (x_j - y_j) \|_2 \tag{2}$$

The distance between t_i and t_j determines the sensitivity Δq, which is $\Delta q = GS$ [5]. After displacing all positions in dataset D_1, the server sends the renewed dataset S back to the client to complete the location service locally at the client.

4.3   Location Retrieval

We input the real WiFi fingerprint $\{RSS_1, RSS_2, ..., RSS_m\}$ and the permuted dataset S, and output the coordinates of the client to be located by location calculation. We choose a modified weighted K nearest neighbor (WKNN) matching algorithm to estimate the client user's location. The localization process is shown below:

Calculate the Euclidean distance between the real-time WiFi fingerprint and the $i(i = 1, 2, ..., N)$-th fingerprint in the data set S. m is the fingerprint vector length, and the equation is as follows:

$$d = \sqrt{\sum_{j}^{m}(RSS_i - rss_{ij})^2} \tag{3}$$

WKNN weighted the inverse of the distance to the K reference point positions to obtain the location of the point to be measured:

$$x = \frac{1}{\sum_{j=1}^{K} d_j^{-1}} \sum_{j=1}^{K} d_j^{-1} x_j \tag{4}$$

$$y = \frac{1}{\sum_{j=1}^{K} d_j^{-1}} \sum_{j=1}^{K} d_j^{-1} y_j \tag{5}$$

x and y are the coordinates of the location of the point to be measured estimated by the algorithm; x_j and y_j are the coordinates of the position of the j-th reference point; d_j is the distance between the fingerprint of the point to be measured and the fingerprint of the j-th reference point.

Output the location coordinates (x, y) of the client to be located.

5   Theoretical Analysis and Experimental Results

In this section, we analyze the security of the experimental protocols, and next we evaluate the experimental performance on the existing dataset. Finally, we have a comparison of the experimental data to confirm the implementability and the optimization of our scheme over the original one.

5.1   Security Analysis

Online Stage Client User Location Privacy Protection. In the AP fuzzification phase, the client to be located collects fingerprints, including the AP number and the appropriate RSS value. However, the client barely sends the AP sample to the server, not the entire WiFi fingerprint. Likewise, no attacker, including the server itself, can obtain the practical fingerprints of the client user and be unable to locate the client by further query. In addition, the location retrieval step is performed locally by the client, and an attacker cannot infer location information by obtaining the dataset sent back by the server.

Optimized DP K-Means++ Centered Noise Addition Algorithm Satisfies Differential Privacy. Given a mechanism χ whose randomness is independent of the specific dataset D_1 and the Laplace distribution, then $\chi(u_j{}' = \frac{sum'}{num'})$ fulfills ε-differential privacy.

According to Laplace mechanism [3], it follows that the Laplace mechanism provides ε-differential privacy protection for cluster centers, i.e., $u_j{}' = \frac{sum'}{num'}$ satisfies ε-differential privacy protection. According to the definition of differential privacy, for the cluster centers D_a, D_b of the neighboring datasets u_1, u_2, we have the formula $Pr[Lap(u_1)] \leq e^\varepsilon \times Pr[Lap(u_2)]$. According to the invariance of transformation, that is, for any algorithm that does not directly use sensitive data, it is applied on the result of an algorithm that has satisfied ε- differential privacy protection, and still satisfies ε- differential privacy protection. So we can get:

$$Pr[\chi(Lap(u_1))] = Pr[Lap(u_1)] \tag{6}$$

$$Pr[\chi(Lap(u_2))] = Pr[Lap(u_2)] \tag{7}$$

From this it follows that:

$$Pr[\chi(Lap(u_1))] \leq e^\varepsilon \times Pr[\chi(Lap(u_2))] \tag{8}$$

5.2 Experimental Performance Analysis

We use the UJIIndoorLoc [11] dataset to evaluate the performance of DP-Loc and do a comparison with the DP3 scheme on this basis. The UJIIndoorLoc database includes three buildings at Jaume I University with more than four floors. We selected one floor to sample and set up 36 AP points with a total of 268 WiFi fingerprint records.

In the overall experiment, we measure the utility of the dataset by considering the distance error (DE) between the replacement location in dataset S and the counterpart location in dataset D_1, as shown in the following equation, where $t_i{}'$ is the position in dataset S with the counterpart of t_i in a particular dataset D_1.

$$DE = \frac{\sum_{t_i \subseteq D_1, t_i{}' \subseteq S} \|(x_i, y_i) - (x_i{}', y_i{}')\|_2}{GS \cdot |S|} \tag{9}$$

To evaluate the utility of DP-Loc for indoor localization measurements and what improvements and enhancements are made in the online stage compared to the first proposed DP3 scheme, we draw conclusions through three approaches: privacy budget, number of iterations, and cumulative error in localization. Similarly, the time required for one localization is one of the important metrics to evaluate the performance of the scheme. In the experiments, the AP fuzzification and location retrieval phases are the same as the traditional WiFi fingerprint localization, and the fingerprint clustering and fingerprint permutation phases take 28 s to process the data set through multiple iterations. Compared to privacy-preserving indoor localization schemes with homomorphic encryption

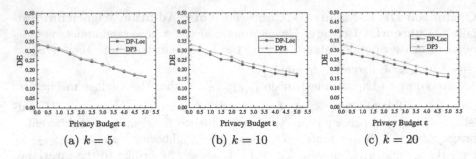

Fig. 2. Comparison of the average error between DP-Loc scheme and DP3 scheme under different privacy budgets with the same number of iterations and different number of clusters k.

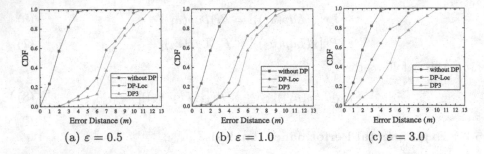

Fig. 3. Cumulative distribution functions of localization errors for three schemes with different privacy budgets.

and secure multi-party computing, the DP-Loc scheme has better timeliness, so this paper does not focus on the experimental comparison of timeliness.

We fix the number of iterations $T = 5$ for fingerprint clustering, and the number of clusters k is set as 5, 10, and 20 to measure the utility of the scheme by analyzing the variation of the mean distance error DE with different privacy budgets ε. We assume that ε is $(0.1, 0.5, 1.0, 1.5, 2.0, 2.5, 3.0, 3.5, 4.0, 4.5, 5.0)$ in order. According to the experimental results in Fig. 2, we observe that the DP k-means fingerprint clustering used by DP3 and the optimized DP k-means++ fingerprint clustering used by DP-Loc both decrease in error as the privacy budget ε increases throughout the online stage. In addition, we clearly see that the fold plots of DP3 and DP-Loc largely overlap when $k = 5$, while the average distance error of DP-Loc is significantly smaller than that of DP3 as the number of clusters k increases, when $k = 10$ and $k = 20$. The reason for this phenomenon is that the number of clustering iterations T is fixed, and in the fingerprint clustering algorithm, the optimized DP k-means++ adds more noise in each iteration than DP k-means, and if the number of clusters k set is small, each cluster has a relatively large range and contains more sampling points, and the fingerprint permutation operation in each cluster will cause a larger error at this time. In addition, because the optimized DP k-means++ algorithm reduces and corrects the impact of errors caused by cluster center deviation, it can still maintain a high level of clustering availability and robustness when the privacy-preserving budget ε is small and the added Laplace random noise is large.

Finally, we compare the localization accuracy of the original scheme DP3 and our proposed DP-Loc scheme, we still choose the iteration number $T = 5$, and choose the privacy budget $\varepsilon = (0.5, 1.0, 3.0)$, respectively, under different privacy budgets, we choose the WiFi fingerprint indoor localization scheme without differential privacy, the original DP3 scheme, and our proposed DP-Loc scheme. Figure 3 represents the cumulative error of localization under different privacy budgets. We can visually see through the above graph that at $\varepsilon = 0.5$, DP-Loc reduces the localization error by 1 m compared to DP3, but still has a significant error compared to indoor localization without differential privacy, but as it gradually increases, we can conclude by comparing the three graphs that DP-Loc is better than DP3 in terms of accuracy while the error with no differential privacy is slowly decreasing. Therefore, we conclude that the DP-Loc scheme can achieve relatively better localization results while choosing the same parameters to achieve privacy protection, and the error is progressively decreasing as the privacy budget ε increases, while still providing good privacy protection in the localization phase.

6 Conclusion

In this paper, we introduce a differential privacy-based indoor localization scheme, DP-Loc, to protect bilateral location privacy. Security analysis shows that the DP-Loc scheme can effectively protect user location privacy during the online location phase. We conducted experiments on the UJIIndoorLoc dataset under existing conditions, and the results confirmed the implementability and optimization of our solution over the original one, which is able to protect the user location privacy from being tested and the server database while guaranteeing the location accuracy.

Acknowledgements. This work was supported by the National Natural Science Foundation of China (62072369, 62072371), the Youth Innovation Team of Shaanxi Universities, Shaanxi Special Support Program Youth Top-notch Talent Program, the Key Research and Development Program of Shaanxi (2021ZDLGY06-02, 2020ZDLGY08-04) and the Technology Innovation Leading Program of Shaanxi (2023-YD-CGZH-31).

References

1. Arthur, D., Vassilvitskii, S.: k-means++: the advantages of careful seeding. Technical report, Stanford (2006)
2. Dwork, C.: Differential privacy: a survey of results. In: Agrawal, M., Du, D., Duan, Z., Li, A. (eds.) TAMC 2008. LNCS, vol. 4978, pp. 1–19. Springer, Heidelberg (2008). https://doi.org/10.1007/978-3-540-79228-4_1

3. Dwork, C., McSherry, F., Nissim, K., Smith, A.: Calibrating noise to sensitivity in private data analysis. In: Halevi, S., Rabin, T. (eds.) TCC 2006. LNCS, vol. 3876, pp. 265–284. Springer, Heidelberg (2006). https://doi.org/10.1007/11681878_14

4. Holcer, S., Torres-Sospedra, J., Gould, M., Remolar, I.: Privacy in indoor positioning systems: a systematic review. In: 2020 International Conference on Localization and GNSS (ICL-GNSS), pp. 1–6. IEEE (2020). https://doi.org/10.1109/ICL-GNSS49876.2020.9115496

5. Hopkins, S.B., Kamath, G., Majid, M.: Efficient mean estimation with pure differential privacy via a sum-of-squares exponential mechanism. In: Proceedings of the 54th Annual ACM SIGACT Symposium on Theory of Computing, pp. 1406–1417 (2022). https://doi.org/10.1145/3519935.3519947

6. Järvinen, K., et al.: Pilot: practical privacy-preserving indoor localization using outsourcing. In: 2019 IEEE European Symposium on Security and Privacy (EuroS&P), pp. 448–463. IEEE (2019). https://doi.org/10.1109/EuroSP.2019.00040

7. Kim, J.W., Jang, B.: Workload-aware indoor positioning data collection via local differential privacy. IEEE Commun. Lett. **23**(8), 1352–1356 (2019). https://doi.org/10.1109/LCOMM.2019.2922963

8. Konstantinidis, A., Chatzimilioudis, G., Zeinalipour-Yazti, D., Mpeis, P., Pelekis, N., Theodoridis, Y.: Privacy-preserving indoor localization on smartphones. IEEE Trans. Knowl. Data Eng. **27**(11), 3042–3055 (2015). https://doi.org/10.1109/TKDE.2015.2441724

9. Li, H., Sun, L., Zhu, H., Lu, X., Cheng, X.: Achieving privacy preservation in WiFi fingerprint-based localization. In: IEEE Infocom 2014-IEEE Conference on Computer Communications, pp. 2337–2345. IEEE (2014). https://doi.org/10.1109/INFOCOM.2014.6848178

10. Roy, P., Chowdhury, C.: A survey on ubiquitous WiFi-based indoor localization system for smartphone users from implementation perspectives. CCF Trans. Pervasive Comput. Interact. **4**(3), 298–318 (2022). https://doi.org/10.1007/s42486-022-00089-3

11. Torres-Sospedra, J., et al.: Ujiindoorloc: a new multi-building and multi-floor database for WLAN fingerprint-based indoor localization problems. In: 2014 International Conference on Indoor Positioning and Indoor Navigation (IPIN), pp. 261–270. IEEE (2014). https://doi.org/10.1109/IPIN.2014.7275492

12. Wang, Y., Huang, M., Jin, Q., Ma, J.: DP3: a differential privacy-based privacy-preserving indoor localization mechanism. IEEE Commun. Lett. **22**(12), 2547–2550 (2018). https://doi.org/10.1109/LCOMM.2018.2876449

13. Zafari, F., Gkelias, A., Leung, K.K.: A survey of indoor localization systems and technologies. IEEE Commun. Surv. Tutor. **21**(3), 2568–2599 (2019). https://doi.org/10.1109/COMST.2019.2911558

14. Zhao, P., et al.: P3-LOC: a privacy-preserving paradigm-driven framework for indoor localization. IEEE/ACM Trans. Networking **26**(6), 2856–2869 (2018). https://doi.org/10.1109/TNET.2018.2879967

A Practical Multi-candidate Voting Protocol on Quantum Blockchain Adapted for Various Tally Principles

Xin Sun[1], Anran Cui[2], Hui Chen[1], and Xingchi Su[1(✉)]

[1] Research Center for Basic Theories of Intelligent Computing, Zhejiang Lab, Hangzhou, China
x.su@zhejianglab.com
[2] Shanghai Key Laboratory of Trustworthy Computing, East China Normal University, Shanghai, China

Abstract. Quantum secure voting aims to provide various approaches to performing electronic voting via quantum technologies, like entangled particles or quantum key distribution, so as to guarantee the security of the voting procedures against forthcoming quantum computers. Beyond the widely studied two-candidate vote, this paper steps to the multi-candidate case. Based on quantum blockchain and quantum secure communication, a class of relatively simple voting protocols is designed. They satisfy several paramount properties regarding secure voting protocols. These protocols can be implemented using presently available technology. Moreover, they show great potential in tallying ballots with respect to different principles, such as Borda rules and maximal lotteries.

Keywords: electronic voting · quantum computation · blockchain · matrix of majority margins

1 Introduction

In the past few decades, electronic voting has been becoming popular in various scenarios, such as state governmental elections in a big scale or decision making in relatively small groups. Many electronic voting protocols based on classical cryptography have been developed and successfully applied in the last two decades [3]. The security of these voting protocols is rooted in the unproven complexity of some computational problems, such as the factoring of large numbers. However, quantum computation is shown to be able to factor large numbers in a short time, which means that classical protocols based on such algorithms are insecure henceforth. To take precautions against the forthcoming quantum computers, a number of quantum voting protocols have been developed in the last decade [8,9,13,15].

It is commonly supposed that a reliable and practically useful voting protocol should meet the following requirements:

1. *Anonymity.* Only the voter him/herself knows how he or she voted.

2. *Bindingness.* Nobody can change his/her submitted ballot after the casting phase.
3. *Non-reusability.* Every voter can vote only once.
4. *Verifiability.* Every voter can verify whether his or her ballot has been counted properly.
5. *Fairness.* Nobody can obtain a partial tally of ballots before the tallying phase.
6. *Self-tallying.* Everyone who is interested in the voting result can tally ballots by himself or herself.

To the best of our knowledge, the protocol proposed by Wang *et al.* [15] is the very first quantum voting protocol which satisfies all requirements above. However, their protocol is difficult to be implemented by the current technology since it involves the manipulation of multi-particle entangled states. Sun *et al.* [12] utilized quantum blockchain studied in [10], which significantly simplifies the protocol and de-centralizes the voting procedure. A quantum bit commitment protocol is also used to ensure some essential properties of voting. There have existed several quantum bit commitment protocols which are highly secure and implementable by the current technology (see [7, 14]). Any of these solutions can be used in our voting protocol.

However, it is more frequent to see multiple candidates involved in voting procedures in our real life. Three or more candidates lead to many subtleties in the classical study of voting theory, e.g. Arrow's impossibility theorem. Reviewing the previous work on quantum secure voting, most of them only focus on two candidates. In order to develop the multi-candidate voting protocols in a quantum setting, we design a Condorcet style voting protocol where the comparison between each two candidates is performed with respect to Sun *et al.*'s protocol. Every voter needs to generate a sequence of nonces to distribute them to every other voters via quantum secure communication. Then voters can construct their own masked ballots and send them to all miners on the quantum blockchain. After all done, each miner can tally the ballots and achieve a common consensus on the final winner. Since our protocol explicitly shows the vote differential between every two candidates, some delicate tally methods proposed to deal with the case of non-unique final winners in voting theory become available, such as Borda rules and maximal lotteries. Furthermore, as these tally methods essentially decide the final winner by a reasonable randomization, every miner each can play the lottery. The more miners there are, the more possible that the candidate assigned with the highest probability to win. Therefore, the structure of blockchain not only de-centralizes the tally procedure, but also improves the accuracy of outputting the most preferred candidate following those tally principles in randomization style.

The protocol designed in this paper meets all the requirements mentioned above by the current technology. Moreover, it also satisfies the Condorcet winner criterion[1], which means that if it always returns the Condorcet winner when one

---

[1] The Condorcet winner is the candidate who is preferred to every other candidate in a pairwise comparison, when the number of candidates is at least three.

exists. Some researchers even find the criterion so compelling that it is necessary when choosing a voting rule [16]. As far as we know, our protocol is the first quantum secure voting protocol that satisfies the Condorcet winner criterion.

The structure of this paper is as follows. We first review some background knowledge on the quantum blockchain and quantum bit commitment in Sect. 2. Then, in Sect. 3, we present our multi-candidate voting protocol. Section 4 shows three different tally principles based on the matrix of majority margins that our protocol adapts to. Related work and comparison with previous studies are discussed in Sect. 5. We finish this paper by Section ??, with conclusions and remarks on the future work.

2 Preliminaries

We next briefly introduce three basic technical components of our quantum voting protocol: quantum secure communication, quantum blockchain and quantum bit commitment. They will not be discussed technically when we illustrate our protocol in Sect. 3 since that does not bring more insightful understandings. But they ensure the communication between voters and miners safe enough to be against the attack from quantum computers.

2.1 Quantum Secure Communication

The quantum secure communication between voters is fulfilled by the famous quantum key distribution (QKD) protocol BB84 [1]. This protocol leverages quantum non-clonability and quantum irreversibility to generate a symmetric cryptographic key for two communicators. Then the two communicators are able to encrypt messages by the symmetric key following the One-Time-Pad (OTD) which is supposed to be uncrackable. In Sect. 3, the communication between voters is based on this type of quantum secure communication. It is naturally immune to attacks from quantum computers.

2.2 Quantum Blockchain

A blockchain is a distributed, transparent, and append-only ledger of cryptographically linked units of data (blocks), which incorporates mechanisms for achieving consensus over the blocks of data in a large decentralized network of nodes/agents who do not trust each other. The concept of quantum blockchain presented in [10] assumes that each pair of nodes is connected by a quantum channel and a classical channel. Every pair of nodes can establish a sequence of secret keys by using QKD-BB84 mechanisms. Those keys will later be used for secure communication via classical channels.

Updates on blockchain are initiated by those nodes that wish to append some new data to the chain. Each miner checks the consistency of the update with respect to their local copy of the database and works out a judgment regarding the update's admissibility. Then all the miners apply a consensus algorithm to the update, arriving at a consensus regarding the correct update.

In this paper, we consider quantum blockchain from a macro view, omitting its inner structure and mechanism, and taking its following desired properties:

1. Every node is a (small scale) quantum computer which can run some quantum computation on a small number of qubits. More specifically, nodes are capable of performing the quantum computation involved in at least one quantum bit commitment protocol.
2. The communication between any two nodes is unconditionally secure.
3. There is a consensus algorithm which can be used by all miners to achieve consensus. A general definition of the consensus algorithm is given below.

Definition 1 (consensus algorithm). *An algorithm among n parties, in which every party p holds an input value $x_p \in D$ (for some finite domain D) and eventually decides on an output value $y_p \in D$, is said to achieve consensus if the algorithm guarantees that the output values of all honest parties are the same. Moreover, if the input value of all honest parties are the same, then the output value of all honest parties equals to the input value.*

The results of the consensus algorithm are always published on the quantum blockchain.

2.3   Quantum Bit Commitment

Bit commitment typically consists of two phases: commitment and opening. In the commitment phase, Alice, the sender, chooses a bit a ($a \in \{0, 1\}$) which she wishes to commit to Bob, the receiver. Then Alice presents Bob some evidence about the bit. The committed bit cannot be known to Bob prior to the opening phase. Later, in the opening phase, Alice discloses some information needed for the reconstruction of a. Then Bob reconstructs a bit a' using Alice's evidence and the disclosure. A correct bit commitment protocol ensures that $a' = a$. A bit commitment protocol is concealing if Bob cannot know the bit Alice committed before the opening phase, and is binding if Alice cannot change the bit she committed after the commitment phase.

The first quantum bit commitment (QBC) protocol was proposed in 1984 by Bennett and Brassard [1]. A number of QBC protocols were designed thereafter to achieve unconditional security. The following is an abstract yet rigorous definition of QBC.

Definition 2 (quantum bit commitment). *A quantum bit commitment protocol consists of the following parts:*

(1) Two finite dimensional Hilbert spaces A and B.
(2) A function   commit : $\{0, 1\} \mapsto A \otimes B$.
(3) Two pure states $|c_0\rangle, |c_1\rangle \in A \otimes B$, in which $|c_i\rangle = commit(i)$ is the commitment of i.
(4) A quantum operation (i.e. completely positive, trace-preserving super operator) Open on $A \otimes B$ such that $Open(|c_0\rangle\langle c_0|) \neq Open(|c_1\rangle\langle c_1|)$.

This QBC protocol is concealing if $Tr_A(|c_0\rangle\langle c_0|) = Tr_A(|c_1\rangle\langle c_1|)$. It is binding if there is no unitary U on A such that $(U \otimes I_B)|c_0\rangle = |c_1\rangle$.

2.4   Voting for Two Candidates

We also show Sun *et al.*'s quantum secure voting protocol on two candidates here as a preparation for illustrating the upcoming new protocol for multiple candidates in the next section.

In the simplest setting for voting, n voters $\{V_1, \ldots, V_n\}$ vote on two candidates Alice and Bob. For the sake of simplicity we assume n is an odd number. Every voter V_i has a private binary value $v_i \in \{0, 1\}$, where $v_i = 0$ means voting for Alice, and $v_i = 1$ means voting for Bob. The protocol consists of two phases: the ballot commitment phase and the ballot tallying phase. Figure 1 presents simplified visualization of our protocol.

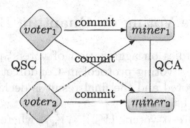

Fig. 1. A network of voters and miners: Voters use quantum secure communication (QSC) to distribute matrix. Voters commit their masked ballots to miners. Miners use quantum consensus algorithm (QCA) to achieve consensus about voters' masked ballot.

1. Ballot commitment.
   (a) For every $i \in \{1, \ldots, n\}$, voter V_i generates the i-th row of an $n \times n$ matrix of integers $r_{i,1}, \ldots r_{i,n}$, of which the sum $\sum_j r_{i,j}$ and 0 are congruent modulo $n + 1$. That is, $\sum_j r_{i,j} \equiv 0 \pmod{n+1}$.
   (b) For every i and j, voter V_i sends $r_{i,j}$ to V_j via quantum secure communication [1]. That is, they first use quantum key distribution to establish share secret keys, then communication by exchanging messages encrypted by the secret keys.
   (c) Now for every i, voter V_i knows the i-th column $r_{1,i}, \ldots, r_{n,i}$. Then he computes his masked ballot $\widehat{v_i} \equiv v_i + \sum_j r_{j,i} \pmod{n+1}$. V_i commits $\widehat{v_i}$ to every miner of the blockchain by a QBC protocol.
2. Ballot tallying.
   (a) For each i, V_i reveals $\widehat{v_i}$ to every miner of the blockchain by opening his commitment.
   (b) All the miners run the consensus algorithm to achieve a consensus of the masked ballot $\widehat{v_1}, \ldots, \widehat{v_n}$.
   (c) The result of voting is obtained by calculating $\sum_i \widehat{v_i}$, which equals to $\sum_i v_i$ because $\sum_i \widehat{v_i} \equiv \sum_i (v_i + \sum_j r_{j,i}) \equiv \sum_i v_i + \sum_{i,j} r_{j,i} \equiv \sum_i (v_i + \sum_j r_{i,j}) \equiv \sum_i v_i \pmod{n+1}$.

(d) Alice is the winner if $\sum_i \widehat{v_i} < \frac{n}{2}$. Bob is the winner if $\sum_i \widehat{v_i} > \frac{n}{2}$.

Example 1. Assume there are 3 voters $\{V_1, V_2, V_3\}$ with $v_1 = v_2 = 1, v_3 = 0$ and the matrix generated by those voters is

$$\begin{pmatrix} 2 & 0 & 2 \\ 1 & 1 & 2 \\ 3 & 0 & 1 \end{pmatrix}.$$

Then $\widehat{v_1} = 1 + (2 + 1 + 3) = 7 \equiv 3 \ (mod \ 4)$, $\widehat{v_2} = 1 + (0 + 1 + 0) = 2 \equiv 2 \ (mod \ 4)$, $\widehat{v_3} = 0 + (2 + 2 + 1) = 5 \equiv 1 \ (mod \ 4)$. Then we have $\widehat{v_1} + \widehat{v_2} + \widehat{v_3} = 3 + 2 + 1 \equiv 2 \ (mod \ 4)$, which equals to $v_1 + v_2 + v_3 = 2$.

3   Multi-candidate Voting on Quantum Blockchain

There are amount of studies on aggregation of voters' preference on multiple candidates. We will give a voting protocol in Condorcet style where each pair of candidates are to be voted and the final result is decided by all comparisons between every two candidates.

Suppose that there are n voters $\{V_1, \ldots, V_n\}$, where n is an odd number, and m candidates $\{c_1, \ldots, c_m\}$. We first break the whole voting into $\frac{m(m-1)}{2}$ binary votings. Each binary vote is a pair (c_i, c_j) where $i, j \in \{1, \ldots, m\}$ and $i < j$. We fix a lexicographical order of these pairs as follows: $(c_1, c_2), (c_1, c_3), \ldots,$ $(c_1, c_m), (c_2, c_3), \ldots, (c_2, c_m), (c_3, c_4), \ldots, (c_{m-1}, c_m)$. Binary variables s_k, where $k \in \{1, \ldots, \frac{m(m-1)}{2}\}$ is used to store the result of voting on the competition of the kth pair in the lexicographical order. For example, s_2 represents the result of the voting on the competition of (c_1, c_3). If $s_2 = 0$, then c_1 is the winner of this competition. Otherwise c_3 is the winner. The winner(s) of the multi-candidate voting is the candidate who wins the binary voting most often.

The voting protocol consists of the following steps:

1. Ballot commitment.
   (a) For every $i \in \{1, \ldots, n\}$, voter V_i generates the i-th rows of $\frac{m(m-1)}{2}$ numbers of $n \times n$ matrices of integers $r_{i,1}^1, \ldots r_{i,n}^1, r_{i,1}^2, \ldots r_{i,n}^2, \ldots, r_{i,1}^{m(m-1)/2},$ $\ldots r_{i,n}^{m(m-1)/2}$, of which the sum $\sum_j r_{i,j}^k$ and 0 are congruent modulo $n+1$. That is, $\sum_j r_{i,j}^k \equiv 0 \ (mod \ n+1)$ for all $k \in \{1, \ldots, \frac{m(m-1)}{2}\}$.
   (b) For every i and j, voter V_i sends $r_{i,j}^1, \ldots, r_{i,j}^{m(m-1)/2}$ to V_j via quantum secure communication.
   (c) Now for every i, voter V_i knows the i-th column $r_{1,i}^k, \ldots, r_{n,i}^k$ for all $k \in \{1, \ldots, \frac{m(m-1)}{2}\}$. Then he computes his masked ballot $\widehat{v_i^k} \equiv v_i^k + \sum_j r_{j,i}^k \ (mod \ n+1)$ for all $k \in \{1, \ldots, \frac{m(m-1)}{2}\}$. V_i commits $\widehat{v_i^k}$, for all $k \in \{1, \ldots, \frac{m(m-1)}{2}\}$, to every miner of the blockchain by a QBC protocol.

2. Ballot tallying.

   (a) For each i, V_i reveals $\widehat{v_i^k}$, for all $k \in \{1, \ldots, \frac{m(m-1)}{2}\}$, to every miner of the blockchain by opening his commitment.

   (b) All the miners run the consensus algorithm to achieve a consensus on the masked ballot $\widehat{v_1^k}, \ldots, \widehat{v_n^k}$, for all $k \in \{1, \ldots, \frac{m(m-1)}{2}\}$.

   (c) The result of voting is obtained by first calculating $\sum_i \widehat{v_i^k}$, for all $k \in \{1, \ldots, \frac{m(m-1)}{2}\}$, which equals to $\sum_i v_i^k$ because $\sum_i \widehat{v_i^k} = \sum_i (v_i^k + \sum_j r_{j,i}^k) \equiv \sum_i v_i^k + \sum_{i,j} r_{j,i}^k \equiv \sum_i (v_i^k + \sum_j r_{i,j}^k) \equiv \sum_i v_i^k \ (mod\ n+1)$. Then sets $s_k = 0$ if $\sum_i \widehat{v_i^k} < \frac{n}{2}$ and $s_k = 1$ if $\sum_i \widehat{v_i^k} > \frac{n}{2}$, for all $k \in \{1, \ldots, \frac{m(m-1)}{2}\}$. Finally, the winner(s) is the candidate who wins binary voting most often, which is determined by the values of s_k, for $k \in \{1, \ldots, \frac{m(m-1)}{2}\}$.

Apparently, a Condorcet winner (if it exists) will always win in our voting protocol. Besides, our voting protocol also satisfies the following security requirements:

1. **Anonymity**. The anonymity is guaranteed because the quantum secure communication prohibits other voters to know the entire matrix. Therefore, other voters can only know the masked ballot, while the original ballot stays unknown.

2. **Bindingness**. The voter cannot change his/her submitted ballot because of the binding property of quantum bit commitment.

3. **Non-reusability**. Miners only accept voters commitment for only once. Therefore, no voter can vote for more than once.

4. **Verifiability**. Every voter can easily check if his masked ballot is successfully uploaded to the blockchain because by design it is a transparent database.

5. **Fairness**. Fairness will be destroyed if somebody can partially tally the ballots before the ballot tallying phase. To achieve this, he or she have to know some masked ballots before the ballot tallying phase. Note that according to the concealing property of quantum bit commitment, even the miners cannot know a single masked ballot before the tally phase. Therefore fairness is ensured.

6. **Self-tallying**. This requirement is satisfied because of the transparency of the blockchain. All data published on the blockchain is accessible to every interested user. Users can tally ballots by some calculation on masked ballots.

7. **Decentralization**. Instead of a single miner, the update of quantum blockchain is managed by multiple miners. Therefore our voting protocol is decentralized in the sense that it does not rely on a single authority.

4   Tallying by Matrix of Majority Margins

Although the protocol introduced in the last section provides a reliable method to elect a winner (winners) in Condorcet style voting, the story is not ending there. Considering the case where the winner is not unique, how to choose one final winner has become an inspiring question for decades. Considering a simple scenario where two voters vote for two candidates while one votes for A and the other prefers B. Randomization is required to decide the winner by choosing one voter randomly and his/her vote decides the final winner (like a dictator). Random dictatorship is put forward aiming to break the tie. Alternatively, faced with these situations where there does not exist one undisputed winner, using lotteries on selecting one winner from a group of candidates goes back to the ancient Greece and also draws a lot of attention in recent decades [6]. Briefly speaking, if there is a probability distribution over the set of candidates which reflects all voters preference, choosing the final winner with respect to this probability distribution makes the lottery more reasonable.

The voting protocol studied in Sect. 3 is based on pairwise majority comparisons between candidates. We next introduce an important notion called *the matrix of majority margins* specifically designed for this type of voting protocols in the classical voting theory.

Definition 3 (Matrix of majority margins [2]).
Given n voters $\{V_1, \ldots, V_n\}$ (n is odd) and m different candidates $\{c_1, \ldots, c_m\}$, we perform a voting protocol as Sect. 3 and for the kth binary vote, $v^k \equiv \sum_i v_i^k (\bmod\ n+1)$. Then the matrix of majority margins $M \in \mathbb{R}^{m \times m}$ of this voting protocol is given as follows:

- *For all $i \in \{1, \cdots, m\}$, let $M[i, i] = 0$;*
- *If $1 \le i \le j \le m$, then let $M[i, j] = (m - v^k) - v^k$ in which v^k denotes the binary competition of (c_i, c_j);*
- *If $1 \le j \le i \le m$, then let $M[i, j] = -M[j, i]$*

Let us elaborate on the definition above. As we know, the value of v^k is the number of voters supporting c_j in the kth binary voting (c_i, c_j). So for arbitrary $i, j \in \{1, \cdots, m\}$, $M[i, j]$ represents the vote differential between candidate c_i and c_j. The vote differential of one candidate him/herself is 0, *i.e.* $M[i, i] = 0$. The value of the skew-symmetric point of $M[i, j]$ is $-M[i, j]$.

Based on the matrix of majority margins, we introduce three different tallying methods on deciding the final winner(s), two of which are to induce probability distributions (lotteries) over candidates. The three different tallying methods yields three new protocols of quantum vote. They share mostly the same steps with the multi-candidate quantum vote in the previous section, the only difference is in step (c) of the Ballot tallying phase, in which we use different methods to determine the finally winners.

4.1   Borda Rules

Borda rules are originally used for scoring all candidates. Alternatively, we can calculate the Borda score of each candidate by a given matrix of majority margins.

Definition 4 (Borda score [2]). *Given n voters $\{V_1, \ldots, V_n\}$ (n is odd) and m different candidates $\{c_1, \ldots, c_m\}$, we perform a voting protocol as Sect. 3 and a matrix of majority margins is obtained. The Borda score of a candidate i is $\Sigma_j \frac{M_{i,j}}{2} + \frac{n(m-1)}{2}$, denoted as $Borda(i)$.*

According to Definition 4, $\frac{n(m-1)}{2}$ is a constant and hence the Borda score of the candidate i is totally decided by $\Sigma_{j \in \{1, \cdots, m\}} M_{i,j}$. Intuitively, $\Sigma_{j \in \{1, \cdots, m\}} M_{i,j}$ denotes the sum of all vote differentials comparing i with every other candidates. It is straightforward to decide the final winner based on the maximal scores.

Definition 5 (The principle $Borda_{max}$). *We perform a voting as Sect. 3 and a matrix of majority margins is obtained. The set of winners is $\{i \mid Borda(i) \in \max\{Borda(i) \mid 1 \leq i \leq m\}\}$.*

According to Definition 5, it is still possible that there exist plural winners with maximal Borda scores, which seems inadequate for us to select the unique final winner. Therefore, we can assign probabilities to each candidate that are proportional to their Borda scores as follows.

Definition 6 (The principle $Borda_{pro}$). *We perform a voting as Sect. 3 and a matrix of majority margins is obtained. Let $p : \{1, \cdots, m\} \mapsto [0, 1]$ be the lottery w.r.t. $Borda_{pro}$ such that for each $i \in \{1, \cdots, m\}$, $p(i) = \frac{Borda(i)}{\Sigma_{j \in \{1, \cdots, m\}} Borda(j)}$.*

It is easy to check that $\Sigma_{i \in \{1, \cdots, m\}} p(i) = 1$. So the function p indeed represents a lottery over the set of candidates. Then every miner produces the winner w.r.t. the lottery induced by the matrix of majority margins according to $Borda_{pro}$. Finally, the miners run the consensus algorithm to output the unique final winner.

4.2 Maximal Lotteries

The main goal is to find a lottery that is reasonable enough to select a final winner. If there is a benchmark for comparing different lotteries, all things go easier. The notion of maximal lotteries goes back to P. C. Fishburn [5]. He provides an approach to comparing two probability distributions as follows:

Definition 7 (Group preference for p over q). *We perform a vote as Sect. 3. Given two lotteries p and q over the set of candidates,*

$$\phi(p, q) = \Sigma_{i \in \{1, \cdots, m\}} \Sigma_{j \in \{1, \cdots, m\}} p(i) q(j) (|\{n \mid i >_n j\}| - |\{n \mid j >_n i\}|)$$

$\phi(p, q)$ is a measurement of voters' preference for lottery p over lottery q.

In Definition 7, the part $(|\{n \mid i >_n j\}| - |\{n \mid j >_n i\}|)$ is identical to v^k when (c_j, c_i) is the kth binary voting. It represents the vote differential between c_i and c_j. According to Fishburn, if $\phi(p, q) > 0$, we say that voters prefer p to q, annotated as $p > q$. If $\phi(p, q) = 0$, we say p and q are equally good.

Definition 8 (Maximal lotteries (original) [5]**).** *A lottery p is a maximal lottery if for all other lottery q, $\phi(p, q) \geq 0$.*

We can also rewrite Fishburn's definition with the matrix of majority margins. When p is a lottery, we can denote it with a m-dimensional vector.

Definition 9 (Maximal lotteries [2]**).** *We perform a vote as Sect. 3 and a matrix of majority margins M is obtained. A lottery p is maximal if for all other lottery q, $p^T M q \geq 0$.*

It is easy to check that Definition 9 is equivalent to Definition 8. Intuitively, a maximal lottery is the most preferred lottery by the whole group of voters with respect to their pairwise majority comparisons between candidates. Our maximal lottery quantum vote is a protocol similar to the voting protocol in Sect. 3, but in step (c) of the Ballot tallying phase, the miners first use the maximal lottery to produce an intermediate winner, and then run the consensus algorithm to produce the final winner.

It worth noting that either $Borda_{pro}$ or maximal lotteries requires all miners to play a lottery with respect to the probability distributions that they induce. In the classical setting, there is only one authority to tally the ballots and therefore the lottery will be played merely once, which will very likely make the candidate assigned with lower probability win the election. That is not desirable. In contrast, our protocol is established over blockchain where multiple miners need to play the lottery independently. The plural times of performing the lottery can make the final winner more closely indicate the candidate assigned with the highest probability. The accuracy of playing the lottery is therefore improved.

All tallying methods introduced in this section require the matrix of majority margins. However, the common idea of previous works is constructing an aggregated ballot in entanglement or superposition by manipulations of each voters. The tallyman will measure the final aggregated ballot to decide the final winner. During the process, the information of individual votes is assured anonymous. Some approaches only output a final winner, which leaves no possibility of finding the vote differentials and thereby they cannot tally the result by the matrix of majority margins [8]. Other approaches can count the number of votes for two candidates. But the multi-candidate case is not considered by them. Hence they are not compatible with the tallying by the matrix of majority margins.

To sum up, $Borda_{max}$ finds the final winners who get the highest Borda score. $Borda_{pro}$ and maximal lotteries are to find a reasonable probability distribution over the set of candidates to which an election goes with respect. To the best of our knowledge, the quantum voting protocols studied in this paper are the first quantum protocols that support tallying by the matrix of majority margins.

5   Related Work and Conclusion

The first quantum voting protocol was proposed by Hillery *et al.* [8] who proposed two voting modes, traveling ballot and distributed ballot to ensure the security voting. Vaccaro *et al.* [13] uses entangled states to ensure that the votes are anonymous and to allow the votes to be tallied. The entanglement is distributed over separated sites; the physical inaccessibility of any one site is sufficient to guarantee the anonymity of the votes.

Since Wang *et al.*'s protocol shares many advantages with ours, here we emphasize the advantages of our protocol on *scalability* over theirs. For an n-voter m-candidate voting, Wang *et al.*'s protocol heavily relies on the m-level, n-particle state $|\chi_n^m\rangle \equiv \frac{1}{\sqrt{m}} \sum_{j=0}^{m-1} F_m|j\rangle \otimes \ldots \otimes F_m|j\rangle$, where F_m is the m-dimensional Fourier transform and the n-level, n-particle state $|S_n\rangle \equiv \frac{1}{\sqrt{n!}} \sum_{s_1 \ldots s_n \in P_n^n} |s_1\rangle \ldots |s_n\rangle$ where P_n^n is the set of all permutations of $\{0, 1, \ldots, n-1\}$. Both $|\chi_n^m\rangle$ and $|S_n\rangle$ are difficult to be implemented by the current technology. Moreover, implementing $|\chi_n^m\rangle$ and $|S_n\rangle$ becomes harder when the number of voters and candidates grow. In contrast, our protocol can be implemented by the current technology and the growth of the number of voters and candidates does not lead to more difficulties in implementation. Therefore, our protocol has better scalability than Wang *et al.*'s protocol.

Another approach to defending voting systems from the attack of quantum computers is to design voting systems based on post quantum cryptography. The first post-quantum voting system is proposed by Chillotti *et al.* [4] making use of fully-homomorphic encryption. Del Pino *et al.* [11] constructed a post-quantum voting system based on zero-knowledge proofs on top of homomorphic commitments. The security of all those post-quantum voting systems still rely on computational assumptions. This is a disadvantage comparing to quantum voting systems. On the other hand, it seems that post-quantum voting systems are better in scalability than quantum voting systems. Therefore, we believe quantum and post-quantum voting should be applied in different scenarios. For scenarios in which the number of voters is not large, quantum voting should be used. Post-quantum voting suits better otherwise.

This paper proposes one main multi-candidate voting protocol based on quantum blockchain which can be adapted for three different tallying principles. Besides of being simple, our protocols are anonymous, binding, non-reusable, verifiable, fair, self-tallying, de-centralized and scalable. Moreover, our protocol satisfies the Condorcet winner criterion, a highly desirable property for all voting systems from a social choice perspective. In addition, the protocols enables tallying by the matrix of majority margin. And hence, it brings about more accuracy in electing the final winner with respect to probability distributions induced by $Borda_{pro}$ and maximal lotteries principles. Besides quantum blockchain, other quantum techniques used in our protocol include quantum secure communication and quantum bit commitment.

References

1. Bennetta, C., Brassard, G.: Quantum cryptography: public key distribution and coin tossing. In: Proceedings of IEEE International Conference on Computers, Systems and Signal Processing, pp. 175–179 (1984)
2. Brandt, F.: Rolling the dice: recent results in probabilistic social choice. Trends Comput. Soc. Choice 3–26 (2017)
3. Chaum, D.: Secret-ballot receipts: true voter-verifiable elections. IEEE Secur. Priv. **2**(1), 38–47 (2004). https://doi.org/10.1109/MSECP.2004.1264852
4. Chillotti, I., Gama, N., Georgieva, M., Izabachène, M.: A homomorphic LWE based e-voting scheme. In: Takagi, T. (ed.) PQCrypto 2016. LNCS, vol. 9606, pp. 245–265. Springer, Heidelberg (2016). https://doi.org/10.1007/978-3-319-29360-8_16
5. Fishburn, P.C.: Probabilistic social choice based on simple voting comparisons. Rev. Econ. Stud. **51**(4), 683–692 (1984)
6. Goodwin, B.: Justice by lottery. Andrews UK Limited (2013)
7. He, G.P.: Simplified quantum bit commitment using single photon nonlocality. Quantum Inf. Process. **13**(10), 2195–2211 (2014). https://doi.org/10.1007/s11128-014-0728-8
8. Hillery, M., Ziman, M., Bužek, V., Bieliková, M.: Towards quantum-based privacy and voting. Phys. Lett. A **349**(1), 75–81 (2006). https://doi.org/10.1016/j.physleta.2005.09.010.   http://www.sciencedirect.com/science/article/pii/S0375960105014738
9. Horoshko, D., Kilin, S.: Quantum anonymous voting with anonymity check. Phys. Lett. A **375**, 1172–1175 (2011)
10. Kiktenko, E.O., et al.: Quantum-secured blockchain. Quantum Sci. Technol. **3**(035004) (2018). http://stacks.iop.org/2058-9565/3/i=3/a=035004
11. del Pino, R., Lyubashevsky, V., Neven, G., Seiler, G.: Practical quantum-safe voting from lattices. In: Thuraisingham, B., Evans, D., Malkin, T., Xu, D. (eds.) Proceedings of the 2017 ACM SIGSAC Conference on Computer and Communications Security, CCS 2017, Dallas, TX, USA, 30 October–03 November 2017, pp. 1565–1581. ACM (2017). https://doi.org/10.1145/3133956.3134101
12. Sun, X., Wang, Q., Kulicki, P., Sopek, M.: A simple voting protocol on quantum blockchain. Int. J. Theor. Phys. **58**(1), 275–281 (2019). https://doi.org/10.1007/s10773-018-3929-6
13. Vaccaro, J.A., Spring, J., Chefles, A.: Quantum protocols for anonymous voting and surveying. Phys. Rev. A **75**, 012333 (2007). https://doi.org/10.1103/PhysRevA.75.012333
14. Verbanis, E., Martin, A., Houlmann, R., Boso, G., Bussières, F., Zbinden, H.: 24-hour relativistic bit commitment. Phys. Rev. Lett. **117**, 140506 (2016)
15. Wang, Q., Yu, C., Gao, F., Qi, H., Wen, Q.: Self-tallying quantum anonymous voting. Phys. Rev. A **94**, 022333 (2016). https://doi.org/10.1103/PhysRevA.94.022333
16. Zwicker, W.S.: Introduction to the theory of voting. In: Brandt, F., Conitzer, V., Endriss, U., Lang, J., Procaccia, A.D. (eds.) Handbook of Computational Social Choice, pp. 23–56. Cambridge University Press, Cambridge (2016). https://doi.org/10.1017/CBO9781107446984.003

Quantum Augmented Lattice Attack on NTRU with Side Information

Qingfeng Cheng, Jinzheng Cao(✉), and Xiangyang Luo

Information Engineering University, Zhengzhou 450001, China
caojinzheng@126.com

Abstract. NTRU is one of the most important lattice-based public key cryptosystems, and a potential candidate for post-quantum cryptography. This paper derives a generic lattice-based attack on NTRU assisted by side information and a quantum augmented lattice basis reduction algorithm. We first exploit the various situations of side information to transforming the NTRU lattice, and produce a smaller lattice basis containing the target vector. Then, we adopt a new variant of BKZ algorithm to solve the NTRU cases, and further construct a quantum augmented version of lattice-based attack with quantum sieve oracles. With the new lattice reduction techniques, our attack only requires a smaller fraction of the secret polynomial's coefficients to successfully recover the NTRU key.

Keywords: NTRU · Side-channel attack · Lattice basis reduction · Quantum algorithm

1 Introduction

The NTRU is one of the most important cryptosystems in the development of lattice-based cryptography. After initially proposed by Hoffstein, Pipher, and Silverman [14], NTRU has been studied on the basis of the worst-case hardness of lattice problems, and has in many ways inspired other lattice-based schemes, for example, the lattice structure and polynomial rings [3,8]. One of the threats to post-quantum cryptography comes from side-channel attacks. The NTRU cryptosystem is known for high speed and small memory requirement, and is thus favored for protecting constrained devices. With the development of internet community and increased popularity of smart devices, the cryptography schemes have been deployed in small resource-constrained platforms. The NIST post-quantum cryptography competition has in particular asked for schemes to focus on performance on Cortex-M4 processor. Recently, more effective side-channel attacks against NTRU are proposed [15,17]. Most of the attacks aim to recover the secret key's coefficients through power-analysis, electromagnetic detection and other techniques. For example, Askeland and Rønjom [2] claimed to recover all -1 coefficient and in total nearly 75% of all coefficients with electromagnetic-probe. Karabulut et al. [15] exploited single-trace vulnerabilities of ω-small polynomial sampling and recover a large portion of coefficients.

C. Ge and M. Yung (Eds.): Inscrypt 2023, LNCS 14527, pp. 317–328, 2024.
https://doi.org/10.1007/978-981-97-0945-8_18

With the acquired information, one of the possible methods to recover the key is to build a more efficient lattice basis and solve the shortest vector problem instance on it. Some attacks require much larger amount of side-information [13].

In this paper, we summarize various possible scenarios of side information about NTRU, and introduce efficient lattice-based attacks accordingly. We base our attack models on transforming and modifying the original NTRU lattice, and analyze how different types of side information will transform the original lattice in various aspects, e.g. to reduce the lattice's rank or increase the determinant. On the basis of merged equations, we use a new lattice reduction method [4] to solve the NTRU cases, and discuss accelerating the algorithm with quantum sieve oracles. Finally, we show in theory and experiments how the information affects the security NTRU schemes for different parameter settings.

2 Preliminaries

We first introduce the basic notations and necessary assumptions about lattice, then discuss the NTRU problem. More details about lattice can be found in [16]. In our work, the vectors are all for row vectors. A lattice $\mathcal{L}$ in field $\mathbb{R}^m$ is a discrete subgroup of $\mathbb{R}^m$, defined as the set of all integer linear combinations of d linearly independent vectors $b_1, \ldots, b_d \in \mathbb{R}^m$. The matrix $B = [b_1, \ldots, b_d]$ form a basis of the lattice. For a given basis B of lattice $\mathcal{L}$, $\pi_i(v)$ is the projections of vector v orthogonal to the span of $b_1, b_2, \ldots, b_{i-1}$. Further, the Gram-Schmidt orthogonalization of basis B is $B^* = [b_1^*, b_2^*, \ldots, b_d^*]$, where $b_i^* = \pi_i(b_i)$. The determinant of $\mathcal{L}$ denotes the volume of the fundamental area, and can be defined as $\det(\mathcal{L}) = \det(B) = \|b_1^*\|\|b_2^*\| \ldots \|b_d^*\|$. The hardness of the Shortest Vector Problem (SVP) is at the centre of estimating the security of lattice-based cryptosystems. Given a lattice basis, SVP asks to find the shortest nonzero vector in the lattice. Such a problem is proved to be NP-hard under certain assumptions. The extended applications of SVP lead to a list of variants, such as approximate SVP and unique-SVP. We define $\lambda_1(\mathcal{L})$ as the length of the shortest nonzero vector in $\mathcal{L}$.

We introduce NTRU and lattice-based attacks. Let n be a prime, q be a positive integer. Two random polynomials $f = \sum_{i=0}^{n-1} f_i X^i, g = \sum_{i=0}^{n-1} g_i X^i$ are sampled with ternary coefficients in $\{-1, 0, 1\}$. In NTRU, we present f, g with vectors $[f_0, f_1, \ldots, f_{n-1}], [g_0, g_1, \ldots, g_{n-1}]$. The secret is the pair $[f, g]$, and the public key is $h = g/f \mod \mathcal{R}_q$, where $\mathcal{R}_q = \mathbb{Z}_q/(X^n - 1)$. The NTRU cryptosystem can be broken if the attacker is able to recover f or g from h. For NTRU encryption, the pair of polynomials $[f, g]$ is the secret decryption key. For most NTRU-based signatures [9,12,18], f, g can form the trapdoor.

While the NTRU scheme is described in the form of polynomials, its security relies on the SVP in an NTRU lattice. Therefore, NTRU is usually considered as a lattice-based cryptosystem. We represent the polynomials as vectors, and define the cyclic matrix of dimension $d = 2n$, and the NTRU lattice basis

$$B = \begin{bmatrix} I & H \\ \mathbf{0} & qI \end{bmatrix}. \tag{1}$$

It is clear that $fH = g \bmod q$, thus the vector $v = [f, g]$ is in the lattice $\mathcal{L}(B)$. The vector v is usually short in $\mathcal{L}(B)$, since secret polynomials f, g have all coefficients in $\{-1, 0, 1\}$. It is also true that rotations are enough to attack NTRU, and are equally short vectors in $\mathcal{L}(B)$. Coppersmith et al. [6] proved finding a vector in the sublattice generated by rotations of $[f, g]$ is already enough to solve the NTRU problem. It also can be accomplished by performing lattice reduction.

3 Constructing Lattice Basis with Side-Information

In this section, we discuss the lattice-based attack on NTRU which integrates various types of side information. The attack transforms the classical NTRU lattice basis with additional equations obtained from side information, which can fit into various scenarios. By merging such information, we convert the task of recovering NTRU keys to finding the shortest vector in lattice basis.

3.1 Known Exact Coefficients

Most side-channel attacks against NTRU recover some (if not all) coefficients of f or g. It is believed when a sufficiently large portion of coefficients are known, there exist polynomial-time algorithms to recover the secret key [17]. Furthermore, when only a few coefficients are known, we can still use the lattice-based method. Askeland et al. [2] suggested that with m coefficients known, the dimension of constructed basis is reduced from $2n$ to $2n - m + 1$, but did not provide a detailed model. In this section, we summarize the information in two categories, called the "zero type" and "non-zero type". In both cases, the dimension of the modified lattice decreases when more side information is known.

Zero Type. Systemizing various kinds of conditions satisfied by the target vector $v = [f, g]$, we find a case where there exists a vector u such that $\langle u, v \rangle = s$, and start with the basic case such that $s = 0$. We consider it as a feasible situation, since many side-channel techniques are able to distinguish the zeros in secret vectors f, g. For example, Suppose the i-th coefficient of f is presumed as zero, then set the i-th element of u as 1 while others as 0. If we know the j-th coefficient is zero, we define the $(n + j)$-th element of u as 1 and others 0. Another important case is that the sum of some coefficients of f or g is 0.

In addition to knowing a single zero element, we also know side information that can be described as sum of coefficients being 0. A direct example is that in some schemes, polynomial g is sampled with equal numbers of 1 elements and -1 elements. In this case, we define a vector

$$u = [\underbrace{0, 0, \ldots, 0}_{n}, \underbrace{1, 1, \ldots, 1}_{n}],$$

then it holds that $\langle u, v \rangle = 0$. Such information is available from the parameter setting of schemes and from side-channel attacks.

Generally, we can introduce a method of modifying the lattice basis with such equations. Suppose we have an NTRU lattice basis $B = [b_1, \ldots, b_d]$, and a hint vector u which satisfies $\langle u, v \rangle = 0$, where v is the target vector. We follow the steps:

1. initiate column list $L = [\langle u, b_1 \rangle, \ldots, \langle u, b_d \rangle]^T$;
2. perform integer combinations, get list $L' = U \cdot L = [t, 0, 0, \ldots, 0]^T$, where U is an unimodular matrix;
3. use U to renew the basis $B' = U \cdot B$;
4. remove the first row of B', and output the basis matrix B''.

Proposition 1. *Matrix B'' is the basis of sublattice $\{z \in \mathcal{L}(B) : \langle z, u \rangle = 0\}$.*

Non-zero Type. Beside the zero type information, we need to support various kinds of information beyond zero equations. For example, side-channel techniques often recover exact values of some coefficients, which are probably non-zero. In addition, in various NTRU-based schemes, the secret polynomials are sampled with deviance $\sigma^2 = 2/3$, and the possible sums of $\{f_i\}, \{g_i\}$ can be guessed around 0. In most situations, however, these coefficients don't add up to zero. We therefore propose a different method to utilize such information. Similar to the first case, we describe the known conditions of the target vector v with a vector u such that $\langle v, u \rangle = s, s \in \mathbb{Z}$.

To recenter the subset $\{z \in \mathcal{L}(B) : \langle z, v \rangle = s, s \neq 0\}$, we presume a non-zero coefficient. Without losing generality, we consider $f_0 = 1$. The basis of the sublattice with known u and $s = \langle v, u \rangle$ is produced following the steps:

1. initiate an auxiliary vector u_a from a known non-zero coefficient and s;
2. define column list $L = [\langle u - u_a, b_1 \rangle, \ldots, \langle u - u_a, b_d \rangle]^T \in \mathbb{Z}^{d \times 1}$;
3. perform integer combinations, get list $L' = U \cdot L = [t, 0, 0, \ldots, 0]^T$, where $U \in \mathbb{Z}^{d \times d}$ is an unimodular matrix;
4. use U to renew the basis $B' = U \cdot B$;
5. remove the zero vector of B', and output the basis.

Besides the dimension decrease, the updated lattice also has different values of determinant. The new volume will affect the complexity estimation of our attack. According to [7], with a hint vector u, the dimension of the lattice $\mathcal{L}(B'')$ decreases by 1, and the determinant of the lattice is multiplied by $\|u\|$. For the zero type, $\|u\| = 1$ will not affect the determinant. For the non-zero type, $\|u\| = 2$, and the determinant will increase. As a result, the Gaussian heuristic of $\mathcal{L}' = \mathcal{L}(B'')$ is explicitly increased, and the gap between $\mathrm{GH}(\mathcal{L}')$ and the target vector v is larger, making it easier to recover the secret key.

3.2   Known Modular Coefficients

The attack model proposed in the first subsection allows us to recover the secret key from known coefficients. However, it is not always feasible to know exact values of coefficients. Recent side-channel analysis tools tend to determine a coefficient based on statistic analysis [15], and there is a possibility that one can only detect if a coefficient is zero or not. For ternary coefficients $\{-1, 0, 1\}$, we are not able to confirm their signs. Therefore, we can not formulate an exact equation. To exploit this kind of side information, we adopt a new method to quantify the known coefficients. Compared with the "exact" case, we put the product of v and u in $\mathbb{Z}_q, q \in \mathbb{Z}$.

Similar to the exact hints, we should create a vector u such that $\langle v, u \rangle = 0 \bmod p$, and find the basis of sublattice $\mathcal{L}' = \{z \in \mathcal{L}(B) : \langle z, u \rangle = 0 \bmod p\}$. For example, knowing two non-zero coefficients f_i, f_j but not sure about their signs, we can describe the situation as $f_i + f_j = 0 \bmod 2$, and present the equation with $u = [0, \ldots, 0, \underbrace{1}_{i}, 0, \ldots, 0, \underbrace{1}_{j}, 0, \ldots, 0]$ and $\langle v, u \rangle = 0 \bmod 2$.

The basis of sublattice $\mathcal{L}' = \{z \in \mathcal{L}(B) : \langle z, u \rangle = 0 \bmod p\}$ can is done by computing the kernel of B in $\mathbb{Z}_p$. We will describe the steps to find the new basis.

1. Define column list $L = [\langle u, b_1 \rangle, \ldots, \langle u, b_d \rangle]^T$;
2. insert a modulus p into L, get $L_p = [p, \langle u, b_1 \rangle, \ldots, \langle u, b_d \rangle]^T \in \mathbb{Z}^{(d+1) \times 1}$;
3. perform integer combinations, get list $L'_p = U \cdot L_p = [t, 0, 0, \ldots, 0]^T$, where $U \in \mathbb{Z}^{(d+1) \times (d+1)}$ is an unimodular matrix;
4. use U to renew the basis $B' = U \cdot \begin{bmatrix} 0 \\ B \end{bmatrix} \in \mathbb{Z}^{(d+1) \times d}$;
5. remove the first row in B', then output the basis matrix B''.

In practice, more efficient operations are possible: one can directly remove the first row and first column of U and get U', then compute $B'' = U' \cdot B$. Besides, we can prove that the acquired matrix B'' is the basis of the sublattice we desire.

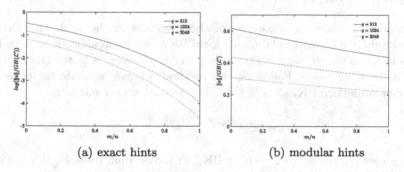

(a) exact hints   (b) modular hints

Fig. 1. Estimated $\|v\|/\mathrm{GH}(\mathcal{L}')$ for different parameters

Proposition 2. *Matrix B'' is the basis of sublattice $\{z \in \mathcal{L}(B) : \langle z, u \rangle = 0 \bmod p\}$.*

The unimodular matrix U is obtained by computing the Hermite normal form of L_p. According to the definition of Hermite normal form, L'_p has only one non-zero element t in the first row, and the transformation matrix U is unimodular. With a modular hint vector u, the dimension of the lattice is not changed, and the determinant of the lattice is multiplied by 2. As a result, the Gaussian heuristic of $\mathcal{L}' = \mathcal{L}(B'')$ is explicitly increased, and the gap between $\mathrm{GH}(\mathcal{L}')$ and the target vector v is larger, making it easier to recover the secret key. Figure 1 illustrates how the $\|v\|/\mathrm{GH}(\mathcal{L}')$ changes with more known exact/modular coefficients.

4   Solving NTRU with Quantum Augmented Lattice Reduction

In Sect. 3, a modified lattice is constructed by merging side information into the basis. The next challenge is to solve these SVP instances and find secret vectors. In this step, choosing efficient basis reduction algorithms is vital for solving the problem. Our attack adopts the algorithm of SubBKZ [4], and we further combine it with quantum sieve. The basic idea of SubBKZ is the existence of short lattice vectors in sublattices.

Definition 1. *(Sublattice) A sublattice $\mathcal{L}_1$ is a subset of $\mathcal{L}$, with basis $B_1 = [b_1, b_2, \ldots, b_k]$, where $k < d$.*

Previous works discussed the $\mathcal{L}_1$ generated from basis $B_1 = [b_1, b_2, \ldots, b_{d/2}]$. This paper extends the idea to generalized k-dimensional sublattices.

Theorem 1 (Under GSA). *For the sublattice $\mathcal{L}_1$ of basis $B_1 = [b_1, b_2, \ldots, b_k]$, $\mathrm{GH}(\mathcal{L}_1) = \sqrt{\frac{k}{d}} \beta^{\frac{d-k+1}{2\beta}} \mathrm{GH}(\mathcal{L})$.*

Theorem 1 states the existence of short vectors in the sublattice $\mathcal{L}_1$. The original SubBKZ algorithm [4] uses a local BKZ reduction subroutine with large blocks in $\mathcal{L}_1$. This strategy is able to recover short vectors faster than running BKZ in the whole basis. Following this method, we can estimate the time complexity of sublattice BKZ-β is $\beta^{\beta/(2e)}$. The output vector has norm

$$\left(\beta^{1/2\beta}\right)^k \cdot \det\left(\mathcal{L}_1\right)^{1/k} = \left(\beta^{1/2\beta}\right)^{d+1} \cdot \det\left(\mathcal{L}\right)^{1/d},$$

which is close to the output norm of BKZ in the original basis B. When we run a local BKZ with larger block size β', the output norm is

$$\delta_{\beta'}{}^k \delta_\beta{}^{d-k+1} \det\left(\mathcal{L}\right)^{1/d}.$$

The SubBKZ algorithm outputs a short vector with relatively low time cost by running sublattice SVP solvers. Here we try to find short vectors with sieve.

Sieve classically solves d-dimensional SVP in time $2^{0.292d+o(d)}$, and can be further accelerated by techniques such as SubSieve [10]. When we run sieve in sublattice $\mathcal{L}_1$, it is expected to produce the vectors shorter than

$$\sqrt{4/3} \cdot \mathrm{GH}(\mathcal{L}_1) = \sqrt{\frac{2k}{3\pi e}} \cdot \delta^{d-k+1} \cdot \det{(\mathcal{L})}^{1/d}.$$

In this way, we get a vector significantly shorter than BKZ by running sieve in a sublattice. However, a problem with sublattice sieve is the cost. In the quantum computing model, the algorithm can be accelerated by quantum sieve and QRAM (Quantum RAM). Chailloux et al. [5] introduce a quantum sieve algorithm with quantum walk that runs in time $2^{0.2570d+o(d)}$, uses QRAM of size $2^{0.0767d}$, quantum memory of size $2^{0.0495d+o(d)}$ and classical memory of size $2^{0.2075d+o(d)}$, while classical sieve requires time $2^{0.2925d+o(d)}$ and classical memory of size $2^{0.2075d+o(d)}$. With the quantum sieve oracle as the SVP solver, we can evaluate the output and cost of SVP in sublattices with size k changing from 0 to d.

Figure 2 illustrates an example of different sublattice SVP solvers on an NTRU with parameters $n = 97, q = 1024$. After preprocessing with BKZ-30, SubBKZ produces shorter vectors than original BKZ. Notably, SubBKZ requires fewer known coefficients to output a vector of certain norm than simple BKZ. As a result, SubBKZ will be more effective in exploiting side information about NTRU.

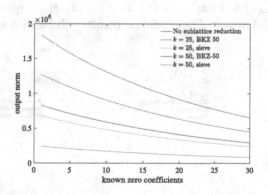

Fig. 2. Predicted SubBKZ norms on BKZ-30 reduced basis

5 Evaluation and Experiments

This section tests the performance of our attack on randomly generated NTRU and NTRU Prime instances. Our lattice reduction algorithms include classical BKZ 2.0 and SubBKZ introduced in Sect. 4. We implement SubBKZ in Sage, and use the BKZ procedure in Fpylll [19]. When solving the NTRU cases, we follow the progressive reduction strategy, which lets the block size increase in each tour, starting from 10. In our analysis, we record the block size required to successfully recover the secret vector as an indicator of complexity of the instance.

5.1   Evaluating the Attack

We first consider predicting the estimated performance of the attack when using BKZ algorithm. To recover the secret vector, we estimate the required BKZ block following the assumption of [1] (under GSA). For d-dimensional lattice $\mathcal{L}$ and an unusually short vector v, BKZ is able to recover v when

$$\sqrt{\beta/d} \cdot \|v\| < \delta_\beta^{2\beta-1} \cdot \mathrm{vol}(\mathcal{L})^{1/d}, \tag{2}$$

where δ is the root-Hermite factor estimated by $\delta_\beta = ((\beta\pi)^{\frac{1}{\beta}}\beta/(2\pi e))^{\frac{1}{2(\beta-1)}}$ and $\delta_\beta^\beta \sim \sqrt{\beta/2\pi e}$. However, for q-aray lattices, the GSA is often modified into ZGSA, which can be summarized as: the head and tail GSO vectors are flat, and middle GSO vectors have decreasing norms. Based on ZGSA, the estimate can be updated.

The BKZ reduced basis of NTRU lattices with merged equations are shown the result in Fig. 3. Although side information may randomize the basis, the reduced basis still roughly follows the ZGSA shape with a flat head part. In the following experiments, we can safely use ZGSA to estimate the behavior of algorithms. Following the description of ZGSA shape in [11] and analysis of the structure of the modified lattice in [7], we estimate the required block size to perform a successful attack. The predicted results will be shown in the following experiments.

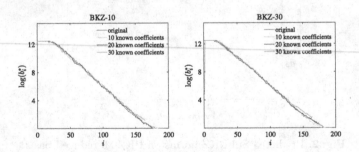

Fig. 3. ZGSA shape of NTRU instances

We now test the efficiency of the attack with values of some coefficients known. For different parameter settings ($n \in \{97, 113\}, q \in \{512, 1024\}$) and different numbers of known coefficients, we run a series of experiments. To test the attack, we run experiments on both NTRU and NTRU Prime instances.

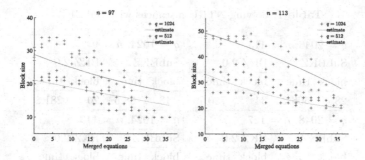

Fig. 4. Attacking NTRU with known coefficients

NTRU. In NTRU lattices, cyclic vectors $[fX^i, gX^i]$ will accelerate recovering the target vectors. In our analysis, however, more presumed coefficients limit the number of possible vectors until only one unique shortest vector remains. Figure 4 shows our experimental results, along with our estimation in Subsect. 5.1. Based on the analysis of finding the shortest lattice vector and the ZGSA assumption, we provide a simulation for required BKZ blocks, which is also shown in the figure.

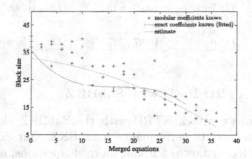

Fig. 5. Attacking NTRU Prime with modular coefficients

Attacks Knowing Modular Coefficients. Besides attacking NTRU knowing exact values of coefficients, we also test the attack with some modular equations. We perform a series of experiments with a fraction of known modular coefficients on NTRU Prime instances ($n = 97, q = 512$). Figure 5 summarizes the results. Attacking with modular coefficients is expected to be less effective since such information does not reduce the dimension of the lattice. Generally, attacking with modular coefficients requires a slightly larger block than the exact case. We also find that attacking classical NTRU with modular hints is not explicitly efficient, because of the cyclic structure.

Table 1. Solving NTRU instances with SubBKZ

q = 2048, n = 113				q = 1024, n = 97			
SubBKZ		BKZ 2.0		SubBKZ		BKZ 2.0	
block	time	block	time	block	time	block	time
28	506.2	34	750.1	13	168.6	20	281.8
q = 2048, n = 127				q = 1024, n = 113			
SubBKZ		BKZ 2.0		SubBKZ		BKZ 2.0	
block	time	block	time	block	time	block	time
46	2329.6	48	2556.7	42	1242.5	44	1540.1

Table 2. Block sizes and time required to find NTRU secrets

merged equations	SubBKZ		BKZ 2.0		merged equations	SubBKZ		BKZ 2.0	
	block size	time(s)	block size	time(s)		block size	time(s)	block size	time(s)
0	15	204.1	24	272.9	12	13	110.6	20	161.0
2	15	131.7	23	233.6	14	12	93.2	19	142.6
4	14	115.3	23	210.7	16	12	87.5	18	139.2
6	14	126.7	23	209.9	18	12	73.6	18	122.7
8	14	84.7	22	201.5	20	11	61.6	16	66.7
10	13	114.6	20	160.7	22	11	50.6	14	57.8

5.2   Reducing NTRU Basis with SubBKZ

In this subsection, we attack NTRU with the SubBKZ algorithm introduced in Sect. 4 and compare its performance with BKZ. Our experiments test the algorithms on NTRU instances without merged equations, as shown in Table 1. For example, with parameters $q = 1024, n = 97$, the SubBKZ method successfully recovers the secret key with an average block size 13 and average time 168 s, while BKZ 2.0 will take block size 20 and time 281 s. With parameters $q = 2048, n = 113$, SubBKZ completes the attack in 506 s with block size 28, and BKZ 2.0 requires 750 s with block size 35. In the following section, we use different algorithms to evaluate NTRU instances with merged equations. An observation is that the new algorithm performs better on overstretched instances, in other words for larger q and smaller n. In such instances, a sublattice is more likely to contain the target vector $[f, g]$ or its cyclic $[fX^i, gX^i]$. For the NTRU instances, we set parameters $n = 97, q = 1024$ and run 200 instances to compare the average block size and time required to solve the cases. We also include merged equations into the NTRU basis to test our algorithm. The results are shown in Table 2. The results indicate that SubBKZ runs faster than BKZ in the same NTRU settings. Specifically, even no equations are merged, SubBKZ can still solve the case in about 200 s, while BKZ will need about 8 merged equations to reach similar time cost.

6   Conclusion

This paper proposes a generic lattice-based attack model of NTRU with side information. We summarize different cases of known coefficients into zero/non-zero and exact/modular types. After merging various types of side information, the determinant of lattice basis is increased, and the dimension may reduce. We test the efficiency of the attack with experiments for solving classical NTRU problem and NTRU Prime. When solving the modified NTRU instances, we adopt a new BKZ variant, SubBKZ, to improve the performance. Further, we discuss using quantum sieve as a local SVP oracle in BKZ and analyze its complexity. By implementing the new reduction algorithm, our attack achieves fast solution to NTRU instances with a smaller amount known information compared with known algorithms.

Acknowledgement. This work was supported by the National Key Research and Development Program of China (Grant No. 2022YFB3102900), the National Natural Science Foundation of China (Grant Nos. 61872449, 62172433, 62172435) and the Science Foundation for the Excellent Youth Scholars of Henan Province (Grant No. 222300420099).

References

1. Alkim, F., Ducas, L., Pöppelmann, T., Schwabe, P.: Post-quantum key exchange—a new hope. In: 25th USENIX Security Symposium (USENIX Security 2016), pp. 327–343. USENIX Association, Austin, August 2016. https://www.usenix.org/conference/usenixsecurity16/technical-sessions/presentation/alkim
2. Askeland, A., Rønjom, S.: A side-channel assisted attack on NTRU. IACR Cryptol. ePrint Arch., p. 790 (2021). https://eprint.iacr.org/2021/790
3. Bos, J., et al.: CRYSTALS - Kyber: a CCA-secure module-lattice-based KEM. In: 2018 IEEE European Symposium on Security and Privacy, pp. 353–367. IEEE (2018). https://doi.org/10.1109/EuroSP.2018.00032
4. Cao, J., Pan, Y., Cheng, Q.: A lattice reduction algorithm based on sublattice BKZ. In: Huang, Q., Yu, Yu. (eds.) ProvSec 2021. LNCS, vol. 13059, pp. 174–189. Springer, Cham (2021). https://doi.org/10.1007/978-3-030-90402-9_10
5. Chailloux, A., Loyer, J.: Lattice sieving via quantum random walks. In: Tibouchi, M., Wang, H. (eds.) ASIACRYPT 2021. LNCS, vol. 13093, pp. 63–91. Springer, Cham (2021). https://doi.org/10.1007/978-3-030-92068-5_3
6. Coppersmith, D., Shamir, A.: Lattice attacks on NTRU. In: Fumy, W. (ed.) EURO-CRYPT 1997. LNCS, vol. 1233, pp. 52–61. Springer, Heidelberg (1997). https://doi.org/10.1007/3-540-69053-0_5
7. Dachman-Soled, D., Ducas, L., Gong, H., Rossi, M.: LWE with side information: attacks and concrete security estimation. In: Micciancio, D., Ristenpart, T. (eds.) CRYPTO 2020. LNCS, vol. 12171, pp. 329–358. Springer, Cham (2020). https://doi.org/10.1007/978-3-030-56880-1_12
8. D'Anvers, J.-P., Karmakar, A., Sinha Roy, S., Vercauteren, F.: Saber: module-LWR based key exchange, CPA-secure encryption and CCA-secure KEM. In: Joux, A., Nitaj, A., Rachidi, T. (eds.) AFRICACRYPT 2018. LNCS, vol. 10831, pp. 282–305. Springer, Cham (2018). https://doi.org/10.1007/978-3-319-89339-6_16

9. Das, D., Saraswat, V., Basu, K.: Lattice signatures using NTRU on the hardness of worst-case ideal lattice problems. IET Inf. Secur. **14**(5), 496–504 (2020). https://doi.org/10.1049/iet-ifs.2019.0580
10. Ducas, L.: Shortest vector from lattice sieving: a few dimensions for free. In: Nielsen, J.B., Rijmen, V. (eds.) EUROCRYPT 2018. LNCS, vol. 10820, pp. 125–145. Springer, Cham (2018). https://doi.org/10.1007/978-3-319-78381-9_5
11. Ducas, L., van Woerden, W.: NTRU fatigue: how stretched is overstretched? In: Tibouchi, M., Wang, H. (eds.) ASIACRYPT 2021. LNCS, vol. 13093, pp. 3–32. Springer, Cham (2021). https://doi.org/10.1007/978-3-030-92068-5_1
12. Espitau, T.: MITAKA: faster, simpler, parallelizable and maskable hash-and-sign signatures on NTRU lattices. In: Emura, K., Wang, Y. (eds.) Proceedings of the 8th on ASIA Public-Key Cryptography Workshop, APKC@AsiaCCS 2021, Virtual Event Hong Kong, 7 June 2021, p. 1. ACM (2021). https://doi.org/10.1145/3457338.3458293
13. Esser, A., May, A., Verbel, J., Wen, W.: Partial key exposure attacks on BIKE, Rainbow and NTRU. IACR Cryptol. ePrint Arch., p. 259 (2022). https://eprint.iacr.org/2022/259
14. Hoffstein, J., Pipher, J., Silverman, J.H.: NTRU: a ring-based public key cryptosystem. In: Buhler, J.P. (ed.) ANTS 1998. LNCS, vol. 1423, pp. 267–288. Springer, Heidelberg (1998). https://doi.org/10.1007/BFb0054868
15. Karabulut, E., Alkim, E., Aysu, A.: Single-trace side-channel attacks on ω-small polynomial sampling: with applications to NTRU, NTRU prime, and CRYSTALS-DILITHIUM. IACR Cryptol. ePrint Arch., p. 494 (2022). https://eprint.iacr.org/2022/494
16. Nguyen, P., Vallée, B.: The LLL algorithm: survey and applications, January 2010. https://doi.org/10.1007/978-3-642-02295-1
17. Ravi, P., Ezerman, M.F., Bhasin, S., Chattopadhyay, A., Roy, S.S.: Generic side-channel assisted chosen-ciphertext attacks on streamlined NTRU Prime. IACR Cryptol. ePrint Arch., p. 718 (2021). https://eprint.iacr.org/2021/718
18. Tang, Y., Xia, F., Ye, Q., Wang, M., Mu, R., Zhang, X.: Identity-based linkable ring signature on NTRU lattice. Secur. Commun. Netw. **2021**, 1–17 (2021). https://doi.org/10.1155/2021/9992414
19. The FPLLL development team: FPyLLL, a Python wraper for the FPLLL lattice reduction library, Version: 0.5.6 (2021). https://github.com/fplll/fpylll

Quantum Attacks: A View of Data Complexity on Offline Simon's Algorithm

Bo Yu[1], Tairong Shi[2,3]($\boxtimes$), Xiaoyang Dong[4], Xuan Shen[5], Yiyuan Luo[6],
and Bing Sun[1]

[1] College of Sciences, National University of Defense Technology, Changsha 410073,
Hunan, China
[2] TCA, Institute of Software Chinese Academy of Sciences, Beijing 100190, China
tairong2018@iscas.ac.cn
[3] PLA SSF Information Engineering University, Zhengzhou 450001, Henan, China
[4] Institute for Advanced Study, Tsinghua University, Beijing 100084, China
[5] College of Information and Communication,
National University of Defense Technology, Wuhan 430010, Hubei, China
[6] School of Computer Science and Engineering, Huizhou University,
Huizhou 516007, Guangdong, China

Abstract. Simon's algorithm has shown a threat to block ciphers in
the quantum setting, especially accelerating attacks with superposition
queries. Sometimes it is difficult for attackers to make superposition
queries, while an easier way is to use classical data then process them on
quantum computers. At ASIACRYPT 2019, Bonnetain et al. proposed
the offline Simon's algorithm. But there is a gap between the classical
queries and a quantum database in their work.

In this paper, we propose an algorithm involving polynomial qubits
that can transform a classical database into a quantum superposition
state without using QRAM. What's more, we analyze the influence of
two approaches called pre- and post-distinguisher methods for Simon's
algorithm attack. Then we run a quantum key recovery attack on Feistel
structure in the Q1 model. For attacking r-round Feistel structure with
n-bit block size and $n/2$-bit subkey, the time complexity of our attack is
$O(l \cdot 2^{n/2+2} + 2^{(r-3)n/4})$ (where l is a constant), and the classical data
complexity is always $O(2^{n/2+1})$, which is much better than the classical
attacks especially for $r > 5$.

Keywords: Block cipher · Quantum key recovery attack · Classical
query · Offline Simon's algorithm · Feistel structure

1 Introduction

Quantum algorithms, such as Shor's algorithm [1], Grover's algorithm [2] and
Simon's algorithm [3], have become powerful tools in cryptanalysis. The security
of classical cryptographic primitives has raised a lot of concerns. Therefore, the
ability of symmetric-key scheme to resist quantum attacks also arouses great

© The Author(s), under exclusive license to Springer Nature Singapore Pte Ltd. 2024
C. Ge and M. Yung (Eds.): Inscrypt 2023, LNCS 14527, pp. 329–342, 2024.
https://doi.org/10.1007/978-981-97-0945-8_19

interest. As a generic attack, the attackers can recover a k-bit key by running Grover search [2] in time $O(2^{k/2})$ on quantum computers, resulting in the security length of the key is halved. Recent studies also have shown that the performance of quantum attacks against some constructions, modes of block ciphers are much faster than classical methods [5,12,17].

In addition to the quantization of many classical cryptanalysis methods are obviously remarkable, a new particular way called Simon's algorithm attack is also efficient. For example, a 3-round quantum distinguisher in the QCPA model is constructed, leading to 3-round Feistel structure can be distinguished from PRPs in polynomial time by using Simon's algorithm (4-round in the QCCA model [7]). Combined with Grover search, the *Grover-meets-Simon* algorithm proposed by Leander and May [4] can be used to make quantum key recovery attacks. Some constructions even become insecure in the quantum setting, such as Even-Mansour construction [9] and FX construction [4].

For quantum cryptanalysis, Zhandry [10] classified two models: one is **the Quantum Model** and the other one is **the Standard Model** (marked as **the Q2 model** and **the Q1 model** respectively by Kaplan et al. [5]). In the Q2 model, the attackers have the ability to query the oracles in superposition, and make offline quantum computation. However, only the online classical query is allowed in the Q1 model, and one can make offline quantum computation.

It should be noted that the assumptions of attacks in the Q2 model maybe too difficult to be achieved considering the scale of quantum computers. A feasible hardware-friendly scenario is running quantum attacks without QRAM in the Q1 model. The two models above are not unrelated, attacks in the Q2 model can be transformed into the Q1 model, i.e., the process of an quantum attack can be simulated by using classical data.

For running Simon's attack in the Q1 model, Bonnetain et al. [14] proposed a new technique called *Asymmetric Search of a Period*. Let $g : \{0,1\}^n \rightarrow \{0,1\}^l$, and $F : \{0,1\}^m \times \{0,1\}^n \rightarrow \{0,1\}^l$ is a family of functions indexed by $\{0,1\}^m$ (denoted as $F(i, \cdot) = f_i$). If there exists only one $i = i_0 \in \{0,1\}^m$ such that $f_i \oplus g$ is periodic, i.e., $\forall x \in \{0,1\}^n$, $f_{i_0}(x) \oplus g(x) = f_{i_0}(x \oplus s) \oplus g(x \oplus s)$ for some $s \neq 0$. Then how to find i_0 and s. The breakthrough is the quantum queries is replaced by classical queries only using polynomial qubits.

To run the asymmetric search successfully, two algorithms are designed in [14], one is called **Alg-PolyQ2** (means using polynomial qubits) in the Q2 model and the other one **Alg-ExpQ1** (means using exponential classical queries) in the Q1 model. Here we give a brief introduction of them. The attack can be divided into online query phase and offline computation phase. For **Alg-PolyQ2**, the attackers firstly make quantum queries to g to prepare the quantum database $|\psi_g\rangle$. Secondly, run the Grover search over $i \in \{0,1\}^m$. Meanwhile, apply a test procedure based on Simon's algorithm to check if $f_i \oplus g$ has a hidden period by using $|\psi_g\rangle$ and making queries to f_i.

The first step in **Alg-ExpQ1** is changed into making 2^n classical queries to g and prepare the quantum state $|\psi_g\rangle$. In detail, start with all-zero state $\bigotimes^{cn} |0\rangle |0\rangle$, then apply Hadamard gates resulting to

$$\bigotimes^{cn}(\sum_{x\in\{0,1\}^n}|x\rangle\,|0\rangle).$$

Next, for each $y \in \{0,1\}^n$, query classically to $g(y)$ then apply a unitary which writes $g(y)$ in the second register if the first one contains y. Finally, output the quantum database of g, i.e.,

$$|\psi_g\rangle = \bigotimes^{cn}(\sum_{x\in\{0,1\}^n}\cdot\,|x\rangle\,|g(x)\rangle).$$

Our Main Contributions. Although the offline Simon's algorithm [14] has been applied, it's still interesting that how to implement such a unitary mentioned in the second step in **Alg-ExpQ1** to prepare the database $|\psi_g\rangle$. Our work can be illustrated as follows.

Table 1. Summary of the key recovery attack on Feistel structure

Round	Classical attacks [11]		Q2 attacks [6]	Q1 attacks (This work)	
	Time	Data	Time	Time	Data
5	2^n	$2^{n/2}$	$2^{n/2}$	$l\cdot 2^{n/2\,|\,2}+2^{n/2}$	$2^{n/2+1}$
6	$2^{3n/2}$	$2^{3n/2}$	$2^{3n/2}$	$l\cdot 2^{n/2+2}+2^{3n/4}$	$2^{n/2+1}$
				2^{n^*} [12]	$2^{n/2}$
7	$2^{3n/2}$	2^n	2^{2n}	$l\cdot 2^{n/2+2}+2^n$	$2^{n/2+1}$
8	$2^{7n/4}$	$2^{5n/4}$	$2^{5n/2}$	$l\cdot 2^{n/2+2}+2^{5n/4}$	$2^{n/2+1}$
15	$2^{7n/2}$	2^{2n}	2^{6n}	$l\cdot 2^{n/2+2}+2^{3n}$	$2^{n/2+1}$

A quantum tradeoff attack against 6-round Feistel structure is proposed in [12]. The result is $T\cdot Q = 2^n$ (where T is the time complexity, Q is the number of qubits) and the classical data complexity is $2^{n/2}$. If Q is limited in polynomials, the time complexity is about 2^n, which is higher than our method.

1. The main task is to design a quantum algorithm for making a quantum super-position state based on some classical data. In this paper, we propose an app-roach to achieve this goal especially without using QRAM, which makes the algorithm viable.
2. Considering the distinguisher has an influence on key recovery attacks, we compare two types, i.e., pre-distinguisher method and post-distinguisher method, from the view of data complexity. Our analysis reveals that only the pre-distinguisher method is recommended in the QCPA setting.
3. As an application, we apply our algorithm to attack Feistel structure in the Q1 model based on the Q2 attack proposed in [6]. For attacking r-round Feistel structure with n-bit block size and $n/2$-bit subkey, the results are shown in Table 1. The results show that our attack is faster than the generic classical attack [11], and the classical data complexity is always $O(2^{n/2+1})$ when $r > 5$, which is much lower especially for long rounds.

2 Preliminaries

2.1 Quantum Algorithms

Simon's Algorithm. In 1994, Simon [3] proposed a quantum algorithm to solve the following problem in polynomial time, which is an exponential speedup than classical ones.

Given a Boolean function $f : \{0,1\}^n \rightarrow \{0,1\}^n$, if there exists a nonzero value s, such that

$$\forall x \in \{0,1\}^n, f(x) = f(x \oplus s),$$

then find s. In other words, the Boolean function f has a hidden XOR period s and we want to find it. To solve Simon's problem, classical method requires $\Omega(2^{n/2})$ calls to the function f. However, Simon's algorithm only need $O(n)$ calls in superposition with the quantum access to f.

Grover's Algorithm. In 1996, Grover [2] proposed a quantum algorithm for searching some marked items over an unordered database. In detail, it has quadratic speedup than classical one. Given a set X where $|X| = 2^n$ including m items are marked, we define the test function f as

$$f(x) = \begin{cases} 1, & \text{if } x \text{ is marked}; \\ 0, & \text{else}. \end{cases}$$

The objective is to find a marked item in X, i.e., one of the preimages of $f(x) = 1$. It can be done classically in time $|X|/m = 2^n/m$. However, using Grover's algorithm, this problem can be solved in time $\sqrt{2^n/m}$ with a high probability.

More details about those two algorithms please refer to [2,3]. For quantum cryptanalysis on block ciphers, they are combined together to recover the keys, as shown in [4].

QRAM. The Quantum Random Access Memory (QRAM) can be regarded as a quantum version of classical RAM, which is an essential device for quantum computer, since many quantum algorithms require the quantum random-access in computing. The QRAM allows us to lookup the memory in superposition and accept superposition answers. But it's hard to build QRAM with huge scale. One of the advantages of Simon's algorithm is no QRAM needed, therefore we expect to maintain it in offline Simon's attack.

2.2   Simon's Attacks on Feistel Structure in the Q2 Model

At ISIT 2010, Kuwakado and Morii [8] firstly studied the Simon's attack on 3-round Feistel structure. Then Dong et al. [6] expanded two rounds and proposed a quantum key recovery attack. The idea of their attack is as follows.

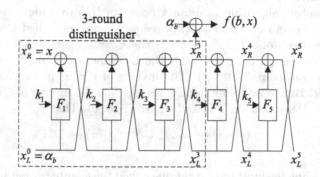

Fig. 1. Quantum key recovery attack on 5-round Feistel structure

Let $x_R^0 = x$, $x_L^0 = \alpha_b$ ($b \in \{0,1\}$) and $\alpha_0 \neq \alpha_1$ are two constants. Define $f : \{0,1\} \times \{0,1\}^{n/2} \rightarrow \{0,1\}^{n/2}$ as $f(b,x) = F_2(k_2, x \oplus F_1(k_1, \alpha_b))$. It is easy to verify that f has a nontrivial period $s = 1 \| F_1(k_1, \alpha_0) \oplus F_1(k_1, \alpha_1)$. Applying Simon's algorithm, a quantum attacker could get the value of s in polynomial time. If (k_4, k_5) is right, we know that

$$f(b,x) = \alpha_b \oplus x_R^3 = \alpha_b \oplus F_4\left(k_4, F_5\left(k_5, x_R^5\right) \oplus x_L^5\right) \oplus x_R^5. \tag{1}$$

Define

$$g(k_4, k_5, b\|x) = \alpha_b \oplus F_4\left(k_4, F_5\left(k_5, x_R^5\right) \oplus x_L^5\right) \oplus x_R^5. \tag{2}$$

Hence, if (k_4, k_5) is right then g has a nontrivial period s.

3   Prepare Quantum Superposition State Based on Classical Database

When using Simon's algorithm to attack a block cipher $\mathcal{E}$, the first step is to construct a quantum distinguisher, i.e., we should find at least one periodic function $f : \{0,1\}^m \rightarrow \{0,1\}^n$ associated to $\mathcal{E}$. By making quantum queries to f, we will obtain a superposition state including all the values of f, that is

$$\sum_{x \in \{0,1\}^m} |x\rangle |f(x)\rangle.$$

Here we omit the amplitude. In fact, we can begin at an m-qubit state $|0\rangle^{\otimes m}$, and apply Hadamard gate on it then query $|x\rangle$ to the oracle of $f(x)$ in superposition and store the values in the second register. Obviously, all values of f are in the superposition state. From this view, to simulate the quantum state of f with classical queries, we need to obtain the truth table $\mathbf{T} = \{E_0, \ldots, E_{2^m-1}\}$ of f by making queries classically over $x \in \{0,1\}^m$, where $f(x_j) = E_{x_j}$. Once we've done this, the next procedure is to transform $\mathbf{T}$ into a quantum superposition state. Especially, we hope the procedure won't use the QRAM. Therefore, we propose a quantum algorithm (a unitary operator $\mathcal{U}_E$) to achieve the goal.

The unitary operator $\mathcal{U}_E$ includes three suboperators, called Create, Delete and Compare operators. The first one is the Create operator (Cre for short). Given an index $i \in \{0, 1, \ldots, 2^m - 1\}$, the Cre operation constructs m qubits $|0\rangle$ separately and maps $|0\rangle$ to $|i\rangle$. The inverse of Cre is in fact itself because $Cre \circ Cre = I$. But to avoid ambiguity, we redefine the inverse of Cre as Delete and named as Del for short. The Del maps $|i\rangle$ to $|0\rangle$. That is

$$Cre : (|0\rangle, i) \mapsto |i\rangle, \quad Del : (|i\rangle, i) \mapsto |0\rangle.$$

Then we define the most important one called the Compare operator ($COMP$ for short) as follows.

$$COMP : (|i\rangle |x_j\rangle |0\rangle, E_{x_j}) \mapsto \begin{cases} |i\rangle |x_j\rangle |E_{x_j}\rangle, & if \ x_j = i; \\ |i\rangle |x_j\rangle |0\rangle, & else. \end{cases}$$

It takes classical input E_{x_j} from a truth table $\mathbf{T}$ indexed by x_j. Given an index $i \in \{0, 1, \ldots, 2^m - 1\}$, if $i = x_j$ then write the value of E_{x_j} into the last register. Otherwise the last register is still in zero state $|0\rangle$. According to the definition of $COMP$, we can verify that

$$COMP : (|i\rangle |x_j\rangle |E_{x_j}\rangle, E_{x_j}) \mapsto \begin{cases} |i\rangle |x_j\rangle |0\rangle, & if \ x_j = i; \\ |i\rangle |x_j\rangle |E_{x_j}\rangle, & else. \end{cases}$$

Consequently, the $COMP$ is a unitary operator. Finally, we define $\mathcal{U}_E$ as

$$\mathcal{U}_E = Del \circ COMP \circ Cre.$$

Obviously, it is unitary because the three suboperators are unitary. Given an index i, we apply $\mathcal{U}_E$ one time on a single quantum state $|x_j\rangle$ resulting in

$$\mathcal{U}_E : (|0\rangle |x_j\rangle |0\rangle, i, E_{x_j}) \mapsto \begin{cases} |0\rangle |x_j\rangle |E_{x_j}\rangle, & if \ x_j = i; \\ |0\rangle |x_j\rangle |0\rangle, & else. \end{cases}$$

If we are given a classical truth table $\mathbf{T}$ (treated as an array), we apply $\mathcal{U}_E$ on a quantum superposition state and $\mathbf{T}$. There is one element E_{x_j} from $\mathbf{T}$ written into the quantum superposition state each time. After running $\mathcal{U}_E$ about $|\mathbf{T}| = 2^m$ times from $i = 0$ to $2^m - 1$, all the values stored in $\mathbf{T}$ are written into the corresponding positions of the quantum superposition state:

$$\mathcal{U}_E : \left(|0\rangle \otimes \sum_{x_j \in \{0,1\}^m} |x_j\rangle |0\rangle, i, \mathbf{T}\right) \mapsto |0\rangle \otimes \sum_{x_j \in \{0,1\}^m} |x_j\rangle |E_{x_j}\rangle.$$

Thus we will obtain a quantum database $|\psi_f\rangle$ of the function f. Once we repeat the process on the final state $\sum_{x_j \in \{0,1\}^m} |x_j\rangle |E_{x_j}\rangle$ we will obtain

$$\mathcal{U}_E : (\sum_{x_j \in \{0,1\}^m} |x_j\rangle |E_{x_j}\rangle, i, \mathbf{T}) \mapsto \sum_{x_j \in \{0,1\}^m} |x_j\rangle |0\rangle.$$

Algorithm 1: Prepare a quantum superposition state.

Input: $|0\rangle \otimes \sum_{x_j \in \{0,1\}^m} |x_j\rangle |0\rangle$, $\mathbf{T} = \{E_0, E_1, \ldots, E_{2^m-1}\}$.

Output: $|0\rangle \otimes \sum_{x_j \in \{0,1\}^m} |x_j\rangle |E_{x_j}\rangle$.

1 **for** $i = 0$ *to* $2^m - 1$ **do**
2   Choose an index $x_j \in \{0,1\}^m$ and get E_{x_j} from $\mathbf{T}$.
3   Construct $|i\rangle$ by using the Cre operator.
4   Apply $COMP$ on the state $|i\rangle |x_j\rangle |0\rangle$:
5   **if** $x_j = i$ **then**
6   Update $|i\rangle |x_j\rangle |0\rangle$ to $|i\rangle |x_j\rangle |E_{x_j}\rangle$.
7   Clear the first register $|i\rangle$ to $|0\rangle$ using the Del operator.
8 **return** $|0\rangle \otimes \sum_{x_j \in \{0,1\}^m} |x_j\rangle |E_{x_j}\rangle$.

To sum up, we can prepare a quantum superposition state based on a classical database $\mathbf{T}$ by applying the unitary operator $\mathcal{U}_E$ about $|\mathbf{T}|$ times. The process of our algorithm doesn't use the QRAM, since we use two operators Cre and Del to control the process from $i = 0$ to $2^m - 1$. Our algorithm only uses polynomial qubits. The description of $\mathcal{U}_E$ is showed in Algorithm 1. Assume that the length of x is m bits and the length of E_{x_j} is n bits, our algorithm needs $(m + n) + m$ qubits in total because there are m auxiliary qubits used in the process.

4   Pre-or Post-distinguisher Method: A View on Data Complexity

The distinguisher affects the complexity of an attack, and two methods are usually used, i,e., **pre-distinguisher method** and **post-distinguisher method**. We define them as follows and give the diagram in Fig. 2.

Definition 1. *Given a d-round distinguisher of an iterative block cipher. If the last $(r - d)$ subkeys are recovered by extending $(r - d)$ rounds afterward the distinguisher, we call the way **pre-distinguisher method** (See Fig. 2(a)).*

Definition 2. *Given a d-round distinguisher of an iterative block cipher. If the first $(r - d)$ subkeys are recovered by extending $(r - d)$ rounds forward the distinguisher, we call the way **post-distinguisher method** (See Fig. 2(b)).*

Many studies have implied that Simon's attack has very low complexity in the Q2 model. For the offline Simon's algorithm, it's necessary to determine the massive way that how a quantum distinguisher should be used to achieve low classical data complexity. In this section, we will discuss it in detail taking the Simon's attack against Feistel structure as an example.

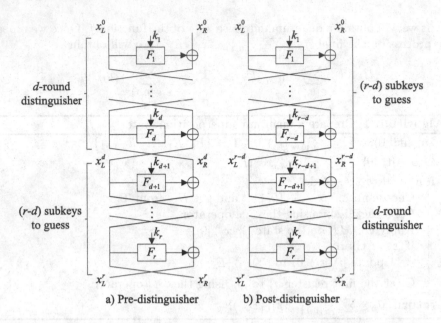

a) Pre-distinguisher   b) Post-distinguisher

Fig. 2. Pre-distinguisher method and post-distinguisher method

4.1 Offline Simon's Attack in the QCPA Setting

Pre-distinguisher Method. The original Simon's attack on 5-round Feistel structure [6] in the Q2 model actually used the pre-distinguisher method (See Fig. 1). The procedures are as follows.

Step 1. Guess the value of (k_4, k_5), and implement a quantum circuit which

1.1 Take (k_4, k_5) and $(x_L^0, x_R^0) = (x, \alpha_b)$ as inputs;
1.2 Qurey (x, α_b) to $\mathcal{E}$ in quantum state to obtain (x_L^r, x_R^r);
1.3 Compute (x_L^3, x_R^3) by decrypting (x_L^0, x_R^0) with (k_4, k_5).

Step 2. Once we get the distinghuisher $f(b, x) = x_R^3 \oplus \alpha_b$, apply Simon's algorithm to check its correctness. If Simon's algorithm returns s, and then output (k_4, k_5). Otherwise continue Grover search.

The subkeys we need to guess are n bits, which can be done by Grover search in time $O(2^{n/2})$. For each (k_4, k_5), we check its correctness using Simon's algorithm in time $O(n)$. So the time complexity to recover (k_4, k_5) in the Q2 model is $\tilde{O}(2^{n/2})$. Similarly, the time complexity to attack r-round Feistel is $\tilde{O}(2^{(r-3)n/4})$ and the quantum data complexity is about $O(n)$.

Following we consider the Simon's attack in the Q1 model. As mentioned in Sect. 3, we should generate a truth table at the very beginning. So the attack has two phases: classical data collection and offline quantum computation.

Step 1. For each $b\|x \in \mathbb{F}_2^{n/2+1}$, query $(x_{b\|x,L}^0, x_{b\|x,R}^0) = (x, \alpha_b)$ classically to $\mathcal{E}$ to get $(x_{b\|x,L}^r, x_{b\|x,R}^r)$, and store it in a table **T**. Based on table **T**, we run Algorithm 1 l times to prepare l quantum superposition states. The formal description is shown in Algorithm 2.

Step 2. Run Grover search for (k_4, k_5), and decrypt x^r with (k_4, k_5) to get $x^3 = (x_L^3, x_R^3)$. Thus we can obtain the distinguisher $f(b, x) = x_R^3 \oplus \alpha_b$. Run Simon's algorithm to solve the period s of f. If Simon's algorithm returns s then output (k_4, k_5). Otherwise continue Grover search.

The attack requires $O(2^{n/2+1})$ classical queries to $\mathcal{E}$. And we can recover (k_4, k_5) in time $\tilde{O}(2^{n/2})$. According to Lemma 4 in [4], let $l = 2(n/2 + 1 + \sqrt{n/2 + 1})$ is enough for the attack with a high success probability.

For attacking r-round Feistel structure, the classical data complexity is also $O(2^{n/2+1})$ and the time complexity is $\tilde{O}(2^{(r-3)n/4})$. Here we omit the time to prepare quantum superposition states.

Algorithm 2: Prepare quantum states for pre-distinguisher method.

1 Do classical query phase.
2 **for** $i = b\|x \in \mathbb{F}_2^{n/2+1}$ **do**
3 $\quad$ Query (α_b, x) classically to $\mathcal{E}$ to obtain $(x_{i,L}^r, x_{i,R}^r)$.
4 $\quad$ Store the value $E_i = (x_{i,L}^r, x_{i,R}^r)$ in **T**.
5 Run **Algorithm 1** to prepare quantum states based on **T**.

Post-distinguisher Method. Now we consider the case of post-distinguisher method. The last 3 rounds of the r-round Feistel structure can be regarded as a quantum distinguisher, i.e.,

$$f : \{0,1\} \times \{0,1\}^{n/2} \to \{0,1\}^{n/2},$$
$$b\|x \mapsto x_R^r \oplus \alpha_b,$$
$$f(b, x) = F_{r-1}(F_{r-2}(\alpha_b) \oplus x),$$

where $x_L^{r-3} = x$ and $x_R^{r-3} = \alpha_b$ ($\alpha_0 \neq \alpha_1$ are constants). And we want to recover $(k_1, k_2, \ldots, k_{r-3})$. In the Q2 model, the complexity is as same as the pre-distinguisher method.

However, the result in the Q1 model is different. Because we can only query the oracle of $\mathcal{E}$ classically, meaning the search for $(k_1, k_2, \ldots, k_{r-3})$ is in a classical method, thus the time complexity is $O(2^{(r-3)n/2})$. For each guessed $(k_1, k_2, \ldots, k_{r-3})$, we need update the truth table **T** for the following offline quantum computation (As shown in **Algorithm 3**). Hence, the classical data complexity is $O(2^{(r-3)n/2} \cdot 2^{n/2+1}) = O(2^{(r-2)n/2+1})$. It implies that the classical data complexity exceeds the scale of plaintext space $O(2^n)$, leading to the key recovery attack in the Q1 model is infeasible.

Algorithm 3: Post-distinguisher method for Simon's attacks in the Q1 model

---

1 **for** $K = (k_1, \ldots, k_{r-3}) \in (\mathbb{F}_2^{n/2})^{r-3}$ **do**
2 | Collect the classical data:
3 | **for** $i = b\|x \in \mathbb{F}_2^{n/2+1}$ **do**
4 | | Decrypt $(x_{i,L}^{r-3}, x_{i,R}^{r-3}) = (\alpha_b, x)$ by K to get $(x_{i,L}^0, x_{i,R}^0)$.
5 | | Query $(x_{i,L}^0, x_{i,R}^0)$ classically to $\mathcal{E}$ to obtain $(x_{i,L}^r, x_{i,R}^r)$.
6 | |__ Store the value of $E_i = (x_{i,L}^r, x_{i,R}^r)$ in **T**.
7 | Run **Algorithm 1** to make quantum states based on **T**.
8 |__ Apply Simon's algorithm to check K. Return K if it is right.

4.2 Offline Simon's Attack in the QCCA Setting

There are two scenarios in the QCCA setting: the quantum attackers have access to the decryption oracle or have the access to both the decryption and encryption oracles. In the former case, the analysis in Sect. 4.1 can be applied directly. For the later case, Ito et al. [7] constructed a quantum distinguisher against 4-round Feistel structure. Based on their work, we can deduce that both the pre- and post-distinguisher methods are infeasible in the Q1 model.

We list the relation between the oracle access and the feasibility of those two methods in Table 2.

Table 2. The relation between the feasibility of Simon's attack and pre-distinguisher method or post-distinguisher method

Setting	Distinguisher	$\mathcal{E}$	$\mathcal{E}^{-1}$	Pre		Post	
				Q1	Q2	Q1	Q2
QCPA	3-round [8]	✓	×	✓	✓	×	✓
QCCA	4-round [6]	✓	✓	×	✓	×	✓

5 Offline Simon's Algorithm Attack Against Feistel Structure in the QCPA Setting

According to our analysis in Sect. 3 and Sect. 4, only the pre-distinguisher method can be used for the offline Simon's attack in the QCPA setting. Following we give a complete description of our attack.

Firstly, we define a function $h : \mathbb{F}_2^{n/2} \times \mathbb{F}_2^{n/2} \times (\mathbb{F}_2^{n/2+1})^l \to (\mathbb{F}_2^{n/2})^l$ with

$$(k_4, k_5, x_1, \ldots, x_l) \mapsto g(k_4, k_5, x_1) \| \ldots \| g(k_4, k_5, x_l),$$

where g has been defined in Eq. (2). Let $\mathcal{O}_h$ be the following quantum oracle

$$\mathcal{O}_h : |k_4, k_5\rangle \left(\bigotimes_{j=1}^{l} |x_j\rangle |E_{x_j}\rangle\right) |0\rangle \mapsto |k_4, k_5\rangle \left(\bigotimes_{j=1}^{l} |x_j\rangle |E_{x_j}\rangle\right) |h\rangle .$$

Algorithm 4: Prepare the quantum database $|\psi_f\rangle$.

Input: Classical query access to $\mathcal{E}$.

Output: The quantum state $|\psi_f\rangle$.

1 Choose two constants $\alpha_0 \neq \alpha_1$, query $(x_L^0, x_R^0) = (\alpha_b, x)$ to $\mathcal{E}$ over $b\|x \in \mathbb{F}_2^{n/2+1}$. The answers are stored in $\mathbf{T} = \{E_0, \ldots, E_{2^{n/2+1}-1}\}$.

2 Start with $(3n/2+1)l$-qubit state $|0\rangle$, i.e.,

$$\bigotimes_{j=1}^{l} (|0\rangle^{\otimes(n/2+1)} |0\rangle^{\otimes n}).$$

3 Apply Hadamard gates on each register $|x_j\rangle$ resulting in

$$|\psi_f\rangle = \frac{1}{2^{l(n/2+1)/2}} \sum_{x_1,\ldots,l \in \mathbb{F}_2^{n/2+1}} \bigotimes_{j=1}^{l} (|x_j\rangle |0\rangle).$$

4 Apply $\mathcal{U}_E$ implemented in **Algorithm 1** on $|\psi_f\rangle$ and $\mathbf{T}$ for $j = 1$ to l.

5 Return the final state $|\psi_f\rangle = \sum_{x_1,\ldots,l \in \mathbb{F}_2^{n/2+1}} \bigotimes_{j=1}^{l} (|x_j\rangle |E_{x_j}\rangle)$.

The first phase is to prepare the quantum database $|\psi_f\rangle$ that we need as shown in Algorithm 4. The offline quantum computation is to recover (k_4, k_5) by combining Grover's algorithm with Simon's algorithm. We run Grover search for (k_4, k_5) and test if it is right by Simon's algorithm. See Algorithm 5 for the formal description.

We call (k_4, k_5) is good if and only if g has a period. Because for any tuple $(k_1, k_2, k_3, k_4, k_5)$, the distinguisher f defined in Eq. (1) is always periodic. But there is only one (k_4, k_5) such that g is also a periodic function when the subkeys are fixed. Under the good (k_4, k_5), we can apply Simon's algorithm to solve the period of g. To run Grover search, we define

$$G(k_4, k_5) = \begin{cases} 1, & \text{if } g \text{ has a period}; \\ 0, & \text{else}. \end{cases}$$

Simon's algorithm will return (k_4, k_5) when $G(k_4, k_5) = 1$.

As shown in Algorithm 5, to prepare $|\psi_f\rangle$, we need query $\mathcal{E}$ classically about $2^{n/2+1}$ times and store the answers in a truth table $\mathbf{T}$. Next, we apply the quantum unitary $\mathcal{U}_E$ to prepare $|\psi_f\rangle$. Finally, we run Grover search $O(2^{n/2})$ times and use Simon's algorithm to recover the right (k_4, k_5).

Algorithm 5: Offline Simon's attack against 5-round Feistel structure.

Input: Classical query access to $\mathcal{E}$.
Output: The right (k_4, k_5).

1 Query classically to $\mathcal{E}$ to obtain a table $\mathbf{T} = \{E_0, \ldots, E_{2^{n/2+1}-1}\}$.

2 Start with $(n + (3n/2 + 1)l + nl/2)$ zero states $|0\rangle$. Prepare the quantum database $|\psi_f\rangle$ by **Algorithm 1**:

$$\sum_{x_j \in \mathbb{F}_2^{n/2+1}} |0\rangle^{\otimes n} |0\rangle^{\otimes n} \bigotimes_{j=1}^{l} (|x_j\rangle |E_{x_j}\rangle) |0\rangle^{\otimes n/2}.$$

3 Apply Hadamard gates on the first $2n$ qubits resulting in

$$\sum_{k_4, k_5 \in \mathbb{F}_2^{n/2}, x_j \in \mathbb{F}_2^{n/2+1}} |k_4\rangle |k_5\rangle \bigotimes_{j=1}^{l} (|x_j\rangle |E_{x_j}\rangle) |0\rangle.$$

4 Apply $\mathcal{O}_h$ to the above state, we get:

$$\sum_{k_4, k_5 \in \mathbb{F}_2^{n/2}, x_j \in \mathbb{F}_2^{n/2+1}} |k_4\rangle |k_5\rangle \bigotimes_{j=1}^{l} (|x_j\rangle |E_{x_j}\rangle) |h(k_4, k_5, x_1, \ldots, x_l)\rangle.$$

5 Apply $\mathcal{U}_E$ on the state again to clear the $|E_{x_j}\rangle$-register in time $2^{n/2+1}$.

6 Run Grover search for $(k_4, k_5) \in \mathbb{F}_2^{n/2} \times \mathbb{F}_2^{n/2}$. Apply Hadamard gates on $|x_1\rangle \ldots |x_l\rangle$ to obtain

$$\sum_{x_j, \mu_j \in \mathbb{F}_2^{n/2+1}; k_4, k_5 \in \mathbb{F}_2^{n/2}} |k_4\rangle |k_5\rangle \bigotimes_{j=1}^{l} (-1)^{\langle u_j, x_j \rangle} |x_j\rangle |h\rangle.$$

7 Compute the $\dim(Span(\mu_1, \ldots, \mu_l))$. Return (k_4, k_5) if and only if $\dim = n/2$, else uncompute Hadamard gates and continue Grover search.

8 After $O(2^{n/2})$ Grover iterations, we can recover the right (k_4, k_5).

In summary, the classical data complexity of our attack is $O(2^{n/2+1})$ and the time complexity includes two parts, applying $\mathcal{U}_E$ in time $O(l \cdot 2^{n/2+2})$ and run Grover search in time $O(2^{n/2})$. To prepare $|\psi_f\rangle$, we need auxiliary $(n/2+1)$-qubit register $|i\rangle$ when implementing $\mathcal{U}_E$. Thus, the attack requires

$$Q = n + (3n/2 + 1)l + nl/2 + n/2 + 1$$
$$= 3n/2 + (2n + 1)l + 1$$

qubits. And our attack is without using the QRAM. For attacking $r \geq 5$-round Feistel structure, the classical data complexity is always $O(2^{n/2+1})$ (See Table 1).

6   Conclusions

In this paper, we analyzed the offline Simon's attack on Feistel structure. The Simon's algorithm is powerful in the Q2 model, but it is limited in the Q1 model from the view of classical data complexity. To achieve lower complexity and make the Simon's attack against Feistel structure effective, the pre-distinguisher method is regarded as the optimal one. The classical data complexity of our attack is always $O(2^{n/2+1})$ for attacking $r > 3$-round Feistel structure, which is better than other classical attacks.

We also designed a quantum unitary operator $\mathcal{U}_E$ that can be used to prepare quantum database in superposition based on classical data. Our method needn't use QRAM by allocating some auxiliary qubits to control the process, leading to only polynomial qubits are involved.

Acknowledgements. The authors would like to thank the anonymous reviewers for their helpful comments and suggestions. This work was supported by National Natural Science Foundation of China (Grant No. 62202493, 61772545, 62072207) and Scientific Research Plan of National University of Defense Technology (No. ZK21-36) and Guangdong Basic and Applied Basic Research Foundation (No. 2022A1515140090)

References

1. Shor, P.W.: Algorithms for quantum computation: discrete logarithms and factoring. In: FOCS 1994, pp. 124–134. IEEE Computer Society (1994). https://dblp.org/rec/conf/focs/Shor94.bib
2. Grover, L.K.: A fast quantum mechanical algorithm for database search. In: Miller, G.L. (eds.) STOC 1996, pp. 212–219. ACM (1996). https://doi.acm.org/10.1145/237814.237866
3. Simon, D.R.: On the power of quantum computation. In: FOCS 1994, pp. 116–123. IEEE Computer Society (1994). https://dblp.org/rec/conf/focs/Simon94.bib
4. Leander, G., May, A.: Grover meets Simon – quantumly attacking the FX-construction. In: Takagi, T., Peyrin, T. (eds.) ASIACRYPT 2017. LNCS, vol. 10625, pp. 161–178. Springer, Cham (2017). https://doi.org/10.1007/978-3-319-70697-9_6
5. Kaplan, M., Leurent, G., Leverrier, A., et al.: Quantum differential and linear cryptanalysis. IACR Trans. Symmetric Cryptol. **2016**(1), 71–94 (2016). https://tosc.iacr.org/index.php/ToSC/article/view/536
6. Dong, X., Wang, X.: Quantum key-recovery attack on Feistel structures. Sci. China Inf. Sci. **61**(10), 102501 (2018)
7. Ito, G., Hosoyamada, A., Matsumoto, R., Sasaki, Yu., Iwata, T.: Quantum chosen-ciphertext attacks against Feistel ciphers. In: Matsui, M. (ed.) CT-RSA 2019. LNCS, vol. 11405, pp. 391–411. Springer, Cham (2019). https://doi.org/10.1007/978-3-030-12612-4_20
8. Kuwakado, H., Morii, M.: Quantum distinguisher between the 3-round Feistel cipher and the random permutation. In: Proceedings of 2010 International Symposium on Information Theory, pp. 2682–2685. IEEE, Austin, Texas, USA (2010)
9. Kuwakado, H., Morii, M.: Security on the quantum-type Even-Mansour cipher. In: Proceedings of 2012 International Symposium on Information Theory and Its Applications, pp. 312–316. IEEE, Honolulu, HI, USA (2012)

10. Zhandry, M.: How to construct quantum random functions. In: 53rd Annual IEEE Symposium on Foundations of Computer Science, pp. 679–687. IEEE Computer Society, New Brunswick, NJ, USA (2012)

11. Dinur, I., Dunkelman, O., Keller, N., Shamir, A.: New attacks on Feistel structures with improved memory complexities. In: Gennaro, R., Robshaw, M. (eds.) CRYPTO 2015. LNCS, vol. 9215, pp. 433–454. Springer, Heidelberg (2015). https://doi.org/10.1007/978-3-662-47989-6_21

12. Hosoyamada, A., Sasaki, Yu.: Quantum Demiric-Selçuk meet-in-the-middle attacks: applications to 6-round generic Feistel constructions. In: Catalano, D., De Prisco, R. (eds.) SCN 2018. LNCS, vol. 11035, pp. 386–403. Springer, Cham (2018). https://doi.org/10.1007/978-3-319-98113-0_21

13. Luby, M., Rackoff, C.: How to construct pseudorandom permutations from pseudorandom functions. SIAM J. Comput. **17**(2), 373–386 (1988)

14. Bonnetain, X., Hosoyamada, A., Naya-Plasencia, M., Sasaki, Yu., Schrottenloher, A.: Quantum attacks without superposition queries: the offline Simon's algorithm. In: Galbraith, S.D., Moriai, S. (eds.) ASIACRYPT 2019. LNCS, vol. 11921, pp. 552–583. Springer, Cham (2019). https://doi.org/10.1007/978-3-030-34578-5_20

15. Kaplan, M., Leurent, G., Leverrier, A., Naya-Plasencia, M.: Breaking symmetric cryptosystems using quantum period finding. In: Robshaw, M., Katz, J. (eds.) CRYPTO 2016. LNCS, vol. 9815, pp. 207–237. Springer, Heidelberg (2016). https://doi.org/10.1007/978-3-662-53008-5_8

16. Boneh, D., Dagdelen, Ö., Fischlin, M., Lehmann, A., Schaffner, C., Zhandry, M.: Random oracles in a quantum world. In: Lee, D.H., Wang, X. (eds.) ASIACRYPT 2011. LNCS, vol. 7073, pp. 41–69. Springer, Heidelberg (2011). https://doi.org/10.1007/978-3-642-25385-0_3

17. Hosoyamada, A., Sasaki, Yu.: Cryptanalysis against symmetric-key schemes with online classical queries and offline quantum computations. In: Smart, N.P. (ed.) CT-RSA 2018. LNCS, vol. 10808, pp. 198–218. Springer, Cham (2018). https://doi.org/10.1007/978-3-319-76953-0_11

FaBFT: Flexible Asynchronous BFT Protocol Using DAG

Yu Song[1], Yu Long[1(✉)], Xian Xu[2(✉)], and Dawu Gu[1(✉)]

[1] Shanghai Jiao Tong University, Shanghai, China
{sy_121,longyu,dwgu}@sjtu.edu.cn
[2] East China University of Science and Technology, Shanghai, China
xuxian@ecust.edu.cn

Abstract. The Byzantine Fault Tolerance (BFT) protocol is a long-standing topic. Recently, a lot of efforts have been made in the research of asynchronous BFT. However, the existing solutions cannot adapt well to the flexible network environment, and suffer from problems such as high communication complexity or long latency. To improve the efficiency of BFT consensus in flexible networks, we propose FaBFT. FaBFT's clients can make their own assumptions about the network conditions, and make the most of their networks based on different network assumptions. We also use the BlockDAG structure and an efficient consistent broadcast protocol to improve the concurrency and reduce the number of steps in FaBFT. The comparison with other asynchronous BFT protocols shows that FaBFT has lower complexity and cancels the dependency on the view change. We prove that FaBFT is an atomic broadcast protocol in flexible networks.

Keywords: Byzantine Fault Tolerance Protocol · Asynchronous Network · Flexible Consensus · DAG

1 Introduction

With the increasing popularity of blockchain and distributed applications, the need for atomic broadcast protocols that can meet real-world scenarios becomes significantly more urgent. To this end, Byzantine fault tolerance (BFT) and distributed consensus have been studied for more than 40 years. BFT consensus enables a group of parties, who do not trust each other, to reach an agreement in permissioned environments. Compared to the permissionless consensus, BFT consensus merits high efficiency and good performance, so it suits better for applications in mission-critical infrastructures.

Most of the conventional BFT protocols [4,19] utilize some time-bound assumption, either synchronous or partially synchronous, to guarantee the achievement of the security agreement. Specifically, [14] proposed the concept of *flexible consensus*, which allows clients to make different assumptions about

This work was supported in part by the Key Research and Development Plan of Shandong Province (No. 2021CXGC010105).

the network condition. In 2021, a flexible BFT protocol, named the Ebb-and-Flow protocol [16], was proposed in the partially synchronous network. Roughly, Ebb-and-Flow utilized two types of ledgers. As one ledger is the prefix of the other, these two ledgers can grow independently with different network assumptions (i.e., either synchronous or partially synchronous), without violating the requirements of the secure BFT. Thus, Ebb-and-Flow can flexibly meet the needs of different clients. Unfortunately, none of these partially synchronous consensus schemes can maintain their security without the time-bound assumption, and all these solutions lack liveness when the network experiences long delays or fluctuations.

In 2016, the first practical asynchronous Byzantine fault tolerance (aBFT), named HoneyBadger BFT [15], was proposed and proven secure without any time-bound assumptions. HoneyBadger does not suffer from network fluctuation and has stronger robustness and responsiveness. Subsequently, a series of works have been proposed [5,11,18,20]. As far as we are concerned, all the existing aBFT solutions utilize a two-phase mechanism, i.e., the *broadcast phase*, followed by the *agreement phase*. In the broadcast phase, the reliable broadcast (RBC) is used typically to guarantee that valid blocks can be delivered by honest parties. In the agreement phase, to bypass the FLP impossibility theorem [7] (i.e., deterministic consistency cannot be achieved in asynchronous networks), a random procedure is required, such as the common coin method [2,3]. Both phases require multiple rounds of communications and complex protocol flows, which make the aBFT protocol less usable. Thus the aBFT has been viewed as a "theoretical" consensus [10], and the early studies on aBFT protocols are not yet satisfactory from the standpoint of realistic applications.

One most critical issues in aBFT lies in the "unbalance" in the two phases, including both the bandwidth and the time requirements. Roughly, the reliable broadcast phase requires $O(n^3)$ times of communications (n is the number of the BFT parties), which leads to high communication overhead. Meanwhile, the agreement phase needs much less bandwidth but a much longer time. Consequently, the different requirements in the two phases result in a big waste of bandwidth. Most recently, some new methods have been proposed to address these issues, basically by applying different consensus strategies under different network conditions. Some of the aBFT schemes, such as [9,13,18], can deal with the "optimistic case". When these protocols detect that the real network is stable or performs better than the "pessimistic case", they can change the consensus strategy to make full use of the network and improve the performance of the consensus. Specifically, BDT [13] utilizes a complex *transformer* in its pace-sync process, which can achieve the switch between the optimistic fast lane and the pessimistic path. Bullshark [18] needs vertexes (blocks) in different networks that have different voting types and uses two types of leaders, i.e., the steady-state leaders and the fallback leaders, to commit blocks. The mechanism of dealing with network switching is highly complex and time-consuming. As such, Bullshark achieves weak liveness only [21]. Ditto [9], which derives from its partially synchronous version named Jolteon [9], uses the asynchronous fallback technique to handle the asynchronous network and view change phase. However, unlike the aforementioned flexible consensus, all these optimistic aBFT solutions maintain only one ledger instead of two, and thus the clients can not make their choice based on their own network assumptions. In other words, all these optimistic aBFT schemes are more suitable to work under the single network assumption. Concerning the performance, some existing (a)BFT solutions adopt the *single chain* structure to form the ledger. For example, in the HoneyBadger BFT protocol [15] or Dumbo-families protocols [10,11,13], only the block that contains at least $n - f$ transaction batches from different parties can be committed in a round. Instead of assembling transactions in blocks to form a single chain, using the *BlockDAG* structure to organize the *DAG chain* can preserve the parties' concurrent blocks, and fully utilize the bandwidth.

In this work, we extend the idea of flexible consensus to the asynchronous BFT and adapt the BlockDAG structure to this setting. Inspired by Ebb-and-Flow [16], our basic idea is to ask the committee parties to maintain two ledgers, including the *safer ledger* (for conservative clients) and the *faster ledger* (for aggressive clients). The clients can make their own network assumptions: either the "optimistic case" or the "pessimistic case". For the conservative clients who think the network condition is the pessimistic case, i.e., the asynchronous case, the safer ledger can be utilized to guarantee a secure consensus. For aggressive clients who believe that their network conditions are as good as the partially synchronous case, the faster ledger can be used to speed up the committing of transactions. In this way, we effectively cancel the time-bound assumption when dealing with the "pessimistic case", and optimize the utilization of the network in the "optimistic case".

To realize this high-level idea, however, there are some technical challenges. In particular, to guarantee a secure consensus, how can we utilize the BlockDAG structure and reduce the unbalance between phases for both ledgers? Moreover, how can we make sure that the safer ledger is the prefix of the faster ledger?

Our Contributions. To achieve secure BFT consensus in the flexible asynchronous network and answer the foregoing questions, we propose FaBFT, an asynchronous BFT protocol using DAG to support flexible consensus. To the best of our knowledge, FaBFT is the first flexible BFT consensus protocol that achieves all of the following properties.

- **Flexible in an asynchronous network.** FaBFT can run in both partially synchronous and asynchronous networks, and the network assumption is totally made by the clients. Thus the clients can make flexible choices independently, without sacrificing security.
- **DAG-based.** FaBFT's committee parties utilize the BlockDAG structure to improve the transaction throughput and network utility.
- **More efficient protocol.** We use the more efficient consistent broadcast (CBC) to design the broadcast phase, which reduces the rounds and thus the time latency. In the partially synchronous/asynchronous case, only 6/12 steps are required to commit blocks, respectively, completely eliminating the view change.

Table 1 compares FaBFT with other related consensus protocols.

Table 1. Comparison of related BFT protocols

Protocol	Network Assumption[a]	Steps[b]	Time Complexity[c]	Communication Complexity[d]	Message Complexity[e]	Structure	DAG Based	View Change
Hotstuff [19]	P-Sync.	6	$O(1)$	$O(n)$	$O(n)$	3-Phase Voting	N	Y
Ebb-and-Flow [16]	Sync.+P-Sync.	N.A.	$O(1)$	$O(n^2|m|)$	$O(n^2)$	Longest-Chain+BFT	N	Y
HBBFT [15]	Asy	Best: 9 Adv.: 13.5	$O(\log n)$	$O(n^2|m| + \lambda n^3 \log n)$	$O(n^3)$	RBC+ABA	N	N
Speeding-Dumbo [10]	Asy	Best: 10 Adv.: 16	$O(1)$	$O(n^2|m| + \lambda n^3 \log n)$	$O(n^2)$	RBC+MVBA	N	Y
BDT [13]	Opt-Asy	Best: 3 Adv.: 63	$O(1)$	$O(n^2|m| + \lambda n^3 \log n)$	$O(n^3)$	CAST/RBC+ BA+ MVBA	N	N
BullShark [18]	Opt-Asy	Best: E(10) Adv.: E(20) [f]	$O(1)$	$O(n^3|m|\log n)$	$O(n^3)$	RBC	Y	N
Ditto [9]	Opt-Asy	Best: 5 Adv.: E(10.5)	$O(1)$	$O(n^2|m|)$	$O(n^2)$	Asy-fallback	N	Y
This work	P-Sync.+Asy	Best: 6 Adv.: 12	$O(1)$	$O(n^2|m|)$	$O(n^2)$	CBC+GPC	Y	N

[a] We use "Sync." for "Synchronous", "P-Sync." for "Partially-Synchronous", "Asy." for "Asynchronous", and "O-Asy." for "Optimistic Asynchronous". Ebb-and-Flow is flexible in the partially synchronous network, and our FaBFT is flexible in the asynchronous network.

[b] We use "Steps" to estimate the approximate time from the block generation to the block commitment. Assume that the message from the sender reaches the receiver in one step. "Best" means that all parties are honest and the network is stable. "Adv." means the asynchronous network with $1/3$ Byzantine parties. E(s) means that the expected value of steps is s.

[c] Time Complexity: The expected number of rounds of communication before the protocol terminates. n is the number of the BFT parties.

[d] Communication Complexity: The expected value of the length of the message generated by the honest node for committing a block. m represents the average bit length of the block.

[e] Message Complexity: The expected value of the total messages that an honest node has generated.

[f] The "wave blocks" will be committed together after two or four rounds.

2 Preliminaries

2.1 BlockDAG Chain and Basic Operations

Instead of the single (i.e., longest) chain rule used in Bitcoin, BlockDAG consensus organizes blockchain into a *Direct Acyclic Graph* (DAG) which can benefit from all blocks created in parallel by honest parties. Through the DAG structure, BlockDAG consensus makes good use of the node's bandwidth and achieves true concurrency. We refer readers to [17] for the definition and operations on DAG.

2.2 Other Building Blocks

We use the *consistent broadcast* and the *global perfect coin* protocols as our building blocks to construct ledgers.

Roughly, the *Consistent Broadcast* (CBC) protocols ensure that only the delivered requests are the same for all receivers, and we refer readers to [1,6] for the definition of CBC. The *Global Perfect Coin* (GPC) protocol is used as a black box in the construction of the safer ledger for asynchronous networks. The GPC protocol is also called the common coin protocol [15], which typically works as a source of randomness for asynchronous BFTs. A secure GPC protocol satisfies the termination, agreement, unpredictability, and fairness properties. We refer readers to [12] for the detailed definitions.

3 Model and Security Definition

3.1 The Security Model

FaBFT runs in the permissioned setting with an initially fixed number of committee parties. Each authorized committee party has its unique public key.

Adversary Model. Without loss of generality, we consider that the committee set consists of n parties indexed by $i \in [n]$, where $[n] = \{1, ..., n\}$ and use f to denote the maximum number of the Byzantine faulty parties. Without loss of generality, we assume that $n = 3f + 1$. That is, no more than $1/3$ committee parties can be corrupted by the adversary $\mathcal{A}$. In FaBFT, we consider the static adversary only.

Network Model. Network communication is point to-point. In this network, adversary $\mathcal{A}$ is capable of delaying or reordering any messages between all the parties, but it cannot drop or modify the messages broadcast by honest parties. By borrowing definitions from [13,16,18], we define the partially synchronous and asynchronous networks as below.

Assume that every party has a local clock controlled by $\mathcal{A}$ and the time of a "tick" is at the speed of the actual network δ. Also assume that there is a global stabilization time (GST), after which all messages can be delivered within time δ. If $GST > 0$ the network is called to be *partially synchronous*, and if $GST = \infty$ the network is called to be *asynchronous*.

3.2 Definition of Security

Since FaBFT focuses on solving the asynchronous Byzantine Atomic Broadcast problem in the flexible network to attain robustness and reduce latency, we utilize the definition of atomic broadcast (ABC) to provide the security definition of FaBFT. We refer to [15] for the detailed definition of ABC.

4 Technical Overview

Current asynchronous consensus cannot meet the requirements of flexible networks. Specifically, in order to guarantee the "pessimistic-case" security, clients are unable to fully utilize their network in reality, especially when their real network conditions are better than the pessimistic-case scenario, which can lead to wasted bandwidth and long-term waits. In contrast, FaBFT introduces the flexible consensus in asynchronous networks, providing more resilient options for different clients. In addition, FaBFT uses BlockDAG to organize transactions.

4.1   Flexible Architecture

In FaBFT, each party may be in one of two different network environments. That is, the client can make different assumptions about the state of the network, i.e., partially synchronous or asynchronous. To reach a secure consensus in this environment, BFT parties run our FaBFT protocol to maintain two types of ledgers, a *faster ledger* for partially synchronous networks and a *safer ledger* for asynchronous networks. Particularly, a safer ledger is a prefix to a faster ledger. The client chooses one of them based on the client's network assumptions.

FaBFT guarantees that both ledgers can meet the security requirements of the BFT protocol regardless of the real network. In other words, clients can take advantage of a flexible network environment for better performance. In addition, by adopting the BlockDAG structure, the throughput of our consensus protocol depends only on the network speed. To illustrate the FaBFT protocol at a high level, we assume that there are n parties, where up to f could be broken by a static adversary $\mathcal{A}$.

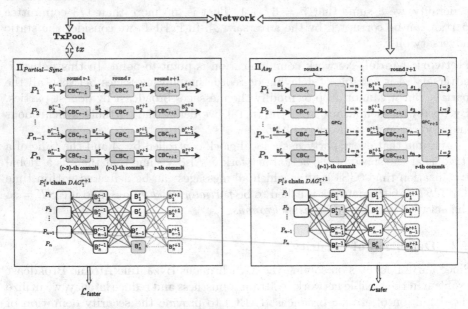

Fig. 1. The FaBFT architecture. FaBFT runs two parallel protocols. 1) The left box denotes the running of the partially synchronous protocol $\Pi_{\text{Partial-Sync}}$. The upper is $\Pi_{\text{Partial-Sync}}$'s running process in round $r+1$. Each green box denotes one CBC instance running smoothly, while the red box denotes one CBC instance with some errors. $P_1's$ chain DAG_1^{r+1} is shown at the bottom. Each solid box denotes a committed block and each dashed box denotes one block which is not arriving or in P_1's block buffer. Since $P_n's$ CBC in round r fails to arrive in P_1, blocks generated in round $r+1$ are added to P_1's block buffer, and then the dashed arrows help P_1 to retrieve B_n^r at round $r+1$. 2) The right box denotes the running of the asynchronous protocol Π_{Asy}. The blue boxes denote the GPC processes. In DAG_1^{r+1}, each yellow box denotes a leader block. Since B_n^r reaches lately and is elected as the leader in round $r+1$, blocks from round $r-1$ to $r+1$ are not committed. When B_n^r arrives, B_n^r and $\text{past}(\text{DAG}_1^r, B_n^r)$ can be committed. (Color figure online)

Flexible Protocol. The FaBFT committee runs two parallel protocols as Fig. 1 shows. The left ledger (i.e., the faster ledger $\mathcal{L}_{faster}$) has aggressive partial synchronous network assumption and runs faster. In this setting, every party's clock is consistent with the network speed and almost unanimously. The protocol is propelled by time. The right one (i.e., the safer ledger $\mathcal{L}_{safer}$) has a conservative asynchronous network assumption and runs slower but safer. Protocol operates at the network flow rate and advances in sufficient "quantities". Both $\mathcal{L}_{faster}$ and $\mathcal{L}_{safer}$ are constantly increased in each round. A two-phase process is required to commit blocks, including the *broadcast phase* and the *agreement phase*. It is worth noting that the two-phase process under the two ledgers is not the same, and the flexibility of FaBFT relies on the second phase, where the client chooses a committing strategy based on his own network assumption.

(1) *The broadcast phase*. During the broadcast phase, every honest party generates one block and broadcasts it. It collects votes from other parties for their blocks to form a broadcast certificate set and also votes for other blocks. Only the block with a legal certificate may be recorded on DAG.

(2) *The agreement phase*. In the agreement phase, an honest party will/will not generate a new block for the $\mathcal{L}_{faster}/\mathcal{L}_{safer}$. Roughly,

> The aggressive clients assuming that they are working in the partial synchronization network use the timeout mechanism similarly to their broadcast phase. That is, the honest parties create new blocks to guarantee that enough blocks can be generated in the current round, to ensure that all blocks in the previous round can be committed safely.

– Conservative clients, who assume themselves in an asynchronous network environment, use a counting mechanism instead of creating new blocks. They start a random process only when enough blocks have been collected, to decide the committed blocks.

BlockDAG Structure. Like [8,18], FaBFT adopts the BlockDAG structure. Specifically, each legal block references at least $n - f$ "parent blocks" generated in the previous round. This way, once a new block is recorded on one party's DAG chain, this party has received not only the certificate of this block but also all the parent blocks referenced by this block. Therefore, the recording of this new block implies that the party has agreed on all the referenced blocks. If this new block is committed, all the referenced ones are committed too. We note that in FaBFT, there are $2f + 1$ (i.e., instead of only 1) initial *genesis blocks* in the first round, and these genesis blocks appear in the past set of any valid blocks in FaBFT. If there are only the genesis blocks on the FaBFT ledgers, then parties only reference them. Otherwise, the parties will reference all (i.e., no less than $n - f$) tips of the DAG in their view.

Transaction Packaging and Block Construction. When receiving transactions from clients, one party puts them into its own buffer pool TransactionPool, and packages the new transactions TX into the blocks. TX's Merkle tree root, denoted as MKroot, is recorded in the head of the block. The resulting blocks, which contain the references to all tips (i.e., end blocks in DAG), are submitted by

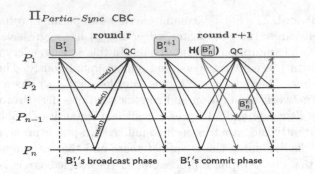

Fig. 2. P_1's CBC phase in $\Pi_{\mathsf{Partial-Sync}}$. 1) In round r, P_1 broadcasts a block B_1^r and collects unambiguous votes to form QC, then P_1 broadcasts QC to other parties. Round $r+1$ is B_1^{r+1}'s broadcast phase and also B_1^r's commit phase. When other parties receive B_1^{r+1}'s QC, B_1^{r+1} is added to their DAG chain, B_1^r can get committed. 2) The red lines denote that P_1 has received a block from some other party, but one of the parent blocks B_n^r is not contained in DAG_1^r, then P_1 calls for help from others. At the end of round $r+1$, all blocks belonging to round r can be committed.

the parties to get recorded on the ledger. FaBFT runs in rounds, and each honest committee generates exactly one block in one round. A block B_i^r submitted by party P_i at the beginning of the r−th round contains the identity information of P_i, the round number r, the transactions TX contained in this block, and the references to parent blocks in the previous round PaB_i^{r-1}. We emphasize that only blocks with certificates can be recorded on the ledger. Specifically, a block's qualified certificate consists of at least $n-f$ *votes* for this block. Each vote of B_i^r is generated by one party's *voting* in the r-th round. For simplicity, we denote a block authorized B_i^r generated by P_i as $B_i^r = \{\mathsf{MKroot}, P_i\text{'s identity}, r, \mathsf{TX}, \mathsf{PaB}_i^{r-1}\}$, and denote the qualified certificate as QC. A block B_i^r with QC is a "legal block".

Block Checking and Voting. When a party receives blocks, it adds them to its local buffer, checks them, and votes for valid ones. Especially, if one party finds a received block containing references to some parent blocks which this party has not received yet, this party starts the "call for help" process for other parties and retrieves the missing blocks if only they really existed. If all checks pass, this party waits for blocks' QCs, and removes a block from the local buffer to the end of the DAG when the corresponding QC arrives. In the partially synchronous network, valid missing blocks will be sent in this step with the QC.

4.2 Two-Phase Consensus in Partially Synchronous Networks

In the partially synchronous network, we can assume that there is a uniform clock. In this environment, the protocol runs round-by-round, and the protocol's rounds are driven by a timer. Each round consists of 3 steps, the timer starts at the beginning of each step, and a step consists of multiple "ticks". A block B_i^r created by P_i at the beginning of the r-th round (i.e., the broadcast phase of

B_i^r) will be committed at the end of the $(r+1)$-th round (i.e., the agreement phase of B_i^r), if B_i^r is correctly formed. Therefore, it takes 6 steps (or 2 rounds) to commit a block.

Broadcast Phase. Generally, the broadcast phase consists of n parallel consistent broadcast (CBC) being run by every party. Each CBC instance consists of 3 steps: (1) Each honest party generates exactly one block at the beginning of the broadcast phase and broadcasts it among the committee. (2) Other parties check the received blocks and return the votes if all the checks pass. (3) Once at least $n - f$ votes for one block have been received, the block's QC has been formed and the creator of this block broadcasts QC. At the end of the broadcast phase, the honest parties add blocks to its DAG chain only if (i) each added block has a qualified certificate QC, and (ii) all the reference blocks appear in this party's DAG view. Otherwise, the blocks are saved in the party's block buffers. Under the partially synchronous assumption, at least $n - f$ new blocks will be added to $\mathcal{L}_{\text{faster}}$ at the end of this phase.

We use an honest party P_1 running at round r as an example to illustrate the CBC phase in Fig. 2. Here the block B_1^r together with its QC are received by other parties at the end of round r. It is worth noting that B_1^r can always be committed until the end of the $(r+1)$-th round.

The Agreement Phase. The agreement phase works in a way similar to the broadcast phase. At least $n - f$ new blocks will be added to $\mathcal{L}_{\text{faster}}$ at the end of this phase, and each of the new blocks references at least $n - f$ legal blocks (i.e., with their QCs) in the previous round. Therefore, at the end of this phase, all blocks before this batch of blocks can be committed. In Fig. 2, block B_1^r is committed when block B_1^{r+1} is recorded on $\mathcal{L}_{\text{faster}}$.

4.3 Two-Phase Consensus in Asynchronous Network

Asynchronous networks do not have the assumption of time bounds, and the advancement of each party depends entirely on the speed of their respective networks. Although the protocol still operates on a round-by-round basis, iterations of rounds are guaranteed by a counting mechanism.

The Broadcast Phase. Each honest party advances into a new round via the CBC process by generating and broadcasting a new block. During each round, each honest party can generate exactly one block, and thus no less than $n - f$ blocks will be recorded on DAG. The most crucial difference in the CBC process under the asynchronous network is that there is no timer. Thus, parallel CBCs belonging to the same round can *not* start at the same time. When a new block is generated, not only more than $n - f$ parent blocks but also all tips(DAG) blocks with no subsequent references should be referenced. Then broadcasts the block. After that, honest parties will keep waiting for more than $n - f$ consistent votes to form and broadcast the QC, instead of utilizing the timeout mechanism. When an honest party adds at least $n - f$ blocks on the DAG, it will advance into both the agreement phase and the next CBC, and organize a new block.

The Agreement Process. When a party admits $n - f$ blocks into its DAG during the CBC process, it will immediately boost the global perfect coin by broadcasting its random signature share, and $f + 1$ random share will invoke GPC. Then a random leader P_l can be elected. If the leader's block B_l has been on DAG and fortunately it is a parent block for more than $n - f$ next-round blocks, B_l block and its history can be committed without ambiguity, which means more than $n - f$ parties have acknowledged B_l's QC and recorded B_l on DAG. Otherwise, there will be no progress in this round. We can prove that once the subsequent available leader's block appears, all these blocks can still be committed. The fact that this protocol can move forward satisfies the liveness and is censorship resistance.

5   Detailed Protocol Description

For the length limitation, we only left the description of each algorithm, and the reader can find the pseudocode for each algorithm in the full version [17].

5.1   Block Generation

At the start of a round, to generate a new block and add it to the BlockDAG, a party needs to refer to all end blocks (no less than $n - f$) in its BlockDAG chain (Here we emphasize that in the asynchronous network, the party needs to traverse its BlockDAG to reference all end blocks reached lately too). Moreover, the party needs to select transactions from its local transaction pool. The selected transactions constitute the body of a block, and the Merkle-tree root of these transactions is recorded in the head of the block. Then the party signs it to create a block. After that, the party broadcasts it instantly to others and then waits to collect enough votes to form a broadcast certificate QC for this block.

5.2   Block Transmission

CBC guarantees that a new block can reach every party consistently. As one of the senders, P_i first broadcasts its newly generated block B_i^r to every other party and collects votes to form QC. More than $n - f$ unanimous votes form a broadcast QC for B_i^r. This QC proves that most of the parties have received B_i^r and acknowledged its correctness. Then P_i also sends the QC to all parties.

When P_j receives the new block B_i^r from P_i, it needs to check its validity, including the transaction's correctness and the signature legality. If all checks pass, P_j returns a vote of this block to P_i. Meanwhile, P_j needs to check if all of the referenced blocks are in PaB_i^{r-1} in DAG_j. If not, P_j needs to call for help from others. In this case, other honest parties will send the corresponding parents' block(s) to P_j. Specifically, the received blocks are first included in the receiver's block buffer. A block B_i^r in P_j's block buffer will be moved out and added to P_j's DAG chain only if (1) B_i^r is correct, (2) B_i^r's QC has arrived, and (3) P_j has received all blocks stated in PaB_i^{r-1}.

5.3   Optimistic Case Block Confirmation

As Fig. 2 shows, when the current CBC_r ends, there are at least $n - f$ blocks on the honest party P_i's DAG chain DAG_i^r, we denote these blocks as B^r. All blocks referenced by B^r on DAG_i^r have corresponding QC and have passed at least two voting processes. They can all be committed and recorded on the faster ledger.

5.4   Pessimistic Case Block Confirmation

If P_i receives more than $n - f$ blocks in round $r + 1$, it will broadcast its signature share and the agreement phase starts. $f + 1$ shares from different parties in round r will invoke the random common coin GPC. A leader P_l will be elected. If there was leader's block B_l^r in round r on the view of DAG_i^{r+1} and B_l^r if referenced by more than $n - f$ blocks from $r + 1$, B_l^r and all its casual history (i.e., blocks belong to $past(DAG_i^{r+1}, B_l^r)$) will be committed legally. Otherwise, if there is progress in round r, we can prove that the next available leader will also commit.

6   Security Analysis

6.1   Security Theorem

We prove that FaBFT satisfies all the proper satisfies all properties of the atomic broadcast (ABC), no matter what the network environment is. Besides, we discuss the censorship resistance of FaBFT. The detailed proofs for Theorem 1 and Theorem 2 can be found in [17].

Theorem 1. *Assuming* $n - 3f + 1$, *FaBFT can meet the total order, agreement, and liveness properties of the atomic broadcast protocol, except for a probability exponentially small in* n.

Theorem 2. *FaBFT is censorship resistance.*

6.2   More Discussions

When the network assumption is inconsistent with the real environment, FaBFT can still guarantee security. In an optimistic network, clients can make any assumptions. Two consecutive CBCs are sufficient to guarantee the safety and liveness of honest blocks. As each honest party generates exactly one block in each round and Theorem 1, the slower $\mathcal{L}_{safer}$ is the prefix of $\mathcal{L}_{faster}$. In particular, when the clients assume that the network is partially synchronous but the real network is pessimistic, the faster ledger may stop increasing, and clients can adopt the safer ledger instead, i.e., $\mathcal{L}_{faster} = \mathcal{L}_{safer}$ in this case. When the network is stable and optimistic, honest parties' DAG views can be synchronized quickly and will continuously increase $\mathcal{L}_{faster}$.

7   Performance Analysis and Conclusion

As shown in Table 1, FaBFT has the merits of low communication complexity and message complexity in flexible asynchronous networks, due to the elegant combination of BlockDAG, CBC, and GPC. Compared with [9], which currently requires the lowest bandwidth and smallest number of messages in the literature, FaBFT costs only one more step in the best case and comparably steps in the asynchronous case, through canceling the costly asynchronous-fallback and view change operations. Even better, FaBFT supports BlockDAG and a flexible network, which makes it more applicable in practice.

References

1. Byzantine broadcasts and randomized consensus (2009). https://dcl.epfl.ch/site/education/secure_distributed_computing
2. Cachin, C., Shoup, V.: Random oracles in constantinople: practical asynchronous byzantine agreement using. In: Proceedings of the 19th ACM Symposium on Principles of Distributed Computing, pp. 1–26 (2000)
3. Canetti, R., Rabin, T.: Fast asynchronous byzantine agreement with optimal resilience. In: Proceedings of the Twenty-Fifth Annual ACM Symposium on Theory of Computing, STOC 1993, pp. 42–51 (1993)
4. Castro, M., Liskov, B., et al.: Practical byzantine fault tolerance. In: OSDI, vol. 99, pp. 173–186 (1999)
5. Danezis, G., Kokoris-Kogias, L., Sonnino, A., Spiegelman, A.: Narwhal and tusk: a DAG-based mempool and efficient BFT consensus. In: Proceedings of the Seventeenth European Conference on Computer Systems, pp. 34–50 (2022)
6. Duan, S., et al.: Dashing and star: byzantine fault tolerance using weak certificates. Cryptology ePrint Archive (2022)
7. Fischer, M.J., Lynch, N.A., Paterson, M.S.: Impossibility of distributed consensus with one faulty process. J. ACM (JACM) **32**(2), 374–382 (1985)
8. Gągol, A., Leśniak, D., Straszak, D., Świętek, M.: Aleph: efficient atomic broadcast in asynchronous networks with byzantine nodes. In: Proceedings of the 1st ACM Conference on Advances in Financial Technologies, pp. 214–228 (2019)
9. Gelashvili, R., Kokoris-Kogias, L., Sonnino, A., Spiegelman, A., Xiang, Z.: Jolteon and ditto: network-adaptive efficient consensus with asynchronous fallback. In: Eyal, I., Garay, J. (eds.) FC 2022. LNCS, vol. 13411, pp. 296–315. Springer, Cham (2022). https://doi.org/10.1007/978-3-031-18283-9_14
10. Guo, B., Lu, Y., Lu, Z., Tang, Q., Xu, J., Zhang, Z.: Speeding dumbo: pushing asynchronous BFT closer to practice. Cryptology ePrint Archive (2022)
11. Guo, B., Lu, Z., Tang, Q., Xu, J., Zhang, Z.: Dumbo: faster asynchronous BFT protocols. In: 2020 ACM CCS, pp. 803–818 (2020)
12. Keidar, I., Kokoris-Kogias, E., Naor, O., Spiegelman, A.: All you need is DAG. In: Proceedings of the 2021 ACM Symposium on Principles of Distributed Computing, pp. 165–175 (2021)
13. Lu, Y., Lu, Z., Tang, Q.: Bolt-dumbo transformer: asynchronous consensus as fast as the pipelined BFT. In: Proceedings of the 2022 ACM SIGSAC Conference on Computer and Communications Security, pp. 2159–2173 (2022)
14. Malkhi, D., Nayak, K., Ren, L.: Flexible byzantine fault tolerance. In: Proceedings of the 2019 ACM SIGSAC Conference on CCS, pp. 1041–1053 (2019)

15. Miller, A., Xia, Y., Croman, K., Shi, E., Song, D.: The honey badger of BFT protocols. In: 2016 ACM CCS, pp. 31–42 (2016)
16. Neu, J., Tas, E.N., Tse, D.: EBB-and-flow protocols: a resolution of the availability-finality dilemma. In: 2021 IEEE Symposium on Security and Privacy (SP), pp. 446–465. IEEE (2021)
17. Song, Y., Long, Y., Xu, X., Gu, D.: FaBFT: flexible asynchronous BFT protocol using DAG. Cryptology ePrint Archive (2023)
18. Spiegelman, A., Giridharan, N., Sonnino, A., Kokoris-Kogias, L.: Bullshark: DAG BFT protocols made practical. In: Proceedings of the 2022 ACM SIGSAC Conference on Computer and Communications Security, pp. 2705–2718 (2022)
19. Yin, M., Malkhi, D., Reiter, M.K., Gueta, G.G., Abraham, I.: HotStuff: BFT consensus with linearity and responsiveness. In: Proceedings of the 2019 ACM Symposium on Principles of Distributed Computing, pp. 347–356 (2019)
20. Zhang, H., Duan, S.: Pace: fully parallelizable BFT from reproposable byzantine agreement. Cryptology ePrint Archive (2022)
21. Zhou, Y., et al.: Dory: asynchronous BFT with reduced communication and improved efficiency. Cryptology ePrint Archive (2022)

Forward Secure Online/Offline Key Policy Attribute-Based Encryption with Keyword Search

Husheng Yang[1], Sha Ma[1(✉)], Pan Zhou[1], Guiquan Yang[1], and Qiong Huang[1,2]

[1] College of Mathematics and Informatics, South China Agricultural University, Guangzhou 510642, China
martin_deng@163.com, zhoupan@stu.scau.edu.cn
[2] Guangzhou Key Lab of Intelligent Agriculture, Guangzhou 510642, China
qhuang@scau.edu.cn

Abstract. Industrial Internet of Things (IIoT) is a cloud-based system that collects data from devices, and key policy attribute-based keyword search (KP-ABKS) scheme enables fine-grained keyword search over the encrypted data obtained from IIoT devices. However, in existing KP-ABKS schemes, the trapdoor's lifetime is generally infinite, meaning that the trapdoor can be used for searching at any time. This poses a risk to the disclosure of the keyword in the trapdoor. Additionally, the inherent computational and storage requirements of KP-ABKS impose a significant burden on IIoT terminal devices. In this paper, we propose a new cryptographic primitive called forward secure online/offline key policy attribute-based keyword search (FS-OO-KPABKS), which supports both forward security and online/offline secret key generation and encryption. We provide a rigorous security model that the FS-OO-KPABKS scheme achieves selective security against chosen keyword attacks (SCKA) in the standard model. Furthermore, theoretical analysis demonstrates that our scheme exhibits remarkable efficiency in online secret key generation and, online encryption and search execution, and hence shows good adaptability in the IIoT thanks to its unbounded attribute universe.

Keywords: key policy · attribute-based encryption with keyword search · forward security · online/offline

1 Introduction

In Industrial Internet of Things (IIoT), each device is equipped with sensors which they can collect data, and then upload this data to cloud servers with powerful computing and storage capabilities. However, cloud servers are typically assumed to be honest yet curious. If the data is sent in plain form, sensitive private data is vulnerable to the cloud, so the sensors should encrypt the data before uploading it. Nonetheless, the availability of encrypted data is greatly compromised. A simple solution is for the user to download all authorized ciphertexts to be accessed and decrypt them, but this undoubtedly consumes an immeasurable amount of computing and storage overhead. Fortunately, public key encryption with keyword search (PEKS) [1] is seen as a viable and effective solution to solve the data availability problem. The sensors embed a keyword of the data when encrypting it, and then upload it to the cloud for storage. When a user wants to search for data, it first generates a trapdoor associated with its interested keyword, and then submits the trapdoor to the cloud. At last, the cloud performs the search operation and returns the search results to the user. In order to achieve the advantages of both fine-grained access control and ciphertext retrieval, a new cryptographic primitive named attribute-based encryption with keyword search (ABKS) [9] is proposed by combining attribute-based encryption (ABE) [6] and PEKS. To prevent malicious cloud servers from using old trapdoors to test newly added ciphertexts and potentially compromising users' privacy, the importance of forward security should also be emphasized in the ABKS scheme. Furthermore, the existing ABKS scheme suffers from efficiency issues due to a large number of pairing operations. Therefore, it is necessary to introduce online/offline ABE technique in foward security ABKS to enhance the IIoT system's operational efficiency, with the vast majority of time-consuming computational operations being performed in the offline phase.

1.1   Contribution

The main contributions of this paper can be summarized as follows:

1) We propose a new concept called forward secure online/offline key policy attribute-based keyword search (FS-OO-KPABKS) to improve the efficiency and enhance the security of ABKS by introducing forward security. The key generation and ciphertext generation phases are divided into offline and online phases, and most time-consuming operations can be completed in the offline phase. What's more, we introduce forward security to guarantee that the trapdoor can only be used for the ciphertexts whose generation time is before the generation time of secret key in trapdoor, which can effectively limit the search power of the server and hence protect the user privacy by preventing it from searching for newly added ciphertext.
2) We present the first practical FS-OO-KPABKS scheme in prime order group using the techonology of 0-Encoding and 1-Encoding and online/offline ABE, and provide security model based on Modified q-2 assumption in the standard model.
3) Compared with the related schemes, the comprehensive performance illustrates that while supporting the dynamic verifiable attribute addition thanks to the large universe, our FS-OO-KPABKS achieves significant efficiency in online encryption generation and online key generation execution and hence shows its applicability in the IIoT system.

1.2   Related Work

Forward Secure Public Key Encryption with Keyword Search. In key-policy attribute-based encryption with keyword search(KP-ABEKS), the keyword ciphertext is encrypted with attributes, and the Attribute Authority (AA) generates the key with access policy for the user. Then the user selects the keywords of interest to generate trapdoors and submits them to the server for search operation. Traditional PEKS schemes are vulnerable to adaptive file injection attacks As a countermeasure, the concept of forward security is proposed [8]. Zhang et al. [8] proposed a forward security PEKS scheme with resistant to quantum computer attacks based on lattice assumptions, which allows users to update private keys at various time period through the key update algorithm and hence the number of trapdoors become linearly dependent with the number of search time periods. In order to address this problem, Kim et al. [4] proposed the FS-PEKS scheme, which uses a search counter to achieve forward security. Although [4] reduces the number of search tokens drastically, every time users search ciphertext, the ciphertext must be re-encrypted with a new search counter and then uploaded to the cloud server, which would not be a small burden for the whole system. Zeng et al. [7] proposed an efficient FS-PEKS scheme to realize forward security function through 0-Encoding and 1-Encoding without updating ciphertext or private key. To the best of our knowledge, there is no scheme to implement the forward security property in ABKS.

2   Preliminaries

2.1   0-Encoding and 1-Encoding

Let $a = a_n a_{n-1}...a_1 \in \{0,1\}^n$ be an n-bit binary string. The 0-encoding and 1-encoding results of a are the sets S_a^0 and S_a^1 of binary strings with at most n elements, respectively, such that

$$S_a^0 = \{a_n a_{n-1}...a_{i+1}1 | a_i = 0, 1 \leq i \leq n\},$$
$$S_a^1 = \{a_n a_{n-1}...a_i | a_i = 1, 1 \leq i \leq n\}.$$

To compare the values of two integers x and y, x is encoded with the 0-encoding algorithm to obtain S_x^0, and S_y^1 is encoded with the 1-encoding algorithm to obtain S_y^1. If the intersection of S_x^0 and S_y^1 is not empty, we say that $x < y$. Otherwise, we denote $x \geq y$. Formally, it is denoted as $S_x^0 \cap S_y^1 \neq \emptyset \Leftrightarrow x < y$.

2.2   Bilinear Pairing

Let $\mathbb{PG} = (\mathbb{G}_0, \mathbb{G}_1, g, p, e)$ be a symmetric-pairing group. $\mathbb{G}_0$ and $\mathbb{G}_1$ are cyclic groups of prime order p. For all $g, h \in \mathbb{G}_0$ and $a, b \in Z_p^*, e : \mathbb{G}_0 \times \mathbb{G}_0 \rightarrow \mathbb{G}_1$ is a map satisfying the following three properties.

1) Bilinear: $e(g^a, h^b) = e(g, h)^{ab}$.
2) Non-degenerate: $e(g, h) \neq 1_{\mathbb{G}_1}$.
3) Computable: $e(g, h)$ can be computed effectively.

2.3 Monotonic Access Structure

Let U denote the universe of attributes. The access construction $\mathbb{A}$ is a non-empty set of U, that is, $\mathbb{A} \in 2^U \backslash \{\emptyset\}$. An attribute set in $\mathbb{A}$ is called an authorized set, otherwise it is an unauthorized set. If for every $C, D \in U$ such that $C \subseteq D, C \in \mathbb{A}$, and then $D \in \mathbb{A}$, an access construction is said to be monotone.

2.4 Linear Secret-Sharing Schemes (LSSS)

Let p be a prime and U be the attribute universe. A secret sharing scheme Π with domain of secrets Z_p^* realizing access policies on U is linear over Z_p^* if

1) The shares of a secret $s \in Z_p^*$ for each attribute are from a vector over Z_p^*.
2) For each access structure $\mathbb{A}$ on U, there exists a share-generating matrix $M \in (Z_p^*)^{\ell \times n}$, and a function ρ that labels the rows of M with attributes from U, which satisfy the following: During the generation of the shares, we consider the column vector $\boldsymbol{y} = (s, r_2, ..., r_n)^\top$, where $r_2, ..., r_n \in Z_p^*$. Then the vector of ℓ shares of the secret s is equal to $M \cdot \boldsymbol{y}$. The share $\lambda_j = M_j \cdot \boldsymbol{y}$ belongs to attribute $\rho(j)$, where M_j is the j th row of the matrix M.

Let S denote an authorized set for the access structure $\mathbb{A}$ such that $S \in \mathbb{A}$, I be the set of rows whose labels are in S, i.e. $I = \{i | i \in 1, ..., \ell, \rho(i) \in S\}$. The reconstruction requirement asserts that the vector $(1, 0, ..., 0)$ is in the span of rows of M indexed by I. Then, there exists coefficients $\{\omega_i\}_{i \in I}$ such that $\sum_{i \in I} \omega_i \lambda_i = s$.

2.5 Modified $q - 2$ Assumption

We will use a Modified q-2 assumption on prime order bilinear groups, which is similar to the Decisional Bilinear Diffie-Hellman Assumption.

Initially the challenger calls the group generation algorithm with input the security parameter, picks a random group element $\hat{g} \xleftarrow{\$} \mathbb{G}_0$, and $q + 3$ random exponents $x, y, z, b_1, b_2, ..., b_q \xleftarrow{\$} Z_p^*$. Then it sends to the attacker the group description $(p, \mathbb{G}_0, \mathbb{G}_1, e)$ and all of the following terms:

1) $\hat{g}, \hat{g}^x, \hat{g}^y, \hat{g}^z, \hat{g}^{(xz)^2}, \hat{g}^{x^2 z}, \hat{g}^{x^3 yz}$,
2) $\hat{g}^{b_i}, \hat{g}^{xzb_i}, \hat{g}^{xz/b_i}, \hat{g}^{x^2 zb_i}, \hat{g}^{y/b_i^2}, \hat{g}^{y^2/b_i^2}, \hat{g}^{x^3 z^2 b_i}, \hat{g}^{xz/b_i^2}$ $(\forall i \in [1, q])$,
3) $\hat{g}^{xzb_i/b_j}, \hat{g}^{yb_i/b_j^2}, \hat{g}^{xyzb_i/b_j^2}, \hat{g}^{(xz)^2 b_i/b_j}, \hat{g}^{(xz)^2 b_i/b_j^2}, \hat{g}^{xzb_i/b_j^2}$ $(\forall i, j \in [1, q], i \neq j)$.

The challenger also flips a random coin $\psi \xleftarrow{\$} \{0, 1\}$ and if $\psi = 0$ it gives to the attacker the term $e(\hat{g}, \hat{g})^{xyz}$. Otherwise it gives a random term $R \xleftarrow{\$} \mathbb{G}_1$. Finally the attacker outputs a guess $\psi' \in \{0, 1\}$. It can be proved that the Modified q-2 assumption is secure, as detailed in full version.

Definition 1. We say that the Modified q-2 assumption holds if all probabilistic polynomial time (PPT) attackers have at most a negligible advantage in λ in the above security game, where the advantage is defined as $\mathbf{Adv}_{\mathcal{A}}^{\text{Modified } q-2}(1^\lambda) = \Pr[\psi' = \psi] - 1/2$.

3 Problem Formulation

3.1 System Model

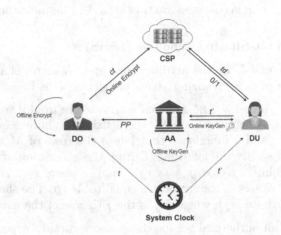

Fig. 1. The system model of our FS-OO-KPABKS scheme.

As seen in Fig. 1, the system model of our FS-OO-KPABKS scheme consists of the following four entities **Data Owner(DO)**, **Attribute Authority(AA)**, **Data User(DU)**, **Cloud Service Provider(CSP)**, assuming that the **System Clock** is an available resource:

1) **Data Owner(DO):** This entity prepares for encryption during the offline phase, and then encrypts its own index plaintext data into ciphertext ct and uploads the ct to the CSP in the online phase.
2) **Attribute Authority(AA):** This entity generates the public key PP and master secret key for the system, and then prepares for secret key generation during the offline phase, and generates secret keys sk for DU according to its role in the system in the online phase.
3) **Data User(DU):** This entity generates trapdoors td with its own sk and keywords of interest, and sends it to the CSP for searching.
4) **Cloud Service Provider(CSP):** This entity has a large amount of storage space and strong computing power. It can store the ct sent by DO, and provide search function for DU.

3.2 The Definition of FS-OO-KPABKS

In formal, a forward secure online/offline key policy attribute-based encryption with keyword search (FS-OO-KPABKS) scheme consists of the following seven algorithms.

1) **Setup(1^λ):** This algorithm is performed by AA. λ is input as a security parameter, and then the global public parameter PP and master secret key MSK are output.

2) **Offline.Encrypt(PP):** This algorithm is performed by DO. Inputting the global public parameter PP, DO calculates the intermediate ciphertext $IT = (IT_{main}, IT_{att})$.

3) **Online.Encrypt(PP, kw, S, t, IT):** This algorithm is performed by DO. Inputting the global public parameter PP, the attribute set S determined by DO, the current time t, the keywords set kw of the document, and the intermediate ciphertext IT, DO calculates the final index ciphertext ct corresponding to the keywords and the current time t.

4) **Offline.KeyGen(PP):** This algorithm is performed by AA. Inputting the global public parameter PP, AA calculates the intermediate key I_{row}.

5) **Online.KeyGen($MSK, I_{row}, \mathbb{A} = (M, \rho), t'$):** This algorithm is performed by AA. Inputting the master key MSK, the intermediate key I_{row}, the current time t', and an access control matrix M with a function ρ, AA calculates a secret key sk for DU according to his role in the system and the current time t'.

6) **TrapGen(PP, sk, kw'):** This algorithm is performed by DU. Inputting the data user's secret key sk and the keyword kw', DU calculates the trapdoor td.

7) **Search(PP, td, ct):** This algorithm is performed by CSP. Inputting the trapdoor td and the index ciphertext ct, CSP calculates the search result 0/1 and returns 1 if and only if the time t' in the trapdoor td is after the generation time t of ct, which is denoted by $t < t'$, the attributes of ct satisfies the access policy of td, and both have the same keyword, otherwise returns 0.

3.3   Security Model

We define a security model for FS-OO-KPABKS in the sense of selective security under chosen keyword attacks between a challenger and an attacker via the following game. The phases of the game are the following:

Initialization: In this phase, the adversary chooses a challenge time t^* and declares a challenge attribute set S^*.

Setup: In this phase, the challenger calls the **Setup(1^λ)** algorithm and sends the public parameter PP to the adversary.

Query Phase 1: In this phase the challenge first calls **Offline.KeyGen(PP)** to generate the intermediate key I_{row}. Given secret key for $(t'_1, \mathbb{A}_1), (t'_2, \mathbb{A}_2)$, ..., $(t'_{Q_1}, \mathbb{A}_{Q_1})$ submitted by the adversary, the challenger calls **Online.KeyGen($MSK, I_{row}, \mathbb{A} = (M, \rho), t'$)** to get sk_i and sends the sk_i to the adversary, for any $i \in [1, Q_1]$, where Q_1 is the number of inquiries in phase 1. There exists a restriction: if $t'_i \geq t^*$, S^* doesn't satisfy any queried policies, i.e. $S^* \notin \mathbb{A}_i$. $\mathcal{A}$ can then use these private keys responded by $\mathcal{C}$ to encrypt any query keyword to obtain legitimate search trapdoors.

Challenge: The challenge first calls **Offline.Encrypt**(PP) to generate intermediate ciphertext $IT = (IT_{mian}, IT_{att})$. Sequentially, the adversary selects two equal-length keywords set kw_1 and kw_2, and sends them to the challenger. Then the challenger flips a random coin $\psi \in \{0,1\}$ and calls the **Online.Encrypt**$(PP, kw_\psi, S^*, t^*, IT)$ algorithm to generate the challenge ciphertext ct. Finally it returns ct to the adversary.

Query Phase 2: This is the same as query phase 1. The adversary continues to query the private key for access constructs $(t'_{Q_1+1}, \mathbb{A}_{Q_1+1}), (t'_{Q_1+2}, \mathbb{A}_{Q_1+2}),$ ..., $(t'_Q, \mathbb{A}_Q)$, where Q is the number of inquiries in phase 2 and the same restrictions hold as in query phase 1.

Guess: The adversary outputs its guess $\psi' \in \{0,1\}$ for ψ.

Definition 2. We say that the FS-OO-KPABKS is selective security against chosen-keyword attack (SCKA) if all PPT adversaries have at most a negligible advantage in λ in the above security game, where the advantage of an adversary is defined as $\mathbf{Adv}^{SCKA}_{\text{FS-OO-KPABKS}, \mathcal{A}}(1^\lambda) = \Pr[\psi' = \psi] - 1/2$.

4   The Proposed Scheme

In this section, we first introduce how to optimize the structure of an access tree to realize the property of forward security. The root node of the access tree is an AND gate, which has two children. Encode the time period t as a set $\mathcal{T} = \{t_1, t_2, ..., t_n\}$, and then transform it to an OR gate as the first child of the root node. The other child node can be an AND gate, OR gate or threshold gate, which can connect some normal attributes, such as Cadillac, female etc., as shown in Fig. 2.

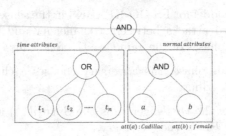

Fig. 2. An access tree paradigm.

1) **Setup**$(1^\lambda:)$ Inputting the security parameters λ, this algorithm generates the public parameters PP and the master key MSK of the system. More specifically, the algorithm gains the description of the group and bilinear pair $\mathbb{PG} = (\mathbb{G}_0, \mathbb{G}_1, g, p, e)$, where p is the prime order of the groups $\mathbb{G}_0$ and $\mathbb{G}_1$. H

is a hash functions on $\{0,1\}^*$ to Z_p^*. The attribute universe U is all elements in the group Z_p^*, i.e. $U = Z_p^*$. The algorithm then selects random elements $g, u, h, w \xleftarrow{\$} \mathbb{G}_0$, and $\alpha \xleftarrow{\$} Z_p^*$ and further computes $e(g,g)^\alpha$. It outputs:

$$PP = (\mathbb{PG}, g, u, h, w, e(g,g)^\alpha, H), \quad MSK = \alpha.$$

2) **Offline.Encrypt**(PP): This algorithm generates any intermediate ciphertext IT_{main} and IT_{att}. It selects a random $s \in Z_p^*$, and then calculates the main module $IT_{main} = (C, C_0, C_w)$, respectively

$$C = e(g,g)^{\alpha s}, C_0 = g^s, C_w = w^{-s}.$$

Meanwhile, random $r, \tilde{x} \in Z_p^*$ is selected, and attribute module $IT_{att} = (r, \tilde{x}, C_1', C_2')$ is calculated, respectively

$$C_1' = g^r, C_2' = (u^{\tilde{x}} h)^r.$$

The intermediate ciphertext is $IT = (IT_{main}, IT_{att})$.

3) **Online.Encrypt**(PP, kw, S, t, IT): This algorithm generates a keyword index ciphertext that embedds time and attributes. Given a set of input keywords $kw = \{kw_1, kw_2, ..., kw_m\}$, and the attribute set of DO $S = \{A_1, A_2, ..., A_k\}$, where m is the number of keywords, k is the number of attributes and the element A_i in S is from Z_p^*. The DO then extracts the current time period t from the system clock and encodes it as a set T_t^0 using 0-Encoding, denoted as $T_t^0 = \{t_1, t_2, ..., t_{|T_t^0|}\}$. Next, to map the set T_t^0 to the Z_p^*, it computes $H(t_i)$ for $i \in [1, |T_t^0|]$ and adds the result to the set S. We denote the length of the new attribute set as $\eta = k + |T_t^0|$, and $\tilde{S} = S \cup T_t^0$. The algorithm randomly selects $\eta + 1$ random $s, r_1, r_2, ..., r_\eta \xleftarrow{\$} Z_p^*$. It selects any one main module IT_{main} and any η attribute module IT_{att}. For each $i' \in [1, m]$, and $\tau \in [1, \eta]$ it computes

$$C_{i'} = e(g,g)^{\alpha s H(kw_i')}, \quad C_0 = g^s, \quad C_{\tau,1} = C_{\tau,1}' = g^{r_\tau},$$
$$C_{\tau,2} = C_{\tau,2}' \cdot C_w = (u^{\tilde{x}_\tau} h)^{r_\tau} w^{-s}, \quad C_{\tau,3} = r_\tau \cdot (A_\tau - \tilde{x}_\tau).$$

The final ciphertext is $ct = (\tilde{S}, \{C_{i'}\}_{i' \in [1,m]}, C_0, \{C_{\tau,1}, C_{\tau,2}, C_{\tau,3}\}_{\tau \in [1,\eta]})$.

4) **Offline.KeyGen**(PP): This algorithm generates any "row" modules. It selects random $\lambda', x, \delta \in Z_p^*$ and computes $I_{row} = (\lambda', x, \delta, K_0, K_1, K_2, K_3)$, where

$$K_0 = g^{\lambda'}, K_1 = w^\delta, K_2 = (u^x h)^{-\delta}, K_3 = g^\delta.$$

The intermediate key is $I_{row} = (\lambda', x, \delta, K_0, K_1, K_2, K_3)$.

5) **Online.KeyGen**$(MSK, I_{row}, \mathbb{A} = (M, \rho), t')$: This algorithm generates the secret key for the DU. t' is encoded into a set $T_{t'}^1$ using 1-Encoding, denoted as $T_{t'}^1 = \{t_1', t_2', ..., t_{|T_{t'}^1|}'\}$. We use the method described at the beginning of this section to obtain a new matrix M' with ℓ rows and n columns and a new function ρ'. Then AA chooses a vector $\boldsymbol{y} = (\alpha, y_2, ..., y_n)^\top$, where $y_2, ..., y_n \xleftarrow{\$} Z_p^*$.

The shared vector is $My = \lambda = (\lambda_1, \lambda_2, ..., \lambda_\ell)^\top$. It then randomly chooses ℓ "row" modules from I_{row} and ℓ random exponents $\delta_1, \delta_2, ..., \delta_\ell \xleftarrow{\$} Z_p^*$, and for each $\tau \in [1, \ell]$ it computes

$$K_{\tau,0} = g^{\lambda'_\tau}, \quad K_{\tau,1} = w^{\delta_\tau}, \quad K_{\tau,2} = (u^{x_\tau} h)^{-\delta_\tau},$$
$$K_{\tau,3} = g^{\delta_\tau}, \quad K_{\tau,4} = \lambda_\tau - \lambda'_\tau, \quad K_{\tau,5} = \delta_\tau \cdot (\rho(\tau) - x_\tau).$$

The private key is $sk = ((M', \rho'), \{K_{\tau,0}, K_{\tau,1}, K_{\tau,2}, K_{\tau,3}, K_{\tau,4}, K_{\tau,5}\}_{\tau \in [1,\ell]})$

6) **TrapGen**(PP, sk, kw'): This algorithm generates search trapdoors for DU. DU picks its interested keyword kw', and inputs his private key sk. For each $i \in [1, n], \tau \in [1, \ell]$, it chooses $z_\tau \in Z_p^*$, and computes

$$td_{\tau,0} = g^{-z_\tau} K_{\tau,0}^{H(kw')} K_{\tau,1}^{z_\tau H(kw')} = g^{-z_\tau + \lambda'_\tau H(kw')} \cdot w^{\delta_\tau H(kw') z_\tau},$$
$$td_{\tau,1} = K_{\tau,2}^{z_\tau H(kw')} = (u^{x_\tau} h)^{-\delta_\tau H(kw') z_\tau},$$
$$td_{\tau,2} = K_{\tau,3}^{z_\tau H(kw')} = g^{\delta_\tau H(kw') z_\tau},$$
$$td_{\tau,3} = K_{\tau,4} \cdot H(kw') + z_\tau = (\lambda_\tau - \lambda'_\tau) \cdot H(kw') + z_\tau,$$
$$td_{\tau,4} = K_{\tau,5} \cdot z_\tau H(kw') = \delta_\tau \cdot (\rho(\tau) - x_\tau) \cdot H(kw') \cdot z_\tau.$$

The trapdoor is $td = ((M', \rho'), \{td_{\tau,0}, td_{\tau,1}, td_{\tau,2}, td_{\tau,3}, td_{\tau,4}\}_{\tau \in [1,\ell]}$.

7) **Search**(PP, td, ct): The algorithm finds the set of rows in M that can provide a share to attribute in $\tilde{S}$, i.e. $I = \{i : \rho'(i) \in \tilde{S}\}$. Then compute a constant vector $\omega = (\omega_1, \omega_2, ..., \omega_i)_{i \in I}$, where ω_i belongs to Z_p^*, such that $\sum_{i \in I} \omega_i M'_i = (1, 0, ..., 0)$, where M'_i is the i-th row of the matrix. If there is such a constant vector, it means that the ciphertext is within the user's search authority. Then it calculates

$$B = \prod_{i \in I} (e(C_0, td_{\tau,0} \cdot g^{td_{\tau,3}}) e(C_{\tau,1}, td_{\tau,1} \cdot u^{-td_{\tau,4}}) e(C_{\tau,2} \cdot u^{C_{\tau,3}}, td_{\tau,2}))^{\omega_i}.$$

If $B = C_{i'}$, output result 1, otherwise output 0.

5 Security

This proof is a direct application of Theorem 1 combined with the result from [3]. We embed the Modified q-2 assumption into the C, and hence the advantage of $\mathcal{A}$ is negligible in breaking our scheme. Please see full version for details.

6 Comparison

In this section, we provide the comprehensive comparison of the FS-OO-KPABKS scheme with related schemes. The frequently used notations are summarized in Table 1.

Table 1. NOTATIONS.

Notation	Description
P	bilinear pairing operation
E_0	exponentiation operation in $\mathbb{G}_0$
E_1	exponentiation operation in $\mathbb{G}_1$
H_0	hash function mapping to $\mathbb{G}_0$ operation
$|\mathbb{G}_0|$	the length of the element in $\mathbb{G}_0$
$|\mathbb{G}_1|$	the length of the element in $\mathbb{G}_1$
$|Z_p^*|$	the length of the element in Z_p^*
l_U	the number of attributes in attribute universe
l_S	the number of attributes in attribute set
l_A	the number of attributes in access policy
l_I	the number of attributes for the final successful search
n	the length of the time slot
m	the number of keywords
π	the maximum number of rows in access policy
$(\cdot)$	efficient operations (e.g., modular addition, modular multiplication)

6.1 Theoretical Evaluation

We select the three most relevant schemes for comparison in our work [2,5,9]. Scheme [9] is a pure ABKS scheme, while schemes [2,5] possess the online/offline property. Table 2 presents the computational costs of **Online.Encrypt**, **Online.KeyGen**, **TrapGen**, and **Search**. Since the tasks in the offline phase can be performed by the data user during their free time, our theoretical analysis focuses only on the computational costs in the online phase. Furthermore, we also present the storage costs of public key PK, secret key SK, trapdoor TD, and ciphertext CT. To facilitate comparison, we set $m = 100$ and $l_S = l_A$.

Table 2. COMPARISON WITH RELATED SCHEMES.

		KP-ABKS [9]	DSF [5]	OO-KPABKS [2]	OURS
Computation	Online.Encrypt	$(4 + l_S)E_0 + l_S H_0$	$\odot$	$mE_0 + mH_0 + E_1 + mP$	mE_1
	Online.KeyGen	$(1 + 2l_A)E_0 + l_A H_0$	$(l_S + 5)E_0$	$\odot$	$\odot$
	TrapGen	$(3 + 2l_A)E_0$	$2E_0$	H_0	$3l_A E_0$
	Search	$l_I E_1 + (2l_I + 2)P$	$(l_I + 1)E_0 + l_I E_1 + (2l_I + 4)P$	$3l_I E_0 + l_I E_1 + (3l_I + 1)P$	$3l_I E_0 + l_I E_1 + 3l_I P$
Storage	PK	$4|\mathbb{G}_0|$	$(l_U + \pi + 1)|\mathbb{G}_0| + |\mathbb{G}_1|$	$4|\mathbb{G}_0| + |\mathbb{G}_1|$	$4|\mathbb{G}_0| + |\mathbb{G}_1|$
	SK	$2l_A|\mathbb{G}_0|$	$(4 + l_S)|\mathbb{G}_0| + |Z_p^*|$	$3l_A|\mathbb{G}_0| + 2l_A|Z_p^*|$	$4l_A|\mathbb{G}_0| + 2l_A|Z_p^*|$
	TD	$(2l_A + 2)|\mathbb{G}_0|$	$2|\mathbb{G}_0|$	$(3 + 5l_A)|\mathbb{G}_0|$	$3l_A|\mathbb{G}_0| + 2l_A|Z_p^*|$
	CT	$(l_S + 3)|\mathbb{G}_0|$	$(3l_A + m + 4)|\mathbb{G}_0| + |\mathbb{G}_1| + l_A|Z_p^*|$	$(2l_S + 1)|\mathbb{G}_0| + (m + 1)|\mathbb{G}_1| + (l_S + m)|Z_p^*|$	$(2l_S + 1)|\mathbb{G}_0| + m|\mathbb{G}_1| + l_S|Z_p^*|$
Feature	Large Universe	✓	✗	✓	✓
	Forward Security	✗	✗	✗	✓

Computation Overhead. In terms of computation overhead, our analysis is as follows:

- Comparison with [9]: Due to our scheme's division of the Encrypt and Key-Gen algorithms into offline and online phases, the majority of the work can be completed in the offline phase. As a result, our **Online.Encrypt** and **Online.KeyGen** exhibit higher efficiency than [9]. Particularly **Online.KeyGen** has almost negligible operations. Although our scheme's computational cost for **TrapGen** and **Search** is slightly higher than [9], it is worth noting that [9] lacks forward security property.
- Comparison with [5]: Our scheme exhibits remarkable advantages in **Online.KeyGen** but lower efficiency in the **Online.Encrypt**, **TrapGen**, and **Search** algorithms. However, it is important to note that [5] is a small attribute universe scheme that requires determining the boundary of the attribute universe during the **Setup** phase. In large-scale IoT systems, when new users constantly join and new verifiable attributes are added to represent their identities, it is possible to exceed the boundaries of the attribute universe. This would necessitate a complete system reconstruction, which is a time-consuming task and makes [5] challenging to expand because of its bounded attribute universe. In contrast, our scheme has the property of large attribute universe, allowing the dynamic addition of attributes, and hence demonstrates good adaptability in the IIoT.
- Comparison with [2]: Our scheme demonstrates significantly better efficiency in **Online.Encrypt**. Additionally, our scheme exhibits lower efficiency in **TrapGen**, but it demonstrates higher efficiency in **Search**. However, it is worth noting that trapdoor generation in [2] may pose some security vulnerabilities. When an adversary intercepts trapdoors for different keywords submitted by the same user, denoted as $Qw_1 = H(w_1) * D$ and $Qw_2 = H(w_2) * D$, it only needs to perform a simple division operation on the two trapdoors to obtain $H(w_2)/H(w_1)$. Furthermore, due to the limited size of the keyword space, the adversary can undoubtedly guess the keyword associated with the trapdoor successfully, which undermines the trapdoor unlinkability described in [2]. In addition, [2] only provides a rough security analysis, while this paper provides a rigorous security proof.

Storage Size. In terms of storage size, our scheme is generally comparable to [2], with significant advantages in the storage cost of TD and CT. Compared to [5], our scheme has higher storage costs for SK and TD, but it demonstrates excellent advantages in the storage cost of CT and PK, especially in the storage cost of PK, as our scheme is a large attribute universe scheme that does not require defining l_U during the initialization phase. Our scheme has a slight disadvantage compared to [9].

7   Conclusion

In this paper, we proposed the first forward secure key policy attribute-based encryption with keyword search scheme (FS-OO-KPABKS), which provides forward security online/offline encryption and secret key generation based on KP-ABKS. We provide the selective security model against chosen-keyword attack (SCKA) of FS-OO-KPABKS in the standard model. Finally, a comprehensive theoretical evaluation shows that our work has significant efficiency of **Online.Encrypt** and **Online.KeyGen** algorithms compared with related work, while achieving forward security. Preferably, our work has good adaptability thanks to the property of large universe, thus indicating the applicability of our FS-OO-KPABKS scheme in the IIoT system.

Acknowledgements. This work is supported in part by the National Natural Science Foundation of China under Grant 61872409, Grant 61872152 and Grant 62272174, in part by Guangdong Basic and Applied Basic Research Foundation under Grant 2020A1515010751, in part by the Guangdong Major Project of Basic and Applied Basic Research under Grant 2019B030302008, and in part by the Science and Technology Program of Guangzhou under Grant 201902010081.

References

1. Boneh, D., Di Crescenzo, G., Ostrovsky, R., Persiano, G.: Public key encryption with keyword search. In: Cachin, C., Camenisch, J.L. (eds.) EUROCRYPT 2004. LNCS, vol. 3027, pp. 506–522. Springer, Heidelberg (2004). https://doi.org/10.1007/978-3-540-24676-3_30
2. Cui, J., Zhou, H., Xu, Y., Zhong, H.: OOABKS: online/offline attribute-based encryption for keyword search in mobile cloud. Inf. Sci. **489**, 63–77 (2019)
3. Hohenberger, S., Waters, B.: Online/offline attribute-based encryption. In: Krawczyk, H. (ed.) PKC 2014. LNCS, vol. 8383, pp. 293–310. Springer, Heidelberg (2014). https://doi.org/10.1007/978-3-642-54631-0_17
4. Kim, H., Hahn, C., Hur, J.: Forward secure public key encryption with keyword search for cloud-assisted IoT. In: 2020 IEEE 13th International Conference on Cloud Computing (CLOUD), pp. 549–556. IEEE (2020)
5. Miao, Y., Tong, Q., Choo, K.K.R., Liu, X., Deng, R.H., Li, H.: Secure online/offline data sharing framework for cloud-assisted industrial internet of things. IEEE Internet Things J. **6**(5), 8681–8691 (2019)
6. Sahai, A., Waters, B.: Fuzzy identity-based encryption. In: Cramer, R. (ed.) EUROCRYPT 2005. LNCS, vol. 3494, pp. 457–473. Springer, Heidelberg (2005). https://doi.org/10.1007/11426639_27
7. Zeng, M., Qian, H., Chen, J., Zhang, K.: Forward secure public key encryption with keyword search for outsourced cloud storage. IEEE Trans. Cloud Comput. **10**(01), 426–438 (2022)
8. Zhang, X., Xu, C., Wang, H., Zhang, Y., Wang, S.: FS-PEKS: lattice-based forward secure public-key encryption with keyword search for cloud-assisted Industrial Internet of Things. IEEE Trans. Dependable Secure Comput. **18**, 1019–1032 (2021)
9. Zheng, Q., Xu, S., Ateniese, G.: VABKS: verifiable attribute-based keyword search over outsourced encrypted data. In: IEEE INFOCOM 2014-IEEE Conference on Computer Communications, pp. 522–530. IEEE (2014)

Differential Privacy Enhanced Dynamic Searchable Symmetric Encryption for Cloud Environments

Peiyi Tu and Xingjun Wang[✉]

Tsinghua Shenzhen International Graduate School,
Tsinghua University, Shenzhen, China
tpy21@mails.tsinghua.edu.cn, wang.xingjun@sz.tsinghua.edu.cn

Abstract. In recent years, the Database-as-a-Service (DAS) model has become increasingly popular for cost-effective data outsourcing to cloud service providers. To ensure data security and functionality, Searchable Encryption (SE) has been introduced. However, many existing SE schemes unintentionally leak access patterns, posing significant privacy risks. While solutions like Oblivious RAM (ORAM) and Fully Homomorphic Encryption (FHE) can mitigate this, they are computationally intensive, limiting their practicality for large-scale databases.

In this paper, we design a dynamic and efficient SE scheme called DPDSE that exploits differential privacy obfuscation of access patterns. Specifically, we obfuscate the ciphertext by deploying Laplace and Randomized Response mechanism. DPDSE strikes a balance between privacy and storage costs, while maintaining compatibility with any SE scheme. We give a formal mathematical proof of the security of DPDSE and conduct experiments on real datasets. The results show that DPDSE is significantly more secure than traditional SE schemes at a storage cost of up to 2.5%.

Keywords: Data Security · Searchable Encryption · Encrypted Database · Differential Privacy

1 Introduction

In recent years, the continually increasing sophistication of technology is shaping the unceasing evolution of data. According to IDC's global datasphere forecast report, by 2025, 163ZB of data is expected to be generated. Handling such volumes of raw data can cause serious management problems for human engineers. To alleviate such burdens, cloud storage service such as the Database as a Service (DAS) model emerges as an important cost reduction option. Nevertheless, DAS model causes concerns about security when it comes to personal privacy or confidential business data. Such concerns still hamper the adoption of cloud solutions. A common solution is to encrypt the data before outsourcing it. However, the data encrypted by the traditional method makes it complicated to perform efficient record retrieval. Hence, Searchable Encryption(SE) [14] is proposed.

C. Ge and M. Yung (Eds.): Inscrypt 2023, LNCS 14527, pp. 368–386, 2024.
https://doi.org/10.1007/978-981-97-0945-8_22

Significant progress has been made in improving the efficiency and functionality of SE over the last decade. Nonetheless, some information is inevitably leaked in these SE schemes, and the common feature is the leakage of access patterns [8]. Regrettably, recent studies [10,16] have demonstrated that an attacker equipped with auxiliary knowledge can exploit this leakage to effectively recover plaintext content, thereby compromising the user's privacy. While Fully Homomorphic Encryption (FHE) [4] and Oblivious RAM (ORAM) [7] techniques offer potential solutions to mitigate this leakage, their practical adoption is hindered by substantial computational complexity and communication overhead.

Differential privacy (DP) [6] is an information-theoretic guarantee that offers stringent privacy assurances for individuals in a dataset, irrespective of the adversary's auxiliary knowledge. It is characterized by a parameter $\epsilon > 0$, where smaller values of ϵ correspond to stronger privacy guarantees. Another appealing feature of DP is its property that any post-processing computation performed on the noisy output of a DP algorithm does not introduce additional privacy loss. Recognizing the growing demand for continuously modified and updated data, the adoption of the continual observations model becomes the new standard in the field of DP.

Based on this vulnerability, we propose DPDSE (Differential Privacy enhanced Dynamic Searchable Encryption), a novel SE scheme that addresses both the protection of access patterns and the satisfaction of the Continual Observations model. Traditional DP schemes are mainly applied to data distribution, where ϵ is used to trade-off the privacy protection degree with the offset of the data, in our scheme, ϵ is used to trade-off the privacy protection degree with the additional storage overhead, which does not affect the consistency of the data. The main idea behind DPDSE is to obfuscate each histogram bin of the data and to generate a new obfuscation for each update, rather than only once when outsourcing the database. Our scheme allows to execute queries against an encrypted database and receive matching documents in the same communication round. At the cost of limited additional storage overhead, DPDSE achieves lower communication overhead than ORAM. While the introduction of false positives (irrelevant records are actually returned) and false negatives (records relevant to the query are not retrieved) is necessary to obfuscate access patterns, the post-processing algorithms designed by our mechanism cull out false positives and false negatives from the result set, guaranteeing the completeness and correctness of query results. Our mathematical analysis and experimental evaluation show that DPDSE significantly reduces the accuracy of known access pattern attacks with reasonable storage overhead and privacy protection.

Summarizing, our contributions are the following:

- We present a static DP-enhanced scheme for dealing with fuzzy access pattern leakage, utilizing the Laplace mechanism. This scheme ensures differential privacy guarantees regarding the data distribution, and effectively conceals the actual retrieval accesses. In our protocol, the introduction of noise with negative magnitude necessitates placing records into a local cache with limited capacity. To adhere to the capacity constraint, we employ mean offset to optimize the storage cost, while a post-processing algorithm ensures accurate retrieval of encrypted records.

- We propose a dynamic DP-enhanced scheme that utilizes randomized response and the Laplace mechanism to handle the update policy for record insertion, deletion, and modification in cloud environments. Prior to updating, we obfuscate the identity of the modified record using the randomized response mechanism. Then, based on this obfuscated identity, we employ the Laplace mechanism to obfuscate the data that requires changes. This approach effectively safeguards dynamic data privacy while maintaining accurate query results for authorized users. Furthermore, our scheme is compatible with any SE scheme operating at the underlying layers, providing a flexible and adaptable solution.

- We implemented DPDSE and rigorously provided formal security proofs in both static and dynamic scenarios and assessing the attacker's guessing probability. Additionally, we conducted a comprehensive evaluation of DPDSE's privacy and cost aspects. To validate its performance, we conducted experiments using real datasets, and the results revealed that DPDSE outperforms traditional SE schemes, offering enhanced privacy protection for data at a limited storage cost. These findings collectively demonstrate the effectiveness and efficiency of DPDSE as a robust solution for data privacy in various practical applications.

The paper is organized as follows: Sect. 2 presents a brief review of related works before we introduce preliminaries in Sect. 3. We provide a detailed description of our system model, static and dynamic DPDSE schemes in Sect. 4. We analyze the privacy, security and cost of our scheme in Sect. 5. Based on this analysis, Sect. 6 shows experimental results on real datasets. In Sect. 7, we discuss the conclusion and future works.

2 Related Work

Searchable Encryption. Song et al. [14] first introduced the concept of SE in 2000. Their implementations include sequential scanning, which leaks a lot of information to the server and is inefficient. However, most SSE schemes reveal which documents are accessed and returned in each query. Leakage of such access patterns is not resistant to strong chosen plaintext attacks.

Attacks Using Access Pattern. Attack methods leveraging access patterns to detect privacy leakage in searchable encryption require the attacker to possess auxiliary background information or additional capabilities. For instance, in 2012, Islam et al. [8] demonstrated an attack known as the IKK attack, where a server can accurately recover the contents of queries with over 90% accuracy.

Zhang et al. [16] proposed a file injection attack where the attacker injects a set of files, each containing selected keywords. After the attack, the attacker can reveal the keywords of any search token. Liu et al.'s frequency attack [10] utilizes query frequency information and search pattern recovery queries.

Fully Homomorphic Encryption and Oblivious RAM. Fully Homomorphic Encryption allows arbitrary computations on the ciphertext that are consistent with the plaintext. In 2009, Craig Gentry proposed the first FHE scheme. Although FHE has made some progress [4] in recent years in terms of ciphertext length and computational efficiency, however, its computational overhead is still unacceptable for database retrieval. Gentry computes the AES function on encrypted data in about 40 min on a block of data, which is more than six orders of magnitude slower compared to the plaintext.

Oblivious RAM can completely hide access patterns by successively transforming and re-encrypting data, but it often results in significant communication overhead [7]. Despite subsequent work optimizing this overhead, ORAM remains difficult to practice.

3   Preliminaries

3.1   Dynamic Searchable Symmetric Encryption

It is assumed that the database consists of $\mathbf{D} = (id_i, W_i)_{i=1}^{d}$ document address and keyword set, where id_i is the i-th document, W_i is the set of keywords contained in the i-th document, and d is the number of documents.

Definition 1 (Dynamic Searchable Symmetric Encryption [5], DSSE). *An DSSE scheme is a collection of the following five polynomial-time algorithms Π:*

- $K_{\mathcal{I}} \leftarrow \text{GenKey}\left(1^{\lambda}\right)$ *: The data owner inputs the security parameters λ and outputs the key $K_{\mathcal{I}}$.*
- $\mathcal{I} \leftarrow \text{BuildEncIndex}\left(K_{\mathcal{I}}, \mathcal{D}\right)$ *:The data owner inputs the key $K_{\mathcal{I}}$ and the plaintext database D, and outputs the ciphertext index I.*
- $T_w \leftarrow \text{GenToken}\left(K_{\mathcal{I}}, w, ind\right)$ *:Inputs the key $K_{\mathcal{I}}$ and retrieval keyword w, and outputs the token T_w.*
- $\mathcal{ID}_w \leftarrow \text{Search}\left(\mathcal{I}, T_w\right)$ *:The input is index I and token T_w, and the output contains document identifiers $\mathcal{ID}_w$ of w. The correctness requires the following properties.*

$$\Pr\left[\text{id}_i \in ID_w \mid d_i \in w\right] = 1, \quad \Pr\left[\text{id}_i \notin ID_w \mid d_i \notin w\right] \geq 1 - \mu$$

where μ is a negligible function.
- $\mathcal{I}' \leftarrow \text{Search}\left(\mathcal{I}, T_u, op\right)$ *:It is executed on the server with the input of ciphertext index I, retrieval token T_u and update operation type op, where $op \in \{add, del\}$, the output of the updated ciphertext index I'.*

Definition 2 (Forward and Type-I Backward Security [3]). *If the update $\mathcal{L}^{Updt}$ and query $\mathcal{L}^{Srch}$ leak function is expressed as*

$$\mathcal{L}^{\text{Updt}} = \mathcal{L}'\left(op, \{(id_i, W_i)\}\right)$$
$$\mathcal{L}^{\text{Updt}}(op, w, \ id\ ) = \mathcal{L}'(op)$$
$$\mathcal{L}^{\text{Sich}}(w) = \mathcal{L}''\left(\text{TimeDB}(w), a_w\right)$$

where op indicates an update operation, $\{(\text{id}_i, W_i)\}$ indicates the number of keywords in all number of keyword W_i updates to document id_i. If $\mathcal{L}^{Updt}$ is state-independent, then an L-adaptive security DSSE scheme is forward-secure. TimeDB(w) indicates the current set of all matching keyword w document identifier set and the point in time when they were inserted, excluding deleted identifiers, a_w is the number of entries matching w inserted in total, $\mathcal{L}'$ and $\mathcal{L}''$ are stateless, then an DSSE scheme is called Type I backward secure.

3.2 Differential Privacy

Definition 3 (Differential Privacy, DP [6]). *Differential privacy gives a mathematically rigorous definition of privacy. For all proximity datasets D and D' and possible outputs O, the mechanism F satisfies*

$$\frac{\Pr[F(D) = O]}{\Pr[F(D') = O]} \leq e^{\varepsilon}$$

then the mechanism F satisfies the ϵ-difference privacy. The ϵ parameter is the privacy budget. a smaller ϵ implies the need to provide very similar outputs for similar inputs, thus providing a higher level of privacy.

Definition 4 (Laplace Mechanism). *Let the function $f : N^n \rightarrow R^k$, then the laplace mechanism satisfies*

$$F(D) = f(D) + \text{Lap}\left(\frac{\Delta f}{\epsilon}\right)$$

where $\text{Lap}(S)$ denotes sampling with Laplace distribution with mean of 0 and scale factor of S, and Δf is the global sensitivity.

Local Differential Privacy (LDP). The local model is another prominent framework within the realm of DP. In this model, each individual modifies their data through a local differential privacy algorithm [15] and transmits the obfuscated data to the aggregator. Randomized response technique is the mainstream obfuscation mechanism for LDP. After initiating a sensitive question, users will not respond directly to the real answer. Suppose that the answer is given with the help of a non-uniform coin with probability p of being heads up, and the coin is tossed, the true answer is given if heads are up, and the opposite answer is given if tails are up.

4 Methods

4.1 System Model

Overview of the proposed scheme is depicted in Fig. 1. Encryption, decryption, indexing, SQL rewriting, and other operations are performed in a proxy manner to achieve transparency to users.

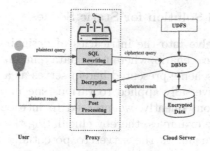

Fig. 1. System Model

Upon the user's initiation of a retrieval or data update request, the agent assumes control over all such requests and executes a series of operations. These operations encompass the reformulation of the retrieval statement, encryption and decryption of the data, and subsequent transmission of the processed query to the server. Notably, the cloud server houses all encrypted data, which includes encrypted table and column names. Moreover, the cloud server offers User Defined Functions(UDFS), which serve as an extensible interface integrated within the database. This interface allows for the expansion of specific functions without necessitating modifications to the database source code, thereby enabling operations on the encrypted text.

Functioning as an intermediary, the proxy server initially possesses the capability to encrypt and decrypt data. When the user inserts data, the proxy server encrypts the provided information and dispatches it to the database for storage. In instances where a retrieval request is sent by the user, the proxy server reconfigures the statement and transmits the revised form to the cloud server for the purpose of retrieving ciphertext data. Subsequently, when the cloud server transmits the retrieval results, the proxy server undertakes decryption and subsequent post-processing, culminating in the final delivery of the results to the user.

The system faces two primary types of security threats, each with its own implications. The first type of threat originates from within the system. The cloud storage service provider, functioning as a custodian of the database, possesses access to all data stored within it. Consequently, there exists a potential for unauthorized tampering with the data, with the provider capable of eradicating any traces of intrusion after gaining illicit access. Consequently, the server is deemed a semi-honest component. While it faithfully executes user requests, it may also attempt to access and exploit the user's private data during the process. The second scenario involves external malicious attackers seeking to steal user data. Once successful, they gain unauthorized privileges and can proceed to steal or even manipulate the data at will. Therefore, it is crucial to employ robust measures to mitigate these risks and ensure the safeguarding of sensitive user information.

4.2   DP-Enhanced Solution for Static Scenes

In this section, we delve into the intricacies of designing DP-enhanced DSSE schemes within a static scenario, wherein the data remains unchanged and devoid of any updates. The scheme presented herein serves as a comprehensive framework that can be universally applied to various specific DSSE schemes at the foundational level. Consequently, we proceed to introduce Bloom filter index schemes as illustrative examples, thereby elucidating the core concept.

The access pattern allows the server to potentially infer the precise data distribution after multiple queries, making it possible for an attacker, armed with some background knowledge, to crack the ciphertext successfully. To mitigate this privacy risk, we introduce a differential privacy scheme.

We present a novel approach to enhance privacy. We introduce recoverable "false-negative" and "false-positive" records within the database system. Trustworthy agents, acting as "false-negative" entities, maintain a limited number of records within their local caches. Simultaneously, they transfer certain "false-positive" records to their respective local caches. The "false-negative" trusted proxy also preserves a restricted number of records in its local cache while injecting some "false-positive" dummy records into the cloud server. The presence of "false-negative" and "false-positive" records contributes to introducing noise and uncertainty, making it challenging for the server to accurately discern the genuine retrieval patterns and the associated data distribution. This differential privacy scheme helps protect against privacy leakage by obfuscating the relationship between the queries and the underlying data.

1) Histogram Bin Generation: Histogram publishing is an important scenario for DP to make applications. An independently sampled Laplace random variable can be added to each bin to satisfy DP.

Let $\Phi \leftarrow (\phi_1, \ldots, \phi_k)$ be the set of non-overlapping ranges that delimit the domain of the queryable attribute A_q. Let the histogram bin b_i denote the number of records in range Φ_i, each b_i corresponds to a record mapping in index I, and the histogram is the set of all b_is in the range of values taken.

2) DP Obfuscation: Let the privacy budget in the static scenario be ϵ_s. For the number of records in bin b_i adding Laplace noise with privacy budget, the number of records in the bin N_i after scrambling is

$$N_i = |b_i| + \text{Lap}\left(\frac{\Delta f}{\epsilon_i}\right) \tag{1}$$

where $\epsilon_i \leq \epsilon_s$.

Let the randomized to noise value be n. If n sampled from the Laplace mechanism is positive, n dummy records are inserted at uniformly random locations in the dataset. Note that each bin is obfuscated individually and the rule applies to each node obfuscated by positive noise. An attacker in the cloud is able to see the main volume of data in the bin. The insertion of dummy records is necessary to hide this information from the adversary. After encryption the attacker cannot distinguish between real and dummy records.

In order to ensure the accuracy of the retrieval results, it is necessary to be able to distinguish dummy records after decryption. Therefore, add a column as a check. The column is generated by Algorithm 1. The check column also needs to be semantically securely encrypted and stored in the cloud server.

Algorithm 1. GenCheck

Input: Primary key $x = (x_1, \ldots, x_k)$ of records in bin b_i
Output: Check value y_i
  while $x_j \in b_i$ **do**
    if $x_j == $ 'dummy' **then**
      $y_j \leftarrow rand()$
    else $\{x_j$ is integer$\}$
      $y_j \leftarrow Hash(x_j)$
    end if
  end while

For the false-negative case, when the sampling noise N is negative, this requires removing some data records from the dataset while still ensuring that they can be retrieved. There will be missing data in the query.

In the proposed setup, positive noise is managed by introducing dummy records. These records are added to the cloud server, which typically possesses high storage capacity. On the other hand, negative noise necessitates the inclusion of actual records in the proxy cache. Since the proxy cache typically has limited capacity, it becomes crucial to address the limited space constraint when dealing with negative noise. One way to achieve this is by reducing the amount of negative noise, which involves adjusting the mean on the distribution axis.

While the mean in the Laplace mechanism does not impact ϵ, a mean of zero provides less obfuscation. Therefore, bringing the mean closer to zero while adhering to the capacity constraints becomes necessary.

Theorem 1. *Let the number of bins be B, C is a capacity parameter indicating the number of records that can be placed into the cache, $\frac{\Delta f}{\epsilon_s}$ is λ and FN is the expected amount of negative noise expected for a single bin. The estimated mean of the Laplace distribution closest to 0 under the constraints of this equation is*

$$\mu = \max\left(-\lambda \cdot \ln\left(\frac{2C}{\lambda \cdot |B|}\right), 0\right) \tag{2}$$

Proof. The mean offset closest to zero under the capacity constraint can be estimated according to the following equation:

$$|FN| \cdot |B| \leq C \rightarrow \left|\frac{1}{2\lambda}\int_{-\infty}^{0} x \cdot e^{-\frac{|x-\mu|}{\lambda}} dx\right| \cdot |B| \leq C$$

Further derivation of this equation gives

$$|FN| \cdot |B| \leq C \rightarrow e^{-\mu/\lambda} \leq \frac{2C}{\lambda \cdot |B|}$$

$$\rightarrow \mu \geq - \cdot \ln\left(\frac{2C}{\lambda \cdot |B|}\right) \rightarrow \mu = \max\left(-\lambda \cdot \ln\left(\frac{2C}{\lambda \cdot |B|}\right), 0\right)$$

3) Build Index and Encrypt: After DP obfuscation and check generation, Bloom filter indexes need to be created. After the scanning of the plaintext dataset, a Bloom filter index is generated for each bin, and the index can be used to create pointers to all the records in the bin (including dummy records) or to directly indicate the corresponding ciphertext. Finally, the records and check columns are encrypted using a semantically secure scheme and sent to the cloud server. The index can be placed in the proxy or in the cloud server.

4) Quey Process: The resulting ciphertext output from the server encompasses both false positive and false negative records. To obtain the accurate set of query results, the proxy undertakes post-processing(See in Algorithm 2) of the ciphertext result. This post-processing entails filtering out any records that fall outside the scope of the query and incorporating the false-negative records.

Algorithm 2. Post Processing

Input: Ciphertext obfuscation result $r' = (r'_1, \ldots, r'_k)$, records in cache $C = (c_1, \ldots, c_n)$

Output: Plaintext accurate result $R = (R_1, \ldots, R_m)$

  while $r'_i \in r$ **do**

    $r_i \leftarrow Decrypt(r'_i)$

    if $r_i.Check == Hash(r_i)$ **then**

      $R_k \leftarrow r_i$

    else $\{r_i$ is dummy$\}$

      CONTINUE

    end if

  end while

  for $i = 1$ to n **do**

    if $c_i.Value == R.Value$ **then**

      $R_k \leftarrow c_i$

    end if

  end for

By applying this post-processing step, the proxy effectively eliminates any records that are irrelevant to the query and includes any missing records (false negatives) that were not initially retrieved by the server. As a result, the final set of records represents the correct and complete query results.

4.3   DP-Enhanced Solution for Dynamic Scenes

This section extends our scheme to support updates. The operations of inserting, deleting or modifying(can be viewed as a delete followed by an insert) the initial data after it is stored by the cloud server also need to satisfy the DP. As with the static scheme, it can be applied to any underlying DSSE scheme.

The server can learn which data has changed while updating. This leakage leads to some risk of dynamic attacks. Therefore, we obfuscate the data using a randomized response algorithm, which guarantees local differential privacy. Assuming a record insertion is requested, this update operation must be handled without compromising privacy. Records cannot be inserted directly from published indexes and databases, as doing so would violate the DP (e.g., inserting a record directly from a database would indicate that the record is not a dummy record). Therefore, the data is updated by first making a randomized response to each bin and proceeding to the next step based on the value after the response. If the response results in 0, the number of that bin does not change, and if it is 1, it needs to change, regardless of what it should actually change.

1) Insert Operation: Figure. 2 shows the insertion process of the dynamic scheme as an example of batch insertion. Single-article insertion can be regarded as a special case of batch insertion. Essentially, an update to encrypted data obfuscated by the Laplace mechanism can be interpreted as an integration of randomized responses to T problems, T being the size of the new bin and the old bin concatenation. Where the i-th problem can be described as 'Does the size of this bin in the cloud server need to be changed?'

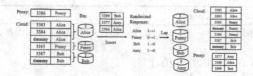

Fig. 2. Insert Example

Suppose that the initially released dataset contains records with specific key values in attribute A_q. Histogram bins of the data are generated using the same approach as the static scheme. When performing an insert operation, assuming that the inserted data intersects with the original data, the intersecting parts are not processed first, and all the different records that do not intersect with each other are created as a new bin alone, with the count set to 0. The final bins are $b = b_1, ..., b_k$.

For each bin, set the 'change' attribute so that if the corresponding data exists in the data to be inserted, this bin is set to 1, indicating that the count of this bin should change. The value of the 'change' bit is obfuscated by randomizing the response, maintaining the original value with probability p and taking the opposite value with $1 - p$. This algorithm is denoted by $c' \leftarrow$ RandRes(c, p), where c denotes the original 'change' bit and c' is the value after randomizing the response.

For a bin with a c' bit of 0, the server should not notice a change in its count. If the data in this bin exists in the dataset to be inserted, it is directly inserted into the proxy cache as a false negative.

For a bin with c' of 1, let its original count be $|b_i|$ and the number to be inserted be v_i, add Laplace noise to the original bin count and the inserted count respectively, and the sum of the two is the final bin count. Let the privacy budget of the dynamic scheme be ϵ_d, the final count N_i' is

$$N_i' = |b_i| + \mathrm{Lap}\left(\frac{\Delta f}{\epsilon_i}\right) + v_i + \mathrm{Lap}\left(\frac{\Delta f}{\epsilon_i'}\right) \tag{3}$$

where $\epsilon_i \leq \epsilon_s, \epsilon_i' \leq \epsilon_d$.

If the new count is greater than the old count, insert a randomly selected portion of the data, and if the number is not enough, it is filled with dummy records. If the new count is equal to the old count, then we add and delete an equal number of records. The deletion can be done by directly deleting the dummy record or by transferring the original record to the proxy cache, and the addition can be done by adding the real or dummy record. If else, the dummy record is deleted, and if it is not enough, the extra record and the record to be inserted are put into the proxy cache. The algorithm is described in Algorithm 3.

Algorithm 3. Insert Operation

Input: Original cloud bins $b = (b_1, \ldots, b_k)$, corresponding count N, bins to be inserted $v = (v_1, \ldots, v_n)$

Output: Final data $R = (R_1, \ldots, R_m)$

  $b.Change \leftarrow 0$, $v.Change \leftarrow 1$
  $b \cup v \leftarrow RandRes(b \cup v, p)$
  for all $b_i.Change == 1$ or $v_i.Change == 1$ **do**
    Calculate N_i' from the above equation, $d_i \leftarrow |N_i' - N_i|$
    if $N_i' > N_i$ **then**
      Insert d_i records to cloud, $v_i - d_i$ records to proxy or $d_i - v_i$ dummy records to cloud
    else if $N_i' == N_i$ **then**
      Randomly insert records in v or dummy records, delete dummy records or migrate records to proxy cache
    else
      Move v_i records to proxy, delete or move d_i dummy or real records
    end if
  end for

Figure 2 needs to insert 'Bob', 'Amy', and 'Alice', the 'Change' bit of these three bins is initially set to 1 and 'Penny' is set to 0. After randomizing the response, the 'Change' bit of 'Amy' becomes 0, and so insert the added record into proxy. 'Alice's' and 'Penny's' 'Change' bits become 1. These two bins are recounted after Laplace scrambling. The count of 'Alice' becomes less by 1, so a dummy record is deleted and the newly added record is inserted into proxy. the record of 'Penny' is increased by 2, and a record from proxy is moved to cloud and newly insert a dummy record.

2) *Delete Operation:* The delete process is similar to the insert process. Again a 'Change' bit needs to be maintained. The bin to be deleted is set to 1. After randomizing the response, the bin with a 'Change' of 1 calculates a new count N'_i

$$N'_i = |b_i| + \text{Lap}\left(\frac{\Delta f}{\epsilon_i}\right) - (v_i + \text{Lap}\left(\frac{\Delta f}{\epsilon'_i}\right)) \tag{4}$$

where $\epsilon_i \leq \epsilon_s, \epsilon'_i \leq \epsilon_d$.

For records where 'Change' is 0 but needs to be deleted, since it can't be reflected in the cloud server, note it as a dummy record in the proxy. For bin with N'_i smaller than the original, delete it in the cloud and move it to proxy if not enough. For the bin where N'_i is larger than the original, delete part of the original record and insert more dummy records.

5 Analysis

5.1 Privacy

Theorem 2. *The DP-enhanced solution satisfies the ϵ_s-DP for the static scenario.*

Proof. After Histogram Bin Generation, the original dataset D is divided into k disjoint bins $b = (b_1, \ldots, b_k)$, which satisfies $b_1 \cup \ldots \cup b_k = D$. The maximum change of 1 is used as the global sensitivity of the sample noise of the Laplace distribution, i.e., $Lap(1/\epsilon_i)$. On each individual bin, its number satisfies ϵ_i-DP and $\epsilon_i \leq \epsilon_s$, denoted $M_1(b_1), M_2(b_2), ..., M_k(b_k)$. According to the parallel combination theorem of DP, these bin combinations satisfy $\max_{1 \leq i \leq k} \epsilon_i$. Therefore, the DP Obfuscation function satisfies ϵ_s-DP. Furthermore, by the post-processing nature of DP, the post-processing of in the scheme also satisfies ϵ_s-DP.

Once the DP-enhanced solution constructs the scrambled bins, it encrypts each data record using a semantically secure DSSE scheme. Semantic security ensures that our computationally constrained adversary cannot distinguish between the encrypted dummy record and the actual record.

For the dynamic scenarios, DPDSE satisfies ϵ_d-DP in terms of hiding the changed data, and still satisfies ϵ_s-LDP in terms of the distribution of the data, and thus both satisfy the continuous observations model.

Theorem 3. *The Randomized Response Mechanism in DPDSE satisfies the ϵ_s-LDP, where $\varepsilon_s = \ln\frac{p}{1-p}$.*

Proof. The Randomized Response Mechanism disrupts the 'Check' bit, where each bin b_i is equivalent to a user, disrupting its answer to 'has my count changed in this update?'. Let the state transfer matrix be

$$\mathbf{P} = \begin{pmatrix} p_{00} & p_{01} \\ p_{10} & p_{11} \end{pmatrix} = \begin{pmatrix} \frac{e^\epsilon}{1+e^\epsilon} & \frac{1}{1+e^\epsilon} \\ \frac{1}{1+e^\epsilon} & \frac{e^\epsilon}{1+e^\epsilon} \end{pmatrix}$$

where $p_{uv} \in \{0,1\}$ and $p_{uv} = P[y_i = u \mid x_i = v]$ $(u,v \in \{0,1\})$ denotes probability that the output is u with v inputs. In our scheme, p is exactly p_{00}, which leads to $\epsilon_s = \ln \frac{p}{1-p}$.

Theorem 4. *The dataset D' after the dynamic DP-enhanced solution update still satisfies ϵ_d-DP.*

Proof. When inserting data, it can be seen as inserting the data into a secondary database $\triangle D$. In $\triangle D$ each bin is also scrambled as in the static scheme, so it satisfies ϵ_d - DP. The updated database D' can be considered as a combination of the original database D and $\triangle D$, which also satisfies ϵ_d-DP according to the parallel combination theorem. Similarly, while deleting it is viewed as first deleting the data into the $\triangle D$.

Both our static and dynamic schemes are shown to satisfy DP, respectively protect the privacy of data distribution and data changes, both of which are independent of each other and thus do not affect each other's privacy budgets. Both of our DPs are satisfied in the continuous observation model.

5.2   Security

Theorem 5. *Both static and dynamic DP-enhanced schemes satisfy semantic security.*

Proof. The adversary's advantage can be defined as: $\text{Adv}_A(\lambda) = |\Pr[\text{win}_{adv}] - \frac{1}{2}|$, where λ is a security parameter that determines the length of the encryption scheme key. The indexes are generated using Bloom filters in DPDSE, and since there is no leakage in the number of hash functions used and the specific mappings, the adversaries cannot be distinguished. After the index is established, both the real data and dummy data are encrypted using the semantically secure underlying DSSE scheme, which are indistinguishable. There exists a negligible function, $negl(\lambda)$, such that $\text{Adv}_A^{\text{IND-CPA}}(\lambda) \leq negl(\lambda)$, and so the algorithm is IND-CPA secure.

Theorem 6. *Dynamic DP-enhanced scheme satisfies forward security and type-I backward security.*

Proof. According to Definition 2, forward security requires that the update algorithm leaks only the number of records corresponding to the index. Due to the randomized response applied in the scheme, the changes in the data are disrupted. The cloud server may be informed of an approximation of the changed number, but cannot be informed of exactly which bins have changed. Therefore forward security is satisfied.

Type-I backward security in Definition 2 only allows disclosure of the total number of search results. Since the requests corresponding to the insertion or deletion of each record are disrupted in the scheme, and there is no way to distinguish between dummy records. Therefore, the correspondence between deletion and insertion operations and the uploading time will not be leaked. For the total number of search results, the server can only get an approximation after Laplace mean shift. Thus type-I backward security is clearly satisfied.

Without any additional protection, an attacker can certainly reveal the ciphertext value through a record injection attack. Denoting the binary vector of whether the data bins have changed or not as $c = (c_1, ..., c_T)$, the probability of correctly guessing the corresponding ciphertext d of the updated data is

$$P_{attack}(D) = \begin{cases} \Pr\left(\hat{d} = d \mid c_d = 1\right) = 1 - \mu, & \text{if } T > 1 \\ \Pr\left(\hat{d} = d \mid c_d = 1\right) = 1 & \text{if } T = 1 \end{cases} \tag{5}$$

where μ is a negligible probability. When $T = 1$, a unique ciphertext record can be determined.

Suppose the obfuscated binary vector c' is, $c' = (c'_1, ..., c'_T)$, which is the attacker can learn.

Theorem 7. *Assuming that the probability that the coin is heads in the randomized response is p, the probability that the attacker guesses the true change in the data is*

$$P_{ranRes}(D) = \mu + p \cdot \frac{1}{\beta + 1} \tag{6}$$

where μ is the negligible probability and β is the number of 1-bits in c' excluding the d-th bit.

Proof. Based on the randomized response algorithm, $P_{ranRes}(D)$ can be calculated as follows:

$$P_{ranRes}(D) = \Pr\left[\hat{d} = d \mid c'_d = 0\right] \cdot \Pr\left[c'_d = 0 \mid c_d = 1\right] + \Pr\left[\hat{d} = d \mid c'_d = 1\right] \cdot \Pr\left[c'_d = 1 \mid c_d = 1\right]$$

From the definition of the randomized response and DSSE, it follows that

$$\Pr\left[c'_d = 0 \mid c_d = 1\right] = 1 - p, \quad \Pr\left[c'_d = 1 \mid c_d = 1\right] = p$$

$$\Pr\left[\hat{d} = d \mid c'_d = 0\right] = \mu, \quad \Pr\left[\hat{d} = d \mid c'_d = 1\right] = \frac{1}{\beta + 1}$$

Substituting all the above parts into the previous equation yields

$$P_{ranRes}(D) = \mu \cdot (1 - p) + p \cdot \frac{1}{\beta + 1} = \mu + p \cdot \frac{1}{\beta + 1}$$

where $\mu \cdot (1 - p) = \mu$ due to the properties of negligible functions.

5.3   Cost

DPDSE stores additional dummy records in the server and false negative records in the proxy cache, whcih increases the storage cost. The DP-enhanced scheme puts as much additional storage as possible in the server instead of the proxy cache according to Theorem 1. For a server, it has a storage cost of

$$FP = \frac{1}{2\lambda} \int_0^{+\infty} x \cdot e^{-\frac{|x-\mu|}{\lambda}} dx = \mu + \frac{\lambda}{2} \cdot e^{-\frac{\mu}{\lambda}} \tag{7}$$

where μ is the mean offset. Similarly, the number of records placed in the proxy cache is

$$FN = \frac{1}{2\lambda} \int_{-\infty}^0 x \cdot e^{-\frac{|x-\mu|}{\lambda}} dx = -\frac{\lambda}{2} \cdot e^{-\frac{\mu}{\lambda}} \tag{8}$$

In dynamic scenarios, in addition to the storage cost, the obfuscated change introduces an additional time cost. The randomized response ensures that the number of changing bins can be correctly estimated.

Theorem 8. *Assuming that the number of bins with "Change" as 1 is k_1, the number of bins with 0 is $k - k_1$, and the true percentage of changes is π. The number of bins that eventually change can be estimated as*

$$K = \hat{\pi} \times k = \frac{p-1}{2p-1}k + \frac{k_1}{2p-1}. \tag{9}$$

where $\hat{\pi}$ is is an unbiased estimate of the true distribution π.

Proof. According to the above statistics, the ratio of changed and unchanged bins is

$$\Pr(c_i = 1) = \pi p + (1 - \pi)(1 - p),$$
$$\Pr(c_i = 0) = (1 - \pi)p + \pi(1 - p).$$

The above statistical proportions are not unbiased estimates of the true proportions, and therefore the statistical results need to be corrected. The great likelihood estimate of π is

$$\hat{\pi} = \frac{p-1}{2p-1} + \frac{k_1}{(2p-1)k}$$

Therefore, the additional time cost is

$$TC = K - k \cdot \pi$$

6   Experiments

6.1   Experimental Design

To evaluate the effectiveness of the scheme, the UCI Census Income dataset [1] was selected, consisting of 32,561 data records. We selected the 'age' attribute for Histogram Bin Generation, and after applying DP to each bin constructed Bloom filter indexes on top of it, and sent them to the cloud server. For efficiency evaluation, we take the extra storage cost as an evaluation metric. We select 300 privacy budget points in the range of [0.3, 0.7] for sampling, set the proxy server to have three different cache capacities, and perform 500 retrievals to obtain the number of dummy records and take the average value. In terms of security, we simulate the frequency attack [10] to test the accuracy of the attack.

6.2 Performance Evaluation

Figure 3 demonstrates all the results of the experiments. Figure 4 (a) shows the histogram of the distribution of the original data, there are a total of 73 bins, ranging between [17, 89]. Figure 4 (b) and Fig. 4 (c) are the expected value of the storage cost and the true value in the experiment respectively, and it can be seen that the true value fluctuates around the expected value, and the regression is basically the same as the expected value, which verifies the correctness of the cost estimation. Where p is the ratio of the number of bins to the proxy cache capacity, the larger it is, the higher the mean offset needed, the higher the storage cost of the cloud server. Except for the effect of p, the storage cost decreases logarithmically with ϵ. This is because the smaller ϵ is, the smaller the difference between the outputs of neighboring datasets, the better the privacy of individuals is protected, and the more costly it needs to be. Figure 4 (d) shows the final dummy number of records as a percentage of the total number of records, again the smaller p is, the smaller ϵ is and the higher the percentage is. With the restriction that ϵ and p are not too small, the storage cost is no greater than 0.025 relative to the whole database, indicating the practicality of the scheme.

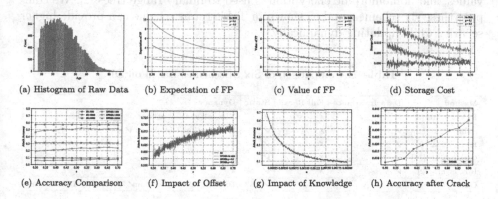

(a) Histogram of Raw Data   (b) Expectation of FP   (c) Value of FP   (d) Storage Cost

(e) Accuracy Comparison   (f) Impact of Offset   (g) Impact of Knowledge   (h) Accuracy after Crack

Fig. 3. Performance of Experiments

The security is evaluated using the accuracy under frequency attack. The attacker can crack with the approximate frequency of the plaintext data(true frequency plus Gaussian noise). Figure 4(e) compares our DPDSE with traditional

SE scheme, and randomly samples 1,000, 10,000, and 30,000 entries respectively data, the results show that no matter how much authority and knowledge the attacker has, the attack accuracy under DPDSE is always lower than traditional SE scheme. As ϵ increases, the attack accuracy gradually improves and approaches that of SE scheme, this is because the Laplace noise added at this time has a higher probability of taking a smaller absolute value, and the obfuscated ciphertext data is closer to the original data. It can also be seen from the figure that the more data the attacker understands, the greater the attack accuracy.

Figure 4(f) shows the accuracy comparison of the attack on the data at full volume. It implies that the mean offset does not affect the security of our scheme, and the results are basically the same no matter how much the offset is, and all of them are more secure than the traditional SE scheme. Figure 4(g) shows how much the attacker's knowledge of the frequency situation differs from the true situation affects the accuracy of the attack. α is the proportion of Gaussian noise added, and the smaller α is, the closer it is to the true value, and the more likely it is that the attacker can correctly decrypt the ciphertext. Figure 4(h) shows the impact on attack accuracy when the attacker has p probability of guessing the dummy record. As p increases, the attack accuracy improves, but even when p is as high as 0.9, the attack accuracy is still lower than the traditional SE scheme. The security of our DPDSE scheme is verified.

There are three options for combining DP with SE: 1) using the Laplace mechanism to generate noise for keywords to be added to the original capacity, which is used in [9,13] and our scheme. 2) representing access patterns as mapped indexes of retrievals and records, and generating obfuscated access patterns to be protected through randomized responses to the indexes or an exponential mechanism, which is used in [11,12]. 3) Laplace noise is added directly to the values, and homomorphic encryption is used to binary range trees [2]. We compare these six schemes, and as shown in Table 1, our scheme can provide higher security while updating dynamically.

Table 1. Comparison of Six SEschemes Based on DP

Method	Data Invariance	Full Recall	Static	Dynamic
Bakas et al. [2]	✗	✗	✔	Numerical Dimension✔
Sahin et al. [13]	✔	✗	✔	Distribution Dimension ✔
Kuzu et al. [9]	✔	✗	✔	✗
Quan et al. [11]	✔	✗	✔	✗
Roy et al. [12]	✔	✗	✔	✗
Ours	✔	✔	✔	Distribution Dimension✔ + Identity Dimension✔

Bakas's scheme adds noise directly to the values, affecting the accuracy of the values. The other schemes changed the retrieval result set and did not perform post-processing, affecting the integrity of result. In terms of dynamics, Bakas switches the counts with each update, which ensures security in the numerical dimension. Sahin maintains the auxiliary database and obfuscated it with DP when it is updated, which ensures distributional dimension security. Our scheme also blurs the identity with randomized responses on top of that.

7 Conclusion

We enhance the security of searchable encrypted data schemes using DP. Our mechanism significantly suppresses the attack accuracy of adversaries and implements DP over data distributions with support for update operations and hiding the identity of updated data. DPDSE is applicable to any underlying SE scheme. We have demonstrated the security of DPDSE and empirically proved its utility and efficiency through extensive experiments on real datasets. Future work includes generalizing the DPDSE approach to other index structures, especially those designed for high-dimensional data.

References

1. Census income dataset (2013) https://archive.ics.uci.edu/ml/datasets/census+income
2. Bakas, A., Michalas, A., Dimitriou, T.: Private lives matter: A differential private functional encryption scheme. In: Proceedings of the Twelfth ACM Conference on Data and Application Security and Privacy, pp. 300–311 (2022)
3. Bost, R., Minaud, B., Ohrimenko, O.: Forward and backward private searchable encryption from constrained cryptographic primitives. In: Proceedings of the 2017 ACM SIGSAC Conference on Computer and Communications Security, pp. 1465–1482 (2017)
4. Brakerski, Z., Vaikuntanathan, V.: Efficient fully homomorphic encryption from (standard) LWE. SIAM J. Comput. **43**(2), 831–871 (2014)
5. Cash, D., et al.: Dynamic searchable encryption in very-large databases: data structures and implementation. Cryptology ePrint Archive (2014)
6. Dwork, C., Roth, A., et al.: The algorithmic foundations of differential privacy. Found. Trends® Theor. Comput. Sci. **9**(3–4), 211–407 (2014)
7. Fuller, B., et al.: Sok: cryptographically protected database search. In: 2017 IEEE Symposium on Security and Privacy (SP), pp. 172–191. IEEE (2017)
8. Islam, M.S., Kuzu, M., Kantarcioglu, M.: Access pattern disclosure on searchable encryption: ramification, attack and mitigation. In: Ndss. vol. 20, p. 12. Citeseer (2012)
9. Kuzu, M., Islam, M.S., Kantarcioglu, M.: Efficient privacy-aware search over encrypted databases. In: Proceedings of the 4th ACM Conference on Data and Application Security and Privacy, pp. 249–256 (2014)
10. Liu, C., Zhu, L., Wang, M., Tan, Y.: Search pattern leakage in searchable encryption: attacks and new construction. Inf. Sci. **265**, 176–188 (2014). https://doi.org/10.1016/j.ins.2013.11.021
11. Quan, H., Liu, H., Wang, B., Li, M., Zhang, Y.: Randex: mitigating range injection attacks on searchable encryption. In: 2019 IEEE Conference on Communications and Network Security (CNS), pp. 133–141. IEEE (2019)

12. Roy Chowdhury, A., Ding, B., Jha, S., Liu, W., Zhou, J.: Strengthening order preserving encryption with differential privacy. In: Proceedings of the 2022 ACM SIGSAC Conference on Computer and Communications Security, pp. 2519–2533 (2022)
13. Sahin, C., Allard, T., Akbarinia, R., El Abbadi, A., Pacitti, E.: A differentially private index for range query processing in clouds. In: 2018 IEEE 34th International Conference on Data Engineering (ICDE), pp. 857–868. IEEE (2018)
14. Song, D.X., Wagner, D., Perrig, A.: Practical techniques for searches on encrypted data. In: Proceeding 2000 IEEE symposium on security and privacy. S&P 2000, pp. 44–55. IEEE (2000)
15. Wang, T., Blocki, J., Li, N., Jha, S.: Locally differentially private protocols for frequency estimation. In: 26th USENIX Security Symposium (USENIX Security 17). pp. 729–745 (2017)
16. Zhang, Y., Katz, J., Papamanthou, C.: All your queries are belong to us: the power of {File-Injection} attacks on searchable encryption. In: 25th USENIX Security Symposium (USENIX Security 16), pp. 707–720 (2016)

Poster

An Efficient Privacy-Preserving Scheme for Weak Password Collection in Internet of Things

Changsong Jiang[1,2], Chunxiang Xu[1,2]([✉]), and Kefei Chen[3]

[1] School of Computer Science and Engineering, University of Electronic Science
and Technology of China, Chengdu 611731, China
[2] Yangtze Delta Region Institute (Huzhou), University of Electronic Science
and Technology of China, Huzhou 313001, China
chxxu@uestc.edu.cn
[3] Department of Mathematics, Hangzhou Normal University,
Hangzhou 310027, China

Abstract. Password-based authentication is widely applied in Internet of Things (IoT) to resist unauthorized access. However, choices of weak passwords, especially popular ones, might violate the privacy of users and lead to large-scale network attacks in IoT. To address the issue, we propose EAGER, an efficient privacy-preserving scheme for weak password collection in IoT. EAGER is mainly constructed on lightweight tools including secret sharing and symmetric encryption, which allows a service provider to identify popular passwords without disclosing unpopular ones in an efficient manner. Furthermore, passwords are hardened via multiple key servers during the collection to thwart offline dictionary guessing attacks.

Keywords: Privacy-preserving · Password-based authentication · Weak password collection · Internet of Things

1 Introduction

Internet of Things (IoT) changes the way people live in various fields, such as home automation. IoT devices can collect real-time data from their surroundings, and exchange or process the data over the Internet to provide users with convenient access to an array of services. The collected data generally involves users' private information [3], and hence prevention of unauthorized access to the data is crucial to preserve the privacy of users. Password-based authentication allows IoT devices to identify users with passwords to address this issue [6]. However, choices of weak passwords, especially popular ones, might violate the privacy of users and even lead to large-scale network attacks in IoT. Collection of popular passwords among IoT devices to establish blacklists via a service provider can effectively prevent the use of weak passwords [5,8]. To protect unpopular passwords during the collection, existing privacy-preserving schemes [7] (e.g., the GC-based scheme and the QR-based one) rely on cryptographic primitives with

C. Ge and M. Yung (Eds.): Inscrypt 2023, LNCS 14527, pp. 389–393, 2024.
https://doi.org/10.1007/978-981-97-0945-8_23

expensive overheads such as garbled circuits and zero-knowledge proofs, which would impose heavy communication and computation burdens on constrained devices and hinder the wide deployment of these schemes.

In this paper, we propose an efficient privacy-preserving scheme for weak password collection in IoT, dubbed EAGER. EAGER is mainly constructed on secret sharing and symmetric encryption rather than expensive cryptographic primitives. Each IoT device encrypts the used password with a symmetric key derived from the password itself to guarantee security. The resulting ciphertext along with a random share of the symmetric key is transmitted to the service provider. If a threshold number of devices or more use the password, the service provider can reconstruct the symmetric key from the shares received for decryption of the ciphertext. Additionally, EAGER employs a group of key servers to harden the password for the key derivation, which defends against offline dictionary guessing attacks (DGA) without the single-point-of-failure problem.

2   Methodology

EAGER involves a set of IoT devices $\{\mathcal{D}_1, \mathcal{D}_2, \cdots, \mathcal{D}_m\}$, a group of key servers $\{\mathcal{KS}_1, \mathcal{KS}_2, \cdots, \mathcal{KS}_n\}$, and a server provider $\mathcal{SP}$. EAGER consists of four phases: **Setup**, **PasswordHardening**, **MessageConstruction**, and **Collection**.

Setup. In this phase, system parameters and keys are generated.

- With the security parameter ℓ, system parameters $\{p, P, G, G_T, e, Enc, Dec, h, h', H, H', F, \kappa, m, t, n, PRG\}$ are determined, where G is an additive group of prime order p with generator P, G_T is a multiplicative group, $e : G \times G \rightarrow G_T$ is a bilinear pairing, Enc is an IND-CPA secure symmetric encryption algorithm with key space $\mathbb{KS}$, Dec is the decryption algorithm, $h : \{0,1\}^* \rightarrow Z_p^*$, $h' : Z_p^* \rightarrow \mathbb{KS}$, $H : \{0,1\}^* \rightarrow G$, $H' : G \rightarrow Z_p$ are secure hash functions, $F : Z_p \times \{0,1\}^* \rightarrow Z_p$ is a pseudorandom function, κ denotes the threshold for the popular password collection, m denotes the number of IoT device, t denotes the threshold for the password hardening, n denotes the number of the key servers, and $PRG : Z_p^* \rightarrow Z_p^{t-1}$ is a pseudorandom generator.

- A secret key sk is randomly selected from Z_p. Let $[n]$ denote the set $\{1, 2, \cdots, n\}$. The secret key share sk_i $(i \in [n])$ for the key server $\mathcal{KS}_i$ is computed, where $sk_i = f(i)$ and $f(x) = sk + a_1 x + \cdots + a_{t-1} x^{t-1}$ is a randomly chosen polynomial over Z_p with degree at most $t - 1$. The corresponding public key share $Q_i = sk_i P$ $(i \in [n])$ and the public key $Q = skP$ are published.

PasswordHardening. An IoT device $\mathcal{D}_j$ $(j \in [m])$ hardens a password pw_j.

- $\mathcal{D}_j$ randomly selects $a \in Z_p^*$, blinds the password as $pw_j^* = aH(pw_j)$, and sends pw_j^* to all key servers.

- For each $i \in [n]$, the key server $\mathcal{KS}_i$ generates a signature on pw_j^*, i.e., $\sigma_{i,j}^* = sk_i \cdot pw_j^*$. The signature $\sigma_{i,j}^*$ is sent to $\mathcal{D}_j$.

- After receiving $\sigma_{i,j}^*$, $\mathcal{D}_j$ verifies its validity by checking $e(\sigma_{i,j}^*, P) \stackrel{?}{=} e(pw_j^*, Q_i)$. If t signatures pass the verification (we denote these signatures by $\{\sigma_{i_1,j}^*, \sigma_{i_2,j}^*, \cdots, \sigma_{i_t,j}^*\}$ and a set $T = \{i_1, i_2, \cdots, i_t\}$), $\mathcal{D}_j$ calculates $\sigma_j =$

$a^{-1}\sum_{k=i_1}^{i_t} w_k \sigma_{k,j}^*$, where $w_k = \prod_{i_1 \leq \eta \leq i_t, \eta \neq k, \eta \in T} \frac{\eta}{\eta-k}$ is the Lagrange coeffi-

cient. $\mathcal{D}_j$ then verifies the correctness of σ_j by checking whether $e(\sigma_j, P) = e(H(pw_j), Q)$ holds.

- $\mathcal{D}_j$ calculates the hardened password $hpw_j = F(H'(\sigma_j), pw_j)$.

MessageConstruction. Each device $\mathcal{D}_j$ ($j \in [m]$) constructs a message M using hpw_j and pw_j. M will be transmitted to the service provider $\mathcal{SP}$.

- $\mathcal{D}_j$ adopts hpw_j to compute three values: $r_{j,1} = h(hpw_j \| 1)$, $r_{j,2} = h(hpw_j \| 2)$, and $r_{j,3} = h(hpw_j \| 3)$. $\mathcal{D}_j$ computes $K_j = h'(r_{j,1})$ as a symmetric key.

- $\mathcal{D}_j$ derives $\kappa - 1$ random elements $\{b_{j,1}, b_{j,2}, \cdots, b_{j,\kappa-1}\}$ in Z_p via PRG, where $r_{j,2}$ is used as the seed. $\mathcal{D}_j$ builds a polynomial $f_j(x) = r_{j,1} + b_{j,1}x + \cdots + b_{j,\kappa-1}x^{\kappa-1}$ over Z_p with degree at most $\kappa - 1$. Then, $\mathcal{D}_j$ samples $\eta_j \in Z_p$, evaluates $y_j = f_j(\eta_j)$, and produces $s_j = (\eta_j, y_j)$ as a random share of $r_{j,1}$.

- $\mathcal{D}_j$ encrypts the hash of pw_j to obtain the ciphertext $c_j = Enc_{K_j}(H(pw_j))$.

- $\mathcal{D}_j$ constructs a message $M_j = (c_j, s_j, t_j)$, where $t_j = r_{j,3}$ serves as a tag.

Collection. The service provider $\mathcal{SP}$ receives messages from IoT devices. If κ IoT devices send the messages constructed from the same password, $\mathcal{SP}$ can reveal the password's hash and add it to a list $\mathcal{E}$ for popular password collection.

- $\mathcal{SP}$ keeps a storage file L to store messages from IoT devices. L is compromised of tags, counts of tags, and messages from IoT devices.

- Each time $\mathcal{SP}$ receives a message $M_j = (c_j, s_j, t_j)$ from device D_j ($j \in [m]$), $\mathcal{SP}$ generates a message $M_j' = (c_j, s_j)$, and checks if the tag t_j is in L. If so, the count of t_j is incremented by one, and M_j' is added to the corresponding messages. Otherwise, $\mathcal{SP}$ creates a new entry $\{t_{\tau'}, Count_{\tau'}, M_j'\}$ and stores the entry in L, where $t_{\tau'} = t_j$ and $Count_{\tau'}$ is set to be one.

- If the count of tag t_τ reaches κ, $\mathcal{SP}$ reveals the password's hash as follows:

1) $\mathcal{SP}$ collects shares $\{s_{\tau_1}, s_{\tau_2}, \cdots, s_{\tau_\kappa}\}$ from the messages corresponding to t_τ. Parse these shares as $\{(\eta_{\tau_1}, y_{\tau_1}), (\eta_{\tau_2}, y_{\tau_2}), \cdots, (\eta_{\tau_\kappa}, y_{\tau_\kappa})\}$ and let $T = \{\eta_{\tau_1}, \eta_{\tau_2}, \cdots, \eta_{\tau_\kappa}\}$. $\mathcal{SP}$ computes $\lambda_k = \prod_{\eta_{\tau_1} \leq \xi \leq \eta_{\tau_\kappa}, \xi \neq k, \xi \in T} \frac{\xi}{\xi-k}$ and $r_{\tau,1} = \sum_{k=\tau_1}^{\tau_\kappa} \lambda_k y_k$.

2) $\mathcal{SP}$ derives a symmetric key $K_\tau = h'(r_{\tau,1})$ from the value $r_{\tau,1}$, and decrypts a ciphertext c_τ corresponding to t_τ to obtain $H(pw_\tau) = Dec_{K_\tau}(c_\tau)$. $H(pw_\tau)$ is added to the list $\mathcal{E}$, which accomplishes the popular password collection.

Security Analysis. The generation of hardened passwords is based on (t, n)-threshold blind BLS signature [1,4], which is of obliviousness and unpredictability. Obliviousness ensures that the key servers learn nothing about a password. Unpredictability means that given a password, an adversary that compromises up to $t-1$ key servers cannot predict the hardened password, which resists offline DGA without the single point of failure. Additionally, EAGER protects unpopular passwords against a semi-trusted service provider assuming the IND-CPA security of symmetric encryption and the share privacy of secret sharing [2].

Performance Analysis. Figure 1 and 2 show the comparison between EAGER and existing schemes in terms of communication and computation costs. Regarding the number of communication rounds between an IoT device and the service

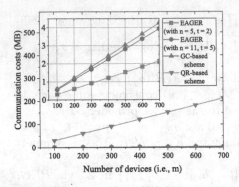

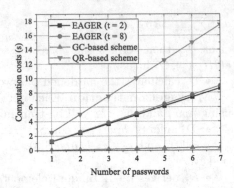

Fig. 1. Comparison of the total communication costs.

Fig. 2. Comparison of computation costs on the device side.

provider, EAGER requires only one round, which outperforms existing schemes. The comparison results demonstrate the efficiency of EAGER.

3   Conclusion

In this paper, we proposed EAGER, an efficient privacy-preserving scheme for weak password collection in IoT. By using lightweight tools, EAGER allows for efficient collection of popular passwords without leaking any information about unpopular ones. Moreover, we employ multiple key servers to harden passwords in the collection, which achieves resistance against offline DGA.

Acknowledgements. This work was supported in part by the National Natural Science Foundation of China under Grant 62272091 and Grant 61872060, and in part by the National Key R&D Program of China under Grant 2017YFB0802000.

References

1. Agrawal, S., Miao, P., Mohassel, P., Mukherjee, P.: PASTA: Password-based threshold authentication. In: Proceedings of ACM CCS, pp. 2042–2059 (2018)
2. Davidson, A., Snyder, P., Quirk, E., Genereux, J., Livshits, B., Haddadi, H.: STAR: secret sharing for private threshold aggregation reporting. In: Proceedings of ACM CCS, pp. 697–710 (2022)
3. Jiang, C., Xu, C., Zhang, Y.: PFLM: privacy-preserving federated learning with membership proof. Inf. Sci. **576**, 288–311 (2021)
4. Jiang, C., Xu, C., Zhang, Z., Chen, K.: SR-PEKS: subversion-resistant public key encryption with keyword search. IEEE Trans. on Cloud Comput. **11**(3), 3168–3183 (2023)
5. Lee, K., Sjöberg, S., Narayanan, A.: Password policies of most top websites fail to follow best practices. In: Proceedings of SOUPS, pp. 561–580 (2022)
6. Li, S., Xu, C., Zhang, Y., Zhou, J.: A secure two-factor authentication scheme from password-protected hardware tokens. IEEE Trans. Inf. Forensics Secur. **17**, 3525–3538 (2022)

7. Naor, M., Pinkas, B., Ronen, E.: How to (not) share a password: privacy preserving protocols for finding heavy hitters with adversarial behavior. In: Proceedings of ACM CCS, pp. 1369–1386 (2019)
8. Tan, J., Bauer, L., Christin, N., Cranor, L.F.: Practical recommendations for stronger, more usable passwords combining minimum-strength, minimum-length, and blocklist requirements. In: Proceedings of ACM CCS. pp, 1407–1426 (2020)

TRGE: A Backdoor Detection After Quantization

Renhua Xie[1], Xuxin Fang[1], Bo Ma[1], Chuanhuang Li[1(✉)], and Xiaoyong Yuan[2]

[1] School of Information and Electronic Engineering, Zhejiang Gongshang University, Hangzhou, China
chuanhuang_li@zjgsu.edu.cn
[2] College of Computing, Michigan Technological University, Houghton, USA
xyyuan@mtu.edu

Abstract. Quantization is evolving as the main technique for efficient deployment of deep neural networks to hardware devices, especially edge devices. However, we observe that quantization hardly has negative impact on backdoor attacks, but leads trigger reverse-based defenses to fail. We argue that the round operation in quantization that blocks the backward propagation of the gradient in the quantized model is the main reason for the failure of the trigger reverse-based approaches. We then propose a novel Trigger Reverse method with Gradient Estimation (TRGE) to synthesize triggers for backdoor detection in quantized models. Experiments on MNIST, CIFAR10, and GTSRB demonstrate that our proposed method is effective in detecting backdoor attacks in quantized models.

Keywords: Backdoor · Trigger Reverse · DNN · Quantization

1 Introduction

Noting that backdoor attacks are a threat to quantitative models, we explore the impact of quantization on backdoor attacks and defense methods. We observe that conventional quantization schemes preserve the features of backdoor attacks, i.e., the backdoor of an infected model remains alive after quantization (Table 1). And existing trigger reverse-based defenses fail to detect in quantized models. Figure 1 shows the potential triggers reversed by Neural Cleanse in quantized models trained with MNIST and CIFAR10 datasets are close to 0. We argue that the main reason is that the quantized round operation blocks the gradients of the backpropagation process of the quantized models. We propose a new trigger reverse method for backdoor attack detection in quantized models by using the estimated gradient instead of backpropagation in the trigger reversion process. Experiments show that our approach is effective to detect backdoors in quantized models.

ⓒ The Author(s), under exclusive license to Springer Nature Singapore Pte Ltd. 2024
C. Ge and M. Yung (Eds.): Inscrypt 2023, LNCS 14527, pp. 394–398, 2024.
https://doi.org/10.1007/978-981-97-0945-8_24

2 Proposed Method

2.1 Gradient Estimation

In practice we found that the trigger reversion lost its detection effect on the quantized model. We argue that the quantized model has a trouble in the back propagation of the gradient during the optimization process. Inspired by Auto-ZOOM [2], we estimate the gradient using a random vector.

$$u = \frac{v}{|v|} \tag{1}$$

$$g \approx \frac{f(x + \alpha u) - f(x)}{\alpha} \cdot u \tag{2}$$

where v is a Gaussian random vector with the same dimension of x, and u is a unit length vector of v. The gradient of the entire input is estimated only once by the random vector gradient estimation, which significantly improves the estimation efficiency. For higher accuracy of estimated gradients, we take an average by sampling n times. Note that n is much smaller than the number of elements in the input.

$$\bar{g} = \frac{1}{n} \sum_{j=1}^{n} g_j \tag{3}$$

2.2 Outlier Detection

Considering the asymmetric distribution of the reversed triggers' norms and the additional noise introduced by the gradient estimation may cause the median absolute deviation to be inapplicable in anomaly detection, we take a simple and effective approach, i.e., standard score [1]. Given a distribution with mean M, standard deviation s and one of the sample points x, the standard score z can be calculated as equation (4). We use the absolute value of the standard score for anomaly detection.

$$z = \frac{(x - M)}{s} \tag{4}$$

3 Experiment and Result

In this section, we experimentally illustrate the impact of quantization on backdoor attacks and trigger reverse-based defenses, and evaluate our proposed approach against backdoor attacks.

- Backdoor attacks: BadNet and TrojanNN.
- Datasets: MNIST, CIFAR10, and GTSRB.
- The percentage of poisoned samples for both attacks is 1%. Triggers are 3×3 squares, located in the upper left corner.

- Quantization methods: post-training static quantization (PTSQ) and quantization-aware training (QAT) in PyTorch on TrojanZoo framework.
- Anomaly detection threshold mentioned in Subsect. 2.2: 1.6 decided through a lot of experiments, as shown in the Fig. 4. (i.e., Labels with an absolute criterion less than 1.6 are infected labels. The model is an infected model.)

Table 1. Model performance before and after quantization. PTSQ, QAT, and Clean Accuracy represent post-training quantization, quantization-aware training, and the prediction accuracy when inputs without triggers.

Attack	Dataset	Attack Success Rate (%)			Clean Accuracy (%)		
		Original	PTSQ	QAT	Original	PTSQ	QAT
BadNets	MNIST	100.00	100.00	99.23	99.27	99.24	99.26
	CIFAR10	100.00	100.00	100.00	92.85	92.40	92.54
	GTSRB	99.98	100.00	100.00	94.91	94.82	94.79
TrojanNN	MNIST	99.97	100.00	100.00	99.34	99.34	99.28
	CIFAR10	99.95	100.00	100.00	92.63	92.40	92.76
	GTSRB	99.87	99.85	100.00	94.99	94.95	95.59

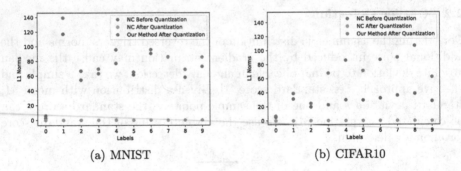

(a) MNIST   (b) CIFAR10

Fig. 1. Norms of potential triggers reversed before and after quantization. NC represents Neural Cleanse. The blue point in label 7 overlaps with the green point. (Color figure online)

Table 1 shows the prediction accuracies before and after quantization of different methods tested and recorded on different models and datasets. The results indicate that most of the attack success rates (especially in TrojanNN attack) after quantization are equal to or even higher than those before quantization. Figure 1 compares trigger norms reversed by Neural Cleanse before and after quantization, and it shows that the quantization model is not friendly to trigger

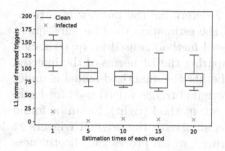

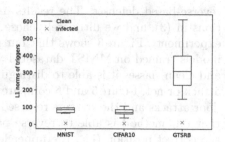

Fig. 2. Norms of different estimation times on MNIST

Fig. 3. Norms of masks from reversed triggers

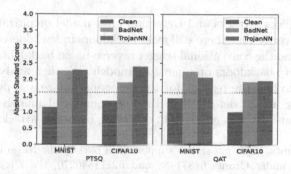

Fig. 4. Outlier detection of PTSQ (left) and QAT (right). The red dotted line is on a scale of 1.6. (Color figure online)

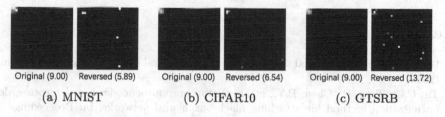

Original (9.00)   Reversed (5.89)   Original (9.00)   Reversed (6.54)   Original (9.00)   Reversed (13.72)

(a) MNIST   (b) CIFAR10   (c) GTSRB

Fig. 5. The original triggers and reversed triggers examples of BadNet. The numbers in brackets indicate the L1 norms of the masks.

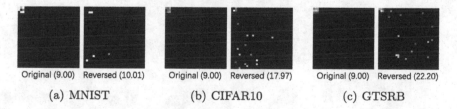

Original (9.00)   Reversed (10.01)   Original (9.00)   Reversed (17.97)   Original (9.00)   Reversed (22.20)

(a) MNIST   (b) CIFAR10   (c) GTSRB

Fig. 6. The original triggers and reversed triggers examples of TrojanNN. The numbers in brackets indicate the L1 norms of the masks.

reverse-based defenses. The results in Fig. 2 determine the number of estimations in (3), and we ultimately chose 10 as the estimation time for subsequent experiments. Figure 3 shows that our proposed method is used for quantization models trained on MNIST dataset. By comparing the L1 norms of the infected and clean classes it is able to distinguish whether the quantized model is under attack or not. Figure 5 and 6 compares the original triggers (left) used for backdoor attacks and the triggers reversed with our method (right). It can be found that our method is able to reverse patterns similar to the original triggers at the correct position (i.e., the upper left corner), which proves the effectiveness of our method.

4   Conclusion

Aiming at Backdoor Attacks and Detection after model quantization. First, we investigate and verify that there still exist backdoors in backdoored models after quantization. And the conventional trigger reverse-based backdoor detections are unable to identify backdoors on quantized models. We then analyse the quantization process to find the reasons for the detection failure and propose TRGE, a new backdoor attack detection method for quantized models. Experiments demonstrate that TRGE is effective in detecting backdoor attacks.

Acknowledgments. This paper was supported in part by the Natural Science Foundation of China under Grants 61871468 and 62111540270, the Zhejiang Provincial Natural Science Foundation of China (LZ23F010003, LQ23F010009), Zhejiang Provincial Key Laboratory of New Network Standards and Technologies (NNST) (No. 2013E10012).

References

1. Howell, D.C.: Fundamental statistics for the behavioral sciences. Cengage Learning (2016)
2. Tu, C.C., Ting, P., Chen, P.Y., et al.: Autozoom: autoencoder-based zeroth order optimization method for attacking black-box neural networks. In: Proceedings of the AAAI Conference on Artificial Intelligence, vol. 33, no. 01, pp. 742–749 (2019)

Improved Homomorphic Evaluation for Hash Function Based on TFHE

Benqiang Wei[1,2] and Xianhui Lu[1,2(✉)]

[1] State Key Laboratory of Information Security, Institute of Information
Engineering, Chinese Academy of Sciences, Beijing, China
luxianhui@iie.ac.cn
[2] School of Cyber Security, University of Chinese Academy of Sciences,
Beijing, China

Abstract. Homomorphic evaluation of hash functions offers a solution
to the challenge of data integrity authentication in the context of homomorphic encryption. The earliest attempt to achieve homomorphic evaluation of SHA-256 hash function was proposed by Mella et al. [15] based
on the BGV scheme. Unfortunately, their implementation faced significant limitations due to the exceedingly high multiplicative depth, rendering it impractical. Recently, a homomorphic implementation of SHA-256
based on the TFHE scheme [1] brings it from theory to reality, however,
its current efficiency remains insufficient.

In this paper, we revisit the homomorphic evaluation of the SHA-
256 hash function based on TFHE, further reducing the reliance on gate
bootstrapping and enhancing evaluation latency. Specifically, we primarily utilize ternary gates to reduce the number of gate bootstrappings
required for logic functions in message expansion and addition of modulo 2^{32} in iterative compression. Furthermore, we demonstrate that our
optimization techniques are applicable to the Chinese commercial cryptographic hash SM3. Finally, we give specific comparative implementations
based on the TFHE-rs library. Experiments demonstrate that our optimization techniques lead to an improvement of approximately *35%–50%*
compared to the state-of-the-art under different cores.

Keywords: TFHE · Hash function · Implementation

1 Introduction

Fully homomorphic encryption (FHE) is a cryptographic technique that allows
performing arbitrary function on ciphertexts without decryption. Since Gentry
[13] proposed ingenius bootstrapping technique to construct the first true fully
homomorphic encryption scheme, extensive research spanning over a decade has
resulted in significant advancements in both theoretical understanding and practical implementations of FHE. Some representative works include BGV [6], BFV
[5,12], CKKS [7,8], FHEW [11], TFHE [9] and Final [4].

The earliest evaluation of hash function can be traced back to Mella et al. [15],
who presented an evaluation of the SHA-256 based on the BGV scheme [6]. However, the main challenge encountered in evaluating SHA-256 homomorphically

© The Author(s), under exclusive license to Springer Nature Singapore Pte Ltd. 2024
C. Ge and M. Yung (Eds.): Inscrypt 2023, LNCS 14527, pp. 399–402, 2024.
https://doi.org/10.1007/978-981-97-0945-8_25

is the extremely high multiplicative depth caused by its significant number of iteration rounds. Compared with the BGV scheme, TFHE [9] has the advantage of not being limited by circuit depth. Recently, Bendoukha et al. [3] evaluated hash functions constructed by lightweight block ciphers such as PRINCE [10], SIMON [14], and LowMC [2] using the TFHE scheme. In this paper, we presented a faster homomorphic evaluation of SHA-256 and Chinese commercial cryptographic hash SM3.

1.1   Contributions and Techniques

In this paper, we revisit the evaluation of SHA-256 in the context of TFHE homomorphic encryption and concentrate on improving the latency of SHA-256 evaluation. We first discuss modifications to the SHA-256 code to make it more friendly to the TFHE scheme. One significant improvement is the utilization of ternary gates, which effectively reduces the number of gate bootstrappings required for evaluating SHA-256. Specifically, the logic functions $\sigma_0, \sigma_1, s_0, s_1$ and Maj required in message expansion can be evaluated with only a single bootstrapping. For the expensive addition of modulo 2^{32}, we present a number of optimization techniques to further minimize the number of required gate bootstrappings. Moreover, we show that our optimization techniques are also applicable to the evaluation of SM3 hash algorithm. Finally, we provide a concrete implementation based on the **TFHE-rs** library. Our experimental results show that our optimization tricks can achieve about *35%–50%* efficiency gains compared with the state-of-the-art under different CPUs.

2   Implementation and Experimental Results

We implement our evaluation method in the TFHE-rs library[1]. All tests were conducted on 12th Gen Intel(R) Core(TM) i5-12500 × 12 with 15.3 GB RAM, running the Ubuntu 20.04 system.

2.1   Experimental Parameter Setting

Now we present our parameter settings in the TFHE scheme. We use parameter sets "DEFAULT_PARAMS" from the TFHE-rs library, as shown in Table 1, which provides at least 128 bits of security and guarantees an error probability bound of 2^{-40}.

2.2   Performance Result

We present the comparison of homomorphic evaluation of SHA-256 and SM3 based on the parameter sets "DEFAULT PARAMS" for different CPU cores in Fig. 1. Experimental results show that for the SHA-256 and SM3 we achieve about 35%–50% efficiency improvement compared to the state-of-the-art work.

---

[1] https://github.com/zama-ai/tfhe-rs.

Table 1. Parameter sets of the TFHE scheme.

Parameter Sets		DEFAULT_PARAMS
TLWE dimension	n	777
TRLWE dimension	k	3
Polynomial size	N	512
LWE std_dev	σ_{LWE}	3.6726×10^{-6}
GLWE std_dev	σ_{GLWE}	3.4525×10^{-12}
PBS base log	$\log_2(\beta_{PBS})$	18
PBS level	ℓ_{PBS}	1
KeySwitch base log	$\log_2(\beta_{KS})$	4
KeySwitch level	ℓ_{KS}	3

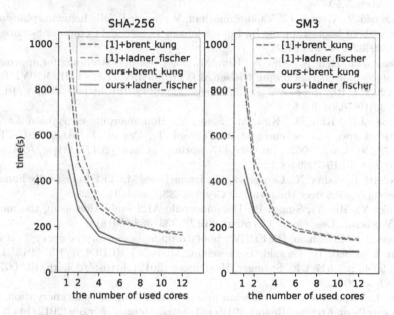

Fig. 1. Comparison of implementations of SHA-256 and SM3 based on parameter set "DEFAULT_PARAMS" from TFHE-rs library under different CPU cores.

Acknowledgement. We thank the anonymous INSCRYPT 2023 reviewers for their helpful comments. This work was supported by the Huawei Technologies Co., Ltd. and CAS Project for Young Scientists in Basic Research Grant No. YSBR-035.

References

1. Homomorphic evaluation of SHA-256. https://github.com/zama-ai/tfhe-rs/tree/main/tfhe/examples/sha256_bool
2. Albrecht, M.R., Rechberger, C., Schneider, T., Tiessen, T., Zohner, M.: Ciphers for MPC and FHE. In: Oswald, E., Fischlin, M. (eds.) EUROCRYPT 2015. LNCS,

vol. 9056, pp. 430–454. Springer, Heidelberg (2015). https://doi.org/10.1007/978-3-662-46800-5_17

3. Bendoukha, A., Stan, O., Sirdey, R., Quero, N., de Souza, L.F.: Practical homomorphic evaluation of block-cipher-based hash functions with applications. In: Jourdan, GV., Mounier, L., Adams, C., Sèdes, F., Garcia-Alfaro, J. (eds.) Foundations and Practice of Security - 15th International Symposium, FPS 2022. LNCS, vol. 13877, pp. 88–103. Springer, Cham (2022). https://doi.org/10.1007/978-3-031-30122-3_6

4. Bonte, C., Iliashenko, I., Park, J., Pereira, H.V.L., Smart, N.P.: FINAL: faster FHE instantiated with NTRU and LWE. In: Agrawal, S., Lin, D. (eds.) ASIACRYPT 2022. LNCS, vol. 13792, pp. 188–215. Springer, Cham (2022). https://doi.org/10.1007/978-3-031-22966-4_7

5. Brakerski, Z.: Fully homomorphic encryption without modulus switching from classical GapSVP. In: Safavi-Naini, R., Canetti, R. (eds.) CRYPTO 2012. LNCS, vol. 7417, pp. 868–886. Springer, Heidelberg (2012). https://doi.org/10.1007/978-3-642-32009-5_50

6. Brakerski, Z., Gentry, C., Vaikuntanathan, V.: (leveled) fully homomorphic encryption without bootstrapping. In: Innovations in Theoretical Computer Science 2012, pp. 309–325. ACM (2012)

7. Cheon, J.H., Han, K., Kim, A., Kim, M., Song, Y.: Bootstrapping for approximate homomorphic encryption. In: Nielsen, J.B., Rijmen, V. (eds.) EUROCRYPT 2018. LNCS, vol. 10820, pp. 360–384. Springer, Cham (2018). https://doi.org/10.1007/978-3-319-78381-9_14

8. Cheon, J.H., Kim, A., Kim, M., Song, Y.: Homomorphic encryption for arithmetic of approximate numbers. In: Takagi, T., Peyrin, T. (eds.) ASIACRYPT 2017. LNCS, vol. 10624, pp. 409–437. Springer, Cham (2017). https://doi.org/10.1007/978-3-319-70694-8_15

9. Chillotti, I., Gama, N., Georgieva, M., Izabachène, M.: TFHE: fast fully homomorphic encryption over the torus. J. Cryptol. 33(1), 34–91 (2020)

10. Doröz, Y., Hu, Y., Sunar, B.: Homomorphic AES evaluation using the modified LTV scheme. Des. Codes Cryptogr. 80(2), 333–358 (2016)

11. Ducas, L., Micciancio, D.: FHEW: bootstrapping homomorphic encryption in less than a second. In: Oswald, E., Fischlin, M. (eds.) EUROCRYPT 2015. LNCS, vol. 9056, pp. 617–640. Springer, Heidelberg (2015). https://doi.org/10.1007/978-3-662-46800-5_24

12. Fan, J., Vercauteren, F.: Somewhat practical fully homomorphic encryption. Cryptology ePrint Archive, Report 2012/144. https://eprint.iacr.org/2012/144

13. Gentry, C.: A Fully Homomorphic Encryption Scheme. Stanford University (2009)

14. Lepoint, T., Naehrig, M.: A comparison of the homomorphic encryption schemes FV and YASHE. In: Pointcheval, D., Vergnaud, D. (eds.) AFRICACRYPT 2014. LNCS, vol. 8469, pp. 318–335. Springer, Cham (2014). https://doi.org/10.1007/978-3-319-06734-6_20

15. Mella, S., Susella, R.: On the homomorphic computation of symmetric cryptographic primitives. In: Stam, M. (ed.) IMACC 2013. LNCS, vol. 8308, pp. 28–44. Springer, Heidelberg (2013). https://doi.org/10.1007/978-3-642-45239-0_3

Power of Randomness Recovery: Tighter CCA-Secure KEM in the QROM

Ziyi Li[1,2], Xianhui Lu[1,2(⊠)], Yao Cheng[1,2], and Bao Li[1]

[1] Institute of Information Engineering, CAS, Beijing 100049, China
[2] School of Cyber Security, University of Chinese Academy of Sciences, Beijing 100049, China
liziyi@iie.ac.cn

Abstract. We propose a novel, efficient and secure Key Encapsulation Mechanism (KEM) transformation in the random oracle model. Furthermore, we demonstrate its security in the Quantum Random Oracle Model (QROM) as introduced by Boneh et al. (CRYPTO 12), supported by a tighter security reduction.

Keywords: Key Encapsulation Mechanism · Quantum Random Oralce Model · Chosen-Ciphertext Attacks

1 Introduction

With the growing threat of quantum computers, there is a great need for secure Key Encapsulation Mechanisms (KEMs) against quantum attacks. Substantial effort has been dedicated to the provable security of KEMs in the Quantum Random Oracle Model (QROM) [2], especially the FO-KEM transformation [1,3–5,7–12]. However, the de-randomization (T transformation) process in the transformation introduces reduction loss to the security proof of the entire transformation. To address this issue, we propose a novel generic KEM transformation which converts an One-Way under Chosen-Plaintext Attacks (OW-CPA) Randomness Recoverable Public-Key Encryption (PKE-RR) [6] scheme into an Indistinguishable under Chosen-Ciphertext Attacks (IND-CCA) KEM scheme in the (Q)ROM. It eliminates the need for de-randomization and achieves tighter security against Chosen-Ciphertext Attacks (CCA) in the QROM.

2 Preliminaries

We review the formal definition of Randomness Recoverable Public Key Encryption (PKE-RR) and its correctness and injectivity.

Definition 1 (PKE-RR, [6]). *A PKE-RR scheme consists of a tuple of PPT algorithms* (Gen, Enc, Dec, Rec) *as follows:*

- Gen(1^λ) → (pk, sk): *The generation algorithm takes the security parameter* 1^λ *as input and outputs a (public key, secret key) pair* (pk, sk).

C. Ge and M. Yung (Eds.): Inscrypt 2023, LNCS 14527, pp. 403–406, 2024.
https://doi.org/10.1007/978-981-97-0945-8_26

- $\mathsf{Enc}(pk, m) \to c$: *The encryption algorithm takes a public key pk and a message m as input and outputs a ciphertext $c := \mathsf{Enc}(pk, m; r)$, where the randomness r is randomly choosen from the randomness space R.*
- $\mathsf{Dec}(sk, c) \to (m, r)/\bot$: *The decryption algorithm takes a secret key sk and a ciphertext c as input and outputs (m, r) or the failure symbol $\bot$.*
- $\mathsf{Rec}(pk, c, r) \to m/\bot$: *The recoverable algorithm takes a public key pk, a ciphertext c and a string r as input and outputs m or $\bot$.*

Definition 2 (key-δ-correctness, [6]). *A PKE-RR scheme* $\mathsf{PKE} := (\mathsf{Gen}, \mathsf{Enc}, \mathsf{Dec}, \mathsf{Rec})$ *with message space M and randomness space R is key-δ-correct if*

$$\Pr[m \in M, r \in R \ s.t. \ \mathsf{Dec}(sk, \mathsf{Enc}(pk, m; r)) \neq (m, r)] \leq \delta(\lambda),$$

and

$$\Pr[m \in M, r \in R \ s.t. \ \mathsf{Rec}(pk, \mathsf{Enc}(pk, m; r), r) \neq m] \leq \delta(\lambda),$$

where the probability is taken over $(pk, sk) \leftarrow \mathsf{Gen}(1^\lambda)$. If δ is negligible, the PKE-RR scheme is almost-all-keys perfect correct.

Definition 3 (key-η-injectivity). *A PKE-RR scheme* $\mathsf{PKE} := (\mathsf{Gen}, \mathsf{Enc}, \mathsf{Dec}, \mathsf{Rec})$ *with message space M and randomness space R is key-η-injective if*

$$\Pr[\exists (m_0, r_0), (m_1, r_1) \in M \times R \ s.t. \ (m_0, r_0) \neq (m_1, r_1), \mathsf{Enc}(pk, m_0; r_0) = \mathsf{Enc}(pk, m_1; r_1)] \leq \eta(\lambda),$$

where the probability is taken over $(pk, sk) \leftarrow \mathsf{Gen}(1^\lambda)$.

3   CCA-Secure KEM Transformation

The transformation TU converts an OW-CPA secure PKE-RR scheme into an IND-CCA secure KEM in the (Q)ROM. More detailed, let $\mathsf{PKE} := (\mathsf{Gen}, \mathsf{Enc}, \mathsf{Dec}, \mathsf{Rec})$ be a PKE-RR scheme with message space M, randomness space R and ciphertext space C, and H is a random oracle. Then the resulting KEM scheme $\mathsf{KEM} := TU[\mathsf{PKE}, H]$ can be described as in Fig. 1.

The security of the transformation in the (Q)ROM is demonstrated as follows:

$\underline{\mathsf{KEM.Gen}(1^\lambda)}$	$\underline{\mathsf{KEM.Enc}(pk)}$	$\underline{\mathsf{KEM.Dec}(sk, c)}$
1: $s \xleftarrow{\$} R$	1: $m \xleftarrow{\$} M, \ r \xleftarrow{\$} R$	1: parse sk into sk' and s
2: $\mathsf{Gen}(1^\lambda) \to (pk', sk')$	2: $c := \mathsf{Enc}(pk, m; r)$	2: $(m, r) \leftarrow \mathsf{Dec}(sk', c)$
3: $pk := pk', \ sk := sk'\|s$	3: $k := H(r, c)$	3: **if** $(m, r) = \bot$
4: **return** (pk, sk)	4: **return** (c, k)	4: **return** $k := H(s, \dot{c})$
		5: **return** $k := H(r, c)$

Fig. 1. Transformation TU. Here, $(\mathsf{KEM.Gen}, \mathsf{KEM.Enc}, \mathsf{KEM.Dec})$ is the resulting KEM.

Theorem 1. *Let* PKE *be an OW-CPA secure PKE-RR scheme with key-δ-correctness and key-η-injectivity, and H be a random oracle. For any PPT IND-CCA adversary $\mathcal{A}$ against* KEM *issuing q_H random oracle queries to H and q_D decryption queries to O_{Decap}, then there exists a PPT OW-CPA adversary $\mathcal{B}$ against* PKE *such that*

$$\mathsf{Adv}^{\mathsf{IND\text{-}CCA}}_{\mathsf{KEM},\mathcal{A}}(1^\lambda) \leq \mathsf{Adv}^{\mathsf{OW\text{-}CPA}}_{\mathsf{PKE},\mathcal{B}}(1^\lambda) + \frac{q_H}{|R|} + \delta + \eta,$$

where R is the randomness space of PKE.

Proof. Here, we provide a proof sketch. For any IND-CCA adversary $\mathcal{A}$ against KEM, we can construct an OW-CPA adversary $\mathcal{B}$ against PKE. The key point of this construction is that $\mathcal{B}$ needs to simulate the decapsulation oracle O_{Decap} for $\mathcal{A}$ without the secret key sk'. In the ROM, $\mathcal{B}$ can simulate O_H via lazy sampling and generate the query list to record $\mathcal{A}$'s queries and corresponding responses. Additionally, $\mathcal{B}$ can check the validity of (r, c) ((r, c) is valid if $\mathsf{Rec}(pk, c, r) = m$ and $\mathsf{Enc}(pk, m; r) = c$) by running the algorithm Rec and re-encryption. Through lazy sampling and validity checking, $\mathcal{B}$ can simulate O_{Decap} without sk'.

Theorem 2. *Let* PKE *be an OW-CPA secure PKE-RR scheme with key-δ-correctness and key-η-injectivity, and H be a random oracle. For any quantum PPT IND-CCA adversary $\mathcal{A}$ against* KEM *issuing q_H quantum random oracle queries to O_H with query depth at most d and q_D classical queries to O_{Decap}, there exists a quantum PPT OW-CPA adversary $\mathcal{B}$ against* PKE *such that*

$$\mathsf{Adv}^{\mathsf{IND\text{-}CCA}}_{\mathsf{KEM},\mathcal{A}}(1^\lambda) \leq 4d \cdot \mathsf{Adv}^{\mathsf{OW\text{-}CPA}}_{\mathsf{PKE},\mathcal{B}}(1^\lambda) + \frac{2q_H}{\sqrt{|R|}} + \delta + \eta,$$

where R is the randomness space of PKE.

Proof. We also provide a proof sketch. Similar to the above proof, $\mathcal{B}$ needs to simulate O_{Decap} without sk'. In the QROM, $\mathcal{B}$ introduces a new independent random oracle H' and modifies $c \rightarrow r \rightarrow H(r, c)$ (decapsulation of valid c) and $c \rightarrow H(s, c)$ (decapsulation of invalid c) into $c \rightarrow H'(c)$. Then, $\mathcal{B}$ can simulate O_H and O_{Decap} with H'. In addition, we need apply the measure-rewind-measure One-Way to Hiding (OW2H) lemma proposed by Kuchta et al. in [9] to deal the reprogramming of O_H.

Acknowledgement. We thank the anonymous INSCRYPT 2023 reviewers for their helpful comments. This work was supported by the National Natural Science Foundation of China (Grant No. 61972391) and the Bureau of Major R&D Programs, Chinese Academy of Sciences (Grant No. ZDRW-XX-2022-1).

References

1. Bindel, N., Hamburg, M., Hövelmanns, K., Hülsing, A., Persichetti, E.: Tighter proofs of CCA security in the quantum random oracle model. In: Hofheinz, D., Rosen, A. (eds.) TCC 2019. LNCS, vol. 11892, pp. 61–90. Springer, Cham (2019). https://doi.org/10.1007/978-3-030-36033-7_3

2. Boneh, D., Dagdelen, Ö., Fischlin, M., Lehmann, A., Schaffner, C., Zhandry, M.: Random oracles in a quantum world. In: Lee, D.H., Wang, X. (eds.) ASIACRYPT 2011. LNCS, vol. 7073, pp. 41–69. Springer, Heidelberg (2011). https://doi.org/10.1007/978-3-642-25385-0_3

3. Fujisaki, E., Okamoto, T.: Secure integration of asymmetric and symmetric encryption schemes. J. Cryptol. **26**(1), 80–101 (2013)

4. Jiang, H., Zhang, Z., Ma, Z.: Key encapsulation mechanism with explicit rejection in the quantum random oracle model. In: Lin, D., Sako, K. (eds.) PKC 2019. LNCS, vol. 11443, pp. 618–645. Springer, Cham (2019). https://doi.org/10.1007/978-3-030-17259-6_21

5. Hofheinz, D., Hövelmanns, K., Kiltz, E.: A modular analysis of the Fujisaki-Okamoto transformation. In: Kalai, Y., Reyzin, L. (eds.) TCC 2017. LNCS, vol. 10677, pp. 341–371. Springer, Cham (2017). https://doi.org/10.1007/978-3-319-70500-2_12

6. Hohenberger, S., Koppula, V., Waters, B.: Chosen ciphertext security from injective trapdoor functions. In: Micciancio, D., Ristenpart, T. (eds.) CRYPTO 2020. LNCS, vol. 12170, pp. 836–866. Springer, Cham (2020). https://doi.org/10.1007/978-3-030-56784-2_28

7. Jiang, H., Zhang, Z., Chen, L., Wang, H., Ma, Z.: IND-CCA-secure key encapsulation mechanism in the quantum random oracle model, revisited. In: Shacham, H., Boldyreva, A. (eds.) CRYPTO 2018. LNCS, vol. 10993, pp. 96–125. Springer, Cham (2018). https://doi.org/10.1007/978-3-319-96878-0_4

8. Jiang, H., Zhang, Z., Ma, Z.: Tighter security proofs for generic key encapsulation mechanism in the quantum random oracle model. In: Ding, J., Steinwandt, R. (eds.) PQCrypto 2019. LNCS, vol. 11505, pp. 227–248. Springer, Cham (2019). https://doi.org/10.1007/978-3-030-25510-7_13

9. Kuchta, V., Sakzad, A., Stehlé, D., Steinfeld, R., Sun, S.-F.: Measure-rewind-measure: tighter quantum random oracle model proofs for one-way to hiding and CCA security. In: Canteaut, A., Ishai, Y. (eds.) EUROCRYPT 2020. LNCS, vol. 12107, pp. 703–728. Springer, Cham (2020). https://doi.org/10.1007/978-3-030-45727-3_24

10. Liu, X., Wang, M.: QCCA-secure generic key encapsulation mechanism with tighter security in the quantum random oracle model. In: Garay, J.A. (ed.) PKC 2021. LNCS, vol. 12710, pp. 3–26. Springer, Cham (2021). https://doi.org/10.1007/978-3-030-75245-3_1

11. Saito, T., Xagawa, K., Yamakawa, T.: Tightly-secure key-encapsulation mechanism in the quantum random oracle model. In: Nielsen, J.B., Rijmen, V. (eds.) EUROCRYPT 2018. LNCS, vol. 10822, pp. 520–551. Springer, Cham (2018). https://doi.org/10.1007/978-3-319-78372-7_17

12. Xagawa, K., Yamakawa, T.: (Tightly) QCCA-secure key-encapsulation mechanism in the quantum random oracle model. In: Ding, J., Steinwandt, R. (eds.) PQCrypto 2019. LNCS, vol. 11505, pp. 249–268. Springer, Cham (2019). https://doi.org/10.1007/978-3-030-25510-7_14

Partial Key Exposure Attack on Common Prime RSA

Mengce Zheng$^{(\boxtimes)}$ (iD)

Zhejiang Wanli University, Ningbo 315100, China
mengce.zheng@gmail.com, mczheng@zwu.edu.cn

Abstract. In this paper, we focus on the common prime RSA variant and introduce a novel investigation into the partial key exposure attack. We are able to identify weak private keys that are susceptible to partial key exposure by using the lattice-based method. Through experimental examinations, we demonstrate the validity of the proposed attacks.

Keywords: Cryptanalysis · Common Prime RSA · Weak Key · Partial Key Exposure Attack · Lattice

1 Introduction

Let us consider an instance of RSA with a public key (N, e) and a private key (p, q, d), where the modulus $N = pq$ is the product of two balanced primes. In the original RSA scheme [3], the public and private exponents e and d are chosen to be inverses of each other modulo $\varphi(N) = (p-1)(q-1)$. However, it is now common to define these exponents modulo Carmichael's lambda function, denoted as $\lambda(N) = \text{lcm}(p-1, q-1)$. In Hinek's design [1], the balanced primes p and q are defined as $p = 2ga + 1$ and $q = 2gb + 1$, where g is a large prime and a, b are positive integers. These primes are referred to as common primes.

The public and private exponents e, d are defined modulo $\lambda(N) = \text{lcm}(p-1, q-1) = \text{lcm}(2ga, 2gb) = 2gab$. The key equation $ed \equiv 1 \pmod{\text{lcm}(p-1, q-1)}$ can be rewritten as

$$ed \equiv 1 \pmod{2gab}, \tag{1}$$

which further leads to $ed = 2gabk + 1$, where k is an unknown positive integer relatively prime to $2g$. In this paper, we use γ and δ to represent the greatest common divisor $g \simeq N^\gamma$ and the private exponent $d \simeq N^\delta$, respectively. Since $2g = \gcd(p-1, q-1)$ for balanced p and q, we have $0 < \gamma < 1/2$. Additionally, the bit-length of e is assumed to be roughly the same as N/g, which implies $e \simeq N^{1-\gamma}$.

The security of common prime RSA has been intensively studied by previous attacks. However, it is worth noting that partial key exposure attacks, which involve the leakage of certain bits of the private key, are particularly relevant in scenarios where common prime RSA is used in constrained environments. Thus, investigating partial key exposure attacks is of great importance, and we present the first investigation of partial key exposure attacks on common prime RSA.

© The Author(s), under exclusive license to Springer Nature Singapore Pte Ltd. 2024
C. Ge and M. Yung (Eds.): Inscrypt 2023, LNCS 14527, pp. 407–410, 2024.
https://doi.org/10.1007/978-981-97-0945-8_27

2　Preliminaries

We apply the specific lattice-based method [2] for our attack scenarios. This particular construction allows for the easier creation of a triangular lattice matrix, while also yielding superior analysis results. The method is specifically designed to solve the problem of finding small roots of extended simultaneous modular univariate linear equations,

$$\begin{cases} f_1(x_1) = x_1 + a_1 \equiv 0 \pmod{u^{r_1}} \\ \vdots \\ f_n(x_n) = x_n + a_n \equiv 0 \pmod{u^{r_n}} \end{cases}$$

The given parameters are positive integers $r_1, \ldots, r_n, r, a_1, \ldots, a_n, U$, and bounding reals $\eta, \gamma_1, \ldots, \gamma_n \in (0, 1)$, where $U \equiv 0 \pmod{u^r}$ for unknown $u \simeq U^\eta$. The goal is to extract all roots $(x'_1, \ldots, x'_n)$ such that $|x'_1| \leq U^{\gamma_1}, \ldots, |x'_n| \leq U^{\gamma_n}$. We present the following lemma. For a detailed explanation, refer to [2, Theorem 10] and its accompanying proof.

Lemma 1. *The extended simultaneous modular univariate linear equations can be solved if*

$$\sqrt[n]{\frac{\gamma_1 \cdots \gamma_n}{r r_1 \cdots r_n}} < \eta^{\frac{n+1}{n}}$$

provided that $\eta \gg 1/\sqrt{\log U}$ and $\gamma_i \leq r_i \eta$ for $1 \leq i \leq n$. The running time is polynomial in $\log U$ but exponential in n.

3　Partial Key Exposure Attack

Let N be the product of two common primes p, q having the same bit-length. Let $e \simeq N^{1-\eta}$ and $d \simeq N^\delta$ satisfy $ed \equiv 1 \pmod{\lambda(N)}$, where $\lambda(N) = \text{lcm}(p - 1, q - 1) = 2gab$. We consider the following attack scenario. Given N, e and MSBs d_M in a $(\delta_M \log_2 N)$-bit block along with LSBs d_L in a $(\delta_L \log_2 N)$-bit block of d satisfying $d = d_M M + \bar{d} L + d_L$, where $M = 2^{(\delta - \delta_M) \log_2 N}$, $L = 2^{\delta_L \log_2 N}$ for known δ_M, δ_L, and unknown $\bar{d}$ is bounded by $|\bar{d}| \simeq N^{\delta - \delta_M - \delta_L}$, the target is to efficiently factor N in polynomial.

According to the property of common prime RSA, we have $N - 1 \equiv 0 \pmod{g}$ and further $\frac{N-1}{2} \equiv 0 \pmod{g}$. We also have $ed - 1 \equiv 0 \pmod{g}$ from Eq. (1). Since $d = d_M M + \bar{d} L + d_L$ for $M = 2^{(\delta - \delta_M) \log_2 N}$, $L = 2^{\delta_L \log_2 N}$ with known δ_M, δ_L and unknown $\bar{d}$, we substitute d into $ed - 1 \equiv 0 \pmod{g}$ and obtain $ed_M M + e\bar{d} L + ed_L - 1 \equiv 0 \pmod{g}$. Hence, we have a modular univariate linear equation,

$$x_1 + a_1 \equiv 0 \pmod{g}, \tag{2}$$

where $a_1 = (ed_M M + ed_L - 1)\left((eL)^{-1} \bmod \frac{N-1}{2}\right) \bmod (N - 1)$ and x_1 represents the unknown $\bar{d}$. Moreover, since $(p - 1)(q - 1) = 4g^2 ab = pq - p - q + 1 = N + 1 - (p + q)$, we have another modular univariate linear equation,

$$x_2 + a_2 \equiv 0 \pmod{g^2}, \tag{3}$$

where $a_2 = N + 1$ and x_2 represents the unknown $-(p + q)$.

Thus, combining two simultaneous modular univariate linear Eqs. (2) and (3), we have the following equation system,

$$\begin{cases} x_1 + a_1 \equiv 0 \pmod{g} \\ x_2 + a_2 \equiv 0 \pmod{g^2} \end{cases} \tag{4}$$

We focus on equation system (4) with roots $x_1' = \bar{d}$ and $x_2' = -(p + q)$. Once discovering an integer pair (x_1', x_2') satisfying (4), we can factor the RSA modulus N via $p + q$. Similarly, since $U \equiv 0 \pmod{g}$ with $g \simeq N^\gamma$, and $X_1 = N^{\delta - \delta_M - \delta_L}, X_2 = N^{1/2}$, we have $n = 2$, $r_1 = 1$, $r_2 = 2$, $r = 1$, $U = N - 1 \simeq N$, $\eta = \gamma$. Therefore, we directly apply Lemma 1 and obtain $\gamma_1 \gamma_2 < 2\gamma^3$. Substituting $\gamma_1 = \delta - \delta_M - \delta_L$ and $\gamma_2 = 1/2$, we finally have $\delta < 4\gamma^3 + \delta_M + \delta_L$.

Moreover, we must ensure that $0 < \delta - \delta_M - \delta_L \leq \gamma$ and $1/2 \leq 2\gamma$, which imply that $\gamma \geq 1/4$ and $\delta_M + \delta_L < \delta < \gamma + \delta_M + \delta_L$. Gathering them together with $0 < \gamma < 1/2$, we derive the final condition: $\delta_M + \delta_L < \delta < 4\gamma^3 + \delta_M + \delta_L$, $1/4 \leq \gamma < 1/2$. For completeness, we conclude partial key exposure attack on common prime RSA with the following proposition.

Proposition 1. *Let $N = pq$ be a common prime RSA modulus with two balanced common primes p and q of the same bit-length. Let $e \simeq N^{1-\gamma}$ and $d \simeq N^\delta$ be its public and private exponents such that $ed = 1 \pmod{\text{lcm}(p - 1, q - 1)}$, where $\gcd(p - 1, q - 1) = 2g$ for a large prime $g \simeq N^\gamma$. Given an approximation of d with known MSBs d_M in a $(\delta_M \log_2 N)$-bit block along with LSBs d_L in a $(\delta_L \log_2 N)$-bit block satisfying $d = d_M M + \bar{d}L + d_L$, where $M = 2^{(\delta - \delta_M) \log_2 N}$, $L = 2^{\delta_L \log_2 N}$ for known δ_M, δ_L and unknown $\bar{d}$ is bounded by $|\bar{d}| \leq N^{\delta - \delta_M - \delta_L}$. Then N can be efficiently factored in time polynomial in $\log_2 N$ if*

$$\delta_M + \delta_L < \delta < 4\gamma^3 + \delta_M + \delta_L, \quad \frac{1}{4} \leq \gamma < \frac{1}{2}.$$

4   Experimental Results

To validate the validity and effectiveness of our proposed partial key exposure attacks on common prime RSA, which exploits Proposition 1, we conducted a series of numerical experiments. These experiments were performed on a computer running a 64-bit Windows 10 operating system with Ubuntu 22.04 installed on WSL 2. The experiments were conducted using SageMath [4].

To execute the proposed attacks, we selected a suitable parameter t to construct a lattice. The experimental results are presented in Table 1. The δ_t column provides the theoretical upper bound of d, while the δ_e column presents the corresponding experimental results. The lattice settings are controlled by t, and the lattice dimension is provided in the w column. The time consumption of the LLL algorithm and the Gröbner basis computation is recorded in the **Time** column (measured in seconds). During each experiment, we collected sufficient polynomials that satisfied the solvable requirements after running the LLL algorithm. We recovered $x_2' = -(p + q)$, which allows us to factorize N by putting obtained integer polynomials into Gröbner basis computation. The common root was successfully recovered in all generated common prime RSA instances.

Table 1. Experimental partial key exposure attacks on common prime RSA

$\log_2 N$	γ	δ_{M}	δ_{L}	δ_t	δ_e	t	w	Time
1024	0.36	0.117	0	0.304	0.252	4	22	0.52 s
1024	0.40	0.127	0	0.383	0.314	4	20	0.35 s
1024	0.44	0.132	0	0.473	0.388	5	25	0.82 s
1024	0.48	0.068	0	0.511	0.422	6	31	1.53 s
1024	0.36	0	0.146	0.333	0.290	5	32	3.20 s
1024	0.40	0	0.156	0.412	0.350	5	29	0.86 s
1024	0.44	0	0.144	0.484	0.412	6	34	3.15 s
1024	0.48	0	0.125	0.567	0.479	7	41	5.57 s
1024	0.36	0.098	0.137	0.421	0.337	3	18	0.13 s
1024	0.40	0.132	0.127	0.515	0.450	5	29	1.56 s
1024	0.44	0.102	0.144	0.586	0.518	7	44	10.53 s
1024	0.48	0.144	0.165	0.751	0.691	10	72	101.46 s

Acknowledgements. This work was supported by the National Natural Science Foundation of China, grant numbers 62002335, Ningbo Natural Science Foundation, grant number 2021J174, and Ningbo Young Science and Technology Talent Cultivation Program, grant number 2023QL007.

References

1. Hinek, M.J.: Another look at small RSA exponents. In: Pointcheval, D. (ed.) CT-RSA 2006. LNCS, vol. 3860, pp. 82–98. Springer, Heidelberg (2006). https://doi.org/10.1007/11605805_6
2. Lu, Y., Zhang, R., Peng, L., Lin, D.: Solving linear equations modulo unknown divisors: revisited. In: Iwata, T., Cheon, J. (eds.) ASIACRYPT 2015. LNCS, vol. 9452, pp. 189–213. Springer, Berlin, Heidelberg (2015). https://doi.org/10.1007/978-3-662-48797-6_9
3. Rivest, R.L., Shamir, A., Adleman, L.M.: A method for obtaining digital signatures and public-key cryptosystems. Commun. ACM **21**(2), 120–126 (1978). https://doi.org/10.1145/359340.359342. http://doi.acm.org/10.1145/359340.359342
4. The Sage Developers: SageMath, the Sage Mathematics Software System (Version 9.5) (2023). https://www.sagemath.org

An Efficient Autonomous Path Proxy Re-encryption Without Pairing for Cloud-Assisted mHealth

Linghui Chen[1], Zhiguo Wan[1], Jun Zhou[2]([✉]), and Carvajal Roca Ivan Edmar[1]

[1] Zhejiang Lab, Hangzhou 311121, Zhejiang, China
{chenlh,wanzhiguo,ivancr}@zhejianglab.com
[2] Shanghai Key Laboratory of Trustworthy Computing, East China Normal University, Shanghai 200062, China
jzhou@sei.ecnu.edu.cn

Abstract. We propose the first construction of an efficient AP-PRE scheme without pairing for data confidentiality in the cloud-assisted Mobile Health (mHealth) system. In our scheme, the user can outsource his encrypted Personal Health Information (PHI) to the Cloud Service Provider (CSP) and share it with a list of doctors ordered in priority, where he has complete control over the transformation of the ciphertext. Based on the Modified Computational Diffie-Hellman (M-CDH) assumption, we prove the chosen-ciphertext security for our proposed scheme in the Random Oracle (RO) model. We demonstrate that our proposed AP-PRE scheme is highly efficient by comparing it with previous AP-PRE schemes based on bilinear pairing.

Keywords: mHealth · Delegation path · Proxy re-encryption · Consensus network

1 Introduction

Mobile Health (mHealth) enables users to collect their Personal Health Information (PHI) and receive healthcare anytime and anywhere with widely deployed mobile devices. Most mHealth systems are cloud-assisted, where PHI is uploaded to clouds for remote storage. This leads to potential challenges to guaranteeing both confidentiality and availability of the PHI. Proxy Re-encryption (PRE) offers a promising solution since it enables the user to encrypt his PHI and delegate the decryption right of the encrypted PHI to some doctors he trusts for a diagnosis. However, as shown in Fig. 1(a), with traditional PREs, the user could only control the selection of the first doctor who can then transform the ciphertexts to someone at his will when he is busy, rather than the user's will. In this paper, we propose an efficient Autonomous Path Proxy Re-Encryption (AP-PRE) scheme with much better fine-grained access control for cloud-assisted mHealth. As shown in Fig. 1(b), the user can make a list of preferred doctors in order of priority, like $Doctor_1 \rightarrow Doctor_2 \rightarrow ... \rightarrow Doctor_n$ and generate the corresponding re-encryption keys $rk_{0\rightarrow1}, rk_{1\rightarrow2}, ..., rk_{n-1\rightarrow n}$ in advance. If

C. Ge and M. Yung (Eds.): Inscrypt 2023, LNCS 14527, pp. 411–415, 2024.
https://doi.org/10.1007/978-981-97-0945-8_28

$Doctor_1$ happens to have no time within the expected diagnostic time, the CSP will autonomically re-encrypt the ciphertext with the re-encryption key $rk_{1\to2}$ to transfer the decryption right to $Doctor_2$.

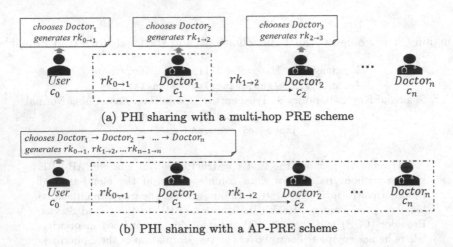

(a) PHI sharing with a multi-hop PRE scheme

(b) PHI sharing with a AP-PRE scheme

Fig. 1. The comparison between PHI sharing with a multi-hop PRE scheme and a AP-PRE scheme

2   Our Proposed AP-PRE Without Pairing

We propose our scheme by extending the conditional PRE scheme proposed in [1]. We extend the re-encryption key generated by the delegator into a set of re-encryption keys in the absence of a condition. The construction of these re-encryption keys is embedded by the private key of the delegator, which ensures that the intermediate delegatees cannot generate a valid re-encryption key or re-encrypt the ciphertext on the delegation path to a ciphertext with meaningful decryption. The use of multiplicative in the construction of E_j^i in the **ReEncrypt** algorithm ensures that the ciphertext C_{j+1}^i can only be converted from ciphertext C_j^i, that is, the delegation can only be carried out in the designated order. Find more details below. Our proposed AP-PRE scheme consists of the following algorithms:

Setup(λ): On input of the security parameter λ, output the system's public parameters $params = (\mathbb{G}, q, g, H_1, H_2, H_3, H_4, H_5, H_6, H_7, l_0, l_1)$:

- Let $\mathbb{G}$ be a cyclic group with a prime order q and a generator g. Choose the following cryptographic hash functions: $H_1 : \mathbb{G} \to \mathbb{Z}_q^*$, $H_2 : \mathbb{Z}_q^* \times \mathbb{Z}_q^* \to \mathbb{Z}_q^*$, $H_3 : \mathbb{G} \to \{0,1\}^{\log_2 q}$, $H_4 : \{0,1\}^{l_0} \times \{0,1\}^{l_1} \to \mathbb{Z}_q^*$, $H_5 : \mathbb{G} \to \{0,1\}^{l_0+l_1}$, $H_6 : \mathbb{G}^4 \to \mathbb{G}$, $H_7 : \mathbb{G}^2 \times \{0,1\}^{l_0+l_1} \to \mathbb{Z}_q^*$. $\{0,1\}^{l_0}$ is the message space M and l_1 is determined by the security parameter λ.

– Output the system's public parameters *params*.

KeyGen($i, params$): On input of the system's public parameters *params* and a user's index i, output the public key and corresponding private key for user i:

– Pick $x_{i,1}, x_{i,2} \in_R Z_q^*$ at random;
– Privacy key sk_i for user i is set to be tuple $(sk_{i,1}, sk_{i,2}) = (x_{i,1}, x_{i,2})$. Public key pk_i is set to be tuple $(pk_{i,1}, pk_{i,2}) = (g^{x_{i,1}}, g^{x_{i,2}})$ correspondingly;
– Output the public key and corresponding privacy key (pk_i, sk_i) for user i.

CreatePath($params, pk_i$): User i is the delegator who selects l_i preferred delegatees. On input of the public key of delegator pk_i, output $(Path^i, l_i)$:

– $Path^i = (pk_0^i = pk_i, \cdots, pk_j^i, \cdots, pk_{l_i}^i)$ is a sequence of ordered public keys, where $pk_0^i = pk_i = (pk_{i,1}, pk_{i,2})$ is the public key of the delegator, and $pk_j^i = (pk_{j,1}^i, pk_{j,2}^i) = (g^{x_{j,1}^i}, g^{x_{j,2}^i})(1 \le j \le l_i)$ is the public key of the j-th delegatee in the delegation $Path_i$. For $0 \le j \ne k \le l_i$, $pk_j^i \ne pk_k^i$.

ReKeyGen($sk_i, pk_i, Path^i, params$): On input of the delegator's privacy key $sk_i = (sk_{i,1}, sk_{i,2}) = (x_{i,1}, x_{i,2})$, public key $pk_i = (pk_{i,1}, pk_{i,2}) = (g^{x_{i,1}}, g^{x_{i,2}})$ and the delegation path $Path^i = (pk_0^i, pk_1^i, \cdots, pk_{l_i}^i)$, the delegator generates the re-encryption key set as follows.

– $z_i = \frac{1}{x_{i,1}H_1(pk_{i,2})+x_{i,2}}$ mod q; for $1 \le j \le l_i$:
– Pick $z_{j,1}^i, h_i \in_R \mathbb{Z}_q^*$, compute $v_j^i = H_2(z_{j,1}^i, h_i)$;
– If $j = 1$, set $z_{1,2}^i = \frac{z_i}{z_{1,1}^i}$ mod q. Else, compute $z_{j,2}^i = \frac{z_i}{z_{j,1}^i \cdot \prod_{t=1}^{j-1} z_{t,2}^i}$ mod q;
– $V_j^i = (pk_j^i)^{v_j^i}$, $W_j^i = H_3(g^{v_j^i}) \oplus (z_{j,1}^i \parallel h_i)$, $RK_{j-1\to j}^i = (z_{j,2}^i, V_j^i, W_j^i)$;
– Output the re-encryption key set $RK^i = \{RK_{0\to1}^i, \cdots, RK_{l_i-1\to l_i}^i\}$.

Encrypt($pk_i, m, params$): Encrypt message m with delegator's public key pk_i:

– Pick $u \in_R \mathbb{Z}_q^*, r' \in_R \{0,1\}^{l_1}$, and set $r = H_4(m, r')$;
– $D_i = (pk_{i,1}^{H_1(pk_{i,2})} pk_{i,2})^u$, $E_i = (pk_{i,1}^{H_1(pk_{i,2})} pk_{i,2})^r$, $F_i = H_5(g^r) \oplus (m \parallel r')$;
– $\bar{D}_i = H_6(pk_i, D_i, E_i, F_i)^u$, $\bar{E}_i = H_6(pk_i, D_i, E_i, F_i)^r$;
– Set $s_i = u + rH_7(D_i, \bar{E}_i, F_i)$ mod q;
– Output the second level ciphertext $C_0^i = C_i = (D_i, \bar{E}_i, F_i, s_i)$.

ReEncrypt($RK_{j-1\to j}^i, C_{j-1}^i (1 \le j \le l_i), params$): On input a ciphertext under the public key pk_{j-1}^i, the algorithm transforms C_{j-1}^i into a ciphertext under the public key pk_j^i using the re-encryption key $RK_{j-1\to j}^i$.

(1) If the ciphertext is the second level ciphertext C_0^i:
   – Parse C_0^i as $(D_i, \bar{E}_i, F_i, s_i)$ and $RK_{0\to1}^i$ as $(z_{1,2}^i, V_1^i, W_1^i)$.

$$- E_i = ((pk_{i,1}^{H_1(pk_{i,2})} pk_{i,2})^{s_i} D_i^{-1})^{H_7(D_i, \bar{E}_i, F_i)^{-1}} = (pk_{i,1}^{H_1(pk_{i,2})} pk_{i,2})^r;$$

$$\bar{D}_i = H_6(pk_i, D_i, E_i, F_i)^{s_i} \cdot (\bar{E}_i^{H_7(D_i, \bar{E}_i, F_i)})^{-1} = H_6(pk_{i,1}, pk_{i,2}, D_i, E_i, F_i)^u;$$

- Check if the ciphertext is well-formed by verifying the following equation:

$$H_6(pk_i, D_i, E_i, F_i)^{s_i} \stackrel{?}{=} \bar{D}_i \bar{E}_i^{H_7(D_i, \bar{E}_i, F_i)} \tag{1}$$

If the condition is not satisfied, the ciphertext is not well-formed and can not be re-encrypted. Hence output '$\perp$'.

- $E_1^i = E_i^{z_{1,2}^i}, F_1^i = F_i$; Output the first level ciphertext $C_1^i = (E_1^i, F_1^i, V_1^i, W_1^i)$.

(2) If the ciphertext is the first level ciphertext $C_{j-1}^i (2 \leq j \leq l_i)$:

- Parse C_{j-1}^i as $(E_{j-1}^i, F_{j-1}^i, V_{j-1}^i, W_{j-1}^i)$ and $RK_{j-1 \to j}^i$ as $(z_{j,2}^i, V_j^i, W_j^i)$.
- $E_j^i = E_{j-1}^i{}^{z_{j,2}^i} = E_i^{z_{1,2}^i \cdots z_{j,2}^i} = E_i^{\prod_{t=1}^{j} z_{t,2}^i}, F_j^i = F_{j-1}^i$;
- $C_j^i = (E_j^i, F_j^i, V_j^i, W_j^i)$. Output the first level ciphertext C_j^i.

Decrypt$(sk_i, C_0^i, params)$: To decrypt a second level ciphertext C_0^i with the private key sk_i of user i, parse C_0^i as $(D_i, \bar{E}_i, F_i, s_i)$, decrypt as below:

$$- (m \parallel r') = H_5(E_i^{\frac{1}{x_{i,1} H_1(pk_{i,2}) + x_{i,2}}}) \oplus F_i.\ \text{Output } m.$$

ReDecrypt$(sk_j^i, C_j^i, params)$: On input a first level ciphertext $C_j^i (1 \leq j \leq l_i)$ and the private key $sk_j^i = (sk_{j,1}^i, sk_{j,2}^i) = (x_{j,1}^i, x_{j,2}^i)$ of the j-th delegatee in the delegation path, parse C_j^i as $(E_j^i, F_j^i, V_j^i, W_j^i)$ and re-decrypt it as follows:

$$- (z_{j,1}^i \parallel h_i) = H_3(V_j^{i^{\frac{1}{x_{j,2}^i}}}) \oplus W_j^i, (m \parallel r') = H_5(E_j^{i^{z_{j,1}^i}}) \oplus F_j^i.\ \text{Output } m.$$

3   Performance and Security Analysis

Except for one scheme proposed in [2] that is based on lattice, other existing constructions [3,4] of AP-PRE are all based on costly pairing operations. Although the constructions in [5,6] are no longer based on pairing operations, they are both single-hop PRE and have no autonomous delegation path. In a nutshell, our scheme satisfies the properties that the preceding schemes do not. Note that the pairing operation is considered to be one of the most costly cryptographic primitives. Through comparison, we prove that our scheme has higher computation efficiency than the previous pairing-based AP-PRE schemes. Besides, it satisfies chosen-ciphertext security under the Modified Computational Diffie Hellman assumption in the random oracle model.

Acknowledgement. This work was supported in part by the National Key Research and Development Program of China under Grant 2022YFB2701400 and in part by the National Natural Science Foundation of China under Grant 62172161.

References

1. Paul, A., Selvi, S.S.D., Rangan, C.P.: A provably secure conditional proxy re-encryption scheme without pairing. J. Int. Serv. Inf. Secur. **11**(2), 1–21 (2021)
2. Xie, W., Weng, J., Tong, Y., Liang, X., Yao, L., Zhao, F.: Lattice-based autonomous path proxy re-encryption in the standard model. Sci. China Inf. Sci. **66**(10), 202101 (2023)
3. Cao, Z., Wang, H., Zhao, Y.: AP-PRE: autonomous path proxy re-encryption and its applications. IEEE Trans. Dependable Secur. Comput. **16**(5), 833–842 (2017)
4. Hu, H., Cao, Z., Dong, X.: Autonomous path identity-based broadcast proxy re-encryption for data sharing in clouds. IEEE Access **10**, 87322–87332 (2022)
5. Shao, J., Cao, Z.: CCA-secure proxy re-encryption without pairings. In: Jarecki, S., Tsudik, G. (eds.) PKC 2009. LNCS, vol. 5443, pp. 357–376. Springer, Heidelberg (2009). https://doi.org/10.1007/978-3-642-00468-1_20
6. Lu, Y., Li, J.: A pairing-free certificate-based proxy re-encryption scheme for secure data sharing in public clouds. Future Gener. Comput. Syst. **62**, 140–147 (2016)

Author Index

Printed in the United States
by Baker & Taylor Publisher Services